D0891828

CANADA'S ODYSSEY

A Country Based on Incomplete Conquests

SASKATOON PUBLIC LIBRARY
36001403000116 **RM**
Canada's odyssey : a country based on in

PETER H. RUSSELL

Canada's Odyssey

A Country Based on Incomplete Conquests

UNIVERSITY OF TORONTO PRESS
Toronto Buffalo London

© University of Toronto Press 2017
Toronto Buffalo London
www.utppublishing.com
Printed in Canada

ISBN 978-1-4875-0204-1

Printed on acid-free, 100% post-consumer recycled paper
with vegetable-based inks.

Library and Archives Canada Cataloguing in Publication

Russell, Peter H., author
Canada's odyssey: a country based on incomplete conquests / Peter H. Russell.

Includes bibliographical references and index.
ISBN 978-1-4875-0204-1 (cloth)

1. Canada – History.   I. Title.

FC500.R87 2017   971   C2017-900215-5

University of Toronto Press acknowledges the financial assistance to its
publishing program of the Canada Council for the Arts and the Ontario Arts
Council, an agency of the Government of Ontario.

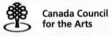

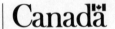

Contents

Part Five: Transformation of the Pillars

Part Six: Seeking a Constitutional Fix

Acknowledgments

I would like to acknowledge the help I received from two groups of students located at opposite ends of the age spectrum. For three years, as I was writing this book, the Department of Political Science at the University of Toronto invited me to teach a seminar course for senior undergraduates and graduate students. The course was organized around the central argument of this book, and enabled me to test my thinking on the significance of the events in the story of Canada that I was developing. The students frequently "took me on" and made me reconsider my ideas. Through their own research, they also provided new grist for my mill. I thank these students for their help and my department for the opportunity it gave me. The other students, of my own age group, were the students in the Later Life Learning Program at Glendon College, who took a course with me in 2011 on Canada in Question. In teaching this course, I began to work my idea about Canada's being best understood as a country based on "incomplete conquests" through all the major episodes, pre-Confederation and post-Confederation, in our country's "odyssey." These senior students were wonderfully responsive. They did not think my thesis was a screwy idea, and many of them encouraged me to turn that course into a book.

In between are scholars and writers who read some or all of the manuscript and made many helpful suggestions – Martin Friedland, Richard Gwyn, Rainer Knopff, Kent McNeil, Ken McRoberts, and Robert Vipond. They corrected me on factual points and challenged my thinking as good colleagues should, but were always encouraging. I thank them very much for that. I also benefited from the feedback of the University of Toronto Press's anonymous readers, who questioned many points, but nonetheless, despite being somewhat put off by my breezy style, were all of the view that the book must be published. I am thankful that, at the University of Toronto Press, acquisitions editor Daniel Quinlan was – enthusiastically – of the same opinion. Dan helped me a lot in preparing the book for publication. I also thank my copy editor, freelancer Barry Norris, not only for his sharp eye, but also for his sympathetic treatment of my work, which much improved it.

I am also much indebted to the many Aboriginal teachers I have had over nearly half a century. My education began on an August day in 1973 when the Dene Nation asked me to come to Yellowknife to consider the constitutionality of the Dene Declaration that was to frame their encounter with Canada over the proposed Mackenzie Valley pipeline. At the beginning of the meeting, a woman elder asked me two questions: what is sovereignty? and how did the queen get it over us? The first question was easy. But the second launched me on an inquiry about Indigenous-settler relations that has been unending. Along the way, many First Nations, Inuit, and Métis friends have helped me. In particular I would like to thank John Borrows, Paul Chartrand, Darlene Johnson, Keira Ladner, and Mary Sellitt. Like so many from my pillar, I may be a slow learner, but I hope that my depiction of the Aboriginal pillar's Canadian odyssey has benefited from their insights and their accounts of the experiences of their peoples.

Finally, there is my wife Sue. As always she has been with me through my struggle with a big project, caring for my material and emotional needs, keeping me within my limits, and helping me to write a book that is a comfortable read for all Canadians seeking to understand their country. Without Sue, my odyssey would have long been over.

CANADA'S ODYSSEY

A Country Based on Incomplete Conquests

Chapter 1

Introduction

In 1990 I wrote *Constitutional Odyssey*, an account and analysis of Canada's constitutional development from Confederation to the mega constitutional struggles that continued into the 1990s. *Constitutional Odyssey*, which has gone through three editions, the latest in 2004, has a disturbing subtitle: *Can Canadians Become a Sovereign People?*[1]

That subtitle has raised many hackles – within Canada's English-speaking majority. It certainly requires an explanation. That explanation, troubling though it may be to many Canadians and puzzling though it surely is to outsiders, is the rationale for writing this second account of Canada's constitutional odyssey. The explanation is that Canadians, all thirty-five million of them, have not agreed that they belong to a single "people" whose majority expresses the sovereign will of their nation.

The holdouts are the French Canadians and members of the nations indigenous to North America whose historic lands are in Canada. For many in both groups, their primary social identity and political loyalty attach to "nations" or "peoples" older than the Canada created by Confederation. These Canadians do not accept that the tide of history has somehow washed away these nations of their first allegiance or diluted their constitutional significance. Their enduring presence as "nations within" Canada is fundamental to understanding Canada, as is the often troubled, uncomfortable accommodation of these "nations within" by the country's English-speaking majority.

That is why the account of Canada that I present here begins a century before Confederation. In that sense it is a corrective to *Constitutional Odyssey*. When I wrote that book, I did not fully appreciate the importance of Canada's pre-Confederation history in shaping the path along which the country would develop after Confederation. In this book I argue that the existence of nations or peoples preceding Britain's imperial presence in Canada, and Britain's decision not to attempt a complete conquest of these peoples, are the crucial facts about Canada's founding.

The book is organized in a historical narrative form, and contains a great deal of historical detail. But it is not a history of Canada, nor am I a historian. The book is an argument about Canadian history and its bearing on Canada today. I have poached shamelessly from the work of Canadian historians and am much indebted to them. But I am a political scientist who believes strongly that an understanding of today's politics requires an appreciation of formative events of the past. If you like academic theorizing (and I do not), some political scientists call this approach a "path-dependency" theory. It is not a theory of historical inevitability. But it is an argument that the changing relationships of Canada's three foundational pillars – Aboriginal Canada, English-speaking Canada, and French Canada – to one another is what drives Canadian history, shapes the country's most important challenges, and marks its successes. Those changing relationships in turn are driven by changes within the pillars. Aboriginal peoples (I use Aboriginal peoples and Indigenous peoples as synonyms), French Canadians, and the English-speaking majority are not fixed entities or frozen cultures. And yet they never disappear as the main protagonists in the Canadian story.

The story I tell unfolds in six parts. In Part One, I examine Canada's three founding pillars. French Canadians come first, not because they are a first people, but because they were the first people to call themselves, and to be called by others, "Canadians." After France ceded New France in 1763, Britain's plan was to convert Quebec into a predominantly English Protestant colony. Although Britain backed off that plan, largely for practical reasons, considerations of principle began to influence its policy in accommodating ethnic and religious diversity. That accommodation was evident in the Quebec Act of 1774, French Canada's magna carta. The principle underlying the Quebec Act was fundamental to the policy of the second British Empire, and remains to this day fundamental to Canada's constitutional culture. Britain's acquiescence in the continuation of a French-speaking, Roman Catholic community with its own distinctive laws is one of the two "incomplete conquests" referred to in the subtitle of this book.

The other "incomplete conquest" of the subtitle refers to the Indigenous peoples. The language of conquest – complete or incomplete – is even more of a stretch in relation to these "nations within." In the many battles and wars between the nations native to North America and European powers in the centuries before the founding of Canada, both sides experienced victories and defeats. But there was certainly no overall conquest of the Indigenous peoples, by the British or by any other European power.

The Peace of Paris, signed by Britain, France, and Spain in 1763, ended the European part of the French and Indian War but not the Indian part. In fact, when news of the treaty reached the western Indian nations and they learned that France purported to hand over the Indian nations' lands to Britain, they took up arms, as never before, against Britain and its American colonies. That war, the so-called Pontiac uprising, ended only when, at Niagara in July 1764, representatives of twenty-four nations native to North America accepted the terms of peace offered by the British monarch's personal envoy, Sir William Johnson. Those terms drew on commitments the British government had made in the Royal Proclamation of 1763 to respect the Indian nations' ownership of their lands and to restrict European settlement to lands acquired by the Crown through treaties with their native owners.

The 1764 Niagara treaty can be regarded as Canada's first Confederation, for it set out the terms on which Britain and many Indian nations agreed to share the country and have peaceful relations. Crucial to that agreement was respect for the Indian nations' political independence and ownership of their lands and waters. Although, over the next two centuries, the terms of peace and sharing with Aboriginal peoples agreed to at Niagara in 1764 were often ignored by Britain and Canada, they remained law in British North America and in Canada. Today the "rights and freedoms recognized by the Royal Proclamation of October 7, 1763" are enshrined in section 25 of the Canadian Charter of Rights and Freedoms.

It is sometimes said that English-speaking Canada, the third pillar of Canada's foundation, was created by the American Revolution. Such a statement is true only if we think of Canada as the territory of Quebec that was loosely referred to at the time as Canada. In what would become Atlantic Canada, there was already a substantial English-speaking population well before the Revolution. But the conclusion of the American Revolutionary War in 1784 led to a migration of Loyalists from the United States and a stream of immigration from Britain that very quickly made the English-speaking people (who make up what I refer to as "English Canada") the dominant European population of the entire Canadian territory. In that sense the American Revolution made "English Canada."

English-speaking Canadians brought more than numbers. They brought a civic culture in which were embedded the seeds of a system of government that would become the common heritage of all Canadians. The three seeds of this embryo civic culture were parliamentary government, the monarchy, and constitutionalism.

The form of parliamentary government first planted in the Maritime provinces in the mid-1700s and later in the century extended to Lower and Upper Canada gave little power to its democratic component: an elected legislative assembly. It would be decades before the principle that government must be responsible to an elected assembly was established in Britain's North American colonies, and many decades more before voting rights were established on a truly democratic basis. Still the seed that would grow into parliamentary democracy was firmly planted on Canadian soil in the aftermath of the American Revolution.

The second vital component of the tradition of government that British settlers and American Loyalists brought with them and planted firmly in Canada was the monarchy. By the time Canada was being formed, the monarchy had become a constitutional one, well on its way to giving over the direction of government to politicians responsible to the elected branch of Parliament. For a country whose founding myth is that it is based on one people, a republican head of state might make sense, but Canada is not such a country. For Canada, a country based on several peoples, the Crown would serve as a unifying institution.

The third seed that grew to become part of Canada's civic culture was constitutional government. This is the idea that those who govern do so according to constitutional rules, written or unwritten, which they cannot unilaterally change. It took many centuries for constitutional government to become firmly established in Britain. But the process of converting an absolute monarchy into a constitutional monarchy and establishing the supremacy of Parliament, made up of the House of Commons, the House of Lords, and the Crown, was completed by the time of the American Revolution.

Constitutional government was not by any means uniquely British. Aboriginal peoples had well-developed constitutional systems long before the Europeans arrived; the Great Law of Peace of the Five Nation Iroquois Confederacy is a leading example. Treaties, mutually binding and fairly negotiated, are the form that constitutionalism has taken in regulating relations between Indigenous nations and the other two pillars. Constitutional government was not part of the heritage of the people who settled in Quebec as subjects of an absolute French monarch, unencumbered by constitutional limitations. But as Canadians they embraced the constitutionalism of the Quebec Act, which recognized their rights to live under their own laws and to practise their religion.

As the Canadian story unfolds, practices and institutional arrangements stemming from these first seeds of a civic culture will be modified, and much will be added. But, I will argue, a shared civic culture provides the glue that holds together a society as ethnically diverse as Canadians are building, and that enables us to work out our differences peacefully, rather than through violent conflict.

The two chapters of Part Two are about the efforts of the English-speaking majority to complete the conquest of the nations within. First comes the sad story of Britain's treatment of His Majesty's Indian Allies. It is a story, not of attempted military conquest, but of political subjugation following the betrayal of allies. Three times Indian nations fought with the British, calculating it was in their interest to do so. Three times the British defaulted on their promises and commitments to their native allies.

The first of these military engagements was the American Revolutionary War. Many of the Six Nations, especially the Mohawks, and the western nations fought on the king's side quite formidably. In the end, although the Iroquois Six Nations people were compensated with land in Canada, in the Treaty of Paris Britain ceded to the United States Indian lands in the northwest, ignoring the commitment made in the Treaty of Fort Stanwix to respect the territory west and north of the Ohio River as Indian territory.

The second war was the struggle of the western Indian nations, egged on by slippery British diplomacy, to resist the US expansion into their territory that was going on in the first decade following the Revolution. After the war had been going for ten years, the British – who had been supporting the Indians with arms and ammunition from ex-French forts they continued to garrison in US territory – suddenly reversed policy. When Indian warriors suffered their first defeat at the Battle of Fallen Timbers in 1794 and sought sanctuary in nearby Fort Miami, the gates were closed to them. In the Jay Treaty that in effect ended the war, Britain agreed to hand over to the United States all of the forts it had maintained in US territory.

In the War of 1812 Britain's Indian allies played an extremely important role in preventing the United States from conquering Canada. To secure that alliance the British had promised to support the western Indian nations' goal of establishing a buffer state between the United

States and Canada. When the war was nearing its end, British diplomats took that proposal to the peace negotiations at Ghent, but dropped it when US representatives firmly rejected it. That was betrayal number three.

After the War of 1812, Britain, no longer in need of Indigenous allies, began to treat the Indian nations as subjects of the Crown. The colonial administrators paid lip service to the 1763 Royal Proclamation by continuing to acquire land for settlement through treaties with their native owners. But the purpose of making treaties was not to establish a continuing relationship of mutual help and the sharing of the country, but to pave the way for British settlers by isolating groups of Indians on tiny reserves, denying them the possibility of carrying on their traditional economy or the opportunity to participate in the new economy on the off-reserve lands they were considered to have "surrendered." The policy behind this approach became clear when the United Colony of Canada passed the Gradual Civilization Act in 1857. Indians were now to be confined to reserves until sufficiently civilized to be "emancipated" from their Indian status and assimilated into mainstream society.

For French Canada, the attempt to complete the conquest also took the form of an effort to use political means to make this "nation within" disappear. This effort was inspired by a leading British statesman, John George Lambton, 1st Earl of Durham. Durham, who was on the radical side of politics, was sent to Canada in 1838 as governor-in-chief of the British American colonies. His commission was to diagnose the cause of the rebellions that had broken out in both Canadas in 1837 and to prescribe a remedy. Durham's prescription was twofold. The first, which was sound, but not implemented until the late 1840s, was that the British North American colonies should be granted responsible government. The second was his solution for the two nations he found warring "within the bosom of a single state." The answer was based on a tenet of the prevailing liberalism of the day that a democratic state could be built only on a single ethnic nation. Therefore, unite the two Canadas into a single state in which, eventually, the backwards French Canadians would, for their own good, be assimilated into the progressive society of the English-speaking majority. This recommendation was implemented immediately. In 1841, the Act of Union melded Lower and Upper Canada into the United Province of Canada.

Fortunately Durham's good idea defeated his bad idea. The British could not figure out how a colonial government could be responsible to its local assembly without breaking the imperial tie. But pushed hard by Joseph Howe in Nova Scotia and Reformers in Canada, the imperial authorities eventually saw the light. In 1848, as democratic uprisings were being suppressed all over Europe, two of Britain's North American colonies, Nova Scotia and Canada, achieved self-government in their local affairs under a system of responsible government. In the 1850s, home rule was extended to New Brunswick, Prince Edward Island, and Newfoundland. Responsible government meant cabinet and party government: governments directed by ministers whose political party commanded the confidence of the elected assembly.

In Canada, Reformers, led by led by Louis-Hippolyte La Fontaine and Robert Baldwin, formed the first such government. An underlying premise of that alliance was the survival of the French nationality. On the issues that mattered most to them, French Canadians would have their own ministers and officials. Indeed, the United Province of Canada was already operating in a quasi-federal manner. And the success of La Fontaine and Baldwin working together for common ends began to put the lie to the liberal assumption that democracy must be built on a single nationality.

Confederation constitutes Part Three of the book. Confederation, the great event of 1867, whose 150th anniversary Canadians celebrate in 2017, did not create Canada. Canada and Canadians existed well before Confederation. What Confederation did was establish Canada as a political society organized on a federal basis, with a system of parliamentary government under the British Crown. In the chapter on Confederation, I examine the event and its implications from the perspective of Canada's three founding pillars – French Canada, Indigenous Canada, and English Canada.

French Canada was surely Confederation's big winner. French-speaking Catholics had survived Lord Durham's plan for their assimilation and established a province in the Canadian federation in which they would be a large majority, with jurisdiction over matters considered essential to their distinct society. In addition, the new Constitution,[2] the British North America Act, 1867 (the BNA Act), guaranteed their right to use French in the federal Parliament and courts – rights not extended to them in the 1840 Act of Union. For English Canada Confederation was more of a compromise. Its leaders had been divided over the merits of federalism. This was certainly true of Canada's first prime minister, Sir John A. Macdonald, who favoured unitary government and viewed federalism as a temporary expedient needed to secure the support of French Canadians and the Maritimes. On the upside

English-speaking Canadians would be a majority in the new federal Parliament – a Parliament that Macdonald considered would take the lead in developing the new Dominion.

The new Constitution also provided a platform for English-Canadian nation building, with a clause preparing the way for the acquisition of the Hudson's Bay Company lands in the north and the west. There was evidence of a new brand of Canadian nationalism in the enthusiasm of many Fathers of Confederation for building a continental British North American nation. A few even spoke of Canada's fostering a new kind of nationality, one that would be neither English nor French but a political nationality that people of all ethnic backgrounds could share.

For the Indigenous peoples in Canadian territory, Confederation was simply a continuation of the colonialist subjugation they had been experiencing since the end of the War of 1812. The idea of involving them in the construction of a new political community never occurred to Confederation's architects. The only mention of Indigenous peoples in Canada's new Constitution was in section 91, listing the exclusive legislative powers assigned to the federal Parliament. In this constitutional instrument Indians were simply a subject matter of laws made by a legislature in which they had no representation. Fortunately there was much more to Canada's constitutional system than the BNA Act. There were numerous treaties made with the British Crown, the Royal Proclamation of 1763, and the common law's recognition of Aboriginal title. It would take more than a century for the tide of imperialism to ebb and for new life to be breathed into these earlier constitutional foundations of Canada's relationship with the unconquered Indigenous peoples.

Part Four of the book deals with the development of Canada from Confederation to the Second World War. During that period Canada became a modern industrial democracy with a continent-wide territory and, except for final control over its formal Constitution, an independent state in the world's community of nation-states. The three chapters of this part examine the experience of each of the three founding pillars in this era of Canada's national development.

The worst comes first: the intensification of the colonial domination of Indigenous peoples, to whom Canada applied the administrative apparatus it was developing as a modern state. For those whom Europeans called Indians, this took the form of a regime of tight bureaucratic control and oppression under the 1876 Indian Act. These policies were sustained by strongly held assumptions of the racial superiority of white, European peoples. Side-by-side with this regime of domination, Canada

continued, somewhat illogically, to use the historic treaty process to acquire land for settlement as it expanded northward and westward. In
British Columbia the provincial government simply thumbed its nose
at the federal treaty process and helped itself to whatever lands it wanted for white settlement and economic development.

For the Métis nation – mostly French, Cree, and Anishinabek – that
had grown up around the northwest fur trade and become the majority of the Red River colony in the Assiniboia territory, the confronta-
tion with Canada took a sharper, more brutal form. Chapter 8 traces
the main lines of this story, beginning with the efforts of Louis Riel's
Provisional Government in 1870 to negotiate the terms on which
Manitoba would become Canada's fifth province to the military defeat
of the Métis at the Battle of Batoche in 1885. When Riel was captured
and hanged, Ontario rejoiced but Quebec mourned, creating Canada's
first crisis of national unity.

For the Inuit people of Canada's far north, Canadian imperialism arrived much later. Britain waited until the 1880s to transfer to Canada
the "sovereignty" it claimed in the Arctic, but Canada did not begin to
govern there until well into the twentieth century. At first that rule was
mostly a policing operation; gradually it grew into an ill-informed and
insensitive colonial administration.

For Indigenous peoples, Canada's first century of development was
stressful and depressing. There was little for them to enjoy in the country's considerable economic and political accomplishments. Yet they
retained a strong enough sense of their collective identity and interests
to negotiate a more just and beneficial relationship with Canada when
Canadian leaders were eventually prepared to listen to them. That time
did not come until after the Second World War.

The story of French Canada during Canada's first century is essentially one of provincialization. After Confederation, contrary to Sir John
A. Macdonald's expectations, Canada became, and has remained, a
deeply federal country – a country with two strong levels of government constantly jousting for jurisdiction and popular support.

Although the emergence of strong provinces gave the French majority in Quebec a strong platform for defending its interests, it also exposed French Canada to the power of English-speaking majorities in all
the other provinces. The Manitoba School crisis in the 1890s showed
that provincial governments controlled by English-speaking Protestants
were, to say the least, not inclined to respect the rights of French
Catholics. There would continue to be French-Canadian intellectuals

and politicians who nurtured the vision of a dualistic French-English Canada from coast to coast. But after the hanging of Riel in 1885 and the Manitoba Schools crisis in the 1890s, French Canada as a political force would be confined to the French majority in Quebec. Canada outside of Quebec could not be thought of as part of French Canada's homeland.

Throughout this period Quebec's governments were constitutionally conservative. Their abiding constitutional aspiration was to protect the powers the province had acquired at Confederation from the encroachments of the federal government. All of this would change – with stressful consequences for Canada's unity – before Canada had completed its first century.

For English Canada the period from Confederation to the Second World War was one of nationalization. Canada became a continental state, with five new provinces, four of them in the west, added to the federation. Its population increased fourfold from three million to nearly twelve million. Much of the English-speaking population's growth came from immigration, and most of the immigrants came from the British Isles. By the 1930s, largely through the exploitation of its natural resources, Canada had developed one of the world's most powerful economies. Canada's Parliament made its own decision to declare war on Nazi Germany in 1939, and the country's contribution to the Allied cause was of crucial importance, especially in the first two years of the war, when Britain and the Commonwealth stood alone against the Nazi tyranny.

Canada matured from a British colony (at least in its external affairs) to an independent Dominion within the Commonwealth of Nations. But along the way, so far as relations with Aboriginal Canada and French Canada are concerned, imperialism left its scars. By the time of Confederation, Britain had transferred to Canada responsibility for dealing with Indigenous peoples. Like the governments of other settler states, Canadian authorities applied much more vigorous control over Indigenous peoples than Britain had ever attempted. Moreover, Canadians who took pride in being part of an empire that ruled "lesser breeds without the law" had no trouble believing that their racial superiority justified their colonial domination of Indigenous peoples.

For French Canadians, Canada's continuing ties to the British Empire were a serious obstacle to their supporting Canada's participation in both world wars. The conscription crises Canada experienced in both wars strengthened a sense of national identity in English Canada, but made it more difficult than ever for French Canadians to embrace that kind of Canadian nationalism. Between the wars, the *Québécois*'s sense that their province must be treated as a homeland for a founding people stood in the way of Canadians' "patriating" their Constitution. English-Canadian leaders – especially on the left side of politics, where there was a desire for a much stronger central government – wanted Canada to have an amending process that made constitutional change relatively easy. This view ran up against Quebec's insistence on a veto over any changes that threatened the powers it had secured in the Confederation deal. The inability of Canadian leaders to agree on how their country's Constitution should be amended in Canada is what induced the British Government to insert a clause in the 1931 Statute of Westminster that kept in place the British Parliament's final control over Canada's Constitution.

And so Canada emerged from the Second World War as an economically strong and, for many of its citizens, proud member of the international community of nation-states. In 1949 Newfoundland became Canada's tenth province, but the referendum majority favouring union with Canada was very small, and based more on hopes for economic gain then sentiments of national loyalty. The country still had not worked out satisfactory relations with the "nations within." After the war, remarkable changes in all three founding pillars would make that a more challenging task than ever before.

Part Five looks at the changes that had Canadians absorbed in constitutional politics for virtually a generation in the latter decades of the twentieth century. Driving the country into strenuous bouts of constitutional politics was Quebec – more precisely, French Quebec. In the 1960s Quebec switched from being constitutionally conservative to being constitutionally radical. Its leaders, instead of being concerned with fending off federal encroachments on provincial powers, sought to expand Quebec's powers so that Quebecers could become *maîtres chez nous*. A movement for Quebec independence began to mobilize support. Although this radical constitutional turn occurred suddenly with the defeat of the conservative Union Nationale government in 1959, the forces behind it had been at work over several generations. The so-called Quiet Revolution had been transforming French Quebec from a largely agrarian society into a much more urbanized, industrial, and secular society. The Roman Catholic Church's declining influence had dramatic consequences for constitutional politics in Canada. In effect nationalism replaced Catholicism as the *zeitgeist* of much of French Quebec.

This surge of Quebec radicalism occurred at the very moment Canada seemed on the brink of completing its great national project: the patriation of the Constitution. In October 1964, Canadian newspaper headlines proclaimed "The Constitution is coming home": federal and provincial leaders had finally agreed on a formula for amending the Constitution in Canada. Then, suddenly, Jean Lesage, Quebec's premier, a Liberal and a federalist, feeling the political pulse of the province, changed his mind. Quebec would not support patriation without constitutional changes that recognized Quebec's special status as a homeland of a founding – and, I would add, "incompletely conquered" – people. The fat was now in the fire. Another prominent Quebecer, Pierre Elliott Trudeau, entered politics in 1965 with a view to countering Quebec nationalism. Within three years he had become leader of the federal Liberal Party and prime minister of Canada. Much of Trudeau's political appeal arose from his offering a constitutional agenda designed to strengthen national unity. Two contending nationalisms now animated the constitutional contest. They would soon be joined by a third.

For Aboriginal peoples the Second World War was a watershed moment, not in changing their concerns and aspirations, but in getting a hearing in the political space of the Canadian state. They had never given up their desire to have their relationship with the white man based on consensual agreements that respected their responsibility for their own societies and their bond with the lands and waters that nurture them. But the war changed the perceptions of white men – well, at least enough of them in leading positions. They became less imbued with that sense of racial superiority which made it a duty to rule "uncivilized" peoples. After all, the Charter of the United Nations, of which Canada was one of the keenest founders, begins by affirming "a faith in fundamental human rights, in the dignity and worth of the human person, in the equal rights of men and women and of nations large and small."[3]

Although Aboriginal peoples did not fundamentally change their political aspirations, by the post-war period a significant number of their leaders had acquired the political skills needed to be heard in the political space of mainstream Canada. In part that was a benefit – surely unintended – of so many of them passing through the residential school system. Like Third World leaders who imbibed the ideologies of Western radicals in the capitals of the empires that had colonized them, Aboriginal leaders who learned the Europeans' languages in residential schools subsequently used their sojourns in Canadian cities to master the vocabulary of modern nationalism and the right to self-determination. So when the Canadian Parliament and media opened their doors – just a bit – to Indigenous advocates, they would hear the cause of the descendants of that other "incomplete conquest" as it had never been articulated before.

The first showdown came in 1969, when Prime Minister Trudeau and Indian Affairs Minister Jean Chrétien, embarrassed by the poor living conditions of Indians on reserves, invited a large group of their leaders to Ottawa to be presented with a new deal. The deal, set out in a White Paper, offered Indians all the rights and opportunities of Canadian citizenship, on condition that they forget about their treaties, their land rights, and their historic nations – in effect, give up being Indians. The First Nations leaders had no difficulty supporting the ending of discrimination against their people in Canadian law and policy and gaining full access to Canada's educational system and economy. But they totally repudiated the condition attached.

After this, Trudeau's government knew it would have to modify its policy, but it took a decision of the Supreme Court of Canada four years later to indicate the direction of change. In the 1973 *Calder* case, Canada's highest court resuscitated the 1763 Royal Proclamation and recognized the existence of native title on land not ceded through treaty to the Crown. The decision ushered in a new era of treaty making with Indigenous peoples, including the Inuit, to settle the terms on which settlement and development could occur on their lands. By this time, First Nations, Métis, and Inuit leaders saw an opportunity, in the constitutional negotiations between Ottawa and the provinces that Quebec had instigated, to better secure their rights in the Constitution. Although they were not given a seat at the constitutional table, Canada's Aboriginal peoples managed to get enough of a hearing to be, ironically, the biggest beneficiaries of the mega constitutional process.

Although the political culture and aspirations of the *Québécois* and the political leverage of Aboriginal peoples were changing dramatically, the nation's third founding pillar, English-speaking Canada, was undergoing a transformation dramatic enough to deserve being called, like that in Quebec, a "quiet revolution." Beginning in the late 1950s, Canada gradually opened its doors to immigrants from all parts of the world, a change in immigration policy that has made the Canada of today one of the most ethnically diverse countries in the world. It is remarkable that a change of this magnitude was not the occasion of a major debate about the future of the country. There were those who challenged the change, and there was lots of discussion about its social and cultural implications, but immigration did not become a hot political issue. The change in policy was supported by consensus among the federal parties. Quebec, though, has taken less than its proportionate share of the new stream of immigrants. The *Québécois*'s determination to maintain their province as a distinct French-speaking society has made them hostile to Trudeauvian multiculturalism, which treats all ethnicities as equal. Quebec's interculturalism welcomes diversity on condition that minority cultures accept the primacy of Quebec's French culture. Aboriginal peoples in Quebec are respected as "nations within" – political entities, not minority cultures.

The "incomplete conquests" made Canadians more open than majorities in any other Western democracy to admitting immigrants from all over the world. Although this proposition is difficult to prove, is there a better explanation of why the immigration that has changed Canada so dramatically has not become as big and divisive an issue as it has in the United Kingdom, other European countries, Australia, and the United States? The social, cultural, and religious diversity resulting from the dramatic change in immigration policy has made Canada a multicultural country. The Trudeau government made that official in 1971. The parliamentary statement that endorsed multiculturalism and the legislation that followed were essentially aspirational, and did not commit the country to specific programs or expenditures. Most Canadians appear to have no difficulty accepting Canada's being a multicultural country.

Less well understood – and the central argument of this book – is that Canada is also multinational. The goals of French Canada and Aboriginal Canada, the incompletely conquered founding pillars of the country, are political and constitutional. These nations within seek more than respect for their cultures. They have governments within Canada to which many of their members give their first allegiance and view as crucial to protecting and advancing their interests. This is not true of the communities of newcomers who are the targets and beneficiaries of Canada's multicultural policy. Accepting the multinational character of Canada can be problematic for its ethnic minorities. Some spurn both multiculturalism and multinationalism, and yearn for an unhyphenated sense of citizenship in a one-nation Canada. Others resent the more privileged place that French Canada and Aboriginal Canada enjoy in the constitutional structure of the country. But accommodating the nations with which "old Canadians" identify has helped make Canada an attractive place in which to settle for "new Canadians."

English Canada's growing diversity, however, has made constitutional consensus more elusive than ever. After René Lévesque's separatist Parti Québécois (PQ) came to power in Quebec in 1976, constitutional politics heated up, the agenda expanded, and the prospects of a constitutional reform acceptable to all parts of the country diminished. Still, Canada did have one success in its quarter-century of mega constitutional politics and the continuing failure to obtain a grand constitutional resolution: the "patriation" of the Constitution in 1982. And it with this success that Part Six deals.

Patriation was a strange and ironic success. Quebec, whose drive for more power had initiated the constitutional struggle, came out of patriation with its powers reduced and its special status denied. Patriation's biggest beneficiary was Aboriginal Canada, which throughout was excluded from the constitutional negotiating table. Despite constituting only 3 per cent of the population, Aboriginals, through their organizations, got enough of a public hearing to secure important constitutional resources, including affirmation and recognition of their Aboriginal and treaty rights. Patriation certainly provided an all-Canadian process for amending the Constitution – essentially, that was what patriation was all about. But the politics of constitutional change became so toxic that the constitutional amending process is virtually unusable. Again ironically, the only time the general amending process has been used since patriation is the 1983 amendment clarifying the Aboriginal rights recognized in the patriation additions to the Constitution.

The most popular part of patriation was the Charter of Rights and Freedoms that it added to the Constitution. Canadians, almost as much in Quebec as in the rest of Canada, have embraced the Charter as a bond of citizenship. It is surely the most significant development in Canada's civic culture since Confederation, The Charter's slightly lower level of popularity in Quebec is more than offset by its appeal to francophone minorities outside Quebec. Pierre Trudeau supported the rights of French Canadians outside Quebec to access government and educate their children in their mother tongue as strenuously as he opposed giving Quebec special status as the homeland of a founding people.

The fact that patriation so clearly reflects the Trudeauvian vision of Canada means that it also fell short of a comprehensive constitutional reform that could bring closure to Canada's intense constitutional wrangling. For Quebec nationalists, patriation was a loss and a betrayal. Nor did the gains made by Aboriginal people in the patriation amendments go far enough in recognizing their inherent right to govern themselves. Atlantic and western provinces both brought concerns to the constitutional table that patriation did not address. And there was growing support among Canadian nationalists for strengthening Canada's economic and social union.

So the country reeled through two more efforts to find a grand constitutional solution. The first, an accord agreed to by Canada's first ministers at Meech Lake in 1987, was primarily a response to Quebec's unsatisfied constitutional aspirations. The Meech Lake Accord was voraciously attacked in English Canada and abandoned when, after three years, it failed to win the support of all ten provincial legislatures. Next came another accord, this one reached at Charlottetown in 1992, again by the first ministers plus, this time, leaders of Aboriginal organizations. The Charlottetown Accord was a messy potpourri of constitutional proposals aimed at meeting all of the constitutional discontents brewing in the land. Because the Meech Lake process had been widely regarded as too elitist, the Charlottetown Accord was put directly to the people in a referendum. In October 1992 the people turned it down by a country-wide majority of 54 per cent and by majorities in six of the ten provinces, including the four western provinces and Quebec. Acting as a "sovereign people," Canadians could only say "no."

By this time the only group in Canada that had any stomach left for constitutional politics was Quebec's separatists, who, once back in power, decided to have another kick at the can. In October 1995 the PQ government invited Quebecers to vote in a referendum to empower the provincial government to take Quebec out of Canada. By the narrowest of margins – just slightly over 1 per cent – a majority turned down the proposal. Quebecers, like Canadians as a whole, found there was no basis for a constitutional consensus within their "sovereign people."

Canada has not returned to the quest for a big bang, popular resolution of all of its constitutional concerns – and let's hope it never does. That kind of constitutional politics may be appropriate for a country based on a single founding people. But Canada, a country based on incomplete conquests, is clearly not such a country. For a country as diverse and complex in its composition as ours, the organic constitutionalism of Edmund Burke is the path along which Canadians can best adjust their relationships with one another. That is the path we Canadians have been following for the past two decades. It is a path of small incremental constitutional adjustments: the occasional amendment of the formal Constitution, federal and provincial laws creating new institutions and modifying old ones, adjustments to the operation of the federal system, clarification and reforms of the practices and conventions of parliamentary democracy, loads of judicial decisions putting flesh on the bare bones of the Charter, new treaties with Aboriginal peoples on land and self-government issues and the renovation of historic treaties, and new international agreements managing Canada's relationships with a dynamic global community.

As the last chapter of the book shows, this is by no means a constitutionally sterile path. Along this path of organic constitutionalism much can change in the way Canadians are governed and relate to one another. The adjustments and changes we make through this process will not settle all our constitutional issues, but they may enable Canada's three foundational pillars – French Canada, Aboriginal Canada, and English Canada – to carry on their extraordinary project of sharing the top half of the North American continent in a relationship of mutual respect, growing justice, and shared well-being.

Unlike Odysseus, our Canadian odyssey does not have a clear final destination. Indeed, what we have learned at this point in our odyssey is that it is unwise to jump to conclusions – either constitutional conclusions or conclusions about one another. As a country or a society, Canada might always be a work in progress. We make the best progress in living well together when we learn more about those we see as "the other" – Canadians not in our own pillar. Canadians are not supposed to think of themselves in grandiose ways – but I do suggest, in closing the book, that what we have learned about living well together could be of value to all of humankind. Multinational, multicultural Canada might offer more useful guidance for what lies ahead for the peoples of this planet than the tidy model of the single-nation sovereign state. Indeed, Canada might be more like a civilization than a nation-state. As an example of how diverse peoples can live together in freedom and peace, this loose, never settled alliance of peoples called Canada could replace empire and nation-state as the most attractive model in the twenty-first century.

PART ONE

The Founding Pillars

Chapter 2

The Incomplete Conquest of New France

As dawn broke on the morning of Monday, 28 April 1760, two columns of soldiers marched out of the gates of Quebec onto the Plains of Abraham. These were British troops sallying forth to stop a French force on its way to take Quebec.[1]

François-Gaston de Lévis, a tough Gascon brigadier, commanded the French troops. After the death of Montcalm and the British occupation of Quebec the previous September, Lévis had rallied and reorganized the French army some thirty miles upriver from the town. As soon as the St Lawrence was clear of ice, Lévis's ships began to arrive at Pointe-aux-Trembles, twenty miles above Quebec, with supplies for his army of over seven thousand French regulars and Canadian militia. It was a force that outnumbered by three to one what was left of the British army commanded by Lieutenant-Colonel James Murray. The second battle of the Plains of Abraham was about to begin. It would be a replay of the first – except with the roles of winners and losers completely reversed.[2]

The battle was over in less than two hours, and it was even bloodier than the first. Murray lost a third of his army before withdrawing behind the walls of Quebec. Lévis's losses were much lighter, and he proceeded to place Quebec under siege.

An account of this second battle on the Plains of Abraham, the one the French and Canadians won and the British lost, comes as a shock to English Canadians. But it is a proud and important moment in French Canada's history. Regular French soldiers made up just over half the force that defeated the British. Both the British and the French referred to the inhabitants of New France as "Canadians." Although the French fought for King Louis XV, the Canadians fought for their home and native land: Canada.[3] That the Canadians prevailed in this battle is an important measure of the incompleteness of the British conquest that rests as a foundation stone of our country.

Of course, the French and Canadians' victory was only temporary. Afterward, Lévis would anxiously eye the St Lawrence to see whether the first ship to enter the Basin of Quebec would be flying the French or the English flag. On 9 May he sighted *Lowestoft* with the Union Jack on its flagstaff. When its sister ships, *Vanguard* and *Diana*, turned up on 15 May, Lévis decided to raise the siege and withdraw his army westward to Montreal.

The arrival of British ships could not have been a surprise to Lévis. In the summer of 1758, a British force led by the "dauntless hero" James Wolfe had captured Louisbourg, the great French fortress at the tip of Cape Breton. In November 1759, at the Battle of Quiberon Bay, off the French coast, a powerful British force under Admiral Edward Hawke destroyed the last operational French squadron on the Atlantic. In the end Britain's naval supremacy would prove to be the decisive factor in its victory over France in the struggle that would be known as the French and Indian War. But in 1760 the end of the wider conflict, to be called the Seven Years' War, was still three years away. And it would be Indigenous nations, the other incompletely conquered player in Canada's founding, that would play a major role in ending the war on the North American mainland.

The attack from the east up the St Lawrence had delivered Quebec and its immediate environs to the British, but west of Quebec the French remained the dominant European power. The British attack from the south up the "Great Warpath" – the waterway of rivers and lakes running from Albany to Lake Champlain and Montreal – was stopped by Lévis's army at the Richelieu River.[4] Jeffery Amherst, the British commander-in-chief, now decided to concentrate on attacking Montreal from the west.

A crucial development in enabling the British to take Montreal was the diplomatic breakthrough of Sir William Johnson, the British monarch's envoy to the northern Indian nations, in rallying Mohawks and other Iroquoian peoples to the British side in the war with France. Johnson had no difficulty persuading Amherst to attack the great French fort and fur-trading post at Niagara.[5] In July 1759 an army of two thousand British regulars, a thousand colonial militia, and about the same number of Iroquois warriors proceeded from Oswego along the south shore of Lake Ontario and put Fort Niagara under siege. The Iroquois warriors' ambush of a large French force on its way to relieve the British siege led the French commander to surrender the fort.[6]

Lake Ontario was now a British lake. In 1758, a daring British colonel, John Bradshaw, had crossed the lake and, in a hit-and-run attack on Fort Frontenac (now Kingston), succeeded in capturing the entire French fleet. In August 1759 Johnson, with fourteen hundred Iroquois warriors fresh from their victory at Niagara, met Amherst, in command of ten thousand British troops, at Oswego. Together they crossed Lake Ontario and proceeded along the St Lawrence towards Montreal. Again William Johnson's diplomacy was crucial in negotiating treaties of neutrality with the Aboriginal communities along the river that had been supporting the French. With the Canadians' native allies providing no protection, Amherst's army rowed on to the west end of the Island of Montreal without firing a shot. On 9 September 1760, the governor, the Marquis de Vaudreuil, surrendered not just Montreal, but all of New France.[7]

Following the military custom of the time, after the surrender of both Quebec in September 1759 and Montreal a year later, formal Articles of Capitulation were determined by the victors (in this case the British) responding to requests made by the vanquished (the French). These Articles of Capitulation reflect the tentativeness of Britain's military leaders as to the long-term future of New France. Indeed, Article XIII of the document contemplates Vaudreuil's possible return if, after the peace treaty, "Canada should remain to his most Christian majesty [that is, the king of France]."[8] Other articles allowed all the inhabitants of New France, except for the officers and soldiers, to remain in their homes and on their farms, if they wished. And most of them did not wish to return to France. Both the Quebec and Montreal Articles granted those who stayed "the free exercise of the Catholic, Apostolic and Roman Religion." For the Canadians this was the most important concession by the Protestant victors, although the British commanders drew the line at allowing the pope to appoint a new bishop. The Articles of Capitulation were non-committal on whether the Canadians should continue to be governed according to the custom of Paris and the laws of the country.

The terms governing New France's surrender were in stark contrast to those on which the British had taken Acadia just five years earlier. Now *that* was a complete conquest! In the summer of 1755 a combined force of New England troops and British regulars laid siege to Fort Beauséjour, on the Chignecto Isthmus connecting what are now Nova Scotia and New Brunswick. Having found three hundred Acadians within the French lines, the British authorities were determined to remove this threat to the security of the colony they had begun to develop in and around Halifax. The Acadians were willing to swear an oath of allegiance to the British monarch, but were not prepared to go so far as to swear they would fight against the French. So Governor Charles Lawrence in Halifax, without consulting the British government, decided to expel the Acadians – all of them – from the lands along the Bay of Fundy that had been their homeland for generations. In all, seven thousand were deported, most of them to the British colonies to the south, from Massachusetts to South Carolina.[9]

A much less well known expulsion occurred three years later, after the final British capture of Louisbourg in July 1758. Six thousand Acadians, over half of them from Île-St-Jean (later Prince Edward Island) were forced from their homes and deported to France.[10] But there remained a French presence in the Atlantic region. Many Acadians managed to evade the British roundup and make their way back to their old homes and some to new locations, including the Magdalen Islands in the Gulf of St Lawrence. Although France – under the terms of the Treaty of Utrecht that ended the War of the Spanish Succession in 1713 – had surrendered its substantial naval and military base at Newfoundland's Placentia Bay, many French fishing settlements continued to function along the Newfoundland coast. In the spring of 1762, in the final North American engagement of the Seven Years' War, France sent a force across the Atlantic that carried out a surprise raid on St John's. The French held St John's until September, when a British force led by Jeffery Amherst's younger brother William came up from Halifax and drove them out.[11] The French had not intended to establish another North American colony; they (and the Spanish) were simply showing their determination and capacity to protect valuable North American fishing rights. France, in fact, retained fishing rights along the Newfoundland coast until early in the twentieth century.

Britain's expulsion of the Acadians helps us understand the motives behind its much softer treatment of the Canadians. The Acadians posed a serious threat to the security of Britain's North American colonies. Their population was small and easy to deport, and their fertile farmlands were coveted by New England and British settlers. The situation with the Canadians was entirely different. After the capture of the major French forts and the defeat and deportation of the French army, the Canadians did not threaten British security. On the contrary, deporting the Canadians, who were nearly ten times more numerous than the

Acadians, would have required a substantial military effort, and might even have driven them to seek help from the American colonies to the south, where there were already rumblings of anti-imperial sentiment. Still, the British were careful not to overcommit: in response to the Canadians' request that they not be forced to take up arms against the French king, the British simply said, "they become subjects of the King" – that is, His Britannic Majesty.

Practical considerations of strategy and prudence largely underlay the relatively generous terms of the Articles of Capitulation and explain Britain's decision to allow a French Catholic society to survive along the banks of the St Lawrence. But an element of principle would soon become evident in Britain's treatment of the Canadians, gradually yielding a constitutional ethic recognizing the value of deep diversity that came to be a defining feature of Canada. We have a very long way to go, however, before we reach that point in Canada's odyssey.

A spirit of decency and Christian charity marked the first government the Canadians experienced under British rule. This was the administration of James Murray, the thirty-nine-year-old Scottish colonel who, after the capture of Quebec in the fall of 1759, found himself appointed governor of the District of Quebec. Murray's immediate concern was military security, so he cleared the town of priests and others he suspected of spying for the French. But he allowed inhabitants of the town who had been rendered homeless by the British bombardment to leave with all their possessions. More than that, through the harsh winter of 1759–60, with barracks full of wounded soldiers and a local population still suffering the shock and devastation of war and defeat, his regime was one of even-handed sensitivity to all human suffering. He had his troops share their dwindling food supplies with the Canadians, while Catholic nuns nursed his soldiers. Fluent in French, he governed in French. And he allowed the Canadians to carry on settling disputes among themselves according to their laws and custom.[12]

Following the capitulation of Montreal in September 1760, General Amherst, the British commander-in-chief, set up a system of military rule for the entire colony of Quebec similar in spirit to Murray's regime. The province was divided into three districts, with a British officer in charge of each district: Colonel Ralph Burton at Three Rivers, Brigadier General Thomas Gage at Montreal, and Murray in charge at Quebec. All three spoke French, and for the hands-on administration were assisted by Canadians.[13] At least at the top, Canada had its first bilingual regime. In all three districts, justice at the local level was administered by Canadian captains of militia acting as justices of the peace. While British officers handled justice at higher levels, they were scrupulous in trying to adhere to Canadian precedents.

All of this was worked out on the spot by the military leaders without policy direction from the home government in London. It was not until December 1761 that General Amherst received a letter from the British secretary of state, Lord Egremont, blessing the arrangements with these words: "nothing can be more essential to His Majesty's service than to retain as many as the French subjects as may be." Egremont went on "to recommend it strongly to them (the different governors) to employ the most vigilant attention and take the most effectual care that the French inhabitants ... be humanely and kindly treated, and that they do enjoy the full benefit of that indulgent and benign government which already characterizes His majesty's auspicious reign and constitutes the peculiar happiness of all who are subjects of the British Empire."[14]

There was plenty of "rule Britannia" in those words, and clearly strategic considerations more than political morality underlay them. But this pragmatic decency contained the seeds of the practice of toleration and accommodation of ethnic pluralism that would become a defining feature of "the second British Empire" and an enduring element of Canadian constitutionalism. That began to become evident when military rule gave way to civil government following the Peace of Paris that, in February 1763, ended the Seven Years' War.

The peace, agreed to by Britain, France, and Spain, reflected Britain's victory over its European rivals in all theatres of the war, as well as its imperviousness to the rights of its native allies.[15] In North America, France transferred to Britain control over all the territory to which it laid claim east of the Mississippi River. The only exceptions were the town of New Orleans and the islands of St Pierre and Miquelon in the Gulf of St Lawrence. Spain transferred to Britain its Florida territory, consisting of the peninsula and the Gulf Coast over to the Mississippi. Article VII drew the line between "the dominions of his Britannic Majesty and those of his Most Christian Majesty" down the middle of the Mississippi River. It apparently did not occur to the European statesmen who made this treaty that nations native to the territory might have significant claims to the lands they were dividing up. The consequences of that inattention will be the subject of the next chapter.

British colonial officials and politicians considered holding on to the island of Guadeloupe, in the Caribbean, instead of New France, but in the end they agreed to restore Guadaloupe to France. The long-term economic prospects of the vast reaches of New France and its value as a military base against a possible uprising of restless American colonies made it worthwhile for Britain to take on the challenge of governing a colony of seventy thousand French-speaking papists. In the era of European imperialism, no other European power had ever attempted this feat of ruling a large colony of a rival's former subjects.

Governmental arrangements for Quebec, as well as for East Florida, West Florida, and Grenada – the new North American and Caribbean colonies Britain had acquired from France and Spain – were set on 7 October 1763 in a Royal Proclamation.[16] Those arrangements take up most of the document; the final six paragraphs, however, do not deal with the governments of new colonies, but state the British Crown's commitments to "the several Nations or Tribes of Indians with whom we are connected" and whose lands lay to the west of Quebec. Although the Proclamation's arrangements for governing Britain's new colonies turned out to be transitional, its commitments to Indian nations – the part dealing with Aboriginal peoples – in effect, constituted the formal beginning of Canada's constitution.

The Royal Proclamation advanced a single plan of government for each of His Britannic Majesty's new colonies: Grenada, the two Floridas, and Quebec. The plan, however, appeared insensitive to the fact that Quebec's population was French and Catholic, with its own well-established system of law. Rather, the plan was geared to attracting English-speaking Protestants to Quebec from the American colonies to the south. Already Americans were moving to Nova Scotia, to which the Peace of Paris had added Cape Breton and Prince Edward Island. With the population of the thirteen colonies exceeding two million and a shortage of good new farmland, a steady stream of American migrants could quickly outnumber the Canadians.

Accordingly the Proclamation called for that essential institution of Anglo-American liberal government: a representative assembly. Governors were to call assemblies "so soon as the state and circumstances of the said colonies will admit thereof." These assemblies were empowered "to make laws for the Public, Peace, Welfare and good Government" of the colonies. Governors were also to establish courts for hearing and determining "all cases, criminal as well as civil, according to Law and Equity, and as near as may be agreeable to the Laws of England."

This plan of government reflected the fact that, in terms of constitutional and representative government, Britain was the most advanced European state of the day. But this did not make it a suitable way to govern Quebec, whose population had no experience or tradition of representative government and whose former mother country, France, was still an absolute, not a constitutional, monarchy.[17] Even worse was the fact that, under British law, Roman Catholics would be barred from being elected to the assembly and could not practise law in the courts or serve on a jury. If Quebec was to be governed according to the Royal Proclamation, its French Catholic inhabitants would be ruled by a handful of British Protestants enforcing an alien political and legal system. Fortunately for the Canadians of that time – and of our time – the British monarch's plan was not put into force. Instead it was systematically subverted.

The chief subverter was none other than James Murray, the military governor of the town of Quebec and its environs, now promoted to the position of civilian governor of all Quebec. It was not that Murray was disloyal or that he opposed a gradual process of assimilation. In fact, naively, he harboured the hope that the Roman Catholic Canadians could eventually be converted to Protestantism. Soon after his appointment he issued a proclamation that resembled a modern immigration poster. Life in Quebec, it proclaimed, was "as healthy as any under the sun, for in no country do people live to a greater age with more uninterrupted good health."[18] Needless to say, these glowing words about the true north strong and free and healthy were not aimed at France – their target was Britain and the American colonies.

Although absorption of French Catholic Canada into a Protestant, English-speaking northern colony might have been an attractive long-term goal, Murray was in no hurry to summon an assembly that, given the bar against Roman Catholics, would represent approximately two hundred households of British and American merchants in Montreal and Quebec. He much preferred to govern Quebec through the small council that his first instructions authorized him to establish. Dominated by Murray's hand-picked people – he favoured French Huguenots and retired military officers who spoke French – the council supported his efforts to secure the trust of the Canadians, and it set the mould for a system of government by appointed council that would govern Canada for the next three decades.

Murray's system of government not only made good practical sense, it also accorded with his social sentiments.[19] He admired the Canadians not because they were French-speaking Catholics, but because they were God-fearing farming people with a deep love of family and respect for social hierarchy. For the British merchants, on the other hand, he had nothing but contempt. In his words they were "the most cruel, Ignorant, rapacious Fanatics, who ever existed." No wonder Murray made no effort to call an assembly that would be dominated by such people. And no wonder he began to pressure the imperial government to grant "a very few Privileges, which the Laws of England do not allow to Catholics at home." By doing this, he argued, the Canadians "must in a very short Time become the most faithful & useful Set of Men in this American Empire."[20]

The key to establishing a judicial process that could "temper the English wind to the French-Canadian lamb"[21] was the Court of Common Pleas, the middle tier of a three-level court structure. In between the Court of King's Bench – presided over by Chief Justice William Gregory, "a needy man of doubtful background" – which heard the most serious cases, and Justices of the Peace (mostly English and American merchants), the Court of Common Pleas became in effect "the Canadian court."[22] Murray staffed the bench of the Court of Common Pleas with three non-lawyers, all of whom had some appreciation and knowledge of the civil law of New France. In her study of the Canadian legal system of this period, Hilda Neatby concludes that "[t]here is indeed every reason to suppose that Canadian civil laws and practices remained practically undisturbed."

Despite his belief in the eventual conversion of the Canadians to Protestantism, Murray worked hard to maintain that other crucial pillar of Canadian society, the Roman Catholic Church. Here was a delicate problem to be resolved. The Canadians had lost their bishop when Henri-Marie Pontbriand, the bishop of Quebec, died in June 1760. Only a bishop could consecrate priests and assign them to parishes. Only the pope could appoint a bishop. A papal appointee serving in one of their colonies was the one thing Britain could not abide. This was an era in which the deepest ideological divide among Europeans was support of or resistance to papism.

Murray, Protestant though he was, understood that the Roman Church was a crucial ally in maintaining British rule over Quebec. He promoted the candidacy of Jean Oliver Briand, whom he had worked with in Quebec, over the senior clergy's choice, Étienne Montgolfier, vicar general of Montreal. With the connivance of British diplomats, Murray managed to get Briand consecrated by the pope as the seventh bishop of Quebec. Although for British purposes his title was "superintendant of the Catholic Church in Canada," he was welcomed back to Quebec in June 1766 "with a great display of joy from both Canadians and British."[23]

The principal accomplishment of James Murray, Quebec's first governor under British rule, was to begin the process of resisting the anglicization of Quebec. This proved of enormous importance in shaping the country Canada would become, but it cost Murray his job. The English party in Quebec, aggrieved that nothing had been done to establish the promised assembly and disturbed by the continuation of Canadian law, never let up its attack on Murray. It besieged government officials in London with complaints and petitions, leading to Murray's being ordered home to give an account of his actions and policies.[24]

Murray left Quebec in June 1766, never to return, even though in London he was completely exonerated. In April 1767 a Committee of Law Lords dismissed the charges against Murray "as groundless, scandalous, and derogatory to the honor of the said Governor, who stood before the committee unimpeached."[25] A year earlier, in April 1766, the government had named Colonel Guy Carleton "Lieutenant-Governor and Administrator of Quebec." Murray remained nominally the governor of Quebec until April 1768, when Carleton, who had arrived in Quebec in September 1766, became captain general and governor in chief of Quebec. Unlike Murray, Carleton would have full civil and military command of the province.

With the shift from Murray to Carleton, the British government was still stumbling along trying to figure out how to govern its new Quebec province. Communications and lobbying by both Murray's supporters and critics indicated deep and growing political tensions about Quebec's future. But neither senior officials nor parliamentary leaders nor, for that matter, the king himself – who still played an important role in imperial policy-making – had a clue about what to do. The hope in appointing Carleton and sending him out to Quebec with a new legal team was that they could make a "clean sweep" in handling the novel challenge to colonial governance that Quebec represented.[26]

But that is not how things turned out. Carleton's regime, rather than reversing the direction in which Murray had begun to take Quebec, built on his policies, gave them greater clarity and coherence, and worked towards giving them constitutional expression in the Quebec Act of 1774. Like Murray, Carleton was a military man with an impressive career but no previous experience in civil government.[27] Like Murray he too had fought in the first battle of the Plains of Abraham. Of Anglo-Irish background, he was, like Murray, not English but British. But while Murray was struggling with the new government of Quebec, Carleton had been pursuing his military career and building powerful connections in London, including George III, who welcomed the nomination of such a "gallant & Sensible Man." From the earliest days of his administration in Canada, Guy Carleton was convinced that it was a mistake for British policy to aim at anglicization. In a 1767 letter to Lord Shelburne, secretary of the Board of Trade, Carleton wrote: "Barring a catastrophe shocking to think of, this country, to the end of time, will be peopled by the Canadian race, who already have taken such firm root and got to so great a height that any stock transplanted will be totally hid amongst them except in the towns of Quebec and Montreal."[28]

Soon after his arrival, Carleton became embroiled in a political feud with some of Murray's supporters, provoked not so much by policy as by his more authoritarian style of governing. Carleton was more aloof and lacked Murray's personal warmth. But he was a more efficient and better-organized administrator. Far from having English law supplant Canadian law, he had his Canadian secretary prepare a digest of ordinances passed under the old regime that gave effect to the custom of Paris. On the religious side he overrode senior officials in London in approving the appointment of a coadjutor (or assistant) bishop, and he supported Bishop Briand in allowing religious orders to continue – even the Jesuits, despite papal bulls dissolving the order. Socially Carleton reached out to the *seigneurs* much more than Murray had done to support their role in Canadian society. Through them he hoped to conciliate "the national spirit" that was resentful of the exclusion of Canadians from official government positions.[29]

For Carleton and his advisers, the ambiguity of the regime unfolding under the Royal Proclamation – on paper, anglicization; on the ground, the survival of French Catholic Canada – was unsustainable. There were also growing doubts about the adequacy of a Royal Proclamation as a constitutional framework for a new British colony as complex and as European in its makeup as Quebec. Was not the outcome of the Glorious Revolution of 1688 the supremacy of Parliament, of which the monarch was a part, but only a part? If so, should not the constitution of Quebec be provided for in Britain's highest legal form, an Act of Parliament? These considerations drove the authorities in the imperial capital inexorably towards a Quebec Act.

In August 1770 Carleton sailed for London. He would remain there for the next four years, working to get the kind of Quebec Act he wanted. The legislation was becoming a hot political issue in British politics. The battle lines were basically drawn over whether the legislation should favour the province's "old subjects" (its small British population) or its "new subjects" (the Canadians). Carleton lobbied hard for an approach designed to meet the concerns of the Canadians. Positively, this meant building in protections for the Canadians' legal system and the position of the Roman Catholic Church. Negatively, it meant resisting the introduction of an elected assembly. "The better sort of Canadians," he claimed, "fear nothing more than popular Assemblies, which, they conceive, tend only to render the People refractory and insolent."[30]

In London Carleton found strong support for his position among senior officials and the government's political leaders. Lord North led a government that had taken over from the Whigs. Its Tory supporters in the House of Commons were considered to be the king's party. As early as 1771 the North government had decided against an elected assembly for Quebec and in favour of retaining key elements of Canadian civil law. In part this policy decision was based on pragmatic considerations. Carleton was right about Quebec's demographics: British settlers were not flocking to the new province. During this period nearly all of the approximately twenty thousand British immigrants arriving in North America each year settled in the American colonies. Keeping the king's "new subjects" loyal was a practical priority, and weighed strongly against anglicization. But by this time arguments based on principle were also beginning to influence the policy of accommodating a French Catholic Canada.

By the time of the Quebec Act, the European Enlightenment was having some influence on political thinking. One idea growing out of the Enlightenment was the concept of natural rights: the view that all human beings, regardless of their race or rank, are entitled to certain rights. This is an idea that would provide philosophical fuel for the American Revolution. But we can also hear the idea at work among British imperial officials such as Carleton when he writes in defence of his policies that, "I take it for granted that the natural rights of men, the British interests on this continent and securing the King's dominion over this province must be the principal points of view, in framing its civil constitution and body of laws."[31]

Respect for human rights generated the idea that a "conquered people" should have the right to carry on their own custom and laws after conquest. This was a principle England's highest judges were applying throughout the British Empire. When Lord Mansfield, chief justice of England, heard that the Proclamation of 1763 purported to replace Canadian law in Quebec, he expressed horror at "so rash and unjust an act." In the 1774 case of *Campbell v. Hall*,[32] which dealt with the application of the Royal Proclamation of 1763 in Grenada, Mansfield enunciated the principle that, in a country conquered by the Crown, "the laws of the conquered people continue in force until they are altered by the conqueror."[33] While the chief justice acknowledged Britain's overriding power to change the law of a conquered people, an assertion of English law by Royal Proclamation did not amount to the parliamentary authorization required for such a rash and unjust act as wiping out a people's laws and customary practices. None of this came close to recognizing a people's right to self-determination, but it shows that considerations of principle early on entered the discussion of Canada's constitutional future.

There was plenty of principle on the other side of the debate. Quebec's English merchants lobbied hard in London for a Quebec Act that respected the historic rights of Englishmen. This struck a responsive cord among Whig politicians on the left side of British politics, the most eloquent of whom was the great political philosopher, Edmund Burke. Speaking against the Act in the House of Commons, Burke thundered, "Give them English liberty, give them an English constitution, and then, whether they speak French or English, whether they go to mass or attend our own communion, you will render them valuable and useful subjects of Great Britain."[34] Although Burke spoke against the proposed Act because it would deny the Canadians the benefits of representative government and guarantees of the sacred English legal rights of *habeas corpus* – the right not to be held by the state without being charged with an offence – and juries in civil trials, he applauded its respect for religious toleration. And religion – the rights and powers that the Act would confer on the Roman Catholic Church in Canada and its failure to make the Anglican Church the established church of the province – was the hot-button issue of the debate. On his way to Westminster to sign the bill, George III was lambasted with cries of "No Popery." He justified his decision to sign the Quebec Act with words redolent with principle and pragmatism: "It [the Act] is founded on the clearest principles of justice and humanity, and will, I doubt not, have the best effect in quieting the minds and promoting the happiness of my Canadian subjects."[35]

The Quebec Act was introduced in the 1774 session of Parliament, but not before that body dealt with legislation responding to the rebellious Boston Tea Party of 16 December 1773. Although the Quebec Act certainly helped fan the flames of the American Revolution, there is no evidence that its main purpose was to secure the loyalty of the Canadians in the event revolution would break out in the thirteen colonies. The Act was drafted in the early 1770s, well before the Boston Tea Party, by officials and politicians who believed it embodied the best way forward for Quebec – whether or not there was an American Revolution. The

possibility that France might launch a revenge attack on Quebec
weighed as much, if not more, on the minds of the Quebec Act's architects than did the prospect of rebellion in the American colonies.

The Quebec Act is often referred to as the Charter of the French
Canadian people because it enshrined their laws and religion, two traditional features of their distinct society. The Act made no mention of
the French language, the third pillar of Quebec's distinct society, because it was obvious that, with an overwhelmingly French population,
French would be the principal language of public life.

On the laws the Act stated: "in all Matters of Controversy, relative to
Property and Civil Rights, Resort shall be had to the Laws of *Canada*, as
the Rule for the Decision of the same."[36] This meant that the Canadians'
law would continue to be the law for settling *civil* suits, a constitutional
guarantee of Quebec's historic civil law that has been carried forward
through Confederation to Canada's constitution today. Nearly a hundred years later, the Constitution that created the Canadian federation
used the language of the Quebec Act in giving all the provinces the exclusive power to make laws relating to "Property and Civil Rights in
the Province." Another clause of that Constitution provides for the possibility of establishing uniformity of civil law in the "common law"
provinces, but that clause clearly does not apply to Quebec. Today the
term "civil rights" is usually taken to refer to fundamental human
rights that protect citizens from government. But in 1774, and ever
since, that phrase in Canada's Constitution refers to the laws that govern private relationships, the fields of law that shape a society: family
relations, inheritance, property, commercial contracts, and civil suits.
Quebec's legal distinctiveness has remained a constant feature of
Canadian constitutionalism for two and half centuries.

On religion the Act not only recognized "the free Exercise of the
Religion of the Church of Rome," it also stated "that the Clergy of the
said Church may hold, receive, and enjoy, their accustomed Dues and
Rights." This was an enormous concession by Britain. It meant that the
Catholic Church in Quebec could levy mandatory tithes on its parishio-
ners, and would thus have the material means to support its clergy and
their activities.

Both of these concessions to the Canadians were offset by anglicizing
clauses. The Act provided that the *criminal* law of England would continue to be the law of the province. It justified this provision by stating
that "the Benefits and Advantages resulting from the use of it have been
sensibly felt by the Inhabitants from an Experience of more than Nine
years." Given the brutal qualities of French criminal law at this time,

this language was not unduly boastful. The Act also made it clear that the powers of the Catholic Church were "subject to the King's supremacy," and that the king could take steps "for the Encouragement of the Protestant Religion, and for the Maintenance and Support of a Protestant Clergy" within Quebec.

The Quebec Act contained two other provisions that, although of temporary duration, had great significance in the short term. One concerned the governance of Quebec. Because, as the Act put it, "it is at present inexpedient to call an Assembly," Quebec would continue with a concilar form of government. A council made up of not more than twenty-three or less than seventeen persons, appointed by the king, was empowered "to make Ordinances for the Peace, Welfare, and good Government" of the province. The council's law-making powers did not extend to levying new taxes or duties, but parliamentary government by this time was so embedded in Britain's constitutional culture that it was unacceptable to have a non-elected body levying taxes. So, in order to provide Quebec with a source of revenue, Parliament, as a companion piece of legislation to the Quebec Act, passed the Quebec Revenue Act, levying a duty on spirits and molasses imported into the province. The Quebec Act was silent on the thorny issue of whether Roman Catholics could serve on the council. But the very mild oath of loyalty the Act required of office-holders implied that Catholics could be appointed. Lord North stated in the House of Commons that the government intended a minority of the council to be Roman Catholic Canadians. In fact, eight of the twenty-two persons named to the council (hand-picked by Carleton) were Canadians, and seven of those eight were Roman Catholics. Although British "old subjects" would be in the majority, the barrier against Catholics holding office had been quietly broken.

Another then-significant provision of the Quebec Act that would soon be overtaken by events was a change in Quebec's boundary. The Act re-annexed Labrador to the province and extended its boundary westward to incorporate all the territory ceded by France in the Peace of Paris. Quebec, in 1774 and for the next decade to the end of the American Revolution, included the southern portion of what was to become Ontario and all the lands around the Great Lakes down to the confluence of the Ohio and Mississippi rivers and up to the Hudson's Bay Company's lands in the north. This did not mean that the British were rescinding the commitment made in the Royal Proclamation of 1763 to recognize and respect Indigenous ownership of land in this western territory. Quite the contrary: a key policy reason for placing this territory under Quebec's jurisdiction rather than that of New York, Pennsylvania, or Virginia was that the British did not trust the Americans to comply with the 1763 Proclamation's commitment to allow settlement only on lands ceded to the Crown through a proper treaty with its Indigenous owners. The states bordering "Indian Territory" were governed by politicians responsive to land-hungry settlers, whereas the main Canadian interest in the western hinterland was carrying on the fur trade. The Indian nations' interests were more secure when Britain's Quebec officials were responsible for regulating the activities of Europeans in this territory.

Although the westward extension of Quebec made good sense in terms of relations with Aboriginal peoples, it enraged the Americans. It seemed designed to confine them inside a fixed frontier while enabling their French-Canadian rivals to dominate the fur trade. As the Quebec Act also denied British subjects (in Quebec) representative government and guarantees of the basic British liberties of *habeas corpus* and jury trials in civil cases, it is clear why the Act is thought to have been one of the causes of the American Revolution. It is much less clear that it was the Quebec Act that persuaded the Canadians not to side with the revolutionaries.

It did not take long for the Americans to test the Canadians' loyalty to Britain. On 21 October 1774, just a few months after the passage of the Quebec Act, the first Continental Congress, assembled in Philadelphia, sent a letter to the people of Britain in which it complained of the "Intolerable Acts" – the closing down of the port of Boston and the Quebec Act denying Canadians fundamental rights and expanding Canada's boundaries. Five days later the Congress addressed a letter to the inhabitants of Quebec. The letter, subsequently translated into French for distribution up north, held out to the Canadians the promise of democracy in a manner that was to become the trademark of American foreign policy: "You have been conquered into liberty, if you act as you ought. This work is not of man. You are a small people, compared to those who with open arms invite you into fellowship. A moment's reflection should convince you which will be most for your interest and happiness, to have all the rest of North America your unalterable friends, or your inveterate enemies."[37]

There it is: the Canadians were to be conquered into liberty.

Back in Canada, Governor Carleton was, to say the least, extremely nervous. He had returned to Canada in January 1775 with a new wife but an old problem. Although he was well received by leading Canadians for his contribution to the Quebec Act, he was confronted by a movement among the British merchants to have the Act repealed. Carleton calculated that there were enough Tories among the British families in Montreal to make them less of a threat than the Canadians to join the rebellious Americans. Consequently he ignored instructions from the British government designed to make the Quebec Act regime more palatable to Quebec's English Protestant minority by allowing English law, including jury trials, to be the rule, at least in part, for decisions and processes in civil suits and commercial disputes. In Carleton's view, if the Canadians got wind of these instructions, their trust in the British regime might be shaken. Not only did he not follow these instructions; he kept them secret. Again, as with Murray, it took a governor confident enough in his assessment of Canadian imperatives to subvert instructions from colonial headquarters.[38]

Within days of the first shots of the American War of Independence at Concord and Lexington in April 1775, the Americans began attacking Canada. Once again the fighting took place along the Great Warpath – the waterway from Albany to Montreal.[39] In May improvised raids of New Englanders led by Benedict Arnold and Ethan Allen easily captured Ticonderoga and Crown Point, British forts on Lake Champlain. In June the Continental Congress appointed George Washington commander-in-chief and authorized an attack on Canada. Politically, the aim was to make Canada the fourteenth state of the American union. Militarily, taking Canada would remove Quebec as a major British naval and military base in the north. Washington planned a pincer attack – one army under Brigadier General Richard Montgomery moving north along the Great Warpath to Montreal and another under Benedict Arnold approaching Quebec from the east by way of the challenging Kennebec River route through Maine, then over the height of land to the Chaudière River.

The American attack appeared to have every chance of success. Before any fighting began, Governor Carleton, heeding calls from General Gage, dispatched most of his regulars to reinforce British garrisons in New York and New England. That left him with about seven hundred soldiers to defend all of Quebec, including the western outposts. The American forces, though mostly untrained farm boys, would greatly outnumber any force he could assemble. Carleton's efforts to raise a Canadian militia through priests and *seigneurs* were so ineffectual that he had to resort to declaring martial law in an attempt to coerce the *habitants* into taking up arms to resist the Americans. Many refused enrolment and hid their firearms in the woods. Carleton had much overrated the subservience of the Canadians to their social superiors and their priests. The lyrics of a song popular among the Canadians at the time mocked Bishop Briand for assuming the American rebels would fail because "they don't observe our holidays, and don't adore our saints" and for believing that denying indulgences was enough to persuade *habitants* to "get their throats cut."[40] In September, when Montgomery's army moved north of Lake Champlain, Carleton became alarmed by reports of the hospitality and services rendered rebel soldiers by Canadian farmers along the Richelieu River. Although few Canadians joined the Americans' cause, many practised a benevolent neutrality that disturbed and disappointed Carleton. He would later say of the Canadians, "I think there is nothing to fear of them, while we are in a state of prosperity, and nothing to hope for when in distress."[41]

In November British forts at St-Jean and Chambly on the Richelieu fell to the Americans. Most of Carleton's regulars were stationed there, and they became the first American prisoners-of-war. At this point Carleton, leaving Montreal with a few dozen troops to defend it, fled down the St Lawrence to Quebec, where he arrived just before Arnold's force reached the riverbank opposite the Canadian capital. On 6 November Montgomery's army marched into Montreal without encountering serious resistance. They would occupy the city for the next seven months.

By early December Montgomery and Arnold had united their forces outside the walls of Quebec. They waited until the morning of 31 December to launch their attack on the city. It was a disaster. The defenders within the Quebec Citadel, including several hundred Canadian militia, were more than a match for the Americans. Montgomery was killed. Arnold was seriously wounded, and the soldiers, their ranks much depleted by arduous travel and suffering through a severe Canadian winter without adequate food or shelter, took heavy losses. Through that awful winter, the Americans continued to lay siege to Quebec, but in May, when the British frigate *Surprise* appeared in the Basin of Quebec, the Americans withdrew and retreated southward. The troops that had remained in Montreal soon followed suit. The first – but not the last – American invasion of Canada was over.[42]

The Americans would go on to win their War of Independence, but they did not win Canada. The Canadians proved no more willing to join forces with their would-be Protestant liberators than they were to fight under the flag of a Protestant king. This allegedly conquered people was now showing signs of a national sentiment that indicated to its

British conquerors a strong – and troubling – determination to control its own destiny.

In their unsuccessful war against the Americans, the British had received support from another people determined to remain in control of their fate: the Indian nations west and north of the frontier of American settlement. These peoples constituted more than half of the population of what Europeans considered to be Canadian territory. Politically, their fate was to be, along with the French Canadians, a pillar of the country Canada was becoming.

It is time we turned to this other incomplete conquest that is part of Canada's foundation.

Chapter 3

The Founding Treaty with Native Peoples

They danced until dawn: Sir William Johnson, King George III's personal envoy to the northern Indian nations and Angélique Cuillerier, the vivacious young daughter of a *coureur de bois*, swirled around the hall of the grandest house in the fortified town of Detroit. It was not their first gay evening together. A week earlier, on the first Sunday in September 1761, when he arrived in Detroit midst great fanfare, Sir William, ever the woman's man, had asked for a ball to be arranged to show off the beautiful women of the French frontier town. Angélique immediately caught Sir William's eye. He spoke no French and she spoke no English, so they flirted in Iroquois, he with an accent from the Mohawk country where he lived and she with the accent of the Wyandot, the traditional Iroquoian ally of the French.[1]

In the week between these festive Sunday soirées Sir William worked on the diplomatic mission that had brought him to Detroit: the pacification of a group of Indian nations aroused to war when news reached them that France had handed over their forts in Indian territory to Britain. Aside from the arrogance in ignoring the Indians' ownership of these lands, there were practical concerns about the British replacing the French as their principal European partner.

For a century and a half, native peoples, mostly Algonquian-speaking, and the French had coexisted in *le pays d'en haut,* that great stretch of North America around the Great Lakes over to the Mississsippi. The French – mostly fur traders, priests, and diplomats – were there in small numbers, not in large settlements, but using trading posts that often attracted native settlement. France certainly assumed that it held sovereignty over *le pays d'en haut,* but that sovereignty was directed at other European powers that might threaten to enter the territory.[2] It was not a claim to rule the native peoples of the area as French subjects. When Indians referred to the French governor as Onontio, or Great White Father, they were showing respect for French power and the expectation that the French would respect and protect their societies. Over the decades there was a great deal of intermarriage (often according to the custom of the country rather than the rites of the Roman church) between Canadian men and Indian women. Indeed some French statesmen, including Samuel de Champlain, envisaged a new civilization emerging from this close alliance of French and native North Americans.[3]

· To the native peoples of *le pays d'en haut*, the British (and their American colonists) represented a much more threatening European presence.[4] The British took land not brides. Their colonists kept arriving in great numbers, most of them intent on farming the fertile lands of the New World. By the 1750s American families were streaming westward through the Alleghenies, settling on lands that had not been acquired through the established policy of purchasing land through treaties with the leaders of the owning native nation. To make matters worse, British policy on the ground was being made by General Jeffery Amherst, commander-in-chief of British forces in America. Amherst had no respect for Indians. He regarded them as uncivilized savages who eventually must succumb to Britain's superior military force. He began to garrison the trading posts that the British had taken over from the French in the northwest, and issued orders cutting off supplies of ammunition and rum to the Indians in the territory. He even gave his blessing to planting smallpox germs in blankets to be traded to the Indians.[5]

Given all this, is it any wonder that by 1761, Amherst, his officers, and Sir William Johnson were hearing the beat of native war drums all along the western frontier? On his way to Detroit, word reached Johnson that a grand council of Indian nations, including Iroquois, Delaware, Shawnee, Mohicans, Mingos, Miamis, Wyandot, Kickapoo, Chippewa, Ottawas, Potawatomi and Neutrals, were gathering near Detroit to form an anti-British confederacy.[6]

Johnson's diplomacy at Detroit quelled a native uprising for the moment. He had promised a continuation of the policies that had enabled him to win Six Nations support for the British in their struggle against the French – respect for Indian land rights, fair and consistent regulation of the fur trade, gift-giving as a way of showing mutual respect and support, and the honouring of treaties with nations who were allies, not subjects of the British Crown.[7] But when Johnson left Detroit, he knew that all of his diplomacy would be for naught as long as

General Amherst directed British policy. Over the next two years Johnson, with his slow but direct line to the Board of Trade in London and to the king himself, did all he could to have Amherst's harsh military approach reversed. The fact that Johnson prevailed in the end is of great consequence for Canada. If he had not, it is doubtful we could treat Aboriginal peoples as one of Canada's foundational pillars.

It is time to say a little bit more about Sir William Johnson. In the previous chapter we saw the pivotal role he and his Iroquoian allies played in defeating the French at Fort Niagara and in the capitulation of Montreal. Who was this remarkable man who played such a key role in the founding of our country – even though he never lived in Canada?

William Johnson arrived in America from Ireland in 1738.[8] He was twenty-three years old and had come to help settle a dozen or so Irish families on lands his uncle Peter Warren, a senior officer and soon to be admiral in the Royal Navy, had acquired on the Mohawk River, the tributary of the Hudson that flows west from Albany across upcountry New York. Uncle Peter's lands were along the south bank of the Mohawk, but it did not take long for his young nephew to observe that all the action was on the north side of the river where the main fur trade trail to the northwest ran to the great trading centre at Albany. Within a year young William had acquired a quarter mile tract of land on the north side where he quickly established himself as a middleman in the fur trade between the Mohawks and other Six Nations peoples and the Dutch and British merchants in Albany. William Johnson quickly became very rich and very Mohawk.

In 1742 he was inducted into the Mohawk nation as a sachem and given the Iroquoian name Warraghiyagey, meaning "man who undertakes great things." Johnson learned the Mohawk tongue and mastered their ceremonies and condolences. In 1746, he took his first formal Indian wife, Caroline, niece of the great Mohawk sachem Hendryk. You might say Johnson had gone native. Indeed the sixth and most recent biography of him is titled *White Savage*. But Johnson retained his ties with the Dutch and British settler communities and built close ties to New York's governing elite. The two great mansions he built on the Mohawk, Johnson Hall and Fort Johnson, were filled with the classics of English literature, European art and musical instruments along with the gifts and artefacts of his Indian friends. Parties and balls were intercultural affairs at which visiting Brits and Iroquois guests whooped it up to all hours of the morning.

Johnson was knighted by George II for his role in defeating the large French army that invaded New York down the Great Warpath from Montreal in 1755, a year before the outbreak of the Seven Years War. Commanding a band of Iroquois warriors and colonial militia, Johnson defeated an army led by one of France's top generals, Baron Dieskau, of over five thousand French regulars augmented by about as many Canadian militia and over one thousand native warriors, at the bottom of Lake George. Following his victory, Johnson was feted in New York City. In January 1756 he was given a new commission as sole superintendent of Indian affairs for the northern colonies, reporting directly to the Lords of Trade and the king.

In the spring of 1763, news of the final peace settlement between Britain, France and Spain reached *le pays d'en haut*. This confirmed that France had ceded all of Canada and Louisiana east of the Mississippi to Britain. Now there were not just rumours of an Indian war, but a real war – the so-called Pontiac uprising. On 27 April 1763 Pontiac, an Ottawa chief, called a council of war of his own people and the Wyandot and Potawatomie, ten miles from Detroit. On 9 May Pontiac led his warriors across the river, killed twenty British soldiers outside the fort, took others captive and laid siege to Detroit.[9] The insurgence then spread like wild-fire, not in any coordinated way but with war belts sent out by other tribal communities all through the *pays d'en haut*. The uprising was fuelled ideologically by the oratory of the Delaware prophet Neolin, who summoned native peoples to make a final stand against the seemingly unending encroachments of the European nations.[10]

This outbreak of war by Indian nations against Britain should not be regarded as a rebellion, for these peoples had never been British subjects. Rather, it should be seen as the one great effort of native North American nations to turn back what seemed to be the inexorable encroachment of Europeans on their societies and their lands. In a short space of time it was astonishingly successful. Within six weeks the western Indian nations had taken all the forts the British had taken over from the French in the northwest and had put Forts Niagara, Detroit, and Pitt under siege. Raiding parties attacked settler communities along the frontiers, killing six hundred Pennsylvanians. One historian has compared the shock and terror of these attacks to Pearl Harbor.[11]

Amherst's reaction, of course, was to put the uprising down with military force. With very thin resources the British, by the end of 1764, were able to recover the forts under siege, but could do no more. By military means they could achieve a temporary stalemate with the Indian nations, but not a victory. The road to peace was paved by Amherst's return to England in November, 1763. His was not a hero's welcome. Sir William Johnson's friends in London were now firmly in charge of policy and they strongly preferred Johnson's peace-making approach over mounting a major military campaign in the *pays d'en haut*.

The key to peace lay in the final six paragraphs of the 1763 Royal Proclamation issued by George III.[12] In the previous chapter, we saw that most of the Proclamation was devoted to setting down the terms on which the British would govern the colonies, including Quebec, that France and Spain had ceded. The drafting of the final paragraphs, on relations with Indian nations, was no doubt influenced by reports of the Pontiac uprising that reached London in the early summer of 1763. But months before this, Lord Egremont, writing to General Amherst on behalf of the Lords of Trade, stated that the king had it "much at heart to conciliate the Affection of the Indian Nations, by every act of strict Justice, and by affording them his Royal Protection from any incroachment [sic] on the Lands they have reserved for themselves, for their hunting Grounds, & for their own Support & Habitation."[13]

It is worth quoting the opening preamble of this section of the Royal Proclamation as it shows so clearly the underlying assumptions and motives of Britain's policy: "And whereas it is just and reasonable, and essential to Our Interest and the Security of Our Colonies, that the several Nations or Tribes of Indians, with whom We are connected, and who live under Our Protection should not be molested or disturbed in the Possession of such Parts of Our Dominions and Territories as, not having been ceded to or purchased by Us, are reserved to them, or any of them, as their Hunting Grounds." Note how explicitly the combination of justice and prudent self-interest is acknowledged. That same mixture of motives was evident as we saw in the accommodation of French Catholic Canadians and remains characteristic of Canada's accommodation of the "nations within" throughout the Canadian story. This means that the justice involved is justice as understood by the dominant party: first, the British Crown; later, the English-speaking majority.

Next note the reference to "the several Nations or Tribes of Indians, with whom We are connected, and who live under Our Protection." The Indian nations are treated here not like the former French colonies to be governed by a colonial British government, but as self-governing allies who are promised Britain's protection. The upside of this from the

Indians' vantage point was that Britain recognized the political independence of the Indian nations and had no intention *at that point* of imposing its direct rule on them. But the downside was that underlying the entire document is an assumption of British sovereignty over the whole of the territory reserved to the Indians. That assumption was implicit in the phrasing that these nations "live under Our Protection" – a rather presumptuous claim, given the Pontiac insurgence. Like the French and other European imperial powers, Britain's main purpose in asserting its sovereignty over the Indians' territory was to exclude other European powers from the territory. Nonetheless, Britain considered that, according to its understanding of its sovereign right, it could, if it wished, introduce its own laws and system of government and impose them on the peoples native to the territory.

Of course the native peoples did not share that understanding of the legitimate scope of British sovereignty. They viewed their nations as independent allies of the British Crown with their relations regulated by mutually agreed upon covenants or treaties. In the aftermath of the Pontiac uprising, the Crown's representatives acted and spoke most of the time in a manner consistent with the Indians' understanding – Sir William Johnson being the leading example. It is doubtful if peaceful relations could have been maintained at that time in any other way. Still, it must be recognized that from the beginning right up to today there has been no agreement between Indigenous nations and Britain or its successor state Canada on sovereignty. Indian nations were self-governing societies when Britain and other European powers arrived in their territory. These Indigenous nations in what was to become Canada had no reason to accept that they and their lands were subject to an overriding British sovereignty. They had not been conquered or defeated in battle and they valued, as do all nations, their political independence.

It might seem that this failure to agree on sovereignty creates an unbridgeable gulf that made it impossible for Britain – and later, Canada – to have a relationship with Indigenous peoples based on mutual consent. But as we shall see, in the years immediately following the 1763 Royal Proclamation and in more recent times, it has been possible to forge mutually beneficial and consensual relations between Indigenous peoples and the British and later the Canadian state without agreeing on sovereignty.

The remainder of the Indian section of the Royal Proclamation dealt mostly with property relations. The opening preamble already quoted made it clear that Britain recognized that the Indian nations were in possession of their lands – or at least the lands reserved to them. Underlying this recognition was the emerging principle of the British Empire that in territories over which Britain asserted its sovereignty the laws – including property laws – of the people indigenous to the territory would continue. This is the root of the common law doctrine of native title. But note that Britain reserved the right to take land owned by a native nation and to "extinguish" native title using its underlying sovereign power. It should do this, however, clearly and explicitly, and preferably through consensual agreements with the native owners. Note again that, for the Indians, this British policy had an upside and a downside. For the time being their ownership of their lands, in some cases dating back hundreds of years, was recognized, but they were vulnerable to the possibility of losing some or all of it through unilateral actions authorized by the British Crown.

The Proclamation made an effort to assure the Indians that, at least in the short run, the Crown was committed to protecting their land rights. It drew a line along the range of mountains where the head-waters of rivers draining into the Atlantic Ocean are located. Everything west of that land was Indian territory. The American colonies were prohibited from carrying out surveys or issuing land patents in that territory. The only settlement permitted in Indian territory would be on land ceded to or purchased by the Crown at "some publick meeting or Assembly" of the Indian nation that collectively owned the land in question. Any colonists who had settled on unceded lands were to be removed. In effect the Royal Proclamation sealed off all the country west of the Appalachians from settlement initiated by the thirteen American colonies. This would soon become one of the important sources of colonial discontent that erupted in the American Revolution.

Because the Royal Proclamation was issued unilaterally in London by the British government, in no way could it itself be considered a treaty with Indian nations. For the Proclamation to have served as a basis for a peace-making agreement its terms and conditions would have to have been submitted to and considered by the Indian nations. With that in mind, Sir William Johnson met with people of the Algonquin and Nipissing nations and persuaded them to send messengers with copies of the Proclamation and various strings of wampum to nations around the Great Lakes inviting them to meet with Johnson at Fort Niagara in the summer of 1764 to consider Britain's terms of peace.[14] This effort bore fruit. In July 1764 canoes began arriving at Fort Niagara from all directions bearing sachems and chiefs of at least twenty-four nations, from Nova Scotia in the east to the Mississippi River in the west. One historian describes it as the most widely representative gathering of American Indians ever assembled.[15]

It was a critical moment for Johnson. He had scores to settle and remonstrances to make, given the warfare that had taken place since the peace settlement he thought he had secured three years earlier at Detroit. But he also had a peace to make and to secure. For this he had brought to Niagara a vast amount of gifts which he distributed liberally. These were mostly for the Algonquian nations of the northwest that had never been allied with the British. The Senecas, the westernmost and most pro-French of the Six Nations, received very different treatment. Johnson bullied them into giving up land on both sides of the Niagara River.[16] The first few days of the gathering were taken up with diplomatic negotiations with individual nations involving exchanges of prisoners, and exchanges of wampum belts to establish new alliances. Gradually Johnson's diplomacy began to establish an atmosphere conducive to a more general kind of peace-making.

When he felt the moment was ripe, Johnson assembled representatives of all the nations and presented the Crown's key commitments as set out in the Royal Proclamation. In return a promise of peace was made by the Aboriginal representatives.[17] Johnson was determined to secure this agreement through Indigenous protocols. So he presented them with a Great Covenant Chain, with figures representing twenty-four nations linking arms with the British Crown. In exchange the assembled nations presented Johnson with a two row wampum belt that had been used many times before by the Haudenosaunee to communicate their understanding of the relationship they wished to have with the British – and before them, the Dutch. Here is how Robert A. Williams, a leading Native American scholar, explains its meaning:

There is a bed of white wampum which symbolizes the purity of the agreement. There are two rows of purple, and those two rows have the spirit of your ancestors and mine. There are three rows of wampum separating the two rows and they symbolize peace, friendship, and respect. These two rows will symbolize two paths or two vessels, travelling down the same river together. One a birch bark canoe, will be for the Indian people, their laws, their customs, and their ways. The other, a ship, will be for the white people and their laws, their customs, and their ways. We shall each travel the river, side by side, but in our own boat. Neither of us will try to steer the other vessel.[18]

When we refer to the Treaty of Niagara, we mean the Crown's commitments in the 1763 Royal Proclamation, to the extent they are consistent with the Great Covenant Chain and the Two Row Wampum. For it is only on that basis that the assembled representatives of the Indian nations agreed to cease their military struggle and become allies of Britain.

The key difference between the Royal Proclamation on its own and acceptable terms of peace with the Indian nations is that the Indians would never have accepted British sovereignty over them. Johnson fully understood this. Writing to General Thomas Gage in 1764, he said "You may be assured that none of the Six Nations or Western Indians ever declared themselves *subjects*, or will ever consider themselves in that light while they have any men or open country to retire to. The very idea of subjection would fill them with horror."[19] The Indians were prepared to share their country with Britain and its colonists not in a relationship of subordination but in a relationship of equality and mutual respect. They could share a Great White Father with Britons, as some of them had with the French, not as fellow subjects of the Crown but more as brothers and sisters.

The trouble was that Johnson's understanding of the relationship forged at Niagara did not have deep roots on either the British or the American side. So, although I refer in the title of this chapter to the agreement reached at Niagara between representatives of the British Crown and Indian nations as "The Founding Treaty with Native Peoples," it is important to understand how vulnerable it was to being undermined and betrayed on the British and later the Canadian side in the years to come.

Nevertheless, the Treaty of Niagara remains of fundamental importance in understanding Canada. It embodies the conditions on which Canada's settler population can share the country with its first inhabitants on terms agreeable to both. This is not just a matter of arcane historical interest. In 1982 when we Canadians patriated our Constitution, we added section 35, which states: "The aboriginal and treaty rights of Canada's aboriginal peoples are hereby recognized and affirmed." We also added the Charter of Rights and Freedoms. That is all relatively well known. But what is much less well known, especially among non-Aboriginal Canadians, is that section 25 of the Charter enshrines "certain rights and freedoms ... that pertain to the aboriginal peoples of Canada including any rights or freedoms recognized by the Royal Proclamation of October 7, 1763," and states that nothing in the Charter shall be construed to derogate from or abridge those rights and freedoms.[20] What those rights and freedoms mean must surely be interpreted in the context of the Treaty of Niagara.

Granted that not long after the Treaty of Niagara there would be much slippage on the part of British and Canadian officials and judges away from the understanding of the Proclamation expressed in the Great Covenant Chain and the Two Row Wampum. But those erroneous interpretations must give way to the original understanding between Sir William Johnson and the Indian nations if Canada is to enjoy a relationship with Indigenous peoples based on consent, rather than on force. That is why I believe Johnson should be regarded as Canada's first Father of Confederation for he was the architect of a constitutional agreement that has the capacity – historically and ethically – to join the founding Indigenous pillar to Canada on a truly honourable basis.

The Treaty of Niagara by no means provided the basis for a complete cessation of war between the western nations and the British. A number of nations did not attend the Niagara meeting. These included the Shawnees and the Delawares who had suffered from Six Nations' aggression against their lands in the Ohio Territory and who did not see Johnson, with his close Iroquois ties, as an impartial arbiter. Also, it was quickly becoming clear that the line the 1763 Proclamation had drawn against settlers moving into Indian territory was not working. The British seemed unable or unwilling to do anything to enforce the policy, so unauthorized settlements continued to be a source of conflict.

Pontiac, moreover, was no longer a major player. Soon after the British relieved the siege of Detroit, Pontiac directed his efforts to promoting peace, and the British hoped that this renowned Ottawa warrior would succeed. But the Pontiac uprising had never been based on a well-formed alliance, and Pontiac soon found that many of the western nations did not accept him as their leader. He did not attend the meeting at Niagara in the summer of 1764, but in 1766 he met Johnson at Fort Ontario, near Oswego, to make his own private peace.[21] His end was tragic. He had fallen out with his own people and retired to the Illinois country where a strong French influence continued. In April 1769 after visiting a trading post in the French village of Cahokia, the nephew of an Illinois chief clubbed him from behind leaving him to die on the road.[22]

In the autumn of 1768, Johnson called together a large meeting at Fort Stanwix, located at the furthest navigable point of the Mohawk River seventy-five miles west of Fort Johnson.[23] Twenty-two hundred Indians were present when the conference opened on 24 October, and their number increased to over three thousand by the time it adjourned two weeks later. The colonies of New Jersey, Pennsylvania, and Virginia were also represented. The main aim of the conference was to set the western boundary of the American colonies. Johnson found himself in a tight corner. His closest ally, the Six Nations, laid claim to a huge stretch of land in the Ohio country. But it was a dubious claim based on their effort to push the Shawnees and Delawares out of their traditional hunting grounds. He was also under instructions from London to keep the colonial boundary as close as possible to the Atlantic seaboard. So what did he do? Well, after several days of difficult negotiations, Johnson purchased from the Iroquois, for £10,000, the lands they claimed on the south side of the Ohio River all the way down to its junction with the Tennessee.

In this case prudence truly triumphed over principle. Johnson defied his instructions because he thought they were unrealistic. The Americans could not be confined to a three-hundred mile strip of land along the Atlantic seaboard. They must have land for western expansion. The new boundary agreed to at Fort Stanwix drew the line between the American colonies and Indian territory along the Ohio River. South of the river extending the frontier of settlement four hundred miles westward was territory that would become West Virginia, Kentucky, and Tennessee. North of the river was the *pays d'en haut*, the lands of most of the nations that had participated in the Pontiac uprising. Although the head of the Board of Trade, Lord Hillsborough, was at first outraged by Johnson's actions, he was soon brought round by other cabinet ministers to accept a boundary change that went down well with political and business leaders in the colonies, including Benjamin Franklin and Samuel Wharton.[24]

Johnson had received as a "gift" from the Mohawks ninety-nine thousand acres of the lands purchased at Fort Stanwix. In his final years he was preoccupied with turning these lands into the new settlement of Markland and filling them with homesteaders who would be his tenants. Johnson was now a land magnate on a grand scale. But he had little time to enjoy peace and prosperity at Johnson Hall where he lived with the love of his life, Molly Brant, half-sister of Joseph Brant, and their six children. The drums of revolution were now beating and they

Johnson Hall (Sir William Johnson Presenting Medals to the Indian Chiefs
of the Six Nations at Johnstown, NY, 1772). Edward Lamson Henry (1841–1919),
oil on canvas, Albany Institute of History & Art Purchase, 1993.44

were not music to the ears of the king's envoy to the northern Indian
nations. Although his health was failing – he had never fully recovered
from a musket ball he took in his thigh at Lake George in 1755 – with
Molly as mistress of the manor, he continued to host parties and hold
council on Indian issues. On 11 July 1774 he received a delegation of
Conojahorie Mohawks with a grievance about a fraudulent land trans-
action. In what might have been his final public utterance he told his
Mohawk friends that such conduct was "disagreeable to the King."[25]
Soon after, Sir William, in a very sickly state, was carried up stairs
where he died two hours later.

It is surely a blessing that Sir William Johnson did not live to see his
family, his friends, his tenants, and his Iroquois allies driven off their
lands north and west to Canada. His son, Sir John Johnson, his nephew
Guy Johnson, his wife Molly, their children and her brother Joseph
Brant would ensure that his legacy lived on in Canada. As Loyalists
they would participate in the building of English Canada, the third
founding pillar of our country.

Chapter 4

Making English-Speaking Canada

The twentieth of April 1783 was a happy day for young Stephen Jarvis, a lieutenant in one of the regiments of The Queen's Rangers that had fought alongside the British army in the American Revolutionary War. After his engagement in the final British defeat in the south, Jarvis managed to reach New York City, where about thirty-five thousand Loyalists had gathered under the protection of Guy Carleton, former governor of Quebec and now Britain's new commander-in-chief, whose main responsibility was to ensure their safe evacuation. But Jarvis was not ready to go into exile. He was determined to get back to his hometown, Danbury, Connecticut, to reunite with his family and, even more important, to marry his fiancée Amelia Glover.[1]

On arriving in New York, Stephen met his brother Sam who had brought a permit that their father had arranged to be signed by all the "respectable inhabitants" of Danbury allowing young Jarvis to return to his home in Connecticut. General Cornwallis had surrendered to the Americans at Yorktown in October, 1781, in effect ending the war. But it took two more years for peace negotiations to be concluded, and during that period, intermittent fighting continued in the form of a low level civil war in communities where victorious patriots and defeated Loyalists lived side by side. Danbury, Connecticut, was one such community.

The day after Jarvis's return, an angry mob of armed patriots stormed into the Jarvis house demanding that he show himself. In many other communities, patriot mobs had tarred and feathered Tories and ridden them out of town backwards on a rail; some were even executed. Was young Jarvis, who had survived nearly five years of continuous fighting, now to suffer such a fate? With the strong support of his family,

Jarvis went downstairs and mixed with the threatening crowd. He probably did not help his cause by announcing to the patriots, "Be assured I have no wish to become an inhabitant of the United States."[2] His father had arranged for Amelia Glover to be in town, and the family planned a church wedding. But in such a dangerous situation, it seemed prudent to marry the couple that very night in the Jarvis house protected by a guard of Loyalist dragoons

The marriage took place without incident. But early the next morning the local sheriff returned to the Jarvis house with a warrant for Stephen Jarvis's arrest. When Sheriff Hunt burst into the bedroom where Amelia and Stephen were enjoying their first post-nuptial night together, Stephen jumped out of bed and threatened to blow the man's brains out.[3] Sheriff Hunt stumbled backwards down the stairs but pulled himself together and soon returned with a posse of patriots. Young Jarvis handled the situation well. He threw enough silver on the ground to pay for a bottle to drink to the bride's health. A strenuous round of toasts and responses ensued which brought peace if not quiet to the streets of Danbury and enabled Jarvis to slip unseen out the back door into the forest.

A few days later Stephen was reunited with Amelia. They intended to emigrate to Nova Scotia, but by this time it was very difficult to secure safe passage. When Amelia became pregnant they risked a return to Danbury so Amelia could have her confinement in the Jarvis home. This was nearly a disastrous mistake. An angry patriot mob again attacked the house. Stephen and Amelia and other members of the family sought safety in the cellar while his sister and father ran into the street calling out "murder! murder!" Eventually a group of magistrates assembled and the crowd dispersed. But Jarvis records in his diary that both his mother and his wife were black and blue from the blows they received defending the cellar door.[4]

In 1784 Jarvis managed to board a ship headed for the new colony of New Brunswick which had just been carved out of Nova Scotia. As a Loyalist soldier he was granted land at Fredericton, and Amelia was soon able to join him there. After twenty-four years as a founding pioneer family of New Brunswick, Stephen and Amelia Jarvis with their six children moved westward to join another new Loyalist settlement at York, the capital of Upper Canada. It is wonderful that this story has such a happy ending for otherwise I would never have been able to marry Eleanor Sewell Jarvis, the great-great-great-grand-daughter of Stephen and Amelia.

Stephen and Amelia Jarvis and their fellow Loyalists were certainly the founders of Upper Canada. But it would be a mistake to credit the Loyalists with being the founders of English Canada. Significant parts of what would become English Canada were well in place along the North Atlantic seaboard well before the American Revolution.

At the end of the Revolutionary War the territory loosely referred to as Canada consisted of the British colony of Quebec, its boundaries expanded by the 1774 Quebec Act all the way to the Ohio River in the south, the Mississippi in the west, and the Hudson's Bay Company's territory in the north. It was populated mostly by French Canadians and Indian nations allied to Britain. In the Treaty of Paris, which ended the war, Britain had ceded to the United States that part of Quebec which lay south and west of the Great Lakes. Once again Britain assumed that the Indian nations' lands were theirs to give away. However, the British continued to occupy the forts they had taken over from the French in *le pays d'en haut* on the pretext that they would hold them while waiting to see if anything came of the clause in the peace treaty that said the individual states might consider providing compensation to the Loyalists – a fairy tale promise if ever there was one. The population of what remained of Quebec was almost entirely French and Indian. That would quickly change with the migration after the war of American Loyalists into a Quebec that, in 1791, would be carved into Upper and Lower Canada.

But we should not forget that there was a sizable English-speaking population in what would become Canada well before the American Revolution. British settlement in what is today's Canada began in Newfoundland, where, in the 1600s, fishers began staying through the winter.[5] By the mid-1700s Newfoundland had seven thousand permanent residents, although Britain did not treat it as an official colony. Instead Nova Scotia became Britain's first official northern colony. In 1749 a British fleet carried over twenty-five hundred settlers to Halifax.[6] Thousands more followed, not all of them from the British Isles. Nova Scotia's fertile farmlands and commercial opportunities attracted significant numbers of New Englanders, as well as Protestant settlers recruited from France, Germany, and Switzerland. As part of the treaty ending the Seven Years' War, what are now Prince Edward Island and Cape Breton Island were added to Nova Scotia, and the province quickly expanded northward into what would become the separate colony of New Brunswick.

Although the Loyalists did not create English Canada, the northern migration of tens of thousands of them to various parts of British North

America in the 1780s ensured that the third founding pillar of Canada, its English-speaking people, would form the country's majority.

There is a lot of mythology about the Loyalists – or, to give them the label so many of them savoured, the United Empire Loyalists. They are often depicted as high Tories, people of considerable wealth and status in colonial society – more British than the British. In fact they were very American, virtually indistinguishable from Americans who supported the revolutionary cause.[7] Many tried to sit on the fence waiting to see which side would prevail in the war but got flushed out of their neutrality by refusing to take a patriot oath or enlist on the rebel side. Stephen Jarvis's story shows how difficult it was for families that were not fervent republicans to survive and prosper in post-bellum America.

Among the Loyalists there were certainly a few powerful and wealthy families, like the Beverly Robinsons and the DeLanceys, but there were many more very ordinary people, including a great many soldiers and sailors, of all ranks, who, like young Stephen Jarvis, had decided to fight for king and country. The Loyalists included merchants, millers, craftsmen, doctors, lawyers, clergymen, tenant farmers, and others of modest means. Nor were they solidly of British ancestry. Among the Loyalists were many Dutch and German families, and Hessian mercenaries brought over by Britain who wished to stay in America but in British territory. Over three thousand Loyalist evacuees were Afro-Americans, most having fled slavery in the southern states, but some still in servitude to northern white masters. And there were thousands of Six Nations people led by Joseph Brant and his cousin John Deseronto who, having fought for King George, sought sanctuary in British territory. They too should be included among the Loyalists.

The big surge of Loyalist evacuees came in 1783 out of New York and the southern ports of Charleston and Savannah. The main destinations for the southern evacuees were British East Florida, and Jamaica and the Bahamas in the British West Indies. For many of these Loyalists, the attraction was the prospect of taking their slaves with them and carrying on the plantation economy they had enjoyed in the American south. Many thousands of other Loyalists returned to Britain, where they became a political lobby pressing Parliament and the government to reward their loyalty with compensation for their property and commercial losses. A commission set up by Parliament took submissions over many months and eventually paid out £3 million, a significant sum for those times, but not nearly enough, of course, to satisfy all Loyalist claims.[8]

But the largest group of Loyalists, perhaps more than half of the one hundred thousand who left America at the end of the war and in the first six years of the peace went to British North America. By today's standards fifty to sixty thousand seems a small number for such a significant migration. But bear in mind that Britain was not then promoting emigration to North America. Far from it: Britain needed to man a huge army and navy during the American Revolutionary War, again during the war that soon followed with revolutionary France, and after that, the Napoleonic wars. Emigration from Britain on a substantial scale would come later, greatly facilitated by the establishment of English-speaking communities in parts of Canada that hitherto had been overwhelmingly French Catholic or without any substantial European settlements. In effect the migration of a few tens of thousands of American Loyalists paved the way for the later arrival of hundreds of thousands of English-speaking immigrants.

The largest group of northward-bound Loyalists, about thirty-five thousand, went to Nova Scotia, which at the end of the Revolutionary War had a European population of about twenty thousand. Soon, perhaps as many as ten thousand other Loyalists were landed at the mouth of the St John River. From there they made their way upriver to St Anne's, soon to be renamed Fredericton. The new settlers formed a strong enough identity to demand their own province. Much to the displeasure of Nova Scotia's governor, John Parr, the colonial authorities agreed, and in 1784 New Brunswick was carved out of Nova Scotia.[9] Much earlier, in 1769, the island known as Île-St-Jean under the French regime, added to Nova Scotia in the Treaty of Paris, had became the separate colony of St John Island – later named Prince Edward Island after Prince Edward, the Duke of Kent. The hundred or so Loyalists who ended up there found to their dismay that the island was controlled by absentee English landowners.[10]

The largest settlement of Nova Scotia Loyalists was at Port Roseway (soon to become Shelburne) on the south coast west of Halifax. The sudden landing of about ten thousand Loyalists on unsurveyed land with almost no shelter, little food and a cold winter coming on was a disaster. There was much hardship and considerable conflict. Many referred to their new home as Nova Scarcity. And a great many did not stay for long, moving quickly to more hospitable destinations. The Afro-Americans who landed were Port Roseway's biggest victims. The general chaos that prevailed there brought out the worst in the white community. Blacks, though most were free British subjects, suffered rank discrimination in the allocation of property and the necessities of life. No wonder, when the opportunity arose, that so many of them opted to sail to Sierra Leone, a colony of freed slaves set up by the British on the west coast of Africa.[11]

By the time the Revolutionary War was over there were already about three thousand Loyalists in Quebec – which at that time included what we now know as Ontario. After the war additional Loyalists did not come in groups as large as those that sailed out of New York, Charleston, and Savannah; most made their own way, family by family, through the forests and along the rivers that flow into the St Lawrence and Lake Ontario. My mother's extended family, Griffins and Smiths, barged across Lake Ontario and founded Smithville on the Niagara Escarpment in 1790.[12] Under the leadership of Frederick Haldimand, the British officer of Swiss background who succeeded Guy Carleton as governor, Quebec was well prepared for an influx of English-speaking Loyalists. For security reasons, Haldimand did not want a settlement of Vermont Loyalists to develop close to the US border. He preferred to see former Americans settle farther north and let the French Canadians provide a buffer against the new republic. Among other things, he purchased a seigneury for Loyalists near the junction of the St Lawrence and the Richelieu, and sent surveyors along the north shore of the St Lawrence to survey lots and organize townships as far west as Kingston.[13] Altogether the so-called late Loyalists, plus those who had migrated to Quebec in the closing years of the war, numbered around ten thousand.

The largest single group of Loyalists to migrate into the western part of Quebec were native peoples led by the Mohawk Joseph Brant. For the Six Nations peoples who had fought fiercely on the British side in the Revolutionary War, Canada beckoned as a safe sanctuary. Brant also had a broad strategic rationale for seeking land for his people in Canada. He envisaged forming a confederacy of western nations that could be a buffer state between the United States and the British Empire. The 1783 peace treaty, like the 1763 peace treaty, totally ignored Indian interests and rights. Indeed, the treaty ceded to New York State large areas of land that the Treaty of Fort Stanwix had awarded to Indian nations. Brant responded to the treaty by organizing a conference of Indian nations at Sandusky in the Ohio Territory to discuss his vision of a buffer state.[14]

When Brant went to Quebec City in 1784 to negotiate a land base for Indian refugees in Canada, he got a reasonably sympathetic hearing from Governor Haldimand. Haldimand was able to purchase from the Mississaugas a large tract of land along the Grand River – six miles on each side of the river from Lake Erie to its source at Shelburne. In October 1784 the Grand River tract, which would be known as the "Haldimand Tract" was granted to the Mohawks "for them and their posterity to enjoy forever."[15] Although it was Brant's Mohawks who were named in the grant, many of the two thousand who arrived at the Grand River over the next year were members of other Iroquoian nations, and some were from Algonquian nations. There were even some Cherokees and Creeks from the American south. Another hundred Mohawks, led by Chief John Deseronto, settled at the Bay of Quinte on land Governor Haldimand had secured for them. Although these new communities of Indian refugees were somewhat pluralistic, they were predominantly Iroquoian and governed themselves according to Haudenosaunee traditional law.

The arrival in the mid-1780s of significant numbers of "His Majesty's Indian Allies" meant that Aboriginal people were by far the majority population of what was soon to become Upper Canada (after that, Ontario). These native inhabitants were on their own lands and were completely self-governing. Within thirty years the demographics would change dramatically, and for the native peoples, disastrously. Through the combination of disease among the Indians and immigration from Britain and America, the Aboriginal people would be reduced to a tiny fraction, perhaps one-twentieth, of the provincial population.

The Loyalists brought more than numbers. They also brought a set of beliefs in principles of government that would shape the civic culture of Canada. A country whose foundations involve such deep ethnic and indeed national diversity as Canada could not hold together unless its key components, its founding pillars, shared a civic culture. A common civic culture is essential if those founding pillars, French Canada, Aboriginal Canada and English Canada, are to negotiate their differences through accepted procedures and institutions rather than through violent conflict or the exercise of the brute force of the majority English-speaking people. Admittedly there have been times, for Aboriginal Canada very long times, when their rights and interests have been subject to the brute force of the majority. But, as the Treaty of Niagara shows, there is the potential to manage relations between Aboriginal peoples and other Canadians according to shared principles if the majority and its leaders have the will to do so.

The civic culture evident in the governmental institutions and political practices of these early British North American colonies was a far cry from the civic culture that would evolve and shape Canada. To begin with, the Loyalists and early British settlers operated a governmental system premised on British imperialism, its institutions designed by colonial officials and legislated for the colonies by British lawmakers. Any liberties Britain granted to the colonists could be taken away. Parliament in London was, in law, the sovereign of British North America and, after Confederation, of Canada until 1982. A liberty fundamentalist – which might include many Americans – would dismiss any system of government so tainted with imperialism as incapable of containing the seeds of a constitutional democracy. But a careful consideration of these early governmental arrangements in British North America shows at least in embryo three elements of what would become the civic culture of a mature and democratic Canada.

The first is a parliamentary system of government, planted first in Nova Scotia in 1749, followed by Prince Edward Island in 1769, New Brunswick in 1784, and Upper and Lower Canada in 1791. The Constitutions of the five colonies differ in detail, but they were shaped by the same colonial cookie-cutter. As William Pitt explained in the House of Commons, the aim was to reproduce as much as possible the British constitution so as "to avoid a repetition of the first great colonial failure" – the rebellion of the American colonies.[16] But despite Pitt's intention, there would be very little power for elected representatives of the people in these arrangements. Legislative authority was vested in the governor or lieutenant-governor acting "with the advice and consent" of an appointed legislative council and an elected legislative assembly. In exercising his executive powers, the governor would be assisted by an executive council whose members were appointed by the governor following Colonial Office instructions. The governor had the power to reject legislation passed by both houses of the legislature or refer legislation to the colonial authorities for possible disallowance by the British government.

This clearly was a very top-heavy, elite-dominated system of government. It meant that government in all five colonies would be led by a British governor or lieutenant-governor whose principal advisers were appointed members of the executive council and the legislative council. The upper house of the legislature, the appointed legislative council, was supposed to replicate the House of Lords. This part of the design was based on the misguided notion that a land-owning aristocracy would soon emerge in the back woods of British North America. There was considerable overlap of membership between the executive and legislative councils. Socializing with the governor and securing some kind of

public office, including judicial office, was a much surer and easier way
to win an appointment to the legislative council than clearing large
tracts of land. At the bottom of the structure was the legislative assembly, typically about twice the size of the legislative council. Lower
Canada began with an assembly of fifty members and a legislative
council of at least sixteen. Much less populous Upper Canada had an
assembly of sixteen and a legislative council of at least seven. The franchise was limited to white males, with a property requirement considerably lower than that required for the British House of Commons.
Despite their lack of power, these elected assemblies would play a decisive role in bringing about democratic change in the colonial governance of British North America.

The model of government described above bears a formal resem-
blance to the institutions of the British Parliament. But in terms of moving closer to parliamentary democracy the parliaments of colonial
Canada were a long way behind Westminster. By the latter half of the
eighteenth century, the British government was being led by prime
ministers most often drawn from the House of Commons. The sovereign, George III, continued to have an important influence on policy,
and personally picked the parliamentary group that would lead his
government, form the ministry, and be his constitutional advisers. But
his choice was shaped by the need to pick people who had a reasonable
chance of winning parliamentary approval and funding for their policies. Over time the Crown learned that it must, in Lord Durham's
words, "carry on the Government in unison with a representative body,
it must consent to carry it on by means of those in whom that representative body has confidence."[17] That practice embodied the principle of
"responsible government," though neither Durham nor British constitutional writers used that phrase. Since the Glorious Revolution of 1688,
when Parliament asserted its supremacy over the monarch, Parliament
had become the hub of government, supplying its leaders and leading
the public discussion of policy. And the elected chamber of Parliament,
the House of Commons gradually but most definitely supplanted the
House of Lords as the most powerful legislative chamber.

Now compare the powerful position the House of Commons had arrived at with the position of the elected houses in the British North
American colonies. Far from being the hub of government these lower
houses were the hub of opposition. Those elected to these assemblies
were totally excluded from government, which was in the hands of the
governor and those who toadied up to him. And yet, the governor had
to win the support of the legislative assembly to get legislation enacted

or funds based on local levies approved. This was the fatal flaw in the Constitutions provided for these colonies. It was also their saving grace. Elected assemblies could use the power given them in the legislative process to hold the governor hostage and force him to pay attention to their demands and grievances. This meant that governors often engaged actively in elections in order to get assemblies that were as friendly as possible. Given the patronage at the governor's disposal, this could lead to considerable corruption of the electoral process.

The governor of Lower Canada (who was also governor-in-chief of British North America) and the lieutenant-governor of Upper Canada faced the toughest challenges. In both colonies the legislative assembly was a forum for one side of a fundamental societal cleavage. In Lower Canada, from the beginning, the French Canadians had a large majority in the Legislative Assembly, and they used that majority to attack the governor and the mostly English "château clique" for the undemocratic way they controlled the Executive and Legislative Councils.[18] The spirit of the democratic age ushered in by the American and French revolutions was beginning to animate both the *habitants* and an emerging French petite bourgeoisie. Because their opponents were *les Anglais*, the Assembly became a platform for French-Canadian nationalism, a development that the British architects of the colony's Constitution clearly did not intend. In Upper Canada the cleavage was based on class not ethnicity. The first lieutenant-governor, Robert Graves Simcoe, in style and ideology an arch Tory, encouraged the development of a local aristocracy based on a few of the most prominent Loyalist families. This coterie of well-connected notables, which became known as the "Family Compact," monopolized the positions of public office and controlled the banking and financial system.[19]

The conflict between the elected assembly and the government elite made Lower and Upper Canada virtually ungovernable and eventually led to armed rebellions in both colonies. In the end responsible government – requiring that government be responsible to the elected branch of the legislature and led by elected members who have majority support in the assembly – would make the system workable. But by the time responsible government was put into practice, as we will see in Chapter 5, the two Canadas were joined together. Although the colonial governments that preceded responsible government were liberal in the sense that their Constitutions divided power but not yet democratic, they firmly planted the institutional structure of parliamentary government as an enduring component of Canada's civic culture. Neither the French-Canadian assemblymen in Lower Canada nor their counterparts

in the Upper Canada, in all of their impassioned attacks on the domination of government by the governor and his friends, ever called for
republican government or a presidential-congressional division of governmental powers along American lines. When they called for republican government, they meant government in which the popular element
directs government. They accepted the parliamentary system with its
tendency towards executive domination of the legislature. They simply
insisted that the executive be directed by political leaders who have the
support of a majority of the people's elected representatives.

The one dimension of parliamentary government in Canada that was
wobbly from the start was the upper house. Upper houses, lacking any
societal or historical base, were eventually eliminated at the provincial
level after Confederation. At the federal level, an appointed upper
house, the Senate, survives. Although a strong principled case for an
appointed upper house can be made,[20] there would be little public support for parliamentary bicameralism so long as political partisanship is
the dominant consideration in appointing senators.

The second contribution implanted in Canada's civic culture by the
English-speaking settlers was constitutional monarchy. What else would
you expect from Loyalists? But there is a much more fundamental reason a monarchical head of state became an enduring part of Canada's
civic culture. For a country whose founding myth is that it is one people,
a republican head of state might make sense, but Canada is not such a
country. Even though, in Canada's case the monarch was British and
thereby closely attached to one of the founding peoples, it could be a
source of unity if it was congenial to the other two founding peoples in
a cultural and historical sense. And that has been the case with both
French Canada and Aboriginal Canada.

For the habitants of New France it was not easy to switch their allegiance from the king of France to the king of Britain. Indeed, to get
them to swear fidelity to His Britannic Majesty, the oath had to be softened to leave out a promise to fight for the British monarch. Troubling
and confusing as the sudden shift of national allegiance was for the
people of New France, the idea of swearing allegiance to a monarch
was not. The fact that the first governors who exercised the powers of
the British Crown in Quebec – Murray, Carleton, and Haldimand –
spoke French and sided with the French majority against the English
minority helped overcome the Canadians' apprehensions about being
ruled by a British sovereign. It also helped that, as Britain felt its way
forward to a more liberal style of imperialism, British monarchs felt

obliged to be sensitive to the interests of the many diverse peoples inhabiting the far flung reaches of the empire. This was evident in George III's support of his emissary, Sir William Johnson, in respecting native rights in America, and later when he ignored anti-papist demonstrators as he rode to Westminster to sign the Quebec Act.

French Canada had its first personal experience of the British royals when Prince Edward, the Duke of Kent, with his regiment of Royal Fusiliers, arrived in Quebec in 1791.[21] Prince Edward was the fifth-born child of George III and Queen Charlotte. The young prince was quite a lad. He had carried on the proliferate lifestyle of a young royal, accumulating mistresses and large debts at a level that was scandalous even in those pre-Victorian times. For this the king sent the prince and his regiment to Gibraltar in 1790 in the hope that his prodigal son might mend his ways in this isolated outpost of empire. In Gibraltar he behaved well enough for his father to allow him to move to Quebec, which had become in effect the capital of British North America. Prince Edward was welcomed to Quebec by Guy Carleton, governor-in-chief of Britain's North American colonies, who now carried the title of Lord Dorchester, conferred on him for his services to the empire.

Prince Edward did not come alone. Not only did he bring his regiment, complete with a full military band; he also brought his newest mistress, the vivacious and elegant and very French Julie de St-Laurent. Because Julie was a Roman Catholic, Edward could not marry her, but Julie was installed discretely in separate quarters from the prince. For several seasons, the prince and his lady, equally congenial to French and English society, were the centre of the social whirl and cultural life of the small, emerging colonial capital.

Prince Edward was very aware of the tension between French and English. When an election dispute in Charlesbourg between French and English candidates for election to Lower Canada's first Legislative Assembly erupted in violence, he rushed to the town. In addressing the rioters he asked: "Can there be any man among you who does not take the King to be the father of his people? Is there a man among you who does not look upon the new constitution as the best possible one for both the subject and the Government? Part then in peace, I urge you to unanimity and concord. Let me hear no more of the odious distinction of French and English. You are all his Britannic Majesty's Canadian subjects."[22] Historians have noted that this is the first recorded use of "Canadians" to refer to both English and French inhabitants of the country.

In 1794 Prince Edward moved to Halifax, where he became commander-in-chief of British military forces in North America. He made a good enough impression in the Maritime colonies that the Legislative Assembly of St John Island changed the province's name to Prince Edward Island. Long after Prince Edward returned to England, he married Princess Victoria of Saxe-Coburg-Saalfeld. After the short reigns of Edward's elder brothers George IV and William IV, his daughter Victoria would become British North America's sovereign in 1837.

The warm relations that early governors and the British royals cultivated with French Canadians were an important factor in winning their support for the British crown. But the real clincher was the French Revolution. The guillotine that beheaded Louis XVI in January 1793 cemented French Canada's loyalty to the British monarch. This had nothing to do with the persona of George III; rather, it reflected a conservative Catholic society's revulsion at the horrors of republicanism. The republicans guillotined not only the monarchy but also the privileges of the Roman Catholic Church. Now that there was no chance of a return of the French monarch, loyalty to the British monarch was the only alternative to the evils of republicanism. So long as the Catholic Church retained its strength in French Canada, and that was a very long time, there was strong support in Quebec for the British king or queen as Canada's head of state. Of course, that would change dramatically with the Quiet Revolution and the rise of secular Quebec nationalism in the 1960s. Even so, republican aspirations have never figured prominently in Quebec nationalists' aspirations. Indeed, Quebec sovereigntists have been exceedingly vague about their proposed arrangements for a head of state in an independent Quebec.

As for the Indian nations, the Crown has been the one institution they have shared with settlers.[23] This has been true under both the French and British regimes. But First Nations peoples have viewed their relationship with the Crown as a family relationship not a state political relationship. Indians traditionally viewed the settlers' monarch as their Great White Father or Mother, not as their sovereign ruler. They never accepted that they were the monarch's subjects. Viewing their relationship with the Crown through the prism of family meant that their relationship with the settlers was understood in kinship terms as being that of brothers and sisters sharing the same father or mother rather than being subjects of the same ruler.

In treaty-making with the Indians, British and Canadian governments portrayed the negotiations as agreements made with the Crown. Although this rhetoric helped win the Indians' trust in the treaty process, it was deeply misleading: as responsibility for relations with native peoples was transferred from Britain to Canada, and as the role of the Crown's representative in Canada adjusted to the imperatives of responsible democratic government, treaties in reality became agreements between Indian nations and the Government of Canada. This meant that implementation of the treaties would be in the hands of political leaders and civil servants in Ottawa whose understanding of the treaties and their purposes differed radically from commitments made in negotiations conducted in the name of the Indians' Great White Mother or Father.

As we saw in the previous chapter, the Aboriginal peoples' foundational agreement for sharing the country with the settlers was with the British Crown. The rights and freedoms of Aboriginal peoples recognized in that agreement are now inscribed in the Charter. Since that agreement, Canada has become a self-governing democracy. Some might say this means that Aboriginal people should adjust to this reality and give up counting on an honourable Crown as their partner in regulating their relationship with Canada. But why should they do that? They were never consulted about these huge changes in the nature of their treaty partner. They were totally excluded from any kind of participation in the discussions and negotiations that led to Confederation and the founding of the Dominion of Canada. For nearly a century after Confederation they were denied any right to participate in the institutions of the new Dominion – including, for a time, its courts. For Canadians who wish to see Canada's relations with Aboriginal peoples based on justice and honour rather than force, the task ahead is to find a way modern-day Canada can replace the Great White Mother or Father with a treaty-making process that Aboriginal peoples can trust but that also meets the imperatives of accountable democratic government.

As we will see in later chapters, since the first English-speaking colonists ensured that constitutional monarchy would be part of Canada's civic culture, the institution has evolved – mightily. It has evolved to be not only compatible with, but also a protector of, parliamentary democracy. It has also evolved to serve a federal, post-colonial country; indeed, it has become the Canadian Crown. That evolution has been facilitated by a constitutional process that is a defining feature of Canada's civic culture.

This brings us to the third civic culture seed planted by the early English-speaking settlers: constitutional government. Constitutional government means more than having a constitution; every country

– even the most tyrannical – has a constitution. Constitutional government means that those who govern do so according to constitutional
rules, written and unwritten – in short, that those who govern take the
constitution seriously. The constitutional rules that bind government
cannot be changed unilaterally by any branch of government. It took
many centuries for constitutional government to become firmly entrenched in Britain. But that process of converting an absolute monarchy into a constitutional monarchy and establishing the supremacy of a
Parliament made up of the House of Commons, the House of Lords,
and the Crown was completed by the time of the American Revolution.

Constitutional government was not by any means uniquely British.
Aboriginal peoples had well-developed constitutional systems long before the Europeans arrived in North America. The Five Nation Iroquois
Confederacy's Great Law of Peace is a leading example, as is the "set of
understandings" through which other Aboriginal peoples organized
their societies.[24] These agreements, which bound communities together,
dispersed power and served as protection against any kind of absolutism. Constitutional government was not part of the heritage of the
French people who settled in Quebec, coming as they did from an absolute monarchy in France. But as Canadians, they embraced the constitutionalism of the Quebec Act, which recognized their rights to live
under their own laws and to practise their religion. As French Canadians
looked ahead and saw themselves becoming a minority people in
Canada, constitutional government offered the prospect of protection
of their rights and interests against simple majority rule.

The constitutionalism that British settlers brought to Canada had a
distinctive form. It was not a constitutionalism based on a single document called the Constitution setting out all the important rules and
principles of government and establishing the country's institutions of
government. The constitutionalism of countries, such as the United
States, that are formed in the context of making a new start after war
or revolution is centred on a single founding constitutional document.
England had such a Constitution after the Cromwellian revolution in
the mid-1600s. After the restoration of the monarchy under Charles II,
followed by James II, England's parliamentarians staged the Glorious
Revolution of 1688 to curb royal absolutism and replace the Stuart
dynasty with William of Orange, a monarch who would accept the
sovereignty of Parliament. From that point on the path of Britain's constitutional development has been evolutionary, not revolutionary.
Along this path have come seminal Acts of Parliament, such as the
1689 Bill of Rights and the 1701 Act of Settlement, setting out the line

of succession to the throne and securing the independence of the judiciary. But many of the most important rules developed as informal "unwritten" conventions embodying principles accepted by all the key players involved in governing and reflecting the spirit of the times. For instance the principle essential to democratizing parliamentary government in Britain – namely, that the Crown must choose as its constitutional advisers politicians who command the confidence of the House of Commons – was based entirely on an unwritten constitutional convention.

Constitutionalism of this kind is based on a philosophy very different from that of the United States and other countries born in the aftermath of war or revolution. The patron saint of the American Revolution was the English philosopher John Locke. For Locke the constitution was a contract between a people and their governors. The people first form a political society in which the majority has "a right to set and conclude the rest,"[25] and then in the Constitution set out the terms on which the people agree to be governed. Such a constitutional philosophy is inappropriate for a country such as Canada, based as it is on three founding peoples who have not agreed to become a single people subject to the will of the majority. Nor has the Canadian constitution arrived in one fell swoop after a war or revolution. Important as is the written Constitution produced by Confederation – the British North American Act; renamed in 1982 the Constitution Act, 1867 – it built on constitutional principles and practices established well before Confederation, and as we shall see, it by no means purported to set out all the important principles of government. In a word, Canada's constitution has been profoundly evolutionary, and so the constitutional theory of another British political philosopher, Edmund Burke, is much more appropriate than that of John Locke.

According to Burke the contract that best ensures good government is an intergenerational contract in which a generation inherits arrangements that have worked tolerably well – in the sense of providing reasonable security, social harmony, and prosperity – and passes on to the next generation its own improvements to that heritage. For a country as complex as Canada, based not on a single people but on several peoples, the Burkean idea of an organic constitutional system working itself out over time has proved eminently more suitable than the Lockean ideal of a single constitutional document expressing the moral beliefs of a single founding people.

Parliamentary government, monarchy, and constitutionalism are the bare beginnings of a civic culture that Canada's founding peoples share. They have evolved over time as they have adapted to changing circumstances and attitudes. And they have been augmented by other practices and institutions such as responsible government, federalism, judicial independence, fundamental social and political rights, and multiculturalism.

But one element of a Canadian civic culture that has taken a very long time for English-speaking Canada to accept is the multinational character of the country. In the next part of this book I examine the efforts of English-speaking Canada as it became the country's majority to build a "one nation" Canada. But first we must address the tragic transition in the status of Amerindian nations in British North America from Britain's allies to marginalized subjects.

PART TWO

Trying to Complete the Conquests

Chapter 5

Three Wars and Three Betrayals
Lead to the Subjugation of
His Majesty's Indian Allies

In August 1794 a ferocious wind storm ripped through the northern Ohio country, felling a stand of tall trees along the Maumee River. On 20 August several hundred native warriors, including Miamis, Shawnees, Delawares, Ottawas, Potawatamis, Winnibegos, and Wyondots, plus seven Loyalist militia from Fort Detroit, crouched behind the fallen timbers, their rifles pointing south, poised to counter the attack of a new American army, the Legion of the United States, under the command of Major General "Mad Anthony" Wayne, advancing northward along the Maumee. They were about to engage in the Battle of the Fallen Timbers, the final battle of the Northwest Indian War.[1]

Most Canadians have never heard of this war. It was provoked by American aggression and British deviousness following the end of the American Revolutionary War in 1783. After the war a priority for the Continental Congress of a bold and victorious United States of America was to occupy all the Indian lands in the northwest, driving the Indians, if necessary, west to the Mississippi and north to Canada. US leaders considered that Britain's cession of these lands removed any obligation to respect native title in the lands north and west of the Ohio River that had been recognized as Indian territory in the 1768 Treaty of Fort Stanwix. The Americans would prefer to absorb the native peoples peacefully into their new republic, but if that proved impossible they were prepared to use military force.

For their part, after the war, the British began to make amends for failing in the peace negotiations to insist on respect for native title in Indian territory. That failure was their first betrayal of their Indian allies after the first of the three wars in which Indian nations fought on the British side. After the Revolutionary War, despite the peace treaty's silence on the matter, Britain took the position that, in ceding the Indian territory north and west of the Ohio River, they had given the United States only the right of pre-emption – that is, the exclusive right to make land cession treaties with Indian nations in that territory. As I reported in the previous chapter, the British hung on to the forts they had taken over from the French in *le pays d'en haut* on the excuse that they were waiting for individual US states to compensate Loyalists for their losses. Not only did Britain hang on to the forts; it garrisoned them and used them as bases for supplying Indians with guns, ammunition, food, and trade goods.[2] In 1793 Governor-in-Chief Lord Dorchester requested John Graves Simcoe, lieutenant-governor of Upper Canada, to build Fort Miami, near present-day Toledo, a mile or two downriver from where the Battle of Fallen Timbers would take place.

British policy-makers in London, and even more so their officers on the ground in British North America, had come to view maintaining a close alliance with the Indian nations of the northwest as essential for the security of Canada. Maintaining this alliance required following a fine line between encouraging the Indians to resist American encroachments, but not doing so in a way that would provoke the outbreak of a full-scale war. The idea of an Indian buffer state between the United States and Canada, extending from the Ohio River north to the Great Lakes and west to the Mississippi, began to garner support among both British officials and Indian leaders. Joseph Brant floated the idea with Governor Haldimand, and when Lord Dorchester took over as governor-in-chief in 1786, he too encouraged officers in the Indian Department in Upper Canada to promote the buffer state idea – but always with the cagey caveat not to push so hard as to get Britain involved in a war against the United States.[3]

Meanwhile Indian nations in the Ohio Territory were forming a military confederacy to resist American encroachment on their lands. They welcomed the material support of the British, but for good reasons were wary of counting on them too much.

Just as the Continental Congress was moving to a more conciliatory Indian policy, native resistance stiffened. In 1789 Indian warriors struck settlements in Kentucky and along the Ohio frontier. The next year full-scale war was under way. The first two engagements were major victories for the United Indian Tribes. In 1790 Miami, Shawnee, Delaware, and Potawatomi warriors repulsed an attack on their villages led by Colonel John Harden, inflicting heavy losses on the Americans. In 1791 Indian warriors led by Shawnee chief Blue Jacket and Miami chief Little Turtle in a battle south of the Wabash defeated an American force led by

Governor Arthur St Clair. American casualties were over a thousand, ten times the Indians' losses.[4]

The Americans now sought peace. Their Indian commissioners were instructed to concede the Indians' "right of soil." The Americans had come over to the British view that, in the northwest, the United States had only the right of pre-emption – the right to purchase lands from Indians willing to sell their land. In 1793 the Indian Confederacy was close to entering into peace talks with the Americans at Sandusky, on Lake Erie. But American unwillingness to commit firmly to honouring the Ohio River boundary agreed to at Fort Stanwix ended the possibility of peace talks. The only alternative now for both sides was war.

These developments convinced President George Washington that the time had come to raise a real army to fight the Indians. He commissioned Major General "Mad Anthony" Wayne, hero of the Revolutionary War, to organize an army of close to five thousand men at Fort Washington (now Cincinnati). On 20 August 1794, a third of that force, including several hundred cavalry led by "Mad Anthony," advanced up the Maumee River towards the Indian warriors, augmented by a few Loyalists, lying in wait south of Fort Miami. Although outnumbered by at least three to one, the Indian warriors acquitted themselves well at the battle of Fallen Timbers. They inflicted greater losses on the Americans than they suffered themselves, but among their dead were a number of chiefs, including eight principal chiefs of the Wyandots and two of the Ottawas. When the warriors fell back to Fort Miami, however, instead of finding sanctuary they found the gates shut in their face.

British policy was suddenly changing. Now that Britain was at war with revolutionary France, it could not afford to be involved in a proxy war with the United States. Later in 1794, under the Jay Treaty, Britain, agreed to abandon all its forts on US territory; Britain's Indian allies, however, received only free passage across the US-Canadian border. Thus ended the second war, with the second betrayal.

A year after the Battle of Fallen Timbers, Shawnee chiefs and their allies negotiated a peace treaty with "Mad Anthony" Wayne at Greenville, Ohio,[5] agreeing to give up their claims to lands in eastern, central, and southern Ohio. In return they would be paid annuities ranging from a few hundred to ten thousand dollars, depending on the size of the community. Notably absent from the Greenville negotiations was a rising young Shawnee chief, Tecumseh.[6]

After the Treaty of Greenville and the handover of the British forts in the northwest in 1796, the United States pushed forward with a new Indian policy of peace and purchase.[7] It was very similar to the policy being pursued by Britain's Indian Department in Upper Canada: acquiring land for settlers by making land purchase treaties with Indians. Although the policy complied with the letter of the 1763 Royal Proclamation, it was a far cry from the understanding conveyed in the 1764 Niagara peace agreement. Peace and purchase meant that, instead of serving as ongoing nation-to-nation agreements on sharing territory, treaties aimed to clear Indians off large parts of their hunting grounds and confine them to small settlements or reserves in the hope they would soon assimilate into mainstream society.

The new American policy was deeply divisive for the First Nations in the Ohio Territory. The Treaty of Greenville opened the floodgates for thousands of settlers to move into the upper reaches of the Ohio Valley. As they moved north and west, there was pressure on Indians still on unceded lands to make land cession treaties. This split tribes such as the Shawnees and Miamis right down the middle. Villages whose leaders were more inclined to accept the white man's ways, including shifting their economy to agriculture, entered into treaties that ceded most of their land in return for an annuity. But other parts of the same nation under anti-assimilationist leadership refused to make treaties, and began to refer to their tribesmen who took treaty as "government Indians."[8]

One such group was the Shawnee village in which Tecumseh and his remarkable younger brother grew up. The younger brother's preaching – he became known as "the Prophet" – had an electrifying affect on native people in the northwest, akin to that of the Delaware prophet Neolin at the time of the Pontiac uprising in 1763. Native people from as far away as the Mississippi and the upper Great Lakes flocked to hear his teaching. By 1808, the Prophet had moved west with many of his disciples to the Indiana Territory, where they established a village that became known as Prophetstown, at the confluence of the Wabash and the Tippecanoe rivers, just south of Lake Michigan. By this time Tecumseh, who had accepted his younger brother's teachings, was well on his way to turning what had begun as a spiritual movement into a political movement. Tecumseh was a born leader, with quiet dignity, enormous energy, and the intelligence of a shrewd political and military strategist. He began visiting native communities along the frontier of American settlement, urging them to join a confederacy that would resist US expansion by establishing their own native American state. Resisting the Long Knives (as Indians referred to Americans) was an easy sell for Tecumseh. It was much more difficult to convince tribes that for centuries had conducted their own affairs to become part of a state – even one that was entirely native.

Tecumseh's effort to build a confederacy of Indian nations became much more significant when the Royal Navy began taking provocative actions against American shipping.[9] Britain's politically insulting and economically damaging actions on the high seas are generally regarded as the main reason for growing anti-British war fever in the United States at the time. But suspicion that Britain was stirring up the Indians on the northwest frontier was, especially for Americans in the western states, becoming an important part of the case for war. The activities of the Prophet and his warrior brother Tecumseh fuelled these concerns. By 1811 a party of "War Hawks," made up of western and southern Republicans, had become the most powerful group in Congress, and pressed for the annexation of Canada, virtually as a divine right: "the Author of Nature has marked our limits in the south, by the Gulf of Mexico; and in the north, by the regions of eternal frost." Whether it was manifest destiny or simply a strategic need for security in the country's northwest, the idea of taking Canada by invading it at its weakest point of defence along the western border of Upper Canada was gathering strength in the United States.

The Americans had reason to be concerned about the threat the British-Indian alliance posed to their security in the northwest. In that fateful year, 1807, Sir James Craig, the new governor-in-chief of British North America, received "secret instructions" from London to refurbish Britain's alliance with the Indian nations.[10] Craig wasted no time passing the word down the line to Upper Canada's lieutenant-governor, Sir Francis Gore, to have the Indian Department polish up the chain of friendship with His Majesty's Indian allies south and west of the Canadian border.

At this time the Indian Department, headed by Sir John Johnson, Sir William's son, employed a number of agents who, like the Johnson family, had strong connections with Indian communities in the United States. Besides the Indian Department's agents, there were hundreds of English and Scottish fur traders in le pays d'en haut who, like the French coureurs de bois before them, had taken Indian wives and maintained close ties with Indian communities. These British agents, official and unofficial, worked their Indian networks with great success. Again, as instructed, they conveyed that cagey British message: we remain your allies, we support your resistance to American encroachments on your lands, and we will supply you with arms and ammunition when the time comes to fight the Americans, but that time is not now, so please don't start a war with the Americans until we are ready.

In the autumn of 1808, over five thousand chiefs and warriors of Indian nations in the US northwest came to Amherstburg, south of present-day Windsor, answering the call to renew the alliance with the British Crown.[11] Among them was Tecumseh, who made a strong impression as the emerging leader of a native confederacy. Two years later Tecumseh returned to Amherstburg, this time leading two thousand Shawnee, Sauk, Winnebago, Ottawa, and Potawatomi warriors. He announced to the Indian Department officials that the tribes he could speak for "are now determined to defend it [our country] ourselves, and after raising you on your feet leave you behind but expecting you will press forward towards us what might be necessary to supply our wants."[12] The British were now scrambling to hold back His Majesty's Indian allies.

The Americans were thoroughly aroused about the danger of attack on their northwest frontier – none more than William Harrison, governor of Indiana Territory. In the fall of 1811, with Tecumseh away in the south on a recruiting mission, Harrison saw a promising opportunity to strike at the heart of the Indian Confederacy. With a force of about a thousand, Harrison advanced up the east bank of the Wabash, crossed over to the west bank, and encamped within a mile of Prophetstown, where the Wabash meets the Tippecanoe. The Indians succeeded in breaking into the American compound and came close to killing Governor Harrison, but the US soldiers rallied and drove the Indians back. The next day, when Harrison and his army marched into Prophetstown, they found the village deserted.[13] The Prophet, his followers, and warriors had disappeared into the forests to the north and west.

Harrison, a politician to the core, did all he could to weave the myth of his great "victory" over the Indians at Tippecanoe into American history. Thirty years later, when he ran successfully for the presidency of the United States, his slogan was "Tippecanoe and Tyler too" (John Tyler was his vice-presidential running mate). Harrison died a month after his inauguration, but the myth of his victory at Tippecanoe lives on. And it is a myth: no side won at Tippecanoe, and both sides suffered only minor losses. Tecumseh's warriors returned to their villages, but it would not take long for the Shawnee chief to restore the confederacy's military force and have it ready to fight along side the British when the United States declared war on Britain on 18 June 1812.

For the third time Indian nations went to war as allies of the British Crown. But not all of them. Some remained neutral, and some Six Nations communities – in particular, Oneida, Senecas, and Tuscaroras, who had remained in New York, although forced onto small reserves – fought on the American side. Indeed the Americans began to recruit them when they saw how valuable Indians were to the British defenders of Canada.[14]

Tecumseh's confederacy was in from the start. When the war began, the Grand River Six Nations were divided. Some of them still collected American annuities for land they had sold in the United States and maintained family ties with American Iroquois communities. They also were divided ideologically over whether they should engage in private real estate transactions or adhere strictly to the Royal Proclamation policy of selling land only to the Crown. Once the drums of war began beating, however, their warrior tradition and the possibility of a native state in the northwest brought them around to renewing their alliance with the Crown enthusiastically.[15] Even the Mississaugas along the Lake Ontario shore – who had entered into land treaties with the British, were deeply embittered by the way the British had excluded them from land they were deemed to have surrendered, and outraged by the brutal murder of their chief, Wabakinine, by two British soldiers[16] – contributed several hundred warriors to the defence of Canada, as did other Ojibwa.

Further east, warriors of the Seven Nations, a confederacy of some Algonquian nations with Mohawks and other Iroquois peoples who had moved north in the eighteenth century to be closer to Catholic missions in the Montreal area, added considerable strength to the British forces that turned back American attempts to invade Canada at Châteauguay and at Lacolle, in the Eastern Townships of Lower Canada. Thirty warriors from Tyendinaga, John Deseronto's small Mohawk reserve on the Bay of Quinte, were part of the force that blocked the Americans' advance into Canada at the crucial battle of Crysler's Farm, near Morrisburg, on the banks of the St Lawrence in Upper Canada.[17]

Across the US northwest all the way over to the Mississippi, Indian nations were defending their homeland, and so naturally allied with the British. The first allied victory of the War of 1812 was the capture on 15 July 1812 of Fort Michilimackinac, on Mackinac Island, in the jaws of Lake Michigan. The presence of four hundred Indians in the attacking forces persuaded the American commander to surrender the heavily manned fort without firing a shot.[18] The capture of Michilimackinac was of great strategic importance: it gave the British control of the upper Great Lakes and the main transportation links to the US and Canadian northwest. News of its capture would quickly have a demoralizing impact on the American side.

On the heels of the capture of Michilimackinac came the capture of an even larger American fort, Detroit. The taking of Detroit was a remarkable operation in which Tecumseh and his confederacy of native warriors played a crucial role. The fortified town, mostly inhabited by French settlers, was the Americans' gateway to Canada. It is the place that ex-president Thomas Jefferson must have had in mind when he said that taking Canada would be "a mere matter of marching." And sure enough, in the opening month of the war, the Americans sent Brigadier General William Hull, governor of the Michigan Territory, with a regiment of US soldiers and three regiments of militia, to bolster the American forces at Detroit and launch an invasion of Canada. On 17 July Hull's army crossed the Detroit River and landed at Sandwich, on the Canadian side, without encountering resistance. Hull proudly announced to the settler community, many of whom had arrived only recently from the United States, that by receiving him peacefully they "will be emancipated from Tyranny and oppression and restored to the dignity of freemen."[19] But he added a stern warning: "No white man fighting on the side of an Indian will be taken prisoner." Whites fighting in alliance with Indians were considered by many Americans to be guilty of racial treason, punishable by death.

Hull's invasion was short-lived. News that General Isaac Brock's flotilla, carrying British regulars, Canadian militia, and Mohawk warriors, was nearing Fort Malden, coupled with news that Fort Michilimackinac had fallen and that the hitherto neutral Wyandot community around Detroit had come over to the Canadian side, convinced a dithering General Hull to turn tail and take his army back to Detroit. When Tecumseh and Brock met at Fort Malden, it was a case of respect at first sight.[20] Tecumseh, famously, turned to his men and said, "Here is a man." Brock said of the Shawnee chief, "a more sagacious or gallant Warrior does not I believe exist." They immediately plotted a strategy for capturing Fort Detroit, the key to which was Tecumseh's crossing the Detroit River with six hundred warriors – mainly Shawnees, Miamis, Delawares, Potawatamis, and Wyandot – and tricking the Americans into thinking they had three times that number. When the British cannon finally found the range and landed a ball inside the fort, General Hull, never a tower of courage, had had enough. The white flag went up, and Brock came forward to negotiate the surrender. [21]

The Americans surrendered twenty-two hundred men, large quantities of weapons, a brig in Lake Erie, and all of the Michigan Territory. Over five hundred US soldiers were sent as prisoners of war on the long trip to Quebec. General Hull was court-martialled and sentenced to be shot, but was saved by President Madison's grant of mercy. The capture of Detroit was the biggest single British victory of the war. It secured Canada's western frontier and lifted the morale of Canadians. Also, it was news of this victory that convinced the Six Nations at Grand River to commit four hundred warriors to the British cause.

The Six Nations warriors were sorely needed to bolster British forces on the Niagara frontier from Fort Erie to Burlington Heights, where the most intense fighting of the war was taking place. Over the better part of two years, the fortunes of war ebbed and flowed as both sides fought for control of this border area. It was here that the Americans made their strongest effort to take Canada. Britain's and Canada's native allies played a crucial role in this campaign. At Queenston Heights, where Brock fell in October 1812, the whooping and hollering of Six Nations warriors led by John Norton terrorized the American soldiers, many of whom chose to jump over the steep embankment of the Niagara River gorge rather than submit to the Indians' tomahawks (the Indians were actually armed with muskets).[22] In April 1813 American forces occupied York, the capital of Upper Canada, as British regulars under Major General Roger Sheaffe blew up the magazine at Fort York, abandoned the town, and fled eastward along the Kingston Road. The Americans were deterred from penetrating beyond York's few blocks, however, by the war dances of Mississauga and other Ojibwa families encamped behind the town making "the cedar woods echo with many savage yells."[23] And in June 1813 it was an ambush staged by five hundred native warriors, more than Laura Secord and her cow, that enabled British forces to win the Battle of Beaver Dams, a turning point in the Niagara frontier campaign.

While the British forces were holding their own on the Niagara frontier, they suffered a severe setback at the southwest edge of the colony. In September 1813 US naval forces won a decisive battle on Lake Erie. This meant they could land troops on the Canadian side of the lake and cut off the British and their Indian allies at Forts Malden and Detroit from allied forces to the east. Anticipating this, the British officer in charge, Major General Henry Proctor, persuaded a reluctant Tecumseh that their forces needed to withdraw into Upper Canada along the Thames River. An American army under the command of William Harrison – the same William Harrison of Tippecanoe fame – followed them somewhat cautiously. When the advancing Americans reached Moraviatown, near present-day Chatham, the British forces, with the Indians on their right flank, turned to face the enemy. The battle was rather perfunctory.[24] After a few exchanges of fire, Proctor decided he was outgunned and that it would be best to withdraw and join the main British force at Burlington. Tecumseh and his men, however, fought on alone, for their homeland. Tecumseh was killed, and the Indians withdrew, as did Harrison, who preferred the safety of Detroit to the risky business of occupying the Canadian southwest.

A very different story unfolded in the northwest, where Robert McDouall, the new British commander at Michilimackinac, leading an army made up mostly of Indians and fur traders, repulsed the US effort to advance up the Mississippi and beyond to the Red River in Rupert's Land.[25] Taking the Americans by surprise, McDouall's force had a relatively easy time capturing Fort Selby, which the Americans had built to protect the village of Prairie du Chien. Sauk, Fox, and Kickapoo warriors blocked an American relief column coming upriver from St Louis. Later in the summer, a larger alliance, including Sioux and Winnebago and led by the great Sauk chief Black Hawk, turned back an American force led by Major Zachary Taylor, another future US president. By the autumn of 1814 the Americans had been swept back to St Louis by a force largely made up of Indians and fur traders. At the end of the War of 1812, for the Indian nations of the far northwest, an independent Indian territory was not a dream; it was a reality.

While all this fighting was going on in the northwest and other theatres, American and British diplomats were gathering at Ghent, then an independent Flemish city, to negotiate the terms of peace. In London, both in Parliament and at the popular level, there was considerable support for the Indians having an independent state in the northwest. Britain's representatives certainly put the proposal on the negotiating table as one of their priorities. They rolled out a map showing the quarter of a million square miles – 15 per cent of then-US territory – they proposed the United States and Britain guarantee as an independent state.[26] The American envoys, John Quincy Adams and Henry Clay, argued that the Indians were neither civilized nor independent, and so could not have a state; besides, they had been given no instructions from Washington on the issue. The British negotiators eventually were instructed to back down. On Christmas Eve 1814 they reluctantly signed a draft treaty that recognized the *status quo ante bellum*: borders would remain as they were before the war; any captured territory would be returned. The only reference to the Indians was in Article XI of the Treaty of Ghent, which called for the cessation of all hostilities against "Indian tribes or nations" and the restoration of "all possessions, rights and privileges" they enjoyed before the war. Article XI at least recognized the Indians as distinct and separate nations. But it fell well short of recognizing the independent homeland that His Majesty's Indian allies had fought for. The third war ended with a third betrayal.

After the War of 1812 Indian nations in Upper Canada found their situation had fundamentally changed. No longer was Britain's Indian Department diplomatically courting them to fight the Americans. Instead of plotting military strategy with their military allies, the Indians found themselves on the receiving end of British policy. It is essential to note that this change in the Indians' situation was not effected through any formal constitutional document. No colonial authority gathered the tribes together and told them they were now all subjects of the Crown. These nations had not been conquered. They had not lost any war. But more and more they were treated not as His Majesty's Allies, but as wards of the colony.

To be sure, the Indians were treated as a distinct category of the population separate from the white settlers. Their governmental relations continued to be primarily with the Indian Department, which reported to imperial headquarters in London, rather than with the government of the colony. But the head office officials who directed the department were in a penny-pinching mode, cutting back severely on its expenditures now that the Indians were no longer essential to the empire's security. The Indian Department, representing the Crown, continued to negotiate land purchase treaties with Indian nations in Upper Canada through a treaty process that implicitly recognized the Indigenous nations' independence and ownership of their lands. After all, the Crown did not make treaties with its subjects or purchase land from peoples who did not own it.

These land cession treaties were flawed by the fundamental inequality of the parties.[27] The Indians no longer had the option of walking away from the negotiations and threatening to resume military hostilities. Their bargaining position was further weakened by their desperate material circumstances and their lack of knowledge of the white man's legal culture. No longer in receipt of the Crown's largesse, with greatly diminished resources from their hunting grounds inundated by the incoming flood of settlers, and continuing to experience the devastating and bewildering impact of disease, many native communities were poor and hungry. The promise of an annual payment of cash or goods and a reserve of land where they could make a fresh start free of settler encroachments was difficult to resist. It is clear that the Indians did not understand that the off-reserve lands, always by far the lion's share of their lands according to the white man's understanding of the treaties, were being sold to the Crown and forever alienated from them. The rhetoric of the Crown's negotiator employed phrases such as "as long as the rivers flow and the sun rises" to assure the Indians that they would be able to pursue their traditional economic pursuits on the lands they were agreeing to *share* with the white man. As native communities quickly discovered, these vast tracts of their traditional country that they were deemed to have "surrendered" would be turned into settlers' farms and towns from which they would be excluded.

The Huron Treaty of 1827 is an example of the inequity of these treaties.[28] The Indian Department was anxious to settle southwest Ontario, the area the Americans had invaded in 1813, in order to secure the border with the United States. After nine years of negotiations through which the Crown's offer kept being reduced, Chippewa chiefs, at Amherstburg, put their marks on a treaty whereby the Crown took over 2.1 million acres in the southwest corner of Upper Canada. In return the Chippewa got four postage-stamp reserves near Sarnia and along the shore of Lake Huron, amounting to less than 1 per cent of their total territory, plus an annual payment of £1,100 in goods, not cash. There was provision to reduce the annuity if the native population declined, but no commitment to increase it if the population grew – which is what happened when Loyalist Potawatomi from Michigan were crowded into the reserves.

The Indian Department lacked the means, and perhaps the will, to enforce the treaties. The earliest treaties were virtually impossible to enforce in any case because of their extremely sloppy and imprecise nature. For instance, through the "Gunshot Treaty" of 1787, in return for agreeing to pay annual gifts to a group of Mississaugas, the British acquired rights to land along the shore of Lake Ontario from the Bay of Quinte to just east of present-day Toronto and extending north as far as the sound of a gun could carry.[29] Even when the boundaries of lands reserved exclusively for Indians were well delineated, settlers would ignore treaty rights and squat on the land. The land ceded by the Mississaugas to the Crown and then granted by the Crown to Joseph Brant's Six Nations people along the Grand River was particularly prone to this kind of squatting. Official inquiries and dubious attempts to purchase the land illegally occupied by settlers resolved very little, leaving a legacy of unsettled land issues, many of which remain unsettled to the present day.

It is remarkable how Upper Canada's First Nations, despite what must have been deep disappointment in their treatment, retained a fundamental loyalty to the Crown. When rebellion broke out in 1837, Ojibwa allies from Lake Huron and Lake Simcoe joined local militia in protecting the Yonge Street transportation route from Toronto to Penetanguishene. About a hundred Six Nations warriors volunteered to serve in a militia regiment under the command of Sir William Johnson's grandson, William Johnson Kerr.[30] Indians retained their respect for their Great White Father and later their Great White Mother, but had little or none for the settler politicians who were coming to play an ever-greater role in the colony's government.

Although a single Indian Department reported to imperial headquarters in London, there was no unified Indian policy for the North American colonies. In Lower Canada and the Atlantic colonies, land purchase treaties were not used to acquire land for settlement. This was so even though the British had entered into treaty relations with Indian nations in these areas well before the American Revolution. Building on earlier treaties in New England, in 1760 the British entered into a series of negotiations with Maliseet, Mi'kmaq, and Passamaquoddy communities across what is now New Brunswick and Nova Scotia. The treaty agreements resulting from these negotiations dealt with peace and friendship matters, including the exchange of prisoners and the continuation of trading relations, but not with the sale of land. As Loyalist settlers poured into the region, the requirement under British law to purchase land through treaties with their native owners was ignored. Native communities were simply pushed out of the way to areas less desirable or less accessible to settlers. Eventually these First Nations settlements would be recognized as "reservations," based not on treaty provisions, but on Orders in Council setting aside the lands to be held in trust for the Indians. In Prince Edward Island a private benefactor set aside land for a Mi'kmaq reserve.[31]

Perhaps the absence of any security threat from the United States accounts for the failure of colonial administrators to adhere to their own law in Lower Canada and the Atlantic colonies. The British also used the argument that, since the French, unlike the English, had never recognized native title or entered into land cession treaties with native peoples, they had in effect extinguished native title, so when Britain took over New France (including Acadia), it had no need to purchase land from the Indians. This was a bogus argument. France, following Champlain's vision of building a partnership with native peoples, never purported to extinguish native ownership. As I pointed out in Chapter 3, the sovereignty France claimed over the territory of New France was aimed at excluding other European powers from having commercial or diplomatic relations with the native peoples in the territory. It was not a claim to rule over the Indian nations as subject peoples. Besides, if the British really believed that France had extinguished the native peoples' ownership of their lands, why did they negotiate land cession treaties with Indian nations in Upper Canada that had also been part of New France and Quebec?

Further evidence of the incoherence of Britain's Indian policy is the establishment in 1849 of its first colony on the west coast, on Vancouver Island. Although the colony's practical rationale was to act as a fur-trading post, the British government also contemplated bringing in settlers, but without making any effort to acquire land for settlement from the island's native inhabitants. Richard Blanchard, the colony's first governor, appeared to have received no instructions as to the rights of native peoples, and indeed "regarded the Indians as essentially irrational."[32] Suspecting Indians of having murdered two company seamen, he led a naval expedition to the top of Vancouver Island, where he destroyed a Newitty village as retribution. His successor, James Douglas, chief factor of the Hudson's Bay Company trading post at Fort Victoria, at least appreciated the crucial importance of establishing friendly relations with native peoples. Douglas entered into fourteen treaties with First Nations on Vancouver Island to acquire land for the British settlers who were beginning to trickle into the colony. However, the direction he received from London was based not on the Royal Proclamation of 1763, but on a very limited mid-nineteenth-century view that Indigenous peoples' ownership of land was limited to the sites where they had villages and enclosed fields. The benefits the Indians received by ceding lands through these treaties were minimal: mainly a few blankets and the reservation of small bits of land for their own purposes.[33] As government in the colony became responsive to the settler population that built up quickly on Vancouver Island and the British Columbia mainland, and as the importance of the fur trade waned, there was virtually no official or popular support for recognizing the rights of native peoples as they were understood when Britain made peace with the Indian nations many years earlier in the eastern part of the continent.

At this time, between the west coast and the Canadas, the only British settlement was Lord Selkirk's tiny band of Scottish Highlanders at Red River, on lands purchased from the Hudson's Bay Company. Although the vast territory of Rupert's Land covered by the charter granted the Company in 1670 was classified under the legal fictions of European law as "conquered territory" or "settled territory," any proprietary rights to the soil were "subject to subsisting aboriginal interests, along with the exclusive right to extinguish such interests by cession or purchase."[34] Before Confederation the Aboriginal peoples with hunting grounds in this territory remained not only unconquered, but, except for trading relations with the Hudson's Bay Company, unconnected to Britain.

The failure of the British government and its administrators in the colonies to respect the rights of native peoples did not escape the notice of Parliament, which, in 1836, set up a select committee to undertake an intensive inquiry into the treatment of Indigenous peoples in Britain's colonies.[35] By this time an Aboriginal Protection Society was active in Britain and, together with the Anti-Slavery Society, the Church Mission Society, and a network of Christian and liberal forces, was able to get concerns about the mistreatment of Aboriginal peoples before a Parliament increasingly committed to the idea that imperialism must be animated by a spirit of liberal benevolence. The select committee sought reports from colonial governments in British North America, and in New South Wales and South Australia. Some, including those in Nova Scotia and New Brunswick, refused to report. Nonetheless the committee received evidence of the mistreatment of native people in British North America, including the extinction of the Beothuk in Newfoundland. The committee rapped the knuckles of those responsible for their unjust and, indeed, illegal treatment of native peoples, but not much more came of it.

Here we meet an iron law of British colonialism: policy-makers in the imperial capital were always far more sensitive than settlers to the rights and interests of native peoples. The settlers experienced first hand the clash of their interests, especially in relation to land, with native peoples' interests, and of their culture with that of the native peoples. Settlers on the ground tended to see respect for native peoples' rights and the accommodation of difference as luxuries that only those in the home country, unfamiliar with the realities of life on the colonial frontier, could afford. A "settler colonialism" thus emerged in British North America, Australia, and New Zealand in the nineteenth century that was much tougher and less liberal in relations with Indigenous peoples than were the official policy and law of the empire.[36] And British imperial policy-makers, still smarting from the loss of the American colonies, were reluctant to interfere with the emergent democracies of English-speaking settlers. This meant that transitioning from imperial control to responsible government in the settler colonies was bad news for native peoples.

We can see this policy shift working itself out in the colonies that would form the Dominion of Canada. In the early 1800s local initiatives in Indian policy came largely from religious organizations. Churches and mission societies in Upper Canada hoped that, by converting Indian communities from hunting and gathering to an agricultural economy, they could convert them to Christianity. There was a long tradition of this kind of Christian colonialism in New France, some of which survived into the British regime. For instance, the *Articles of Capitulation of Montreal* promised the Iroquoian and Algonquin peoples who had settled on lands near the seminary of St-Sulpice, just west of Montreal, that they could remain on their lands except for those areas that had been formally surrendered to the Crown. Christian colonialism proceeded with the consent of native peoples, and in that sense respected their political independence. But it also had its downside. For First Nations it could be very divisive, separating Christian converts from native traditionalists, and sometimes involving a battle for souls among competing Christian denominations.[37] A lot of the latter was inflicted on native communities in Upper Canada. Also, an assimilationist purpose underlay Christian efforts to help native peoples. Christians of this era assumed they had a lock on religious truth, and consequently lacked respect for Amerindians' spiritual traditions and were intolerant of their spiritual pluralism.

By the 1830s the Indian Department's activities in Upper Canada had changed from a military to a civil administration in which the initiative in policy-making passed to local authorities. This meant that Indian policy was directed by the colony's lieutenant-governor, who was largely unaccountable to the Legislative Assembly and totally unversed in the law and practice of relations with native peoples. The worst example was Sir Francis Bond Head, who served in the viceregal office from 1836 to 1838 and whose only credential was his service as a Poor Law commissioner in England. The constitutional historian W.P.M. Kennedy comments that Bond Head's regime was "almost tragic in its fatuity."[38] Bond Head got it into his head that Indigenous peoples could not be "civilized" through Christianity and farming, so they should be pushed north out of Upper Canada's fertile farmland to Manitoulin Island, where they could carry on their traditional life in isolation and eventually fade into oblivion.[39] This resulted in a number of Ojibwa communities being pushed off lands they were farming successfully to the rocky terrain of the Laurentian Shield.[40]

Following Bond Head, Upper Canada – and later, the United Colony of Canada – launched a number of inquiries into the "Indian problem." Lieutenant-governors, backed by popular sentiment, were now strongly committed to a policy of "civilization." Indians on reserves needed protection from the bad influences and encroachments of settlers while they were prepared for the transition to civilized society. The last of these commissions, chaired by Richard Pennefather, mapped out a strategy for achieving "civilization" that was quickly translated into law by the 1857 Act to Encourage the Gradual Civilization of the Indian Tribes in this Province. Under the Act, voluntary "enfranchisement" – that is, freedom from Indian status – was available to an Indian male considered by a board of examiners to be of good character. The enfranchised Indian could detach fifty acres of reserve land for his private use and settle there with his wife and children.[41] The legislation was thoroughly – and wrongly – patriarchal in its assumptions about native societies.

Although the Gradual Civilization Act applied only in the United Colony of Canada, it was clearly the precursor of the post-Confederation Indian Act that would apply to all Indians in Canada. It ignored the rights of Indigenous peoples recognized in the 1764 Treaty of Niagara; instead, in the words of legal historian Sydney Harring, "it defined an inferior legal status for Indians, creating a system of legal dualism, denying them the franchise, and placing them in a distinct legal category, under the paternalistic protection of the government."[42] Thus was accomplished the political subjugation of the peoples who were His Majesty's Indian allies – in the white man's law. In the twenty years between the Gradual Civilization Act and the Indian Act, only one Indian, Elias Hill, opted for enfranchisement – a strong indication of what the peoples of the unconquered Indigenous nations thought of the white man's freedom.[43]

Chapter 6

Rebellions and the Plan
to Assimilate French Canada

"The Province must be converted into an English Colony or it will be lost to England."[1] These are the words of Jonathan Sewell, the chief justice of Lower Canada from 1803 to 1838. Sewell was no bigot. He was a liberal-minded Loyalist lawyer who, after coming to Quebec in 1789, became fluent in French and acquired a "mastery of French law," which helped earn him appointment as attorney general in 1796.[2] (I should add that he is yet another great-great-great-grandfather of my wife, on her mother's side.) What was primarily on Chief Justice Sewell's mind, as the last words in the quote indicate, was the French majority's growing nationalism and the fear it would lead to a break with Britain.

Back in Guy Carleton's day, the slightest indication of a sense of nationalism among the *habitants* sent shivers down the spines of British officials in Quebec. But the concessions made through the Quebec Act seemed to be rewarded when, at the time of the American Revolution, the *Canadiens* spurned American blandishments to be "conquered into freedom." Colonial officials thought that reorganizing Quebec as Lower Canada (1791), thereby giving the French Canadians a popular assembly, might be the icing on the cake. A grateful people, it was hoped, would receive the gift of representative government "with profound respect" and, "having done so, would seek union with Upper Canada."[3]

The very opposite happened. The French Canadians used Lower Canada's elected Legislative Assembly as a platform to secure and advance the interests of their nation. This horrified the British officials and alienated many members of the province's English minority. The flaw in the new system of government introduced by the 1791 Constitutional Act – giving the majority a representative institution but excluding it from the executive branch of government – exacerbated the situation. The French majority had voice but no power, no share in the responsibility of governing. The English governed, the French protested. This was a recipe for the ethnic conflict that eventually erupted in violent rebellion.

The context in which these events unfolded was the age of nationalism. The French Revolution lit the flame of democratic nationalism. As Hans Kohn put it, "The absolute sovereignty of the king was replaced, as the Revolution progressed, by the absolute sovereignty of the people."[4] And the people formed the nation. The force of that ideology – one people, one nation, one state – which in the early decades of the nineteenth century was stirring popular uprisings against imperial powers in Europe, would now be felt in Canada. This kind of nationalism – on both the English and French sides – was the underlying driving force behind the battle that was now to take place, in Lord Durham's memorable phrase, between "two nations warring in the bosom of a single state"[5] and the attempt to settle that battle by the absorption of one nation into the other.

The French majority's determination to use its majority in the Legislative Assembly to secure its people's interests was evident from the Assembly's very first meeting, when it used its numbers (a majority of thirty-four to sixteen) to elect a French-speaking speaker, Jean-Antoine Panet. The French party – for that is what it was becoming – followed this up by carrying a motion that gave the French language the same status as English in the records and publications of the Assembly and, in effect, established French as the language of debate.

The *Canadiens'* leaders in the Assembly quickly learned the "power of the purse" – the classic role of the popular house in the British parliamentary tradition to supply the Crown with the moneys needed to run the government. But Britain was not prepared to grant the popular assemblies of its colonies in British North America the control over government revenues and expenditures that the House of Commons exercised in the mother country. The Assembly could try to exercise its control over public spending by voting supply, but the governor had direct access to Crown revenues from the sale of lands and other commissions, and to the proceeds from custom duties and licences under the Quebec Act. Nor did the governor concede the Assembly's right to control public expenditures. Besides, anything passed by the French-dominated elected Assembly was almost certain to be rejected by the

English-dominated appointed Legislative Council. So ethnic conflict frequently resulted in fiscal paralysis.

By the early 1800s the battle between the English party and the French (or Canadian party) was spilling over into public life outside the legislative chambers. In 1804 the English party established the *Quebec Mercury*, "the first bone fide party organ in provincial history."[6] An early issue of the *Mercury* proclaimed that "This province is already too French for a British colony ... Whether we are at peace or war, it is essential that we should make every effort, by every means available, to oppose the growth of the French and their influence."[7] The Canadian party responded by establishing *Le Canadien*. At first relatively moderate in tone, it concentrated on defending the French against their English enemies, rather than attacking the British government. The new journal's motto, *"Notre langue, nos institutions et nos lois,"* captured the traditionalism in the nationalist aspirations of French Canadians.[8]

British officials, at head office in London and on the ground in Canada, did not have a clue about how to manage the emergence of a strong sense of French-Canadian nationalism. When Sir James Craig arrived in Quebec in 1807 as governor, his reaction was that of a military man. He feared the French Canadians were waiting for a victory of Napoleon over the British and would possibly support an American invasion of Lower Canada. Craig resorted to force to control French Canada, inaugurating what some historians refer to as "the reign of terror." He had a number of the leaders of the Canadian party dismissed as militia officers; later, on the pretext of irregularities, he prorogued the Legislative Assembly. In 1810 he seized the press of *Le Canadien* and jailed its printer and principal editors, including Pierre Bédard, a leading member of the Assembly.[9] Craig's "reign of terror," instead of having its intended result, fanned the flames of French-Canadian nationalism.

Craig's successor, Sir George Prévost, arrived just in time to shift to a more conciliatory approach that helped to ensure French Canada's loyalty and support for the British cause in the War of 1812. Among other things, Prévost restored the Canadian militia officers whom Craig had cashiered, and not only released the *Le Canadien* editors and writers from prison, but made Pierre Bédard a judge. Prévost was followed by an equally conciliatory governor, Sir John Sherbrooke. But by this time the French Canadians' position in the Assembly was hardening. In 1819 the Assembly refused to support a permanent "civil list" guaranteeing remuneration for senior officials, including judges. Instead it now insisted on going carefully through all the estimates, even reducing salaries and censuring officials.

The toughening of the French party's position in the Assembly had much to do with the emergence of Louis-Joseph Papineau as its leader. Papineau was first elected to the Assembly in 1812 at the age of twenty-six. Three years later he was elected speaker; but for one short intermission, he held that position for the next twenty-two years, until the outbreak of the rebellion. He turned down Sherbrooke's offer of a position on the Executive Council, choosing to exercise his leadership of the Canadian party by remaining speaker of the Assembly. In his early years of leadership, Papineau's focus was mainly that of a constitutionalist, insisting on the Assembly's having the same powers the House of Commons exercised under the British constitution. But then the English party made a move that would remove any trust Papineau might have had in British rule and turn him into a rebel.

In June 1822 the under-secretary for the colonies introduced a bill in the House of Commons to unite the legislatures of the provinces of Lower and Upper Canada. The bill was primarily the work of the English party in Lower Canada and its supporters in Britain. John Richardson, leader of the English party and a member of Lower Canada's Legislative Council, through his uncle, Edward Ellice, an MP in the British House of Commons with large commercial interests in Lower Canada – he had brought a *seigneurie* and had interests in the Northwest Company – persuaded Colonial Office officials that the only way to break the political deadlock in Lower Canada was to reunite the two Canadas.[10] Each section of the reunited province would have sixty members in the assembly, but a clause empowering the governor general to establish new counties in the Eastern Townships and to add their representatives to the new assembly was designed to ensure that French representatives would be in a minority.[11] The bill's assimilationist objective was evident in clauses that required Roman Catholic priests to obtain the governor's written consent to collect tithes, and that made English the only official language of the Legislative Council and Legislative Assembly, eliminating French as a language of debate within fifteen years.

As soon as news of the Union bill reached Lower Canada, a storm of public meetings erupted. French Canadians, in the words of historian Alfred Decelles, saw in the bill "a menace to their national existence."[12] Papineau and John Neilson, a Scottish immigrant who had become editor of the bilingual *Quebec Gazette* and a strong supporter of the

Canadian party's constitutional position, were appointed agents to go to London to fight the bill. This they did – successfully. With the help of James Mackintosh, a prominent Whig MP, they managed to get the Union bill withdrawn. The Tories, it turned out, did not relish a major parliamentary debate over the Canadian question. A Canada Trade Act was passed that set out a way of dividing customs duties between the two Canadas that protected Upper Canada's interests. For the time being the plan to merge the two Canadas was dropped.[13]

The Union bill, though aborted, deeply affected French Canada's political leaders, none more so than Papineau. After that episode, even though he had been well received in the imperial capital, Papineau moved steadily away from working for reform within the existing constitutional system and towards a complete break with Britain. The party he led in the Assembly became known as the *Patriotes*. Driving their politics was an increasingly strident French-Canadian nationalism.

Like virtually all nationalist movements, French Canada's surge of nationalism was led by middle-class politicians. Papineau himself was a lawyer, and most of the *Patriote* leaders in the Assembly were lawyers, notaries, doctors, or surveyors. It is men of this kind who acquire the literary and oratorical skills needed to mobilize the masses. The social and economic vision of these middle-class nationalists was not that of a developing commercial society, but that of the traditional and very distinctive agricultural society of historic Quebec.[14] This meant using their power in the Assembly to protect the seigneurial system and their ancient civil law, *le coutume de Paris*. The myth at the centre of French-Canadian nationalism right up to the time of the Quiet Revolution in the 1960s was traditionalist: the preservation of a socially conservative, highly Catholic, largely agricultural and rural society. This nationalism was fuelled by the economic collapse of the traditional agricultural economy. The farming lands along the St Lawrence had been badly managed and could no longer support a rapidly expanding French-Canadian population. Meanwhile, lumbering, shipbuilding, and commercial trading were coming on strong, but were dominated by the English. The *habitants* felt excluded from these new sources of economic progress, and were thus susceptible to nationalist rhetoric that gave their economic plight an ethnic spin: their declining circumstances were caused by the flood of English immigrants arriving in their province. Fernand Ouellet reports that, between 1815 and 1840, four hundred thousand immigrants arrived at the ports of Lower Canada.[15] Most were just passing through on their way to Upper Canada and the

United States. But many stayed, and made their presence felt by purchasing *seigneuries*, settling in the Eastern Townships, and becoming
the dominant elites in the cities of Montreal and Quebec.

The nationalism of Papineau and the *Patriotes* also had its progressive side: they were very strong democrats. Despite the conservatism
of the classical education they received from clergy in the seminaries
and colleges of the province, they were exposed to the ideas of Montes-
quieu, Rousseau, and other writers of the European Enlightenment.
The Ninety-Two Resolutions the *Patriote* leadership introduced in the
Assembly in 1834 bristle with the surging democratic spirit of the era.
The thirty-seventh resolution identifies the *Patriotes* with the party of
"liberals, constitutionalists, republicans, whigs, reformers, radicals and
similar appellations" that "overspreads all America." The *Patriotes'* opponents, on the other hand, are portrayed as aligned with a party of
"serviles, royalists, tories and conservatives" that is "on this continent,
without any weight or influence except what it derives from its
European supporters, and from a trifling number of persons who become their dependents for the sake of personal gain."[16]

Among the democratic reforms the Ninety-Two Resolutions called
for were an elected upper house (the Legislative Council) and the elected Assembly's full control over the province's finances. Although the
resolutions complained about the underrepresentation of the French
majority among the province's salaried officials, it is interesting to note
that they did not put forward the principle of responsible government
as the solution to Lower Canada's undemocratic governance. This
might reflect Papineau's propensity for opposition and his reluctance
to participate in the government of a British imperial regime he had
come fundamentally to distrust. On the one occasion he was offered a
position in the Executive Council, he refused the invitation, and he for-
bade assembly members to accept government posts.[17]

The hardening of the French party's position under Papineau's leadership began to win concessions from the British government. A new
school of imperialism that believed Britain's interests were most effectively advanced through peaceful means, trade, and overseas investment
was beginning to take hold in London.[18] From a strategic perspective,
Britain's North American colonies were most important as a check on
American expansion, and the greatest threat to those interests was the
latent disloyalty of the French Canadians.

The conciliatory shift in policy began with a House of Commons
committee that confirmed French Canadians' continued enjoyment of

their religion, laws, and privileges.[19] Baron Matthew Aylmer became
Lower Canada's governor in 1830, with instructions to proceed with a
conciliatory policy. Aylmer recruited French Canadians for both the
Executive Council and the Legislative Council, agreed to strengthen
judicial independence by removing all judges (except Chief Justice
Sewell) from the executive and legislative councils, and granted the
Assembly greater control of fiscal policy. The latter concession was facilitated by the passage in London of the 1831 Canadian Revenue
Control Act, giving the legislatures of both Canadas control over Crown
revenues, including all customs and import charges.[20] But there was
still one crucial point on which Lower Canada's imperial masters
would not yield: the assembly must support the governor's permanent
civil list of senior officials and judges. The British were not prepared to
yield on a matter they saw as essential to maintaining both Crown prerogative and imperial control. The assembly, for its part, was not prepared to yield on a point that by this time was key to ensuring
government by persons the majority could trust.

With the Ninety-Two Resolutions tabled in the Assembly on
21 February 1834, the *Patriotes* threw down the gauntlet. Although there
were enough expressions of wounded loyalty to Britain to attract some
English-Canadian support, in the middle of the lengthy review of past
and present injustices were resolutions with rebellious intonations.
Number 48, in particular, stands out. After stating that "this House and
the people whom it represents had always cherished the hope and expressed their faith that His Majesty's government in England did not
knowingly and wilfully participate in the political immorality of its colonial agents and officers," the resolution went on to lament that things
had come to such a pass as to leave the people with "only the hard alternative of submitting to an ignominious bondage, or of seeing those
ties endangered that unite them to the mother country."[21] All but six
of the Assembly's members, including many of its anglophone members, supported the resolutions.

With the Ninety-Two Resolutions as their manifesto, Papineau and
his followers swept the 1834 election. None of the English party's members was returned to the Assembly from the cities or *seigneuries*, while a
significant number of English-speaking candidates were elected under
the *Patriotes*' banner.[22] The imperial government responded in a way
that will bring a smile to the faces of many contemporary Canadians:
it recalled Governor Aylmer and dispatched a Royal Commission to
Lower Canada. The appointment of Royal Commissions when things

go wrong and no one has the answers, for better or worse, has become a fixture of Canada's civic culture.[23] Lord Gosford, "a good-natured and innocuous Irishman" who chaired the commission, tried his best to ingratiate himself with the French Canadians.[24] But in the end, with no give on the *Patriotes'* basic political demands, Gosford returned empty-handed to England.[25]

The Royal Commission's report was tabled in the House of Commons on 2 March 1837. Four days later Lord John Russell, chancellor of the exchequer in a Whig administration led by Lord Melbourne, gave the British government's response by way of Ten Resolutions. The Ten Resolutions were incendiary: they rejected the Assembly's constitutional proposals and authorized the governor to pay arrears of civil service salaries out of public funds without the Assembly's consent.[26] When news of the passage of Lord Russell's Ten Resolutions reached Canada, "Papineau and his friends began to set the heather on fire."[27] It would be November before the first shots were fired, but the organization of armed rebellion was now under way.

At this point in the evolution of its empire, Britain was unwilling to grant self-government to its colonists. It would take insurrection and the statecraft of Lord Durham to induce this most liberal of empires to take that next step.

By the time rebellion was brewing in Lower Canada, all of the other British North American colonies were experiencing the tension inherent in their constitutional arrangements between the democratic spirit springing from an elected assembly and the reality of rule by British governors and their hand-picked local supporters. In Upper Canada this tension threatened to erupt in violence. Elsewhere, in New Brunswick, Nova Scotia, Prince Edward Island, and Newfoundland, the innate Loyalism of English-speaking settlers served as a break on armed insurrection.

In Upper Canada after the War of 1812, new streams of immigration from Britain and the United States began to change the composition of the province's English-speaking people in ways that had a polarizing impact on its politics. Among the immigrants from England, Ireland, and Scotland were increasing numbers of the lower classes, who hoped to find in the New World a society free of the domination of an aristocratic governing class. These new Upper Canadians would find their spokesman in William Lyon Mackenzie, a failed, twenty-five-year-old Scottish shopkeeper who was deeply influenced by the democratic ideals of English radicals such as William Cobbett. Mackenzie arrived in

Louis-Joseph Papineau addresses the Assemblée des six-comtés.
Charles Alexander (artist), *L'Assemblée des six comtés à Saint-Charles-sur-Richelieu,
en 1837*, oil on canvas, 300 x 690 cm, Musée national des beaux-arts du Québec,
1937.56; photo: Jean-Guy Kérouac

Upper Canada in 1820 and, through his journalism, began to set the agenda for a constitutional reform movement.[28] The post-war American immigrants were mostly attracted by cheap land, and while they tended to be less radical than Mackenzie, the snobbish ways of Upper Canada's governing elite and its tendency to treat criticism as sedition would drive many of them into the reform camp.

The reformers' opponents were the network of early Loyalists and their descendants known as the "Family Compact," a term that can be misleading. Although there were plenty of family connections among the socially prominent Loyalist families, it would be more accurate to refer to the political leaders who worked closely with the lieutenant-governor, holding most of the positions on the Executive Council and the appointed Legislative Council, as a "court party" or an incipient Tory party.[29] Many of the Tory opponents of democratic reform who served on these appointed bodies were social upstarts, and their power was based more on their control of economic institutions such as the Bank of Upper Canada – a private bank with a state-created monopoly over the issuing of credit – and the Canada Land Company than on their family pedigree. The undoubted leader of these Tories was not an old Loyalist but an Anglican cleric, John Strachan, who had come to the province originally to teach the first Loyalists' children.

By the 1820s Strachan, a converted Presbyterian, had become the Anglican archdeacon of York. With a seat both on the Executive Council and in the Legislative Assembly, he was a force in Upper Canada's governance. Strachan's enduring contribution to Upper Canada was his work as an educator,[30] but his efforts to develop a better-educated population came with a sharp Anglican edge. Strachan and the Family Compact were deeply committed to making the Church of England the established state-supported church in Upper Canada. This was part of the constitutional vision of the province's first lieutenant-governor, John Graves Simcoe. But it never suited the province's circumstances. Even in the province's earliest days, it is doubtful that a majority of its people was Anglican. By the 1820s Anglicans were clearly a minority, and the idea that the state would favour their church was particularly offensive to Methodists, Congregationalists, and adherents of other Christian faiths who harboured strong convictions about the need to keep religion separate from the state.

The focus of religious controversy was the clause in the 1791 Constitutional Act that set aside reserve lands "for the support and maintenance of a protestant clergy."[31] Even though the language of the clause seemed clear enough, the Anglicans claimed that these lands and the revenue they might yield belonged exclusively to their church. Ironically, these reserves, set aside to foster loyalty, became "a chief cause of political unrest."[32]

Almost as divisive as clergy reserves were the efforts of old Loyalists to disenfranchise American immigrants to Upper Canada. Those arriving after 1783 came as American citizens. At this time in neither Britain nor Canada was "citizenship" the concept that designated eligibility to participate in the political community. Indeed, it was not until after the Second World War that citizenship became a legal status for Canadians; "citizen" was too republican-sounding a term to be acceptable in Britain or any of its imperial appendages. The 1791 Constitutional Act stipulated that, to be a member of the Legislative Council or the Legislative Assembly or to vote, a person had to be a natural-born subject of the king or be naturalized as a subject by British legislation.[33] By the 1820s conservatives were using this constitutional provision as a political weapon to keep American immigrants from taking seats in the Assembly. Officials in London wanted to see this issue settled locally.[34] But in the end they had to have Upper Canadian legislation aimed at American immigrants disallowed, and instructed Lieutenant-Governor Sir Peregrine Maitland to introduce a new bill that would naturalize all persons who had at any time received grants of land from the province, had held public office, or had taken an oath of allegiance to the king.[35] This episode demonstrates how anxious British policy-makers were becoming about holding on to their Canadian colonies.

By the 1830s the battle between the forces of conservatism and reform was reaching a climax over the undemocratic character of Upper Canada's system of government. The conflict had its source in the separation of the executive branch of government, led by a British-appointed lieutenant-governor, from the elected chamber of the legislative branch. In all of Britain's North American colonies, this system operated more like the American system of a separation of powers than the parliamentary system with an executive formed by majority leaders in the legislature. The struggle of reformers to make the executive responsible to the popular branch of the legislature went on in the shadow of the Mother of Parliaments at Westminster where, gradually, over many decades, monarchs had learned that their political survival depended on entrusting ministers who had the confidence of the House of Commons and, for the most part, had seats in that House, to lead the various departments of government. But this evolved system had never been spelled out in a precise formula of constitutional legitimacy called "responsible government." It was not firmly in place until after the House of Commons moved closer to becoming a democratic institution with the 1832 Great Reform Bill's expansion of the franchise.

The difficulty in transferring to Canada the British system of government by ministers responsible to the elected assembly was that it would mean, in effect, home rule for the colonists: the British governor would no longer answer to the Colonial Office in London, but to the representatives of a majority in the local legislature. The majority of British parliamentarians was not yet ready for such a weakening of imperial ties. Nor were many colonists. In resisting the reformers, Upper Canada's Tories played the loyalty card. Responsible government, they argued, would lead to an American-like break with the British Empire. One response to this Tory cry was that of Canadian Whigs, who, like their counterparts in England, believed in a balanced constitution of king, lords, and commons. The leading representatives of the Whig tradition in Upper Canadian politics were William Warren Baldwin and his son, Robert. Although both were professional men (Baldwin senior was both a doctor and a lawyer, and his son was a lawyer) with extensive land holdings, they were critical of the concentration of power in the hands of the governor and his entourage. The Baldwins insisted that the one constitutional change the colony needed was to make the

Executive Council responsible to the Assembly by establishing the practice "that the executive council should resign or be altered when it lost the confidence of the majority of the Assembly."[36]

"Firebrand" William Lyon Mackenzie led a more radical branch of the reform movement.[37] First as editor of the *Colonial Advocate*, the province's first anti-establishment newspaper, then as an elected member of the Assembly, and finally in 1834 as the first mayor of the newly incorporated City of Toronto, Mackenzie was a virulent critic of Upper Canada's governing elite. His sharp pen and shrill voice certainly got under the skin of the Family Compact. In 1826 some of the younger members of York's finest families broke into his shop, smashed his press, and scattered the type in Lake Ontario.[38] His political opponents called him a "reptile," and had him banished five times from the Assembly.

Undeterred, Mackenzie steamrolled ahead and used his position as chairman of the Assembly's Committee on Grievances to invite members of the public into the legislature to express their concerns about the government's incompetence and lack of accountability. Mackenzie was all for responsible government and was an articulate advocate of it. He had the investigative journalist's ability to expose the waste and inefficiencies that result when government does not have to account to the people for its activities. Like the *Patriotes,* he believed the Legislative Council should be elected, and was a strong advocate of judicial independence, protesting the lieutenant-governor's removal without due process of King's Bench judge John Walpole Willis in 1828.[39]

When two thousand copies of Mackenzie's Grievances Committee's reports printed found their way across the Atlantic and came to the attention of King William IV and his colonial secretary, Lord Glenelg,[40] the response was to dispatch a new lieutenant-governor, Sir Francis Bond Head, with instructions to calm things down somehow without making concessions to the reformers' constitutional demands. This was a recipe for political disaster. By this time the political cauldron of Upper Canada was reaching the boiling point. Mackenzie had established strong ties with dissenting religious communities, organizers of stock companies, and mechanics' institutes building more cooperative forms of economic enterprise, and immigrant groups resisting the economic domination of the Bank of Upper Canada.[41] But Tory forces were also gathering strength at the grassroots level. A flood of immigration in the early 1830s increased Upper Canada's population by nearly 50 per cent. Many of these new arrivals belonged to the Orange Order, and were readily wooed to the conservative side of politics by charges that the reformers were disloyal republicans.[42] Elections were closely contested, with the pendulum swinging back and forth between reformers and Tories.

The 1836 election, forced by the new governor, Bond Head, was a prelude to rebellion. When he appointed reform leaders Robert Baldwin and John Rolph to the Executive Council, it looked as if the governor was introducing responsible government. But when he refused to seek the Executive Council's advice on policy matters and appointments, Baldwin and Rolph resigned. The Assembly, with its reform majority, then refused to vote supply. Bond Head fought back, not just by calling an election, but by leading the government side in the campaign, which was bitterly fought, with more than the usual amount of violence and voter intimidation. The secret ballot, though advocated by the reformers, would not be instituted in Canada for many decades, so citizens voted under the gaze of their employers, creditors, and government agents, making free and fair elections impossible. Beneath all the factors that told against the reformers was an underlying base of loyalty. In the words of historian William Kilbourn, "Those people in Upper Canada who prized the British connection, for whatever reason, above all the other political values, were stirred to action by the call of Governor Head."[43] Bond Head and his supporters won a landslide victory. Willie Mackenzie, the Baldwins, and John Rolph all lost their seats.

This electoral defeat was followed by a second blow: Lord Russell's Ten Resolutions in March 1837 confirming the control of government by the lieutenant-governor and his advisers. The reformers likely would have attempted to recover from these setbacks along a nonviolent political path had it not been for the firebrand Mackenzie and the influence of the *Patriotes* in Lower Canada. Mackenzie had established a bond with Papineau: he visited Lower Canada several times in 1837, and had been infected by the momentum of rebellion. By October 1837, encouraged by the move of the entire British garrison out of Toronto to Montreal, Mackenzie began making soundings in reform communities about support for an armed uprising to remove Bond Head. He set 7 December as the date when five thousand armed men would assemble at Montgomery's tavern at the corner of Yonge Street and Eglinton Avenue, at the time about two and a half miles north of the city.

The first shots of the Lower Canada rebellion were fired in November 1837, when Sir John Colborne, now commander-in-chief of British forces in North America, sent six companies of British regulars under

Colonel Charles Gore to attack the *Patriotes* at St-Denis on the Richelieu River. Colborne's action was triggered by communal fighting in Montreal between partisans of the *Canadiens* and English Loyalists, and a series of large public meetings, culminating in a gathering of five to six thousand at St-Charles, a few miles upriver from St-Denis, which produced "a declaration of independence drawn directly from the American Declaration."[44] The battle of St-Denis on 23 November was the *Patriotes'* one and only victory. Under the leadership of Wolfred Nelson, with Papineau notably absent, the *Patriotes* forced Colonel Gore to retreat, with six of his soldiers dead and eighteen wounded.[45] News of that victory spurred Mackenzie's rebellious organizing in Upper Canada. But just three days later British forces, now outnumbering the rebels, struck back and won a decisive victory at St-Charles. Papineau and other *Patriote* leaders fled to the United States. The final and bloodiest battle took place on 13 December at St-Eustache, in the Two Mountains area northwest of Montreal, where Colborne's force of two thousand regulars, including a detachment of cavalry and eight artillery pieces, overwhelmed a badly led group of *Patriote* defenders. At least seventy rebels were killed and more charred bodies were later recovered from the ruins of a church set aflame by British soldiers.[46]

In comparison the rebellion in Upper Canada was a comic opera affair.[47] For the rebels it was a case of Murphy's Law: virtually everything that could go wrong did go wrong. Mackenzie jumped the gun, and instead of waiting for all the rebel forces to congregate at Montgomery's tavern on 7 December, he decided to attack Toronto on 4 December. The day before, Mackenzie, out on patrol, captured a Loyalist alderman, John Powell, but as a man of honour allowed him to keep his pistol. Powell quickly took advantage of Mackenzie's generous nature and shot and killed Captain Anthony Anderson, the only person with military experience among the rebels. That evening, a few hundred North York farmers, after slogging through a bitterly cold wintry day, arrived thirsty and hungry at Montgomery's tavern, only to find that Montgomery had sold his tavern and the new owner wanted cash on the barrelhead before he would give them anything to eat or drink. As well, the guns promised by Mackenzie had not arrived. The next day – D-day – the rebel leaders frittered away hours dithering about what to do. Dozens of men went home when they found there were no muskets. So it was a very motley band of unhappy and frightened rebels, many armed with nothing more than sharp pikes affixed to long sticks, pitchforks, and beechroot clubs that began the advance down Yonge Street in the twilight of Monday, 4 December. Meanwhile government "forces" were also in a state of chaotic disorganization. Until the very last moment, Governor Bond Head remained in total denial that a rebellion of his loyal people was possible. He categorically refused to authorize Colonel James Fitzgibbon, a hero of the War of 1812, to organize the Toronto militia, the only available defenders of the provincial capital. It was not until late Monday night that Fitzgibbon was able to prevail on Bond Head's housekeeper to get the governor out of bed and convince him that an insurrection was in progress. Even then Bond Head dithered. His only decisive actions that day were to complete his toilette and park his family on a ship in Toronto harbour. Without his permission, a picket of Loyalists under a leading Family Compact member, Sheriff William Botsford Jarvis, took up a position in Mrs Sharpe's garden at what is now College Street, just west of the future site of Maple Leaf Gardens, to guard the entrance to Toronto. As the rebel column approached the city in the gathering dusk, Sheriff Jarvis's twenty-seven musketeers let loose their first volley. It turned out to be their last volley. The front rank of the rebels returned the fire and then dropped to their knees to give the line behind a clear shot. That was enough to panic the ranks behind, who thought the kneeling men had all been shot, so they all turned and fled. So did Sheriff Jarvis's men, when they realized they were greatly outnumbered. Willie Mackenzie, with six greatcoats rapped around his five-foot frame, galloped off on his white pony across the American border, ending armed insurrection in Upper Canada. Had the rebels been more professionally led, they might well have taken Toronto, so lightly was it defended. But it is most unlikely that they could have held it for long. Mackenzie's band of North York farmers could not have prevailed against Upper Canada's widespread Loyalist base and the military experience available to lead it. In Lower Canada the popular base for the rebel cause was much greater. The fact that the hierarchy of the Roman Catholic Church stood firmly against the uprising is credited with weakening the *Patriotes'* appeal. But parish priests close to the communities engaged in fighting the British army did not abandon their people. The military mismatch between Britain's professional army and a French-Canadian force led by middle-class professionals with no military experience would seem as important an explanation of the *Patriotes'* defeat as the Church's support for the established order.

In November 1838, just three days after Lord Durham left Canada to return to England, a small band of *Patriotes* who had taken sanctuary in the United States, led by Robert Nelson, crossed the Vermont border into Lower Canada and attempted to rally support for another insurrection. But though four thousand insurgents answered the call, the promised American arms and soldiers failed to arrive and the second Lower Canada rebellion fizzled out, put down by local English- and French-speaking militia before the arrival of Colborne's army.[48]

The rebellions of 1837 and 1838 are serious breaches in the Canadian myth of being a "peaceable kingdom." Because of this, there is a tendency to dismiss them as historical aberrations, but to do so is to miss their enduring importance in the development of our country. For French Canada, the *Patriotes* uprising, even though there were English-speaking Canadians in their ranks and at the leadership level, consolidated its sense of nationhood. At this time it was a socially and economically conservative sense of nationhood, but one that would prove strong enough to withstand the most determined effort ever made to destroy French Canada, a threat that the *Canadiens* were about to face in post-rebellion Canada. For all of Canada, these pre-Confederation rebellions showed the strong and growing popular support for democratic government. Without the armed rebellions, Lord Durham would not have come to Canada. His coming provided the prod Britain needed to permit democratic self-government in its North American colonies.

It was the news of the armed uprisings in Canada that reached England just before Christmas 1837 that persuaded John George Lambton, Earl of Durham, to accept the queen's commission to go to Canada with virtually dictatorial powers. Durham had returned from a difficult ambassadorial mission to Russia in the summer of 1837, just as a teenage Queen Victoria ascended the throne. Before that he had carried out an equally challenging diplomatic mission to Belgium. He was in poor health, and at age forty-five ready to settle down on his ancestral estates and resume his position as a leading Whig in Parliament. Hence his reluctance to accept the Canadian commission when it was offered to him by Lord Melbourne, the Whig prime minister.[49] But once Durham heard that Britain's North American colonies, the pride of its empire, were in danger, duty called, and early in the new year he accepted the young queen's commission.

Lord Durham was one of the greatest British statesmen of his day. As a young twenty-year old, he had been elected to Parliament in 1812, and held that seat until his elevation to the peerage in 1828. He became a leading member of the liberal Whigs who pushed through the Great Reform Bill. He was very much a child of the European Enlightenment.

Socially he was an aristocrat who believed strongly that his class had to make way for democracy. In international affairs he was a liberal imperialist who believed that the lesson to be learned from the loss of the thirteen American colonies was that the British Empire would survive and flourish only by recognizing that settler colonies could not be denied the liberty enjoyed in the mother country. This put him on the left side of the Whig parliamentary group and considerably left of his prime minister. Indeed, one of Lord Melbourne's incentives in pushing Durham, whom he regarded as a dangerous ideologue, to accept the Canadian commission was to keep him from rallying the radicals in Parliament against him.[50] Melbourne knew only too well that Durham was widely regarded as his most likely successor. In carrying out his Canadian mission, Durham never had the Melbourne ministry firmly behind him.

Lord Durham arrived in Quebec City on 29 May 1838. He came with his wife, Lady Durham, a recently appointed lady-in-waiting to the queen, an entourage of advisers and officials, and a double mandate. As captain general and governor-in-chief of Britain's North American colonies, he was given, in the words of Colonial Secretary Lord Glenelg, "a general superintendence over all British North America," and he was to consider any proposals he might think "conducive to the permanent establishment of an improved system of government in her majesty's North American possessions."[51] So not only was Durham given the usual job of royal commissioners to analyse the problem and recommend solutions; he was also to govern. Most of his governing would be done in Lower Canada, which the imperial authorities recognized was at the heart of the crisis and where there was no lieutenant-governor.

As soon as he arrived in Quebec City, in order not to be encumbered by past quarrels, Durham replaced all the locals, English and French, on the Executive Council with members of his own staff. And then, showing his abundance of energy and reforming zeal, he set up commissions on public lands, immigration, and municipal government. His most notable decision in these early days was the ordinance he issued in June 1837 concerning the insurgents General Colborne had imprisoned and those, such as Papineau, who had fled to the United States. By the time Durham arrived, only 72 of the 326 men Colborne had incarcerated remained in prison. Under Durham's ordinance, eight of these were transported to Bermuda, while the rest were released.[52] Warrants were issued against the sixteen *Patriotes* in exile, including Papineau, but they could return with the governor's permission. Compared

John George Lambton, 1st Earl of Durham. Replica by Thomas Phillips,
oil on canvas, 1820 (1819) © National Portrait Gallery, London

with the punishment meted out after the second rebellion (and after Durham's departure) – 850 *Patriotes* imprisoned, 99 condemned to death (12 of whom were hanged), 58 deported to Australia, 2 banished, and 27 released under bond for good behaviour – Durham's ordinance was extremely lenient.[53] For their participation in the much lighter Upper Canada rebellion, two reformers, Samuel Lount and Peter Mathews, were hanged behind the courthouse on Toronto Street, and seven others were transported to Australia.[54] Although Durham's leniency did much to ingratiate him with French Canadians, it was strongly criticized by British parliamentarians. The Melbourne government's failure to stand behind him would lead to his resignation in September 1838.

Lord Durham spent most of his short time in North America in Quebec City, Lower Canada's capital, where, in the words of his biographer, Chester New, "he hardly came at all into personal contact with the French-Canadians, while he had many conversations with the British leaders."[55] In July he spent five days in Montreal, where he laid out his plan for a federal union of the British North American colonies before a group of English bourgeoisie selected by Peter McGill. He continued on to Upper Canada for a very short visit – in fact he spent almost as much time visiting Buffalo as he did in Toronto. A distinguished British lord showing obvious admiration for their democracy impressed the Americans. The most important event in his twenty-four-hour visit to Upper Canada's capital was receiving from Robert Baldwin a copy of the letter Baldwin had written to Lord Glenelg setting out as clearly as anyone ever had the case for responsible government.[56] Durham did not venture east to the Atlantic provinces, but he did invite their lieutenant-governors to meet with him in Quebec City. Nova Scotia's Sir Colin Campbell, New Brunswick's Sir John Harvey, and PEI's Sir Charles Fitzroy all met with him in August. Harvey and Campbell warned Durham that the people of their provinces would oppose joining a federal union – opposition that stemmed largely from hostility to French Canada.[57]

On the very day Durham began his return voyage to England, the second rebellion broke out. When news of the uprising reached him, he began to realize that delay in putting together a British North American federation would be dangerous. When he arrived in England, it was clear that the imperial government was in no mood to leave the rebellious French Canadians in control of a legislative assembly, which would be an essential feature of a federal union.[58] It was also clear that the Atlantic colonies were not ready for such a federation, so legislative union of the two Canadas is what Durham prescribed in his famous report. He worked feverishly through the Christmas holidays to finish the report, and presented it officially to the Colonial Office on 4 February 1839. A week later it was tabled in the House of Commons.

Lord Durham's report is widely regarded as a great work. Constitutional historian W.P.M. Kennedy writes that it "remains the greatest state paper in colonial history."[59] Certainly the report bristles with bright ideas on how to make the British North American colonies more progressive and harmonious: the constitutional foundation of clergy reserves should be terminated and proceeds from their sale turned over to the local legislature; lands should be developed and public works established to make British North America economically competitive with the United States; institutions of higher education and a sound system of municipal government were greatly needed, as was a Supreme Court of Appeal for British North America. But the report is remembered most for its two fundamental constitutional recommendations: first, the principle and practice of responsible government – that government should be directed by the political leaders who command the confidence of the elected legislature – should be extended to the British North American colonies; and second, Lower Canada and Upper Canada should be reunited to form the Province of Canada.

Durham put forward a hard-hitting critique of the constitutional arrangements that Britain had put in place for all its British North American colonies. The fundamental flaw in these arrangements was establishing elected legislative assemblies but denying them executive power. "It is difficult to conceive what could have been their theory of government," he thundered, "who imagined that in any colony of England a body vested with the name and character of a representative assembly could be deprived of any of those powers which, in the opinion of Englishmen, are inherent in a popular legislature."[60] He referred to the classic principle of the English constitution that should be applied in Canada not as "responsible government," but as "the true principle of representative government," which means "entrusting the management of public affairs ... to the persons who have the confidence of the representative body."[61] Although it was a stretch for Durham to say that this "wise principle" had been secured in England since the Glorious Revolution of 1688, it was clearly established there in the eighteenth century.[62] Durham's argument that the principle should now be enjoyed by Britain's North American colonists was based both on his view that it was an inherent right of Englishmen and on the prudential calculation that, if it were not granted, Britain's remaining colonies in America were sure to go the same way as the thirteen former colonies to the south.

But Durham remained a British imperialist, albeit a liberal imperialist. He drew a line between colonial affairs and imperial affairs. He considered it outrageously foolish to think that officials and a parliament far away across the ocean could manage the practical local problems of the colonies better than the locals. But he reserved a sphere of policy that imperial authorities should continue to control. This included the constitution and form of government, foreign relations, foreign trade, and the disposal of public lands.[63] The colonists' willingness to continue to enjoy the benefits of the imperial connection, he argued, would not be strengthened by the British government's vexatious interference in their internal concerns.

The case Durham made for colonial self-government is his lasting legacy to Canada and the British Empire. His other big idea – legislative union of the Canadas – is important because it failed. At the time he was writing, the only alternative to bringing the French and English together to govern through a system of responsible parliamentary democracy was English despotism over the French in Lower Canada. There was no way Britain would entrust power to a French majority, but Durham had larger and deeper reasons for advocating the union. He saw French Canada's becoming part of a unitary and democratic province with an ever-increasing English majority as the *Canadiens'* salvation. In his view French Canadians were hopelessly backward. In what is surely the most infamous passage of his famous report, he wrote: "There can hardly be conceived a nationality more destitute of all that can invigorate and elevate a people, than that which is exhibited by the descendants of the French in Lower Canada."[64] On the other hand, "[t]he superior practical and political intelligence of the English cannot be, for a moment, disputed."[65] Ergo, put the English and French together in a democratic union, grow the English population, and all will thrive together.

Although, after the passage cited above, Durham stated that French Canadians were "a people with no history, and no literature," it was their economic backwardness that he fastened on. Instead of supporting the public works, canals, financial institutions, and land registry system that would develop the colony, "they looked on the Province as the patrimony of their race ... not as a country to be settled but as one already settled."[66] If they did not assimilate to English (and American) ways, the greater part of them was destined "to be labourers in the employ of English capitalists."[67] His model was the state of Louisiana, where French-speaking Americans were blending into a progressive English-speaking society. There were signs that this was already under way in Lower Canada: his inquiry into education indicated "that there are ten times the number of French children in Quebec learning English, as compared with the English children who learn French." Louisiana also showed how French civil law and English common law could be amalgamated to secure the best of both systems. As for Catholicism, that other fundamental pillar of French-Canadian culture, it played no part in Durham's assimilation plan. Quite to the contrary, he praised the Catholic Church for having "presented almost the only semblance of stability and organization ... and the only effectual support for civilization and order"[68] – and, Durham might have added, the strongest base of loyalty to the British Crown.

Lower Canada's 150,000 English speakers combined with Upper Canada's 400,000 would result in an English-speaking majority of 550,000 over 450,000 French Canadians.[69] Thus Durham saw no reason to recommend anything but representation based on population for the legislative assembly of the reunited province. French Canadians would be a minority from the start, and become an ever-smaller minority as British and American migrants flooded into a prospering and self-governing English-speaking province. It was Durham's dream that in this new framework, French Canadians would flourish, abandon their old nationality, and acquire a new English-Canadian nationality.

In envisaging Canada's future as a country based on a single English-speaking nation, Durham reflected the liberal orthodoxy of his time. No less a theorist of liberal democracy than John Stuart Mill insisted that a democratic state must be based on a single nationality. "Free institutions," Mill wrote, "are next to impossible in a country made up of different nationalities."[70] The clash of nationalities within a state, the argument went, would make it impossible for the people of a democracy to work together on their common problems. Louis-Joseph Papineau was equally convinced that a democratic French Canada must be based on a single nationality – that of *les Canadiens*.

Another English liberal of the era, Lord Acton, challenged the doctrine that political liberty was possible only in states based on a single ethnic nation. Acton saw as potentially tyrannical "the perpetual supremacy of the collective will, of which the unity of the nation is the necessary condition, to which every other influence must defer and against which no objection enjoys authority." He contended: "The co-existence of several nations under the same state is a test, as well as the best security of freedom."[71] In the middle of the nineteenth century, and for a long time afterwards, Acton's was a liberal voice crying in the wilderness. But in the long run it is Acton's ideal of the peoples of a multinational state sharing a liberal democratic civic culture that charts the path along which Canada would develop and flourish.

Of Lord Durham's two core ideas, it was the one destined for failure – assimilation of French Canada into a unitary English-speaking politi-cal community – that the British government wasted no time in imple-menting. But it was his good idea about responsible government that, although it took a decade to implement, would be the instrument for defeating his bad idea.

The Union Act was passed by the British Parliament in July 1840 and came into force on 10 February 1841.[72] Unlike in 1822, there was no French-Canadian delegation in London to oppose union. However, a strong delegation from Upper Canada that included John Strachan and John Beverley Robinson did turn up to lobby against their English Protestant province's being joined to a predominantly French Catholic province. The British parliamentarians largely ignored the Upper Cana-dians, and the bill sailed through with little debate. Lord Durham, by this time on his deathbed, saw a copy of the bill and his supporters in Parliament enthusiastically endorsed it. Durham's friend Charles Poulett Thompson – the French called him *poulet* (chicken) – who had served as president of the Board of Trade and had arrived in Canada in 1839 as its governor-to-be, had a large hand in drafting the Union legislation.

The Union Act reunited the two Canadas to form the Province of Canada, but departed in two significant ways from Lord Durham's recommendations. First, instead of trusting in British immigration to en-sure an English-speaking majority and basing representation on popula-tion, the Act gave each section of the province – the former Lower Canada and Upper Canada – an equal number of members (forty-two each to start with) regardless of population. This meant that Upper Canada (now referred to as Canada West) for a few years would be over-represented in the legislative assembly. Later on, when Canada West's population came to exceed Canada East's, the Upper Canadians would become religious about representation-by-population, making it a burn-ing issue of constitutional reform. Second, the Act left out provisions requiring the establishment of the strong system of local government that Lord Durham believed was badly needed to provide Canadians with valuable political training and to elevate parliamentary life by keeping local log-rolling politics at the local level. Responsibility for developing municipal institutions was left with the new governor, Poulett Thompson, soon to be dubbed Baron Sydenham of Sydenham and Toronto. Sydenham was able to put in place some of the groundwork for local government before the Union Act came into force, but his scheme fell far short of full municipal self-government, as it left local bodies largely under the control of centrally appointed officials.[73]

The formal structure of government provided for by the Union Act was much the same as it had been under the 1791 Constitutional Act. An elected lower house would continue to share legislative power with an appointed upper house. The governor general was empowered to summon, in the queen's name, no less than twenty persons to serve for life in the Legislative Council. Durham and the British government, strong believers in the Whig principle of a balanced constitution, totally dismissed the Canadian reformers' agitation for an elected second chamber. Executive power would continue to be exercised by the governor "with the Advice or with the Advice and Consent" of "such Executive Council, or any Members thereof, as may be appointed by Her Majesty ... or the said Governor."[74] The governor would exercise these executive powers according to the instructions of Her Majesty's government in London.[75] The instructions Governor Sydenham received did not amount to what Canadian reformers considered to be "responsible government."

The dispatch sent to Sydenham in October 1839 by Lord John Russell, who had now become colonial secretary, played down responsible government as a principle, but instructed the governor to come very close in practice to meeting the expectations of responsible government.[76] He was to form an executive that could act in harmony with the Legislative Assembly. The governor's appointments to the Executive Council and to senior positions in government should be based on politics – that is, they should be designed to win favour with the majority in the elected Assembly. Now this was getting close to responsible government, but was still not full cabinet government. Senior officials who were not from either house of the legislature could still manage government departments. Moreover, there was still no clear recognition that responsible government meant party government – that is, a government led by ministers associated with the political party that has a majority in the Assembly. Indeed, under the Sydenham system, maintained by his next two successors, Sir Charles Bagot (1842–43) and Sir Charles Metcalfe (1843–45), the governor functioned as a prime minister, constantly scrambling to keep together an executive that could avoid defeat on a non-confidence vote in the Assembly.[77]

The impetus for moving to full responsible government came not from imperial headquarters, but from reform politicians in the colonies: Joseph Howe in Nova Scotia and Louis-Hippolyte La Fontaine and Robert Baldwin in Canada. In 1839 Howe, the fiery editor of the *Novascotian* and leader of the reform movement in the Nova Scotia Assembly, wrote four open letters to Sir John Russell, the new colonial secretary. In passionate tones, Howe swore his loyalty to Crown and Empire, but insisted that prudence and justice required that "the Colonial Governors must be commanded to govern by the aid of those who possess the confidence of the people, and are supported by a majority of the representative branch."[78] Howe's letters were republished in almost every Canadian newspaper, and sent as a pamphlet to British newspapers and to every member of Parliament.[79] Howe's letters, along with Lord Durham's report, stand as the most eloquent plea for Canadian self-government in domestic affairs. Through the 1840s, Howe joined with J.B. Uniacke to push for full responsible government in Nova Scotia.

La Fontaine, a well-educated lawyer from a *habitant* family, who had pleaded the *Patriotes'* cause in England and served some prison time after the second rebellion, emerged in 1839 as the key *Canadien* leader in rallying French Canada out of the deep sulk brought on by the Union Act. In February 1841, as the first election under the Act approached, La Fontaine published his *Adresse aux électeurs de Terrebonne* in the newspaper *L'Aurore*. He was critical of the Union in principle, especially the section of the Act making English Canada's only official language. But he argued that it was only through union that the British would allow responsible government, and that it was only by working with Upper Canadian reformers and using the machinery of responsible government that French Canadians could secure through politics what was essential to their survival as a nationality.[80] La Fontaine established strong links with Upper Canadian reformers and their leader, Robert Baldwin. The Baldwin-La Fontaine alliance would turn out to be of crucial importance in drawing together democratically minded French and English Canadians in a common struggle to win home rule for Canada.[81]

What Baldwin and La Fontaine did for each other helped to seal their alliance. In the first election under the Union Act, in March 1841, French candidates who were not *vendues* (collaborators with the English) did not do well. Governor Sydenham conducted a vigorous campaign, and most *Canadiens* were still very negative about participating in the politics of a union they abhorred. In Terrebonne riding, La Fontaine withdrew from the election when sleighloads of Protestant road workers and a group of Upper Canada militia threatened to attack a column of seven hundred French voters led by La Fontaine, who were walking to the voting station in the English corner of the riding. Baldwin, who recognized La Fontaine as Canada's reform leader, quickly came to the rescue. Under the election law of that day, a candidate could run in more than one riding. Baldwin won in Belleville and in North York, necessitating a by-election in one of the ridings. Robert Baldwin persuaded his father to step aside so that La Fontaine could run in the North York by-election. Not only did La Fontaine run, but the English Protestant farmers of North York, on 19 September 1841, elected the French Catholic reform leader with an overwhelming majority.[82]

La Fontaine and the francophone reformers soon had an opportunity to reciprocate. When Baldwin agreed to accept the position of solicitor general for Canada West in Sydenham's Executive Council, as a newly elected member of the government he had to resign his seat, under the constitutional practice of that day, and run in a by-election. (The rule would plague Canadians right up to the Byng-King crisis of 1926.) Twenty-five members of the French party in Canada East offered to resign so that Baldwin could run in their riding. In October, when Michael Borne officially resigned from his Rimouski seat, Baldwin was entered as the reformers' candidate and won the by-election by acclamation. When Baldwin, accompanied by La Fontaine, came to meet his constituents, all along the road from Lévis to Rimouski every farmhouse had put out bunting and, as Baldwin's carriage passed, *habitants* ran behind it, shooting fireworks, unfurling banners, and shouting their acclaim.[83] French Canada was now engaged in the politics of the hated union.

By this time it had become clear that the only way the united province could be governed was in a quasi-federal manner. The governor would function as head of government for all of Canada, but some responsibilities would be divided between separate ministers for Canada East and Canada West. Sydenham did not include any French Canadians in his government, and tried to govern with the support of a coalition of anglophone conservatives from both sections of the province. Although Sydenham quarrelled with Baldwin over the requirements of responsible government, he did introduce a ministerial system that "placed the officers of the permanent public service ... under a set of political heads who could account for them in parliament."[84] Sydenham died on 20 September 1841, following a carriage accident in Kingston, the new Canadian capital.

The next two governors who followed Sydenham, Sir Charles Bagot and Sir Charles Metcalfe, were sensitive to the need to govern the province in a dualistic, bicultural manner. Bagot never flinched when La Fontaine gave his maiden speech in the Assembly in French. He took care that there were separate Canada East and Canada West superintendants to administer the Commons School Act. He welcomed La Fontaine and Baldwin to seats in the cabinet, each as attorney general for his respective section of the province. And he moved the provincial capital to Montreal. Metcalf was more of a Tory in not trusting former rebels with executive positions, and chose to govern through a double majority system that entailed different policies for each section of the province. But both governors continued to operate as their own prime minister, deciding who could be in their cabinet.[85] Full responsible government would come only under the regime of Metcalfe's successor, Lord Elgin.

The winds of change were now blowing firmly in the direction of self-government – at least for Britain's white colonies. In 1846 Parliament's repeal of the Corn Laws meant the end of preferences for colonial products, the economic glue of the empire.[86] Britain's North American colonies were now free to set their own tariffs. The settling of the Oregon dispute that same year removed the fear of hostilities with the United States, and made it easier for Britain to accept a Canadian government "whose devotion to the imperial connection seemed less than certain."[87] With democratic revolutions breaking out all over Europe, building up to a big explosion in 1848, and the American republic flourishing on the other side of the Canadian border, British leaders knew this was no time to be suppressing democracy in their North American colonies. When the Conservatives divided over Prime Minister Sir Robert Peel's free trade policy, a Liberal-Whig administration under Lord John Russell came to power and appointed Earl Grey, Lord Durham's brother-in-law, colonial secretary. In August 1846 Grey appointed the Earl of Elgin, Durham's son-in-law, to be Canada's next governor. The scene was now set for taking the final step to full responsible government.

The breakthrough came first in Nova Scotia. On 3 November 1846 Earl Grey wrote a dispatch to Sir John Harvey, Nova Scotia's

lieutenant-governor, in effect instructing him to follow the precepts of responsible government: "The object which I recommend to you ... is that of making it apparent that any transfer which may take place of political power from the hands of one party in the province to those of another is the result not of an act of yours but of the wishes of the people themselves."[88] When Harvey tried to put together his own political co-alition, an approach he had had success with as lieutenant-governor of New Brunswick, Grey made it clear in a dispatch of 31 March 1847 that he had meant that "the Government should be carried on by an Executive Council supported by a majority of the Assembly i.e. by a party."[89] The Nova Scotia electorate settled the matter when it gave the Liberals a clear majority in the August 1847 election, and the Liberal leadership rejected Harvey's blandishments to form an all-party government. When the Assembly met at the end of January 1848 and the incumbent Conservative government of J.W. Johnston was defeated on a non-confidence vote, it resigned, and Lieutenant-Governor Harvey swore in a new Liberal government led by J.B. Uniacke and Joseph Howe.

When Lord Elgin arrived in Canada in January 1847, he inherited a shaky Conservative Executive Council. By November the Conserva-tives decided they could procrastinate no longer and advised Elgin to dissolve the legislature. The mid-winter election resulted in a landslide victory for the reformers. La Fontaine could count on the support of all but four or five of the Canada East members, and Baldwin, with consid-erable help from George Brown's *Globe* newspaper, led a much enlarged reform contingent from Canada West. The combined reform forces now had close to a thirty-seat majority in the Assembly. When the Conserva-tive ministry met the House on 4 March 1848, it was defeated, fifty-four to twenty, on a non-confidence vote and immediately resigned. Elgin, who, unlike his predecessors, played no role in the election, did not hesitate to call on La Fontaine and Baldwin to form a new ministry. La Fontaine became attorney general for Canada East, with primacy in government since he led the larger reform group, and Baldwin as-sumed that role for Canada West.[90]

Elgin communicated to Grey the lesson his first year in Canada had taught him. "I must confess," he wrote, "that I for one am deeply con-vinced of the impolicy of all such attempts to denationalize the French. Generally speaking they produce the opposite effect from that intend-ed, causing the flame of national prejudice and animosity to burn more fiercely ... Let them feel on the other hand that their religion, their hab-its, their prepossessions, their prejudices if you will, are more respected

here than in other portions of this vast continent ... and who will venture to say that the last hand which waves the British flag on American ground may not be that of a French Canadian?"[91] Elgin told La Fontaine and Baldwin "that they might count on all proper support and assistance of me."[92] The governor's promise was quickly put to a most difficult test.

One of the La Fontaine-Baldwin government's first pieces of legislation was the Rebellion Losses bill, compensating French-speaking families for damages inflicted on them by British forces in the 1837 rebellion. For hardline English Loyalists, it did not matter that property losses in Upper Canada had been approved earlier. Already infuriated by the handover of power to a government led by former rebels, the bill whipped them into a frenzy. After the bill went through the legislature on 3 March 1849, the Tories counted on the governor general to do the right thing and refuse to sign it. But Elgin knew his duty better than did his Tory critics. On 25 April he came to the parliament building in downtown Montreal through streets packed with surging crowds of angry Tory protestors and signed the bill. On the way back to his Monklands home, his carriage was pelted with stones and rotten eggs. The Montreal *Gazette* rushed out a special evening issue with a banner headline proclaiming, "THE DISGRACE OF GREAT BRITAIN AC-COMPLISHED – CANADA SOLD AND GIVEN AWAY." [93] Later that night an angry mob broke into the parliament building with the Assembly in session, smashed the windows, broke up the furniture, and set the building ablaze. Canada's parliament building burned to the ground that night, but responsible government was firmly in place in the not so peaceable kingdom.

Responsible government, in its full sense of government directed by a cabinet formed by the leaders of the political party with majority support in the elected Assembly, did not arrive in New Brunswick until Grey indicated to New Brunswick's lieutenant-governor, Sir William Colbrooke, that he wanted the system of responsible government he had endorsed for Nova Scotia also to apply in that colony. On 24 February 1848 New Brunswick's House of Assembly debated the principles set out in Grey's dispatch of March 1847, and without great enthusiasm, but with some "merriment," gave its approval to those principles. But it was not until Liberals under the leadership of Charles Fisher in 1854 won a majority in the House of Assembly and formed a government that responsible government was established in New Brunswick.[94]

The island colonies, Prince Edward Island and Newfoundland, also achieved responsible government in the 1850s – but not without a struggle. PEI's absentee landowners lobbied hard in England to prevent self-government on the island. An 1847 Islanders' petition directly to the queen did not move the home authorities. But following the election of George Cole's reformers in 1850, the Colonial Office relented, and in March 1851 a new governor, Sir Alexander Bannerman, crossed the Northumberland Strait on an ice-boat with instructions to accept responsible government.[95] There was even more resistance by the imperial authorities to granting Newfoundlanders self-government. In 1848 Earl Grey stated that, "until the wealth and population of the Colony shall have increased considerably … the introduction of what is called Responsible Government will by no means prove to its advantage."[96] But in 1855 the British government announced that it had changed its mind, allowing P.F. Little's Liberal government, elected on 7 May of that year, to take over as Newfoundland's first home-rule government.

The achievement of home rule by the British North American colonies in the middle of the nineteenth century was an extraordinary development. It is too often seen as simply a generous move by a relatively liberal empire. Not enough weight is given to the democratic spirit of the colonists themselves. Lord Durham's report and the liberal drift in imperial policy were unquestionably important. But without the push of the people themselves, including the resort to arms in the Canadas, it is doubtful that Britain would have moved as quickly as it did to grant its colonists what most of them wanted, and what they denied to Indigenous peoples: control over the running of their own societies. While 1848 was a year in which authoritarian rulers in Europe put down popular democratic uprisings, Britain acceded to the colonists' demand for self-government, making that year a landmark along Canada's path to democracy.

The democratization of Canada's settler societies in the first half of the 1800s marks an important development in the civic culture shared by two of Canada's founding pillars – English Canada and French Canada. But the structure of parliamentary democracy that came with responsible government had two features that were problematic then and remain so today. One was the executive's domination of the legislature. Placing control of government in the hands of politicians who command the confidence of a majority in the elected chamber of the legislature ensured that government was responsible to the representatives of the people. But it also greatly increased the power of Members

of Parliament who form the ministry and diminished the power of ordinary MPs. Under responsible government, ministers, as the Crown's constitutional advisers, exercise the power that flows from the parliamentary rule that the Crown must initiate any measure to raise or spend money. Responsible cabinet government is an executive-centred form of democracy

The second problematic feature of responsible government was the emergence of political parties as the instruments for bringing coherence and discipline to parliamentary politics and cabinet government. In the early days of responsible government, political parties – reforming Liberals and their Conservative opponents – were wobbly institutions with little organization outside of Parliament and not much discipline within. What discipline there was depended mainly on the promise of patronage: the handing out of government positions to party supporters. Imperial officials held their noses about this aspect of colonial home rule, but they were not so hypocritical as to deny the colonists what they knew was well-established practice in the mother country. Political parties, nowhere mentioned in constitutional documents, would quickly become the institutions that control the exercise of constitutional powers. This, too, for better or worse, is a permanent component of Canada's civic culture.

Responsible government, Lord Durham's good idea, enabled French Canada to defeat his bad idea, the assimilation of French Canada into a dominant English Canada. The genius of La Fontaine's leadership was to convince his people that *la survivance* of their nationality would be best ensured by allying with progressive English Canadians in the politics of parliamentary democracy. French Canadians of both political hues, *bleus* and *rouges*, were proving Durham wrong by showing that theirs was not a frozen national culture. Although the English continued to dominate industry and commerce in Lower Canada, French Canadians were beginning to make their mark in this realm. One of Montreal's wealthiest merchants, Joseph Masson, launched a new steamboat line; George-Étienne Cartier was becoming a leader in the bourgeoning railway sector; and Côme-Séraphin Cherrier became president of the Banque du Peuple. By mid-century French Canadians were ready to ditch the seigneurial system, with its debilitating tangle of obligations. They strongly supported an "Act for the Abolition of Feudal Rights and Duties in Lower Canada."[97]

Once French Canada came out of the funk of failed rebellion and the Union Act, it underwent a cultural reawakening. Étienne Parent gave

lectures urging the *Canadiens* to move forward and become leaders in Canada's social and economic life. François-Xavier Garneau rebutted Durham's charge that French Canada had no history by producing a new four-volume national history of his people.[98] *Instituts canadiens* sprung up in Quebec City and Montreal, providing meeting places for French-Canadian writers and intellectuals and access to books proscribed by the Catholic Church. The Church itself, while retaining control of education and great influence over francophone society, was undergoing a reawakening, strengthening its ties to Rome, and "injecting into the *Canadien* mood the full fever of ultramontanism."[99] And the Church was learning a new kind of politics: instead of currying favour with the British governor and his officials, the Church would now support conservative *bleu* forces in democratic politics.

In the 1840s French Canada resisted the attempt to conquer it by political manipulation as successfully as it had survived military conquest eighty years earlier. What was its political destiny now? Given that the nationalist forces led by La Fontaine had prevailed against more radical separatists such as Papineau, as well as against defeatists who supported annexation by the United States, and given also the quasi-federal way in which the United Province of Canada was governed, some form of federal union with English Canadians seemed the most obvious path to follow. The coexistence of English and French Canada in the United Province was based much more on pragmatism than on a shared ideology of diversity. Yet, in the way English Protestant farmers and French Catholic *habitants* reciprocated in supporting the other group's political hero, there was a trace of Lord Acton's appreciation of the freedom that can flow from two nations working together for common ends within a single state. But it was still clear – tragically clear – that there was no room in that ethical vision for Aboriginal Canada.

PART THREE

Confederation

English Canada Gets a Dominion, French Canada Gets a Province, and Aboriginal Canada Gets Left Out

"By amalgamation we do not understand swallowing up; we mean the union of relative natures, fit and proper to be united, in the fruits of which each constituent is represented by the good qualities he contributes to the common stock."[1] These were the words of Thomas D'Arcy McGee, the only Father of Confederation who gave his life for the cause of establishing the Canadian federation. McGee wrote these lines as an Irish Catholic immigrant to the United States. It was the freedoms and rights enshrined in the US Constitution that attracted him to the American republic. But it was the failure to find respect for the Irish Catholic minority in the United States that attracted McGee to Canada.

McGee came to admire Canada's educational system, which, unlike the assimilationist US system of common schools, provided public funding for separate religious schools. He was the most eloquent and best informed of the English-speaking Fathers about the depth and breadth of French Canada. Speaking in the debate on the Quebec Resolutions in the United Province of Canada's Legislative Assembly, McGee reminded the house that French Canadians had been prominent in every one of the founding colonies. Addressing himself to "gentlemen of French origin," he added: "we propose to restore these long-lost compatriots to your protection."[2] McGee's pluralism extended beyond his enthusiastic embrace of French Canada. As his biographer, David Wilson, points out, "McGee was sufficiently progressive to place the 'aboriginal tribes' at the heart of Canadian history and to insist that they were an integral part of the country's identity."[3]

The other facet of his political character that marked McGee's contribution to Confederation was his pragmatic moderation, a cast of mind to which he was a late-in-life convert. He had grown up in Ireland as a

Thomas D'Arcy McGee. William Notman, Library and Archives Canada,
C-016749

fervent Irish nationalist, and when he returned to Ireland in 1846 he
enlisted in the anti-British guerrilla warfare that led in the direction
of Fenianism. He was forced to return to the United States to escape
imprisonment or worse at the hands of the British government. But
he embraced "a pluralistic form of nationalism, which would embrace
all regions, religions, 'races' and classes,"[4] and the party he joined in
Ireland was the Irish Confederation, which called for an independent
Irish legislature in a British federation. It was the intolerance he experienced as an Irish Catholic in the United States that slowly turned him
into a socially conservative liberal. As his biographer sums up his transition, "In Ireland, McGee had been an extreme republican; in the
United States, he had been an extreme Catholic; in Canada, he would
be an extreme moderate."[5]

When McGee migrated with his family to Canada in 1857, he came as a believer in the good and full life possible in a country evolving, as was Canada, under the aegis of the British Empire. The absolute political truths of the Enlightenment no longer had any attraction for him. He now grasped the value of "a middle way, in which firm convictions coexisted with generosity of spirit, in which people realized the wisdom of Edmund Burke's dictum that the possible best is the absolute best."[6] In the political context of Canada, that would translate into the view that, among people deeply diverse not only in their religion, language, and culture, but also in their views on political justice and their local allegiances, a harmonious political union could be achieved only through accommodation – making a deal in which everyone gives up some of what they hold dear.

This chapter on Confederation opens with McGee not because I think he was typical of the Fathers of Confederation, but because the principles of pluralism and pragmatism that McGee wrote about and spoke about so eloquently, and in which he had come to believe so fervently, were essential to the success of Confederation and the possibility of the Canada we live in today. The tragedy is that this man who knew so well what we Canadians must be about fell victim to an assassin's bullet before the Dominion of Canada was a year old. McGee had come to be hated by the Fenians for abandoning the Irish republican cause. Although Patrick James Whelan, the man who hanged for murdering McGee, denied he was a Fenian, there is much evidence that he lied and that McGee died for the moderation he had come to espouse.

The idea of a federal union of the British North American colonies had been around for a very long time. Quebec's chief justice, William Smith, had suggested such a scheme in the 1780s. Lord Durham, as we have seen, had considered such a plan. McGee applauded arguments for a federal union put forward by Thomas Chandler Haliburton. Indeed, there was a sense that, if the British colonies north of the American border were to remain independent from the United States, the day would come when some sort of amalgamation of the colonies would have to take place, and given their diversity and local loyalties, the union would most likely take a federal form.

In 1858 Alexander Galt, finance minister in the Tory-*Bleu* government led by John A. Macdonald and George-Étienne Cartier, put forward a resolution that the "irreconcilable difficulties" of managing the very disunited United Province of Canada "demanded a federal union of

Canada East and Canada West, which should be widened and strengthened by the inclusion of the North-western and Hudson's Bay territories and the Maritime Provinces."[7] Amid the bickering over locating the
capital of the Canadas in Ottawa and the defeat of the Macdonald-
Cartier ministry, Galt's motion was never brought to a vote. But Cartier
and John Ross, president of the Legislative Council, joined Galt on a
mission to London to interest the British government in Galt's idea of a
federal union of British North America. The colonial secretary, Lord
Lytton, told the delegation that Britain could not possibly take action
on such a proposal until the other provinces showed some interest.

By the mid-1860s there was reason to think that the time for a federation of Britain's North American colonies had come. As the American
Civil War reached its culmination, the threat of a victorious Union government sending its large, powerful army north to pick off Britain's
colonies one by one loomed large. Certainly from Britain's point of
view, that threat could be dealt with much more effectively if the colonies were united. The leaders of a Liberal administration in London,
while not prepared to dump their colonists into the Americans' lap,
were anxious to see them assume a greater share of the defence burden,
and that could best be done through union. And to the west, how much
longer could the Americans' sense of their continental manifest destiny
be held back? A union of the Canadas and the Maritimes would provide a stronger platform for saving the northwest for Canada and resisting American expansion. But even with the playing out of these
geopolitical factors, Confederation would not have taken place when it
did had those "irreconcilable difficulties" in the United Province of
Canada not reached crisis proportions.

The balmy days of Baldwin and La Fontaine did not last long. By
1851 both men had retired from politics. What came next was an utterly
dysfunctional politics. With conservative *Bleus* the strongest party in
Canada East and Liberal reformers the strongest in Canada West, there
was no basis for a stable majority government. Most often government
was in the hands of wishy-washy Conservative-Liberal coalitions constantly scrambling to escape non-confidence votes. Increasingly the political divide in the province had a sharp ideological edge. When the
1861 census disclosed that Upper Canada, with nearly a million and a
half people, exceeded Lower Canada's population by close to half
a million, the reform Grits of Canada West exploded with cries of political injustice. They would not accept a constitution under which
they could be ruled by a *Bleu* Conservative government that did not

represent a majority of the province's electorate. After the removal in 1854 of the requirement of a special two-thirds majority of each house of the Canadian parliament to change the number of representatives in the Legislative Assembly, Upper Canadian reformers threatened to achieve representation-by-population by simple majority vote.[8] *Bleu* support for a separate school system, fuelled by ultramontane Catholic clergy, clashed with the dominant Protestantism of Canada West, which viewed religious faith as resting on an individual's voluntary belief and which called for a secular school system.

It was George Brown, editor of the Toronto *Globe* and leader of the Canada West Liberals, who broke the Gordian knot of colonial Canada's politics. But it was an older George Brown who had moved away from the hard-edged ideological ways that marked his earlier days as a journalist and politician. By the 1860s Brown had abandoned the assumption of Lord Durham and other Liberals that French Canadians must some day be assimilated. In the words of his biographer, Maurice Careless, "he was prepared to let the French-speaking community go its own way, to concede the cultural duality of Canada, and, at the most, to see valuable attributes in the French Canadians that made possible a constructive future partnership of peoples."[9] That change in the thinking of English-speaking Canadian leaders on the left side of politics was essential for the future of a harmonious Canada.

After returning from a period of foreign travel and winning a by-election in 1863, Brown introduced a motion to establish a committee of the house to consider the constitutional issue. Brown's motion was cleverly constructed to appeal across party lines. It called for consideration of the dispatch that Cartier, Galt, and Ross had addressed to the British government in 1859 about the "irreconcilable differences" that were plaguing Canada and the need for a constitutional solution. When Brown's motion finally was voted on in May 1864, it passed with a clear majority of fifty-nine to forty-eight. And the really good news was that John A. Macdonald, by now the undisputed Conservative leader, supported the motion.

When the twenty members of Brown's committee assembled in a chamber of the legislature building in Quebec City, Brown locked the door. For once, legislators from both sides would be free to discuss their common problem of a dysfunctional political system and to consider solutions free from the public gaze. The committee met eight times. Brown delivered its report to the house on 14 June. It was short and to the point: "A strong feeling was found to exist among members of the committee in favour of changes in the direction of a federative system, applied either to Canada alone or to the whole British North American Provinces."[10] Only three committee members signed their names in opposition. One of these was John A. Macdonald, a strong adherent of unitary government, who had not yet accepted the federal principle. But when the government of Macdonald and Étienne-Paschal Taché lost a non-confidence by two votes, instead of pouncing on the parliamentary defeat of his political opponents as an opportunity to defeat them in an election, Brown sent a message that he was interested in cooperating with them to use the crisis as a way of resolving the constitutional impasse. Governor General Charles Monck was enthusiastic about exploring a reconstruction of the government, rather than having another election. Macdonald also saw discussing a possible coalition with the Liberals as worth trying, even though it would mean accepting some kind of federation. When Macdonald rose in the house on Friday, 17 June 1864, to announce that he and Galt were making progress in talks with the member for South Oxford (George Brown) and then Brown rose to acknowledge this, the speaker left the chair to join a scene of joyful pandemonium. Could this really be the end of the Province of Canada's seemingly endless political gridlock?

It took a few days of intense negotiations to construct a coalition cabinet. Brown himself hung back from taking a cabinet position, but encouraged by many supporters to join and a note from McGee saying his personal participation was essential, he agreed to form a coalition government with his political opponents. He also accepted his Liberals having only half of the Canada West seats in the new ministry, even though they much outnumbered Macdonald's Tories. Lower Canada's *Rouges* were the only party missing from the "Grand Coalition." In explaining to the house how he could justify entering government with politicians who had been his bitter opponents, Brown made a statement that many Canadians would welcome if they heard it today: "Mr. Speaker, party alliances are one thing, and the interests of my country are another."[11]

The making of the Grand Coalition in June 1864 to govern the Province of Canada was the first of the two "deals" that made Confederation. Fundamentally it was a deal between George Brown and George-Étienne Cartier, the leaders of the two largest political blocs in the Canadas: the Liberals of Canada West and the *Bleus* of Canada East. Brown gave up his party's constitutional reform priority, a rep-by-pop assembly in the Province of Canada. In return he gained the prospect of having the general government of a new federation based on rep-by-pop. Cartier took on the risk of his people, the French Canadians, being governed by a new general government dominated by the English-speaking majority. In return his people would be the majority in a province with a government he believed could protect French Canada's vital interests. All participants could look forward to a political venture that, if successful, would produce a new country, which some dared to call a new nation. That is what induced John A. Macdonald to accept the federal principle. It was the only way he could realize his national dream.

The second deal now lay immediately ahead: bringing the Maritime provinces into a federal union of British North America. The seed for this task was first planted by New Brunswick's activist lieutenant-governor, Arthur Gordon. In 1862, soon after taking office, this young and ambitious son of a former British prime minister, the Earl of Aberdeen, proposed to the colonial secretary that preparation be made for a union of the Maritime provinces. This was by no means a new idea, but growing tensions between Britain and American Union forces lent some urgency to the proposal.

Gordon proposed that the Maritime governors and their premiers meet in Charlottetown to consider a Maritime legislative union. The young British aristocrat apparently had not caught up with the fact that Britain's colonies in North America were into their second decade of responsible government. But Nova Scotia's premier, Charles Tupper, who had become interested in a federal union of British North America, latched onto Gordon's proposal, as at least a first step in that direction. Tupper understood well that, by this time in the evolution of the "colonies," constitutional initiatives must come from politicians responsible to elected legislatures. On 28 March 1864 Tupper moved in the Nova Scotia Assembly for power to appoint five delegates to confer with representatives of New Brunswick and Prince Edward Island "for the purpose of arranging the union of the three provinces under one government and legislature."[12]

Union was far from being a popular cause among the people of the Maritime provinces. Aside from a widespread sense of being British and wanting to remain so, political loyalties were very parochial. It was assumed that Halifax, the capital of the senior province, would be the capital of a united province, but New Brunswickers, always somewhat jealous of Nova Scotia, did not take kindly to the prospect of being governed from Halifax, rather than from Fredericton.

Charlottetown was chosen as the meeting place for the Maritime union conference because the proposal seemed of so little interest to the people of the island. Indeed an Island historian wrote that a political union of the Maritime colonies "held no attraction" for most Islanders."[13] Newfoundland, the fourth British colony on the Atlantic coast, was not invited to Charlottetown because of the general belief that it would not be interested.[14] Still, plans for the conference went ahead. When Governor General Monck wrote to Nova Scotia's lieutenant-governor to see if he could wangle an invitation for Canadian politicians to attend the Maritime conference, the reply came back that, although Canadians would be cordially welcome to attend the conference, their participation would be "entirely unofficial." The time of the meeting, 1 September, was soon settled. The conference was a go.

Canada's coalition government seized on Charlottetown as its chance to push for a larger union, but it had only a month to prepare a plan to take to the meeting. On 4 August the coalition cabinet began a series of meetings in Quebec City to work out its plan for a federal union. Through those hot summer days the cabinet met eight times. Canadians of today should not be surprised to learn that the fundamental issue the coalition ministers grappled with was the division of powers between the two levels of government in the new federal union they hoped to construct. They were not yet at the stage of working out lists of powers, but were focused on the general balance between the federal and provincial governments.

On this topic the centralists were definitely in the ascendancy. George Brown had swung around from the position he had taken at the convention held by Liberal reformers in Toronto's St Lawrence Hall in 1859. On that occasion, in talking about a federal union of the two Canadas, Brown had minimized the role of the central government to a few matters of mutual interest. Now, as he contemplated a central government with the power and authority to build a new continental nation governed in its most important endeavours by a government controlled by representatives of the English-speaking majority, he went the other way: provinces need have nothing more than municipal-like responsibilities for a few matters of local concern. John A. Macdonald, a strong believer in the superiority of unitary government, did not need Brown to persuade him that a British North American federation should be highly centralized. George-Étienne Cartier, the other coalition member, equal in importance to Brown and Macdonald, who, in the words of historian

Christopher Moore, had made himself "chief of the French-Canadian nationality," did not assert himself strongly in these discussions. So long as the Lower Canadian province had responsible parliamentary government, Cartier was confident it would have the power to protect what was essential to its French Catholic majority.

On the same day that the coalition cabinet began its constitutional planning in Quebec City, a party of about a hundred Canadians left for the Maritimes. Their mission was to warm up the "lower provinces" to the prospect of political union with the Canadas. Their leader and troubadour, the only cabinet minister in the group, was that relatively new Canadian, Thomas D'Arcy McGee. McGee, who had visited the Maritimes several times, managed to wangle invitations from its three leading cities, Saint John, Fredericton, and Halifax. Although the Canadians encountered plenty of scepticism about the proposed federal union, they were warmly received at the social level. The greeting of the Saint John *Telegraph* at their first stop was typical: "You come proud sons of a noble state / Too long estrang'd and too long unknown."[15]

The toasts exchanged at the gala dinners put on in the three cities glossed over constitutional concerns. Warmed by good food and plenty of alcohol, Canadians and Maritimers at the elite level were getting acquainted and finding out that they could enjoy each other's company. Through intensive newspaper coverage of these affairs, some of this social camaraderie was trickling down to ordinary voters. McGee and his fellow ambassadors were performing a function essential to a successful constitutional negotiation: they were building the social union without which there could be no political union.

The group of twenty-three colonial politicians who came together at Charlottetown on Thursday, 1 September 1864 – eight from Canada, five from each of the Maritime provinces – was remarkably inclusive in it political composition. Although Nova Scotia's Conservative premier, Charles Tupper, failed to induce his greatest rival, Joseph Howe, to be a delegate, Howe's successor as Opposition leader, Adams Archibald, and Jonathan McCully, a prominent upper house Liberal, agreed to join the Nova Scotia delegation. New Brunswick's Liberal premier, Leonard Tilley, included two prominent Conservatives in his province's delegation. The Prince Edward Island five who were selected by Lieutenant-Governor George Dundas included George Coles, a former Liberal leader, and Andrew Macdonald, another prominent Liberal, as well as the premier, Colonel John Hamilton Gray, and two other members of his Conservative government. And, of course, the Canadian delegation was a coalition of political leaders that excluded only the Lower Canadian *Rouges*.

This political inclusiveness is in marked contrast to the exclusion of Opposition leaders from the meetings in our own time at Meech Lake and Charlottetown that attempted major constitutional restructuring. As Christopher Moore has so forcefully argued, political leaders at the time of Confederation had not yet succumbed to the belief that, between elections, Parliament is an unwelcome impediment to presidential rule by the prime minister and his partisan colleagues. I would add that political inclusiveness in constitutional negotiations greatly improves the prospect that the product of the negotiations will win broad political support.[16]

The political and social success of the short conference that took place in Charlottetown in the first week of September 1864 entitles Prince Edward Island to be considered "the cradle of Confederation." The Maritime delegates opened the conference in the afternoon of 1 September before the government steamer carrying the Canadians reached Charlottetown. But the next day, when the Canadian delegates crowded into PEI's small Legislative Council chamber and the meeting got down to business, the Canadians took over. They had a plan they were anxious to sell, and the Maritimers who had given little thought to Maritime union were more than willing to hear about it. Canada, in George Brown's words, "opened her batteries."[17] Macdonald and Cartier began with the general scheme of Confederation, and they made a great tandem, John A. waxing eloquent about the nation they were building and the strong government that would lead it, balanced by Cartier's sharing his confidence with members of provincial parliaments that a provincial parliament could secure his people's interests. Creative ambiguity, a vital ingredient of success in constitutional negotiations, was there in abundance.

Over the next three days, with just a break for Sunday observance, the plan was fleshed out, mainly by Galt and Brown. Galt laid out the financial aspects, including the assumption by the central government of the provinces' debts. Brown dealt with details of the governmental structure, providing a proposed list of each level's legislative powers and sketching in the structure of the central parliament's upper house. The Canadians' plan for the latter was a senate based on sectional equality – twenty-four senators for each of the new country's principal divisions – the Maritimes, Ontario, and Quebec. Given the possibility of a Maritime union, this made more sense than an upper house based on the US model of equal representation for each state. By Wednesday, 7 September, the Maritime delegates were ready to meet alone to consider their options. In a letter to his wife, Brown reported that their message to the Canadians was "that they were unanimous in regarding federation of all the Provinces to be highly desirable, if *the terms of union could be made satisfactory*, and that they were prepared to waive their own more limited question until the details of our scheme could be more fully considered and matured."[18]

These five days of intense constitutional discussions were punctuated by a steady diet of convivial social events. The delegates wined and dined at sparkling parties in the homes of their Islander hosts. On the second-to-last night of the conference, Lieutenant-Governor Dundas hosted a ball at Government House. The company of the Islanders' wives and daughters did much to soften and warm relationships among the men. And the hospitality was not all one way. The *Queen Victoria* had come – somewhat optimistically – laden with champagne. On Saturday the delegates were invited to a luncheon gala in the stateroom of the Canadians' ship. And it was quite a party! The champagne flowed freely. At one point a delegate called out, "If any one can show just cause or impediment why the Colonies should not be united in matrimonial alliance, let him now express it or forever hold his peace."[19] No one appeared to oppose the marriage banns. As Maurice Careless, Brown's biographer, writes, "There, in the chief stateroom of the *Queen Victoria*, amid the wineglasses and cigar smoke, twenty-three men had warmly agreed to found a new nation. Other states might have a more dramatic start – but few, surely, a more enjoyable one."[20]

On Friday, 9 September, the delegates sailed from Charlottetown to Pictou and then on to Halifax where they assembled in Nova Scotia's Legislative Council chamber. Here there was another round of meetings at which the Maritime leaders resolved to accept the Canadians' invitation to participate in a conference at Quebec City to work out acceptable terms for a federal union. At a public dinner on 12 September, for the first time the Confederation-makers announced what they were up to. The meetings on Prince Edward Island, while by no means secret, had been private: no press had been invited and no public announcements made. Indeed the Charlottetown Conference had to compete for press coverage and hotel space with the visit of the Slaymakers and Nichols circus to the Island capital.[21] But after the Halifax dinner and a visit of the delegates to Saint John, New Brunswick, there was a great

deal of press coverage and public interest as the Fathers of Confederation prepared to meet in Quebec City. Canadians, actual and future,
and their political leaders were now engaged in a mega constitutional
project – one when all other public business is eclipsed by the politics of
constitution-making.

On Monday, 10 October, the Quebec Conference got under way in the
reading room of the Legislative Council in what was then Canada's capital. The United Province's capital had bounced around from Kingston
to Montreal to Toronto to Quebec City like a ping-pong ball – an incon-
venient and expensive consequence of the United Province's fundamental lack of political unity. Queen Victoria, on the suggestion of Governor
General Edmund Head, aided and abetted by John A. Macdonald, had
"chosen" Ottawa as the permanent capital because it appeared to be
politically "the least objectionable" of all the contenders.[22] Construction
of a new parliament building was already under way in Ottawa when
the Quebec Conference opened. The question now was, would this fine
new edifice being erected on the Ottawa River house the parliament of
the old Province of Canada or the central parliament of a new Canadian
federation? The answer would be determined by the outcome of the
Quebec Conference.

Robert Harris's iconic portrait of the Fathers of Confederation somewhat glamorizes that Quebec parliamentary reading room where the
Canadian constitution-makers did their work.[23] Instead of those grand
arched windows in the Harris painting, the room had a pedestrian row
of rectangular windows. Perhaps that had the advantage of not allowing a panoramic vista of the St Lawrence to detract the gentlemen from
their statecraft.

Thirty-three delegates found places in the somewhat crowded reading room. New Brunswick and Prince Edward Island added two each
to the delegations of five that represented them at Charlottetown. Nova
Scotia stood pat with five. The full Canadian Grand Coalition cabinet
of twelve attended, which meant adding four to the eight who were at
Charlottetown. Two delegates from Newfoundland, the colony not invited to Charlottetown, rounded out the potential founding fathers.
The numbers in each delegation did not matter very much, as it was
agreed at the opening meeting that voting would be by provincial
blocks. Canada, because of its large size, would have two votes, while
the other colonies would have one each.

Hewitt Bernard, who was John A. Macdonald's chief clerk in his
attorney general's department and would later become his brother-
in-law, served as "executive secretary," sitting at a small side table

recording motions and votes. There was no one there to take shorthand notes, and certainly no journalists were allowed entry. We owe most of what we know about the discussions and debates that went into making Canada's Constitution to the memoirs, letters, and biographies of leading participants. Étienne Taché, the titular head of the Grand Coalition government, served as the presiding chairman at the middle of the long table that dominated the room.

It took sixteen days, with time off on Sundays, for the Fathers of Confederation to complete their work – a relatively short time to create the constitution of a large and complex new state. It helped that much of the drafting was done in advance by members of the Canadian cabinet. The Maritime delegates let the resolutions introduced by the Canadians form the agenda. In the end the conference agreed on seventy-two of these resolutions, a number of them amended through debate. These, known as "the Quebec Resolutions" or the "Quebec Plan," would become, with very few changes, the substance of Canada's founding Constitution, the British North America Act, 1867.

Thomas D'Arcy McGee credited Macdonald with the authorship of fifty of the seventy-two resolutions.[24] Certainly as a drafter of legal texts and a communicator of their rationale, John A. had no peer among the Fathers. But important as his drafting and leadership skills were in making the Constitution, it is a mistake to identify his intentions and hopes with the meaning of the document. On some crucial points there was bound to be some "creative ambiguity" in our founders' constitution-making, leaving scope for the Constitution's meaning to be shaped by political developments and judicial interpretation.

There was one crucial matter on which the Fathers of Confederation assumed they had little work to do. That matter was nothing less than the nature of democratic government in Canada and its provinces. They did pass a resolution that the general legislature should have a House of Commons.[25] Another resolution vested "Executive Authority or Government" in the British sovereign. But none spelled out the House of Commons' relationship to the executive branch of government. That relationship, of course, would be governed by the principle of responsible government. Delegates from all the provinces had fought for and practised the principle that the Crown's representative must act in accordance with the policies of the political leaders who command the confidence of the elected branch of Parliament. They saw no need, however, to have that principle written into the Constitution. They were content with adding to the resolution vesting executive authority in the sovereign the words "to be administered according to the well understood principles of the British Constitution by the Sovereign personally or by the Representative of the Sovereign duly authorized."

Because of the assumption that there was no need to write responsible government into Canada's Constitution, the Constitution Canadians got in 1867 and still have is silent on how Canada's system of parliamentary democracy is supposed to work. The preamble of the British North America Act, 1867 simply states that "the Provinces of Canada, Nova Scotia and New Brunswick have expressed their Desire to be federally united into One Dominion under the Crown of Great Britain and Ireland, with a Constitution similar in principle to that of the United Kingdom." The Constitution does not mention the office of prime minister or the cabinet or political parties, let alone the basic rule that, in exercising its executive powers, the Crown and those who act in its name must act on the "advice" of the politician who leads the party (or coalition of parties) that commands the confidence of the House of Commons. Nor does Canada's written Constitution say anything about the operation of responsible government at the provincial level. This vital democratic part of Canada's constitutional system is said to be regulated by "unwritten constitutional conventions."[26]

It might have been true that, in the 1860s, the principles regulating the relationship between executive and legislative power were, as the fourth of the seventy-two resolutions stated, "well understood." After all, the political leaders and the representatives of the sovereign had agreed on them and practised them, and the politically active people of the colonies had been engaged in the political struggle to establish them. But such a statement could not be made today. These principles are not taught in Canada's schools, and only slightly in its colleges and universities. In 1926 a crisis arose over Governor General Lord Byng's rejection of Prime Minister William Lyon Mackenzie King's request to dissolve Parliament and hold an election. In 2008 debate took place over granting Prime Minister Stephen Harper's advice to prorogue Parliament and over the legitimacy of coalition government. Both these cases demonstrated a lack of consensus among political leaders on matters supposedly regulated by unwritten constitutional conventions.[27] Moreover, a poll taken during the 2008 constitutional crisis indicated that a majority of Canadians believe that the electorate, not Parliament, decides who is to be prime minister.[28] New Zealand and the United Kingdom have moved away from a total reliance on unwritten principles by establishing written cabinet manuals that provide succinct guidelines accessible on the Internet to basic principles and practices of their parliamentary democracies.[29] Until Canada does something similar, a legacy of the work of the Fathers of Confederation is a serious democratic deficit.

If the principles of parliamentary democracy were underworked in the drafting of Canada's Constitution, the details of the federal division of powers were overworked. Article 1 of the US Constitution gives a short list of the legislative powers of Congress. All other legislative powers were retained by the states. The leading English-speaking architects of Canadian federalism, especially John A. Macdonald and George Brown, wanted Canada's Constitution to reverse this aspect of the American. They believed that confining the national legislature to a limited set of assigned powers and leaving the residue of law-making in the country to the states was a key source of weakness in the American federation and a factor in the outbreak of civil war. But instead of providing a short list of provincial legislative powers and simply leaving the residue of all law-making powers to the new federal parliament, the Canadian drafters produced lengthy lists of the legislative powers of both levels of government. In their quest for certainty, they inflicted on Canada competing shopping lists of federal and provincial powers that have forever plagued constitutional interpretation and the politics of the Canadian federation.

One of the seventy-two Quebec Resolutions (#29) does begin with proposing a broad grant of power for the general parliament "to make Laws for the peace, welfare and good Government of the Federated Provinces," but it then adds, "and especially respecting the following subjects." An enumerated list of thirty-seven powers follows. It is interesting to note that this proposed general grant of power to the federal legislature uses the phrase "peace, welfare and good Government," whereas the general grant of power in section 91 of the text of Canada's Constitution is phrased as the power "to make laws for "the Peace, Order and good Government of Canada." This was one of the changes made at the final constitutional drafting conference in London in 1866. We do not know why. It more likely reflects a drafting preference of Colonial Office lawyers than a shift of policy priorities among Canada's founding fathers.

In any event the Quebec Conference's list of the federal parliament's specific legislative powers contained all the powers assigned to Parliament in the final constitutional text. And it is a formidable list that covers pretty well all the principal domestic functions of government in that era: the regulation of trade and commerce, defence, all forms of taxation, currency, banking, navigation, country-wide transportation and communication works, Indians and land reserved for Indians, immigration, agriculture, fisheries, marriage and divorce, criminal law, and penitentiaries. The list of eighteen powers proposed in resolution #43, for the "Local Legislatures," was also extensive. It included direct taxation, borrowing money, education, hospitals, municipal institutions, local public works, property and civil rights, and the administration of justice. Another resolution (#56) left all Crown lands, mines, minerals, and royalties in the hands of the provinces. Clearly the provinces, despite the rhetoric of centralist-minded Canadians, were to be much more than mere municipalities.

On the fiscal side the Quebec Conference approved a very imbalanced system. The provinces would be fiscally dependent on the federal government. The one kind of taxation assigned to them, direct taxation, in an age that had not yet invented direct taxes on individual or corporate income, would yield very little revenue. In consideration of this, resolution #64 called for the federal government to pay to each of the provinces "an annual grant-in-aid" equal to 80 cents per head of population. In a spirit of laughable optimism the resolution added that these payments "shall be in full settlement of all future demands upon the General Government." Then, as a harbinger of the fiscal federalism follies to come, the following resolution (#65) supported an additional payment of $63,000 for ten years to New Brunswick.

The judicial provisions proposed for the new federation were also highly centralized. The federal government would be able in the future to establish federal courts for "the due execution of its laws" (#30), but in the meantime the superior and county courts of the colonies would simply carry on as the principal courts of the country. Although the provincial governments would have the responsibility of maintaining and organizing these courts, resolution #31 put the power of appointing provincial judges and the responsibility of paying them in the hands of the federal government. It would be nice to report that underlying this unusual judicial scheme was a vision of a national judiciary that would protect the citizens of a federal Canada when they travelled outside their province from exposure to the parochial bias of locally appointed judges – a problem that had troubled the American federation. Alas, the evidence is that, rather than being inspired by such a statesmanlike vision, the desire to control patronage appointments was the principal motivation of the Fathers of Confederation in proposing that the new federal government, in which many of them looked forward to being ministers, be empowered to appoint the judges of the senior provincial courts.[30]

The good news is that resolution #37 stipulated that judges of the superior courts "shall hold their office during good behaviour, and shall be removable only on Address of both Houses of Parliament." This language was taken directly from the 1701 English Act of Settlement, which established judicial independence for that country's highest judges. The political discontent that stirred the British North American colonies in the 1830s included the demand that judges enjoy security of tenure. The Act of Settlement's terms of judicial tenure were secured for Nova Scotia and the Province of Canada in the 1840s.[31] Now this fundamental principle of liberal government, a crucial part of the civic culture of British North Americans, was to be inscribed in Canada's Constitution. It is a pity that it would not apply for many years to the lower courts – the courts presided over by magistrates and justices of the peace – where most Canadians have their first-hand experience with the administration of justice.[32]

The only attention the drafters at Quebec gave to the top echelon of the judicial system was highly centralist in its implications. The federal parliament was empowered to establish "a General Court of Appeal for the Federated Provinces." There was no concern about the need for a neutral judicial arbiter to resolve disputes between the two levels of government. The lawyers among the delegates, and there were not as many as we would expect today, knew that a court comprised of law lords was the final court of appeal for all parts of the British Empire, and that would include the new Canadian federal state they were designing. But the enormously important role that the US Supreme Court was playing in interpreting the American Constitution does not seem to have made any impression on Canada's founders.

The feature of the federal design agreed to at Quebec that appears to have the greatest centralizing potential is the federal government's power to interfere with provincial legislation. The Quebec Resolutions (#50 and #51) built into the Canadian Constitution the imperial legislative powers that Britain continued to exercise over its North American colonies – namely, the power of the sovereign's representative to refuse to give Royal Assent to legislation that had passed through the colonial parliament and instead reserve it for the sovereign's consideration, and if Assent were not given the bill would be disallowed. The Quebec Resolutions proposed the extension of these powers to the operation of the Canadian federation. The governor general would be empowered to reserve bills that had passed through Parliament for consideration in London and possible disallowance, while provincial lieutenant-governors could reserve for the consideration of the governor general in Ottawa bills passed by the provincial legislatures, and if Royal Assent were not given within a year, the bill would be disallowed. These arrangements were being proposed in an era of constitutional monarchy, when the distinction between what Walter Bagehot referred to as the "dignified" and "efficient" elements of the constitution was well understood.[33] This distinction meant that it was not the monarch or the governor general who would exercise the powers of reservation and disallowance, but the ministers who "advised" them. In other words, to call a spade a spade, the British government could veto legislation passed by the Canadian Parliament, and the Canadian government could do the same with provincial legislation. And to underline the power this would give Ottawa, provincial lieutenant-governors would be appointed by the governor general in Council – that is, the federal cabinet.

For those, such as John A. Macdonald and George Brown, who believed that the general government in the Canadian federation must be the senior level of government, it was logical to apply British imperial controls to Ottawa's relationship with Canada's provinces. But what about others at the Quebec Conference who were not so centralist minded? Cartier, the chief representative of French Canada, went along with these arrangements, even though he did not believe that provinces should be subordinate to the federal government. Christopher Moore has put his finger on what was likely the reason Cartier kept his powder dry. "Responsible government," Moore writes, "was the sovereignty of the 1860s."[34] Cartier and his *Bleu* colleagues were counting on the political power responsible government had given their people to secure their vital interests through a provincial parliament in which French Canadians were bound to be the dominant force. Had they been present at the Quebec Conference, *Rouge* politicians would not have been nearly as complacent about the threat the federal powers of reservation posed to provincial autonomy. Maritimers might be expected to have been more astute in protecting their provincial legislatures from federal intrusions, but in this their first serious encounter with federal issues, they were ill-prepared to debate the imperatives of federalism. Besides they had not found that these powers Britain retained over them seriously compromised their enjoyment of self-government. Might not Ottawa be similarly restrained? So this double-decker arrangement of imperial power – Britain over Canada, Ottawa over the provinces – went through, and has remained in Canada's Constitution to the present day.[35] As we shall see in later chapters, however, the forces of Canadian nationalism and provincial autonomy rendered the powers politically unusable many years ago.

The most contentious element of the Canadian federation the Quebec delegates were designing was the federal parliament's upper house – the Legislative Council, as the British North Americans continued to call it.[36] As we have seen, second chambers were a badly designed feature of the parliamentary regimes Britain designed for its North American colonies. Reformers in Lower and Upper Canada had pressed to make their legislative councils elective. That view prevailed in the United Province of Canada when its Constitution was changed to hold elections to fill Legislative Council vacancies created by the death of life members.[37] Prince Edward Island had also acquired an elected Legislative Council in 1862.[38] The case for an elected upper house was made by several delegates, including Oliver Mowat, an Upper Canadian reformer in the Grand Coalition government and a future premier of Ontario, but its proponents lost the debate.

John A. Macdonald said his "own opinion will be made up on having arguments on both sides of the questions, as my mind is open on the subject."[39] It was a reformer, George Brown, who launched the strongest attack on an elected senate. Brown's attack was based on his strong commitment to responsible government: with two elected chambers claiming a democratic mandate, to which one would the government be responsible? Brown did not want an upper house that could challenge the elected House of Commons. And yet the appointed senate that the delegates favoured and that made its way into the Constitution was legally endowed with the same powers, with one exception, as the House of Commons. No bill can become law until it is passed by both the Senate and the House of Commons (and receives Royal Assent), but bills for the raising of money by taxation or for the spending of money must originate in the House of Commons and be "recommended by Message of the Governor General" (resolutions #48 and #49). In reality this meant ministers responsible to the elected chamber of Parliament would control fiscal policy.

The main rationale for having an upper house was, as the hackneyed phrase puts it, to serve as a chamber of sober second thought. John A. Macdonald spelled out what this should mean: "It would be an independent house, having a free action of its own, for it is only valuable as being a regulatory body, calmly considering the legislation initiated by the popular branch and preventing any hasty or ill-considered legislation which may come from that body, but it will never set itself in opposition against the deliberate and understood wishes of the people."[40] Although Macdonald spoke these words a few months after the Quebec Conference, when the Province of Canada's Parliament was debating the resolutions, they sum up as well as anyone ever has the fundamental reason for bicameralism in a parliamentary democracy. Note that Macdonald banked on senators' self-restraint: their recognition that, in a democratic era, the role of non-elected legislators is to improve legislation, not to block legislation for which there is a strong popular mandate. The Canadian Senate, through the course of its history, has not let Macdonald down. It has rarely used its legislative veto power.[41] On several occasions when it has refused to pass major government initiatives, such as the free trade agreement with the United States, it was simply to hold them up until their popularity could be tested in a general election. But where the Senate has not lived up to Macdonald's standard is its capacity to be an "independent body."

When the Fathers of Confederation at Quebec voted to have members of the Legislative Council appointed for life by the Crown (resolution #11), they spoke entirely in terms of the Constitution's "dignified" component, ignoring its "efficient" reality: the prime minister would tell the governor general whom to appoint. Resolution #14 would have taken these patronage appointments away from the first batch of Senate appointments and empowered the provinces' legislative councils to select the senators from their province. But this idea did not survive the London Conference. Section 24 of Canada's Constitution simply states: "The Governor General shall from Time to Time, in the Queen's Name, by Instrument under the Great Seal of Canada summon qualified Persons to the Senate." Of course the reality is that the prime minister decides who gets the royal summons, and usually that has meant the prime minister's telling the governor general to summon his political friends. If a party holds power for several terms, its supporters will have majorities in both houses, seriously compromising the Senate's capacity for political independence.

The qualifications required for Senate appointees were that they must be "of the full age of thirty" and own $4,000 worth of property free of debts and other obligations (resolution #12). In those days thirty-year-olds were well into adulthood, and owning $4,000 of real estate was a respectable amount of property.[42] In these provisions we see a whisper of the classic liberal vision of the balanced constitution in which the more established interests of the community act as a check on the radical tendencies of the demos represented in the House of Commons. The Quebec Resolutions did not stipulate that the senators' property must be in their home province, or that senators must be resident in the province for which they are appointed. Perhaps those requirements were implicit in the resolution that had the first senators appointed by provincial upper houses. Be that as it may, for the provincial delegates at Quebec the most important function of the Senate was to balance the dominant position that rep-by-pop gave the most populous sections of the federation in the House of Commons by giving equality of representation to the country's less populous regions in the upper chamber. It was over this sectional representation that the Quebec Conference had its biggest row.

It was the presence of Newfoundlanders, who were absent at Charlottetown, that gave rise to the conflict. The Canadians' proposal stuck with the formula of twenty-four senators each for the Maritimes, Ontario, and Quebec, squeezing Newfoundland's representation into the allotment for the "Lower Provinces." Much to the displeasure of the Maritime delegates, such an arrangement would clearly mean reducing the number of senators from New Brunswick, Nova Scotia, and Prince Edward Island. In retrospect it might be difficult to understand how a dispute over this issue could have taken up so much of the Quebec Conference's time. It is a measure of the importance that the smaller provinces attached to their representation in the Senate. It is also a reminder, which Canadians need from time to time, that Newfoundland is not one of the Maritime provinces. The issue was resolved at Quebec by retaining the formula of twenty-four senators each for the Maritimes, Ontario, and Quebec (resolution #8) and adding four for Newfoundland, if and when it entered the union (#9).

Given the popular tendency to portray Confederation as a pact between English and French Canada, one would expect to see some evidence of that idea in the deliberations at Quebec City in 1864. In fact, at this time French Canada was taken to be coterminous with the French Canadians of Lower Canada.[43] No *Acadien* was present at Quebec. The *Acadiens* did not think of themselves as French Canadians, nor did French Canadians identify with a community that included French-speaking Maritimers. What was essential for French-speaking delegates at Quebec in securing the interests of their people was a province that had power and autonomy and in which they believed French Canadians would always be a majority. Cartier and his *Bleu* colleagues could not be sure that they had achieved this at Quebec, and they would have a struggle convincing their compatriots that they had.

French Canada's representatives in the Confederation negotiations did not visualize a French-English dualistic country stretching from coast to coast. They did confirm the right to use French in Parliament, which they had secured under the Act of Union, and they supported a reciprocal right for the English-speaking minority to use their language in the Quebec legislature (resolution #46). French Canadians were also to enjoy the right to use their language in federal courts, but not in the courts of other provinces, while Quebec's English minority would have the right to use their language in the courts of Quebec. The asymmetry of these linguistic provisions indicates how little interest there was at this time in making all of Canada a home for French Canadians. Similarly, although the education rights of Ontario Catholics and Quebec Protestants to continue to enjoy their denominational school rights were protected (resolution #43), no such protection was afforded Catholic minorities in the Maritimes.

A further indication of the distinct place contemplated for Quebec in the Canadian federation was inclusion in the list of federal jurisdictions the power to render uniform the laws relating to property and civil rights in all or any of the provinces except Quebec (#29). Parliament could use this power, however, only with the permission of provincial legislatures, a permission that has never been forthcoming from a single "common law" province. Nonetheless the exclusion of Quebec from this uniformity-of-law provision shows the consensus among Canada's founders that Quebec was not to be "a province like the rest."

Three remaining aspects of the constitution-making at Quebec relate to the kind of state the Fathers of Confederation believed they were building. The first of these is resolution #68, committing the general government to completing "without delay" the Intercolonial Railway from Rivière-du-Loup, Quebec, to Truro, Nova Scotia. This was a most important hook in bringing the Maritimes into Confederation. Railway-building was the biggest policy issue of the day in New Brunswick and Nova Scotia, and even though there was much interest in establishing a rail connection to the United States, a commitment to complete the Intercolonial was a much-needed selling point for the delegates of the two mainland Maritime provinces. The commitment to a rail link between the Canadas and the Maritimes also speaks to the founders' ambition to build an economic union. At the time, interprovincial trade in

British North America was minuscule compared with the provinces' trade with Britain and the United States.[44] An intercolonial rail link would be a key step to offsetting this, as well as making it easier to defend Canada along hundreds of miles of its border with the United States. More fundamentally the resolve to have Canada's new central government build a railway shows that Canada's founders expected government to play a robust role in the country's economic development. That was an important component of their shared civic culture. Canada's founders were not committed to laissez-faire economics.

A second element was the Fathers' assumption that they were founding a continental federation. Resolution #10 states: "The North-West Territory, British Columbia and Vancouver Island shall be admitted to the Union, on such terms and conditions as the Parliament of the Federated Provinces shall deem equitable." The vision was not yet of a country stretching from sea to sea to sea because the northerly range of the colonists' vision at this time stopped well south of the Arctic. The North-West Territory covered all the lands between Canada and British Columbia, never mind that nearly all of this vast territory was the homeland of Indigenous nations – at the time, settler peoples and their governments gave no heed to this fact. The Fathers of Confederation, especially those from what is now Ontario, saw a continent-wide Dominion as their manifest destiny. They were in a hurry to make the North-West Canadian before the United States made it American.

An embryo Canadian nationalism stirred that geopolitical ambition. But in the Confederation movement and proceedings there was only the slightest evidence of a sense of *Canadian* nationalism, and it was pretty much confined to the Upper Canadians. When the Quebec Resolutions were debated in the colonial Canadian legislature, Cartier famously answered those who questioned the possibility of creating a new nationality by extolling the virtues of a new kind of political nationality based on ethnic pluralism. "In our own federation," he said, "we should have Catholic and Protestant, English, French, Irish, and Scotch, and each by his efforts and his success would increase the prosperity and glory of the new confederacy."[45] Cartier's pluralist vision of Canadian society was very much in line with Lord Acton's view, noted in the previous chapter, that a society of different ethnic nationalities could support a strong and liberal state. But, like Lord Acton, Cartier was a voice crying in the wilderness. His championing of ethnic diversity elicited mostly silence from his French and English political colleagues. The very concept of a *Canadian* nationality raised hackles in the

Maritime provinces, whose people had never thought of themselves as Canadian. Even more problematic was reconciling the idea of a new nationality with loyalty to the British Empire. "A British subject I was born, and a British subject I will die," thundered John A. Macdonald. Like that of so many of Canada's founders, Macdonald's primary national identity was British.

Retaining a strong tie with Britain is the final element of Canadian constitution-making that must be recognized. Canada's founding fathers were anxious to ensure their constituents that establishing a federal union did not mean there would be a break with the British Empire. The third resolution adopted at Quebec stated that, in "framing a Constitution," the Conference was doing so "with a view to the perpetuation of our connexion with the Mother Country." But the Fathers of Confederation knew that this was a mother country in which "little Englandism" had become the prevailing view. For the colonies populated by British settlers, this meant a loosening of controls and responsibilities. Britain's principal motive in encouraging Confederation was the hope and expectation that a union of its North American colonies would enable them to assume a larger share of the burden of holding off a territorial advance by the American republic. Hence the statement in the preamble of Canada's founding Constitution, which is still there, that a federal union "would conduce to the Welfare of the Provinces and promote the Interests of the British Empire."

Self-government in domestic affairs had been solidly won by the colonists before Confederation. The imperial government's power to veto Canadian legislation would quickly fall into disuse – though it remains in the Constitution to this day. There would remain one real limit on Canadian independence: Britain would continue to control Canada's foreign affairs. Resolution #30 gave the general government and Parliament "all powers necessary or proper for performing the obligations of the Federated Provinces, as part of the British Empire, to Foreign Countries, arising under Treaties between Great Britain and such Countries." It would be many decades before Canada could act as an independent country in the community of nations.

After sixteen days at Quebec, the constitution-makers had completed their work. They had agreed on the architecture of a federal union of Britain's North American colonies, governed through the institutions and practices of British parliamentary government. They recognized the distinct place of Quebec in that federation, provided for the federation's continental expansion, and settled details of finance and infrastructure. A few changes would be made later at a conference in London, the imperial capital, but the main elements of Canada's Constitution were now in place. The work that remained to be done by the founders was political: selling the Constitution to their constituents. But before turning to that, it is important to address the position of one of our country's three foundational pillars, the Aboriginal peoples.

Aboriginal peoples did not ask to participate in Confederation, and the colonies' political leaders, representatives of the Crown, or the British government did not consider including them in the Confederation process. Why? The short answer is Aboriginal peoples, though treated as British subjects, were regarded as "wards" of the Crown, excluded from mainstream British North American politics and society. The more fundamental reason is that, for more than a century, the nations to which the Aboriginal peoples belonged had used treaties to regulate their relations with the Crown, and whatever British North America's new Constitution was, it was not a treaty between the British sovereign and First Nations.

Although Britain, without consulting Aboriginal peoples, had by the 1850s delegated responsibility for relations with native peoples to colonial governments, these governments continued to use treaties to order relations with First Nations along the advancing frontier of settlement and industry. Two major treaties were negotiated by William Robinson on behalf of the Crown with Ojibwa communities with homelands across the watershed of the rivers flowing southward into Lake Superior and Lake Huron.[46] The Robinson treaties became prototypes for the series of post-Confederation treaties negotiated with First Nations as Canada's frontier moved north and west. In the early 1850s William Douglas, governor of the Vancouver Island colony, negotiated fourteen treaties with Indian peoples on the island.[47] As I noted in Chapter 3, nation-to-nation treaties between the Crown and First Nations as the means of settling land issues and securing peaceful relations have their constitutional foundation in the 1764 Treaty of Niagara and the 1763 Royal Proclamation. The Treaty of Niagara has never been rescinded by either of its parties, and the part of the Royal Proclamation relating to the nations and tribes with whom the Crown is connected remains law to the present day.

There was not a trace, however, of the treaty relationship with Indigenous peoples in the work of Canada's founders. The only mention of Indians in the Quebec Resolutions is the listing of "Indians and Lands reserved for Indians" among the legislative powers of the federal Parliament (#29). That language suggests that the Fathers of Confederation saw Indians not as members of independent nations with whom the Crown makes treaties, but as subjects of the Canadian government. The prevailing colonist vision of future relations with the Indians was incorporated in the Gradual Civilization Act, which John A. Macdonald as attorney general for Canada West had introduced in the legislature of the Province of Canada in 1857.[48] That vision looked forward to the complete disappearance of Indians as distinct peoples. The Gradual Civilization Act was the precursor of the 1876 Indian Act, which would attempt to apply its program of total assimilation to all of Canada.

In the two decades between the Gradual Civilization Act and the Indian Act, only one Indian opted for enfranchisement,[49] and the Indian peoples did not disappear. The Government of Canada continued to negotiate treaties with Indian nations while at the same time appointing Ottawa bureaucrats to run their societies. There was no logic in this: a government does not make treaties with persons it regards as its subjects. But the Canadian federation was formed at the high tide of European imperialism, when white people – and this most certainly included the Fathers of Confederation – believed fervently in their racial superiority and, in the words of Edward Said, "the almost metaphysical obligation to rule subordinate, inferior, less-advanced peoples."[50] Through its first century, Canada's policies with respect to native peoples would move along this contradictory path – treaties for getting their lands, imposing white officials as their rulers – with tragic consequences for Indigenous peoples and an enormous legacy of broken promises and distrust.

Approval of the Quebec Resolutions by the colonial parliaments was the expected means of bestowing political legitimacy on the constitutional plan for the new federation. For the colonies' political leaders and their people, this democratic step in constitution-making was based much more on their successful struggle for responsible government than on the theories of political philosophers. It was also a step that colonial administrators in London understood and supported. They did not want to be asked to give legal effect to a constitution that did not have popular support in the colonies. It was common ground for both the colonists and the British government that the proposed Constitution could become law only by being enacted by the British Parliament. Canada's founding fathers readily agreed to leaving their Constitution in the custody of that Parliament not only because that was where their constitutions had always come from, but also because British imperial policy had evolved to the point that they could trust

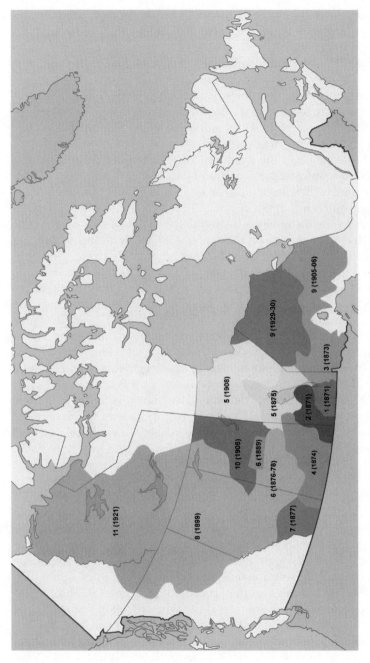

Map of Numbered Treaties of Canada
Source: Wikimedia Commons

British parliamentarians not to impose their will on the Canadian people and to respond to well-supported requests they received from Canadian authorities.

Leaving formal legal control over Canada's Constitution with the Parliament in London was convenient for the Fathers of Confederation. But it side-stepped and left unresolved what is perhaps the most challenging question for a constitutional democracy: who should have the right to make changes in its highest law, the Constitution? Their new Constitution contained no amending formula, no rules spelling out what was required for a request from Canada to be well-enough supported to require implementation by the British Parliament. An attempt to resolve that issue at Quebec in 1864 would probably have blown the conference apart. It is as difficult to envision the delegates from French Canada agreeing to anything less than a veto over constitutional changes touching on the powers of Quebec as it is to imagine the delegates from English Canada agreeing to such a veto. One hundred and fifteen years later, the patriation process failed to reach an agreement between Quebec and the rest of Canada on that crucial issue. Canada's English-speaking pillar has had difficulty accepting that Canada is a multinational society in which there is not a single people whose majority can exercise sovereign constitutional authority.

The fullest parliamentary debate on the resolutions agreed to at Quebec took place in both houses of the legislature of the United Province of Canada. The debate opened early on 3 February 1865 when John A. Macdonald moved that the lower house adopt the Quebec Resolutions, and it concluded on 13 March. In the end the resolutions carried with a large majority, ninety-one votes to thirty-three. Much of the majority was provided by Canada West, whose members voted fifty-four to eight in favour. Although the division among Canada East members was narrower, they still voted thirty-seven to twenty-five in favour. Among French-Canadian members, the resolutions secured a majority of just four.[51] In the upper house a vote to postpone a final vote on the resolutions until after an election had been held was defeated by large majorities from both sections of Canada. In debating the Quebec Resolutions, Canadian legislators were in a situation that is inescapable after a successful constitutional negotiation among political elites: they were faced with a done deal they could not pick apart but had to approve or disapprove in its entirety. Those who are not in on making the deal are never happy about that. This was certainly true in the Canadian Parliament's debate on the Confederation package. The most trenchant criticisms came from the French-Canadian *Rouges* and Canada West members who did not support Brown and Macdonald's Great Coalition. The *Rouge* leader, Antoine-Aimé Dorion, argued that a real confederation would give the largest powers to the local governments and merely a delegated authority to the general government.[52] Christopher Dunkin, an independent Conservative, accused the supporters of Confederation of being misleading and perverse in claiming they had combined the advantages of a legislative union and a federal union in one system. He cited as evidence "the grand power of disallowance of the federal government, which we are told, in one and the same breath, is to be possessed by it, but never exercised."[53]

Macdonald and Brown, the hard hitters on the government side, were eloquent and statesmanlike in presenting the case for the constitutional scheme drawn up at Quebec. They emphasized how the federal union they proposed reversed the excessive powers of the states in the American union. In what are perhaps the most famous lines in Macdonald's speech, he claimed that, "Here we have a different system. We have strengthened the general government. We have given the general legislature all the great subjects of legislation. We have conferred on them, not only specifically and in detail, all the powers which are incident to sovereignty, but we have expressly declared that all subjects of general interest not distinctly and exclusively conferred upon the local governments and legislatures shall be conferred upon the general government and legislature."[54] Brown, following Macdonald, explained that a federal union had been forced on him and his Upper Canadian colleagues by Lower Canada and most of the delegates from the Maritime provinces: "We had either to take a federal union or drop the negotiation." That was their compromise. In return they had drawn up a federal scheme that had "all the advantages of a legislative union."[55] And he went on to itemize the centralizing features of the Quebec Resolutions.

In the legislative debate, the Lower Canada friends of Brown and Macdonald did not argue against the spin their Upper Canadian colleagues were putting on the nature of the proposed federal union. To have done so would have threatened the unity of the coalition government. The counter to the Upper Canadians' centralist vision of Confederation came in the *Bleu* newspapers of Canada East. In an era when newspapers were highly partisan and influential, Confederation's French-Canadian advocates used their newspapers to overcome *Rouge* efforts "to inflame the French population against the Scheme."[56] Typical was *Le Courier du Canada*, which acknowledged the difficulty in agreeing on the division of powers between the two levels of government, but said the problem had been solved by leaving "*aux gouvernements locales des garanties suffisantes pour les protéger contre toute tentative d'impiétement de la part du gouvernement central.*"[57] These journalistic defences of the proposed federal scheme were not carefully crafted constitutional analyses, but they expressed well the constitutional expectations of the supporters of Confederation in French Canada. Although these expectations were markedly different from those of Macdonald and Brown, they turned out to be realized in practice much more than those of the English side of the Grand Coalition.

In Atlantic Canada the Confederation cause encountered much stormier waters. In all four provinces there was widespread support among the political elites and the public for the general idea of a union of Britain's North American colonies. There was also strong support for the union in the mother country. The London *Times* speculated that the proposed union "will be only a state of transition, marking the passage of British America from colonial tutelage to national independence."[58] And it was clear where the British government stood: the colonial secretary, Edward Cardwell, was pushing hard for passage of the Quebec Resolutions through the colonial legislatures. Objections to the "Quebec scheme," rather than opposition to union of the colonies, built support for the anti-Confederation cause. That plus party politics soon began to threaten to sink the good ship Confederation in the seaboard provinces.

Prince Edward Island was the first to withdraw from the Confederation scheme. Edward Palmer, a crusty conservative and the province's attorney general, broke the unity of the Island's delegation a few weeks after the end of the Quebec Conference. On returning to Charlottetown, Palmer turned on his pro-Confederation colleagues for not working hard enough to get better terms for their province – in particular, settling for just five MPs in the rep-by-pop federal House of Commons and failing to secure a commitment to finance buying out PEI's absentee landlords, the province's truly existential problem. George Coles, a former Liberal premier and a member of the PEI delegation at Quebec, soon joined Palmer in attacking Confederation. William Henry Pope, the strongest unionist in the government, and Edward Whalen, an Irish Catholic Liberal, found themselves the only delegates supporting the Quebec scheme. On 17 December 1865, Premier Gray, feeling the tide of opinion running against union, resigned. For the time being, the Confederation cause was dead in Prince Edward Island. In May 1866, both houses of the Island's legislature voted against consideration of the Quebec Resolutions.[59]

In Newfoundland, for a while – a very short while – Confederation's prospects looked better. When Newfoundland's two "observers" at the Quebec Conference, Frederick Carter, a prosperous Protestant merchant, and Ambrose Shea, a Catholic reformer, returned to St John's, they said they were "bringing back the bacon."[60] The Speech from the Throne opening Newfoundland's Assembly in January 1865 struck an optimistic note: Confederation was a matter of "the deepest interest to the whole community," and the "future beneficial consequences of union would not escape the inquiry of the House."[61] But in the ensuing debate it was clear that many of the assemblymen did not find those consequences so alluring. The prospect of giving up their own provincial sources of revenue and having a high Canadian-designed tariff inflicted on them was particularly odious. Canada had no markets to offer for the colony's main product: fish. Newfoundlanders' commercial arrangements and vision were transatlantic, not continental. Conservative premier Hugh Hoyles soon got the message and moved cautiously with assurances that the matter would not be forced through the House. Charles Fox Bennett, an influential leader of the St John's business community, led the anti-Confederation cause. Consideration of the seventy-two Quebec Resolutions was shelved. The denouement came in the 1869 election, when anti-Confederation candidates swept the board. A poem celebrating the election result speaks eloquently to the public mood: "And now Confederation a shameful death has died, / And burnt up at River Head beneath the flowing tide, / And may it never rise again to bother us I pray, / "Hurrah, me boys!" for liberty, the Antis gained the day."[62] Unlike in Prince Edward Island, Confederation in Canada's other island province would be dead for a very long time.

With the withdrawal of Prince Edward Island and Newfoundland, Confederation's fate was in the hands of New Brunswick and Nova Scotia. If you were looking to lay a bet at the beginning of 1865 and knew something about the state of politics in those two provinces, you would not have put your money on Confederation.

Much would depend on the political skills of Leonard Tilley and Charles Tupper, the Conservative premiers of New Brunswick and Nova Scotia, respectively. On their return from Quebec both premiers soon encountered a rising tide of opinion not so much against the general idea of union, but against the "Quebec scheme." They hesitated to emulate their Canadian colleagues and put the Quebec Resolutions before their legislatures.

In New Brunswick the aggressive and ambitious Lieutenant-Governor Arthur Gordon leaned on Tilley to ask for dissolution so that the Confederation scheme could be put to the people in a general election. Gordon was no fan of the proposed federal union – what position would there be for viceregal officers like himself if the provinces were reduced to mere local governments? So let the people decide, and as far as he was concerned they could turn Confederation down. Tilley, an even-keeled, rather phlegmatic man described by one historian as "unblushingly pedestrian," relented and in January 1865 called an election.[63] The result was a disaster for the Confederation cause. The government, which had been in power for almost ten years, was tired and tainted with charges of corruption. The western railway extension from Saint John to Shediac had more immediate sex appeal than union with Canada. When the votes were tallied in early March, Tilley lost his own seat and his supporters were reduced to eleven in a House of forty-one.[64] This was discouraging news to the Canadian leaders who were just winding up their debate and approval of the Quebec Resolutions in the Canadian Parliament, and it was downright alarming to Charles Tupper and his government next door in Nova Scotia. Tupper's government began to see its majority crumble as the anti-Confederation cause gathered strength across the province.[65] Tupper was a more audacious political leader – indeed, he was something of a bully in pushing his views forward – but with the cautionary tale of Tilley's defeat in New Brunswick and the anti-Confederation drums beating loudly, he adopted a cautious, delaying approach. He was in no hurry to submit the resolutions to the province's legislature, let alone to its electorate.

Tupper had something to contend with that was absent from the New Brunswick political scene: a renowned and charismatic Opposition leader. For the generation that achieved responsible government, Joseph Howe was Nova Scotia's outstanding leader. By the 1860s he had become Liberal premier and the best-known colonial statesman in the British Empire – indeed, reforming the empire to accommodate self-governing colonies had become his constitutional project. In 1862 his lobbying in London for an imperial position paid off when he was appointed an imperial fishery commissioner under a British-US reciprocity treaty with the task of mapping the exclusive fisheries in the river mouths and estuaries of the United States and British North America. The following year his Liberal government suffered a resounding defeat; he himself failed to carry the Lunenburg riding.

It was Tupper's good fortune to have his chief opponent out of the Assembly and away on imperial business at a critical time for the Confederation cause. Not that Joseph Howe was deeply opposed to union with Canada. In the past he had spoken eloquently in favour of British North American union, and he would be a cabinet minister in Ottawa two years after Confederation. But like so many others he was bothered by the strange stew of British and American elements in the plans for a federal union. His "Bothersome Letters," published in the Halifax *Morning Chronicle*, exploited public confusion about the Confederation plan, which he attacked as "neither fish, flesh or good red herring."[66] Above all Howe kept clanging the bell about the undemocratic way Tupper and the pro-Confederation people were resisting submitting the Quebec Resolutions to the judgment of the Assembly or the people.

Howe was pushing a strong grassroots anti-Confederation movement from behind. The Tupper government's majority in the Assembly was crumbling.[67] The province's business community began to turn against Confederation. Tupper had no Galt, or Brown, or even a Tilley to defend the fiscal side of Confederation. There was a natural resistance in a province that regarded itself as the senior British North American colony to becoming a junior partner in a Canadian union.

By the fall of 1865 there were signs that the tide was turning. Arthur Gordon returned to Fredericton with a new wife and his backbone stiffened by the Colonial Office to push hard for the Confederation cause. In November, the victory of Charles Fisher, a feisty Conservative notable, in a New Brunswick by-election was "hailed by the Confederate papers as a victory," and the psychological effect was considerable in both provinces.[68] George Brown's visit to the Maritimes was effective in softening Liberal opposition to federal union. The decisive factor in making 1866 a winning year for the Confederation cause in the Maritimes was geopolitical and external, truly a *deus ex machina*: the Fenian attempt to invade New Brunswick.

The Fenians were Irish nationalists dedicated to liberating Ireland from British rule. Many who had emigrated to the United States served on the Union side in the Civil War. After the war the Fenians set their sights on the soft underbelly of the British Empire: they would strike the first blow against Britain by invading and conquering its North American colonies. The US government formally adhered to a strict policy of neutrality, but did nothing to stop the Fenians, many of them hardened and well-armed veterans of the Civil War, from congregating at places along the British North America border. One of these places was Eastport, Maine, where about five hundred Fenians arrived for a "convention" in April 1866. The British responded by dispatching a fleet of five warships to the waters off the coast of Maine and assembling a force of over six hundred British and New Brunswick troops.[69]

Overkill for sure, but eye-catching, alarming, and opinion-shaping for the Maritime people and politicians in the midst of a political debate about belonging to a stronger union of their provinces.

In the end the Fenian "invasion" amounted to five Fenians, on 14 April, making their way onto New Brunswick territory: Indian Island, in the estuary of the St Croix River. But pro-Confederation leaders in New Brunswick and Nova Scotia seized the day, taking advantage of the panic created by the threat of a Fenian invasion to reverse the fortunes of their cause. In New Brunswick, Governor Gordon inveigled Liberal premier Albert Smith to include in the Speech from the Throne a commitment to have the legislature consider federal union. When Smith indicated that he remained opposed to the Quebec scheme, the Conservative Opposition moved a vote of non-confidence. On 6 April New Brunswick's upper house, the Legislative Council, voted in favour of union on the basis of the seventy-two Quebec Resolutions. On 10 April, with a non-confidence motion pending in the Assembly, the Smith government resigned. Using his prerogative power, Gordon dissolved the legislature in May. In the ensuing election, with the help of a lot of money from his pro-Confederation Canadian allies, Tilley swept back to power, inflicting a worse defeat on the anti-Confederation side than he had suffered a year earlier.

On 10 April, the very day that Smith's government resigned in New Brunswick, Charles Tupper submitted a resolution to the Nova Scotia Assembly calling for the appointment of delegates to arrange a "scheme of union" that would "effectually ensure just provision for the rights and interests of Nova Scotia."[70] The anti-Confederation side's insistence that, before proceeding with union, there must be an election or a plebiscite could not overcome the pro-unionists' case for the need to strengthen British North America's defences against the threat from the south. On 17 April Tupper's resolution carried, thirty-one to nineteen. Tilley wasted no time putting a similar resolution before the New Brunswick legislature. On 21 June 1866 the province's Assembly approved, thirty-one to eight, a motion supporting a union "upon such terms as will secure the just rights and interests of New Brunswick." The New Brunswick resolution added the requirement of "immediate construction of the Intercolonial Railway."[71] The legislatures of the two Maritime provinces had given their support not to the seventy-two Quebec Resolutions, but to an effort to negotiate better terms for their provinces than the Quebec scheme offered. The third and final Confederation conference, to be held in the imperial capital, would now determine what changes could be made to the plan agreed to at Quebec twenty months earlier.

Much to the chagrin of the Maritime Confederation leaders – especially Tupper, who had to face an election legally required by May 1867 – John A. Macdonald, now the acknowledged captain of the Confederation ship, dilly-dallied about setting a date for the London Conference. During the hot summer of 1866, John A. was going through one of his periods of heavy drinking, carousing to all hours with Thomas D'Arcy McGee. Responding to the disgust of his soberer colleagues, he is reported to have told his drinking companion, "Look here, McGee, this Cabinet can't afford two drunkards, and I am not quitting."[72] But there was also some strategic thinking behind his delay: Macdonald wanted the shortest possible time between the London Conference and the opening of the British Parliament so that there would be as little time as possible for changes to the Confederation "pact" to stir up a political row back home. With a session of Parliament scheduled to begin in February 1867, Macdonald called for the Canadian and Maritime delegates to meet in London in December 1866.

The five-person delegations from New Brunswick and Nova Scotia were much the same as those that went to Quebec in 1864, the most notable change being the inclusion of R.D. Wilmot, a New Brunswick Liberal who had converted to the pro-Confederation side. The Canadian delegation of six was half the size of its representation at Quebec, but it included three of the big four: Macdonald, Cartier, and Galt. Notably absent was George Brown, who had left the coalition government not because of any decline in his support for Confederation, but because of his disagreement with the government's approach to renewing the reciprocity trade deal with the United States. Hector-Louis Langevin, a rising French-Canadian political star more than made up for the absence of the aging Canadian premier, Taché.

On 4 December 1866 the sixteen delegates met in a room at the Westminster Palace Hotel, where the Canadians were staying. For this stage of the London Conference the colonial delegates were on their own, without any British officials present, to consider possible changes in the Quebec Resolutions. Now this, to say the least, was a delicate operation. Had the resolutions agreed to at Quebec City in 1864 not been presented to the Canadian Parliament in 1865 as a pact or treaty whose terms could not be altered? But the Maritime delegates had been authorized by their elected legislatures to get better terms in London. And it was not only the Maritimers who were looking for changes.

Alexander Galt was anxious to improve the protection of the Protestant minority's educational rights in what was to become the province of Quebec. Galt, although a member of the Canadian delegation, had resigned from the government on this issue. Despite what seemed to be a contradictory situation, the delegates coughed and wheezed and blushed, and then proceeded to review the seventy-two resolutions, one by one. Pragmatism won the day over principle.

Although the delegates did a lot of talking, and worked away on the resolutions right up to Christmas Eve, they made very few changes to their draft constitution. Two issues took up most of their time and attention. One was the protection of the educational rights of religious minorities. Galt was not the only one for whom this was a major concern. Archbishop Thomas Louis Connelly of Halifax had been lobbying hard in London for the right of Roman Catholics in the Maritimes, many of whom were *Acadiens*, to have separate schools. The delegates heard him, and agreed that constitutional protection of minority school rights should apply in all provinces to denominational schools established in law both before and after union – a mark of Canada's distinctive pluralism in its founding Constitution.

Then, of course, there was much discussion of the Senate. Some of the more liberal delegates pressed once again, to no avail, for an elected upper house. The New Brunswickers and Nova Scotians, not without some strenuous pushing, increased their Senate representation to twelve each, gobbling up the four places allotted at Quebec to Prince Edward Island. Agreement was also reached on a provision for breaking deadlocks between the two houses of Parliament by adding more senators. A small move to deliver better terms to the Maritime provinces was to make the resolution concerning the Intercolonial Railway more binding.[73]

It is interesting how little consideration was given to the very crux of the federal union: the division of powers between the two levels of government. Jurisdiction over "Sea Coast and Inland Fisheries," which at Quebec had been assigned to both the federal Parliament and the provincial legislatures, was removed at London from the provincial list of powers. This points to another change in the division of powers that turned out to be extremely important in the operation of Canadian federalism, although it seems to have just snuck its way into the final text of the Constitution. In section 91 of the British North America Act, 1867, the twenty-nine matters listed as examples of the federal Parliament's general power "to make Laws for the Peace, Order and good Government of Canada" are declared to be under "the *exclusive* Legislative Authority of the Parliament of Canada," while section 92 states that,

"In each Province the Legislature may *exclusively* make Laws" with respect to the sixteen mattes the section enumerates.[74] The exclusivity of federal and provincial powers would turn out to be a major generator of litigation in the new Dominion and the constitutional basis for a powerful provincial rights movement.

In January 1867 the second stage of the London Conference got under way when the delegates met with Lord Carnarvon, the new colonial secretary, to transform their resolutions into the text of a bill to be submitted to the British Parliament. The hard work of drafting was interrupted by the most important social event of the London Conference. On 16 February the delegates gathered at St George's Church in Hanover Square to attend the wedding of the chairman of their conference, John A. Macdonald. The bride was Agnes Bernard, the sister of Herbert Bernard, his private secretary, who had also served as the secretary for the Quebec Conference. For the widower Macdonald, the delegates, and the members of their families who had accompanied them to London, it was a joyous occasion – a reminder of the primacy of family life even for statesmen establishing a new country.

Three days later Agnes and John A. watched from the gallery of the House of Lords as Carnarvon moved the second reading of the British North America bill. The British government insisted on only one change in the London resolutions that John A. Macdonald passed on to Lord Carnarvon: Canada would be christened a "Dominion," rather than a "Kingdom." Britain feared that "Kingdom" would be too offensive to the United States, where a congressional committee had declared that a confederation "founded upon monarchical principles" endangered the great republic's "most important interests."[75] Leonard Tilley had fished "Dominion" from the words of the seventy-second Psalm: "He shall have "dominion also from sea to sea and from the rivers unto the ends of the earth." Queen Victoria was not terribly happy with it, but it did speak to the founders' continental ambition, and perhaps it would not make Americans too nervous. The bill sailed easily through both houses of Parliament. The only scary moment came when radical MP John Bright began his speech by protesting that the bill was being pushed through against the wishes of Nova Scotia. But in the end Bright did not oppose it, and the bill received Royal Assent on 29 March 1867. The British North America Act would come into force as Canada's Constitution on 1 July 1867.

There was no dancing in the streets of London with the enactment of Canada's Constitution. The *Times'* statement that "We look to Confederation as the means of saving this country from much expense and

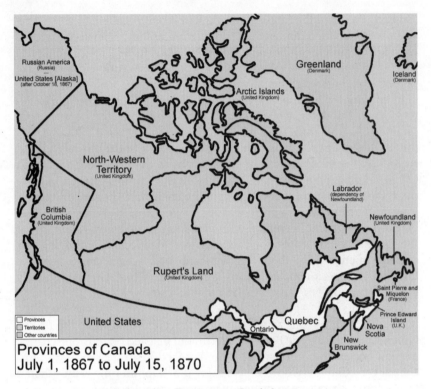

Canadian Territory at Confederation
Source: Wikimedia Commons

much embarrassment" was about as enthusiastic as opinion in the mother country would get. This lack of enthusiasm was disappointing to the Fathers of Confederation, who would have to wait until they returned home to receive some applause for their efforts. For some, especially Charles Tupper and his Nova Scotia colleagues, a political row awaited, and for all of them hard work lay ahead in making the world's first parliamentary federation a successful political enterprise. Their pragmatism and pluralism had served their constitution-making well. Canada's French-speaking pillar had secured a province in which it would be the dominant force. The new country's English-speaking pillar was larger than ever, albeit with an uncertain sense of being Canadian. Both pillars shared a civic culture of parliamentary democracy, constitutional monarchy, the rule of law and an independent judiciary, and maybe federalism, although it was not at all clear that English and French Canada shared a common understanding of what federalism should mean. One of the first challenges for the infant Canadian federation was its relations with the absent pillar, the Indigenous peoples. The Dominion of Canada's approach to this challenge would show, tragically, the limits of both its pluralism and its pragmatism.

PART FOUR

The Three Pillars to the Second World War

Chapter 8

The Colonization of Indigenous Canada

At the end of her epic account of the life of Ahtahkakoop, the Plains Cree chief who was born "about 1816" and died in 1896, Deanna Christens sums up his life as follows: "Ahtahkakoop was both a visionary and a realist. A noted buffalo hunter and warrior. Ahtahkakoop had been blessed with special spiritual powers. He had been a member of the *mitewiwin* (a secret Cree medicine society). He was a respected chief, and a man known for his intelligence and reasoned mind. Faced with the final destruction of the buffalo and relentless waves of newcomers to the land he shared with other plains people, Ahtahkakoop took the steps he believed necessary for the survival of his people."[1]

In the eighty years he lived on what came to be known as the Canadian prairies, Ahtahkakoop had experienced extraordinary change. Born into a free and independent people who had migrated south and west to compete with other Amerindian nations – most often Blackfoot and Sioux – in exploiting the bounty of the buffalo hunt, he ended his life helping what remained of his people to survive on an unpromising small parcel of prairie land subject to the rule of Canadian government officials.

Ahtahkakoop had experienced the establishment of Hudson's Bay Company trading posts intent on commercializing his material life and the arrival of Christian missionaries dedicated to taking over his spiritual life. He suffered the shock of the sudden collapse of the buffalo herds and was puzzled by the approach of a new Canadian government claiming sovereignty over him and his people. Then from the Red River came the mixed-blood Métis, settling along the South Saskatchewan River, followed by white European families establishing farms on the most fertile prairie lands. With them came the North-West Mounted Police to keep the peace, and steam engines along a railway built across Cree lands to deposit even more European farming families on those lands.

As Ahtahkakoop's abilities earned him a leadership role among his people, he used his authority not to resist these changes, but to accommodate them as best he could. This meant that he responded positively to invitations of Canadian officials acting in the name of the British sovereign to enter into a treaty that would set out how the Cree and the white settlers would share the land. And he led his people in converting to the life of a farming community, and at least nominally to Christianity. In 1885 when the Métis took up arms in the second Riel uprising, Ahtahkakoop's people remained loyal to the Crown, with which they had made a treaty. The Plains Cree's reward for that loyalty was the imposition on them of the Indian Act, Canada's legislative instrument of colonization, under which Indian agents would direct the management of their affairs, their traditional recreations would be prohibited, and their children removed from them to be educated in residential schools in an all-out effort to destroy their culture and identity.

At the time of Confederation there were about a hundred thousand Indigenous people spread unevenly across Canada.[2] Demographers estimate that, at the time sustained contact with Europeans began, the Indigenous population had been at least half a million.[3] The decline was almost entirely in eastern Canada, and was mainly the devastating result of disease. The Mi'kmaq and Maliseet in Nova Scotia and New Brunswick, the Montagnais, Cree, Algonquin, Abenaki, and Iroquoian peoples in Quebec, the Anishinabek and Iroquoian peoples in mid- and southern Ontario – all these nations through centuries of contact with Europeans suffered greatly diminished numbers through disease and warfare. At the time of Confederation they were reduced to tiny minority communities confined to reserves, some based on treaties, others on allocations of lands unwanted by the settlers.

The focus of the new Canadian state's Indian policy would be those lands west of Ontario, where Amerindian nations were by far the majority population. Canada did not have to invent the two policy instruments – treaties and legislation – it would employ in this, its first imperial venture. These had been the instruments of pacification, land acquisition, and the project of civilization used in eastern Canada before Confederation. But before Canada could deal with the Indians, it had first to deal with a newly formed nation of mixed blood people, the Métis, who stood at the gateway to its western thrust.

The easy part of acquiring the lands for Canada's western expansion was arranging to obtain Rupert's Land from the Hudson's Bay

Company. Rupert's Land was a vast tract of land comprising the entire Hudson Bay drainage system extending north of the northern watershed from Labrador to Lake Superior, all of what will become Manitoba, most of the prairies, and the north-west.[4] The Company held a fur-trading monopoly under the Royal Charter it had received in 1670, and exercised a thin veneer of governance at a few places in the northern and western reaches of Rupert's Land. With settlers pouring into the American Northwest and a railway connection completed to the Minnesota Territory, Britain was keen to see Canada take charge of the British North American northwest. So it responded positively when Canada's new Parliament passed a resolution empowering the government to buy Rupert's Land. In October 1868, Prime Minister Macdonald dispatched two members of his cabinet, George-Étienne Cartier and William McDougall, to London to negotiate a deal for Canada's takeover of Rupert's Land. After several months of negotiations, the Hudson's Bay Company agreed to surrender its interests to the Crown for £300,000 plus substantial reserves of lands around its 120 trading posts and the right to claim one-twentieth of the cultivable prairie land.[5] The Canadian Parliament agreed to the deal, which would be financed by a British loan, and an understanding was reached for the formal transfer of Rupert's Land and the North-West Territories on 1 December 1869.[6]

Now for the hard part: establishing an effective system of government for the new territory Canada was about to take over. Britain did not help with this transition. On the Pacific coast, where there was a critical mass of settlers on Vancouver Island and the British Columbia mainland, Britain had established a Crown colony in 1858 and elevated James Douglas, an activist Hudson's Bay Company factor, to be its first governor. But such a relatively smooth path from company to colony to province was not open in what was soon to become Manitoba. Along the Red and Assiniboine Rivers, in the basin of Lake Winnipeg, a volatile mixture of Métis, Indians, settlers, and militant Canadian expansionists, plus an ineffective governor, created a situation that Britain was only too happy to hand over to the newly minted Dominion of Canada.

In anticipation of its new responsibility, the federal Parliament passed legislation providing a temporary government for the North-West Territories and the western portion of Rupert's Land, once it was united with Canada. This government would consist of nothing more than a lieutenant-governor who would "administer justice and establish laws, institutions, and ordinances subject to their ratification by Parliament."[7] The fledgling national government in Ottawa clearly knew virtually nothing about acting as a colonial government. To compound its incompetence, it appointed to the lieutenant-governor position a member of the cabinet, William McDougall, who, in the words of Richard Gwyn, was "utterly unfit" for the job. "Wandering Willy," as his unadmiring colleagues referred to him, was a blustering "Canada First" nationalist, dedicated to building a Canada that was Protestant and English. He described the Métis, the most powerful people in the colony he was sent out to govern, as "semi-savages and serfs of yesterday."[8] Soon after his appointment, McDougall was heard to remark that he had just been crowned "King of the North-West."[9]

On 21 October 1869, when the "King," with his entourage, an ornate throne chair, and 350 Enfield rifles, reached Pembina, a town in the Minnesota Territory just inside the US border, he was handed a note from Louis Riel, secretary of the Métis National Committee, ordering him not to enter the North-West Territory without the committee's permission. McDougall at first ignored the message and proceeded up the Pembina Trail towards the Red River. But on 31 October he was compelled by a mounted and armed party of Métis sent by the National Committee to turn around and go back to Pembina.

The Métis, the largest element in the Red River settlement, were the descendants of families formed by French and Scottish fathers and Sauteux, Cree, and Assiniboine mothers. Through decades of experience working together to defend their rights in the fur trade, they had formed a strong sense of identity and a belief that they were a "new nation."[10] When Colonel John Dennis, leading a wagon train carrying a party of six surveyors, trotted into the Red River settlement on 20 August, alarm bells had gone off in the Métis community. They immediately feared for the security of their strip farms that lined the banks of the Red and Assiniboine rivers. The Canadian surveyors seemed to be on a mission to lay out lots that ignored the farms the Métis had developed over generations. More profoundly, it seemed that their country was about to be annexed to Canada without so much as a "how do you do" to its inhabitants. No one in the survey party spoke a word of French. So a party of Métis galloped off to enlist the services of the best-educated man in the community: Louis Riel.

Louis was the son of Jean-Louis Riel, a leader of the Métis who had stormed the courthouse outside Fort Garry in 1849 when Guillaume Sayer and three other Métis were put on trial for trading furs with Indians without a licence from the Hudson's Bay Company. Sayer and his compatriots were found guilty, but sentence was not pronounced and the accused swarmed away shouting "trade was free."[11] The Sayer "trial" was in effect the end of the Hudson's Bay Company's monopoly and an indicator of where power lay in the Red River settlement. Its bishop, Alexandre-Antonin Taché, had hand-picked young Louis at the tender age of fourteen to study for the priesthood at the prestigious Collège de Montréal, where he received the finest classical education available in Canada at that time. Riel could trace his roots in Quebec to his ancestor Jack Reilly, who emigrated to Quebec from Ireland shortly after the Conquest.[12] Young Riel excelled in his studies, but in 1864, just four months short of receiving his baccalaureate, his erratic behaviour led to his dismissal from the College.[13] A romantic tryst with a lady named Marie Guernon seems to have convinced him that he "lacked a priestly temperament."[14] Also he was extremely distressed by news that his father had died. After working in Montreal for a year or so, taking the first steps towards a legal career and indulging his passion for poetry, he moved to the United States. In 1869 the twenty-five-year-old Riel returned to the Red River to help his widowed mother manage the family farm and raise his five younger siblings.

On the day the Métis riders arrived at his farm, Louis had been home less than a month. Despite his bookish nature he did not hesitate to saddle up and ride off with his neighbours to confront the survey party. With Riel explaining that they were trespassing on the Marion farm and the enormous Janvier Richot stomping on the surveyor's chain when Colonel Dennis blurted out that he was acting on the authority of the Canadian government, the surveyors did not need an order from the colonel to pack up their equipment. The Red River resistance had begun.

The resistance unfolded in a three-act tragedy. Act I was all Riel. Through the early weeks of autumn Riel made his rounds of the villages, rallying his people to resist the imposition of Canada's rule. On 16 October 1869 two representatives from each parish met at St Norbert to form a National Committee, with John Bruce as president and Riel as secretary. This organization was modelled on the governance of the buffalo hunt.[15] Two days after representatives of the National Committee stopped McDougall at the US border, armed Métis occupied Fort Garry, the strategic hub of the Red River settlement, just south of Winnipeg. It was a pre-emptive occupation aimed at preventing forces under Canada Firster Dr John Christian Schultz from seizing the fort. Schultz had arrived in the settlement in 1861 after graduating in medicine from Queen's University. He quickly became the most dynamic entrepreneur in the bourgeoning frontier town of Winnipeg, buying up land and the settlement's only newspaper, the Nor'wester. Schultz ardently believed in Canada's western expansion. In the words of Maggie Siggins he was "an aggressive, obnoxious bigot – he despised Métis, Indians, Catholics and French-speakers in that order."[16] Once Schultz hooked up with Colonel Dennis and began building an arsenal of firepower in his Winnipeg house, the dark clouds of civil war began to gather over the Red River settlement.

Riel recognized the need to reach out to the more settled English-speaking people in the area if the resistance he was leading was to avoid communal violence. A week after the occupation of Fort Garry, the president and representatives of the French-speaking population of Rupert's Land issued a proclamation inviting "our friendly fellow inhabitants" to send twelve representatives (one each from ten parishes and two from the town of Winnipeg) to join the twelve members of the French council "to consider the present political state of the country, and to adopt such measures as may be deemed best for the future welfare of the same."[17]

On 16 November the English settlers came to meet with Riel and his council in the courthouse chambers outside Fort Garry. With armed Métis circling the courthouse, it was a tense and tumultuous meeting. There was great uneasiness about supporting an insurrection not only among the English delegates, but also within Métis ranks. There was, after all, a government in place. Not a British or a Canadian government, but a Hudson's Bay Company government: the Council of Assiniboia set up by the company in 1834.[18] Even though it provided only a veneer of governance and its company-appointed council was not representative of the community, its existence was enough to instill respect for established authority and make delegates reluctant to join the provisional government proposed by Riel. A letter from William Mactavish, the Hudson's Bay Company governor, written from his sickbed, brought proceedings to a crisis point. Mactavish charged the Métis with committing unlawful acts, and ordered them to lay down their arms and leave Fort Garry immediately "under the pains and penalties of law."[19]

The Métis held their ground. Riel called for a resumption of the English-French convention in a week's time. On 24 November, after a day of fruitless wrangling, James Ross, son of a leading anglophone half-breed family who had been sent east to study at the University of Toronto, turned to Riel and asked what the French really wanted. Ross was surprised when the Métis leader returned after a two-hour adjournment with a well-formed answer: "I believe we want what every

French parish wants, indeed, what Red River needs to survive. It is of our opinion that we should form a provisional government, a democratic authority that will serve for our protection and lend us a legitimate voice to negotiate with Canada."[20] Riel invited the English to join a government that would be made up equally of French and English – a generous offer considering the French considerably outnumbered the English in the settlement. He presented the English delegates with a written "List of Rights" that included the people's right to elect their own legislature, that their government should be bilingual, that concerns about land title should be tackled, that treaties should be negotiated with the several tribes of Indians in the territory, and that the new province should have a fair representation in the Canadian Parliament.[21] It was the first proposed charter of rights in Canadian history, and its contents were agreeable to both the English and the French delegates. But it is important to note that the List of Rights differentiated the Métis from Indian tribes. Recent historical research indicates that it was strongly influenced by Catholic priests who saw the Métis as fundamentally a French Catholic society, not an Aboriginal people.[22]

The problem now was what to do about Wandering Willy McDougall, the wannabe lieutenant-governor lingering down at the US border. On 1 December, the day he believed Canada was officially taking over in Rupert's Land, McDougall and six flunkies bundled themselves into sleighs and drove to an abandoned Hudson's Bay Company post just north of the border, where, in one of the great comic opera scenes in Canadian history, he unfurled a Dominion flag and, addressing a snowbank, read a "Royal Proclamation" declaring that he was now lieutenant-governor of the territory. He had written the proclamation himself, forging the queen's name. The reading done, he high-tailed it back to Pembina. McDougall's mischief went well beyond uttering a phony document. He declared Colonel Dennis "conservator of the peace," authorizing him, ironically, to "attack, arrest, disarm, or disperse" the Métis armed force.

Dennis worked fast on his commission. By 5 December he had 380 Sauteux and Sioux Indians (the Métis' buffalo hunt rivals), half-breeds, and Canadians training at the abandoned stone fort twenty miles north of the settlement. At the same time Schultz's followers in Winnipeg were transforming their leader's house and warehouse into Fort Schultz.

While all this was going on in Red River, back in Ottawa John A. Macdonald – now *Sir* John A., having been knighted in 1867 – took an action that pulled the rug out from under William McDougall. On

22 November he cabled London to ask that the payment of the money for taking over Rupert's Land from the Hudson's Bay Company be postponed.[23] The Canadian prime minister had heard enough about the tumultuous events in Red River to convince him that this was not the time for Canada to assume responsibility for governing the North-West Territory. The British government agreed, somewhat grumpily, to postpone the transfer, leaving the Hudson's Bay Company nominally in charge.[24] A letter advising McDougall of his decommissioning was sent by ordinary post, arriving long after his ridiculous declaration of authority in the snow.

Riel wasted no time showing who was now in charge at Red River. On 7 December three hundred armed Métis surrounded Fort Schultz, giving the Canadians inside fifteen minutes to surrender.[25] Out they all filed, and were marched down the main street to the waiting jail cells at Fort Garry. Two days later Colonel Dennis, showing better judgment than his commander McDougall, issued a peace proclamation ordering all his recruits at the Stone Fort to stand down. Dennis made his way back to Pembina disguised as an old Indian woman.[26] On 10 December Riel issued a grandiloquent declaration that the people had established a Provisional Government, which was now the only lawful authority in Rupert's Land and the North-West.[27]

The first act thus ended with Riel very much in command at Red River, but with his authority based more on military might than on the broad-based consent of the people.

Act Two took place through a fierce winter. There was a broadening of support for the conditions on which Red River would become part of Canada. In a shrewd move to calm things down, in late December Sir John A. sent three emissaries to the troubled settlement: Jean-Baptiste Thibault, a Catholic priest who had taught at St-Boniface College and might help make up for Bishop Taché's absence in Rome; Colonel Charles de Salaberry, who had considerable experience in the North-West and was known to be liked by the Métis; and, as mediator, Donald Smith, the Hudson's Bay Company's chief factor. Although this was Smith's first trip to the North-West, he was married to a charming Métisse, Isabella Hardisty. Choosing Smith, who turns up in Canada's history fifteen years later as Lord Strathcona, driving the famous last spike that completed the Canadian Pacific Railway (CPR), was a smart decision. He was foxy, smooth, and tough, a "clenched fist in a velvet glove."[28]

The wily Smith bided his time before addressing the public – with Riel's permission. On 19 January over a thousand people from all over the settlement congregated inside Fort Garry's walls.[29] With the temperature at twenty below zero, they listened for five hours as Smith presented what Canada had to offer. Among the official documents he read to the half-frozen multitude were Secretary of State Joseph Howe's letter commissioning Smith to consult and take whatever steps seemed expedient to win the settlement over to joining Canada, and a letter from Canada's governor general, Sir John Young, reporting that Queen Victoria, though upset by the happenings in Red River, was willing to listen to her subjects' grievances. Young himself promised an amnesty to all who would lay down their arms and cease their resistance.[30] It was not exactly what the Métis wanted to hear, but Smith had greased enough palms with the pile of cash he brought with him to keep the crowd from erupting. When the meeting resumed the next day, Riel proposed "that a Convention of Forty be assembled of twenty elected representatives from the English population and twenty from the French," and concluded the meeting with a speech of conciliation.[31]

While progress was being made towards conciliation, Schultz's Canada Party was once again stirring up violence. The Métis proved to be much better mounted riflemen than jailers. On 9 January there was a major breakout by a number of the Schultz mob, including the fiery young road worker Thomas Scott and Schultz's close friend Charles Mair, the Canadian poet and journalist. On the frigid night of 23 January, Schultz himself made his escape, all six-foot-four and 250 pounds of him, falling into a snowbank when his buffalo-skin braided rope broke loose from his third-floor window.[32] Though badly injured, the Canada First doctor was now free to rally his forces against the Métis and their "disloyal" English collaborators.

Despite this gathering storm, elections were held, and the forty-person Convention assembled for its first meeting on 25 January. It spent a few days working on a second List of Rights much like the one Riel had produced two months earlier. When Riel lost some important votes and it looked as though the Convention was coming apart, the Hudson's Bay Company governor, Mactavish, admonished English-speaking delegates from his sickbed to "[f]orm a government for God's sake, and restore peace and order in the Settlement."[33] In the end Riel was successful in securing unanimous support for a provisional government to preside over the settlement while its terms of union were being settled in Ottawa.

Just as peace and concord were being secured at Fort Garry, militant Canadians once again were on the warpath. In the last week of February, a force of 360 led by Dr Schultz, Charles Mair, and Major Charles Boulton, who had come to Red River as second-in-command of the surveying crew, advanced towards Fort Garry. Riel ordered a full mobilization of the Métis militia, but realizing that releasing a force of five hundred against the poorly armed Canadians would result in a dreadful bloodbath, he sent a letter to the insurgents stating that "peace and our British rights we want before all."[34] This was enough for most of the Canadians to disperse, but a small group of fifty led by Boulton and Scott continued towards Fort Garry. When they got close enough to see the hundreds of Métis rifles pointing at them, they surrendered. The ringleaders, including Boulton and Scott, were taken prisoner, charged with treason, and sentenced to be executed.

Donald Smith was able to talk Riel out of having Boulton executed. But Thomas Scott would not let up, pouring out a steady stream of racially insulting invective at his Métis jailers. Riel, as president of the Provisional Government, allowed Scott's trial to go forward. He played no part in the proceedings except to give some testimony about Scott's rabid recalcitrance and to ask the tribunal to show mercy. In the end the tribunal, chaired by Ambroise Lépine, voted four to two to have Scott executed.[35] Donald Smith warned Riel that the Canadians would never forgive him for Scott's execution. Never were more prophetic words spoken. Shortly before noon on 4 March 1870, Scott was led out of his cell into a bright blue Winnipeg winter day and shot dead by a Métis firing squad. Thus endeth Act Two with Riel's one great mistake, which would haunt him until the day he too faced a sentence of death.

In the final act we witness the consummation of the triumph, the peaceful entrance of Manitoba into the Canadian federal union; and the culmination of the tragedy, Riel's exile from Canada.

On 23 March, as a late snowstorm swept through the settlement, the three men chosen by the Provisional Government to negotiate the terms of union with Canada bundled into ox-drawn carts and headed south on a circuitous route to Ottawa.[36] What an unusual threesome they were! Judge John Black represented the English and Father Noel-Joseph Ritchot, a confidant and counsellor of Riel, the French. The third man was Alfred Scott, an American bartender at Winnipeg's O'Lone's Saloon, but it's not clear whether he represented Americans or the settlement's drinkers. The three delegates set out with yet a third List of Rights. Bishop Taché had finally returned to Red River just four days after Scott's execution, and his hand can be seen in a touching up of the list that came out of the January Convention. The most important changes were demands for provincial status and the payment of the Provisional Government's debts.[37]

By the time Red River's delegates reached Ontario, the province was seething with anger over Thomas Scott's execution. "Handbills and posters screaming RED RIVER OUTRAGE – A ROPE FOR THE MURDERER RIEL were plastered everywhere."[38] Dr Schultz and Charles Mair were hailed in Toronto as conquering heroes. When a crowd of five thousand tried to cram into St Lawrence Hall to hear them, the rally had to be moved to City Hall, where more than ten thousand aroused citizens turned out.[39] Ritchot and Scott skirted Toronto to avoid a lynch mob. But on reaching Ottawa, at the instigation of the Canada Firsters, they were arrested twice on the same day by the Ottawa police on a charge of murder. Fortunately, an Ottawa magistrate dismissed the charges for lack of evidence.[40]

In the capital, Sir John A. kept the delegates waiting for several weeks before he would negotiate with them. Canada's first prime minister was into the country's first national unity crisis. Macdonald could hear the hue and cry of anti–French Catholic hatred from Orange Ontario. But he could also hear opposing noises from the other side of the Ottawa River. "How much hatred there is in these Anglo-Saxon souls against everything which is French and Catholic," thundered L'union des Cantons de l'Est.[41] On 25 April Macdonald and Cartier finally sat down with Father Ritchot, the one delegate who could really speak for Red River.

The negotiations were tough, and Father Ritchot had to make some major concessions. A province of the Canadian federation called "Manitoba" – Cree for "Spirit Strait" – would be carved out of the North-West Territory. But it would be a postage-stamp-sized 11,000 square miles – about the same size as Prince Edward Island. And unlike the other provinces, its public lands would be controlled by the federal government "for the purposes of the Dominion" – namely, for railway-building and land settlement.[42] The federal government would also own and control the vast reaches of the remainder of the North-West. So Riel had his province, but what a truncated province it was!

Still, there would be some tangible benefits for the Métis and Red River's soon-to-be-swamped French Catholic majority. The Métis and other settlers would be guaranteed title to their lands along the banks of the Red and Assiniboine rivers. In addition, 1.4 million acres of land would be made available to the unmarried children of the "halfbreed residents."[43] This represented a big chunk of the province, although it was not the reserved block of land that Riel and other Métis leaders hoped to have as a homeland for their people. Moreover, the absence of any provision for its immediate distribution led to a delay in enabling young Métis families to enjoy their benefit. One hundred and forty-two years later the Supreme Court of Canada would recognize the unreasonableness and injustice of that delay – a bit too late for compensation to be effective.[44] The Manitoba Act would contain provisions for the cultural dualism of its European settlers: English and French could be used in the legislature and courts of the new province, and rights to denominational schools held by law or practice at the time of union were recognized.[45] Once English Protestants became a majority, however, these guarantees would prove not worth the paper they were printed on. Indeed, these concessions to the French Catholics were much too much for William McDougall, who moved to reject the government's bill for the founding of Manitoba. But the sore loser's motion was rejected by a vote of 120 to 11, and the Manitoba Act was passed and given Royal Assent on 12 May 1870. Because of doubts about the Canadian Parliament's power to establish new provinces, the British Parliament was asked to validate both the Act and the Canadian Parliament's power to enact legislation establishing new provinces. This was done, and on 15 July Manitoba became Canada's fifth province.

Sir John A. Macdonald had always had a two-pronged strategy for Canada's western expansion: to negotiate a peaceful union of the Red River settlement with Canada, then to send a military expedition to Red River to squash any action by American annexationists and to show the "peaceable kingdom's" flag to its new subjects.

The second part of Macdonald's policy rolled out in the summer of 1870. It took the form of four hundred British regulars and eight hundred Canadian volunteers, most of them fired up with the desire to avenge Thomas Scott's execution, under the command of Colonel Garnet Wolseley, a distinguished British imperial officer. After reaching Fort William by ship, Wolseley's soldiers slogged their way over fifty muddy portages, laden with cannon, ammunition, and food, through one-hundred-degree summer heat, swatting mosquitoes.[46] When the army reached Red River on 23 August, its men were in an ugly mood. Louis Riel, still acting as head of the Provisional Government as it awaited the installation of the new Canadian provincial regime and advised by Bishop Taché that an amnesty was on its way, was tipped off that Wolseley's Canadians were looking for him. He ordered the evacuation of Fort Garry and slipped out himself, so that when

Wolseley's force arrived it walked into an empty fort. Wolseley and his British soldiers left after a week, but Canada's volunteers, brimming with Orange hatred, "began a long reign of terror" in which two Métis were killed.[47]

Louis Riel was twice betrayed on the promised amnesty. First by the Government of Canada, which passed the matter over to Governor General Young to take up with the British government, and then by Young, who led Father Ritchot and Bishop Taché to believe he would recommend the amnesty requested by George-Étienne Cartier. But in his communiqué to Britain, Young supported the Canada Firsters' version of events, with the result that Queen Victoria declined to pardon Riel and the Provisional Government.[48]

Although Riel was now a man many Canadians wanted to be tried for murder – Ontario offered a $5,000 reward for his capture – he remained in Red River, somewhat furtively, to test how much his people wanted him to represent them in the Canadian Parliament. He was nominated to run in Provencher, one of Manitoba's four seats in the House of Commons, in the 1872 federal election. But when the shocking news reached Manitoba that Cartier, Riel's best friend in the Macdonald cabinet, had lost his seat – Quebec voted weeks before Manitoba – Riel agreed to step aside and let Cartier run unopposed in Provencher. A year later, after Cartier died of kidney disease in London, Riel won the Provencher by-election by acclamation. He travelled east, but was advised for security reasons not to take his seat in the House. He won Provencher again – in absentia – in the 1874 election brought on by the Pacific Scandal. This time, despite threats on his life, Riel dared to take his seat as an independent in the House of Commons. It would be a gross understatement to say that his presence in the House caused a buzz. Indeed, on 9 April, on a motion moved by Mackenzie Bowell, a Grand Master of the Orange Order and future prime minister, Louis Riel was banished from the House.

In October 1874 Ambroise Lépine, who had presided over the court that passed the death sentence on Thomas Scott, was himself sentenced to die, having been found guilty of murder by a Winnipeg jury made up equally of English and French members. This verdict enraged Quebec,[49] and its legislature passed a unanimous resolution calling for clemency. Liberal prime minister Alexander Mackenzie, just like Sir John A. Macdonald, now found himself caught in a crisis of national unity. After waiting for Oliver Mowat's Liberals to win the Ontario election, Mackenzie announced a general amnesty for all Métis except Lépine and Riel. Lépine's sentence was commuted to a two-year jail term; Riel was banished from all British territory for a period of five years.[50]

And so the curtain comes down on the final act of this tragedy. But it would not be the end of the story of Louis Riel, nor by any means the final chapter of his people's history. The attempted conquest of the Métis nation would not be completed. They, and their leader, would soon return to centre stage in Canadian history. And although this would end Riel's earthly sojourn, the Métis nation would live on as an important component of Canada's Aboriginal pillar.

With the Métis out of the way, at least for the present, the Canadian government was free to open up the west and pursue what was becoming the national dream of its English-speaking majority. On 20 June 1871, with the support of its legislature and the offer of very generous terms of union, British Columbia became the Dominion of Canada's sixth province.[51] One of the inducements offered to British Columbia was a commitment to commence, within three years, the building of a railway connecting Canada to the Pacific.[52] So the plan now was to build the railroad and bring in Canadians and Europeans to populate the vast area that lay between Manitoba and British Columbia's eastern border along the foothills of the Rocky Mountains. The only serious obstacle to executing the plan was that the vast majority of people who lived in that territory were not Canadians, but members of Amerindian nations with whom Canada had no formal relations.

The Canadian government's choice of treaty-making as its policy instrument for dealing with the Aboriginal peoples of the North-West was not automatic or inevitable. The Macdonald government was "willing to consider alternatives to treaties in order to deal with the perceived obstruction that Indians represented to expansionism."[53] The alternative was to follow the other English settler countries and turn to warfare. The United States, after the Civil War, had begun the project of settling its west with an intense period of treaty-making. But in 1871 the US Congress passed a resolution declaring that "No Indian nation or tribe within the territory of the United States shall be acknowledged or recognized as an independent nation, tribe, or power with whom the United States may contract by treaty."[54] Treaties were seen as an expensive and uncertain way of clearing the path for settlement. So the American government shifted to using military force to move Amerindian nations into areas unwanted for the time being by the American people. If Canada had possessed anything like the military power of the United States, its government too might have preferred that alternative.

In New Zealand, a country founded on the 1841 Treaty of Waitangi between the Maori and the British Crown, warfare had broken out in the 1860s when the country's settler government refused to respect the treaty-based land rights of the Maori people.[55] Australians and the settler governments responsible to them had never used treaties to regulate their relations with Aborigines. As New South Wales, Queensland, and Tasmania advanced their frontiers of settlement through the nineteenth century, warfare and tough policing were their policy instruments for dealing with Aboriginal peoples who got in the way.[56]

In the latter decades of the nineteenth century, planet earth was experiencing the high tide of European imperialism. The Indigenous peoples native to Australia, Canada, New Zealand, and United States had no place in the white democracies British settlers were building – unless as individuals they became totally assimilated into the civilization of the Europeans. Belief in the superiority of European civilization was now being fortified by a scientific Darwinian racism – junk science, to be sure – that relegated Indigenous peoples to the lower rungs of the evolutionary ladder.[57] Fervent belief in Christianity's lock on spiritual truth imbued imperial rule over native peoples with moral passion.

Canadian policy was distinctive in this era in employing treaties with native peoples as the means of clearing the way for the country's development to its "open spaces." But Canada's imperial motivations and prevailing racism made it impossible for its treaty-making to be built on anything close to a meeting of minds. It cannot be said that Canadian authorities regarded treaty-making with Indigenous peoples who held title to their lands as a constitutional imperative. The 1763 Royal Proclamation *in theory* was still good law. But, as we shall see, Canadian courts – including the country's and the British Empire's highest court, the Judicial Committee of the Privy Council – in this imperial age showed no understanding of the common law doctrine of native title that underlay the Royal Proclamation. Moreover, while the time would come when Canada's judiciary would give force to Aboriginal rights as a constraint on the powers of Canadian governments, that time was more than a century away when Canada embarked on its treaty-making project. Sir John A. Macdonald and company knew well the benefits of treaty-making for advancing the frontier of settlement in Canada's west. It must have struck them as a much less costly and more decent way of acquiring the lands of western Canada for settlement than relying entirely on *force majeur* – so long as the native peoples were willing treaty-partners.

The First Nations of the prairies and the northern woodlands were willing – indeed, in some cases, anxious – to make treaties with the Crown. The nations Canada would make treaty with between 1871 and 1877 were experiencing the end of the buffalo-hunt economy that had sustained them for over a century. On top of that, they were beginning to be hit in large numbers by the diseases the white man brought with him – smallpox, measles, influenza, tuberculosis – diseases their immune systems could not handle and for which they had no effective medicines. Although in aggregate they outnumbered the Canadians migrating into their territory and would do so for some time, their political divisions inhibited a united stand against the newcomers and their government. The Plains Cree had assisted the Ojibwa from the north and east in their migration onto the prairies, allowing them access to the buffalo hunt. As buffalo hunting contracted, it became focused on the Cypress Hills, bringing these two nations allied with the Assiniboine into conflict with the nations of the Blackfoot Confederacy.[58] The arrival of part of the powerful Sioux nation in southern Manitoba, pushed north by the US Army, strengthened the case for making treaty, rather than war. Tribal chiefs, band leaders, and sachems for some time had sensed that an irreversible alien force was coming upon them. Under these circumstances, the best course of action was to try through a treaty relationship to get immediate help from the queen's representatives for their economic problems and to establish arrangements for sharing their lands with the newcomers that would enable them to live on their own, apart from the white man, while retaining access to the lands and waters that had traditionally sustained them.

The Ojibwa and Swampy Cree peoples living close to the Red River settlement were the first to make treaty. Settling land issues with these First Nations through a treaty process was included in the Riel Provisional Government's List of Rights. For these Aboriginal peoples, the threat of a flood of Canadians migrating into their lands had become a reality, although Yellow Quill's band of Sauteaux had turned back settlers who tried to go west of Portage.[59] It is doubtful that Canada's western expansion could have proceeded without warfare had Canada shunned the treaty process.

The first treaty was negotiated at the Stone Fort, just north of Fort Garry, in August 1871; the second later that month at the Hudson's Bay Company trading post on Lake Manitoba. These were the first of what came to be known as "The Numbered Treaties."[60] (See map, page 151.) Treaties 1 and 2 cover most of what was at that time the province of

Manitoba. The lead negotiator for the Crown was the province's first lieutenant-governor, Adams Archibald. Archibald had little feel for the treaty process. He did not understand the importance of the Crown to the Indians, and delegated most of the negotiating to Ottawa's Indian commissioner, Wemyss Simpson.[61]

Archibald's successor, Alexander Morris, who negotiated the next four treaties, was better prepared for treaty negotiating. Although he had federal officials to assist him, Morris was always very much in charge of the process. He was a close political ally of the prime minister, and served in the Macdonald government as minister of internal revenue. He had a law degree from McGill, and before entering politics had spoken passionately about the importance for Canada of annexing the North-West. Although he had a strong intuitive sense that Canada had a legal claim to the territory, he recognized that "[t]he rights of Indians are to be thought of and protected."[62] He was disappointed when Macdonald chose McDougall instead of him to be Manitoba's first lieutenant-governor – and Canadian history might have taken a very different direction had it been Morris who dealt with Riel. In 1872 Morris finally wangled an appointment to the North-West when he was appointed chief justice of Manitoba. A few months later Macdonald appointed him lieutenant-governor of Manitoba and the North-West Territories.

The North West Angle Treaty, Morris's first treaty, was negotiated at Lake of the Woods in September 1873. Most of the territory in the treaty would turn out to be in Ontario. But it stretched into the southeast corner of Manitoba covering the route along which Wolseley's army had slogged three years earlier and which would be a crucial lap for the CPR. Indeed, failure to deal with the Saulteaux, the Ojibwa people who owned the territory, when Canada was opening up a transportation corridor through their lands was an issue the Saulteux brought to the table. Morris had a good feel for the ceremonial aspect of treaty-making. He appreciated the pomp and circumstance needed to signify the seriousness he, as the queen's envoy, attached to the occasion. He presented himself in formal regalia, recognized the importance of gift-giving, and at the opening of proceedings smoked the pipe of peace. He brought a military contingent with him to show the flag and his government's strength, and two of his daughters to show his humanity.

Morris's first treaty drew on the two pre-Confederation treaties Commissioner William Robinson had negotiated in 1849–50 with the Ojibwa peoples along the north shore of Lake Superior and Lake Huron.[63] Treaty 3, in turn, became a template for the numbered treaties that followed. The key to all of these treaties was their threefold provision with respect to land.

The first provision, the one that led off the text of every treaty because it was essential for the Government of Canada, was the statement that the Indian signatories "do hereby cede, release, surrender and yield up to the Government of Canada for her Majesty the Queen and Her successors forever, all their rights, titles and privileges whatsoever, to the lands included within the following limits."[64] The text went on to describe in precise geographical terms the entire territory of the Indigenous owners. The native owners are purported to have ceded, released, surrendered, and yielded up all their rights, titles, and privileges to all of this territory. The government's lawyers must have loved those four killer verbs – cede, release, surrender, and yield up. They are in all the numbered treaties. Morris, however, certainly did not use these words, and neither did any other government negotiator.[65] Indeed there is no evidence they were used or explained in any of the numbered treaty negotiations. If they had, it is very doubtful that any Aboriginal leader would have accepted them as accurately expressing what the Indian signatories agreed to. Indigenous representatives had no mandate to sign away all of their people's birthrights.

The second part of the land deal was that, in return for "surrendering" all their land to Canada, the queen agreed to set aside reserves for the Indians. Treaty 3 set the amount of land to be reserved at no more than one square mile for each family of five, or in that proportion for smaller or larger families. This was considerably more than the 160 acres per family of five (about the size of a family farm in the Red River area) that Archibald was permitted to set aside for reserves in Treaties 1 and 2. One square mile per family of five remained the standard for reserve lands in the subsequent numbered treaties. Given that this worked out to considerably less than 5 per cent of the lands "surrendered," it can hardly be regarded as a generous allotment, particularly when one takes into account the third element of the land deal: access to the 95 per cent-plus of the "surrendered" lands outside the reserves.

On this point Her Majesty agreed that the Indian signatories "shall have the right to pursue their avocations of hunting and fishing throughout the tract surrendered as hereinbefore described, ..." Now, except for the reference to "surrendered" lands, that sounds great, and it was certainly an assurance that the First Nations people had to have. Some of them might convert to a more agricultural economy, but none was willing to give up traditional economic pursuits. But note the comma – the fatal comma – that comes after the quoted words. Here are the words that follow: "subject to such regulations as may from time to time be made by Her Government of Her Dominion of Canada, and saving and excepting such tracts as may, from time to time, be required or taken up for settlement, mining, lumbering or other purposes by Her said Government of the Dominion of Canada, or by any subjects thereof duly authorized therefore by the said Government." Those qualifying words created an enormous loophole in the promise made to First Nations that they would enjoy continuing access to their traditional territory. Although the Indigenous peoples were prepared to share their lands with the newcomers – and the treaty negotiations resonated with the language of sharing – there is no evidence that they agreed to be locked into small reserves and excluded, at the whim of an alien government, from participating in the economy – traditional, agricultural, or industrial – throughout their territory. This highly qualified promise to the Indians that they would be able, in Adams Archibald's words, to "continue the chase," was not contained in the texts of Treaties 1 and 2, which he negotiated, but was one of the "outside promises" made in the oral negotiations. It became a standard "boilerplate" item in the treaties that followed Treaty 3, and was later included in the revisions of Treaties 1 and 2.

There is a profound difference between what the Government of Canada and its lawyers believe was accomplished through the treaties and what First Nations believe their forebears agreed to. As the Treaty 7 Elders put it, "[o]ne of the crucial differences between the perspectives of the Canadian government and the First Nations is that the government side has privileged the written form of representation, while the First Nations side has relied (and still does) on an oral discourse."[66] As we shall see in a later chapter, it was not until the 1980s that the Supreme Court of Canada insisted that, in interpreting the treaties, an effort had to be made to probe beyond a literal reading of the written text to make it possible "to choose from among the various possible interpretations of common intention the one which best reconciles the interests of both parties at the time the treaty was signed."[67] The trouble is that, on fundamental issues of rights and title to land, there probably was no "common intention."[68] That leaves for today's Canadians – Aboriginal and non-Aboriginal alike – the challenge of working out an application of the treaties that is fair and mutually beneficial.

On the treaties' monetary terms there was less room for a misunderstanding. After all, money is money. The treaties provided for two kinds of cash payment, a one-time-only "gift" and an annuity. The first was the continuation of a long-established tradition of gift-giving that European powers had found conducive to establishing friendly and respectful relations with native peoples whose lands they had entered. One would not know this, however, from a reading of the treaty text, which stated, somewhat cheekily, that the money was given "with a view to show the satisfaction of Her Majesty with the behaviour and good conduct of Her Indians." At the Lake of the Woods meeting, this gift money was set at $12 for every man, woman, and child of the signatory bands. Morris showed his strong connections to Ottawa by getting considerably more than Archibald, who could offer only $3 in negotiating Treaties 1 and 2. That became the standard for subsequent treaties.[69]

The general annuity was $5 for "each Indian person." In addition, each chief would receive $25 "as an annual salary," and "subordinate officers" $15. Every three years, these First Nations officials would receive "a suitable suit of clothing." The annuities and the annual event at which they would be paid were basically ceremonial, a tangible reminder of the treaty relationship. But referring to the payments to chiefs and subchiefs as "salary" carried with it the troubling intimation of the colonial relationship that would soon be imposed on First Nations. "Salary" was dropped from subsequent treaties; the policy of colonial subjugation was not.

The numbered treaties also promised to provide teachers and schools for Indian children. The need for education in the skills to function effectively in a setting that would soon be dominated by the white man was common ground for the Canadian government and the First Nations leadership. But the schools were understood to be on reserves, not distant residential schools, and there was no expectation on the Indians' part that the fundamental aim of the education their children would receive was to destroy their Indian identity.

The innovative part of Morris's first treaty negotiation – the part that was not in the government's plan, but was seen as essential by the First Nations – was assistance in the shift to a more agricultural economy. Farm implements, carpentry tools, livestock, yokes of oxen, and funds for the purchase of ammunition and twine for fishnets were added to the first three treaties at the Indians' insistence. The Saulteaux of the North-West Angle were not willing to enter into negotiations on Treaty 3 until Morris agreed that this practical kind of economic assistance would be included.[70] All the numbered treaties that followed promised this kind of help. Indeed some of the toughest negotiations were over the extent of this assistance, and the most frequent grievance of First Nations with respect to the government's failure to deliver on the treaties' "sweet promises" concerned this economic assistance.[71] In short, Canada's plan for western expansion gave little weight to the economic development of Indigenous peoples, even on the bits of land reserved for them.

The four numbered treaties that followed Treaty 3 were negotiated between 1874 and 1877. They covered part of what would become northern Manitoba and all of the prairies over to the foothills of the Rockies. Treaty 4, negotiated at Qu'Appelle in 1874 with Plains Cree and Saulteaux people, covered the southern prairies from the western boundary of Treaty 2 in present-day Manitoba to the southeast corner of what would become Alberta. It included the Cypress Hills, where American traders had been in open warfare with the plains nations, raising the spectre of American annexation. Travelling by steamboat, Morris negotiated Treaty 5 with the Ojibwa and Swampy Cree around the northern reaches of Lake Winnipeg. That treaty involved the smallest number of Indians, but Treaty 6, Morris's last, negotiated a year later with the Plains Cree at Fort Carleton, involved the largest number of Indigenous people and the greatest amount of land: the central area of what would become Saskatchewan and a large part of the future province of Alberta. This was Ahtahkakoop's treaty, and the first negotiation at which Morris used an escort of a hundred red-coated North-West Mounted Police to impress on the Indians not only his government's authority but also the Mounties' intended role – to be friends of the Indians – which contrasted so sharply with that of the US Army.[72]

David Laird, a Prince Edward Islander who left his position as minister of the interior in Alexander Mackenzie's Liberal government in 1876 to become lieutenant-governor of the North-West Territories, led the Treaty 7 negotiations with the nations of the Blackfoot Confederacy at Blackfoot Crossing in the fall of 1877. A meeting in August that year between Blackfoot chief Crowfoot and Lakota chief Sitting Bull, whose people were being driven north into Canada by the US Army, quickened Canada's interest in making a treaty with the Blackfoot Confederacy.[73] The negotiations were tough, but in the end they produced a treaty covering the southwest of what would become Alberta: the territories of the Blood, Nizitapi, Peigan, Siksika (Blackfoot), Stoney, and Sarcee nations.[74]

Through the treaty process, Canada, in six years, peacefully and at a very low financial cost, gained access for its people and its railway to the great western plains a vital part of its national dream. It had done this with the consent of the Indigenous peoples who constituted the vast majority of the territory's population. That consent, however, was not based on a common understanding of the First Nations' status. The treaties stated that the Indians promise "to conduct themselves as loyal subjects of Her Majesty the Queen" and that they will "obey and abide by the law." The writers of the treaty texts assumed that the law to be obeyed was Canadian law, and that, somehow, well before the treaties, the Indians had become subjects not just of the queen, but also of the Government of Canada. The First Nations did not share these constitutional assumptions. Nevertheless, while the treaties were being negotiated, federal legislation – the other instrument of Canada's Indian policy – was giving effect to the unshared assumption that the Indian nations had surrendered their political independence.

As I noted in the previous chapter, British parliamentarians were wary of handing over responsibility for relations with Aboriginal peoples to colonial assemblies. They viewed settlers as having a conflict of interest in dealing with the land rights of Aboriginal peoples and, in fact, recommended that, as far as possible, British colonists should not control relations with Aboriginal peoples. That advice was ignored before Confederation, and obviously had no influence on the Confederation constitution-makers either. The Dominion's founding Constitution gave the federal Parliament exclusive legislative jurisdiction over "Indians and Lands reserved for the Indians." The new Parliament wasted no time in exercising that power in a way that reflected exactly what the British parliamentarians feared.

In April 1869, early in the second session of the new Canadian Parliament, Minister of Public Works Hector Langevin introduced the bill that would become Canada's first major piece of legislation relating to Indians, the Gradual Enfranchisement Act. This Act clearly built on the Gradual Civilization Act, the 1857 legislation of the United Province of Canada. The legislation continued to offer any Indian man who passed a morals test the opportunity to "migrate" from an Indian community into Canada with his family and fifty acres of land, give up his Indian identity, and enter into mainstream society. Unlike the Gradual Civilization Act, however, the Gradual Enfranchisement Act was a direct assault on tribal self-government. Under the Act, the superintendent general of Indian affairs (who would be a cabinet minister) could direct bands to adopt a municipal type of government by chiefs and councillors elected for three-year terms.[75] At first this system would not apply in western Canada, as native peoples there had only recently been in contact with Europeans and were not considered sufficiently "advanced" to operate such institutions. The elective band councils would have a limited power to make by-laws on such matters as public health, order, and decorum at public meetings, maintaining roads, bridges, ditches, and fences, and constructing and maintaining schools and dog pounds. These laws, to be effective, required the consent of the governor-in-council – that is, the cabinet.[76] The bands had no enforcement powers – the real ruler on the reserves would be federal officials, "Indian Agents," who would police elections and could remove elected band leaders for "dishonesty, intemperance or immorality."

Sir John A. Macdonald gave the clearest statement of the new legislation's dual purposes. The national goal, he told Parliament, was "to do away with the tribal system and assimilate the Indian people in all respects with the inhabitants of the Dominion, as speedily as they are fit to change."[77] Whereas enfranchisement was a process of individual assimilation, imposing the political institutions of the dominant society on Indian peoples was aimed at collective assimilation. Ottawa decision-makers knew virtually nothing about how Indian nations had governed themselves through the centuries before the white man arrived, but their officials in the field told them how troublesome "tribal governments" could be in resisting the new Dominion's authority. Although English-speaking Canada's crucial accommodation in Confederation was allowing French Canada to have a province in which its distinct society could survive, at this point in Canada's odyssey there was no interest in making such an accommodation with Aboriginal Canada. For both English and French Canada, the vision of Aboriginal Canada's future was for it to disappear, in Macdonald's words, "as speedily as possible." In the United States in 1832, the country's great chief justice, John Marshall, had bestowed on Indians the status of "domestic, dependent nations."[78] Although that doctrine subjected Indian tribes to the plenary power of the US Congress, it gave them some protection from the states. But in Canada at this time, there was not an ounce of respect in either the political or judicial branches of government for Indigenous peoples' right to govern themselves.

Consistent with the Canadian Parliament's assumption of political authority over Indians was its assumption of the power to define who was an "Indian." Section 6 of the 1869 Act stated that "any Indian woman marrying any other than an Indian shall cease to be an Indian within the meaning of this Act, nor shall the children of such a marriage be considered as Indians." The same rule did not apply to Indian men who married non-Indian women. This patrilineal policy went directly against the matrilineal structure of many Indigenous societies. Its practical effect was to force families with Indian mothers but non-Indian fathers to leave the reserve. Many of the families that fell victim to this rule became an underclass, living close to the reserve but forced to live apart from the community to which they felt they belonged. It would take Canada more than a century to begin to address that problem. Women were also excluded from any role in the municipal "democracy" imposed on First Nations. Although that was totally in line with Canadian and European political culture at the time, it was contrary to the long-standing practices of the many Amerindian nations that gave women an important role in governance. Canadian legislation, in tune with the racial theories of the day, also began to define Indians in terms of their blood: a "blood quantum," initially set at 25 per cent, remained part of the Indian Act until 1921.[79]

The Indian Act, passed by Parliament in 1876, was mainly a consolidation of laws already enacted, many of them rooted in pre-Confederation statutes of the Province of Canada. But now Canada was poised to apply the legislative apparatus of control to Indians in all parts of the country. David Laird, the first minister of the interior, laid out the underlying rationale of individual emancipation and strict control of reserves: "Indians must be either treated as minors or white men."[80] Laird was minister in Alexander Mackenzie's Liberal government, but the Indian Act and the thinking behind it were strongly supported on both sides of the House. Indeed the sharpest critics of the Act, William Paterson and Gavin Fleming, were both Liberal MPs. Paterson wanted to see the money from the sale of Indian lands turned over to the Indians, while Fleming complained that the "the system of tutelage in which they were kept deprived them of the spirit of self-reliance and independence."[81] It was no accident that these two MPs represented the two constituencies bordering the Six Nations reserve near Brantford, Ontario. Clearly they had been lobbied by the Six Nations, who were bitterly opposed to the legislation.

The Indian Act became a toolbox for holding legislative instruments of control and suppression. A major revision that took place in 1880 established the Department of Indian Affairs. The minister of the interior continued to serve as the new department's minister with the title of superintendent general of Indian affairs. The real significance of this change was that it laid the foundation for building what would become a huge bureaucracy for controlling every aspect of people the

Government of Canada considered to be Indians. The Indians' real ruler was the deputy superintendent general – in effect, the deputy minister of the department; the superintendent himself did not have time to direct the extensive system of controls. Sir John A. Macdonald, after returning to government in 1879, added the position of superintendent general to his prime ministerial responsibilities, but it was the deputy who was the real commander-in-chief of what was, in effect, a colonized society within the state.

Almost every year the Indian Act was amended to add new measures of control, many of them requested by the government's agents in the field. In twenty-five pages of its report, the Royal Commission on Aboriginal Peoples laid out in detail the "oppressive measures" that were added to the Act right up until 1951. They included the power to force bands to use the municipal election model of government and to police elections so that chiefs and other traditional leaders could be disqualified for office. Indian agents were given the power of justices of the peace, extending their control to the justice system. Enfranchisement, that ticket to the white man's freedom, was forced on Indians who obtained university degrees and later on Indian leaders mobilizing resistance to their people's oppression. The totalitarian ambition of the Act was manifest in its attack on traditional ceremonies and festivals such as the potlatch and the sun dance. Even dress was regulated when a 1914 amendment prohibited Indians from wearing, without permission, "Aboriginal costume" in any "dance, show, exhibition, stampede or pageant."[82] The land base of bands was steadily reduced through government pressure to surrender land to real estate developers and municipalities. In 1911 public authorities were given the power to expropriate reserve lands without a surrender.[83] It was a criminal offence for Indian farmers to sell their produce without the Indian agent's permission. That permission was frequently denied.[84] And to make sure Indians did not challenge any of this in the white man's courts, a 1927 amendment made it a criminal offence to solicit funds for taking claims to court without a licence from the superintendent general.

Of all the "oppressive measures," the one best known and most regretted by non-Aboriginal Canadians is the residential school program. It is the one thing we Canadians did to Aboriginal peoples for which we have made an official apology. Prime Minister Stephen Harper, speaking in the House of Commons on 11 June 2008, said, "I stand before you today to offer an apology to former students of Indian residential schools. The treatment of the children in Indian residential schools is a sad chapter in our history. We are sorry."[85] Justices of Australia's High Court concluded in the *Mabo* case that British settlers' denial that the Aboriginal peoples they encountered were fully human and their insistence for over two centuries that they arrived in a *terra nullius* (an empty land) "constitute the darkest aspect of the history of this nation."[86] Canada's residential school program for Aboriginal children is surely "the darkest aspect" of Canada's history.

The "manifesto" for the residential school program was Nicholas Flood Davin's *Report on Industrial Schools for Indians and Half-Breed Children*.[87] Educational facilities for Indians, including residential schools, had been established in Upper Canada well before Confederation.[88] But those schools were not inspired by the ideological dogma of the new Dominion's program. The core beliefs of that dogma were twofold: first, that adult Indians were hopelessly and irretrievably "savage"; second, that there was some hope for their children if "the influence of the wigwam" could be eradicated.[89] Hence separation of the children from their families was absolutely essential.

The program was a potent brew of political power, religious zeal, and racism. The power was that of a newly formed state whose government viewed the complete assimilation of Aboriginal peoples as part of its nation-building efforts. The new state's partners were the major Christian denominations – Anglican, Catholic, Methodist, and Presbyterian – that, fired up to do good, would provide at low cost the teachers for the program. The racism was a social Darwinism that saw the schools as vehicles for quick-starting the evolution of people who, "a few years ago, were roaming savages" and had suddenly been bought into an advanced civilization.[90] At least it can be said that this was a more optimistic way of thinking than the strict racism that guided policy in Australia, where full-blood Aborigines were considered "a doomed race" for whom the state could do no more than provide a soft pillow for its final years while doing what it could to remove and educate children in whom some white blood could be detected.[91]

From the 1880s to the 1930s, the residential school program expanded rapidly. By 1931, eighty schools had been built. In 1920 Duncan Campbell Scott, deputy superintendent of Indian affairs, concluded that voluntary attendance was not working, and had the Indian Act amended to make it mandatory for every Indian child between ages seven and fifteen to attend school, with a criminal penalty for noncomplying parents.[92] Scott, who held the deputy superintendent's position from 1913 to 1933, became a legendary figure for his stern and ideologically driven management of Indian affairs, a role that is hard to square with his achievements as one of Canada's leading poets.[93] Residential schools were built in every province and territory except Prince Edward Island, New Brunswick, and Newfoundland.[94] By 1948 60 per cent of the Indian school-age population was in residential schools.[95] The program was Aboriginal, not just Indian: children from Métis families were included from the outset, and in the 1950s, when Canada began to engage actively in the development and colonization of the far north, a string of "small hostels" were built mainly for Inuit children in the Arctic. By this time there was enough internal criticism of the residential schools to make these "hostels" less brutal and even to involve Inuit people in their housekeeping aspects.[96]

The worst damage the residential schools inflicted directly on Aboriginal children resulted from the schools' deplorable physical conditions and the cruelty of their custodians. Persistent underfunding produced terrible overcrowding, poor sanitation, and grossly inadequate diets. For many children, this meant death. In 1907 Dr P.H. Bryce, the Indian Affairs Department's medical inspector, reported that the death toll of children in the fifteen schools he surveyed was 24 per cent. That figure would have been considerably higher had children been tracked for a few years after returning home to their reserves. The magazine *Saturday Night* commented that, "even war seldom shows a percentage of fatalities as does the educational system we have imposed upon our Indians."[97] The biggest killer was tuberculosis – the failure to detect it and to treat it properly. Duncan Campbell Scott himself admitted that "fifty per cent of the children who passed through these schools did not live to benefit from the education they had received therein."[98]

As for discipline, the Royal Commission on Aboriginal Peoples commented that "there was a dark contradiction, an inherent element of savagery in the mechanics of civilizing the children." Children were punished for speaking their native language. Some died attempting to escape their captivity. Much of this – maybe all of it – stemmed from "the failure to regard children as persons capable of responding to love."[99]

Children who survived the schools all too often found that the discrimination they encountered in mainstream society made it impossible to use their education. Besides, the industrial part of the curriculum denied students the opportunity to learn how to use the mechanized equipment that was coming to dominate Canadian industry and agriculture. Nonetheless the academic program's training in the three "r's" – reading, writing, and arithmetic – ironically enabled three generations of Aboriginals to acquire skills essential to defend their peoples' interests in the political space of their colonizers. But these skills could have been acquired without the grief and suffering of the residential schools.

The residential schools spectacularly failed to accomplish their purpose of "killing the Indian in the child." If anything, they strengthened Aboriginal peoples' sense of their own native identity, and produced leaders with the determination and skills to restore their peoples' nationhood. But the program left a legacy of dysfunctional families and communities and a great deal of distrust that is still with us and remains an obstacle on the path to reconciliation.

For the Indians and Métis of the western plains, the eight years that followed the signing of Treaty 7 in 1877 were the meanest and leanest period in their relations with Canada. The rapid disappearance of the bison herds was a dreadful economic and social blow. Malnutrition, amounting often to starvation, increased the native peoples' vulnerability to disease, which for many meant death. It was precisely in anticipation of such a calamity that Ahtahkakoop and other Cree chiefs had insisted on a clause in Treaty 6 stating: "In the event hereafter of the Indians comprised within this treaty being overtaken by any pestilence, or by a general famine, the Queen ... will grant to the Indians assistance of such character and to such extent as her Chief Superintendent of Indian Affairs shall deem necessary and sufficient to relieve the Indians from the calamity that shall have befallen them."[100] When famine came within a year of signing the treaty, the Canadian government provided some relief, but not nearly enough to avoid the plains peoples' being in a constant state of hunger. It was administered on a work-to-eat policy in a setting where there was no work. In the words of James Daschuk, a leading scholar of this tragic episode, the government's provision of relief "illustrated the moral and legal failures of the crown's treaty commitments."[101]

Tuberculosis, relatively rare on the plains before the treaties, was reported to be the biggest killer of Indians on the treaty-created reserves. The much more compact lifestyle on reserves seems to have been a major factor in spreading this highly infectious disease. Bringing cattle into the bison-emptying plains also brought diseases such as anthrax. An outbreak of a deadly mountain fever, traced to the rotting carcasses of cattle and buffalo polluting the rivers and streams, broke out in the southwest. In 1880 there was a horrific outbreak of diarrhea and dysentery among 1,500 Cree camped in the Cypress Hills. The "medicine chests" that Treaty 6 required to be at the home of each Indian agent were pitifully incapable of coping with this massive spread of disease.

Lieutenant-Governor Alexander Morris, who tried to use his influence in office to get effective famine relief, was followed by much more compliant federal administrators. Indian Commissioner Edgar Dewdney adhered to a policy of fiscal restraint, and was not above using starvation as a lever to force Indians to submit to treaty.[102]

None of this did anything to persuade plains Indians who had not yet taken treaty that they had made a mistake. The three biggest holdouts were two of the largest bands in the Saskatchewan River area, led by Big Bear and Little Pine, and the Cree/Assiniboine from the Qu'Appelle region led by Piapot. These leaders saw through the Canadian government's divide-and-conquer strategy, and in the early 1880s brought their peoples to encamp near Fort Walsh, in the Cypress Hills in the southern part of the Assiniboine District. Together the people in this encampment made up more than half the total Indian population of the Treaty 4 and Treaty 6 areas.[103] Such a massing together of Indigenous people posed a serious economic and security threat to Canada. The CPR's cross-prairie route had been moved south to pass through Medicine Hat and on to Calgary. Thousands of non-treaty Indians encamped just south of that route might interfere with building the line, and would certainly be an unwelcoming setting for the flood of settlers the railway was expected to bring. Talk of the Cree and Assiniboine allying with their traditional enemies, the Blackfoot, conjured up the spectre of a major Indian war.

So Canada pushed back – strenuously. Indian Commissioner Dewdney decided that the best way to get the Indians out of Fort Walsh, where the North-West Mounted Police were dispensing food to the starving Indians, was to close the fort.[104]

The pressure worked. With the close of Fort Walsh in the spring of 1883, the Cree were forced by the threat of starvation to leave the Cypress Hills, Piapot's people east to Indian Head, in the Treaty 4 region, and Big Bear's and Little Pine's people north to where the Treaty 6 reserves were located. All were pressured into "taking treaty" to have access to the famine relief offered by the Canadian government. "Taking treaty" did not mean making new treaties but signing "adhesions" to existing treaties. This meant, for Big Bear, Little Pine, and Piapot, arch-critics of the numbered treaties, that the cost of keeping their people alive was to abandon any effort to secure better terms. As Big Bear's biographer, Rudy Wiebe, puts it, "Sir John A. Macdonald's government had won its battle to subjugate the Plains People, even the most independent and self-reliant band of Cree, by a deliberate use of convenient starvation."[105]

The Canadian government continued its divide-and-conquer strategy in controlling the choice of reserves. Big Bear and Little Pine wanted reserves for their bands to be close to that of Poundmaker, one of the strongest Cree chiefs. They still harboured the idea that a large contiguous grouping of Indian settlements could form an Indian territory and be a source of political strength. Little Pine was allowed to choose a reserve along the western boundary of Poundmaker's, but Indian Agent Rae insisted that Big Bear's be at Frog Lake many miles to the north. The treaty commitment to consult with bands in locating their reserves turned out in Big Bear's case to be an empty promise. This did not prevent Big Bear and Little Pine from holding a thirst dance near Battleford in the spring of 1884, nor that summer participating in a council of Cree leaders that took place at Duck Lake. The council was attended by chiefs such as Ahtahkakoop, thought by Dewdney to be loyal and docile, as well as by Big Bear and Poundmaker. The chiefs produced a litany of broken treaty promises, and expressed their determination to "take whatever measures necessary short of war, to get redress."[106] These events made government officials so fearful of a pan-Indian alliance that Ottawa was persuaded to introduce a pass system requiring Indians to obtain the local Indian agent's permission to leave the reserve.[107]

The swirling storm of Indian discontent was by no means the only challenge the "peaceable kingdom" faced on the prairies at this time. In May 1884 Métis, English-speaking half-breeds, and angry white settlers in the Saskatchewan River area agreed to send a delegation to summon Louis Riel back to Canada. Riel was now an American citizen, married with two children, and teaching at a small Jesuit mission school in Montana. Gabriel Dumont, a renowned warrior and Métis leader, led the delegation, but could neither read nor write. Riel was wanted for his ability to draft the petitions so necessary for negotiating with the Government of Canada.

Riel accepted the call. Indeed he regarded it as a mission that was "divinely ordained."[108] In June he arrived in Batoche, the centre of the St-Laurent parish along the South Saskatchewan River. Many of the Métis in this community of about fifteen hundred had come from Red River, where, after 1870, they had quickly become a small, marginalized minority without a land base for their growing population. The sudden decline of the buffalo herds meant the St-Laurent Métis economy had come to depend on cultivating the traditional river lots they had settled on along the South Saskatchewan. Lacking any recognized title to these lands, once again Métis felt threatened when the new Dominion's surveyors turned up with plans to lay out a grid of square lots over their narrow riverfront strips.

Soon after his arrival in Batoche, Riel was invited to address a white audience in Prince Albert, the burgeoning commercial capital of the region. Five hundred people packed the town's largest hall to hear his call for responsible government in a new province created out of the three regions of the North-West Territories. In a similar effort to build unity, he had talks with the Cree leaders who met at Duck Lake. The first item in the petition Riel and the Métis drew up to send to Ottawa was a plea to increase food relief to the starving Indians. The petition also called for a reduction of tariffs on farm equipment for the white farmers who were experiencing desperate times in getting started on their homestead properties, land patents for the Métis farms plus grants of land based on native title, and, for all residents, responsible government and provincial status.[109] There was no way this effort at inclusiveness would work as well as it had in Red River fifteen years earlier. Although white settlers might well be interested in constitutional reform, there was never any possibility of their rallying behind a famous rebel leader. Besides, unlike the situation in Red River, there was now an established Canadian government in the North-West Territories, albeit a highly unrepresentative setup of a lieutenant-governor advised by an appointed council. As for the Indians, they would take any help they could get in relieving their hunger, but politically they had their own agenda and leadership, and most of them were loyal to the Crown.

It was a combination of the Macdonald government's bungled reply to the Métis petition and Riel's absorption in being a new Messiah that brought on the North-West Rebellion in the early months of 1885. Macdonald's government was not prepared to recognize that the Métis had a native-title-based land claim, but it was willing to appoint a commission "with a view to settling equitably the claims of half-breeds."[110] This decision was communicated in a badly worded telegram to Commissioner Dewdney, not directly to Riel.

When news reached Riel on 9 February that Canada was offering nothing more than a commission of inquiry, he slammed his fist on the table and roared, "In forty days Ottawa will have my answer."[111] Forty days was the duration of Jesus Christ's temptation in the wilderness. Riel was now deeply into his Messiah persona. The very charisma that was bestowing on Riel the status of sainthood in much of the Métis community was alienating the local Catholic clergy, who now saw him as a dangerous heretic. The provisional government he proclaimed on

19 March was totally unlike the inclusive body of 1870 that had sent delegates to negotiate Manitoba's entry into the Canadian Confederation. Its council was called the Exovedate, meaning roughly "those who have left the flock," a term that, as Joseph Boyden observes, "the Métis who have gathered around Louis and Gabriel have a difficult time pronouncing – or understanding."[112] Riel took no office in this government, "as befitted a prophet whose authority stemmed not from man but from God."[113]

The match that ignited the North-West Rebellion was Lawrence Clarke's chance meeting with some Métis on 17 March. Clarke, the Hudson's Bay Company's chief factor at Fort Carleton, was on his way home from Winnipeg. Asked if the government would do anything about land claims, Clarke replied that "the only answer you will get will be bullets," and he told them that, on the way north from Regina, he had passed a camp of five hundred policemen preparing to capture the half-breed agitators.[114] Clarke's words were a gross exaggeration, but news of them spread like wildfire. Later that evening, when Dumont asked a huge crowd gathered in front of the church of St-Antoine-de-Padoue in Batoche whether they were in favour of taking up arms, they rose as one. There were cries of joy, and they yelled, "if we are to die for our country, we will die together."[115] The North-West Rebellion had begun.

Although the rebellion went on for nearly two months, demography and technology meant that its outcome was never in doubt. The new Dominion had the population and the nascent patriotism that enabled it to raise a large citizen army. By the time the rebellion was over, eight thousand young Canadians, most of them from Ontario and Quebec, had signed up. As for getting them to the west, the rebellion was a heaven-sent opportunity for the Macdonald government to draw on patriotism to salvage its financially troubled railway scheme and complete the CPR line across the prairies. These factors alone spelled eventual defeat for the three hundred or so warriors from the Métis families along the South Saskatchewan. The rebellion would have been a much greater challenge for Canada had it truly been the Indian-Métis uprising Canadians so deeply feared.

That combination of native forces did not occur. Riel and Dumont tried hard to get the Indians to join them in resisting Canadian authority. But the chiefs rejected these appeals. Some younger warriors resisted the authority of their chiefs and fought along side the Métis. It is estimated that, at most, 4 per cent of the Cree, Assiniboine, Blackfoot, and a handful of desperate Sioux refugees from the United States joined the rebellion.[116] Most of the chiefs of bands that had taken treaty took seriously the promise they had made to be loyal to the Crown. Ahtahkakoop and Mistawasis, chiefs of two of the largest Treaty 6 bands, "were determined to honour the treaty."[117] To prevent their people from getting caught up in the fighting along the South Saskatchewan, they moved them across the North Saskatchewan to camp near Prince Albert. In the summer of 1884, Dewdney arranged for Crowfoot and other Blackfoot leaders to be taken by train to Winnipeg so that they could see the strength and wealth of the society they would be up against if they took to the warpath.

Big Bear and Poundmaker did not need that train ride to realize the time had long passed when they could secure their peoples' interests through warfare. But these chiefs were not always able to restrain young warriors who were dismayed and fired up by the failure of their leaders to obtain relief for the dreadful conditions in their communities. On three occasions warrior factions from these bands engaged in acts of violence.[118] When Cree and Assiniboine, on the heels of the Métis defeat of Mounted Police in the opening battle of the war at Duck Lake, came to Poundmaker's reserve outside Battleford, the townsfolk thought they were being attacked and abandoned the town. Some young Assiniboine men took advantage of the situation to carry out a revenge killing of farming instructor James Payne, blamed for a death of a girl. In early April, with Big Bear absent, two officials at Frog Lake who refused to open a food storehouse were murdered by Cree, setting off a round of violence that resulted in the deaths of eight other white men in the camp. The deaths of the nine white men became known as the "Frog Lake Massacre." Later in April Canadian troops under the command of Colonel William Oliver, sent to relieve "the siege" of Battleford, attacked Cree sleeping in teepees on Poundmaker's reserve. The Cree fought back, and at Cutknife routed the Canadians. Only Poundmaker's restraint averted a real massacre.

The Métis won all the small battles, but not the final big one at Batoche, which ended the rebellion. The Canadian commander, General Frederick Middleton, planned a pincer attack. The Hudson's Bay Company's steamboat, the *Northcote*, carrying a troop of artillery, would steam along the South Saskatchewan River and attack Batoche from the north, while Middleton's army would attack from the south. Gabriel Dumont smelled this out, and with thirty riflemen along both banks of the river riddled the gunboat with bullets, sending it careering along the river with its smokestacks sliced off, till it came to rest two miles upstream from Batoche. There it sat for the duration of the battle.[119] Thus ended the only naval battle ever fought on the Canadian plains. For three days Métis marksmen, now down to about 175 in number, firing from pits dug around the village, held off Middleton's army of 800, augmented by 175 North-West Mounted Police. On 12 May, the fourth day, the Canadians finally broke through, and the Métis resistance was crushed. Three days later Riel surrendered to Middleton. Dumont fled to the United States.

With the rebellion put down, the Canadian justice system took over. In what is probably the most famous trial in Canadian history, Riel was tried for treason before a magistrate and an all-white jury in a Regina court. The government chose to have the trial in Regina to avoid the mixed jury that could have been demanded had the trial been held in Manitoba. Riel refused to follow his lawyer's advice and accept an insanity plea. He certainly suffered from extreme religious delusions, but in his lucid moments, and there were plenty of them, he desperately wanted to explain the justice of his people's cause. On 1 August the jury delivered its verdict of guilty but with a recommendation of clemency. The Macdonald Conservatives, caught between the wrath of Ontario and the sympathy of Quebec, and with no medical basis for finding Riel insane, decided against reducing his sentence to life imprisonment. On 16 November 1885 Louis Riel was hanged.

Cree chiefs Little Arrow, Poundmaker, and Big Bear also went to trial for treason in the same Regina court. Little Arrow, accused of having been seen talking to Riel, was found guilty, even though he testified that he had been taken to Batoche as a prisoner.[120] He was sentenced to three years in Stony Mountain Penitentiary in Manitoba. Poundmaker and Big Bear, despite all they had done to restrain their people, were also found guilty and sent to Stony Mountain for three years. Both died within a year of their release. Forty-two other Indians were charged with various offences and convicted in trials that were not very carefully conducted.[121] Some were tried at Battleford by Judge Charles Rouleau, who had narrowly missed being murdered along with farm instructor Payne. Two of the six Indians tried for their role in the "Frog Lake Massacre" were hanged. A section was added to the Stony Mountain Penitentiary to accommodate the twenty-five Indians and eighteen Métis sentenced to prison.[122]

For Canada the west was now won. But this chapter of its "national dream" was surely a nightmare for its native peoples.

The time had now come for Canada to turn its expansionist gaze northward. Indians north of the treatied areas were interested in securing treaty relations with the Crown primarily to gain the recognition and protection of their interests against the white man's encroachments into their territories that they saw coming, and also to get material help and relief for needs arising from the depressed condition of the fur trade and the diseases missionaries and traders brought with them. The Canadian government, however, was in no hurry to make treaties with the northern Indians. So far as it knew, their lands were not good for agriculture, so there was no need to pave the way for floods of settlers. Besides, treaties cost money. Better to provide a little help and relief to needy Indians on an ad hoc basis and wait until a government policy priority indicated a treaty relationship would be useful.

The numbered-treaty process did not resume until the end of the century. Treaty 8 was negotiated with Cree and Athapaskan (or Dene) people, including Beaver, Chipewyan, Slavey, Dogrib, and Yellowknife bands in the watershed area of Great Slave Lake in 1899. The first signing of Treaty 9 with the Cree and Anishinabek people of northern Ontario came in 1905. Treaty 10 with the Cree and Chipewyan people of northern Saskatchewan came the following year. Treaty 11, the final numbered treaty, with the Dene people of the Mackenzie Valley, was negotiated in 1921. Each treaty had its own story and its own wrinkles, but they all used the basic template of the earlier numbered treaties. In the eyes of the Canadian government, they were first and foremost "land cession" treaties, extinguishing native title in return for money. The Indians' role in them is aptly referred to as "taking" treaty, rather than making treaty, reflecting the domineering approach of the Canadian government's treaty commissioners.

The discovery of gold on the Klondike River in the Yukon in 1896 precipitated Treaty 8. The North-West Mounted Police blazed a trail to the Yukon from Edmonton through the Peace River region. In June 1898 five hundred Indians at Fort St John in British Columbia refused to let the police or miners enter their territory until a treaty was signed. The treaty covered all the land in what would become Alberta north of the Treaty 6 area and the land in what is today the Northwest Territories up to Great Slave Lake, as well as the northeast corner of British Columbia.

From the time it entered Confederation until the 1990s, British Columbia was a rogue province so far as respecting native title ownership of land is concerned. The BC government refused to have anything to do with the Treaty 8 process. Federal officials got around this by allocating reserves on the "Peace River Block," which the province had earlier turned over to federal ownership for railway development and agriculture. The other novel feature of the Treaty 8 negotiations was that Clifford Sifton, Sir Wilfrid Laurier's minister of the interior, authorized the treaty commissioner to issue transferable scrip for either $240 or 240 acres of Crown land to Métis who had not received scrip at Red River in 1870. This was not the first time Canada did something to settle the land claims of the survivors of Batoche.[123]

Treaty 9, encompassing the traditional territory of Cree and Anishinabek peoples in northern Ontario, reflected the growing power of provincial governments in the Canadian federation. In 1884 Ontario won a boundary dispute with the federal government, securing a ruling from Canada's highest court, the Judicial Committee of the Privy Council, that defined its boundary as extending westward to the Lake of the Woods and north to James Bay and the Albany River.[124] Ontario, showing no respect for native title, wasted no time in encouraging the exploration for minerals in its newly defined territory. The Indian peoples in the area had family and trading relations with bands that were parties to the Robinson treaties and Treaty 3. So they knew about treaties, and began to communicate their interest in treaty-making to federal officials. They were also experiencing an escalation in the scale of white contact resulting from the building of the CPR around the top of the Great Lakes, giving white trappers and hunters ready access to their hunting grounds and exposing them as never before to diseases such as measles, influenza, and pneumonia.

In responding to the northern Ontario Indians' interest in taking treaty, the federal government had a new problem. In the 1889 *St Catherine's Milling* case, the Macdonald Conservative government had lost another major court battle with Oliver Mowat's Liberal Ontario government.[125] The case arose out of Ontario's challenge to a lease issued by the federal government to a lumber company to cut down and remove a million feet of timber from lands that Ottawa considered the Saulteaux Ojibwa had surrendered to the Crown in Treaty 3. Ontario claimed that the Saulteaux had surrendered their land not to the federal Crown, but to the provincial Crown, so Ottawa had no business leasing timber rights on it. The Judicial Committee and the three courts that heard the case in Canada all decided in Ontario's favour, giving it control over huge tracts of land and their natural resources. But in Manitoba, where the federal government retained public lands and resources, as well as in Saskatchewan and

Alberta, where the same policy was applied, this decision would not take effect until the 1930 Natural Resources Transfer Agreement.

The Saulteaux were afforded no opportunity to participate in the proceedings. The case proceeded entirely as a federal-provincial dispute, excluding the people who had been promised in the treaty process continuing access to the lands at issue. The Saulteaux would have been affronted to see themselves referred to as "heathens and barbarians" and as "rude red men" in the judgment rendered at trial by Chancellor John Alexander Boyd, a senior Ontario judge. Boyd considered the Saulteaux as "a more than usually degraded Indian type." The logic of his language, as legal historian Sidney Harring observes, "is that 'degraded' peoples could not hold title to land."[126] Boyd's judgment is indicative of the racism permeating Canadian relations with Aboriginal peoples at this time.

In the Supreme Court of Canada, the majority took the view that, before the arrival of the Europeans, peoples native to the continent did not really own their lands but only enjoyed the right to use their lands. They were too primitive to possess anything like ownership rights or have title to their lands. Only the two dissenting justices, Strong and Gwynne (both from Ontario), recognized the native title and ownership underlying the 1763 Royal Proclamation. When the case went on appeal to the Judicial Committee, Ontario's premier Mowat and Edward Blake, leader of the Liberal Opposition in the federal Parliament, went over to London to brief the English barristers who would argue the case. Although Mowat and Blake did not go so far as to support Chancellor Boyd's total denial of Indians' having a legal interest in land, they did get their English QCs to sell the British judges on the view that "the tenure of Indians was a personal and usufructuary right, dependent on the good will of the Sovereign." The next year, Lord Watson, who wrote the judgment in *St Catherine's Milling*, applied this diminished, racist view of the land rights of Aboriginals to Australia.[127] We are now indeed at the high tide of racist imperialism.

After Ontario's win in the courts, Ottawa decided that the province would have to participate in future treaty-making. Ontario would be concerned about the location of reserves, as these would be the only bits of the "surrendered" lands they would not control. Also, since the province would get such a huge benefit from the treaty, it ought to assume some of the treaty costs. So, in the summer of 1905, when the treaty party started out on its long journey through the rivers and lakes of the Albany River watershed, one of the men in the canoes was

Dr George McMartin, a Perth doctor, representing Ontario in the negotiations. Ottawa's lead negotiator was none other than Duncan Campbell Scott, at this point a senior official in the federal Indian Affairs
Department, whose poetic juices would be stirred by the glorious land-
scapes of northern Ontario while making his way to sell his soothing
version of a treaty, already printed and agreed to by Ontario, to native
settlements along the way. He later wrote that, even if the treaty text
could have been interpreted (which it was not), the Cree and Ojibwa
would never have understood the concepts.[128]

The commissioners had to return the following summer to get other
communities to take the treaty. The final adhesions to Treaty 9 came
in 1929 and 1930, after the 1912 extension of the Manitoba-Ontario
boundary to the sixtieth parallel and Hudson Bay. In all thirty-nine Cree
and Ojibwa communities became parties to Treaty 9.[129] The written text
of the treaty has all the standard boilerplate, killer words declaring that
the native signatories "cede, release, surrender and yield up ... all their
rights, titles and privileges whatsoever ...," but is just a little bit meaner
and leaner than other numbered treaties. The annual annuity that
Ontario agreed to pay would be $4 per person, a dollar less than pro-
vided for in the other treaties, and the gift on signing day was reduced
from $12 to $8. There would be no suits of clothes for the leaders nor
fishing nets and twine for the people, and, at Ontario's insistence, lands
with a hydro-electric potential were excluded from reserves.

The impetus for Treaty 10, which followed close on the heels of Treaty
9 in 1906, was the carving of two provinces, Alberta and Saskatchewan,
out of the North-West Territories in 1905.[130] Given the emerging role
of provinces in treaties, the federal government did not want treaties to
cross provincial boundaries. So the Cree and Chipewyan peoples of
northern Saskatchewan, instead of being asked to sign adhesions to
Treaty 6, were offered a new treaty. Treaty 10 did not offer equipment and
materials for agriculture, or famine relief. Other than that, its terms were
similar to those of Treaty 6. As with the Treaty 8 process, the treaty commissioner offered Métis scrip worth $240, redeemable for 240 acres. Most
of the scrip ended up in the hands of Saskatchewan land speculators.[131]

The trigger for Treaty 11, the last of the numbered treaties, was
Imperial Oil's striking a rich deposit of oil on 25 August 1920 at Norman
Wells, about forty-five miles north of Fort Norman on the Mackenzie
River. This was well down the Mackenzie, just west of Great Bear Lake.
The Mackenzie River Valley is the traditional territory of the Dehcho
Dene (the Dene of the Great River). The Dene were concerned about

settlers moving into their territory, and were experiencing high levels of disease. Their close ties with the peoples who had signed Treaty 8 generated their interest in the possibility of a treaty with Canada.

After the oil discovery at Norman Wells, the Canadian government was keen to clear the path for the oil industry by extinguishing the Dene's title to their land, and appointed Henry Anthony Conway as treaty commissioner. Conway began his work of inducing the Dene to take treaty in early July 1921 at Fort Providence. In the course of the summer, Conroy visited eight other communities as far north as Arctic Red River and as far south as Fort Liard, near the Alberta border. The commissioner was under strict instructions from Duncan Campbell Scott "to adhere strictly to the terms of the Treaty made in Ottawa."[132] And those terms, to be sure, did not deviate from the numbered-treaty formula. Because it was the last of the numbered treaties, some of its eyewitnesses survived into the era when Indians had access to Canada's courts, where they were later able to challenge the legitimacy of the treaty.

With the signing of Treaty 11, Canada, through the treaty process, completed the process of pacifying the Indians in Ontario, the prairie provinces, and the western part of the Northwest Territories up to the edge of the Arctic Circle. By the 1920s, through the machinery of the Indian Act, Canada was imposing its colonial rule not only on Indians who were parties to "land cession" treaties, but on First Nations peoples in all parts of the country. The Métis had been defeated at Batoche, and although, like the Red River Métis, they retained a strong sense of their national identity, it would take them decades to reorganize as a nation within.

There remained a third component of the Indigenous peoples that would come to be part of Canada: the Inuit, as they refer to themselves, or Eskimos as the white man for so long called them. It was not until the 1920s that Canada began to assert its authority over these people.

The Inuit are descendants of people who originally migrated from Siberia to Alaska and then spread across the Arctic as far as Greenland. The first wave, referred to by anthropologists as Dorset people, came around 2500 BC and were followed by a later migration of Thule people around 1000 AD.[133] The Inuit stayed in the north, above the treeline, where ecologically it makes sense to live in small groups based on a few families on lands that cannot be cultivated and from which the yield of food is so limited.[134] The Inuit people's small-scale groupings meant that they did not live in societies large enough to form armies or to support the specialization of labour that would allow for a social hierarchy or leadership cadre. Consequently no sense of nationhood developed among them. They certainly experienced conflict with other native peoples, such as the Dene and the Innu, and on occasion with the white man – or Qallunaat, as they referred to the whites they encountered. But they lacked the political structures that treaty-making required.

The Royal Charter that Charles II granted to the Company of Adventurers Trading into Hudson Bay in 1670 was premised on England's assumption that it had sovereignty over the vast territory of "Rupert's Land." The northern boundary was vaguely described as "all territories whose waters eventually reach the seas within Hudson Strait, and possibly even further afield."[135] A century earlier, the Elizabethan explorer Martin Frobisher, searching for the northwest passage to Asia, had sailed into waters north of Hudson Bay. For the English, Frobisher's "discovery" would entitle their sovereign to claim sovereignty over the territory, to which it granted the Hudson's Bay Company a trade monopoly. Britain's claim to sovereignty was contested by France in the 1700s when Hudson Bay became a scene of warfare between the two European powers. The French cession of New France in 1763 consolidated Britain's rule over Rupert's Land. And then, in 1869, as we have seen, Britain agreed to have Canada purchase Rupert's Land from the Hudson's Bay Company. Although the boundaries of Rupert's Land remained uncertain even in 1869,[136] its Arctic areas embraced the Inuit's lands. Britain, France, and their fur trade companies certainly knew about the Inuit – after all, with whom were they trading? But in the age of European imperialism, it never occurred to them that the Inuit should be informed or consulted about the changing political status of their lands.

In 1874, when the Foreign Office sent a secret dispatch to Canada's governor general, Lord Dufferin, offering to hand over the Arctic islands to Canada, Canadian politicians were surprised:[137] they had assumed that all of the High Arctic was part of Rupert's Land. But inquiries the British had received from Americans about purchasing land on Baffin Island's Cumberland Sound for a mining development made them nervous about sovereignty in the area. The Canadians might be in a better position to resist American claims in the Arctic Archipelago – a dubious assumption, given that young Canada had neither a navy nor a coast guard. The 1880 Order in Council transferring responsibility for the area to Canada was deliberately vague about its boundaries. Canada was in no hurry to exercise its authority in the Arctic islands. At this time, it had no strong economic interests in its

Arctic domain or the capacity to govern the area. Not until 1895 did Canada pass an Order in Council formally incorporating the transferred lands into the newly created District of Franklin.

Until well into the twentieth century, Canada was content to leave relations with the Inuit to fur traders and the missionaries who followed in their wake. In the early 1900s, having lost the dispute with the United States over the Alaska-Yukon boundary and wary of American whaling activities in what it hoped were Canadian waters, Canada established North-West Mounted Police outposts at Herschel Island in the western Arctic and at Fullerton Harbour in Hudson Bay. But for a long time it did nothing more to "show the flag" in the land of the Inuit.

It took reports that Robert Janes, a Newfoundland fur trader, had been killed by Inuit near Pond Inlet, on Baffin Island, to convince the government of William Lyon Mackenzie King that the time had come to show the world – in particular, the Americans, Danes, and Norwegians who were showing interest in the Arctic islands' resources – who was in charge up there. In July 1923 the Canadian Coast Guard ship *Arctic* sailed out of Quebec for Baffin Island with a full justice crew aboard: judge, prosecuting and defence lawyers, ten members of the Royal Canadian Mounted Police, as the North-West Mounted were now called, and six of the ship's officers to serve as jurors. The trial of the three Inuit accused of murder began at Pond Inlet on 25 August. The three men pleaded guilty, although it is doubtful they had any idea what that meant. For them the trial was simply another chance to tell the truth about what had happened.

As Shelagh Grant's detailed account of the trial shows, despite the clash of cultures, the basic story of how and why Janes was killed filtered through.[138] Janes, who had been living with Inuit people during the winter of 1919–20, ran out of trade goods and became desperate when the Inuit trappers refused to hand over their furs to him. When he came to a camp of Inuit families in igloos at the top of Baffin Island, he threatened to shoot their dogs and kill the hunters. The community talked about what should be done. Although there was no formal meeting, most agreed that Janes must be killed, and to do the deed they chose Nuqallaq, Janes's interpreter, who had spent a good deal of time with the fur trader. On several occasions Janes had threatened to kill him, and had physically attacked his father. Although Nuqallaq fired the gun that killed Janes, in effect he carried out a communal execution. Afterwards the Inuit took the body to Pond Inlet, where they built a coffin for it, to be picked up by the first boat that arrived in the spring.

The trial lasted five days. The jury delivered its verdict on 30 August. Aatitaaq was found "not guilty" for lack of evidence. Ululijarnaat, who had lured Janes out on the ice to be shot, was found guilty of manslaughter, but the jury recommended clemency. There was no clemency, however, for Nuqallaq, who was found guilty of manslaughter and sentenced to ten years in Stony Mountain Penitentiary, Manitoba. At Stony Mountain Nuqallaq became severely ill with tuberculosis. In the summer of 1925 he was returned to Pond Inlet by ship, in isolation below deck so as not to infect the crew. On being released at Pond Inlet, he was allowed to sleep with his family. This resulted in a tuberculosis epidemic and the deaths of many of the Inuit in the area. Canada's use of a trial of people who did not know they had become Canadians in order to display its sovereignty over them and their lands had truly tragic and entirely avoidable consequences.

In the period before the Second World War, Canada's administration of the far north was tentative and uncertain. A bill introduced in Parliament in 1924 proposed to bring the Inuit under the Indian Act. But it was strongly opposed by Arthur Meighen, leader of the Opposition, who objected "to degrading them into wards of the nation: Canada had signed no treaties with them, and should leave them alone."[139] Theoretically the Inuit were just ordinary citizens of Canada, although in reality they did not participate in Canadian life on anything like an equal footing with other Canadians. In the 1930s Canada and Quebec disputed who was responsible for Inuit in the north of the province, each wanting to pass the responsibility on to the other. The dispute was referred to the Supreme Court of Canada, which decided that, for constitutional purposes, Inuit were to be considered Indians and thus would come under federal jurisdiction.[140] Quebec "won" the case by being able to deny jurisdiction – surely a first (and last) in Canadian federal history and a marker of how little either of Canada's French and English founding pillars thought about the Inuit part of the county's Indigenous pillar.

Major revisions of the Indian Act in 1951 brought the Inuit nominally under its provisions, but government policy in relation to the Inuit was moving in the opposite direction of the assimilation program imposed on Indians. Policy-makers in Ottawa wanted to reverse the trend towards Inuit families settling near Hudson's Bay Company trading posts and get them back on the land, living according to their traditional lifestyle. In the words of one official the policy was "to keep the native, native."[141] It was not only European equipment, ammunition, clothes, and food that drew Inuit families to the trading posts, but also the education that missionaries were eager to provide their children. Making the Family Allowance and Old Age Security programs available to Inuit in the form of store food added another incentive for families to settle near trading posts. When prices crashed, many of the Inuit who had moved in off the land became economically dependent on welfare handouts. The discipline and structure of the Inuit's traditional life did not easily survive in newly formed larger communities smitten with the temptations of Western materialism.

In response to this situation, the key policy-makers – the Department of Resources and Development in Ottawa and the Eskimo Affairs Committee advising the commissioner of the Northwest Territories, neither of which included any Inuit people – concluded that it would be better for the Inuit and easier (that is, cheaper and less troublesome) for the government if the Inuit returned to living in small groups out on the ice and snow. And so they adopted a bold program of social engineering: relocating Inuit in the High Arctic.

The largest of these operations took place in 1953 and involved relocating fifty-four Inuit from Inukjuak, a substantial settlement in northern Quebec on Hudson Bay. Inukjuak had a Hudson's Bay Company post, police post, church missions, school, nursing station, weather station, radio station, and a port facility. Resolute Bay and Craig Harbour/ Grise Fiord, north of Devon Island in the High Arctic, where the Inuit were relocated, possessed none of the amenities available at Inukjuak. The only other people in the vicinity of where the Inuit were dropped off were three families relocated from Pond Inlet, hundreds of kilometres to the south. A deputy minister's 1956 memorandum was hopeful that the relocation was going fairly well – at least those relocated were not demanding to be sent back. But the Inuit "were seldom in a position to demand anything."[142] In fact they were suffering grievously. In the 1990s the Royal Commission on Aboriginal Peoples interviewed many of the Inuit, and found that relocation had been a horrible experience. It had taken them away from their families and friends, and torn them away from the life they had come to experience and appreciate in Inukjuak. The government had promised they would be joined by others and that they could return home if they were unhappy. Those promises were crucial in what seemed to be their consenting to relocation. But neither of those promises was kept. The Royal Commission report is full of their sorrowful and angry stories. John Amagoalik, who, twenty years later, would become a leader of the Inuit lands claim movement, begins his account with the following words: "The first ten years in Resolute were the most terrible years of our lives."[143] Although the report found no mention in the relocation planning documents of the need to strengthen Canada's claim to sovereignty in the High Arctic, the commissioners found it hard to believe that sovereignty was not at least part of the motivation behind the program.

At this point we leave the Indigenous peoples pillar, with all three of its components thoroughly "colonized" by the nation-building energy and achievements led by Canada's English-speakers. At this point in the Canadian story, the Indigenous peoples have no enduring place in Canadians' vision of their country. That would come later, when the Indigenous peoples effectively enter the mainstream's political space and gain a hearing for their vision of their future in Canada. But now let us turn to French Canada's experience, which for nearly a century after Confederation focused on conserving its national identity within the province of Quebec.

Chapter 9

The Provincialization of French Canada

On 22 November 1885 the greatest mass meeting ever held in Quebec up to that time took place on the Champs-de-Mars in Montreal. It was less than a week after Louis Riel was hanged in Regina. Many thousands, of all political stripes, came together to voice their angry protests. Sir Hector Langevin, Sir Adolphe Caron, and Adolphe Chapleau, three French-Canadian members of Sir John A. Macdonald's government, were burned in effigy. "Henceforward," screamed *La Presse*, "there are no more Conservatives nor Liberals nor Castors, there are only PATRIOTS AND TRAITORS." Even Wilfrid Laurier proclaimed: "If I had been on the banks of the Saskatchewan, I too, would have soldiered my musket."[1]

It was the announcement of Riel's sentence that had worked French Canadians into a frenzy of nationalist fervour. Before that they "seemed embarrassed, ambivalent, changing" in their attitudes to the North-West Rebellion.[2] Young French Canadians in significant numbers had joined the militia to put it down. At the same time there was much criticism of the Macdonald government's failure to respond sympathetically to the Métis' grievances. French Canadians were virtually unanimous that Riel was mad, and that he had not been given a fair trial. But what aroused French Canadians' nationalist rage, more than anything else, was their belief that the underlying reason for Riel's execution was English Canada's hatred of French Catholics. The joy expressed in Ontario over Riel's hanging convinced many Quebecers that anti-French-Canadian sentiment was sweeping through English Canada. The editorial reaction in the Ontario press the day after the mass rally on the Champs-de-Mars did nothing to dispel that impression. The Toronto *Mail* warned its readers that French Canadians were "now seeking to compel us to recognize their right to suspend the operation of the law when a representative of their race is in the toils," and went on to threaten that, "rather than to submit to such a yoke, Ontario would smash Confederation into its original fragments."[3]

The man of the moment was Honoré Mercier, leader of the Liberals in Quebec's Legislative Assembly. Mercier's family had been staunch supporters of Papineau in the 1837 rebellion, and he himself was steeped in the *Patriote* ethos. He began his political career by being elected to the House of Commons under the banner of the Parti National, a loose alliance of Conservatives and Liberals who were willing to "put the national interest" ahead of party interest.[4] The national interest, of course, was that of French Canada. Now, back in Quebec provincial politics, Mercier used the outrage aroused by Riel's execution as a platform for mobilizing Quebecers to support a new manifestation of the Parti National. In his speech at the Champs-de-Mars, he pleaded for the union of all true patriots to punish those who were guilty and, in the words of historian Mason Wade, "succeeded in imposing his doctrine of a racial party founded on the newly made grave of Louis Riel."[5] In the October 1886 Quebec election, Mercier was able to unite enough Conservatives, ultramontanes (anti-liberal Catholics), and his own Liberal *Rouges* under the Parti National banner to hold the balance of power in the Assembly and have himself installed as premier in January 1887.

Mercier's political victory consolidated the process of identifying the French Canadian nation with the province of Quebec. The Riel execution brought French Canadians to grasp more deeply that, when there was a French-English issue, Canada's English-speaking majority would determine the outcome in Ottawa. That realization, as Ramsay Cook observes, "caused French Canadians to look inward and to fall back on their provincial government as the one bastion protecting them against the English-speaking majority."[6] French Quebecers would continue to pay attention to the political scene in Ottawa, but their primary interest in federal politics would be to protect the interests of French Canada, and for most of them that would mean Quebec. The government they could control in Quebec was now seen as their national government. They would elect strong leaders such as Wilfrid Laurier to the Parliament in Ottawa. But Laurier, a staunch believer in an unhyphenated Canadian identity, and French Canadians of his persuasion found themselves up against an English-speaking majority that continued to think of Canada as a British country.

With Quebec now clearly the homeland of French Canada, protecting it from interference by the federal government became a priority of Quebec politicians of all stripes. Provincial autonomy was the first plank in Honoré Mercier's election platform. But it was not Mercier or Quebec that would lead the provincial rights movement across the federation. That role was taken by Ontario and its premier, Oliver Mowat. It was Mowat and Ontario whose constitutional activism would turn Canada into the kind of federation that, although far from Sir John A. Macdonald's vision, was one that could accommodate French-Canadian nationalism.

The province that might have been expected to lead the provincial rights movement was neither Quebec nor Ontario, but Nova Scotia. In the first federal election Charles Tupper was the only government member to win a Nova Scotia seat; anti-Confederation candidates won the other eighteen. In 1868 Joseph Howe led a delegation to London seeking repeal of the union. But Sir John A. Macdonald quelled Nova Scotian separatism by offering Howe a cabinet seat and then negotiating a deal to grant Nova Scotia better financial terms than were provided for in the British North America Act.[7] This move angered Edward Blake, the Liberal reform leader in the Ontario legislature. Blake was a strong constitutionalist who did not think that the new Dominion's Constitution could be casually amended. Blake's position might seem obvious today, but politicians such as Macdonald were accustomed to the British constitutional tradition in which there is no constitutional text with the status of a supreme law that cannot be changed by a simple majority of parliament. Blake introduced thirteen resolutions in the Ontario Assembly attacking any change in the terms of the BNA Act without consulting all the provinces.[8] In effect Blake was enunciating what would come to be known as the "compact theory," according to which Confederation was an agreement among the provinces and therefore the consent of all the provinces was required for any change in the terms of Confederation.

Edward Blake narrowly won the snap election of 1871 called by Ontario's Conservative premier John Stanfield Macdonald in the midst of the furor over the execution of Thomas Scott by the Red River Métis. The following year the system of dual representation that allowed a politician to hold seats in both the federal and provincial legislatures was abolished, forcing Edward Blake and Alexander Mackenzie to make a choice. Both chose to pursue their careers at the national level. This paved the way for Ontario reform leaders to persuade Oliver

Mowat to leave the judicial post to which his former law partner, Sir
John A. Macdonald, had appointed him and return to the political arena.[9] In October 1872 Mowat was sworn in as Ontario premier, a position
he would hold for the next twenty-four years.

Mowat quickly came round to Edward Blake's constitutional philosophy. Although he had been closely allied with Sir John A. through the
Confederation conferences and debates, as Ontario premier he did not
see himself leading a government subordinate to Ottawa. There was
also a partisan side to Mowat's championing provincial rights. He was
a Liberal reformer, not a Conservative, and his party's coming to power
in Ontario was part of a pattern that would repeat itself all through
Canadian history: the party forming the government in Ottawa would
find its political opponents winning power in the provinces. Mowat
combined shrewd political instincts – he ran a mighty patronage machine – with a first-class legal mind. He was stubby, somewhat cross-
eyed, bespectacled, and exceedingly bland. Sir John A. Macdonald
seriously underestimated him, referring to him as "the mere jackal to
Blake's lion."[10]

The issue that immediately brought Macdonald and Mowat into
constitutional conflict – the position of the Crown in provincial government – might seem arcane today. Section 17 of the British North
America Act (since 1982, the Constitution Act, 1867) states that the
Parliament of Canada consists of the queen, the Senate, and the House
of Commons, but the queen is not mentioned in the sections dealing
with the provincial legislatures of Ontario and Quebec. The Act simply
refers to the lieutenant-governor as a component of the legislatures of
Ontario and Quebec, and states that the "Constitution of the Legislature" of each of New Brunswick and Nova Scotia would continue to
exist as they were at the Union (sections 69, 71, and 88). Although the
Act is silent on who appoints the governor general of Canada, it was
assumed that the queen would continue to do so, as she had been appointing the governors and lieutenant-governors of the British North
American colonies before Confederation. But section 58 of the Act provides that the governor general in council (legalese for federal cabinet)
appoints the lieutenant-governors of the provinces. For Macdonald
that meant the lieutenant-governors were representatives, not of the
queen, but of the federal government – they were Ottawa's agents
in provincial governments. This was part and parcel of the view of
the provinces he enunciated in 1868: "the General Government or
Parliament should pay no more regard to the status or position of the

Local Governments than they would to the prospects of the ruling party in the corporation of Quebec or Montreal."[11]

Oliver Mowat would have none of that. A provincial government was not a mere local government with the status of a municipality. A provincial government had all the paraphernalia of responsible parliamentary government, and part of that paraphernalia was a representative of the queen as titular head of government. That was what the self-governing British North American colonies had before Confederation and what the provinces must have within Confederation. Mowat was anxious to show that the constitutional provision empowering the federal government to appoint provincial lieutenant-governors had not squeezed every ounce of royal jelly out of that office.

Edward Blake, before he gave up the Ontario premiership, had instructed Ontario's lieutenant-governor to confer the title of QC (queen's counsel) on leading members of the Ontario bar. On 23 December 1872 Prime Minister Macdonald wrote to Mowat, in confidence, advising him that the colonial secretary, Lord Kimberley, was of the opinion that a lieutenant-governor did not have the power to appoint QCs, but that a provincial legislature could confer that power on the lieutenant-governor. Mowat took up part of Macdonald's suggestion and had provincial legislation on QCs enacted that, instead of conferring on the lieutenant-governor the power to appoint QCs, declared that the lieutenant-governor already possessed it as part of his share of the Royal prerogative. Mowat similarly battled Ottawa over escheats (estates left without wills) going to the provincial Crown. After Edward Blake became a minister in Ottawa in the Liberal government of Alexander Mackenzie, Mowat's position prevailed, with a helpful decision from a Quebec court.[12]

Another obvious field of battle for Macdonald and the provincial rights movement was the power of the lieutenant-governor to refuse to sign a bill passed by a provincial legislature and reserve it for the federal government's consideration, and the federal government's power to disallow (that is, veto) legislation passed by a provincial legislature. These powers of reservation and disallowance were modelled on tools of control that Britain had exercised over its colonists' legislatures. But after the achievement of responsible government, Britain seldom used them in British North America because they interfered with home rule in these colonies. The BNA Act retained the governor general's power to reserve bills passed by the federal Parliament for consideration in London and the British government's power to disallow Acts passed by the federal Parliament (sections 56 and 57). After Confederation, Britain had the good sense to make almost no use of these powers. Only one Canadian Act was disallowed, in 1873, and it was clearly unconstitutional.[13] The last time a Canadian bill was reserved for consideration in London was 1878. The powers remain in Canada's Constitution even though, at the 1926 Imperial Conference establishing Dominion autonomy, British authorities declared disallowance of Dominion legislation and reservation by the governor general to be obsolete.[14]

The same fate awaited Ottawa's imperial powers over the provinces – except it would take a little longer for federal politicians, especially Sir John A. Macdonald, to accept the incompatibility of these powers with the kind of federal country Canada was becoming. Between 1867 and 1873 lieutenant-governors reserved twenty-four provincial bills for consideration, and Macdonald's government refused Royal Assent to sixteen of these. Most of the provincial bills killed in Ottawa were of doubtful constitutional validity, although a few were well within provincial jurisdiction.[15] The idea that it is the judiciary's job to decide whether legislation is constitutional was coming, but in the federation's early days it was not widely accepted or well understood. Macdonald instructed lieutenant-governors to sign every bill passed by provincial legislatures "unless satisfied that it is beyond the jurisdiction of the Local Legislature or is contrary to the instructions received from the Governor-General."[16] Of course, the governor general's instructions would be those of the federal government.

When Macdonald returned to power in 1878, his government made much less use of reservation and disallowance than during its first term in office. Macdonald instructed lieutenant-governors to reserve bills only in cases of "*extreme necessity*," and added that, "with the facility of communication between the Dominion and provincial Governments *such a necessity should seldom ever arise*."[17] Ottawa did not need reservations by lieutenant-governors to exercise its power to disallow provincial Acts. At Confederation, the view was advanced by George Brown, among others, that the general government's veto power over provincial legislation would serve to protect individual and minority rights. That is why Oliver Mowat moved its adoption in the Quebec Resolutions. But the federal government failed to comply with that principled basis for the federal veto. One of the fiercest battles Macdonald and Mowat fought was over the use of disallowance primarily for partisan purposes, rather than for the protection of high principles.

The battle grew out of a commercial squabble between a prominent Ontario Conservative, Peter McLaren, who had built a dam and slide to float his logs down eastern Ontario's Mississippi River to the lumber mills on the Ottawa River, and Boyd Caldwell, owner of timber rights on the Mississippi and a strong Liberal. When McLaren obtained an injunction stopping Caldwell from using the improvements he had made on the river, the Mowat government stepped in and passed the River and Streams Act.[18] The Act aimed at preventing a private entrepreneur from monopolizing the commercial use of a public resource such as a river. It set up a system of tolls, with some compensation for the person who had paid for the improvements. Prime Minister Macdonald, who also served as his government's justice minister, regarded the Ontario Act as a violation of an individual's property rights, and promptly disallowed it. This was the first time the federal disallowance power was used to strike down a provincial Act that was clearly constitutional. Mowat was enraged, and promptly had the Rivers and Streams Act re-enacted, only to have Macdonald promptly disallow it again.

The exchange of Mowat's punch and Macdonald's counterpunch was repeated a third time on the eve of the 1883 Ontario election, a hard-fought battle between Mowat's Liberals and the Ontario Conservatives revved up by Sir John A.'s appeal to national interests. Mowat won, but with a reduced majority, despite riding a series of legal victories in the courts and going toe-to-toe with the prime minister in defence of the province's right to control the use of its own natural resources. This was not an indication of a lack of strong popular support for provincial rights, but a demonstration that there was popular support both for strong provinces and for a strong national government. This would be an enduring feature of the politics of the Canadian federation: the competition between the federal and provincial governments for popular support. This adds up to a lot of government at both levels. After the election the Ontario legislature passed the Rivers and Streams Act for a fourth time. Macdonald finally threw in the towel – he would allow the damned Ontario law to stand. In 1884 the Judicial Committee of the Privy Council ruled that, under a pre-Confederation Canadian law, the right to float logs downstream included streams made floatable by dams and slides – vindicating the Ontario Act.[19]

All the time Mowat and Macdonald were duelling over the provincial Crown and disallowance, another fight was going on with something much more tangible at stake: Ontario's northwest boundary. At issue was the land between Port Arthur and Fort William, at the

western end of Lake Superior, and the Lake of Woods, the so-called
North-West Angle, the very land covered by Treaty 3 in 1873. After
Manitoba's entry into Confederation, its border with Ontario remained
uncertain. Ontario coveted the North-West Angle for what it would
add to the province's natural resources. Macdonald did not want
Ontario to have it because that would make Ontario too big and too
powerful. He wanted the territory to belong to Manitoba, whose terms
of union left its public lands under Ottawa's control.

We know from the last chapter that this struggle ends with a huge
win for Ontario by way of a ruling of Canada's highest court, the
Judicial Committee of the Privy Council (JCPC). To appreciate how big
a win it was for Ontario, think of Ontario's western boundary ending
at today's Thunder Bay, nearly two hundred miles east of where the
JCPC set it, and run that line all the way up to Hudson Bay. No wonder
Mowat crossed the Atlantic twice to support his province's case in
London, and no wonder Ontarians welcomed him back as a conquering hero after his victory. By this point Macdonald must have been
wondering if it was such a good idea for Canada to retain the JCPC as
Canada's supreme court.

The Judicial Committee of the Privy Council is one of those eccentric
institutions that grew out of British history. It was created by an Act of
Parliament in 1833 to hear appeals from the colonies as well as from
admiralty courts and ecclesiastical cases.[20] As Britain extended its empire around the world, the JCPC offered British colonists access to a taste
of British justice in the form of an appeal to "the foot of the throne." In
practice, this meant that a committee of Britain's highest judges heard
appeals from its colonies, including those of British North America. In
theory, when they were hearing appeals from the colonies, the British
judges were not sitting as a royal court of justice but as the judicial part
of the Privy Council giving advice to the Crown. In reality the lord chancellor, the highest judge in the realm, would form a panel, typically of
five law lords, that would hear appeals from a colony's highest court. In
keeping with the mythology that it was just giving advice to the Crown,
the JCPC met informally around a table in a committee room, the judges
not bedecked in wigs and gowns but wearing business suits or tweeds.
However much the law lords wrangled in reaching a decision, it was
always rendered as unanimous – it simply wouldn't do to confuse the
monarch or show anything but a firm hand to the colonies.

The Fathers of Confederation did not need to create a supreme court
for Canada, as they already had one in the JCPC. As we have seen,

however, they thought that a Canadian supreme court eventually might be established, and inserted section 101 of the BNA Act, empowering the federal Parliament to establish "from Time to Time ... a General Court of Appeal for Canada." That time did not arrive until 1875, when Parliament passed an Act creating the Supreme Court of Canada. With jurisdiction to hear appeals in all matters of law from the provincial courts, the Supreme Court of Canada could save litigants a good deal of time and money, even though it might rob Canadian lawyers of a nice, client-financed trip to London to brief the British barristers who argued Canadian appeals before the JCPC.

In the parliamentary debate on the Supreme Court Act, there were two contentious issues, both with a nationalist flavour. A number of Quebec MPs were opposed to a court in Ottawa dominated by jurists from English-speaking common law provinces having the power to overturn the decisions of Quebec courts in cases concerning Quebec's distinct system of civil law.[21] Quebec MPs on both sides of the House supported amendments that would forbid appeals to the Supreme Court in civil law matters. Quebec lawyers did not have the same objection to the JCPC's hearing Quebec civil law appeals. They regarded the British law lords, rendering justice as they did for a vast and diverse empire, as more sophisticated and cosmopolitan than the backwoods colonial lawyers who would serve on Canada's Supreme Court. The only concession to this Quebec concern was the adoption of a provision that at least two of the six places on the Supreme Court would be filled by members of the Quebec bar or bench. But with a quorum of four and panels of five hearing most appeals, the two civil law justices could be – and indeed frequently were – outvoted by justices from common law Canada on civil law cases from Quebec.

The other concern was voiced by MPs, mostly Macdonald Conservatives, who feared severing Canada's link to the high court of the British Empire. The British connection was still a vital part of their sense of national identity. This sentiment did not stop the House from passing an amendment to the Act, moved by Liberal backbencher Aemilius Irving, that made the Supreme Court's judgments final in all but special "prerogative" appeals to the JCPC. That would seem to have accomplished pretty much what Macdonald and other Empire Loyalists feared. But it didn't! Lord Cairns, the English lord chancellor (and the JCPC's presiding judge), took the view that "the appeal to the Sovereign in Council is one and indivisible."[22] Edward Blake, the Canadian minister of justice, eventually came to accept Lord Cairns's position as correct. The British government decided not to disallow the Irving amendment. On both sides of the Atlantic it was accepted that the appeal to the Privy Council was unchanged.

This meant that Canada's Supreme Court was supreme in name only. From its creation in 1875 until the abolition of Privy Council appeals in 1949, the Supreme Court of Canada would function as an intermediate court of appeal. Not only could its decisions be appealed to the JCPC in London, but Canadian litigants could bypass the Supreme Court and appeal directly to the JCPC from the highest court in their province. The significance of the Supreme Court's subordinate status for the interpretation of its Constitution would soon become evident.

At its first opportunity to show how it would interpret Canada's Constitution, the Supreme Court of Canada showed its centralist colours. In the 1878 case of *Severn v. The Queen*,[23] the Court upheld a federal challenge to Ontario licence fee on brewers. Canada's first chief justice, W.B. Richards, opened his opinion with a thundering statement that must have been music to Sir John A. Macdonald's ears. Referring to what the framers of the BNA Act had learned from the US experience with federalism, Richards said they "knew the difficulties that had arisen in the great Federal Republic ... They knew that the question of State rights as opposed to the authority of the General Government was frequently raised, aggravating, if not causing, the difficulties arising out of their system of government, and they evidently wished to avoid those evils." The chief justice went on to say that Ontario was claiming a power to interfere with the Dominion Parliament's authority in matters of trade and commerce that was "so pregnant with evil" and "so contrary to the manifest intention of the framers of the British North America Act" that it could not be conferred on a province.[24] Justice William Henry, who had been a Nova Scotia delegate at the Charlottetown and Quebec Confederation conferences, contrasted the US Congress's trade and commerce power, which is confined to international commerce, interstate commerce, and trade with the Indian tribes, with the "unlimited" trade and commerce power conferred on Canada's national Parliament.

The JCPC began interpreting Canada's Constitution as early as 1873. In its first decision on the division of powers, the 1881 case of *Citizens' Insurance Company v. Parsons*,[25] it took a markedly different approach from that of the Supreme Court of Canada. This case again involved a challenge, based on the federal Parliament's trade and commerce power, to Ontario legislation – this time a statute regulating fire insurance policies. Instead of considering the views of Canada's founding fathers, the British law lords approached the case as a routine exercise of statutory interpretation. The methodology of statutory interpretation was not to look at the legislators' intentions, a task that would require delving into political history, but to assume that the legislators must have been rational and intended that every part of a statute must have some substance. Applying that logic to the BNA Act, the law lords concluded that the federal Parliament's power over trade and commerce in section 91 must have some limits, otherwise it would simply absorb provincial powers that were bound to relate to trade and commerce, including the power to legislate on matters relating to "property and civil rights in the province." Contracts of insurance were surely matters of property and civil rights. So the JCPC excluded from the federal trade and commerce power "the power to regulate by legislation the contracts of a particular trade or business" in a province. Sir Montague Smith, who wrote the decision in *Parsons*, said that the federal trade and commerce power included international and interprovincial trade, and perhaps "general regulation of trade affecting the whole Dominion."[26] The opinion seemed rather tentative, but it quickly hardened into a binding limitation of federal power.

Hard on the heels of the *Parsons* case came three more constitutional rulings of the JCPC, all of them relating to booze. *Russell v. The Queen* in 1882 seemed to be good news for the federal government. The law lords upheld the Canada Temperance Act, which set up a Canada-wide system of local prohibition, enabling any city or county in the country to vote itself dry. They saw this legislation as a proper use of the biggest federal power: its general power "to make Laws for the Peace, Order, and good Government of Canada." Although the *Russell* case kindled some hope among Macdonald centralists, the next two cases conveyed a different message. In the 1883 case of *Hodge v. the Queen*, the JCPC rejected a challenge to Ontario legislation licensing taverns and shops to sell intoxicating beverages in those parts of the province that had not voted to go dry. The law lords rejected the argument that their decision in *Russell* meant that the entire subject of liquor was under federal jurisdiction. The lesson to take from their decision in *Parsons* was "that subjects which in one aspect and for one purpose fall within sect. 92, may in another aspect and for another purpose fall within sect. 91." The "aspect doctrine" suggested that the JCPC was inclined to be generous to both levels of government and disinclined to overturn federal or provincial legislation. But then along came the *McCarthy Act Reference* case.

In the ongoing duel between John A. Macdonald and Oliver Mowat, legislation drafted by a parliamentary committee chaired by Macdonald's colleague Dalton McCarthy provided for a country-wide system of liquor licensing just like Mowat's Ontario law that was upheld in *Hodge*. To expedite the process of testing the validity of the federal law, Macdonald referred the question of the McCarthy Act's constitutionality directly to the Supreme Court of Canada. The provision for such "reference cases" was an innovative feature of the Supreme Court Act. The result was a shocker for Macdonald and his government. Now, for the first time, the Supreme Court of Canada had to apply precedents set by the JCPC. Although the court did this somewhat grumpily – Justice Strong complained about "judges sitting in a foreign country who know nothing about our laws and institutions"[27] – they fell into line. The Supreme Court found the federal Act *ultra vires* – that is, outside the jurisdiction of the federal Parliament – and therefore unconstitutional. The Court refused to give reasons for its decision. Justice Strong exclaimed that a decision of his Court would be alluded to "only for the purpose of offensive criticism."[28] On appeal to London the JCPC, without giving its reasons, upheld the Supreme Court's verdict.

The die was now cast: the Supreme Court of Canada was a "captive court" subservient to an imperial tribunal developing a view of Canada's federal structure that, while at odds with that of Sir John A. Macdonald, was more in line with the balance of power and opinion in the country. Mowat had bested Macdonald in the courts. Provincial rights had found a significant measure of judicial recognition. The federal-provincial struggle now shifted to the political arena in a setting designed by the premier of Quebec.

In 1887 Honoré Mercier was riding high in Quebec. He sensed that it was time for the provincial rights movement to show its strength throughout the country. With that in mind he issued invitations to the provincial premiers to meet with him in Quebec City to discuss questions relating to provincial autonomy, the financial arrangements of the federation, and other matters of mutual concern. Although the meeting was billed as an interprovincial conference, Mercier also invited Prime Minister Macdonald. In his curt reply declining the invitation, Sir John said, "it would answer no good purpose to send representatives."[29] But the premiers of four of the six provinces accepted Mercier's invitation. New Brunswick's Andrew Blair, Nova Scotia's W.S. Fielding, and Ontario's Oliver Mowat all led Liberal governments. Manitoba's John Norquay was a Conservative but glad to attend the conference, as his government was brawling with Macdonald over the disallowance of Manitoba's railway legislation. The Conservative premiers of British Columbia and Prince Edward Island declined the invitation. Still, the provinces that attended represented over 90 per cent of the Dominion's population.

No premier accepted Mercier's invitation with more alacrity than Oliver Mowat. In bearing and style no one could have been more of a contrast with the flamboyant and almost regal Mercier than the squat, scholarly Ontario premier. But the premiers of the two largest provinces hit it off very well. Mercier agreed that Mowat should chair the conference, and with his mastery of constitutional detail Mowat dominated the discussion. The premiers brought ministers with them – eight in all plus seven from Quebec. When the delegates assembled for a photo opportunity at the Quebec parliament buildings, they looked not unlike earlier pictures of the delegates to the Confederation conferences. Mercier made sure the red carpet was rolled out for the premiers and their ministers with a number of spectacular social events.

After a week of deliberations, the conference agreed to seventeen resolutions all aimed at strengthening the provinces' position in Confederation. At the top of the list was the number one concern of the provincial autonomists: abolishing the federal government's power to disallow provincial legislation. Right behind it was an item that should not be surprising, given what we have seen about the emergence of the courts as arbiters of federal disputes: the provinces should have the same facility as the federal government to refer questions about the constitutionality of legislation to the courts. Number three in the list of resolutions was a proposal to have the provincial governments appoint half the senators – an idea that would resurface in Canada's constitutional debates a century later. After that came proposals to increase provincial powers (for instance, in bankruptcy law), or to reduce federal power (for instance, the power to take over "Local Works and Undertakings" declared by Ottawa to be for "the general Advantage of Canada"). The final resolution – Premier Mercier's top priority, but not Mowat's – was an increase in federal subsidies to the provinces.

The premiers took these resolutions home for approval by their provincial legislatures. After that the idea was to submit those that required amendment to the BNA Act to the British Parliament to be enacted into law. The only provinces that took that step were New Brunswick and Nova Scotia, but of course the British officials refused to take any action on a request for a constitutional amendment that was not supported by the Dominion government.

Although none of the constitutional changes called for by the Inter-Provincial Conference materialized in constitutional amendments, its resolutions showed which way the winds of constitutional change were blowing. The very fact that the premiers thought they could have Canada's Constitution changed without the federal government's participation indicated the growing strength of the "compact theory" of Confederation. That theory, which had long been an underlying premise of many Quebec leaders, was worked into a full-blown theoretical statement by Quebec judge Thomas-Jean-Jacques Loranger just before Mercier's election as premier.[30] Its central argument was that Confederation resulted from a compact entered into by the provinces, which had delegated certain powers to the new central government. It followed that the provinces, far from being subordinate to the federal government, were equal to it. The "compact theory" was ideology, not law, but it was a potent ideology that soon began to have some effects. Even before Sir John A. Macdonald died, his justice minister, Sir John Thompson, demonstrated a less aggressive use of the disallowance power. Thompson also responded to the second of the premiers' resolutions with amendments to the Supreme Court Act providing for greater use of reference cases by having the Court hear additional evidence and submissions from all interested parties before giving its reasoned decision.[31] Two decisions of the JCPC would soon show how in tune judicial power was with the provincial rights cause.

The first of the two JCPC decisions came in a mundane commercial dispute. The Maritime Bank of Canada had gone bankrupt, and first in the line of creditors requesting payment from what remained of the bank's assets was the government of New Brunswick. New Brunswick was relying on long-established English law carried over into Canada that gives the Crown priority over other creditors in bankruptcy proceedings. The argument against New Brunswick's claim was that Confederation had severed any connection between the Crown and the provinces. As we have seen, that was a crucial issue in the constitutional jousting between Macdonald and Mowat. The JCPC totally rejected Macdonald's position. Its decision, written by Lord Watson, the Scottish lord chancellor, stated that "a Lieutenant Governor when appointed is as much the representative of Her Majesty for all purposes of provincial government as the Governor-General Himself is for all purposes of Dominion government."[32] The British law lords justified their decision in broad theoretical terms about the nature of the federalism underlying the BNA Act: "The object of the Act was neither to weld the provinces into one, nor to subordinate provincial governments to a central authority, but to create a federal government in which they should all be represented, entrusted with the exclusive administration of affairs in which they had a common interest, each province retaining its independence and autonomy."[33]

This view of Canadian federalism was clearly not in accord with Sir John A. Macdonald's thinking at the time of Confederation. In the Confederation debates he had said that "[t]he true principle of Confederation lay in giving to the General Government all the principles and powers of sovereignty," and referred to the provinces as "subordinate" to the federal government. Sir John had died in 1891, a year before the JCPC delivered this decision. Some think Lord Watson's words had him rolling in his grave. Perhaps – but Sir John A. was an adaptable politician. He had moved some way from his original opposition to any kind of federalism for Canada, and being the successful politician that he was, he might have adapted to the reality of provincial governments' insistence on being treated as more than mere municipalities.

Of two things we can be relatively certain. On the nature of Canadian federalism, Macdonald never spoke for the French-Canadian participants in Confederation. Indeed it is doubtful that he spoke for a majority of Canada's founding fathers. Second, by the 1890s, the views Macdonald expressed in the Confederation debates did not represent the views of a majority of Canadians. Most Canadians had come to accept the rough equality of status between the two levels of government espoused by Lord Watson. Later on the British judges would go further in diminishing the federal government's powers than was acceptable to most Canadians. The excessively decentralizing jurisprudence of the JCPC in the first part of the twentieth century would not stand for long. But its view of Canadian federalism – sometimes referred to as "classical federalism" – as a division of powers between two levels of government equally sovereign in their allotted fields remains to the present day a fundamental constitutional principle for Canadians. Through the first twenty-five years of the Dominion of Canada's history, the combined forces of law and politics added federalism, understood as the JCPC articulated it, to parliamentary democracy, monarchy, and constitutionalism as a component of Canada's shared civic culture.

The second JCPC decision, the 1896 *Local Prohibition* case, completed the fourth and final round in the constitutional struggle over the regulation of booze.[34] It was won by Ontario, making provincial power triumphant in three of the four rounds. At issue was Ontario legislation restoring a power to municipalities they had enjoyed before Confederation: the power to pass by-laws prohibiting the sale of liquor subject

to the by-law's being approved by the electors. The Ontario Act dupli-
cated the Canada Temperance Act's local option system that the JCPC
upheld in the *Russell* case, except it operated through municipal governments. Following their decision in *Russell*, the British judges considered the federal Parliament's general power to legislate for the peace,
order, and good government of Canada (POGG) as the only possible
basis for the Canada Temperance Act. But then the JCPC added a twist:
the POGG power was weaker than the twenty-nine enumerated powers that, "for greater Certainty," were listed after it. Those specific powers, such as regulating trade and commerce, could encroach on the
exclusive powers of the provinces, but POGG could not. Lord Watson
explained that the federal Parliament's general power must be limited
in this way because any other interpretation of it would "not only be
contrary to the intendment of the Act, but would practically destroy the
autonomy of the provinces."[35] The British lord chancellor left a glimmer
of hope for Canadians who want their national government to have the
constitutional capacity to deal with national problems: Their Lordships,
he said, "do not doubt that some matters, in their origin local and provincial, might attain such dimensions as to affect the body politic of the
Dominion, and to justify the Canadian Parliament in passing laws for
their regulation or abolition in the interest of the Dominion."[36]

For the French majority in Quebec, judicial recognition of provincial
autonomy as a fundamental principle of Canada's Constitution must
have been reassuring. The province in which the French minority in
Canada was a majority would have its powers protected. But what
about provinces in which French Canadians were a minority? Developments in Manitoba would soon answer that question.

In the fifteen years following the Riel uprising, Manitoba had under-
gone an extraordinary demographic revolution. In 1870 Métis accounted
for 82 per cent of the enumerated population of Canada's newest province.[37] The 1886 census recorded French Métis as 4 per cent of Manitoba's
population and the total French population of the province as 10 per cent.
By 1886 Manitoba's population had tripled to 152,000, and two-thirds
of the population was now of British extraction. There were as many
Manitobans of German origin as French, and the province had acquired
an Icelandic population half the size of the French Métis. There was also
a large Aboriginal population in and near the province on the territory
covered by the first three numbered treaties, but Canada was too racist
and imperialist at this time to include the people indigenous to the country as part of its citizenry. The province's English Protestant majority did

not take long to flex its political muscle – with devastating consequences for Manitoba's French Catholic minority.

In 1890 the Manitoba legislature passed the Official Language Act, making English the official language of the province. It prohibited the use of French in the records and journals of the legislature and in court proceedings, and stipulated that provincial Acts be printed and published in English only. The Act was directly contrary to section 23 of the Manitoba Act, incorporating the agreement of Riel's Provisional Government that English and French be used in the legislature and courts of the province. The legislation was soon successfully challenged in the courts. In 1892 Judge Prud'homme of the St Boniface County Court found the Act unconstitutional, but the government of Manitoba simply ignored this judicial ruling. It did so again after the St Boniface County Court made the same ruling in 1909. Not until 1979 would a judicial decision ruling that Manitoba's Official Language Act was unconstitutional reach and be upheld by the Supreme Court of Canada.

A modern-day reader will have difficulty understanding this story. How could a law that clearly contravened the Constitution and was found by a court to do so, stay in force for nearly ninety years? In answering that question, there is much to learn about the evolution of our country.

Vindicating constitutional rights in the courts is a relatively recent liberal democratic practice. This is so even in the United States, the country that has led the world in establishing this practice. It was not until the 1920s, when the United States Supreme Court decided that the Bill of Rights in the US Constitution applies to the states, that the "rights revolution" really got under way in that country. There is much more to the "rights revolution" than having the rights of individuals and groups written into constitutional documents, and the odd judge here and there taking them seriously.[38] A real, grounded "rights revolution" requires a large and accessible legal profession well educated in and supportive of constitutional rights, mass media that follow rights litigation closely at all levels, and a democratic electorate that respects the role of the judiciary in upholding rights claims even when that means overturning the will of legislative majorities. The socio-political infrastructure essential for the "rights revolution" did not exist in Manitoba or anywhere else in Canada until the 1970s. Its arrival would be yet a further addition to the nation's shared civic culture.

Another thing missing in Manitoba of the 1890s was public support for mutual respect between English and French Canada. The seeds of such respect had been sown by Confederation leaders such as Cartier and Macdonald. But the passions stirred by Riel's uprising and execution were pushing hatred – "race hatred," to use the language of the times – to the forefront. What else can explain the popular support of Anglo-Saxon Manitoba for eliminating French language rights? In 1879, when the provincial legislature passed a bill banning the printing in French of all public documents except statutes, a French-Canadian lieutenant-governor, Joseph Cauchon, reserved the bill for consideration in Ottawa. In 1890, Manitoba's lieutenant-governor had no difficulty giving Royal Assent to the much more extreme Official Language Act because he was none other than John Christian Schultz, the personification of anti-French Orange sentiment in Ontario, who had voted against the Manitoba Act when it was debated by the federal Parliament in 1870.

The coupling together of language and religion was fuelling "race hatred" between English and French Canadians. When Honoré Mercier settled a long-standing dispute about estates confiscated from the Jesuit order after the fall of New France by asking the pope to divide up a modest amount of money provided by Quebec, all hell broke loose in the Parliament of Canada. A group of Ontario MPs urged the federal government to disallow Quebec's Jesuit Estates legislation.[39] Visceral Anglo fear of popery raised its ugly head. Sir John A. Macdonald was able to withstand the pressure for disallowance. But the passions unleashed by the legislation animated Manitoba's English Protestant majority to turn on Roman Catholic schools in the province as vigorously as it attacked the French language.

Terminating the school rights of Manitoba Catholics was a tougher nut to crack than removing French as one of the province's official languages. That is because section 22 of the Manitoba Act of 1870, the province's terms of union with Canada, enshrining the right to denominational schools, contained a political remedy – the very same remedy written into section 93 of the BNA Act to protect the school rights of religious minorities in the four founding provinces: the Protestant or Roman Catholic minority could appeal to the federal government from any Act or decision of the provincial legislature affecting their denominational school rights. The federal government, in turn, could require Parliament to pass "remedial legislation" to ensure proper observance of the right. Here we see how Canada's founders looked to political institutions, rather than to the judiciary, to protect constitutional rights.

Soon after the Manitoba legislature passed the Public Schools Act, establishing a system of non-denominational schools, Catholic families in Winnipeg challenged the legislation in the courts. The challenge was successful in the Supreme Court of Canada. The senior Canadian judges recognized that the voluntary system of Catholic schools that had existed before union with Canada would be undermined if Catholic parents had to pay local taxes to support the public school system.[40] But that decision was overturned by the Judicial Committee of the Privy Council. The British judges took a narrower view of the minority right: yes, Roman Catholic parents would have to pay for public schools on top of the cost of maintaining Catholic schools, but they were still *legally* free to operate their voluntary school system at their own expense. The law lords expressed their concern about not erecting barriers to "the establishment of a national system of education upon a non-sectarian basis."[41]

With their case lost in the courts, the Catholic parents resorted to their right of appeal to the federal cabinet. This time the Supreme Court of Canada denied that they had such a right, but the JCPC reversed the Supreme Court and upheld their right of political appeal.[42] The cat was now squarely among the Ottawa pigeons. For the Conservative government, the dilemma of responding to the Manitoba Catholics' appeal could hardly have come at a worse time. Following Sir John A. Macdonald's death in 1891, Senator John Abbott took over as prime minister, and was soon succeeded by the much more capable Sir John Thompson. But when Thompson died suddenly while visiting the queen at Windsor Castle in 1894, his successor, Sir Mackenzie Bowell, a past grand master of the Orange Lodge, was hardly the man to respond to a plea for help from Manitoba Catholics. The resignation of seven of Bowell's cabinet colleagues forced the return of Sir Charles Tupper from his position as Canadian high commissioner in London at the end of 1895. Tupper took over the leadership of the Conservatives in the House of Commons and soon became prime minister. With an election pending he had to decide whether his government would enact the remedial legislation demanded by Manitoba's Roman Catholics.[43]

Tupper did not hesitate. He drafted a remedial bill with the intention of driving it through the House of Commons. But – surprise! surprise! – Wilfrid Laurier, leader of the Liberal Opposition, working with Ontario Orangemen, held it up. Laurier was playing a cagey game. He did not want to vote against the bill, nor would he commit to using remedial legislation if he became prime minister. Laurier preferred conciliation to coercion. He would respect provincial autonomy and work with Manitoba's premier to establish favourable school conditions for the French Catholic minority. The remedial bill still had not passed when the life of Canada's seventh Parliament ran out. The Manitoba Schools Question was the central issue in the June 1896 election. Despite fierce opposition from Catholic clergy in Quebec, Laurier's Liberals took forty-nine of the province's sixty-five seats, and defeated the Conservatives by seventy-nine to seventy-two in the seats outside Quebec. In an election that pitted provincial rights against ethnic minority rights within the province, the Canadian people, including Quebecers, came down firmly on the side of provincial rights.

After the election, the Laurier government reached agreement with the Manitoba Liberal government of Thomas Greenway to provide a modicum of religious instruction in the last half-hour of the school day if authorized by the local school trustees or requested by parents of forty children in urban schools and twenty-five in rural schools. This much religious teaching was available to both Protestants and Catholics. The Laurier-Greenway agreement also authorized some instruction in French or in any other language when ten students spoke that language.[44] All of this was too much for the Orange Order and much too little for the Catholic clergy. But Laurier's "sunny ways" went down reasonably well with most English and French voters. The country had avoided a national unity crisis, but at the cost of making western Canada inhospitable to Quebec migrants and French Canada more provincial than ever. Worse was soon to come.

With Canada's first French-Canadian prime minister in office, and a first minister with such sunny ways, it would seem that smooth sailing lay ahead. But that was not to be. In fact the quarter-century following the 1896 election was the most troubled period in English-French relations the young Dominion had yet encountered. The raw, emotional distrust of the "two races" for one another that marked Canadian politics in this period makes one question how far Canadians had come since Lord Durham observed two nations warring within the bosom of a single state. André Siegfried, the well-known French geographer and political commentator, opened his 1907 book on *The Race Question in Canada* with the observation that "Canadian politics are a tilting ground for impassioned rivalries. An immemorial struggle persists between French and English, Catholics and Protestants."[45] It is doubtful Siegfried would have seen Canada that way in 1867.

The deterioration of relations between Canada's French and English pillars was primarily the result of a change in English-speaking Canada. English-Canadian politicians and many of their supporters, for a short time, became enamoured of their role in the British Empire. The empire they now wanted to be closely bound up with was not the Little Englanders' empire that was happy to wave goodbye to Canada at the time of Confederation, but an empire that now wanted its colonists' support and participation in an era of competitive European imperialism. By the late 1800s Britain saw its colonies, and above all those inhabited and run by British settlers, as its greatest asset in the struggle for global power with its European rivals.[46] The largest and closest of these was Canada.

A vague plan to embrace Canada and other colonies in some form of imperial federation spearheaded by Colonial Secretary Joseph Chamberlain began to emanate from British statesmen. Canadian leaders of British ancestry were open to that embrace. So was Wilfrid Laurier – up to a point. At Queen Victoria's diamond jubilee in 1897, Laurier accepted a knighthood and, next to the queen, was the star of that remarkable pageant. But the challenge of his premiership would be placating English Canada's imperial fever without alienating French Canada. It was a challenge that in the end defeated him.

In meeting that challenge Laurier had no greater thorn in his side than Henri Bourassa. And what an ironic thorn he was! Henri Bourassa, a grandson of Louis-Joseph Papineau, and manager of the Papineau *seigneurie* at Montebello, was a protégé of Laurier. Laurier encouraged young Bourassa, when he was still in his twenties and mayor of Montebello, to run for Parliament in the 1896 election.[47] Bourassa won the election, and began his parliamentary career as a strong supporter of the Laurier Liberal government. Like his leader Laurier, Henri Bourassa was a strong Canadian nationalist. Their French Canada was not confined to Quebec. French Canadians, in their vision, were equal partners with English-speaking Canadians in building a strong and independent Canadian nation. Bourassa, as a rookie MP, had gone along with the Laurier-Greenway compromise, with its reduction of the rights of the French Catholic minority in Manitoba. It was the last of Laurier's compromises he would accept.

Pressure on Laurier to support Britain in the Boer War led to Bourassa's first break with the prime minister. Soon after the war broke out in 1899, British authorities and a new and militaristic governor general, the Earl of Minto, who had served as General Middleton's chief of staff in the 1885 North-West Rebellion, made it clear that Canada was expected to dispatch a contingent of soldiers to South Africa. Laurier quickly found himself in a bind. Orange Ontario was in a frenzy to support the mother country. For French Canadians Britain's war with the

Dutch settlers in South Africa was an imperial venture that had nothing to do with Canada.

Laurier's initial reaction was to put Britain off by insisting that Canada's military support required parliamentary approval. But when he measured the depth of opposing sentiments in Ontario and Quebec, he backed away from a parliamentary debate that would have been dangerously divisive. His compromise was to draft an Order in Council authorizing funds for the arming and transportation of Canadians who volunteered for service in South Africa. When Laurier met with leaders in Montreal to sell them his compromise, it was Bourassa who led the resistance. When the prime minister told Bourassa the circumstances were difficult, young Henri replied, "It is because they are difficult that I ask you to remain faithful to your word. To govern is to have courage, at a given moment, to risk power to save principle."[48] That exchange encapsulates the difference between these two great Canadian nationalists. Bourassa would not compromise his belief in an independent, dualist Canada, governed through parliamentary democracy, even if it meant bringing on a political storm that could rip the country apart and lead to his party's loss of power. Laurier was just as strongly convinced that holding a deeply divided country together was worth temporarily failing to live up fully to principles he shared with Bourassa.

Bourassa resigned from his seat in Parliament and in doing so emerged as a powerful leader of French Canada. On 30 October 1899, 1,150 Canadian volunteers, known unofficially as the Canadian Contingent, sailed for South Africa to fight in the Boer War. Lord Strathcona, the former Hudson's Bay Company factor Donald Smith, who thirty years earlier had stood in the snow outside Fort Garry negotiating with Louis Riel, was now able to dip into the profits of his Canadian Pacific Railway to finance a second contingent that was on it way in January 1900. The Laurier Liberals were able to win the 1900 election with an increased majority. In that sense Sir Wilfrid's compromise paid off. But he now had to do battle with a formidable opponent for the soul of French Canada.

The next round in the Bourassa-Laurier duel concerned the rights of the French Catholic minority in the two provinces Canada was about to carve out of the Northwest Territories. The 1905 legislation creating Alberta and Saskatchewan was referred to as the Autonomy Acts, reflecting how deeply the principle of "provincial autonomy" had sunk into Canada's constitutional culture. The most contentious issue in the Acts was section 16, dealing with the education rights of French

Catholics. In 1904 Laurier, perhaps pumped up by his third election win – with an even larger majority than in 1900 – decided to make a "grand gesture" by providing for the same system of constitutionally entrenched school rights that the Fathers of Confederation had built into the BNA Act. This was not only a "grand gesture" but a very bold one. The two new provinces were now overwhelmingly English-speaking and Protestant. The French Catholics were barely 5 per cent of the population. The Northwest Territories Council had cut back on separate schools and established a system similar to the after-school-hours program in the Laurier-Greenway agreement in Manitoba. And one must add that the Canada of 1905 was not the Canada of 1867: at this time there was little sign, especially in English-speaking Canada, of the spirit of accommodation and compromise that had been so essential to the success of Confederation.

Laurier found this out as soon as he exposed his separate school plan to his cabinet and Parliament. His bold gesture immediately cost him the resignation of Clifford Sifton, his most powerful western minister and author of the immigration policy that was doing so much to build the country.[49] He could feel the hot hatred of Ontario Orangemen seething in the House, and was threatened with other losses from his cabinet, including Finance Minister William Fielding. Laurier quickly backed down. The Autonomy bills were amended. There would be no separate schools for francophone Catholics in the new provinces, just religious classes after school hours, with the provincial government in control of the curriculum. Laurier was able to carry all but two members of his Quebec caucus with him in supporting the amended bills. The two dissenters were Bourassa and his kindred spirit, Armand Lavergne. Behind them was a battery of new Quebec newspapers and organizations such as the Ligue nationaliste and the Catholic Association of French Youth, fired up by Bourassa's rhetoric addressed to "angry young men" speaking for a "beleaguered people."[50]

When the Liberals won the federal election again in 1908, Sir Wilfrid Laurier joined Sir John A. Macdonald as the only prime ministers to win four straight majority governments. But this time the Liberals' majority was slightly reduced, and the squeeze on the government by the contending forces of nationalism and imperialism soon showed signs of making a fifth victory unlikely. Laurier would try to steer a moderate Canadian nationalist course between these forces. Soon after the election, his government had to respond to the naval arms race building up between Britain and Germany. Germany's mighty dreadnoughts threatened Britain's naval supremacy, the key to its imperial strength, and the colonial dominions were expected to help out. Laurier's response was to develop a small Canadian naval force to patrol Canadian waters until an imperial war broke out. Then Canada's navy would be at the service of the empire.

Laurier's plan seemed reasonable enough. It was not opposed by Robert Borden, leader of the Conservative Opposition, and it fitted in with the British Admiralty's plans.

But on 10 January, two days before Laurier's naval bill was introduced in the House of Commons, Henri Bourassa's new newspaper, *Le Devoir*, published its first issue. Bourassa launched a fierce attack on Laurier's naval policy, claiming that it was "a betrayal of his own people."[51] Not only would it commit Canada to participating in Great Britain's imperial wars, but it was also likely to lead to that nightmare possibility – conscription. While Laurier's naval policy was taking these blasts from francophone Quebec, it was being ridiculed in English-speaking Canada for starting up a "tin-pot" navy that fell far short of the direct support a loyal and patriotic Canada should give Britain in building dreadnoughts for the Royal Navy. Laurier's firm statement that "When Britain is at war, Canada is at war" was not enough to appease Canadian imperialists, but it was sickening to the legions of French Canadians whom Bourassa addressed.

The Laurier Liberals might have survived had it not been for a second policy initiative that touched the most tender of nerves in Tory Canada. This was a proposal to enter into a trade deal with the United States aimed at a reciprocal lowering of tariffs. Interest in making the US market more accessible to Canadians was the most long-standing policy difference between Liberals and Conservatives. John A. Macdonald's attack on the Liberal proposal of an unrestricted reciprocity agreement with the United States was crucial to his electoral triumph over Laurier in 1891. The Liberals' trade policy ran up against the Tories' faith in a protective tariff as the best way of developing Canadian industry, and it brought out the lingering strength of loyalty to Britain in English-speaking Canada. It was in Macdonald's final election campaign that the Liberals' advocacy of increasing trade with the Americans inspired the cry, "A British subject I was born – a British subject I will die."[52] Over the next few years the issue went away, as the United States turned to more protectionist policies. But Laurier leapt on the opportunity created by the 1908 election of William Taft, a Republican much less attached to protectionism than Teddy Roosevelt. In January Laurier concluded an agreement with President Taft for a limited reciprocal lowering of tariffs. Customs duties on agricultural and natural resources would be eliminated or substantially reduced, while tariffs remained substantial on manufactured goods.[53] Although it seemed like a "win-win" for Canada, the Laurier-Taft deal turned out to be a "lose-lose" for Laurier.

In July 1911, after returning from a seven-week visit to England for the Coronation of George V and his fourth Imperial Conference, an overconfident Laurier called a September election. Laurier's long overseas absence had given the Conservatives time to regroup and launch a full-scale anti-American attack on the Laurier-Taft trade deal, not for its economic aspects but for its alleged threat to Canada's independence. American supporters of the trade proposal did not help the Liberal cause by expressing, as one congressman did, the hope "to see the day when the American flag will float on every square foot of the British North American possessions, clear to the North Pole."[54] On the Quebec front Laurier was under blistering attacks from Henri Bourassa's forces for his naval policy's betrayal of French Canada. As Laurier put it, "I am branded in Quebec as traitor to the French, and in Ontario as a traitor to the English."[55] By this time Bourassa had organized a nationalist movement that, though not a political party, challenged Laurier Liberals in many Quebec ridings. Bourassa promised Borden the *nationalistes'* support to defeat Laurier. In return he received $200,000 from Conservative financiers, tripling the assets of the publishing company that owned *Le Devoir*.[56]

The only surprising thing about Laurier's loss in the 1911 election, considering the strength of the unnatural Borden-Bourassa alliance, was that somehow he managed to lose only seventeen seats in Quebec and retain half of the Liberal seats in Ontario. But the Borden Conservatives were now in charge, and the country was headed for its deepest crisis of national unity since Confederation.

The crisis that lay ahead was conscription. When Bourassa's *nationalistes* threw their support to the Borden Conservatives, the Great War was nearly three years away. But in the years leading up to the war, relations between the "warring races" deteriorated, making the conscription crisis, when it came, more divisive than it might otherwise have been. In 1913 Ontario's Education Department issued Regulation 17, restricting instruction in French in areas of French settlement in the province, including in the constitutionally protected Roman Catholic separate schools. The controversy over Regulation 17 swirled on into the war years, poisoning English-French relations. A ruling in 1917 by the Judicial Committee of the Privy Council that the education rights protected by section 93 were for the benefit of religious minorities and had nothing to do with language[57] did not soften the blow to French Canada or increase French Canadians' enthusiasm for participating in a war effort so strongly endorsed by English-speaking politicians and the English-language press.

When war broke out, voluntary enlistment, the norm in most countries, worked well. Over two hundred thousand men signed up for military service in the first two years of the war. But 63 per cent of these recruits were British born. As Jack Granatstein observes: "The reality was that, through 1915, most native-born Canadians evidently had little desire to volunteer to fight for king and Empire."[58] Much more was made of the low levels of enlistment by French Quebecers than of the low response of their English-speaking, born-in-Canada compatriots, especially in rural areas, to the call of the recruiters. As the war wore on and turned into a much longer and more challenging struggle than had been anticipated, the Borden government came under pressure, most urgently from his military commanders, to adopt more vigorous forms of recruitment. For a long time Borden and R.B. Bennett, the Conservative MP from Calgary who had taken over as director general of recruiting, resisted moving to a compulsory system of recruitment. In a speech in Toronto in December 1916, Bennett denounced conscription because it would divide the country and endanger national unity.[59]

The turning point was Prime Minister Borden's trip to London in February 1917 to take part in a meeting of the Imperial War Cabinet. Participation in the War Cabinet gave him access for the first time to military intelligence and made him aware of the dangerous situation of the Allies. The "privilege of looking into the eyes of tens of thousands of men at the front" made him resolve to provide the manpower needed to fill the depleted ranks of the Canadian Corps and achieve the victory for which so many Canadians had made their sacrifice.[60] Borden's decision to introduce conscription was his own. He was not brow beaten into it by the Imperial Cabinet. For him, participation in the Imperial Cabinet was essential for giving Canada an adequate voice in war policy and to ensure, to use British prime minister David Lloyd George's words, that the Canadians were fighting, not for Britain, but with Britain.[61]

On 24 May a protest riot broke out in Quebec City, confirming the Borden government's worst fears about the danger of imposing conscription on Quebec. Borden tried to reduce that danger by inviting

Laurier to enter a coalition government in which the Liberal leader could name half the ministers.[62] Laurier turned him down. He was not convinced that conscription was necessary, and he feared that if he joined a coalition government he would turn Quebec over to Bourassa's *nationalistes*. Borden soldiered on. In early June, with the Canadian victory at Vimy Ridge and its staggering losses just two months behind him, he introduced the Military Services bill into Parliament. It was a carefully crafted measure. It made all males between twenty and twenty-four years of age liable for military service overseas, but provided liberally for exemptions, including conscientious objectors, with tribunals across the country to settle disputed cases.[63] A Liberal motion calling for a referendum on conscription was defeated. The bill passed with a substantial majority that included a number of Liberals. It became law at the end of August, but the government postponed putting the Military Service Act into force until October.

Even though Laurier had turned him down, Borden continued to work away at building a coalition government with pro-conscription Liberals he could detach from Laurier. He was convinced that a coalition government was needed to lead Canada through the divisive times brought on by conscription and to give the government all the political strength it could muster for the tremendous effort Canada would have to make to ensure victory in the war. In the small hours of the morning on 12 October, Borden wrapped up the details of a coalition with Thomas Crerar, a leading Liberal westerner, and Newton Rowell, the Liberal leader in Ontario. Exclusive of the prime minister, the new Unionist government would have twelve Conservatives, eight Liberals, and one representative of labour.[64] The stage was now set for the wartime election Borden had been determined to avoid. But the Liberals would not consent to postponing the election for a second year. So it was called for 17 December 1917.

To ensure victory the Unionist government passed two pieces of legislation that constituted an egregious abuse of power. The Military Voters Act gave the vote to all British subjects serving in the Canadian Expeditionary Force, including British soldiers and British subjects who had been living in the United States. These soldier voters could designate any place in Canada where they had resided as their electoral district. In effect the legislation created a floating vote that the government could direct to districts where it would improve its candidate's chances.[65] The Wartime Election Act was even more cynical. It enfranchised immediate female relatives of members of the armed forces and disenfranchised new Canadians who had arrived since 1902 from countries that were now enemies. Even some of the leaders of the women's suffrage movement were outraged at the blatant attempt to capture the votes of women most likely to support the pro-conscription Union government.[66] Borden promised that full women's suffrage would come later, and delivered on that promise in 1918.

In the 1917 federal election, the Canadian electorate divided on ethnic, English-French lines more sharply than in any election before or since. The Union government swept English-speaking Canada, taking 139 of the 159 seats outside Quebec. The Laurier Liberals swept French Canada, taking all but 3 of Quebec's 65 seats. Canada's federal union could not long endure such a sharp political rift between its English-speaking and French-speaking citizens. Nor could parliamentary democracy in Canada long endure such a cynical manipulation of the electoral system.

In the early months of 1918 the Germans launched a major offensive. The Canadian Corps held the line at Ypres in a valiant defensive stand, but suffered heavy losses. In response to pressure to step up the pace of conscription, the Borden government increased efforts to arrest defaulters. The biggest pressure point was Quebec City, where rioting broke out over the Easter weekend. Crowds stormed the offices administering the Military Service Act, smashing equipment and dumping papers into the streets.[67] The federal government put the riot down with a firm hand. Eight hundred troops from the local garrison were reinforced by a thousand more from Toronto. Using its powers under the War Measures Act, the government suspended *habeas corpus*. The jails were filled, and in street skirmishes at least four civilians were killed.[68] The government also removed the exemption for farmers, provoking anger in the rural communities of English-speaking Canada.

Neither Laurier nor Bourassa supported resistance to the Military Service Act. That bloody Easter weekend in 1918 added just a little more to the English-French animosity that had been building up for two decades The more enduring damage from conscription was to the Conservative Party, virtually killing it for several generations in Quebec and weakening it in rural Canada. But as J.L. Granatstein points out in his analysis of how Canada was able to play the lead role in the Allied counteroffensive that finally ended the First World War, the vigorous enforcement of conscription "did produce the reinforcements that the Canadian Corps needed to finish the war."[69]

Two developments brought the dark, dangerous period of English-French relations to an end. The first of these was the reuniting of the Liberal Party. Sir Wilfrid Laurier died in 1919, on the eve of a Liberal

Party convention. His death turned what had been planned as a policy convention into a leadership convention – the first in Canadian political history. William Lyon Mackenzie King, the grandson on his mother's side of Willie Mackenzie, leader of the Upper Canadian rebels, won the Liberal leadership on the third ballot.[70]

King, a leading English-speaking Liberal who had not deserted Laurier in the conscription crisis, could heal the party's wounds. He had built his career on his skills as a conciliator in industrial disputes between labour and management. King would use his aptitude for conciliation to knit the Liberal Party back together and avoid the national unity crises that had plagued the country for a generation. As Quebec and western Liberals returned to the Liberal fold, the Unionists came apart. In the 1921 election King faced a Conservative Party led by Arthur Meighen, who had been chosen in the traditional way by the government caucus. The Liberals won the election, coming within two seats of a majority. Meighen's Conservatives won only fifty seats, finishing third behind the Progressives, who took most of the western seats and twenty-four Ontario rural ridings.[71]

The 1921 election was a major turning point in Canadian politics, which no longer would revolve around the "war of the races." Industrial and ideological cleavages would now cut across ethnic divisions. It also marked the end of the two-party system in federal politics. This would have important consequences for parliamentary democracy. Thomas Crerar, the Progressives' leader, refused King's invitation to join a Liberal government, making King's a minority government, the first of many more to come.[72] And this was the first federal election in which Canadian women were fully enfranchised.

The second development that would foster better relations between Canada's French- and English-speaking pillars was ideological and constitutional. After the First World War, English-speaking Canada moved away from its attachment to the British Empire towards an aspiration for Canadian autonomy that could be shared with French Canada. On the British side, too, there was a growing realization that the dream of imperial federation was over. Through the 1920s, the British Empire would become the Commonwealth of Nations, at least for its "white dominions," and those dominions would move along the road from colony to nation. It was a road that English and French Canada could travel together.

The breakthrough came in foreign affairs, the realm in which Britain, though willing to consult with the dominions, strove to maintain a single imperial policy. Canadians participated in the negotiations that led to the Treaty of Versailles after the war, but only as members of the British delegation. Prime Minister Borden, however, secured a separate membership for Canada in the League of Nations and in its affiliate, the International Labour Organization. The League's covenant gave Canada the right to be represented by three delegates, in the same manner as the British Empire.[73] The key test of whether Canada could pursue its own policies in international affairs or be bound by a common British imperial policy came in 1922, when Turkey, under the leadership of Mustapha Kemal, drove the Greeks out of Asia and confronted British forces at Chanak, in the Dardanelles. The colonial secretary, Winston Churchill, warned Turkey publicly that, if war broke out, it would be war with all the Commonwealth nations.[74] In response, Prime Minister King refused to commit Canada to any measure of cooperation with Britain without a decision of the Canadian government or Parliament. This was classical King: cautious, dithering, but democratic. His position contrasted sharply with Conservative leader Arthur Meighen's "ready, aye ready," and asserted Canada's freedom to make its own foreign policy.[75]

"Empire" and "Commonwealth" continued to be used interchangeably until 1926. The Imperial Conference of that year marked the formal beginning of the Commonwealth. Pressure for a clarification of their independence was particularly strong from South Africa and Eire (the self-governing Irish Free State). But Australia, Canada, and New Zealand certainly supported the other two dominions. The conference produced a statement called the "Balfour Declaration," named after Arthur Balfour, the former British prime minister and foreign secretary who chaired the conference, recognizing Australia, Canada, Eire, Britain, New Zealand, and South Africa as self-governing members of the British Commonwealth. The relationship between these countries was defined as follows: "They are autonomous Communities within the British Empire, equal in status, in no way subordinate to one another in any aspect of their domestic or external affairs, though united by a common allegiance to the Crown, and freely associated as members of the British Commonwealth of Nations."[76] The declaration also stated that the governors general would no longer be representatives or agents of Britain and that the British government's power to disallow dominion legislation and the reservation of bills by the governor general was obsolete.

The change from empire to commonwealth came about in the traditional manner of the British constitution. There was no formal legal text or treaty. The Balfour Declaration was a political agreement, a constitutional convention stating a principle agreed to by all the relevant actors. Some legal matters remained to be settled more formally. That would come five years later with the Statute of Westminster. The fundamental freedom of Commonwealth countries was now clearly established. But it is important to note that this grant of national freedom had racial limitations. It applied only to the countries in the British Empire with white rulers, and by no means did it apply to the Indigenous peoples colonized within the autonomous dominions.

Tidying up the legal loose ends of dominion autonomy posed a challenge to the autonomy of the Canadian provinces. The principal legal impediment to the dominions' full independence was the British Colonial Laws Validity Act, which rendered invalid any colonial law inconsistent with British law. The superior status of British law surely had to go. But Canada's Constitution, the BNA Act, was an Act of the British Parliament. If Canada were no longer bound by British law, would the federal and provincial legislatures no longer be bound by the BNA Act? Would it not be more fitting that the Constitution of a fully independent Canada no longer be a statute of the UK Parliament but be "patriated" to Canada? For that to happen, Canadians would have to answer a question the Fathers of Confederation had put off in 1867: how should the Constitution be amended in Canada? That was a truly difficult question on which Canadians could no more agree in 1867, or in the 1920s, than in the 1980s, when the country finally did patriate its Constitution – but without the agreement of Quebec.

Although the question of who should have the authority to amend a country's constitution is often posed as a technical legal matter, it is one that touches something deep and profound for all citizens. The written Constitution of a constitutional democracy is the country's highest law, binding not only on its citizens, but also on its elected legislatures. Determining who can change the Constitution means deciding who or what is truly sovereign. And how one answers that question depends very much on what kind of country one believes one lives in or wants to live in. For instance, thinking of Canada as fundamentally an association of equal citizens favours a constitutional amending system very different from that favoured by a person who sees Canada as fundamentally a federation of equal provinces, or a union of two founding peoples.

The federal-provincial conference of 1927, called to celebrate Canada's sixtieth anniversary, was the first attempt to answer this most challenging of questions. In this first round of discussions on how to amend the Constitution in Canada, there was an interesting reversal of roles. Ernest Lapointe, the federal minister of justice and King's chief Quebec lieutenant, proposed that only a few sensitive subjects, such as language and religion, should require unanimous provincial consent and that otherwise the consent of two-thirds of the provinces would suffice.[77] But Ontario's Conservative premier Howard Ferguson weighed in with the "compact theory": since Confederation was a treaty among the founding provinces, any change in the treaty required the consent of all the provinces.

While this debate was going on in Canada, in London the Statute of Westminster was being drafted to terminate the Colonial Laws Validity Act's application to the self-governing dominions. When a draft of that statute was discussed in the Canadian Parliament, it was the new Conservative leader, R.B. Bennett, who expressed the most concern about the danger it posed to the provinces if it contained no clause protecting their powers under the BNA Act.[78] The Bennett Conservatives' defeat of the King Liberals in the federal election held in the summer of 1930 meant that it was Bennett who represented Canada at the Imperial Conference called to approve the final version of the Statute of Westminster in the fall of that year. Bennett persuaded the conference to postpone final approval of the statute so that he could consult with the provinces. At a dominion-provincial conference in April 1931, he proposed an amendment to the Statute of Westminster making it clear that it conferred no new powers on the federal or provincial governments. Quebec's Liberal premier, Louis-Alexandre Taschereau, joined Ontario's new Conservative premier, George S. Henry, in extracting a commitment from Bennett to call a meeting in the near future to consider a Canadian amending formula.[79]

Bennett's proposal for protecting the constitutional status quo in Canada was included in the Statute of Westminster (section 7) when it was finally enacted by the British Parliament in December 1931. British law would no longer trump Canadian law – except for the BNA Act. Canada was an "autonomous community," but its highest law remained an Act of the British Parliament, not because Britain refused to let go of Canada's Constitution, but because the Canadians had not yet agreed on how to take custody of it.

Not only would Canada's Constitution remain in British custody; its interpretation would remain in the hands of British judges. Again this was not because of any lingering British interest in maintaining imperial ties, but because ending Privy Council appeals and making the

Supreme Court of Canada truly supreme was controversial in Canada. The Canadian Parliament did abolish appeals in criminal cases in 1933, and its power to do so was upheld by the Judicial Committee of the Privy Council in 1935.[80] But appeals in civil and constitutional cases remained, and were very much valued by advocates of provincial rights, especially in Quebec, where British judges were seen as more reliable protectors of provincial rights than a Canadian court dominated by English-Canadian jurists.

On one issue – the status of women – the British judges had shown a greater ability than Canadian judges to adapt Canada's Constitution to changing circumstances. In 1930 the JCPC overturned the Supreme Court of Canada and ruled that women should be considered to be "persons," and thereby become eligible for appointment to the Canadian Senate.[81] But this capacity for wise adaptation deserted the judges when it came to interpreting the division of powers in the Canadian federation. In a series of cases through the first three decades of the twentieth century, the British judges rolled back federal power enormously. The JCPC reduced the federal Parliament's trade and commerce power to a mere auxiliary power that could be used only to back up other powers,[82] and reduced the other major federal power to legislate laws for the peace, order, and good government of Canada to an emergency power.[83] After supporting the federal Parliament's power to pass legislation implementing Canada's commitments under treaties entered into by an independent Canada, it ruled that the federal power to pass legislation implementing treaties was confined to treaties binding Canada as part of the British Empire.[84] In the memorable words of Lord Atkin: "While the ship of state sails on larger ventures into foreign waters, she still retains the watertight compartments which are an essential part of her original structure."[85] The Government of Canada at the executive level could sign international treaties, but when the subject matter fell under provincial legislation, Ottawa would have to call on the provinces to pass the supporting legislation.

This decentralizing jurisprudence was welcome in Quebec and other provincial capitals. But it was anathema to policy-makers in Ottawa and constitutional scholars in English-speaking Canada. To deal with the economic crisis of the Great Depression, Bennett, the Conservative prime minister, fashioned a legislative package modelled on Franklin Delano Roosevelt's New Deal. Before moving forward with the Canadian New Deal, the ever-cautious King, whose Liberals defeated the Bennett Conservatives in the 1935 election, referred the legislation to the Supreme Court of Canada for an opinion on its constitutional validity. The Supreme Court and, on appeal, the JCPC found that most of it fell outside the federal Parliament's jurisdiction.[86] In the mid-1930s a spate of law journal articles written by eminent scholars such as Frank Scott and W.P.M. Kennedy argued that the Judicial Committee's emasculation of federal powers was rendering Canada incapable of dealing effectively with the social and economic malaise the country faced in the Great Depression.[87]

A study commissioned by the Senate contended that the JCPC had distorted the true meaning of the constitutional text.[88] In 1937 the King government established a Royal Commission to investigate whether the balance of legislative powers and fiscal resources between the federal and provincial governments needed adjustment to deal with the challenges facing Canada as a modern industrial society. The commission, headed first by Ontario Chief Justice Newton Rowell and later by Quebec notary Joseph Sirois, and known as the Rowell-Sirois Commission, recommended a major restructuring of the federation in a centralizing direction.[89]

The pendulum of constitutional politics had now swung away from provincial rights towards strengthening the powers of the federal government. This put Quebec very much on the defensive. The primary concern of Quebec leaders was to protect the powers the province had secured in the BNA Act and their interpretation by the British law lords from encroachment by the federal government. This constitutional conservatism fitted in well with Quebec governments of the era. Under the Liberals, who held office through the 1920s and first half of the 1930s, and the conservative Union Nationale government that took power under Maurice Duplessis in 1935, government remained small. In Quebec, government, in the words of Hélène David, "avoided any responsibility for economic development, restricting itself to the creation and maintenance of conditions favouring the unfettered expansion of capitalism."[90] As a predominantly rural and agricultural Quebec was being urbanized and industrialized, the province's governmental institutions were not being adapted to the modernization of its economy and society. English-speaking Canadians and Americans controlled its industrial and financial institutions, while the Roman Catholic Church remained the province's most important provider of education and social services.

For the time being French Canada was thoroughly and quietly provincialized. But the contradiction between the profound socio-economic changes taking place in Quebec and the conservatism of its governments was building the foundation for a constitutional eruption to come.

Chapter 10

The Nationalization of English Canada

On 1 July 1918 the Canadian Corps' four divisions gathered on the fields of Tincques, a small village in northeast France, to celebrate Dominion Day. With the help of conscription, the units of the corps had been rebuilt and retrained. They were now ready to fight as never before. The celebrations included interdivisional games, a concert, and tattoo with massed bands. It was, in the words of historian Desmond Morton, "an outpouring of national pride that would have been impossible three years earlier."[1]

Morton's statement underscores the significance of Canada's military performance in the First World War in generating a sense of Canadian nationalism at the mass level. But equally it reminds us of how long it took for this sense of being Canadian to develop. After all, this outpouring of national pride, which could not have taken place in 1915, occurred half a century after Confederation. The founding Constitution refers to Canada in various sections, but was entitled the British North America Act, not the Constitution of Canada. "Canada" is a name derived from the Huron-Iroquois word for village or settlement.[2] As was noted in the opening chapter of this book, the inhabitants of New France were the first people to call themselves *Canadiens*. English-speaking settlers in Lower and Upper Canada did not begin to refer to themselves as Canadians until after the War of 1812. Even then, for the great majority their political identity continued to be that of British subjects, not Canadian nationals. The same was true of Maritimers, who at the time of Confederation tended to think of Canadians as residents of the United Province of Canada.

The very concept of nation was problematic for the country's founders. In Europe the age of nationalism saw peoples with a single culture and language attempting to break away from empires and assert their right to self-government. That is why the aspiration to be a "nation" had so much appeal for *Canadiens* and was so frightening to their British governors. The legacy of that tension was still felt at the time of Confederation. For John A. Macdonald and other English-speaking leaders, there was a touch of disloyalty to Britain in talking about founding a new nation. For many Quebecers the nation to which they gave their allegiance was French Canada. George-Étienne Cartier's concept of a political nationality based on ethnic pluralism certainly had the potential of being the basis of a nationality and a sense of nationalism that all Canadians could share. But most Canadians – British, French, and Aboriginal – were not there yet.

At the popular level there was a sense of national identity in English-speaking Canada that was neither political nor ethnic, but based on climate and geography. It was Canada's cold climate, its northerliness, and its rugged landscape that distinguished the country they had settled from both Europe and the United States. Surviving and prospering in this forbidding northern clime could be a strong source of pride. This idea reverberates in the work of William Henry Taylor, one of Canada's early poets:

Hail! Monarch, Northern Winter, hail!
Come! Great Physician, vitalize the gale;
Dispense the ozone, thou has purified,
With Frost and Fire, where Health and age reside,-
Where Northern Lights electrify the soul
Of Mother Earth, whose throne is near the Pole.[3]

There could be an element of racial Darwinism in this celebration of making out in the north. A series of papers on *The Climate of Canada and Its Relation to Life and Health*, published in the 1880s by William Hales Hingston, a professor of surgery at the Montreal School of Medicine, advanced the idea that Canada's harsh climatic conditions would enable the distinct nationalities of Europe to fashion a "Canadian people" based on a homogeneous race that would result from the struggle for survival. Dr Hingston made the straight-faced observation "that those frozen to death display on their visages a look of contentment achieved only by successful religious mystics."[4]

Canada's land and waters and seasons have continued to be a distinctive theme in the country's arts and letters. These physical elements of their surroundings will always be a vital part of Canadians' shared identity. Similarly, the sharing of a civic culture, an agreed-upon set of principles about how we are governed, has been building up, as we have seen. At this point in Canada's odyssey, it includes parliamentary democracy, constitutionalism, and monarchy, to which, by the 1890s, federalism can be added. But still missing is respect for ethnic diversity and multinationalism – the only basis on which the country's three founding pillars can, in full freedom, form a political community.

In geopolitical terms the Dominion of Canada moved quickly after its founding to become a continental state. Arthur Lower refers to Canada as "the first colonial state." That is a more apt term than "nation-state" for Canada at this stage of its evolution. After Confederation, Canada was still not fully independent. Besides controlling Canada's foreign affairs, the British government appointed the representative of its head of state, the governor general, who in Canada's first few decades was not above interfering in its domestic politics. Britain's judiciary managed and staffed Canada's highest court, and the British Parliament had legal custody of its Constitution. On top of all that is the plain fact that the people and their elected leaders did not share a common sense of nationality.

But this still somewhat colonial Canada performed as a strong state, with a governmental organization that could assert its authority and get big things done. It grew quickly from four provinces huddled together around the Great Lakes, the St Lawrence River, and the Atlantic seaboard to a large federal state spanning the North American continent. Manitoba was added in 1870, British Columbia in 1871, and Prince Edward Island in 1873. Once Métis resistance was put down and the prairie First Nations cabined and controlled on reserves, two additional provinces, Alberta and Saskatchewan, were added. Railways were built first to the Atlantic and then to the Pacific, providing the bands of steel that would tie the continental nine-province federation together and provide its people with rapid transit across the land without going through the United States. All this was done before Canada's thirtieth birthday.

The political motivation driving this continental state-building was less a sense of Canada's manifest destiny than a determination to keep Canada from falling into the hands of a more dynamic, populous, and powerful United States of America. This kind of thinking was certainly challenged in English-speaking Canada. Goldwin Smith, who had made his mark in England as Regius Professor of History at Oxford

before moving to Toronto and becoming one of the young country's
leading public intellectuals, argued that Canada's destiny was to become part of the United States. In the 1890s, observing the sluggishness
of Canada's economy and worsening relations between English and
French, Smith wrote that Canadian nationalism was "a lost cause" and
the ultimate union of Canada with the United States appeared to be a
"moral certainty."[5] But the Loyalist legacy remained strong in English
Canada, and arguments such as Smith's made little headway against it.
In French Canada, on the other hand, British Empire Loyalism had never been strong and, as Henri Bourassa's career shows, became a divisive, rather than a unifying, force in Canada. For French Canada, the
counterpart of English-Canadian fear of assimilation with the United
States was its fear of assimilation by English Canada.

A much more important force than public opinion in Canada's early
burst of state-building was the administrative strength of the Dominion's first prime minister. Sir John A. Macdonald is famous for his political savvy, his personal charm, his humour, and his drinking. But he
should also be known for his administrative skills. In an important new
study, political scientist Patrice Dutil shows how gifted Macdonald was
in the arts of public administration.[6] Macdonald filled the positions of
deputy ministers, the civil servant heads of government departments,
with a team of top bureaucrats, most of whom he had worked with in
the United Province of Canada. Some of these were outstanding French
Canadians. These included Étienne Parent, whom we met at the end
of Chapter 6 as a rising intellectual star in Canada East, and Joseph
Bouchette, who as a young *Patriote* had been imprisoned and exiled to
Bermuda in 1837. Macdonald did not let partisan patronage, of which
he was a grand master, interfere with building an English-French civil
service based on merit – at least at its highest levels.

Macdonald was also a professional cabinet-builder. He invited political heavyweights to join his cabinet, including Nova Scotia's Joseph
Howe, the leading opponent of Confederation; his Confederation colleagues, New Brunswick's Leonard Tilley and Nova Scotia's Charles
Tupper; George-Étienne Cartier and Hector Langevin from Quebec;
plus a number of Ontario politicians who, like Francis Hincks and
Christopher Dunkin, had strong independent political bases of their
own. Even with this kind of talent in his cabinet, there could be no truth
to the saying that the prime minister was *primus inter pares*: Sir John A.
was *primus* and his cabinet colleagues were *pares*.

Our first prime minister kept the most challenging files in his own hands. He created and managed Canada's first secret service so that the country could respond intelligently to Irish Fenian efforts to provoke a war between Britain and the United States.[7] As the only Canadian in a British delegation to Washington, negotiating a wide-range of issues affecting Canadian-US relations, he was the country's chief diplomat.[8] As we have seen, the prime minister made the key decisions on acquiring the Hudson's Bay Company's territory for Canada's western expansion and negotiating with representatives of Red River's Provisional Government the terms of Manitoba's entry into the federation. As his own justice minister he functioned as a central agency in giving legal expression to all of the departments' initiatives. He presided over the creation of the North-West Mounted Police, a distinctive device for providing a police presence in the vast, expanding reaches of Canadian territory. And, of course, as prime minister *and* Conservative Party leader, he presided over the greasy manoeuvres to secure Canadian funding for the completion of the Canadian Pacific Railway that in 1873 led to his one and only election defeat.

This strong and highly centralized form of government was not just a concoction of the Macdonald Conservatives. When Alexander Mackenzie's Liberal government took office, it built on the system it found in place. In its five-year mandate, the Mackenzie government added significant elements to the Canadian state's infrastructure, including the Royal Military College at Kingston, which could begin preparing Canadians to lead the country's armed forces, and the Supreme Court of Canada, which, though not supreme on the big constitutional issues, had the potential to be a unifying force in the criminal, civil, and administrative law of a very federalized country.

Although Prime Minister Mackenzie was not as dominating a figure as Macdonald had been, power in his government was still highly centralized. That centralization was simply a consequence of the executive's dominant position in parliamentary assemblies. Herein lies parliamentary democracy's greatest virtue, and its greatest vice. By putting the direction of government in the hands of politicians who control the legislature, the parliamentary system can get things done much more easily than the American system with its sharp separation of powers – but at the expense of reducing the deliberative role of the legislature. The emergence after Confederation of two well-disciplined political parties increased the prime minister's and cabinet's control of Parliament. The parliamentary system was also producing strong governments at the provincial level. The Canadian state was developing on a thoroughly federal basis, with strong governments in provincial capitals competing with a strong government in Ottawa for popular support, resources, and jurisdiction. Canada was a federal state before it was a nation-state.

The National Policy as a political slogan – today we would call it a brand – emerged in the election campaign that brought the Macdonald Conservatives back to power in 1878. At first it focused on using tariffs and custom duties not just for raising revenue, but also for protecting vulnerable new Canadian industries from the destructive gale of mostly American and British international competition. The tariff increases were carefully designed by Leonard Tilley, Macdonald's finance minister, to apply only to imports that competed with goods manufactured in Canada. Macdonald had a tricky time selling this policy in Britain, where free trade had been a policy dogma for a generation. British exporters lobbied the Colonial Office to reverse the program. The fact that the colonial secretary responded by sending the message that the fiscal policy of Canada was a matter for the Dominion legislature to decide[9] shows how far Canadian autonomy had advanced. Given that US tariffs remained much higher than Canada's even after the introduction of the National Policy, Macdonald did not fear American reprisals – although he had to fend off the Liberals, with their policy of seeking a reciprocal lowering of trade barriers to open US markets to Canadian farmers and natural resources.

John A. Macdonald had been brought up to believe in the virtues of free trade, but his political instincts told him that, in the context of the economic depression Canada and the world were experiencing in the 1870s, raising tariffs would be good policy. The National Policy meant that his government was not standing by hoping that things would improve, but was doing something to try to help people experiencing hard times. This interventionism and unwillingness to rely on the free play of market forces was becoming characteristic of Canadian governments on both sides of the political spectrum. The early burst of government-led nation-building conditioned Canadians to think of their country, with its small population strung out from east to west north of the US border, as an artificial construct that needed government action to counter the more natural north-south flow of commerce and people. The National Policy might have been dubious economics, but it was very successful politics. It enabled Macdonald to return from the political wilderness to which he had been exiled after the disgrace of the Pacific Scandal – the sleezy way Macdonald's government financed the building of the CPR – and win a landslide victory over the Liberals in the 1878 federal election

After the election the National Policy came to be associated with a whole set of "nation-building" policies, including the purchase of Rupert's Land, the building of railways, and land policies designed to attract immigrants. There has been much debate about the economic benefits of the National Policy. It fostered a branch-plant economy whereby large American, British, and other foreign firms established branches in Canada to be sheltered from international competition by Canada's tariffs, and it might well have lowered Canadians' standard of living by favouring population increase over increasing per capita income.[10] By protecting Canadian manufacturers of farm machinery in central Canada, whose high-cost products were sold to prairie farmers, the policy engendered resentment in western Canada. Recent reassessments, however, have thrown doubt on the belief that the deficiencies of the western regional economy were caused by the National Policy.[11] The economic debate about the National Policy goes on, but there can be no question about its political significance. It ensured that the northern half of the North American continent would be Canadian, not American, and although, as Macdonald's biographer Richard Gwyn puts it, "[i]t may not have made Canadians richer ... it made them more Canadian."[12]

The National Policy needed people to fulfil its objective of building a continental nation-state. It needed them most of all in the western prairies, whose Indigenous peoples had greatly declined in number and who were not viewed as an enduring part of the state Canadians were building. That vast "empty" space between Ontario and the Rocky Mountains was to be filled with European settlers.

The first efforts after Confederation to attract immigrant settlers were very disappointing. Between 1867 and 1892 one and a half million immigrants arrived, but most of them were in transit to the United States. Indeed in every decade until the turn of the century, the outflow of emigrants exceeded the inflow of immigrants.[13] Canada's population grew from 3.4 million at the time of Confederation to 4.8 million in 1891, but that growth rate was below its natural rate of growth. Lots of born-in-Canada Canadians were emigrating to the United States.[14]

It was not for lack of trying that Canada experienced difficulty in attracting and keeping new immigrants. The federal government, in cooperation with provincial governments, worked hard to recruit immigrants in Britain and continental Europe. As early as 1872 the Dominion Lands Act offered immigrant families 160-acre homestead lots for a $10 registration fee.[15] The main impediments were economic and climatic. Canada's cold climate was a serious handicap in competing with the United States and the other British dominions for immigrants. Also, it didn't help that France and Germany, anxious to build their own numbers for the nationalist wars that loomed ahead, took steps to restrict Canadian recruitment of their citizens. Beginning in 1873 Canada experienced a serious economic downturn as part of a worldwide recession. Establishing successful farms on the arid Canadian prairies before the discovery of strains of wheat good for dry-farming was a challenge requiring large investments of capital and labour before making a decent return. Immigration advertising was often very misleading about what it took to be an economically viable prairie farmer. No wonder so many immigrants lured by false advertising left for the United States. Most immigrants went to Ontario and Quebec, and most of them sought work in the cities, especially Toronto and Montreal. With the economy in recession, the supply of labour exceeded the demand, driving many Canadians in the Maritimes and central Canada across the border to the United States. In these years there was a considerable migration of French farming families into New England, where they formed strong communities that reduced the incentive to return to *la belle province*.

Patterns of migration never develop along straight lines. They fluctuate enormously in response to changes in global conditions and local policies. This is certainly true in Canada's case. Between 1891 and the outbreak of the Great War in 1914, Canada experienced a huge surge of immigration. Over that period Canada, with fewer than five million people, attracted three million immigrants, and most of them stayed.[16] In the final year of the surge, 400,000 immigrants arrived, the largest annual intake in Canadian history. Higher prices for Canadian staples such as lumber and mining products attracted more investment and more people. Advances in knowledge about dry-area farming made Canada's prairies a viable agricultural region. Although promoting immigration had been very much part of the Conservatives' National Policy, the energy and commitment of Clifford Sifton, the Liberal immigration minister from 1896 to 1905, contributed significantly to this dynamic period of Canadian immigration The only other period like it in Canadian history is the years immediately following the Second World War.

Clifford Sifton intensified Canada's efforts to recruit immigrants. He increased the number of agents abroad and of the departmental support staff, improved advertising brochures, and offered bonuses to shipping companies, railways, and colonization organizations to bring in immigrants. These efforts paid off with an eightfold increase during his tenure as immigration minister.[17] Sifton recognized that Britain and the United States, traditionally considered the most desirable sources of immigrants, would not yield the numbers needed to settle the prairie farmlands. So he expanded Canada's recruitment efforts into eastern and central Europe. He described his ideal immigrant in a memorable statement: "I think that the stalwart peasant in the sheepskin coat, born to the soil, whose forefathers have been farmers for ten generations, with a stout wife and half-dozen children is high quality."[18] The United Kingdom continued to be the largest source of immigrants, but they tended not to go in for farming. The immigrants settling in western Canada were mostly Ukrainians, Germans, and other groups from continental Europe. A third of those settling in the Canadian prairies during this period were Americans.

Sifton's policy was driven by practical economic considerations, not ideology about the nature of Canadian society. But his willingness to recruit immigrants from continental Europe had its limits. He harboured the Canadian nationalist bias in favour of hardy and morally sound immigrants from northern climes. Neither he nor his successor Frank Oliver supported government efforts to recruit immigrants from southern Europe. Private employers had no such inhibitions. For example, during this expansive period of immigration 6,500 Italian labourers arrived each year, on average, many of them finding work in the bourgeoning mining industry of Ontario and Quebec, or with the CPR.[19] All of this was beginning to modify the English-French character of Canada's settler population. At the time of Confederation, the ancestry of just 7 per cent of Canada's non-Indigenous people was in continental Europe. By 1921 the proportion of Canadians with European backgrounds neither British nor French had more than doubled, to 15 per cent.

Canada was becoming more multicultural in a descriptive sense, but not in a normative or principled sense. Frank Oliver was so committed to the vision of Canada as a homogeneous Anglo community that he informed the public that his department would stop promoting the immigration of continental Europeans.[20] As we have seen, the migrants from Ontario who dominated prairie politics were set on building a Canada that, outside Quebec, would be English-speaking and Protestant. The relative absence of vigorous recruitment of French-speaking

immigrants added fuel to deep feelings of distrust building up in
Quebec during this period. The colonization of Quebec's hinterland by
French Catholic families was French Canada's response to English
Canada's efforts to make the hinterland outside of Quebec unwelcom-
ing to French Catholic Canadians. Cartier and Bourassa's vision of a
Canada not based on a single ethnicity had still not penetrated the mass
of English-speaking or French-speaking Canadians. The mindset of
most Canadians was "one nation – one state." For English-speaking
Canadians that state was a homogeneous English-speaking, largely
Protestant Canada; for French-speaking Canadians it was a French-
speaking, Catholic Quebec. If these conditions prevailed, Canada's odyssey would soon be over.

Race-thinking was now adding to the drive for social and cultural
homogeneity. In the latter half of the nineteenth century and the first
half of the twentieth, theories about biologically determined cultural
characteristics and capacities held sway among European intellectuals
and many politicians in Europe and its colonies. The influence of racial
thinking can be seen in the importance attached to colour in gathering
information about Canadians. The federal government's instruction to
its civil servants responsible for carrying out the 1901 census was to
designate each household by letters: "w" for white, "r" for red, "b" for
black, and "y" for yellow. The instructions explained that "[t]he whites
are, of course, the Caucasian race, the reds are the American Indian, the
blacks are the African or Negro, and the yellows are the Mongolian
(Japanese and Chinese)." The instructions went on to stipulate that
"only pure whites" will be classified as whites."[21]

Asiatic peoples became the primary targets of racial thinking in immigration policy – first Chinese, then southeast Asians, and finally
Japanese. Chinese immigrants were the first to be singled out for discriminatory treatment because they had been arriving in British
Columbia in relatively large numbers since the California and colonial
BC gold rush days. In British Columbia's early years, Chinese men –
there were almost no immigrant Chinese women – constituted a significant proportion of the province's population, at one point reaching
40 per cent. They came first to the gold fields, many of them having
begun their North American sojourn in California. Later on they provided much of the labour to complete the CPR. There were enough of
them to arouse deeply ingrained Sinophobic fear of the "yellow peril"
among the white population. The Macdonald government responded
by appointing a Royal Commission that recommended a tax of $10 on

every Chinese resident and a tightening of immigration admissions. With the CPR nearing completion, Chinese workers were no longer needed for railway building, but Macdonald and the British Foreign Office were concerned that a total exclusion of Chinese immigration would harm commercial relations with China. The $10 head tax was duly imposed on all Chinese immigrants except diplomats, students, tourists, and merchants by the Chinese Immigration Act of 1885.

In that same year, Parliament passed the Electoral Franchise Act establishing for the first time a uniform set of rules for federal elections. Up to that time, provincial electoral laws were used for federal elections. The debate on this important piece of legislation determining who could vote in elections to the national Parliament sheds interesting light on political thinking of the time. An indication of the strength of racial thinking is the support of a large majority of MPs for a provision in the opening definitions section of the Act defining a "person" as "a male person, including an Indian and excluding a person of Mongolian or Chinese race."[22] Macdonald favoured adding widows and spinsters to the definition of "person," but could not find a majority for this early bit of female suffrage.[23] But his enlightened view about equality of the sexes was not matched by support for racial equality.

In making his case for excluding the Chinese from the franchise, Prime Minister Macdonald spoke of the Chinese as "sojourners" who came to Canada only to make money. "He has no common interest with us," Macdonald explained, "and is valuable, the same as a threshing machine or any other agricultural implement ... a Chinaman gives us his labour and gets his money, but ... does not invest it here, but takes it with him and returns to China."[24] Several MPs objected to this argument, pointing out that the Chinese were industrious people with as good a right to vote as any other British subjects of foreign extraction. Macdonald endeavoured to bolster the case for exclusion by shifting to a race-based argument. If the Chinese came in great numbers, he exclaimed, "they might enforce those Asiatic principles, those immoralities ... which are abhorrent to the Aryan race and Aryan principles, on this House."[25] He went on to expound a race theory supported by many prominent Europeans, notably the French diplomat and writer, Arthur de Gobineau.[26] "If you look around you," Macdonald told the House, "you will see that the Aryan races will not wholeheartedly amalgamate with the Africans or the Asiatics. It is not denied that they should come; that we should have a mongrel race; that the character of the future of British North America should be destroyed by a cross or crosses of that kind."[27]

Belief in a superior, genetically determined white Aryan race was a much more rigid basis for discrimination than concerns about cultural adaptation.[28] In Macdonald's case, he believed that Indigenous peoples if properly educated could be prepared for Canadian citizenship. That indeed was the underlying logic of the Indian Act and of giving the vote to Indian men who lived off-reserve and owned enough property. It was also the logic of limiting the Indian franchise in the 1885 Act to those who lived east of Manitoba and had many more years of exposure to the mainstream culture. Even so, a Liberal government took that limited franchise away from Indians in 1898. But whether the discriminatory treatment of groups was based on race theory or cultural stereotyping, the policy result was the same. Bad science and ill-informed, often hysterical generalizations produced bad and hurtful policies. There were certainly Canadians at this time who were generous of spirit and intelligent enough not to buy into the prevailing race thinking. Alexander Mackenzie, for example, the first Liberal prime minister, rejected a motion to exclude Chinese immigration, arguing that such a resolution was "unprecedented in its character and altogether unprecedented in its spirit, and at variance with those tolerant laws that afforded employment and an asylum to all who came into our country, regardless of color, hair or anything else."[29] But, sad to say, most Canadians, a century or so ago, were committed to building a white Canada.

Animosity against Asians reached a crescendo in the early years of the twentieth century. Between 1900 and 1915 more than 50,000 immigrants of Chinese, East Asian, and Japanese ancestry arrived in Canada.[30] Although this represented only 2 per cent of the immigration flow into the country in this period, for the white people of British Columbia, where most Asians settled, it seemed like a flood, a frightening flood. Most of the East Asians came from the Punjabi part of India, where the density of population was causing severe poverty in rural areas. Young sons of large landowning families were encouraged to come to Canada, where they could earn money to send to the family back home.[31] The Japanese were also economic migrants, many of them arriving from Hawaii to take up contract work with corporate employers.[32] Some took up farming in the Okanagan Valley, while others secured fishing licences and quickly became major participants in the Fraser River salmon fishery.

White British Columbia's deep-seated xenophobic fear of Asians was expressed in a slew of discriminatory provincial laws. In 1884, before the federal Parliament enacted the Chinese head tax, the provincial legislature passed its own Immigration Act prohibiting Chinese from entering the province. The federal government's disallowance of that legislation did not stop the provincial legislature from re-enacting it. The re-enactment and six other exclusionary provincial Acts were also disallowed.[33] But Ottawa allowed most of the province's discriminatory legislation to stand, including amendments to its Provincial Elections Act denying Chinese, East Asian, and Japanese persons the right to vote in provincial elections. In the *Tommy Homma* case, decided by the Judicial Committee of the Privy Council in 1902, these discriminatory provisions were declared constitutionally valid.[34] In reaching this decision the British law lords overturned two BC courts and ignored their own decision, made two years earlier, in the *Union Colliery* case that found legislation banning Chinese from working in BC mines unconstitutional. In that decision the JCPC held that the federal Parliament's power over naturalization and aliens gave it "exclusive authority in all matters which directly concern the rights, privileges, and disabilities with the class of Chinamen who are resident in the provinces of Canada."[35]

Sir Wilfrid Laurier was squeezed by the pressures of domestic politics and foreign policy concerns. The Liberal MP for Vancouver, R.G. Macpherson, told Laurier, "I would like very much to keep this country White and I would also like to keep it Liberal."[36] He urged Laurier to take strong measures to put a stop to Asian immigration. Pressure from Joseph Chamberlain in London made Laurier aware of the danger that tough measures against migrants from India posed – after all, Indians, like Canadians, were British subjects. He was also under pressure not to offend Japan, a rising military power – especially after Japan's victory over Russia in 1905. A sudden upsurge of Asian arrivals in July 1907 – 2,300 in one month – heightened the xenophobic fever gripping white Vancouver. Rioting broke out in early August when a large crowd assembled at city hall, whipped up by hate-mongering racist orators, poured into Chinatown and the Japanese quarter of the city. It took the police four hours to bring the rioters under control. No one was killed, but there were minor injuries plus thousands of dollars of property damage, and the riot left "thousands of Chinese and Japanese quivering with rage and fear."[37]

In response to the Vancouver riot, Prime Minister Laurier did that classic Canadian thing: he appointed a Royal Commission of inquiry. This was a one-man commission, and that one man was none other than William Lyon Mackenzie King, who at the time was deputy minister of labour. King awarded thousands of dollars of damages to the Chinese and Japanese riot victims and, characteristically, made some cautious recommendations about slowing down Asian immigration. His minister, Rodolphe Lemieux, was already in Tokyo, where he persuaded the Japanese government to restrict immigration to Canada. With mounting pressure in Parliament from both sides of the House, the Laurier government took steps to limit the Asian inflow by an Order in Council that on its face did not appear to be racially discriminatory: all immigrants to Canada would be prohibited entry unless they came directly by "a continuous journey and on through tickets" purchased in their home country. This would stop Japanese from immigrating via Hawaii. The CPR was the only shipping company at the time that offered a continuous passage from India to Canada. To curtail this means of migrating to Canada from India, the government prohibited CPR outlets in India from selling through tickets to Canada.[38] Another Order in Council required that all Asian immigrants arriving in Canada possess at least $200.[39] Chinese immigration was sharply curtailed by raising the head tax to $500 in 1903.[40]

As these various measures took effect in cutting down Asian immigration into British Columbia, Vancouver's "nativist" hotheads simmered down. But on the eve of the First World War a remarkable event brought the city's xenophobia once again to fever pitch. On 23 May 1914 the *Komagata Maru*, carrying 376 Indian immigrants, most of them Sikhs, sailed into Burrard Inlet. The *Komagata Maru* was a Japanese ship, chartered by a wealthy Indian living in Singapore for the purpose of challenging the "continuous journey" restriction on Indian immigrants to Canada. It sailed from Hong Kong, taking on more passengers at Shanghai and Yokohama before crossing the Pacific to Vancouver. With strong support from the Borden government in Ottawa, BC's premier Richard McBride made it clear that the passengers could not disembark. "Hindu Invaders Now in City Harbour," screamed the *Vancouver Sun*.[41] For two months, with little food or fresh water, the men, women, and children sweltered on board while a legal team mounted a court challenge against the "continuing journey" Order in Council. Anti-immigrant politicians whipped up fear and resentment in the city, none more than Conservative MP H.H. Stevens, who told a packed hall that Asiatic immigration threatened the nation's destiny: "[W]hat we face in British Columbia and in Canada today is this – whether or no the civilization which finds its highest exemplification in Anglo-Saxon British rule shall not prevail in the Dominion of Canada."[42]

Soon after, the court case was lost, and the *Komagata Maru* weighed anchor and headed back to Hong Kong with all of its would-be immigrants aboard. When it reached Calcutta, because of suspicion that Indian rebels aboard were planning to kindle resistance against British rule, a gunboat prevented it from landing. In the ensuing melee nineteen passengers were killed. At this stage in our odyssey, Britain was as set on maintaining white rule in India as its Canadian colonists were on maintaining white rule in Canada.

Immigration to Canada almost stopped completely during the Great War, and failed to return to pre-war levels afterward. The 1915–30 period saw a 50 per cent reduction of immigration compared with the first fifteen years of the century. When the Great Depression hit, immigration fell even more precipitously, reaching a low of 11,000 in 1936.[43] The Europeanization of the immigrant flow continued through the 1920s. With the Americans experiencing boom times and Britain better times, those favoured sources of new Canadians were drying up. On the other hand, Ukrainians escaping communism, Mennonites seeking religious freedom, Jews escaping pogroms, and other Europeans willing to start up farms or work in the resource industries or on assembly lines found Canada an attractive destination. As a proportion of Canada's most preferred immigrants, continental European immigrants rose from 27 per cent in 1914 to 46 per cent in 1929, while Americans fell from 35 to 15 per cent.[44]

The English-speaking pillar was becoming multicultural, but was remaining as white as the Government of Canada could keep it. The government used the ample discretion it had under the Immigration Act to exclude what its ministers and officials considered to be undesirable applicants. Immigration officials had long been resistant to admitting black-skinned people to Canada, be they Afro-Americans or Caribbean blacks. They justified this policy on the absurd grounds that "it had been observed that after some years of experience in Canada [Negroes] do not readily take to our climate on account of the severe winter."[45] Policies to exclude Asians were also ramped up in the 1920s. In 1923 the Chinese head tax was replaced by a nearly total ban of Chinese immigration except for merchants, students, and diplomats. That same year, an Order in Council excluded Asians from the list of admissible classes of immigrants. Chinese and Japanese were not covered by this regulation because Chinese were dealt with directly by the Chinese Immigration Act and the government preferred to use diplomatic means to stifle Japanese immigration.[46] The bias in Canada's immigration policy extended well beyond the racism of skin colour. Armenians fleeing the Turkish genocide had difficulty gaining admission because they were not considered to be Europeans. The government also worked hard at restricting the immigration of Jews, even those who were fully sponsored by Canadian families. Despite these restrictions, forty thousand Jews managed to gain entry to Canada in the inter-war years. After the Second World War broke out, Canadian immigration policy, tragically, became even more vigorous in preventing Jews from entering.[47]

In the wake of Pearl Harbor, racist fears gave rise to passionate public demands that something be done about the thousands of Japanese Canadians who had settled in British Columbia. The King government's decision to evacuate all the Japanese families from the west coast and confiscate their property was based as much on fear of an outbreak of communal violence as on military security concerns. Using powers available under the War Measures Act, over twenty thousand Japanese Canadians were rounded up and removed, some to internment camps in British Columbia and Ontario, others to work on prairie farms. The *Vancouver Sun* expressed the hope that British Columbia was "Saying Good-bye, Not Au Revoir."[48] The good news is that the removal of the Japanese did not go on without protests, notably from that new political party on the left, the Co-operative Commonwealth Federation (CCF). It would be nearly two decades after the end of the Second World War before these seeds of ideological change about the kind of nation-state Canadians want to build would bear fruit in a more liberal and humanitarian immigration policy.

The First World War marked a turning point in English-speaking Canadians' sense of their national identity. It is probably safe to say that, by the end of the war, most Anglo Canadians thought of themselves primarily as Canadian citizens, rather than as British subjects. This was so even though Canada was still technically not a fully independent nation-state, and the formal introduction of Canadian citizenship lay three decades ahead. How people think of their national identity depends more on the community they feel they belong to and to which they attach their primary allegiance than on formal legal definitions of citizenship or nationhood.

That outpouring of national pride in the celebration of Dominion Day at Tinques in 1918 came mostly from English-speaking Canadians, many of whom had been born in Britain. In principle, French Canadians should have been able to share in that national pride – after all, their forebears were the first to think of themselves as Canadians. But the Canadian armed forces at this time did little to recognize the French fact in Canada.

Only 17 of 254 officers in Canada's Permanent Forces were francophones, and no efforts were made to encourage English-speaking officers to be bilingual.[49] Added to this were the mistreatment of French Catholic minorities outside Quebec and the scars of the conscription crisis.

It was not just the men and women in the ranks who began to harbour feelings of Canadian nationalism. The war gave their officers and political leaders a heightened sense of Canada's having interests and loyalties that differed from those of Britain. Jack Granatstein describes Sir Arthur Currie, who took command of the First Canadian Division in the final stages of the war, as "a nationalist, an officer who believed that the Canadians had to stay together because they fought better when all four divisions were in the field under a single Corps command."[50] Currie insisted on getting his own way against British military brass in tactical and strategic decisions on how his Canadian army would be used. After the Canadians took heavy losses in a meaningless second battle of Passchendaele in the fall of 1917, Sir Robert Borden backed up Currie by telling British prime minister David Lloyd George that, if there is ever another Passchendaele, "not a Canadian soldier will leave the shore of Canada so long as the Canadian people entrust the government of my country to my hands."[51] Even a relatively pro-British Canadian Conservative prime minister would not allow Canadian troops to be cannon fodder for British generals.

The nationalism required for breaking the shackles of empire came more naturally to Liberals. The King Liberals' victory in the 1921 election accelerated the process of Canada's asserting control of its foreign affairs. Canada had long enjoyed a large degree of independence in the commercial side of foreign relations – trade deals, customs, and tariffs. In 1859 Britain had allowed the United Province of Canada to control its own tariff. After Confederation a Canadian "plenipotentiary" was included in any British mission negotiating trade issues affecting Canada, and the Canadian member of the imperial team – Macdonald at Washington; Tupper, Canada's first high commissioner in London, joining a number of British trade missions – was usually able to get his way when Canadian interests were directly involved. In 1914 Britain agreed that Canada would be bound by British trade agreements only if Canada agreed.[52] Once Canada began to use tariffs not just as an instrument of economic policy, this control over its trade policy became a crucial aspect of self-government.

Britain's siding with the United States against Canada in settling the Alaska boundary dispute made Sir Wilfrid Laurier acutely aware of the need for Canada to control the political side of its foreign relations. In 1909 he introduced legislation creating a secretariat of external affairs.[53] Note the imperialism-lite vocabulary: Canada was not to have "foreign affairs," but external affairs, and although it could have a high commissioner in London, certainly Canada could not yet be represented by ambassadors. Until King came to power, imperialism-lite prevailed.

Although Joseph Chamberlain's dreams of imperial federation were over, the British government, in the early 1920s, struggled to keep alive the idea of the British Empire's having a common foreign policy, with the white dominions having full rights of consultation on what that policy should be. Periodic imperial conferences were the vehicle for making that policy. At the 1921 Imperial Conference, Arthur Meighen, who had succeeded Borden as prime minister, and his principal adviser Loring Christie, resisted British plans to forge a new alliance with Japan because the Canadians knew how hostile the United States was to such an alliance. In the end the British backed away from a move that risked a rift with the United States, and the Canadians went home thinking that a common imperial foreign policy could work.

The big break came at the 1923 Imperial Conference. King, who was his own minister of external affairs, attended the conference with two strong nationalist advisers, J.W. Dafoe, the eloquent editor of the *Winnipeg Free Press*, and O.D. Skelton, who had advised Laurier on external affairs and was now deputy minister of the department.[54] Buoyed by the popularity of his refusal to support Britain in the Chanak crisis without the approval of the Canadian Parliament, King argued, in his cautious, logical manner, that just as it made no sense for the dominions to interfere with one another's foreign affairs, "it is equally impossible or undesirable for the Dominions to seek to control those foreign affairs which primarily affect Great Britain."[55] King's clear but gracious dissent from the idea of a common foreign policy for Britain and the dominions was in effect a declaration of independence in foreign affairs. The denouement came three years later at the 1926 Imperial Conference, with the Balfour Declaration that Britain, Australia, Canada, Eire, New Zealand, and South Africa were "autonomous ... members of the British Commonwealth of Nations."[56]

Well before the Balfour Declaration, Canada was acting like a sovereign nation-state. Canada took part in the Paris Peace Conference, signed the Treaty of Versailles, joined the League of Nations with its own seat in its assembly, and became a member of the League's affiliate, the International Labour Organization. But it did all this technically as part of the British Empire, not as a sovereign nation-state.[57] In 1923 Canada negotiated, on its own, a treaty with the United States about the halibut fishery. Before attending the Imperial Conference in 1926, King planned to establish a legation in Washington, and designated Vincent Massey, a rich industrialist and strong Liberal Party supporter, to lead that legation. Massey accompanied King to the conference before taking up his post in the US capital as Canada's first ambassador to a foreign state. In 1952, Vincent Massey, Canada's first foreign ambassador, would become the first Canadian to hold the position of governor general.[58]

Beyond keeping out of Britain's European entanglements and maintaining a watchful eye on the United States, Canada could not be said to have a distinct foreign policy at this time. In the words of John Holmes, "Mr. King had acquired for us the right to a national foreign policy and built up the resources to exercise it, but he was more concerned with defending the right than using it."[59] When pressed to explain how he intended to use Canada's new independence, "King implied that his single purpose was to maintain national unity."[60] Isolationism would best describe Canadian foreign policy in these early years of independence. Given how divisive Canada's participation in British imperial activities had been, staying out of international conflicts was a good recipe for maintaining good relations between French and English Canada. Canadians were still a long way from having a sense of the role they could play in the world.

While Canada was acquiring the capacity to govern its foreign relations, it was also taking important steps to build the internal links it needed as one of the world's largest nation-states. Canadian governments were always somewhat jittery about the viability of their enormous continental state. They tended to be fixated on a vision of the country as a thinly populated, three-thousand-mile-long strip of land just north of a much more populous, wealthier, and more powerful United States. There was no place in this vision for the Indigenous peoples, the dominant population of the north, as part of Canada's strength. The concerns driving this strengthening of Canada's sea-to-sea connections were a dedication to keeping the country from being gobbled up by Uncle Sam and vague fears about national unity, arising from English-French duality.

The organization of the Canadian National Railway (CNR) after the First World War gave Canada two transcontinental instruments for moving people and goods across the country. But it remained for the new telecommunication technologies to give Canadians the capacity to talk to one another individually and on a mass basis from coast to coast. By 1921 Canadians had a million telephones, second in the world only to the United States. Both the CNR and the CPR were stringing thousands of miles of telegraph lines beside their tracks, lines that could carry both telephone messages and radio broadcasts. A key event was the celebration of Canada's Diamond Jubilee, its sixtieth birthday, in 1927. Wartime conditions had ruled out a big celebration of its fiftieth in 1917. On 1 July 1927 ten thousand school children assembled on Parliament Hill to sing "O Canada" and "God Save the King" in English and French. Hundreds of thousands of Canadians, through what Prime Minister King gushingly referred to as "the wizardry of radio," heard the children sing. This meant for King that the question of Canadian unity had been answered: in that Diamond Jubilee radio broadcast, "all Canada became, for the time being, a single assemblage, swayed by a common emotion, within the sound of a single voice."[61]

In January 1932 the Trans-Canada Telephone System was inaugurated, connecting Canadians by telephone from Halifax to Victoria. In that same year the Conservative government of R.B. Bennett introduced the Canadian Radio Broadcasting Act, bringing radio broadcasting under a Canadian-wide regulatory scheme. Both of these initiatives were hailed as major contributions to national unity. The Toronto *Globe*'s headline called the Trans-Canada Telephone System "a new force for unity."[62] Introducing the radio legislation, Prime Minister Bennett said that broadcasting must be an agency by which "national consciousness may be fostered and sustained and national unity still further strengthened."[63]

The country's highest court cleared away any doubts about the constitutional basis for asserting control of the new media. There was some doubt about the issue, because, of course, there was no mention of radio (or telephones) in the BNA Act. So the question of whether the Parliament of Canada had jurisdiction to regulate and control radio communication was put to the Supreme Court. On appeal from a very muddy decision by the Court, the federal government got all it could have hoped for from the Judicial Committee of the Privy Council – which must have been somewhat of a surprise coming from a tribunal that had shown so much solicitude for the provinces' powers.[64]

Policy-making on radio broadcasting was initiated in a vintage Canadian way – by a Royal Commission. The commission was established in 1928 by the King government, with Sir John Aird, president of the Canadian Bank of Commerce, as its chairman. When the

commissioners visited New York, they were shocked by how easily
the heads of the US networks assumed Canada was within their orbit.
They went on to London, and were enormously impressed by the
British Broadcasting Corporation. After touring Canada and finding
that, above all, "Canadian radio listeners want Canadian broadcasting," the commission concluded that "the Canadian nation could be
adequately served only by some form of public ownership, operation,
and control."[65]

In Canada's grappling with the new communication technologies we
can see evidence of a political economy that continues to differentiate
the county from the United States. Canada is fundamentally a capitalist
country, but one that senses it cannot let the free play of market forces
govern its national policies. Worshipping free enterprise, which is the
dominant creed of American political economy, would result in American corporations controlling much of Canadian life. R.B. Bennett saw
the primary purpose of his government's broadcasting legislation as
assuring "complete Canadian control of broadcasting ... free from foreign interference or influence."[66] Bennett's legislation did not establish
a publicly owned broadcaster – that would come later, in 1937, when
the King Liberals established the Canadian Broadcasting Corporation
– but even though he was a Conservative, Bennett did not shy away
from public ownership. It was Bennett's government that, in defiance
of Canada's private bankers, created the Bank of Canada in 1934, establishing a central government agency with the power to manage the
country's money supply and set its exchange rates. In broadcasting, as
in other sectors, profit-seeking private corporations play a large role in
satisfying consumer demand, but they often operate alongside publicly
owned "Crown corporations." Political parties would differ on the degree to which government should involve itself in economic activities,
but the public sector was fated to remain proportionally significantly
larger in Canada than in the United States.

Building the material means of connecting the country together was
hardly the same thing as building a national union of hearts and minds.
Maurice Chartrand argues that this kind of nationalism is a "technological nationalism" that "depends on the empty experience of media
commodities rather than on presumably real ties of language, culture
or blood."[67] Although Chartrand might undervalue the new communication technologies' potentiality for Canadians, from east to west,
English and French, to share a common space of political and social
action, his scepticism about national unity's immediately springing

from these new communication technologies is well founded. In the inter-war period, French-Canadian nationalism, rather than embracing Henri Bourassa's dualist pan-Canadian vision, was drawn to the Quebec-centred vision of intellectual leaders such as Lionel Groulx, the editor of *L'action française*. The reality of French-Canadian, English-Canadian dualism was captured poignantly in Hugh MacLennan's classic novel, *Two Solitudes*. On the Island of Montreal, he saw that "[t]wo old races and religions meet … and live their separate legends, side by side."[68] At the popular level French and English came together, perhaps more than anywhere else, in sharing a passionate interest in the fate of their teams in the National Hockey League. But they rooted for different teams, listened to separate broadcasts in their mother tongues, and the league wasn't national at all: most teams played for American cities.

As Abraham Rotstein has taught us, although the new electronic means of mass communication can be tools for mobilizing and enhancing nationalism, at the same time they integrate nations with the wider world.[69] Through these new technologies, to use Marshall McLuhan's phrase, we come to belong to "a global village." In the Canadian case, this international village we belong to through communication technologies is overwhelmingly American. An enduring challenge for Canadian nationalists is how to participate in the global village without losing our Canadian identity. That challenge is much more a concern of English-speaking Canadian nationalists than it is for French-speaking Canadians, whose language provides a framework for maintaining a distinct culture.

At the end of Chapter 9 we saw how, in the 1930s, the momentum in Canada's constitutional politics shifted away from provincial rights to concerns about strengthening the federal government's capacity to deal with the kind of economic shocks Canada experienced during the Great Depression. King's Liberal government responded to these centrifugal forces in a cautious manner that showed its sensitivity to the delicate balance in the politics of Canadian federalism.

The only area in which King's government sought constitutional change was with respect to unemployment insurance. At the depth of the Depression, with levels of unemployment rising above 30 per cent, several of the provinces faced bankruptcy through their efforts to provide some measure of relief for unemployed workers and farmers, particularly in the drought-stricken prairies. A national scheme of unemployment insurance would not provide immediate relief for the unemployed, but it would give all Canadians a minimum level of social security. In one of its decisions on Canada's "New Deal" legislation, the JCPC had ruled that the federal Parliament did not have the power to introduce a mandatory scheme of unemployment insurance.[70] The Rowell-Sirois Royal Commission strongly recommended that the Constitution be amended to reverse that decision.[71] Still, King proceeded cautiously, and did not go ahead with a request to the British Parliament to add unemployment insurance to the list of federal powers in section 91 of the BNA Act until he had secured the agreement of all nine provinces. And then, cautious as ever, his Quebec lieutenant, Ernest Lapointe, told the House of Commons that he and Mr King had never said unanimous consent of the provinces was necessary, but that "it may be desirable."[72]

King was equally cautious in leading Canada into the Second World War. He kept to his commitment that Canada must not engage in overseas wars without the consent of Parliament. Parliament assembled on 10 September 1939, a week after Britain declared war and, with only two Quebec nationalists and J.S. Woodsworth, the leader of the CCF, dissenting, supported Canada's entering the war.[73] In the lead-up to the vote, the prime minister told the House that "[t]he present government believes that conscription of men for overseas service will not be a necessary or effective step. No such measure will be introduced by the present administration."[74] King fortified his position by calling and winning an election in 1940. The Liberals took 51 per cent of the popular vote – the first time that had been done since the Unionist government's victory in 1917. With substantial numbers of Liberals elected from all provinces and 181 out of 245 seats in the House, King did not have to think about forming a wartime coalition.

King's promise that there would be no conscription of Canadians for overseas duty haunted the country throughout the war years. By 1942, under pressure from military leaders, the Conservative Opposition, and English-Canadian public opinion to provide more Canadian help to a besieged Britain, King decided to hold a plebiscite requesting the Canadian people to release his government from the commitment it had made not to introduce overseas conscription. Two-thirds of the Canadians voting in the April 1942 plebiscite agreed to release the government from that commitment, with majorities as high as 80 per cent in British Columbia and Ontario. But the vote in French Canada was 72.9 per cent *non*.[75] A subsequent Gallop Poll showed that 90 per cent of French Canadians opposed conscription.[76] King and the country were now caught in the awkward bind of "conscription if necessary, but not necessarily conscription." Canadians who were unwilling to volunteer for overseas service could be conscripted under the National Resources Mobilization Act (NRMA) for home defence. Those who were mobilized under NRMA were called "zombies," and although only 20 per cent of NRMA soldiers were French-speaking, popular opinion in English Canada tended to associate the "zombie" term with French Canadians.

The conscription crisis came to a head in the fall of 1944 when the minister of national defence, J.L. Ralston, on returning to Canada from a tour of the front lines in Europe, told King and the cabinet that conscription was now necessary to provide the reinforcements needed to sustain the advance of Canadian and Allied forces. King responded by firing Ralston and replacing him with General Andrew McNaughton, chief of the general staff. McNaughton was convinced he could persuade enough NRMA men to volunteer to join the struggle in Europe. But when McNaughton reported that the voluntary system would not get the men who were needed, King had the excuse he needed to reverse his position and order conscription of the so-called zombies to join the forces overseas. King's about-face shocked Quebec. He immediately lost a key Quebec minister, Chubby Powers, and on a vote of confidence in the House only twenty-three French-Canadian Liberals supported the government. But the King government survived, and went on to win the 1945 election with a reduced but still solid majority.

French Canada's resistance to conscription to fight overseas shows how deeply rooted in North America is the *Canadien* nation. French Canada, not the United States, is truly America's first new nation. The resistance also displayed the lingering conservatism of French Catholic Quebec. A young Pierre Elliott Trudeau, an outstanding product of the classical education offered in Quebec's leading Catholic academies, enthusiastically embraced the anti-war movement in Quebec.[77] When the King government used the votes of Canada's English-speaking majority to support breaking its promise to Canada's French minority, Trudeau, as a young law student, joined the protestors. Forty years later, as Canada's prime minister, Trudeau would be on the receiving end of a similar sense of betrayal when he proceeded with constitutional changes to Quebec's powers without the province's consent.

No one was more sensitive to the tender trust on which harmonious relations between English and French in Canada depend than William Lyon Mackenzie King. In the end he risked breaking that trust for the greater good of ensuring the defeat of the enemies of democracy. But the way he did it – the delays and the dithering – softened the blow and reduced the damage to the country's unity.

The conscription crisis that so disturbed Canada's domestic politics in the war years should not blind us to the impressive – indeed, the magnificent – contribution Canada made to the Allies' victory. Canada might have delayed its entry into the war for a week so that the elected representatives of its people could approve, as they overwhelmingly did, the decision to join Britain, France, and other western European countries in resisting Hitler's Third Reich. But once the country was in, it was really in: Canada moved quickly to overcome its lack of military preparedness and provide the men and material needed to defend Britain against the advancing German forces. In 1941, with Hitler in control of much of Europe and his army poised to cross the English Channel and invade Britain, Canadian forces were the only armed and trained divisions between London and the south coast of England.[78] The Canadian nation-state, with all of its deep diversity, showed that it had the strength and the will to play an important role in the defence of freedom. This is an achievement in which all Canadians should take pride.

Canadians learned through their war effort that their country could make a difference in the world, but what kind of difference was far from clear. Winds of change were blowing in the country and in the world that would dramatically change Canada's three founding pillars and their relationships with one another. The deep societal changes generated by industrialization and urbanization in Quebec would suddenly manifest themselves in a burst of radical and democratic political activism. Ironically, as a secular, less conservative Quebec came closer to resembling the rest of Canada, it posed the greatest challenge ever to the country's unity. As a founding member of the United Nations, based on a charter whose first principle is the self-determination of peoples, Canada would have to come to terms with the application of that principle to Aboriginal peoples within its borders. And after a war that so severely exposed the evils of racism and ethnic intolerance, English-speaking Canadians would have to reconsider their commitment to keeping the country white and European. How Canada responded to these winds of change is the focus of the next section of the book.

PART FIVE

Transformation of the Pillars

Chapter 11

Quebec Becomes Constitutionally Radical

On Sunday evening, 13 February 1949, eighteen hundred asbestos miners, members of the Canadian and Catholic Confederation of Labour (CCCL), met in St-Aimé Hall in the town of Asbestos, Quebec, to decide whether to go on strike or submit the dispute with their employers to arbitration. On the surface it seemed to be a tough decision. As CCCL Secretary General Jean Marchand explained, a strike without attempting arbitration, under Quebec law, would be illegal. But if the employers and the Quebec government expected the *Canadiens'* traditional conservatism and deference to authority to prevail, the asbestos workers wasted no time dashing those hopes. When Marchand suggested a twenty-four-hour delay to give him time to convey the workers' decision to the minister of labour, the workers drowned him out with shouts of "No, no" and "On with the strike."[1]

And it was a mother of a strike! Its epicentre was Asbestos, a small, one-industry town where 90 per cent of the population depended on employment connected to the mining of asbestos. The strike spread to Thetford Mines, East Broughton, and other communities in Quebec's Eastern Townships where asbestos was mined, but it was in Asbestos that violence occurred and the strikers virtually took over the town.[2] The mine at Asbestos was owned by Canadian Johns-Manville, a branch operation of a huge American corporation that did not hesitate to bring in strikebreakers to keep its mine going. The striking miners took to the streets to prevent the scabs from accessing the mine. On 4 May – "bloody Thursday" – they attacked the police sent in by the Quebec government to clear the way for the strikebreakers, overturning their cars, beating a number of officers into unconsciousness, and holding a dozen captive in the basement of the church of St-Aimé. The Asbestos syndicate was the last to settle, returning to work after a 1 July settlement with Johns-Manville reached through the mediation of Monseigneur Maurice Roy, the archbishop of Quebec.

Quebec had witnessed many work stoppages and strikes as the province industrialized through the first half of the twentieth century, but none attracted the attention that the asbestos strike received in the Quebec and American media, and none posed such a challenge to Quebec's political establishment. Father Jacques Cousineau predicted that it would live "as one of the most important events in Quebec history."[3] Historian Irving Abella referred to it as the "first shot of the Quiet Revolution."[4] The asbestos strike did not bring on Quebec's Quiet Revolution, but it gave expression to the forces of social and political change that had been building up for decades and that, when fully unleashed, would produce the Quiet Revolution.

This was most evident in the role played by the Catholic Church in the strike. The union that staged the strike was a syndicate of the CCCL, a confederation of Catholic unions. The inspiration for a denominational union organization was the Roman Catholic Church's fierce opposition to international communism. The thinking behind the CCCL also contained a touch of European corporatism – the idea of eliminating class warfare by linking owners and workers together in a top-down, state-controlled structure. By the late 1930s the CCCL had become as militant as its rival organizations in the province, the Trades and Labour Congress (TLC) and the Canadian Congress of Labour (CCL). The Church was learning, especially its priests in the cities and industrial towns, that for their flock to keep the faith it had to protect workers and their families from the hardships that could be inflicted on them by the profit-maximizing, English-speaking capitalists who owned the factories, mills, and mines in which they toiled. The top demand of the strikers at Asbestos was elimination of the asbestos dust inside and outside the mills that was now known to have life-threatening consequences. Although there were rifts in Church ranks over supporting the strikers, the priests on the ground and most of the senior clergy – none more than Monsignor Joseph Charbonneau, chairman of the Episcopal Committee on Social Issues and archbishop of Montreal – knew that failure to support the strikers with material support and moral encouragement would show that a Catholic trade union movement could not defend the vital interests of industrial workers and their families.[5]

The workers led, their church supported them, but their provincial government strongly opposed the strike. Maurice Duplessis's highly conservative Union Nationale party had returned to power in 1944. It had first won power in 1935, ending thirty-nine consecutive years of Liberal government, but was defeated when Duplessis called a snap election in 1939. The Union Nationale would govern Quebec for the next sixteen years. Quebecers were playing the federal political game of balancing a Liberal government in Ottawa with a conservative regime in Quebec City. Duplessis's political economy was to manage economic development in collaboration with the owners of industry. The asbestos workers rejected arbitration because they knew from past experience that government-appointed mediators and arbitrators were bound to be pro-management. On Sunday, 7 May, when the strikers prevented company scabs from accessing company property, the Duplessis government did not hesitate to send massive police forces into Asbestos, read the people the Riot Act as they made their way home from Mass, and make dozens of arrests in the streets and dozens more by searching the workers' houses.[6]

The Union Nationale's conservatism went well beyond the management of industrial relations. It appealed to a nationalism built on nostalgia for the simple virtues of an agrarian life that was fast fading into history. Confronted by the aggression of a federal government using its dominant fiscal powers to build a welfare state in post-war Canada, the Duplessis government used the classic Canadian instrument of reaction: in 1953 it appointed a Royal Commission of inquiry. The Tremblay Commission's basic conclusion was that the federal government's encroachment on provincial autonomy must be checked if Quebec was to enjoy its fundamental right under the Confederation compact to preserve its distinct society. And it identified the "three great traditions" of that society as "family, autonomous work and the parish."[7] The idea that French Canadians' primary identity and loyalty lie with Quebec would carry on, but a new cadre of political leaders – liberal, bourgeois, and secular – with profound consequences for Canada's constitutional politics, would soon be pouring new wine into this nationalist vessel.

The new breed of Quebec nationalists were not the only Quebecers rejecting the reactionary, anti-modernist aspects of the Duplessis regime. The classical, conservative Quebec nationalism had no fiercer or more eloquent critic than a young rising star in Quebec's intellectual firmament, Pierre Elliott Trudeau. In 1949 a thirty-year-old Trudeau returned from his world travels just in time to accept an invitation from his friend Gérard Pelletier, a reporter at Le Devoir, to drive down to

Asbestos to join the cause of the striking workers. Trudeau marched with the strikers and made a fiery speech to five thousand miners denouncing the Quebec police. Although he was in Asbestos for only two days, he made a strong impression on Jean Marchand, the union leader. Indeed, at Asbestos, Trudeau, Pelletier, and Marchand bonded, staying close friends for the rest of their lives.[8] A decade and a half later, that troika would be summoned to Ottawa to strengthen Canada's response to the new kind of Quebec nationalism.

Seven years later, Trudeau accepted an invitation from McGill University's Frank Scott, one of Canada's leading professors of constitutional law, to edit a book of essays on the asbestos strike. Trudeau used the opportunity to write his first major piece on the nature of Quebec society. It took the form of an introductory essay to the volume, and was a devastating critique of the nationalism inflicted on Quebec by its political and clerical leadership. The result, he claimed, is that "our political life, by concentrating its energies on nationalism, has never evolved beyond the level of emotional response, and finds itself incapable of dealing with ideas."[9] He attacked Duplessis for winning elections by manipulating that nationalism to make French Canadians feel obliged to "save the race" from the Ottawa centralizers. The asbestos strike, he argued, occurred "because the industrial workers of Quebec were suffocating in a society burdened with inadequate ideologies and oppressive institutions."[10]

In the 1950s Quebec was emerging from its suffocation and coming alive with intellectual ferment. The journal of opinion, *Cité libre*, emerged as an influential platform of dissent from the conservatism of the Duplessis regime. From the very first issue in June 1950, Gérard Pelletier and Pierre Trudeau were listed as members of its editorial team. The liberalism of the French-Canadian writers contributing to *Cité libre* covered a broad spectrum of thought. Many, including Trudeau, were practising Catholics whose liberalism was shaped more by French personalism than English utilitarianism.[11] Although personalism has no defining ideology, it generally aims at balancing individual liberty with communal values, and is more favourably disposed to the welfare state than rugged free enterprise. Pelletier and Trudeau formed a small circle of political thinkers and activists who began to meet regularly at Pelletier's Westmount house. In the late 1950s, a young broadcaster whose Radio-Canada television show *Point de mire* had quickly elevated him to celebrity status in Quebec, joined the group. His name was René Lévesque. Lévesque was neither a writer nor an intellectual, a fact that Trudeau's "snotty-nosed behaviour" did not let him forget. But Lévesque would show that the liberalism stirring Quebec in the 1950s could lead in a very different direction than that which the three musketeers of the asbestos strike, Pelletier, Marchand, and Trudeau, would take.

It was not the asbestos strike but the December 1959 strike of producers at Radio-Canada that turned Lévesque into a political activist. When Michael Starr, the labour minister in John Diefenbaker's Conservative government, told the producers there was nothing his government could do for them, and TV screens would simply have to stay blank in Quebec, for René Lévesque the penny dropped. "If CBC producers had gone on strike in Toronto," he later recounted, "Parliament would have acted without delay so as to not disrupt programming for the English-speaking public."[12] The seed was planted for seeking a country in which French Canadians could not be made to feel like second-class citizens.

On 3 September 1959, on a visit to Schefferville to visit the iron ore mines on Quebec's North Shore, Maurice Duplessis had a stroke. He died four days later. His hand-picked successor, Paul Sauvé, turned out to be a surprise. On taking over as premier, Sauvé announced his commitment to modernize the province's institutions. Within months he steered over sixty bills through the Legislative Assembly. Whereas the Duplessis government (with support from Pierre Trudeau) had refused to accept federal grants for higher education, Sauvé found a way of getting Quebec's share of revenue for higher education without compromising provincial autonomy or overburdening Quebec taxpayers. He negotiated an arrangement under which the federal government would reduce its corporate taxes in Quebec, leaving room for the province to raise, through its own taxes on corporations, an amount roughly equivalent to what Ottawa was granting directly to other provinces for universities. His simple slogan for change was a phrase he kept repeating: *Désormais* (from now on).[13] A 2009 documentary marking the fiftieth anniversary of Paul Sauvé's government called him "the unexpected hero of the Quiet Revolution."[14]

Paul Sauvé died suddenly in January 1960 after only 112 days in office. His successor, Antonio Barrette, who was minister of labour during the asbestos strike, lacked Sauvé's political talent. Barrette and the Union Nationale were defeated in the election he called for June by Jean Lesage, who had served in the cabinet of Louis St-Laurent's Liberal government in Ottawa and returned to provincial politics to lead a rejuvenated provincial Liberal Party to victory. Quebec voters, once again, were adhering to the classical pattern: with the Diefenbaker Conservatives in power federally, they retuned a Liberal government to power in Quebec City.

The Liberals' win in the 1960 election was not a sweep: they increased their share of the popular vote by 5 per cent to 51 per cent. Given the tendency of English Quebecers to vote overwhelmingly Liberal, this probably means the Liberals were not supported by the majority of French voters in the province. Social revolutions can be driven by the masses or by leadership at the top. Quebec's Quiet Revolution was led by the province's francophone elites: political leaders, journalists, and intellectuals. Nonetheless the changes wrought by the Lesage government to Quebec institutions were immense.

Compared with other North American and European jurisdictions, these changes might be considered merely a matter of catching up. This is especially true of the change with the deepest implications for Quebec society: reform of education. In 1964 the Lesage government brought the entire system of education under the control and direction of a new Ministry of Education.[15] Up until then, the Roman Catholic Church had been responsible for the education of most Quebecers. The school system would continue to be organized on a Catholic-Protestant denominational basis, as provided for in the Constitution, but the role of church committees would be confined to confessional matters – the Ministry of Education would control the content of education. Secular government control of education was old hat virtually everywhere else in the developed world. But in the Quebec context it meant a profound reduction in the power of the Catholic Church. Quebec's first minister of education, Paul Gérin-Lajoie, also introduced a distinctive new educational tier between high school and university that became Quebec's CÉGEPs (Collèges d'enseignement général et professionel).

The most spectacular of the Lesage government's reforms was led by its minister of natural resources, René Lévesque. Lévesque brought all the private electricity companies in the province under the aegis of Hydro-Québec, the public corporation created by the Godbout Liberal government in the 1930s to provide electricity to the Island of Montreal. With a young economist, Jacques Parizeau, as his aide, Lévesque sought financing for the project from the Anglo business community. Turned down in Montreal, Lévesque and Parizeau found the $300 million they needed in New York.[16] Irony of ironies, it took American capitalists to finance a huge project of nationalization in Canada! The nationalization of the hydro-electric industry was the lead issue in the 1962 Quebec election, which the Liberals won easily, increasing their majority in the Assembly with 56 per cent of the popular vote.

The Lesage government's slogan, *Maîtres chez nous* (masters in our own house), had been the nationalist war cry of Lionel Groulx back in the 1930s. Under this rubric Lesage and his team of talented and dynamic ministers set themselves to building the machinery of a powerful centralized state. The government brought Church-related social welfare agencies under its regulatory control. It introduced a hospital insurance scheme and subjected hospitals to provincial standards. In 1964 it established a compulsory contributory pension plan, and the following year created the Caisse de dépôt et placement du Québec to manage the funds generated by the plan. In the economic realm, except for the hydro-electric industry, the Lesage Liberals left privately owned firms alone under English-speaking managers and owners. To increase the French presence in the economy, it established the Société générale de financement to provide funding for small, often family owned businesses – an initiative that had some embarrassing results. The biggest boost to French power in the province came through recruiting thousands of technologically trained francophones into a rapidly expanding civil service. In the period between 1960 and 1965, Quebec's public service grew by 42.6 per cent – and that was exclusive of public enterprises such as Hydro-Québec.[17]

The fact that Quebec was able to carry out this flurry of state-building initiatives under the existing Constitution seemed to demonstrate that Quebecers did not need any new provincial powers to be *maîtres chez nous*. In the surge of nationalist pride that was building the "state of Quebec," there were some overtones engendering fears that a serious threat to Canadian unity was in the making. But at this point Quebec's Quiet Revolution had not produced a constitutional crisis.

For the federal government Quebec's participation in federal-provincial affairs was troublesome but manageable. In the post-war period Ottawa had continued to use its domination of the fields of direct taxation to collect more money than it needed to fund its own constitutional responsibilities so that it could partner with the provinces in sharing the cost of new programs in health, social welfare, and post-secondary education, policy fields that the provinces regarded as under their exclusive jurisdiction. No province objected to this so-called co-operative federalism and its encroachment on provincial autonomy more than Quebec. The Lesage government took a leaf out of Paul Sauvé's book and embraced the policy of opting out of shared-cost programs with the federal government and in return getting tax room to fund programs with its own revenues. The biggest opt-out was creating and funding its own Quebec Pension Plan, while the rest of Canada would be under the federal government's Canada Pension Plan. Establishing a Canada-wide pension plan was an important plank in the party platform that returned the Liberals to power under Lester Pearson in the 1963 federal election. At a federal-provincial conference in Quebec City in 1965, Premier Lesage wheeled out the Quebec Pension Plan, with better benefits than Ottawa was offering and a lucrative source of investment funds for the provincial government. Pearson and his entourage were totally taken by surprise. On the plane trip back to Ottawa, some passengers were talking about the death of Confederation.[18]

Opting out of federal-provincial programs was giving Quebec a de facto special status in the Canadian federation. The question was: Would this be enough, or would a constitutional restructuring of Confederation be necessary to satisfy the state-building nationalism stirring Quebec? That question was soon to be answered by the collision of Quebec nationalism with the Canadian nationalist project of completing Canada's constitutional independence from Britain.

Nineteen forty-nine was a banner year in Canada's state-building process. It produced a bumper crop of three major developments: a tenth province, Newfoundland, was added to the federation; the Supreme Court of Canada became the country's supreme court in function as well as name; and the first step was taken towards an all-Canadian constitutional amendment process with a mini-patriation of parts of the Constitution.

Newfoundland (now Newfoundland and Labrador) joined Confederation through what for Canada was an uncharacteristically democratic constitutional process, although it was in line with the democratic constitution-making that established new democracies in West Germany and Italy after the Second World War. The people of Newfoundland and Labrador were treated as a sovereign people who could determine their constitutional destiny by majority vote. Britain certainly put pressure on the Newfoundlanders to join Canada – it was eager to rid itself of the burden of financing Newfoundland and the responsibility for its governance – and the Government of Canada worked hard to make the option of joining Canada as materially attractive as possible. But in the end the decision was made by the Newfoundlanders.

In 1934, at the depth of the Great Depression, Newfoundland, like some Canadian provinces, found itself unable to pay its debts. When

Britain stepped in to manage its finances, it temporarily suspended its status as a self-governing Dominion and placed it under the rule of a British commission. In 1946, lacking an elected legislature, Newfoundlanders elected a National Convention to determine their constitutional future. The delegates considered three options: continuation of British commission government; reversion to being a Dominion, with responsible government; or Confederation with Canada. British pressure and Canadian money (mostly from the federal Liberal Party) helped to ensure that Confederation was on the referendum ballot that would determine Newfoundland's future.

The June 1947 referendum campaign was a bitterly contested battle that sometimes exploded in violence. The result was close, but in the end responsible government – that is, an independent Dominion – edged out Confederation by 45 to 41 per cent. The third option, continuation of commission government, received little support.[19] During the campaign, a fourth option – economic union with the United States – divided the responsible government side. But when Chesley Crosbie (the father of Conservative John Crosbie), the economic union leader, and other supporters visited Washington, they got the brush-off. Had this division of the independence forces not occurred, responsible government's margin of victory over Confederation might well have been larger. In the runoff referendum that took place a month later, Confederation narrowly defeated a return to responsible government, 52 to 48 per cent.

On the Canadian side of union with Newfoundland there was no matching referendum of a sovereign people. In November 1948 a delegation of Newfoundland leaders, including Joseph Smallwood, soon to become the province's first premier, flew to Ottawa to meet a group of federal cabinet ministers headed by Prime Minister King and Justice Minister Louis St-Laurent, who would soon succeed him, to put the final touches on Newfoundland's Terms of Union. There was not much to negotiate, as Newfoundland was joining the federation as set out in the 1867 Constitution. Two small special clauses were added: one leaving sanctions to redress violations of denominational school rights (Newfoundland had six different Christian school systems) with the courts, rather than with the federal government, and the other ensuring that Newfoundland did not export oleomargarine to the rest of Canada so long as the federal government was enforcing a policy aimed at protecting the country's dairy farmers from butter's competition. (It is sad to report this embarrassing detail.)

Throughout, the main negotiations were about fiscal matters – the Newfoundlanders anxious to get out from under a massive debt load and on to a more promising future, the Canadians knowing that it was in Canada's national interest to add Newfoundland to the Dominion, but not wanting to antagonize the existing provinces by being too generous. In the end the terms agreed to were fairly generous: Canada assumed responsibility for Newfoundland's accumulated debt, allowed it to keep a current surplus, promised $50 million of transitional grants to be paid over a ten-year period, extended the federal tax rental system to provide the provincial government with new revenues without having to levy new taxes of its own, and gave the citizens of the new province full access to Canada's burgeoning welfare state. David Mackenzie's summation seems fair: by joining Canada, "Newfoundland was able to achieve a degree of development and rise to a standard of living that any government in an independent Newfoundland would have been extremely hard pressed to match."[20] Newfoundland probably would not have entered Confederation without a strong financial offer. But this does not mean that its allegiance to Canada is simply based on what Quebec premier Robert Bourassa would later call "profitable federalism." Newfoundlanders' strong sense of identity is based on their being a distinct and independent society for almost as long as have French Canadians, not on any repudiation of Canada.

Even though adding a new province was a matter of interest and concern to the existing provinces – among other things, it meant adding the six senators promised to Newfoundland in 1867 – the King government rejected Conservative Opposition leader George Drew's motion that the government was "required to consult" with the provinces before proceeding to add a new province to the federation. Both houses of the Canadian Parliament passed resolutions supporting an address requesting the British Parliament to make the necessary changes in the British North America Act on the basis of the negotiated Terms of Union. The British Parliament complied, and on 31 March 1949 Newfoundland became Canada's tenth province.[21]

The second major state-building event of 1949 was the termination of judicial appeals from Canada to the Judicial Committee of the Privy Council, making the Supreme Court of Canada truly the country's highest court. The motivation in taking this important final step in Canada's becoming a fully independent nation-state was nationalist in two senses. First, it was in keeping with the sense of Canadian national independence shared by the great majority of Canadians – anglophone and francophone alike – to cease relying on a foreign tribunal for resolution of the country's most important legal disputes. But, second, Canadian nationalists in English-speaking Canada hoped that a supreme court, staffed by Canadian judges and no longer required to comply with precedents set by British jurists, would interpret Canada's Constitution in a manner much less favourable to provincial rights and much more supportive of the powers of the federal government.

Even though by the late 1930s there was all-party support for abolishing appeals to the Privy Council, in 1940 King, always super cautious about any move that might have national unity implications, referred to the Supreme Court the question of whether the Canadian Parliament had the power to abolish Privy Council appeals. The Supreme Court gave an affirmative answer to that question, but Quebec, joined by British Columbia, New Brunswick, and Ontario, decided to appeal the Court's decision. Given the divisive nature of the case, the JCPC postponed hearing the appeal until after the war, but in 1947 it had no difficulty in finding that the Canadian Parliament could use its power under section 101 of the BNA Act to provide a general court of appeal for Canada to make the Supreme Court of Canada the country's final court of appeal in all matters of law.[22] The British judges' rationale – "to secure through its own courts of justice that the law should be one and the same for all citizens" was "a prime element in the self-government of the Dominion" – seemed to take little heed of the federal structure of Canada.

Once Louis St-Laurent had taken King's place as leader of the Liberal Party and prime minister, the dithering was over. With a win in the June 1949 election behind him, St-Laurent forged ahead with legislation ending Privy Council appeals. Perhaps he felt that, as a distinguished Quebec lawyer and a French Canadian, he could answer any Quebec concerns. In any event, in the parliamentary debate on legislation making decisions of the Supreme Court in all cases "final and conclusive," there was no significant support among advocates of provincial rights from Quebec or other provinces for retaining Privy Council appeals. The Conservative Opposition put forward a motion to make the Judicial Committee's past decisions forever binding on the Supreme Court. This foolish idea was supported mainly by English-speaking lawyers who claimed they were acting on behalf of the Canadian Bar Association. Fortunately the motion was defeated, but Stuart Garson, St-Laurent's justice minister, had the challenging task of explaining (with a straight face) that the Conservative motion was unnecessary because the emancipated Supreme Court would simply apply the law of the Constitution.

But there was concern about how the Supreme Court should be organized to deal with constitutional disputes. Léon Balcer, a Conservative MP from Quebec, thought it questionable that a tribunal that would be settling disputes between the two levels of government would be so thoroughly a creature of the federal government. "We find it inconsistent," he argued, "that only one of the parties to a pact should ... arrogate to itself the right to determine alone what tribunal will decide on disputes with the other party."[23] Another Quebec MP, Wilfrid Lacroix, proposed that four Supreme Court justices (on a nine-judge court) be nominated by provincial governments and that the Supreme Court must be unanimous in decisions affecting provincial rights.[24] Lacroix's proposals were voted down, but the question of the Supreme Court's legitimacy as the federation's judicial umpire would continue to be an issue in Canada's constitutional politics.

The amendment to the Supreme Court Act ending Privy Council appeals added two justices to what since 1927 had been a seven-judge court. The Act continued to recognize Quebec's special status by stipulating that three of the Court's nine justices must be from the bar or bench of Quebec. But the governor-in-council – which, in fact, means the cabinet – would continue to appoint the Court's justices. Unlike other federal judicial appointments, by constitutional convention the selection of Supreme Court justices is entirely the prerogative of the prime minister.[25] Canada would come to stand out among the world's federations as the only one that left the selection of members of its highest constitutional tribunal to the unfettered power of the central government's political CEO.

The Supreme Court of Canada was now one of the most powerful national high courts in the world. The jurisdiction of the US Supreme Court extends only to disputes arising under federal laws and the US Constitution. Disputes involving state laws can be heard by the Supreme Court only if they involve some aspect of the Constitution. State Courts of Appeal are the final adjudicators of disputes about state laws and constitutions. In contrast, as a general court of appeal, Canada's Supreme Court is the final court of appeal in all matters of law, including provincial statutes, municipal by-laws, common law, and Quebec's distinct system of civil law. The Supreme Court may be selective in deciding the appeals it will hear from provincial courts, but it has the potential to be a major force for unifying Canadian law. The scope of the Supreme Court's jurisdiction, combined with the federal government's power to appoint the judges of the higher provincial courts, gives Canada a more unified judicial structure than that of most federal countries.

The third state-building event in 1949 was a sleeper. It was nothing less than a mini-patriation of the Canadian Constitution – although that was not the language used in 1949. What Prime Minister St-Laurent presented to the House of Commons in October 1949 was a request to the British Parliament to add to the enumerated powers of the federal Parliament the power to amend the Constitution of Canada – except for certain matters – without going to Britain and without the consent of the provinces. The main exceptions were the provinces' legislative powers, denominational school rights, and the right to use English and French in federal, Manitoba, and Quebec institutions. Also exempted were two important features of parliamentary democracy: the requirement that there be a session of Parliament every year, and that no Parliament continue beyond five years in length.[26] St-Laurent argued that the proposed amendment would simply enable the federal government to catch up with the provinces. Section 92(1) of the BNA Act gave provincial legislatures the power to amend the "Constitution of the Province, except as regards the Office of Lieutenant Governor." His proposed amendment would give the federal Parliament the power to amend those parts of the Constitution that are of concern only to the federal government.

It was not a good argument. It is far from clear which parts of the Constitution are of exclusive concern to the federal government. For example, what about the Senate? The Senate is a chamber of the federal Parliament, but it is also an institution designed to represent the regions of the country and protect smaller provinces from the power of the more populous provinces in the House of Commons.

In 1949 Senate reform was not the issue. The opposition Conservatives and provincial governments were concerned about something more fundamental: dividing up the Constitution into different parts subject to different amending procedures. They wanted a more holistic approach to constitutional amendment, and objected to the federal government's unilateralism. Some premiers, certainly Quebec's Duplessis, but also Ontario's Leslie Frost, Alberta's Ernest Manning, and Saskatchewan's Tommy Douglas, coupled their opposition to Ottawa's unilateralism with pressure to delay the abolition of Privy Council appeals until the agreement of the provinces was secured. Douglas suggested

that "measures should be adopted to make the Canadian Supreme
Court more representative than it is at present."[27]

Opposition to the St-Laurent government's aggressive, centralizing
actions was mostly at the level of political elites. At this point in the
country's odyssey, the Canadian public was not deeply engaged in constitutional politics. Constitutional amendment issues and Privy Council
appeals could not compete with the euphoric nationalism engendered
by victory in the war, the building of the post-war welfare state, and a
booming economy. St-Laurent felt strong enough to override the opposition and press ahead with the mini-patriation. Both Houses passed
the resolution asking the British Parliament to give the federal government the power to amend Canada's Constitution, with some notable
exceptions. The Parliament at Westminster, without controversy or debate, dutifully complied with the Canadian Parliament's request.[28]

In January 1950 St-Laurent called a federal-provincial conference to
devise a method of amending all of the Canadian Constitution in
Canada. The conference turned the project over to a committee of attorneys general who beavered away on it for a while before running
out of steam. It was now clear that some of the provinces, especially
Quebec, wanted a much more inflexible formula for amending the
Constitution than federal officials found desirable. It was equally clear
that, at this time, patriating Canada's Constitution, politically speaking, "did not have legs."

The 1950s was a period of constitutional quiescence. The federal government, under both Liberal and Conservative administrations, forged
ahead with its state-building activities using the dominant powers it
had then and has now over the Canadian fiscal system. The "feds" certainly encountered some resistance to the aggressive use of their fiscal
powers not only from Quebec, but from other provinces whose motivation was not protecting a distinctive culture but building the provincial
state. Fiscal federalism, not constitutional politics, was the name of the
game, and it preoccupied both levels of government throughout the decade – strong governments competing for taxpayers' dollars and votes.

Canada's Constitution gives both the federal and provincial governments the power to levy direct taxes such as personal and corporate
income taxes and inheritance taxes, without any guidance on how
the two levels of government should divvy up the tax fields. During the
Second World War the provinces were "persuaded" to "rent" their tax-
ing powers to Ottawa so that Canada's central government could be in
full control of the economy. After the war, not surprisingly, the federal

government hoped to continue these arrangements that, in the words of J.A. Corry, had had "a strongly centralizing effect, increasing the leverage of the national government on the policies of the provincial governments as well as on the economy of the country."[29] Also, not surprisingly, the provinces with the two largest economies, Ontario and Quebec, refused to participate in the agreements that continued tax-renting after the war from 1947 to 1952. But after George Drew, a staunch enemy of the federal Liberals, went to Ottawa to lead the Conservative Opposition and was succeeded as Ontario premier by the much more pragmatic and phlegmatic Leslie Frost, Ontario agreed to enter the tax rental agreements when they were renewed for 1952 to 1957. Quebec, of course, was another matter. By 1954 Duplessis's government was finally delivering enough services to the Quebec people to see the need for a little chunk of income tax – about 10 per cent of the federal tax. To accommodate him, and to avoid subjecting Quebecers to double taxation, St-Laurent agreed to reduce federal income taxes in Quebec by 10 per cent.[30] The process of Quebec's acquiring special status in the federation without any constitutional restructuring was under way.

On the expenditure side, fiscal federalism began to generate a plethora of federal-provincial shared-cost programs. Some, such as the building of the Trans-Canada Highway, were Ottawa's initiatives in a field where the federal government clearly had some constitutional responsibility ("works and undertakings" connecting the provinces). Even here, Quebec refused to take Ottawa's highway-building money until 1961, when money overcame constitutional scruple.[31] Others that were squarely in fields of exclusive provincial jurisdiction were not solely federal initiatives. A leading example was hospital insurance. In 1947 Tommy Douglas's Saskatchewan CCF, heading Canada's first social democratic government, introduced North America's first universal hospital insurance scheme. A year later, a Liberal-Conservative coalition government in British Columbia brought in a similar plan. In Ontario, where a Progressive Conservative government was feeling the heat from the CCF on its left, Leslie Frost became a convert to hospital insurance. With Ontario on side, Paul Martin, a left-Liberal minister (and father of his namesake, the future prime minister), was able to secure the St-Laurent government's support for the Hospital Insurance and Diagnostic Services Act. Under the Act, which received unanimous support from the House of Commons in May 1957, Canadians would be publicly insured for in-patient and out-patient services at hospitals,

most of which were privately owned. It was the country's first step towards a universal, publicly funded health care system. Although at the
beginning only five provinces joined the scheme, by 1961 all ten provinces were participating.

The country as a whole, including Quebec, buoyed by post-war prosperity and a growing sense of egalitarianism, had moved to the left. The
ideological consensus on social policy dampened constitutional fric-
tions. This can be seen in the one constitutional amendment enacted
in the 1950s: an amendment empowering Parliament to make laws in
relation to old age pensions. The amendment was occasioned by post-
war agitation to improve the old age pension scheme that the King
Liberal government had introduced in 1927. That scheme was limited
to persons over age seventy who passed a means test. The egalitarian
spirit of the day now found a means test degrading. A parliamentary
committee recommended a universal pension plan for those over age
seventy and a means-tested pension for those between sixty-five and
seventy. Because social welfare was regarded as a provincial responsibility, it was felt that a constitutional amendment was necessary to remove any doubts about federal legislation improving a national pension
plan. The federal government waited until it had secured the agreement of all the provinces before asking the British Parliament to enact
the amendment that added section 94A to the Constitution. The provinces readily agreed. Although the amendment established the federal
Parliament's power to legislate in the field of old age pensions and
supplementary benefits, it recognized the paramountcy of the provincial legislatures in the field.[32] The amendment, in effect, made pensions
a concurrent field of legislation, but in the event of a conflict between a
federal law on pensions and a provincial pension law, provincial law
prevails – the very opposite of the two concurrent fields in the founding
Constitution, immigration and agriculture, where federal law is paramount.[33] The swing of the political pendulum from Liberals to Conservatives in 1957 showed a continuing consensus. John Diefenbaker's
government enriched a number of shared-cost programs, notably old
age pensions, and introduced at least fifteen minor shared-cost programs and five major ones.[34]

Canadian federalism has its moods. Cooperative federalism would
soon enough give way to the more combative ways that marked its
early days. The mood changes have much to do with the personalities
of leaders and the health of the economy. But a lasting legacy of the fiscal federalism of the 1950s and early 1960s was the principle of equalization, introduced in 1957. The basic aim of equalization is to ensure

that all of Canada's provinces are able to provide a reasonable level of essential public services without resorting to exceptionally onerous levels of taxation. The instrument for serving this aim is a system of federal grants calculated to bring the revenues of so-called have-not provinces up to what the more affluent provinces can collect per capita from a number of major tax sources. Although the details of equalization have passed through many iterations, the principle has endured, and a quarter of a century after its introduction, as we shall see, it was written into the Constitution.[35]

Fiscal equalization gives a social democratic character to Canada's federal system that is by no means unique to Canada but does distinguish it from the United States. In Canada equalization provides some shelter for provinces with sagging economies, whereas US states are much more exposed to the free play of market forces. When a US state's economy slumps, its citizens have much more incentive to pull up stakes and move to other parts of the country than do the citizens of a Canadian province that is not doing well economically. Fiscal equalization is an important enough principle to be considered an addition to our shared civic culture – the glue that holds the Canadian political community, with its deep diversity, together. It provides a practical reason for the *Québécois* to stay in Canada. In 1995 the Royal Commission on Aboriginal Peoples recommended applying fiscal equalization to self-governing Aboriginal communities, but non-Aboriginal Canadians and their governments have not yet moved far enough along the path of reconciliation to recognize the merits of that proposal.

Another idea, with even bigger consequences for the life and spirit of the country, was creeping into Canada's civic culture. This was what Michael Ignatieff has referred to as "the rights revolution."[36] The Holocaust and other evils inflicted by the Axis powers on their own and other peoples created a widely shared feeling after the war that all human beings, regardless of colour, creed, ethnicity, age, sex, or state of economic development, have fundamental rights and freedoms that must be respected and protected. The United Nations Charter, signed by its fifty-one founding members in June 1945, begins by affirming "a faith in fundamental human rights, in the dignity and worth of the human person, in the equal rights of men and women and of nations large and small."[37] This was followed by the UN General Assembly's endorsing the Universal Declaration of Human Rights in 1948. Although Canada, as a leading UN founder, was actively involved in these developments, its government was less than enthusiastic about these international codifications of human rights. It was worried that signing on to the Universal Declaration might somehow undermine parliamentary sovereignty in Canada and encroach on provincial rights. The King government's instructions to Lester Pearson, who led Canada's UN delegation, at first were to abstain from voting for the Universal Declaration. When Pearson announced Canada's reversal of its position and voted in favour of the draft Declaration, he made it clear that "the federal government of Canada does not intend to invade other rights which are important to the people of Canada, by this I mean the rights of the provinces under our federal constitution."[38]

In the immediate post-war years the King government also came under pressure from a movement within the country for a Canadian bill of rights. The federal government's outlawing of the Communist Party, Duplessis's anti-bolshevist Padlock Law, and the racist policies of both levels of government first gave rise to a Canadian civil liberties movement in the 1920s and 1930s. The internment of dissidents and the dispossession and relocation of Japanese Canadians, followed after the war by the Gouzenko espionage inquiry's gross violation of civil liberties, broadened support for the movement. But it was the United Nations developments that convinced the Liberal government that it had to do something about all the rights talk. For once the Royal Commission response was not adopted. Instead the government chose to have a special parliamentary committee look into the Universal Declaration of Human Rights and how Canada should respond.

The two joint parliamentary committees and a Senate committee that considered rights issues in the late 1940s opened the door for individuals and groups who believed the time had come for Canada to adopt its own charter of rights and freedoms. John George Diefenbaker, a rising star in Canadian politics, and CCF leader M.J. Coldwell were leading parliamentary spokesmen for the cause. The Liberal government's response was to have Justice Department officials deliver sanctimonious homilies on the sacrosanct status of parliamentary sovereignty, the danger of adopting the economic and social rights that had found a place in the Universal Declaration, and how well civil liberties were already protected in the British common law tradition. With a majority in the House of Commons, the Liberals could prevail in pouring cold water on the bill of rights idea. But evidence that the idea had considerable public support came in February 1949, when CCF MP Alistair Stewart presented to the House an eleven-foot stack of six hundred thousand signatures, gathered by the Toronto Civil Liberties Association, calling for a national bill of rights.[39]

Although parliamentary consideration of a bill of rights abated after 1950, the newly emancipated Supreme Court of Canada was being stirred by the rights revolution. In the 1950s the Supreme Court decided seven cases in which it reversed the Quebec Court of Appeal and upheld claims of political and religious minorities against the Government of Quebec.[40] Some of these "civil liberties" victories turned on the traditional techniques of common law judges: narrowing the scope of criminal offences and police powers or applying judge-made doctrines of administrative law. The most spectacular of the latter was *Roncarelli v. Duplessis*,[41] in which the Supreme Court found that denying a restaurant a liquor licence because its proprietor was putting up bail for Jehovah's Witnesses went beyond the premier's discretionary power. Others involved bits and pieces of what was coming to be known as "the implied bill of rights." In *Saumur*,[42] four of the Court's five-judge majority, which found that a Quebec City by-law requiring permission from the chief of police to distribute pamphlets in the streets could not apply to the Jehovah's Witnesses, rested its decision on the argument that the phrase in the preamble to the BNA Act stating that Canada was to have "a Constitution similar in principle to that of the United Kingdom" removed from provincial legislatures the power to suppress religious freedom. In *Switzman*,[43] the Court struck down Quebec's notorious Padlock Law that authorized the police to close down the premises of an organization propagating communist ideology. Five members of the eight-judge majority held that, in criminalizing communism, Quebec encroached on the federal Parliament's exclusive power over criminal law. The other three invoked the BNA Act's preamble and its provision of parliamentary government that, in the words of Justice Ivan Rand, "means ultimately government by the free play of public opinion of an open society."[44]

The theory that Canada's existing Constitution contains an implied bill of rights was too ethereal and uncertain to blunt the desire for an explicit bill of rights. At no point did a majority of the Supreme Court join together in expounding a clear version of the theory and the rights that flow from it. And it certainly did not ignite a great deal of public interest in civil liberties, which seems to have waned in the 1950s. A 1957 Gallup poll reported that 63 per cent of Canadians felt their rights were fully protected, compared with only 37 per cent who thought so ten years earlier.[45] The game-changer was John Diefenbaker. Dief's early and eloquent advocacy of a bill of rights and his jowl-shaking attacks on the civil rights abuses of the Liberal government, more than anything else, propelled him to the top of the party that since 1942 had called itself the Progressive Conservative Party.

In the 1957 general election, the Diefenbaker-led PCs surprised everyone, including themselves, by winning the most seats and forming a minority government, ending twenty-two years of Liberal rule. The following year Diefenbaker called a snap election and swept the country, winning 54 per cent of the popular vote and a huge majority in the House of Commons. Diefenbaker waited until his majority government was intact to unveil his Canadian Bill of Rights. But it was a very anemic bill of rights. Dief had fallen under the spell of the cautious legal beagles in the Justice Department. His bill would be an ordinary statute, not an amendment to the Constitution, and it would apply only to the federal level of government. Its rights and freedoms basically would be guidelines for judges to use to interpret federal statutes and regulations, as far as possible in a manner that did not conflict with the rights and freedoms listed in the Bill of Rights. Its final part was all about how the Bill would not apply if Parliament declared that "war, invasion, real or apprehended, exists," bringing into force the War Measures Act.

Diefenbaker's Canadian Bill of Rights was a huge disappointment to civil rights advocates in and outside Parliament. The federal Liberals, now in opposition, did a flip-flop. Now they would settle for nothing less than a strong constitutional bill of rights binding on both levels of government. The Diefenbaker government held to the Liberals' former position that a bill of rights should not be imposed on the provinces – above all, not on Quebec. Diefenbaker was mightily embarrassed when a new Liberal Quebec premier, Jean Lesage, turned up at a dominion-provincial conference in Ottawa in July 1960, just a few weeks after the final version of his Bill of Rights had been presented to the House of Commons, and announced that human rights were not adequately protected in Quebec, and that "a Bill of Rights would have much greater value, in reality and symbolically, if it were part of our constitution."[46] The Bill of Rights movement had met the Quiet Revolution! But Diefenbaker ploughed ahead. His Canadian Bill of Rights was passed by Parliament on 4 August 1960.

At the same conference at which Jean Lesage made his surprising announcement, Diefenbaker announced his intention to return to the project of working with the provinces on a system of amending Canada's Constitution in Canada. "More and more Canadians are coming to realize," he claimed, that this change must take place "if Canada is to assume her place as an independent nation within the Commonwealth."[47]

The first ministers agreed to have their attorneys general work on drafting an amending "formula" that would make possible what was now being referred to as "the repatriation of the Constitution." For a country whose Constitution since its founding had been in the custody of the British Parliament, the word "repatriation" did not make much sense.

So the attorneys general and their deputies beavered away, meeting after meeting, to reach a consensus on an amending formula. E. Davie Fulton, Diefenbaker's attorney general and minister of justice, presided over the process when it began, and then gave way to Guy Favreau, Pearson's minister of justice after the Liberals returned to power in 1963. By 1964 it appeared that the eleven governments were close enough together to have what was referred to as the Fulton-Favreau formula considered at a federal-provincial conference in Charlottetown to celebrate the centennial of the first meeting of the Fathers of Confederation.

The Fulton-Favreau formula was a messy and complex set of rules for amending Canada's Constitution.[48] No other constitutional democracy in the world has anything like it. Only a well-trained lawyer could unravel this convoluted document. Although, as we shall see, it was not adopted in 1964, its basic elements foreshadow the formula that was finally adopted in 1982. The formula divided the Constitution into various components. Amending the parts considered most important, including the provinces' legislative powers and English and French language rights, would require unanimous agreement of all the provinces and the federal Parliament. Other components, relevant to the country as a whole but not so important, would be amendable by the federal Parliament and two-thirds of the provinces representing at least 50 per cent of the Canadian population. Bits that concern only one or several provinces or only the federal level of government could be changed by the legislatures of the relevant provinces and the federal Parliament. It was a more rigid formula than the one finally adopted because it required unanimity for any changes in the division of legislative powers. Its technical intricacies, like the fine print in a legal contract, might seem out of keeping with the supreme law of a constitutional democracy, but the formula resonates with the spirit of compromise and accommodation essential for consensus in Canada.

The Fulton-Favreau formula was well enough received by the first ministers at Charlottetown to have their attorneys general put the final touches on it – which they did, in Ottawa. On 14 October 1964 headlines in Canadian newspapers proclaimed that the Constitution was coming home. At long last the struggle to find an acceptable way of amending

Canada's highest law in Canada was over. Or so we Canadians thought for a while, until Premier Lesage encountered a storm of criticism for appearing to have signed off on constitutional reform.

It might seem strange that there was so much criticism of an amending formula that provided everything a constitutionally conservative Quebec could have asked for. But Quebec was becoming constitutionally radical. All the talk of being *maîtres chez nous* was generating aspirations for Quebec to obtain additional powers and constitutional recognition of its special status in the federation as the homeland of a founding people. Daniel Johnson, leader of the Opposition Union Nationale, argued that it would be a strategic error to accept an amending formula that, once in place, would be a constitutional straitjacket for constitutional reform. Under such a rigid amendment formula, Quebec would find it impossible to secure the restructuring of the federation required for its nation-building project. Lesage felt the heat. In January 1966 he informed Prime Minister Pearson that "the government of Quebec has decided to delay indefinitely the proposal for constitutional amendment."[49]

The fat was in the fire. Quebec's nation-building project had collided with the completion of the Canadian nationalist objective of becoming a fully independent state. Canadians did not know it at the time, but now they were in for a lengthy period of the heaviest constitutional politics since the founding of the country in 1867.

The evolving roles played by the two principal protagonists, René Lévesque and Pierre Trudeau, in this first season of heavy constitutional politics, show how the stakes in the struggle quickly became nothing less than the future of the country. The battle between Lévesque and Trudeau has to be set in the context of the times: the 1960s, a turbulent decade when change and the promise of change in the way people lived and in the structures of the states and empires they lived in was in the air everywhere. Internationally, in the Third World the rise of nationalism was dismantling the European empires. In 1960 the UN General Assembly adopted the Declaration on the Granting of Independence to Colonial Countries and Peoples. Canada supported the Declaration, but without any consideration that its principles might apply to the colonized Indigenous peoples within its borders.[50] It would take another half-century for the UN and its colonizing member-states to recognize the rights of Indigenous peoples. Within Canada, nationalist sentiments in French Quebec and among Indigenous peoples were being stirred up by these global winds of change. But it was in Quebec that they had their first major impact, in the emergence of a separatist movement.

There has never been a time since "the Conquest" that the idea of forming a separate French-speaking state has not had some followers in Quebec. For some *Québécois* it has always been an option, the numbers rising and falling with the times. In the 1960s the Quiet Revolution, combined with international influences, was not so much increasing the number of Quebec separatists as spurring them to political organization. Nineteen sixty saw the founding of the Rassemblement pour l'indépendance nationale (RIN) by a small group of mostly young Quebec francophones. Its small number of adherents did not stop the RIN from making a lot of noise. A few weeks after its founding, a flamboyant young actor, Pierre Bourgault, joined the RIN, and in 1961, Marcel Chaput, a National Research Council chemist and a founding member, published *Pourquoi je suis séparatiste*, which became an immediate bestseller. The emergence of the RIN made René Lévesque uncomfortable. He was a Quebec nationalist but not yet a separatist – at least, that was not his first option. In May 1964, speaking at a student conference, he said that the appropriate status for Quebec was that of an "associate state" within Canada, but if that could not be negotiated with the rest of Canada, then "we should separate."[51]

The RIN and Chaput's book made Pierre Elliott Trudeau much more than uncomfortable. The Quebec separatists made him angry, very angry. In "The New Treason of the Intellectuals," published in a special 1962 issue of *Cité libre*, Trudeau poured out his anger in a passionate critique not just of the Quebec separatists, but of Quebec nationalists. He accused the liberal-minded Quebec activists who had brought on the Quiet Revolution of being distracted by their nationalism into turning inwards and abandoning what should be French Canada's destiny: the building of a dualist Canadian state. Trudeau had become a Canadian nationalist, with Henri Bourassa's vision of a Canada, from coast to coast to coast, that is equally a home to French- and English-speaking Canadians. For him that meant, following Lord Acton, rejecting the idea that a state must be based on one ethnic nation. Looking back on recent history, Trudeau argued that one nation/one state nationalism led to international conflict and war.

Lévesque and Trudeau were moving along sharply divergent paths. Where their trajectories would take them – the political leadership roles they would take on – would be worked out in the middle years of the 1960s, perhaps the most turbulent political period of politics in the country's history.

In the 1963 federal election Lester Pearson's Liberals fell four seats short of winning a majority government, but gained enough to displace the Diefenbaker Conservatives and form a minority government. From the beginning of his prime ministership, Pearson was acutely aware of the crisis building in Canada. Besides the emergence of a separatist political party, a separatist organization using terrorist methods was setting off bombs in Montreal mailboxes. The assassination of President John F. Kennedy south of the border heightened the sense of impending crisis. One of the Pearson government's first acts was to establish the Royal Commission on Bilingualism and Biculturalism (the B & B Commission) and to invite André Laurendeau, editor-in-chief of Le Devoir and host of a popular Quebec public affairs television show, to co-chair it. Laurendeau had called for such a commission to study and report on how Canada could become a bilingual and bicultural federation. In their initial 1965 report on English-French relations, the commissioners said that "Canada without being fully conscious of the fact, is passing through the greatest crisis of its history."[52]

Despite its success on the policy front – the Canada Pension Plan, in tandem with the Quebec Pension Plan, was followed a year later by a national medicare scheme embracing the whole country – the Pearson government was under constant attack for smelly scandals. In hindsight the scandals seem small – cabinet ministers accepting free furniture, helping an escaped thug avoid extradition – but the media dine out on scandals, and the string of embarrassing news stories was draining the cabinet of spirit and forcing Quebec ministers and MPs to resign. All of the scandals involved Quebecers, including Guy Favreau, the capable justice minister who carried the constitutional file. This development had crucial consequences for Pierre Trudeau. With the New Democratic Party (NDP), the CCF's successor, strongly supporting their social policy initiatives, the Pearson Liberals were in no danger of defeat in the House. Nonetheless after only two years of minority government Pearson called an election. The only reason for the election was the Liberals' thirst for majority government. To win the election Pearson knew he had to shore up his Quebec flank. Three days after the 7 September 1965 election call, those three Quebec amigos who had first come together in the asbestos strike, Jean Marchand, Gérard Pelletier, and Pierre Trudeau, held a press conference at the Windsor Hotel in Montreal to announce that, in response to the prime minister's call, they would stand as Liberal candidates in the election.[53]

The 1965 election has gone down in history as the election that marked the least change in the electorate's choices. The Liberals and Conservatives both gained two seats, while the NDP gained five.[54] The big losers were Social Credit, now split into an Alberta rump and Réal Caouette's Créditistes in Quebec. So it was back to minority government for the Pearson Liberals. Marchand, Pelletier, and Trudeau all won their ridings, but although Marchand, the prominent labour leader, was the biggest fish in the catch of new Liberals, it was Trudeau who got the plum job: Pearson made him his parliamentary secretary. In April 1967 Trudeau succeeded Lucien Cardin, battered by a spy scandal, as Pearson's justice minister.

As Trudeau's political star was rising, René Lévesque's was falling. In 1966 Quebec premier Jean Lesage, whose grip on his cabinet and caucus was failing, called an election – which he lost to the Union Nationale led by Daniel Johnson. The Liberals' loss indicated the limit to the Quiet Revolution's penetration of Quebec society. The power and influence of the Roman Catholic Church were declining, one clear sign of which was Quebec's plummeting birthrate: from a high of nearly 4 children per family in 1959, by 1972 it had fallen below the 2.1 per family required to maintain the population size.[55] Yet conservative attitudes continued among the working class and in rural areas. There was also considerable opposition among voluntary organizations to the establishment of a Ministry of Education. The Liberals also lost votes to those who felt the Quiet Revolution had not gone far enough. Two separatist parties ran candidates in the election: the RIN, which won 6 per cent of the vote, and the Ralliement national, which garnered 3 per cent. Lévesque won his seat, but was now moving into the political wilderness as a restless Opposition member of the Legislative Assembly.

Nineteen sixty-seven was a momentous year for Canada. A wave of nationalism swept the land as the country celebrated its centenary by hosting Expo 67 in a Montreal bedecked by the new Canadian flag the federal Parliament had adopted in 1965. The festive mood was suddenly shattered by an ugly event. French president Charles de Gaulle, invited like other world leaders to join the centennial festivities, chose to pee on the Canadians' parade. On 24 July de Gaulle concluded what was choreographed as a triumphal drive along the St Lawrence from Quebec City to Montreal with a speech from the balcony of the Hôtel de Ville, Montreal's city hall. With outstretched arms and in a carefully measured cadence, his voice rising with each phrase, the old French general hollered out to half a million people thronging the square and streets below: *"Vive Montréal! Vive le Québec! Vive le Québec libre!"*[56] René Lévesque was not impressed. For him it was an act of unwelcome benevolent imperialism. A true French Canadian, he considered his people already to be free and in no need of help from the country that had abandoned them three centuries ago. As for Trudeau, his advice was crucial in steeling his diplomatic prime minister to issue a stiff rebuke to the French president.

In the fall of 1967 the country was abuzz with constitutional conversation. At the Conservative Party convention in September, called to challenge Diefenbaker's leadership, there was much discussion of Dief's opposition to the idea of a "two nations" Canada. The convention rejected the "two nations" concept, but elected Robert Stanfield, who supported the idea, as their new leader; Diefenbaker finished in fifth place. Restructuring Canada on dualistic, English-French lines was the central idea in *Égalité ou indépendence*, the book Daniel Johnson had written as his manifesto for becoming Quebec's premier. The not-so-veiled threat of separation coming from the more conservative side of Quebec politics was a key factor in moving Ontario's premier John Robarts to invite his fellow premiers to a November meeting in Toronto. The purpose of the Confederation of Tomorrow Conference would be to see if the premiers could work out a plan of constitutional reform that would keep Quebec in the federation. The decisive moment for René Lévesque came at a policy convention of the Quebec Liberal Party in October at the Château Frontenac in Quebec City. Lévesque laid out his proposal for a sovereign Quebec in a continuing association with Canada. When the convention rejected his proposal by a large majority, Lévesque walked out. He would now sit as an independent in the Legislative Assembly. And what was Pierre Trudeau doing? Well, the new federal justice minister was cooling his constitutional heels, holding back his government from participating in constitutional politics dominated by Quebec nationalists.

In 1968 Pierre Trudeau became Prime Minister of Canada and René Lévesque became leader of a new political party, the Parti Québécois. Lévesque did not waste much time licking his wounds from his defeat at the Liberal Party convention. In November 1967, along with other disaffected Liberals at a meeting in a Dominican monastery in Montreal, he founded the Movement Souveraineté-Association (MNA). Lévesque followed this with publication of *Option-Québec*, fleshing out his sovereignty-association position. Despite its name the MNA harboured out-and-out separatists who had no time for Lévesque's more moderate sovereignty-association idea. At the MNA's first convention, held in April 1968 in the Maurice Richard Arena, Lévesque found an opportunity to purge his movement of its fundamentalist wing. Supporters of François Aquin, who approved de Gaulle's liberation call, brought forward a motion to eliminate public funding for English schools in an independent Quebec. "The Quebec I want," Lévesque countered, "will be pluralist, tolerant, and respectful of minorities." Lévesque won the debate, and established his brand of moderate separatism. In October the MNA and the Ralliement national, at a meeting of their followers in Quebec City's Coliseum, joined together to form the Parti Québécois (PQ). A few days later, Pierre Bourgault, leader of the RIN, the other separatist party, announced he was joining the Parti Québécois.

In those same first four months of 1968 that saw René Lévesque establish his brand and his leadership of the Quebec separatist movement, Pierre Trudeau established his brand of constitutional reform and his leadership of Canadians committed not just to saving the Canadian federation, but to strengthening it. The high level of public interest in Robarts's Confederation for Tomorrow Conference convinced Prime Minister Pearson that the federal government could not stay out of the constitutional game. So he invited the provincial premiers to a constitutional conference in Ottawa in early February 1968. Although Pearson chaired the conference, his justice minister, Trudeau, dominated it. Trudeau made sure that the Ottawa meeting would not focus on the question that had framed the Robarts conference: what does Quebec want? On the eve of the conference, the federal government issued a glossy booklet entitled "Federalism for the Future," which put forward a program of constitutional reform that went well beyond patriation.[57] It argued that reforms designed to unify the country, such as guaranteeing the rights of Canadian citizens and strengthening central institutions of government – in particular, the Senate and the Supreme Court – must take priority over the division of legislative powers. In a dramatic televised exchange with Quebec premier Daniel Johnson, Trudeau tore into the Quebec nationalist perspective: his people, the French Canadians, would secure their future not through an autonomous homeland, but as citizens of a Canada-wide community guaranteeing their language rights from sea to sea.

Trudeau's performance at the February 1968 constitutional conference was dazzling. Canadian federalists had found their hero – and a French Canadian at that! There can be no doubt that it was the talent Trudeau displayed for federalist constitutional leadership – to a huge television audience – that propelled him so rapidly up the greasy pole of politics. Prime Minister Pearson had announced in December that his failing health would force him to retire. At the convention to choose a new Liberal leader in the first week of April 1968, the upstart Trudeau, in just his third year of politics, defeated a star-studded roster of experienced Liberals, winning the leadership on the fifth ballot. Trudeau called a federal election for 25 June, and won it with an impressive majority, with his biggest bloc of seats coming from Quebec. The day before the election, when the annual Jean-Baptiste Day parade in Montreal erupted into violence, with rioters hurling bottles and stones at Trudeau on the reviewing stand, the prime minister held his place and did not flinch. This display of courage surely helped to seal his victory in the election the next day. It was also an occasion for Lévesque to show his decency. He was outraged and more determined than ever to achieve Quebec sovereignty by non-violent, democratic means.[58]

Now at the helm of the federal government, Trudeau pressed ahead with his program of constitutional reform. The instrument for doing this was executive federalism: meetings of federal and provincial political leaders and senior officials. Between February 1968 and June 1971 the federal-provincial meeting had its greatest workout in Canada's history. The late Richard Simeon, the leading scholar of federal-provincial diplomacy, recorded for that period seven "summit" meetings of first ministers, nine meetings of ministerial committees, fourteen of a continuing committee of officials, fifteen of officials' subcommittees, plus innumerable informal interactions.[59] Executive federalism is a form of elite accommodation that theorists of "consociational democracy" have argued is the only way decisions can be made in deeply divided political communities.[60] Political leaders and their senior advisers meeting in private out of the public gaze can make accommodations and compromises with one another that would be impossible to make at the popular level. As we have seen, a capacity for compromise among the elites of the day was crucial in making Confederation possible. Since Confederation the Canadian people have developed a much more democratic ethos. That fact – the democratization of Canadians – would prove a serious obstacle to remaking their Constitution in the late twentieth century.

The prospects of accommodating Quebec looked more promising with the shift in power in Quebec provincial politics that occurred in 1970. The Union Nationale leader, Daniel Johnson, died in 1968, and his lacklustre successor Jean-Jacques Bertrand was no match for the new Liberal leader, Robert Bourassa. In the 1970 Quebec election the Liberals scored their biggest victory since 1931, taking 81 of 108 seats. But that victory was based on only 45 per cent of the popular vote.[61] The PQ won only six seats, but garnered 23 per cent of the popular vote. The distortions of the first-past-the-post electoral system were preventing the true state of public opinion from being represented in the provincial assembly.

Robert Bourassa was a cool pragmatist with a good grounding in economics – he taught public finance at the Université de Montréal and Université Laval. It was his concern about the position of Quebec in a monetary union with Canada that kept him from signing with Lévesque's sovereignty-association movement. Bourassa approached constitutional negotiations not with a nationalist's passion, but with the aim of getting the best possible deal in terms of power and money for his province. The priority for his government was to break away from the patchwork quilt of federal-provincial policies in the field of social policy and secure for Quebec full control over all aspects of social welfare, so that Quebec, with a new generation of university graduates trained in the administrative sciences, could build its own welfare state.

The preoccupation of the federation's two central provinces, Ontario and Quebec, with constitutional reform was not shared by the other provinces. The eastern and western provinces were far more concerned with bread-and-butter economic issues – especially the fiscal side of federalism. Here there were cross-cutting regional interests. Provinces with growing economies and tax bases were pushing to reduce the federal presence in the direct tax field so that they could pursue their own policies with their own money. British Columbia's W.A.C. "Wacky" Bennett pressed for the total withdrawal of the federal government from the personal and corporate income tax fields. At the other end of the country, the Atlantic provinces were anxious for the federal government to retain its fiscal dominance so that it would continue to be in a position to redistribute money from rich provinces to provinces with declining economies. Nor was the one quasi-constitutional policy that the Trudeau government felt it could introduce without a constitutional amendment a consensus builder. This was the Official Languages Act of 1969 establishing English and French as Canada's "official languages." The most important practical consequence of the Act was to require that federal government services be available in all parts of Canada in English and French. This policy had little salience for western premiers with tiny francophone minorities nor, with the exception of New Brunswick, was it of much interest to the Atlantic premiers.

The quiet work of federal-provincial diplomacy came to an abrupt halt in October 1970 when the leaders of the Front de liberation du Québec made their last, climactic attempt to change Canada by terrorist means. For a few days Canada and the world watched the October Crisis play out: the kidnapping of James Cross, the United Kingdom's trade commissioner, from his home in Montreal; the kidnapping and subsequent murder of Pierre Laporte, labour minister in the Bourassa government; the federal parliament's invocation of the War Measures Act; the calling in of the Canadian army by the Quebec premier under the aid-to-the-civil-power provisions of federal legislation; and the departure of Cross's kidnappers to Cuba, having negotiated their freedom in exchange for the British diplomat's release.

During the crisis the police used their powers under the War Measures Act to round up 436 citizens, most of whom had only the vaguest connection with Quebec nationalism and separatism, and imprisoned them without charging them with any offence. This program of preventive detention was a flagrant breach of the fundamental right of *habeus corpus* – the right not to be imprisoned without being charged and brought before a judicial officer – which traces its ancestry back eight centuries to Magna Carta. Nonetheless public opinion polls showed that the Canadian government's actions in the 1970 October Crisis were supported by 87 per cent of Canadians, with no significant difference between English and French.[62]

René Lévesque's response to the October Crisis was equivocal. On the one hand, he was appalled by the violence – particularly the murder of Pierre Laporte, who, as a fellow journalist and colleague in the Quebec Liberal cabinet, had been a close friend for many years. But he joined with *Le Devoir* editor Claude Ryan and other liberally minded Quebecers in speaking out against the Trudeau government's use of force. In the end the October Crisis benefited Lévesque and the PQ by consolidating support among separatist-minded *Québécois* for the non-violent, democratic route to Quebec independence. It took a while for the federal government to accept the legitimacy of trying to gain Quebec's independence through the ballot box. The Macdonald Royal Commission on security and intelligence later revealed that, from 1970 to 1976, the RCMP Security Service's spying and disruptive actions against separatist organizations did not distinguish between those using violence and the Parti Québécois.[63] But in 1976, the Trudeau government put organizations pursuing Quebec's independence by democratic means off-limits for the Security Service, a decision that was later accepted by Progressive Conservative leader Joe Clark. Canada was the first of the federal democracies to have the courage to entrust the unity of the country to the will of its people.

After the October Crisis, the federal government resumed constitutional discussions with a little more vigour. The provincial governments and the general public were getting fed up with the endless succession of first ministers' conferences with nothing to show for them. Justice Minister John Turner was Trudeau's point man, touring the provincial capitals to find ground on which there might be consensus. In the late spring of 1971 there seemed to be enough progress to call the first ministers to a conference in Victoria. Trudeau, the provincial premiers, and their officials bargained away for four long days in British Columbia's legislative chambers. They had hoped that the final day, 17 June, would be a televised session. Instead the first ministers met in private in a marathon session from 10 a.m. to past midnight. They finally emerged with a document, a "Canadian Constitutional Charter, 1971," which came to be known as the Victoria Charter. It was a tentative agreement – indeed a very tentative agreement – that the leaders would bring back to their capitals for formal approval by their cabinets and ratification by their legislatures.

Although the Victoria Charter would soon be consigned to the dustbin of history, its contents are worth recalling for what they tell us about the state of play among the participants in Canada's constitutional politics at this stage of the game. The main point of contention between Quebec and Ottawa, the point that turned out to be the deal-breaker, was the proposed addition to section 94A of the Constitution. It is doubtful that more than a handful of Canadians – then and now – have the slightest idea of what section 94A is all about. Readers might even have forgotten meeting section 94 earlier in this chapter. It is the section added to the Constitution by a 1951 amendment recognizing federal legislative power in the field of pensions, but subordinating the federal power to a paramount provincial power in relation to pensions and supplementary benefits. What Quebec wanted now was to extend section 94A to the whole field of social welfare. That would mean giving the federal Parliament some new powers, such as youth allowances and occupational training, in the social policy field but recognizing the provinces' constitutional paramountcy in all fields of social policy. The social policy clause in the Victoria Charter was a compromise: it did not include Quebec's full list of social policy fields to be subjected to provincial paramountcy and it did not provide fiscal compensation for a province that preferred its own plan to one funded by federal taxpayers. This was not enough to satisfy Quebec's aspiration to be *maîtres chez nous*, but it was too much for the English-Canadian left, which very much wanted Canada's national government to retain its leadership role in building the welfare state.

The Victoria Charter showed how far the federation was from embracing Trudeau's constitutional agenda. In pride of place at the top of the Charter was the recognition of fundamental rights and freedoms – but in a most emaciated form. Only the freedom of thought, conscience, expression, association, and assembly made the cut, and legislatures would be able to abridge these so-called fundamental freedoms in the interests of public safety, order, health, morals, or national security. Thankfully the governments were prepared to guarantee universal suffrage, elections every four years, and annual sessions of their legislatures. English and French would be recognized constitutionally as Canada's official languages, but the treatment of minority language rights was an embarrassing checkerboard. Seven provinces would allow English and French to be used in their legislatures, but the three westernmost provinces were unwilling to allow the use of French in theirs. Only Ottawa, Quebec, New Brunswick, and Newfoundland would commit to having official documents available in both languages. Only New Brunswick and Newfoundland would join Quebec and Manitoba in permitting the use of French in their courts. Nova Scotia joined all four western provinces in refusing to recognize the right of their French-speaking citizens to communicate in their mother tongue with the head offices of provincial ministries and agencies. So much for a bilingual country from coast to coast!

As for strengthening the federation's institutions, the Victoria Charter did not touch the Senate, but made a concession to the provincial anxiety about the Supreme Court of Canada's centralizing tendencies. A cumbersome set of procedures for giving provincial governments some input in the selection of judges was agreed to, plus a smidgeon of Quebec's special status: a constitutional guarantee that three of the Supreme Court's nine justices be from Quebec and that these three form the majority in cases involving Quebec's distinctive civil law. The Charter also contained an attempt to capture the social welfare aspect of Canadian federalism in a pledge on the part of both levels of government to promote "equality of opportunity and well-being for all individuals in Canada" and to reduce regional disparities. There was not yet a consensus on fiscal equalization – British Columbia, in particular, was not on board – but we were getting closer.

Finally, there was agreement on a formula for amending the Constitution in Canada. Provincial unanimity would not be required for any amendment. The general formula for amending provisions concerning the entire federation would be approval by the federal Parliament, plus provinces with 25 per cent or more of the population (assuring Ontario and Quebec a veto even if Quebec's population later declined below that level), at least two of Atlantic Canada's four provinces, and at least two of the four western provinces with 50 per cent of western Canada's population (which came close to giving British Columbia a veto). Also included was the usual provision for amendments concerning one or more but not all provinces to be made by Ottawa and the provinces concerned. This was the most flexible amending formula that ever won federal-provincial approval. This probably reflects the fact that, at this point in the constitutional odyssey, a radical Quebec seeking constitutional changes was more interested in constitutional change than in protecting the powers it already had.

On returning to Quebec City, Robert Bourassa was met with a storm of criticism. Newspaper advertisements proclaimed that accepting the Victoria Charter would return Quebec to the days of conscription: "the answer must be NO to Ottawa's ultimatum ... There must be a general mobilization of the people of Quebec."[64] Bourassa got the message. On 22 June, after an all-night meeting of his cabinet, he telephoned Trudeau to say that his government had rejected the Victoria Charter. Claude Ryan, who would later succeed Bourassa as Liberal Party leader, claimed that Bourassa's *non* professed the profound convictions of the whole Quebec people.[65] Ryan surely overstated the negative consensus in Quebec, but the Bourassa government's rejection was enough to kill the Victoria Charter. At this point in Canada's odyssey, the federal government recognized that it should not proceed with a major constitutional change that was opposed by the Government of Quebec.

Thus ended the first round of what I refer to as "mega constitutional politics."[66] Constitutional democracies are constantly engaged in debating constitutional issues, but this normal kind of constitutional politics concerns one or two specific issues. Constitutional politics reaches the mega level when what is at issue is a fundamental remake of crucial parts of the Constitution. At that level, more important than the merits of specific constitutional proposals is a fundamental question about the nature of the political community on which the Constitution is based. The Victoria Charter was rejected in Quebec because it did not provide strong enough recognition of the province's special status as a homeland of a founding people. It did not provide that recognition because such a view of Canada was not shared by the political leaders

of English-speaking Canada or by francophone federalists such as
Pierre Trudeau.

Constitutional politics at the mega level tends to touch citizens' sense
of identity and self-worth. That is why it is an exceptionally emotional
and intense kind of politics. If Quebec is recognized as a special province with a special status in Confederation and not a province like the
rest, the implication for non-Quebecers is that they and their province
are not special. Canadians with a deep understanding of their country's
history might be able to embrace Quebec's special status. After all, there
are elements of it in the founding Constitution and, as we have seen,
Quebec nationalism was accommodated in building the post-war
Canadian welfare state by arrangements that gave the province more
special status. But the new immigrants flowing into Canada at this time
were basically ignorant of this history. Many of them deeply resented
the B & B Commission's dualist vision of Canada. Why, they asked,
should Canada's French minority be privileged over other ethnic minorities? Not that the older part of English-speaking Canada was better
versed in Quebec's history or more committed to recognizing Quebec as
French Canada's homeland. English-speaking Canadians were inclined
to join with Trudeau in embracing an inclusive Canadian nationalism
that favoured no ethnic minority. Differences of the kind that underlie
mega constitutional politics are about identity and status and vision,
matters that are more difficult to resolve than issues of power or money.
That is why mega constitutional politics is the politics of frustration: the
very divisions of the political community that fuel constitutional politics of this intensity make consensual resolution just about impossible.

After the debacle of the Victoria Charter, neither the Trudeau government nor Canadians in general were in a hurry to return to the constitutional table. The government had learned that the constitutional
politics in which it had just engaged tended to monopolize the public
agenda and divert attention away from all other matters. Canada was
facing serious economic issues in the early seventies that demanded the
government's attention. A measure of the public's lack of interest in
constitutional issues was the deafening silence that greeted the 1972
report of the Special Joint Committee of the Senate and House of
Commons on the Constitution of Canada.[67] The Molgat-MacGuigan
Committee – named after its chairs Senator Gildas Molgat and MP
Mark MacGuigan – was the country's first effort at popular participation in constitution-making. The committee toured the country, holding
meetings in 47 cities attended by 13,000 Canadians and receiving

submissions from 1,486 witnesses. The parliamentarians' conclusion was that "Canadians now want a new constitution." Really?

Although the Molgat-MacGuigan report was yet another grand constitutional review destined for the dustbin of history, there is one good reason to take notice of it. Buried in the report in very uncertain language was a reference to Canada's Indigenous peoples, who up until this point had been entirely left out of Canada's constitutional discussions. The report acknowledged that the federal government's plan simply to extend the rights of Canadian citizens to individuals with a native background might not be working. The report observed that an alternative approach, viewing "the native peoples as collectivities ... does appear preferable to many of the native peoples themselves." The report certainly got that point right. Aboriginal Canada's voice was now about to get a hearing in Canada's constitutional politics.

Chapter 12

Aboriginal Peoples Get a Hearing

In 1974 George Manuel, in collaboration with Michael Posluns, published *The Fourth World: An Indian Reality*.[1] George Manuel was a former chief of the Neskonlith band of the Shuswap nation in the interior of British Columbia. At the time of writing his book he was the president of the National Indian Brotherhood. Michael Posluns, a freelance broadcaster and writer, was reporting for the magazine *Akwesasne Notes* on Indigenous peoples' concerns throughout Europe and North America. The collaboration of these two men, one Aboriginal and the other non-Aboriginal, in writing an insightful account of George Manuel's personal story and the story of native peoples in Canada, in a book published by a mainstream publisher, was indicative of the key change taking place in the political situation of Aboriginal peoples. They were beginning to be heard and to be a presence in the white man's political space.

To show how difficult it had been in the past, Manuel tells us about the first native person's effort to get a hearing in the Canadian Parliament. In 1926 Andrew Paull, representing the Allied Tribes of British Columbia, appeared before a Joint Parliamentary Committee on Indian Affairs. Paull asked the committee to consider how the Indian nations in British Columbia could have their claim to native title heard by Canada's highest court, the Judicial Committee of the Privy Council. When Howard Bostock, the Senate speaker, suggested that the way to begin was to let the Indians present their case, he was cut off by Indian Affairs Minister Henry Stevens, who thought the committee should hear first from his deputy minister, Duncan Campbell Scott. Scott gave a lengthy account of how well the Indians were being treated in British Columbia, and cautioned the committee that pursuing their claim to native title in the courts might be to the Indians' disadvantage. When

Scott was finished, Andrew Paull was given twenty minutes to deal with the question of Aboriginal title. He did his best, but in the end the committee concluded that, "the petitioners have not established any claim to the lands of British Columbia based on aboriginal title or other title."[2] In March 1927, to make sure that Indian tribes did not resort to the courts to test their claim, Parliament amended the Indian Act to make it a criminal offence to raise funds for the purpose of pressing any Indian claim.

After the Second World War, Aboriginal peoples began to have more success in getting a hearing in Canadian institutions and media. A key reason for this was that large numbers of native people developed the skills needed to defend and advance their interests in the dominant society. In the residential schools many Indians, Inuit, and Métis had learned to read and write and communicate effectively in English. Acquiring these communicative skills would prove to be beneficial to native people in defending and advancing their interests – although it is a tragedy that so much unnecessary pain and suffering was experienced in obtaining this benefit. Throughout the colonized world, mastering the colonizers' political technologies should be seen as "the ironic wages of success in the decolonising struggle."[3] If you cannot beat the colonizers on the battlefield, then you will have to become adept in dealing with them through their institutions, including their courts. That was the lesson George Manual's generation had imbibed. And it is an ironic lesson, because operating effectively in the colonizers' political and legal institutions is bound to involve some assimilation into their culture.

To be effective George Manuel and other Aboriginal leaders of his generation needed to learn much more than the reading, writing, and arithmetic taught at the residential schools. Learning how to form organizations extending beyond your home community, how to lobby government, how to get your message heard in print and electronic media, how to use the courts to advance your political agenda – none of that kind of learning went on in residential schools. George Manuel's book gives a fascinating account of how he developed these skills – becoming chummy with the secretary of the local chamber of commerce, travelling around British Columbia with a native defence lawyer, serving as a community development officer in an Indian community, sparking enough media attention to provoke a cabinet minister's visit to the community and a commitment to build new houses on the reserve. All of this went into preparing him for the leadership role he took on as president of the National Indian Brotherhood (precursor of the Assembly of First Nations) and a Canadian Aboriginal ambassador to the world.

The new capability of Aboriginal leaders to function effectively in the white man's political world would have made little difference had there not been an ideological shift among the European colonizers. The shift was basically a wavering of belief in white Europeans' cultural and racial superiority, a belief that was the justifying rationale of European imperialism. The experience of the war had much to do with this change. The horrors inflicted on the world by Nazis and Fascists made it difficult to sustain the belief that white Europeans were the bearers of a superior civilization. The horrors of the Holocaust showed what racial bigotry could lead to, and prompted a search for less ethnocentric, more universal principles on which a world order could be based. The first product of that search was the Universal Declaration of Human Rights adopted by the United Nations in 1948. Before that, the first article of the United Nations Charter pledged "respect for the principle of equal rights and self-determination of peoples."[4]

Canada was front and centre in these international developments. As we saw in the last chapter, the Universal Declaration of Human Rights triggered the birth of a human rights movement in post-war Canada. Even if Canadian governments did not connect the anti-racist language and commitment to universalism in those UN documents – in particular, the reference to the self-determination of peoples – to Aboriginal peoples, their ethical tone began to have an important influence on Canada's relations with them. It was now more difficult to shut the door on Aboriginal people when their representatives appeared in the country's political space with a message that the representatives of non-Aboriginal Canadians did not want to hear. Articulate native leaders, like George Manuel, critical of Canada's treatment of their people, could not just be shoved aside as misguided troublemakers.

If Canada's government did not connect the dots between the UN's fostering of decolonization in the Third World and the situation of Aboriginal peoples in the First World, Canada's Aboriginal leaders certainly did – and none more than George Manuel. It was an African diplomat in Canada who first gave Manuel the idea that Aboriginal people are a Fourth World within developed countries with experience that has many parallels with colonialism in the Third World.[5] In the early 1970s Manuel visited Tanzania as part of a Canadian government delegation. A few months before the trip, the Tanzanian high commissioner to

Canada addressed the General Assembly of the National Indian Brotherhood. George Manuel recounts that the high commissioner "did not belabour the evils of colonialism ... There was no need to tell fifty-six Indian leaders what was wrong with someone else running your life."[6] In Tanzania he had an opportunity to spend some time with President Julius Nyerere, and was impressed by his determination to use his people's independence to build a society that was not "a darker imitation of the world of their colonial masters."[7]

Manuel's first trip out of North America was as a member of a parliamentary delegation to New Zealand and Australia in 1971. George was struck by the contrast between the progress the Maori had made in New Zealand in asserting their treaty rights and becoming a political force in New Zealand life and the situation of the Aborigines in Australia, whom he could not meet without a government official being present. What Manuel learned from this trip was the essence of a new Indigenous international movement. By visiting Indigenous peoples in other counties and on other continents, Indigenous leaders could get ideas about what could be done to get out from under the colonialism inflicted on them. Working together internationally would help to compensate for their small numbers in the countries where they found themselves embedded. Modern technology was a great boon to Indigenous internationalism. Jet travel, long-distance telephone communication, and later the Internet made it possible for Indigenous peoples around the world, numbering in the millions, to work together as never before to redress their situation.

Canadian governments and the great majority of Canadian citizens did not view Aboriginal peoples through the colonization/decolonization lens. Many do not see them through that lens today. Prime Minister Stephen Harper once pronounced that Canada has never had any colonies. Certainly decolonization of the Fourth World cannot have the same outcome as in the Third World: European colonization of the Third World ended with the physical withdrawal of the imperial rulers, who were never more than a tiny minority, and full legal independence for the formerly colonized society. Decolonization for Aboriginal peoples cannot have a similar ending. The colonizing power, the dominant settler society, has become the great majority in the countries of Aboriginal peoples, and it is not about to depart. Chief Justice Antonio Lamer surely spoke for all non-Aboriginal Canadians when he wrote, in the Supreme Court of Canada's decision recognizing Aboriginal title, "We are all here to stay."[8] That said, Aboriginal peoples have had the same experience as the colonized peoples of the Third World in having the rule of an alien power imposed on them and their lands, and like those Third World peoples they would like to recover responsibility for governing their societies and the lands that sustain them. Aboriginal self-government and control of traditional lands cannot go as far as Third World decolonization because Aboriginal peoples must share the land and its resources with the settler society. Aboriginal governments also must operate in harmony with federal, provincial, territorial, and municipal governments, and Aboriginal people must share citizenship with all Canadians. That is why Aboriginal decolonization, ideologically, is more challenging than Third World decolonization. There is no precise formula for working out how far Aboriginal self-government and control of homelands can go or should go. For Canada and many other countries around the world, it remains a work in progress

But in Canada, for the first quarter-century after the Second World War, decolonization was not on the agenda of improving relations with native peoples. Indeed, Canada's governments and citizens did not yet recognize Aboriginal peoples as enduring *political* societies within Canada. The reform on offer was essentially a policy of extending the Canadian welfare state and the benefits of Canadian citizenship to individual native people.

Interest in human rights and the mood of egalitarianism unleashed by the founding of the United Nations, combined with recognition of the remarkable contribution of Indian servicemen to Canada's war effort, led to growing public interest in Indian affairs at the end of the Second World War. The Inuit were still pretty much out of sight on the northern frontier, and the Métis, in the urban and rural places where they lived, were not yet visible as a "nation within." In non-Aboriginal Canada unease about the discriminatory aspects of the Indian Act and the unsatisfactory conditions on Indian reserves gave rise to a growing awareness that the policy pursued by government for three-quarters of a century was a failure. Over time the Indians were supposed to leave the reserves and disappear into the general population as civilized Canadians. But 80 per cent of status Indians remained on reserves. Fewer deaths in childbirth and enhanced resistance to European diseases meant reserve populations were growing while Indian Act policies shrunk reserve lands. And the Indians retained a strong sense of their tribal identity, despite the strenuous efforts to destroy it.

This was the context for establishing a Joint Senate and House of Commons Committee to examine the administration of Indian affairs in 1946. From the outset there was a disconnect between the approach to policy reform favoured by parliamentarians and the message they heard from First Nations representatives. For the MPs, senators, and department officials, the aim was to speed up the transition of Indians from their condition of wardship on reserves to citizenship in mainstream Canada. The Indian problem would be solved by the disappearance of the Indians. For Indians the priority was to get out from under the rule of Ottawa bureaucrats, retain their distinct historic identities, and return to a nation-to-nation treaty relationship. This disconnect would remain through the various joint parliamentary committees that worked on "the Indian problem" right up to 1969, when Indians' rejection of the Trudeau government's policy reform led to Aboriginal peoples' setting the reform agenda.

The 1946 joint parliamentary committee began with a repeat of the 1926 episode recounted earlier. The committee decided it wanted to begin by hearing from government officials and experts, but was willing to make an exception and hear what the redoubtable Andrew Paull had to say. Paull's message had basically not changed from his submission in 1926. He urged the committee to make Indian self-government its priority and to "give Indians a greater control over their own lives, free of government interference."[9] A motion to permit five Indian observers from across Canada to monitor the committee was defeated. Many Indian bands and associations who wanted to be heard were denied funding to appear in Ottawa – although some did make an appearance. Others had to be content with writing letters. Although the views presented to the committee included many who pushed for honouring treaties – examining treaty obligations was at the top of the committee's agenda – and restoring nation-to-nation relations, others focused not on ending the Indian Act, but on reforming it. Indeed the main result of this first post-war consideration of the "Indian problem" was to move ahead with Indian Act reform.

The federal government signalled where it intended reform to go by linking Indian policy to its new emphasis on Canadian citizenship. Following the passage of the Canadian Citizenship Act in 1946, Indian Affairs was moved into the Department of Citizenship and Immigration. In 1950 Citizenship Minister Walter Harris introduced Bill 267, stating that its purpose was "the integration of the Indians into the general life and economy of the country."[10] The bill was withdrawn when Indians and Opposition MPs complained about going ahead with the legislation without any consultations with Indians. The next year, in consultation with nineteen Indian representatives from various parts of the country, the government undertook a clause-by-clause review of the Indian Act. For the first time in Canadian history, Indians were consulted on legislation affecting them.

The result of the 1951 revision has been characterized as returning the Indian Act closer to its original 1876 version. Some of the coercive elements added over the years were removed. These included the prohibition of traditional dances and potlatch ceremonies and the criminalizing of raising money to litigate land claims. Although the powers of the minister and federal government to govern Indian bands were reduced, a formidable array remained, including making regulations in areas otherwise covered by band council by-laws. Ottawa retained the odious power to permit a province, municipality, or local authority to expropriate reserve land without band consent. Ottawa also retained its control over band membership – in effect, its power to define who could be an Indian. The reference to "Indian blood" was replaced by a registration system "with a strong bias in favour of descent through the male line."[11] The Act's male bias remained – writ large. Although the oxymoronic process of forced enfranchisement was made more difficult for Indian men, under a new "double mother" provision a child would lose Indian status and have to move off the reserve if his or her mother and grandmother had obtained their own status through marriage. Giving women the vote in band elections was scant compensation for this discriminatory measure.

The 1951 revision also introduced a new provision to the Act. Section 88 would for the first time make provincial laws "of general application" apply to Indians in the province. Provinces could not pass laws specifically aimed at Indians, but so long as a provincial law did not conflict with treaties or a federal law relating to Indians, including the Indian Act, provincial laws would apply to Indians. Indians found this innovation very troubling. It seemed designed to take Canada in the same direction as the United States, where a "termination" policy was gathering support in Congress.[12] The US policy aimed at terminating Indian reservations and relocating their population to cities. In part termination was a reaction to what Republicans considered to be the overspending of Roosevelt's New Deal. When "termination" was completed, there would no longer be a need for the Bureau of Indian Affairs in Washington and its offices across the country. Indians would disappear into the general population and the final solution of the "Indian problem" would be achieved. Canadian Indians were right in fearing that the new section of the Indian Act was the cutting edge of a policy aimed at reaching a similar final solution in Canada. The one thing they were intent on not losing was their distinct identity. That common aspiration was the key to the absence of any call – even among more nationalist leaders – for the termination of the Indian Act.

It was under John Diefenbaker's watch that an important change was made in the status of Canada's Indians. Diefenbaker completed what Sir John A. Macdonald had begun: in 1960, status Indians were given the right to vote in federal elections. Diefenbaker also appointed James Gladstone, a Cree from the Blood reserve in Alberta, to the Senate – the first Aboriginal person to sit in Parliament. Status Indians had been given the option to vote in 1950, but only on condition that they give up the tax exemption they enjoyed on-reserve. Now this condition of their federal enfranchisement was removed. Inuit, Métis, and non-status Indians had never been denied voting rights, but most provinces had followed Ottawa in denying status Indians the vote. Beginning in 1949 with British Columbia and ending with Quebec in 1969, the provinces extended the franchise to Indians. Nova Scotia had never denied status Indians the vote, and Newfoundland did not have status Indians until the federal government recognized the Miawpukek band of Conne River in 1984.[13] For many First Nations people, being able to vote in federal and provincial elections, like being granted Canadian citizenship, was problematic. "Enfranchisement," a word that for more than a century meant giving up one's Indian identity, could hardly be a welcoming concept. At a time when there was no recognition of their own nations, Canadian citizenship and enfranchisement implied that the political destiny of Indian people was meant to be nothing less and nothing more than to be citizens of Canada. That was a destiny few Indians could accept, then or now.

When a third joint parliamentary committee, sitting from 1959 to 1961, came up with few ideas on how to advance the reform agenda, the government turned to social scientists for some answers. The social sciences were just coming into their own at Canadian universities, so there was a significant talent pool from which to draw. In 1965 Indian Affairs officials commissioned Harry Hawthorn, a New Zealander who had had close contact with Maori before joining the University of British Columbia as its first professor of anthropology, to organize a team of social scientists to conduct a survey of Indians in all parts of Canada. Hawthorn's team numbered fifty-two and included scholars such as Alan Cairns in political science, Stuart Jamieson in economics, and

Kenneth Lysyk in constitutional law, who were becoming leaders in their disciplines. The first of two Hawthorn reports, published in 1966 after first being leaked to the *Globe and Mail*, had the biggest impact.[14] It reported the deplorable living conditions on reserves all across the country, and focused on economic development of Indian communities and enhancement of the skills needed for participation in the mainstream economy as policy priorities. But these liberally minded academics did not favour an assimilationist final solution. Remaining an Indian, holding on to one's historic identity, is a matter of choice that should be respected. Everything possible should be done to ensure that Indians have equality of opportunity in the mainstream society but the rights of Indians as "charter members of the Canadian community" should be respected.[15] Indians should be treated as "citizens plus."[16]

The Hawthorn report brought to the attention of the Canadian public as never before, in stark, unsentimental terms, the harsh living conditions of Indians on- and off-reserve. The social scientists documented double-digit percentage gaps between Indians and mainstream Canada in everything from employment and school completion rates to decent housing and life expectancy. They saw improving Indians' access to provincial government services as the main path forward. The report showed that Indian communities were not self-governing, but administered largely by Ottawa. It supported a form of self-government that would amount to that of provincial municipalities, with powers devolved on them by senior levels of government. These scholarly investigators did not see treaties as the basis of the Amerindian nations' relationship with Canada. For them, as for virtually all non-Aboriginal Canadians, section 91(24) of the BNA Act, which made Indians and their lands a matter of exclusive federal jurisdiction, defined the constitutional status of Indians. The academics' analysis was strongly of the view that this exclusive federal power left plenty of room for provinces to participate in providing services to Indians.

While the Hawthorn researchers were doing their work, Indian policymakers and policy-takers were getting caught up in a swirl of social activism. "Doing your own thing" and "citizen participation" were the popular nostrums of the day, and they were certainly having an affect on Indian Affairs in Ottawa, which by 1966 was now in its own Department of Indian Affairs and Northern Development (DIAND). Reserve communities were being animated by Ottawa-"trained" community development officers, some of whom, like George Manuel, were Indians themselves. It was frustrating when community development officers ran up against the conflict between community aspirations and the limited outlook of the established bureaucracy in Ottawa.

The long-simmering conflict between the federal government and Indians about the direction reform should take came quickly to a head once the Trudeau Liberals were in power. Pierre Trudeau brought to government an optimistic energy that saw no issue as too difficult to solve. The "Indian problem" had been around for a long time. By Trudeau's time it had become a policy issue attracting a good deal of attention in the media and in Parliament. It was time that the problem got some fresh thinking and a solution.

The "Indian problem" was not the only thing Trudeau would fix; he and his closest advisers would also fix government by making it more efficient and disciplined. This would be done by strengthening the levers of control at the centre of government – the Prime Minister's Office (PMO) and the Privy Council Office (PCO).[17] The Trudeau government saw a nearly fourfold increase in PMO personnel, making it by far the largest prime minister's office in the Westminster world. This enlarged PMO would be staffed not by experienced public servants, but by "political staffers," mostly young people with skills in marketing and advertising, and devoted to the leader and the political success of his government. The PCO would continue as the administrative headquarters of government, staffed mostly by senior civil servants, but under Trudeau the PCO's policy-making role was enhanced and closely harnessed to the PMO. These two central agencies, one political and the other governmental, both reporting to the prime minister, would play a major role in coming up with a new federal Indian policy.

In Trudeau's first year of government, the "Indian problem" was one of his most important files. He left the policy-making work to his advisers in the PMO and PCO and the ministers and staff in Indian Affairs, but the policy they eventually would come up with was bound to be influenced by Trudeau's thinking and the larger context of the Canadian political scene at the time. As we saw in the last chapter, when he took office Trudeau was fully engaged in a struggle to divert constitutional change in Canada from the divisive path of nationalism and separatism favoured by Quebec governments. His efforts in that arena were bound to spill over into his government's handling of the Indian file. Trudeau's logical cast of mind inclined him to disregard history in making contemporary policy. As Sally Weaver put it, "[b]asically, Trudeau did not believe that the future should be fettered to the chains of the past."[18] Indian peoples politically mobilized to seek redress of historical injustices to their nations likely would not welcome a policy in tune with Trudeau's anti-nationalist, anti-historical point of view.

From the beginning policy-making on the Indian file was caught up in a struggle between DIAND and members of the PCO and PMO. It was also caught up in a struggle between two ministers. Trudeau gave the Indian Affairs portfolio to Jean Chrétien, a thirty-four-year-old lawyer from Shawinigan Falls. It was Chrétien's first major portfolio. At the same time he appointed Robert Andras, a northern Ontario businessman and a relatively new MP, to be "minister without portfolio" in Indian Affairs. Ministers without portfolio were a Trudeau innovation intended to bring extra cabinet heft to departments taking on a major policy challenge. Andras attached himself closely to the process of consulting with Indians on Indian Act reform, a process inherited from the Pearson government. In all, between July 1968 and May 1969, eighteen well-publicized public meetings co-chaired by a departmental official and an Indian delegate were held in different cities across the country. Discussion was allowed to deviate from the Indian Act reform agenda, which it often did, getting into land claims and honouring treaties. Chrétien opened the first consultation meeting in Yellowknife, heralding it as "an attempt at consultative democracy."[19] Although departmental responsibilities prevented Chrétien from attending most meetings, Andras stuck with the process and became a strong advocate of a consultative policy-making process.

Inside government, in a process totally detached from the public consultations on the outside, the real policy-making was taking place. Chrétien and his deputy minister, John A. MacDonald, were much involved in this, interacting with key people in the PMO and PCO. The department had the expertise and the political responsibility, the PCO and, even more, the PMO had new ideas and day-to-day contact with the prime minister. The department and the centre agreed with the Hawthorn report's emphasis on equality of opportunity for Indians in the mainstream economy and greater access to provincial services. Differences arose over the "plus" in Hawthorn's "citizens plus" formula. For Indian Affairs officials and their minister, the special rights and benefits of Indians had to include a process for dealing with their treaty and land rights claims. Chrétien had made a strong public commitment to going ahead with the much-mooted idea of an Indian claims commission. For him and his departmental advisers, the grievances to be dealt with by such a commission would include government's failure to comply with specific terms of treaties, such as providing reserve lands and paying annuities. But they would also include the claims of First Nations that had never signed so-called land cession treaties. These claims were based on the belief that Aboriginal title allowed them to enter into treaties on the terms and conditions of sharing their lands with Canada.

Recognizing the legitimacy of the grievance of Indian peoples who had not entered into land treaties with Britain or Canada was the crucial underlying constitutional difference between the Trudeau government and the Indian peoples – the nations within. The legal foundation of the Indians' position was the concept of Aboriginal title. This concept is embedded in 1763 Royal Proclamation, which, as we saw in Chapter 3, recognizes the Indian nations' ownership of their territories. Under British law, Aboriginal title could be "extinguished" through an agreement ceding or selling land to the Crown or, if necessary, by force, but until it is "extinguished" it exists as a legally enforceable right. Recognition of native peoples' land ownership continues under Canadian law so long as it is not rescinded by Parliament, and it is the basis of a right – an Aboriginal right – that only peoples indigenous to Canada possess. A policy that recognized Aboriginal title would amount to Indians' being Canadian citizens with a very big plus.

At the time the Trudeau government was wrestling with Indian policy, there was virtually no understanding of Aboriginal title within the Government of Canada. The Royal Proclamation was buried in the distant past. Even those who did know about it were not at all sure whether it applied to the whole country. A law case initiated in 1967 by the Nisga'a nation in northwest British Columbia claiming that their native title had never been extinguished was about to change all that. The trial of the Nisga'a claim opened in the Supreme Court of British Columbia in April 1969, just as the Trudeau government's Indian policy initiative was coming to fruition.[20] It is the Supreme Court of Canada's final decision in this case four years later, not Trudeau's policy, that would set the course for a fundamental change of direction in Canada's Aboriginal policy.

Although the Nisga'a lawsuit, important as it would turn out to be, was virtually ignored by the national media, a lot of noise was being made about the Indian issue by Indian leaders and their white supporters in various public meetings. Besides the consultation meetings organized by Indian Affairs, universities were hosting conferences and discussions. A notable one was held at York University's Glendon College in October 1968. The Toronto *Telegram*'s headline – "Red power

Nisga'a Pts'aan Raising: Nisga'a chiefs, elders, matriarchs, youth, and guests celebrate the raising of a Pts'aan (totem pole) in Gitwinksihlkw. Nisga'a Lisims Government / Gary Fiegehen

whoops it up" – catches the passion and excitement of the occasion.[21] The villain of the conference was the Department of Indian Affairs and Northern Development, whose deputy minister, John A. Macdonald, was constantly hissed and booed. Walter Rudnicki, a Trudeau appointee to the PCO, and Robert Andras did not come to the department's defence. Instead they aligned themselves with speakers calling for a more collaborative policy-making approach and the need to get Indians out from under the department's rule. The star of the show was Harold Cardinal, twenty-three-year-old president of the Alberta Indian Association. Cardinal hammered the department and laid down the essential condition for a policy reform that could have the consent of Indians: "Firstly, the Canadian Government will have to commit itself morally, philosophically and legislatively to honouring *fully* its agreements under Treaties signed with Indians, or where Treaties do not apply, to recognize and accept the *aboriginal* rights of these people."[22] The Christmas season was the occasion of two gala events in the nation's capital that drew attention to the Indian issue. At a human rights conference, Harold Cardinal made much the same speech he gave at Glendon College. In an elegant ballroom setting, the Indian Brotherhood broke bread with Prime Minister Trudeau. This event, managed by the PMO's Jim Davey, produced mostly polite words in the holiday spirit. This did not fool George Manuel and his colleagues, who feared something was brewing inside government that they would not like.

The Indian leaders were certainly right about that. The key idea that was now driving policy-making within government was equality, full equality – meaning ending any negative discrimination against Indians, but also any positive discrimination that gave Indians rights or benefits that other Canadians did not have. In a nutshell, Indians were to be treated the same as any other disadvantaged ethnic minority. This focus had a simplicity about it that was attractive to the spin doctors in the PMO. One victim of simplicity was any effort to produce an Aboriginal policy that would embrace the Inuit and Métis as well as Indians, something very much favoured by Gordon Robertson in the PCO, but with too many complexities to survive Jim Davey's razor in the PMO. A focus on equality not only had the merit of simplicity; it was very much a core ingredient of the prime minister's brand.

It took a while for Indian Affairs to change direction from consultative Indian Act reform and come on board with the PMO's full-equality approach, but in the end they did. In February 1969 cabinet approved "full participatory non-discrimination" for Indian people in Canada as the key aim of the new policy.[23] In effect this was a termination policy: a policy for terminating any recognition of Indians (or their historic nations) as a special part of Canada's population. In March the policy process was put in the hands of a PCO-PMO task force, and the decision was taken to produce a White Paper, rather than a fully worked out policy. White Papers have a range of uses, but generally they are policy probes aimed at stimulating public discussion of the direction government is seriously considering taking.

Jean Chrétien presented the White Paper to the House of Commons on 25 June 1969.[24] It was a glossy, ten-page production, painstakingly wordsmithed to sound simple – almost obvious – and decent. Instead of using "termination" as the catchword for the policy, the paper used "separation." Separation was bad: the separate legal status of Indians and the policies flowing from it have "kept the Indian people apart from and behind other Canadians."[25] A page later, the paper declared: "We can no longer perpetuate the separation of Canadians."[26] The connection with the politics of national unity was clear. Ending the separation of Indians would be accomplished by four bold measures: repeal of the Indian Act, winding up the Department of Indian Affairs, removing Parliament's power in relation to Indians from the Constitution, and giving Indians ownership of their reserve lands. The goal was "the full and equal participation of Indians in the cultural, social, economic and political life of Canada."[27] The services that Ottawa had been providing Indians – education, health, welfare, housing, and so on – would now be provided by the provinces just as they are to other citizens. To facilitate the transfer of responsibility, Ottawa would hand over all the funds it was currently spending on Indians, and work out equitable arrangements with the provinces "to ensure that services could be provided in full measure commensurate with the needs."[28] It would also provide a substantial economic development fund for Indian communities. And what about the "plus," the extra bit that Indian citizens would get? Well, Indians, just like other ethnic minorities, would be encouraged to preserve and develop the "folklore, art forms and concepts of community life"[29] so crucial to their distinct identity. In addition the government was committed to appointing a commissioner, in consultation with Indian representatives, who "will inquire into and report" upon how claims "arising in respect of the performance of the terms of treaties"[30] may be adjudicated. The government saw this commitment not as recognition of Indians' having special rights, but simply as a matter of meeting its contractual legal obligations.

The initial reaction to the White Paper in the House of Commons and the media was fairly positive. Two provincial premiers, Ontario's John Robarts and Saskatchewan's Ross Thatcher, were quick to give it a thumbs-up. But the Indians who had gathered in Ottawa caucused on 26 June and produced a press release expressing firm and measured rejection. Quickly, in the days following, the volume of Indian rejection became louder and its tone angrier. The National Indian Brotherhood declared that the White Paper would lead to "the destruction of a Nation of People by legislation and cultural genocide."[31] As the Indian rejection set in, federal and provincial politicians shut up – they had no stomach for forcing policy down Indians' throats.

It took a year for the Trudeau government to withdraw the White Paper officially. Towards the end of 1969, Harold Cardinal published his *Unjust Society*, which immediately became a manifesto for rejecting the White Paper's proposals.[32] In June 1970 Indian leaders gathered in Ottawa to present a "Red Paper" to the Trudeau government. The meeting of Indian leaders with the full cabinet in the Railway Committee Room in the Parliament buildings, with many of the Indians in full regalia, was a historic and colourful occasion. Cardinal's statement to the cabinet, as so many times before, stressed that a new Indian-government relationship was contingent on recognizing treaty and Aboriginal rights. The Red Paper was respectful and constructive. It welcomed support for education and economic development. The Indians were prepared to examine the federal proposal to hand over control of their land to Indian peoples, but not by accepting that Indian lands would be subject to Canadian property concepts. They proposed a review of the Indian Act, not its abolition. And whatever was done must be done through consultative mechanisms. In response, Trudeau was statesmanlike and – this might surprise readers – somewhat humbled. He admitted that "we were very naïve ...We had perhaps the prejudices of small 'l' liberals and white men at that who thought that equality meant the same law for everybody." Back in August 1969, when he was defending the White Paper to a Vancouver audience, Trudeau had said that, "[w]e can't recognize aboriginal rights because no society can be built on historical might-have-beens." Now he seemed to be having second thoughts, which the Supreme Court of Canada would soon help him crystallize. On 17 March 1971 Jean Chrétien, in a speech at Queen's University, announced that the Government of Canada did not intend to force progress along the lines of the White Paper.

The withdrawal of the White Paper was the first political victory of native people in Canada since the resumption of treaty-making after Confederation. That victory – convincing Canada to make treaties before proceeding with western settlement – was, as we saw in Chapter 8, based more on the military power of the native tribes in western Canada than on the Canadian government's accepting the legal and moral reasons for treaty-making. It would be nice to record that, a century later, the government's decision to withdraw the White Paper was based on agreement about the legal and ethical foundations of treaty-making. But at this point in the odyssey, that cannot be said. What can be said is that, within Canada's political and societal elites, there was a growing recognition that Indians are more than a disadvantaged ethnic minority – that they are members of long-standing *political* societies that are here

to stay. That is the essence of the Indians' victory in 1969. Had they accepted the White Paper, they would have consented to the settlers'
completing the conquest and eliminating Canada's Aboriginal pillar.

The nationalism that mobilized Indians to reject the White Paper had
its counterpart in other countries where British settlers had come to
dominate Indigenous peoples. By the late 1960s Indigenous peoples in
all three of these countries – Australia, New Zealand, and the United
States – were using the political techniques of modern western democracies to bring their grievances before settler majorities. Their grievances, as in Canada, focused on land rights and treaties. South of the
border, the occupation of Alcatraz Island in 1969 by Indian activists was
followed by the occupation of lands and buildings all over the country.
The most spectacular event by far was the "Trail of Broken Treaties
Caravan" organized in 1972 by the American Indian Movement (AIM).
The caravan was four miles long by the time it culminated in the occupation of the Bureau of Indian Affairs building in the middle of Washington, DC. At the top of AIM's agenda was a request that Congress
restore the treaty process and establish a commission to review treaty
commitments and violations.[33] AIM's efforts ended in violence a year
later when its leaders answered a call from Oglala Sioux to protect the
little that remained of the reservation in South Dakota that had been set
aside for the Sioux nation in the Treaty of Fort Laramie after the Indian
nations' victory in the Red Cloud War of 1866–68. National Guardsmen
and US marshals encircled AIM leaders, many Sioux, and members of
sixty-four other nations. The siege was broken after ten weeks by gun-
fire, leaving 185 Indians charged with criminal offences and two Indians
dead on a hillside called Wounded Knee. The Nixon White House sent
a curt note saying, "[t]he days of treaty making with American Indians
ended in 1871."[34]

There was no denying treaty rights in New Zealand. The country was
founded on the 1840 Waitangi Treaty between the Maori and Britain.
But through war, the imposition of settler law, and the refusal of courts
to take the founding treaty seriously, the Maori had lost 95 per cent
of their land.[35] By the 1970s Maori were staging political actions to stop
the process of dispossession and to recover land and resources. In 1975,
led by Whina Cooper, first president of the Maori Women's Welfare
League, five thousand Maori marched down the North Island to
Wellington to present a petition signed by sixty thousand Maori to the
prime minister. The petition called for the preservation of Maori lands
in Maori hands. Soon after that, Maori protesters occupied Bastion

Point near Auckland to block the use of their land for a subdivision designed to give wealthy suburbanites undisturbed harbour views. After seventeen months of occupation, they were forcefully removed by the biggest police operation in New Zealand history.[36] The New Zealand Parliament, in which the Maori were allotted a quota of seats, responded with legislation establishing the Treaty of Waitangi Tribunal, which, though initially denied any power to consider past violation of the Treaty, would later become a significant instrument for establishing more just relations with the Maori.

Among the British settler countries, Australia was at the other end of the spectrum. From the arrival of its first colonists, Britain had treated Australia as *terra nullius*, a land of no one. The official line was that the black people who resisted white settlers were not sufficiently human to own land. So there was no recognition of native title nor any land cession treaties. By the mid-twentieth century, Australia's Aborigines and Torres Strait Islanders were responding to those same winds of change that were mobilizing decolonization nationalism in the Third World and the Fourth World, and the white majority was beginning to hear the message. In a 1967 constitutional referendum, the largest majority in Australian history voted in favour of removing the provision in Australia's Constitution that said native people should not be counted as part of the country's population. Aboriginal leaders pressed on from this official recognition of their existence to demand recognition of their land rights. In 1972 a group of Sydney-based Aborigines drove to Canberra and, with a beach umbrella and some plastic fencing, erected an Aboriginal embassy on the lawns of the Parliament building. Their placards proclaimed, "Land rights now." The Tent Embassy – which still stands in the nation's capital – was a galvanizing event.[37] It stirred the Labor opposition in Parliament, led by Gough Whitlam, to call for a national inquiry into land rights. When Labor won the election later in the year, Australia was launched on the road to effective recognition of Aboriginal title.

Canada was witnessing a similar series of Indian protest events in the same period. Indigenous internationalism was working – the television age was seeing to that. In the summer of 1973, Indian youth occupied DIAND offices in Ottawa. The occupation of Anishinabe Park in Kenora, Ontario, followed in 1974, and later that year a Native Caravan completed a trek from Vancouver to Ottawa for a demonstration on Parliament Hill. After the rejection of the White Paper, DIAND and PCO officials continued to work with the National Indian Brotherhood on a consultative process, but Indian policy had slipped from the top of the Trudeau government's agenda as it prepared for the 1972 election. The government did honour one commitment it made in the White Paper: in December 1969, Lloyd Barber, vice-president of the University of Saskatchewan, was appointed claims commissioner. Barber was a person sensitive to Indian concerns and knowledgeable about their history. But his mandate to examine and report on ways of settling treaty and other claims barred him from considering claims based on Aboriginal title. Not surprisingly, Indians boycotted his office.[38] But it was the Supreme Court of Canada, not Indian protesters, that was about to push the Canadian government down a policy path premised on the recognition of native title.

In 1911 Sir Wilfrid Laurier travelled to Prince Rupert to meet with a deputation of chiefs of Indian nations of the northwest British Columbia coast. The chiefs wanted the courts to consider their contention that, under Canadian law, they held Aboriginal title to their lands. The prime minister was sympathetic to that request. "Courts of law are just for that purpose," he said.[39] But Laurier knew that the BC government was opposed to doing this, and he was not sure he could force the provincial government into court. Later in 1911 the Laurier Liberals lost the election, and the Borden Conservatives were not interested in pursuing the matter. *Calder et al. v. Attorney General of British Columbia*, the case that went to trial in 1969 just as the Trudeau government was producing its White Paper, finally dealt with the matter the Indians had being trying for decades to litigate in the courts.

The Nisga'a were one of the nations represented at the 1911 meeting with Laurier. Numbering about five thousand, they live in four villages in the mountain-ringed valley through which the Nass River flows out to the Pacific Ocean. Frank Calder, president emeritus of the Nisga'a Tribal Council, served for twenty-six years as a member of the BC Legislative Assembly. He was the first status Indian to be elected to the provincial legislature or serve as a minister of the Crown. Elected first as a CCF member, he subsequently switched to Social Credit. At his side was Thomas Berger, who had been both an NDP MP in Ottawa and MLA in Victoria and for a time leader of the NDP in British Columbia, and who had become one of Canada's leading civil rights lawyers. Together, Calder and Berger made a formidable team. Still, they were fighting a case that many at the time felt was hopeless.

The question that Calder and his fellow Nisga'a Council members submitted to the British Columbia Supreme Court (the province's highest trial court) was simply this: had the Nisga'a people's Aboriginal title ever been lawfully extinguished? The trial judge, Mr Justice Allan Gould, took no position on whether there is such a thing as Aboriginal title, but decided that, if it had existed, it was extinguished implicitly by pre-Confederation legislation of the colony of British Columbia that provided Crown land grants and other forms of tenure on lands where Indians lived without any mention of Aboriginal title. The Nisga'a fared even worse when they appealed Gould's decision to the British Columbia Court of Appeal. The appellate judges' decision was redolent with the ignorance and racism that had prevailed in common law courts worldwide for more than a century. In the view of Chief Justice William Davey, the Nisga'a "were undoubtedly at the time of settlement a very primitive people with few of the institutions of civilized society, and none at all of our notions of private property."[40] Thomas Berger observes that Davey was "one of British Columbia's finest judges," but he did not understand how native peoples without a written language could have sophisticated concepts of legal relations and legal rights. Since the Nisga'a did not have Aboriginal title, there was no need to deal with the question of extinguishment.

Fourteen months after their defeat in the BC Court of Appeal, the chiefs of the four Nisga'a villages, together with elders decked out in traditional regalia, came to Ottawa for the final hearing of their case in the Supreme Court of Canada. They had to wait until 31 January 1973 for the Supreme Court's decision. And it was a puzzle: the Nisga'a had not won, but neither had they really lost. One of the seven judges who heard the case, Justice Louis-Philippe Pigeon, decided that the case had a procedural flaw that prevented him from dealing with the substantive issues in the case. All six of the other judges agreed on one fundamental point: Aboriginal title existed under British and Canadian law. On that point they overturned the British Columbia Court of Appeal. But the six divided down the middle on the question of whether Aboriginal title had been extinguished in British Columbia. Three judges, in an opinion written by Justice Wilfred Judson, agreed with British Columbia's argument that the province's legislation relating to land – both before and after Confederation – that was inconsistent with native title implicitly extinguished Aboriginal title. Three others – a group that included future Supreme Court Chief Justice Bora Laskin – in an opinion written by Justice Emmett Hall, took the opposite position that native peoples' ownership of their land could be considered to be extinguished by the Crown only if the Crown could provide proof of its "clear and plain" intent to extinguish native title, either through an agreement consented to by the native owners or by legislation – and in the case at hand, the Crown had provided no such proof.[41]

The common ground among the six Supreme Court justices is extraordinarily important. Native peoples' ownership of their land at the time of European settlement is a fact. As Justice Judson put it, "the fact is that when the settlers came, the Indians were there, organized in societies and occupying land as their forefathers had done for centuries. This is what Indian title means."[42] The justices reminded Canadians of the policy and law of the British Empire, which, as we saw in Chapters 2 and 3, was to respect the institutions and laws of the peoples living in the territories over which Britain asserted its sovereignty – always with the qualification that, if local practices interfered with Britain's interests, Britain (according to its law) had the sovereign power to impose its will. The 1763 Royal Proclamation did not create native title, but it assumed native ownership of their lands. This was clear when George III acknowledged that the lands the Indians lived on were in their possession. The British and, subsequently, the Canadian practice of acquiring lands for settlers by making treaties with their native owners would make no sense if the native people did not own their land. As Justice Hall pointed out, what are the rights the Indians are purported to have surrendered through the treaties if not their ownership rights over their lands? The Supreme Court decision in *Calder* clearly established that Aboriginal title is recognized in Canadian law as part of its British common law legacy. That legal recognition does not create Aboriginal title, but it builds a bridge, a connecting link, between the settlers' legal system and native peoples' legal systems.

On the question of extinguishment, all six judges agreed that native title could be extinguished with the consent of the native owners through treaties or by legislation. The judges split on whether extinguishment requires explicit legislation, expressing the clear intent of the sovereign to put an end to native title, or whether extinguishment could be accomplished much more casually simply by treating lands native peoples live on as if the inhabitants did not own their homeland. Which of those contending judicial views would guide Canada's relations with Indigenous peoples would depend on politics and, above all, on one politician, Pierre Elliott Trudeau.

Trudeau found Justice Hall's opinion so persuasive that he called Frank Calder himself to tell him that his government would enter into negotiations with the Nisga'a people. Gérard La Forest, a lawyer working in the federal Justice Department who would later become a Supreme Court judge, found that he was virtually the only person in the department who thought the government should accept Hall's opinion. However, when Donald Thorson became deputy minister in March, La Forest, to his surprise, was handed the file; he also found he had a very congenial boss.[43] On 9 August 1973 Jean Chrétien announced that the federal government was willing to negotiate claims of Aboriginal title wherever it could be established. Both the Conservatives and the NDP supported the government's decision to be guided by the Hall opinion. That was certainly important for the Trudeau government, having lost its majority in the 1972 federal election. But Trudeau's decision was not based simply on the need for his minority government to win the opposition parties' support. With six Supreme Court justices finding that Aboriginal title is a right in Canadian law, Trudeau's respect for the Court and for rights would surely incline him away from a policy of overriding native title in a casual, offhand manner. Trudeau reversed his position on Aboriginal title one hundred and eighty degrees. It is the mark of a statesman to be able to change positions when he or she learns principled reasons for doing so.

The Supreme Court of Canada's decision in *Calder* indicated two ways the federal government could extinguish Aboriginal title: by legislation or by agreement. The Trudeau government, with full support of the opposition parties, did not hesitate to proceed by making agreements with Aboriginal title-holders. That legislating the termination of Aboriginal title was not the chosen course is probably a mark of progress. The generations that passed the Indian Act and added assimilationist elements to it might well have opted for termination legislation. Still, for the federal government, the aim of agreements was extinguishment. The Supreme Court did not say Aboriginal title *had* to be extinguished, but none of the justices talked about leaving it in place. Common law judges conceptualize Aboriginal title as a "burden" on the underlying sovereign title of the Crown.[44] Burdens are best not borne. The primary goal of the land claims negotiations the Government of Canada entered into after *Calder* was to get the burden of Aboriginal title off its back.

In 1981 the federal government set out its policy on land claims negotiations in a glossy booklet entitled "In All Fairness." One thing clear about the policy is that it was anything but fair. To begin with, the policy was made without any discussions with Aboriginal title-holders. Surely a requirement of fairness in negotiating is that one party not impose the negotiating process on the other. The aim of what were termed "comprehensive land claims negotiations" was the extinguishment of Aboriginal title. In the government's view that is what the historic "land cession" treaties before and after Confederation had done and would now be accomplished through agreements – which at this stage the government would not dignify as "treaties" – with Aboriginal peoples still living on their unceded traditional lands. Extinguishment of Aboriginal title, in the government's view, was necessary to establish the legal clarity needed for investment and development. There was too much uncertainty about what conditions might attach to lands with the cloud of Aboriginal title hanging over them. In return for surrendering their land, the title-holding group would own a small parcel of it in "fee simple" – that is, according to the white man's law. The former title-holders would also get a pile of money, theoretically as compensation for past encroachments on their lands, but practically for economic development, and opportunities to participate in the management of the lands and waters of their traditional territory. Needless to say, this was not an attractive negotiating framework for First Nations.

The policy's failure to recognize Aboriginal peoples' right to self-government added greatly to its unattractiveness. For Aboriginal peoples, ownership of their lands cannot be separated from their responsibility for the well-being of the people who live on those lands. In July 1975, at Fort Simpson in the Northwest Territories, a meeting of the Joint General Assembly of the Indian Brotherhood of the NWT and the Métis Association of the NWT passed the Dene Declaration. The Dene – pronounced denay and meaning "we" or "us" in the Athabaskan language – constituting most of the native people in the Mackenzie Valley, declared "the right to be regarded by ourselves and the world as a nation." The Declaration called for "independence and self-determination" within Canada.[45] Other Amerindian nations in Canada with long histories as nations or tribes shared the goal of recovering responsibility for governing themselves on their lands. Local government powers and opportunities to participate with other governments in the management of traditional harvesting and resources beyond their villages fell far short of the self-government rights First Nations were seeking.

Under the government's policy, an Aboriginal people could submit its Aboriginal title claim to the Office of Native Claims in the Department of Indian Affairs. That office would decide whether or not the submission was supported well enough to be accepted for negotiations. It would also control the queue of claimants and the scheduling of negotiations. Given the complexity of the negotiations and the limited resources the government was willing to devote to them, a First Nation might have to wait many years to begin negotiating its claim. The Office of Native Claims also dealt with what were called "specific claims" – submissions that government had failed to meet a "a lawful obligation" under an existing treaty or legislation. These were the kind of claims that Lloyd Barber, the claims commissioner, was mandated to investigate.

With either comprehensive or specific claims, claimants had the option of going to court. But litigating claims would be a long and expensive process and the outcome uncertain. Although Aboriginal peoples would be charged for the costs of negotiating comprehensive land claims – costs that could easily reach seven figures – they did not have to pay their expenses up front. The government would pay for their expenses through a loan to be paid back by a deduction from the financial compensation in the final settlement. The first native people to obtain an acknowledgment of their Aboriginal title through the courts was the Tsihlqot'in nation in 2014.[46]

The comprehensive land claims process had the potential of settling land issues in every part of Canada except the prairie provinces, where numbered treaties cover the entire provincial territory. In British Columbia, aside from portions of Vancouver Island covered by the Douglas treaties and the northeast corner of the province included in Treaty 8, dozens of First Nations, including the Nisga'a, were living on unceded lands. In Ontario the Algonquin nation was still living on unceded lands in the Ottawa Valley. In eastern Canada many Aboriginal peoples might make Aboriginal title claims, as there had been no land cession treaties east of the Ottawa River.

Common law native title applied to Inuit as well as Indian nations. Inuit communities in northern Quebec, northern Labrador, and the Northwest Territories could, and eventually would, use the process. All of the more than dozen First Nations in the Yukon could claim native title, and because of legal doubts about the validity of land sessions under Treaty 11 and the portion of Treaty 8 relating to Dene lands in the Northwest Territories, the comprehensive claims process was available to the Dene.

The 1975 James Bay and Northern Quebec Agreement was the first land claim agreement to be negotiated, and it was a whopper. The native parties to the agreement were the Grand Council of the Cree of Quebec (representing eight Cree communities in northeast Quebec) and the Quebec Inuit Association (representing the Inuit people in

Ungava Bay, along the Hudson Strait, and on the eastern shore of
Hudson Bay, a territory the Inuit call Nunavik). The settler parties were
the Government of Canada, the Government of Quebec, Hydro-Québec,
the James Bay Energy Association, and the James Bay Development
Corporation. The agreement covered a vast area of just over a million
square miles. At stake was the industrial flagship of Quebec's Quiet
Revolution, a mammoth hydro-electric development, planned without
any consultation with the Cree and Inuit peoples who were the territory's majority population. This was the first thrust of Quebec's governance into the northern lands that were added to the province after the
1912 boundary extension. To resist it, the Cree and Inuit went to court
in 1972 and were successful in getting Judge Albert Malouf to issue an
injunction to cease the development because it interfered with the
rights of the people who had been living in and using the land "since
time immemorial."[47] A week later the Quebec Court of Appeal overturned Malouf's decision. In response the Cree and Inuit created an
uproar, staging loud and colourful demonstrations in Ottawa, Montreal,
and Quebec City. Then along came the Supreme Court of Canada's decision in *Calder*, followed by the federal government's decision to negotiate with native groups claiming title on unceded lands. So Ottawa and
Quebec City agreed to negotiate an agreement with the Cree and Inuit.
   The government lawyers went back to those killer words of the historic treaties and made sure the agreement stated that the Cree and
Inuit "cede, release, surrender and convey all their Native claims, rights
titles and interests, whatever they may be, in and to land."[48] What did
the Cree and Inuit get in return for agreeing to the extinguishment
of their Aboriginal title over all of their lands? Each Cree and Inuit community maintains ownership of small parcels of surrounding land, but
the ownership is under Quebec property law, not native law. These
community allotments are for the exclusive use of the native people,
and subject to municipal and regional governments administered by
the Cree and Inuit. In a second category, constituting just over 5 per
cent of their lands, the Cree and Inuit have exclusive hunting, fishing,
and trapping rights and a share in land and resource management. The
remainder of the surrendered lands, over 90 per cent of it, are provincial public lands on which both Aboriginal and non-Aboriginal people
may hunt and fish, although the Aboriginal peoples have exclusive
rights to certain species and the right to participate in land administration and development. The Cree and Inuit share in a cash settlement of
$225 million over twenty years and economic development assistance.[49]

In 1978 the Naskapi Band of Quebec (Innu people) signed the North-eastern Quebec Agreement with the same settler government parties to the James Bay Agreement, extending the regions to which that agreement applies.

It would be six more years before another comprehensive land claims agreement was signed. The nations and peoples who were eligible to negotiate under the federal policy found its terms and conditions so insulting and so insensitive to Aboriginal understanding of treaty relations that they stayed away from it until it appeared to be their only defence against a pending resource development on their lands. For Amerindian nations, treaties were a way of structuring an ongoing nation-to-nation relationship, not a once-and-for-all real estate deal in which one party bought out the other's rights. The very refusal of the federal government to call these agreements treaties – even though that is what they surely are, as Canada acknowledged when it amended the Constitution in 1983 – was mean-spirited and off-putting.

With the defeat of the White Paper, the *Calder* case, and the beginning of a modern treaty process, the country had changed direction and taken a step – from the Aboriginal peoples' perspective, a baby step – towards having an honourable and consensual relationship with its Aboriginal pillar. The next step would be taken when Aboriginal peoples were heard at Canada's constitutional table.

Chapter 13

English Canada Becomes Multicultural

"There will, I am sure, be general agreement with the view that the people of Canada do not wish, as a result of mass immigration, to make a fundamental alteration in the character of our population."[1] These were the words of Prime Minister Mackenzie King, as he addressed the House of Commons in 1947. His government's policy was "to foster the growth of the population of Canada by the encouragement of immigration." Being the cautious fellow he was, King wanted to assure Canadians that encouraging immigration would not mean flooding the country with people of colour from strange parts of the world. Canada would remain a white country of British, French, and northern European settlers. He hastened to add, being the liberal he was, that this did not mean accepting any blatantly discriminatory legislation. His government was committed to rescinding the legislation banning Chinese immigration that an earlier government of his introduced in 1923. Being the smoothie he was, he did not add that his government would do nothing to facilitate Chinese immigration.

Nineteen years later, Jean Marchand, that union activist and spear carrier of Quebec's Quiet Revolution and now immigration minister in a Pearson Liberal government, presenting *his* government's immigration policy to the House of Commons, explained: "It establishes principles and procedures that can and will operate entirely without regard to race, colour or creed."[2] This was a very different perspective than King's, but like King's commitment to preserve a white Canada, Marchand's promise of a non-discriminatory immigration policy was not controversial. Over two decades, something had happened in Canada that would lead to a remarkable change, to use King's phrase, in the "character of our population." That change was so remarkable that it deserves to be called Canada's "other Quiet Revolution."[3]

The vehicle of this second quiet revolution was a huge increase in immigration to Canada after the Second World War. The surge cannot match the period between 1891 and 1914, when three million immigrants came to live in a demographically much smaller Canada. But the numbers are still impressive: between 1946 and 1962 Canada's immigration intake averaged over one hundred thousand a year, totalling over two million – and, as with the pre–First World War immigration surge, most of the immigrants stayed in the country.[4] In that same period Canada admitted nearly a quarter of a million refugees.[5] The immigration numbers dipped in the economic slump of the early sixties, but began to pick up again later in the decade, rising to over two hundred thousand a year by the mid-seventies.[6] Among the New World countries Canada was second only to the United States in its immigrant intake numbers. In terms of immigrants as a proportion of the total population, it became the world leader. Over the three decades of the 1940s through the 1960s Canada, with one-tenth the US population, admitted slightly more than half the number of immigrants who arrived in the United States during that period.[7]

After the virtual shutdown of immigration during the Depression and war years, the return to high annual immigrant intakes was certainly remarkable, but calling it revolutionary has much more to do with the change in the sources of immigration than with the numbers. At first, it was the same old story: the preferred sources were the United Kingdom, the white Commonwealth, and the United States. In 1948, with an election pending, the government conferred the same preferred status on French citizens as British subjects enjoyed. But the immigration stream rapidly broadened out to western and eastern Europe. The late 1940s saw a big surge of German immigrants with the removal of the enemy alien list, and then a surge of Italian immigrants into the 1950s. In 1947 Canada accepted 169,000 of the one million "displaced persons" living in refugee camps in Europe, a fifth of them Jews.[8] In 1956–57, Canada led all other countries in admitting thirty-seven thousand Hungarians fleeing the Soviet Union's invasion of their country. As the immigration steam was broadening, the old sources of immigration were not drying up. In 1957 lines of Britons were forming outside Canadian immigration offices in London, many of them fleeing the class system that reduced the opportunities for those who spoke with the wrong accent. On flights provided by the government's Air Bridge to Canada, British immigrants found themselves sitting beside Hungarian refugees.[9] Young, talented Americans fleeing McCarthyism and later being drafted to fight in Vietnam also sought refuge in the peaceful suburb to the north. Then, in the 1960s, Canadian immigration policy, as we can see in Jean Marchand's statement, replaced the hierarchy of preferred nationalities and races with a universal points system that opened up the country as never before to people of all creeds and colours. A points system that gives weight to education, technical skills, and a knowledge of English or French is universal only in a formal sense. It took quite a while for Asians, Africans, and West Indians to take advantage of the changes in Canadian immigration policy. But by the mid-seventies the impact of the policy change was becoming visibly evident on the streets of Canada's big cities.

By 1961 Canada's two dominant cultural and linguistic groups, British and French, together still made up almost 74 per cent of the population.[10] The 2011 census indicated that this figure had fallen to about 66 per cent. This compares with about 90 per cent in 1891 (and 93 in 1867). A decline of about 25 per cent in the demographic dominance of the British and French in Canada might not seem revolutionary until one takes into account where most of the newcomers live and how they make their presence felt. Most of the "new Canadians" have settled in the big cities. That is where jobs and opportunities are most abundant and where they are most likely to find kith and kin who came to Canada before them. In the cities they have changed dramatically what Canadians eat and drink, enriched our arts, enlivened our entertainment, excelled in the professions, and become a force in politics.

But what is truly revolutionary is that English Canadians have come to value the diversity these new Canadians have brought to the country. As we saw in earlier chapters, the first generations of English-speaking Canadians envisioned a country that could properly be referred to as British North American. The French fact could be tolerated because without it there could be no Canada. But as the country developed westward, French Canada was increasingly cabined in Quebec. English-speaking Canada did not share Cartier's or Bourassa's dream of an ethnically diverse Canadian nationality. Clifford Sifton's immigration policy diversified Canada as a fact, but not as something to be celebrated. Non-British immigrants would be tolerated as an economic necessity, with the hope that as quickly as possible they would blend into the dominant society. The same aspiration applied to Aboriginal Canadians.

The turnaround did not come easily. There were plenty of stresses and strains. In the movie, *My Big Fat Greek Wedding*, there is a telling scene. The son of a very Anglo middle-class family brings his fiancée, the daughter of a Greek immigrant family, to meet his parents. Mother and father sit opposite the young couple. To break the ice, mother leans forward, her face brimming with earnest friendliness, and asks Toula, "Does your name mean something special in your culture?" Never mind that the movie, though shot mostly in the Danforth area of Toronto, is actually set in Chicago – it could have happened anywhere in North America. The nice, very mainstream mother, in her comically awkward way, was trying to stifle any misgivings she had – and it is clear that she and her husband had plenty – about the woman their son had chosen to marry and welcome the Greek girl into the family. It was far from fully convincing, but Mrs Miller was trying! That trying is the very heart of the revolution.

It was a quiet revolution in the sense that it occurred without big battles, with no ringing proclamation or memorable, climactic moment. The legal instrument for facilitating the change in the composition of the Canadian population was not the Constitution, but the federal Immigration Act. There could hardly be a duller, more opaque piece of legislation than Canada's Immigration Act. That is because it was designed to leave to the executive branch of government all the substantive decision-making about who gets in, who is kept out, and who is kicked out. The Act vests enormous power in the cabinet to make rules over the admissibility and deportation of "aliens." The rules took the form of Orders in Council – the very phrase makes one's eyes glaze over – that in practice are written by the minister and departmental officials. The rules approved by cabinet tended to be very general, leaving a great deal of discretion with immigration officials in the field. Even though the really substantive immigration policy was not on view in an Act of Parliament, this did not keep it from being discussed and critiqued by parliamentarians and interest groups. Indeed, as this quiet revolution rolled along, it generated a large array of organizations in the private sector with a focus on immigration policy, and made immigration a frequent topic of parliamentary discussion and debate.

A combination of economic and humanitarian concerns was the driving force behind Canada's post-war immigration surge. In many cases these motives were intermixed. For instance, the King government's decision to admit four thousand demobilized Polish soldiers in 1946 was largely motivated by the country's need for farm workers. The Polish veterans were assigned as employees of Canadian farmers for their first year in Canada.[11] Sometimes, as with admitting seven thousand Ugandan Asian refugees in 1972, Canada has been accused of cherry-picking the most able people in the refugee pool. Tension between economic and humanitarian considerations has been most evident with respect to the admission of family-sponsored immigrants. During much of the post-war period Canadians could sponsor a wide range of relatives, and these relatives in turn could sponsor other relatives "in a rapid process of chain migration."[12] Sponsored relatives did not have to meet any skills or education criteria, and tended to congregate in self-contained ethnic enclaves, notably in Toronto and Vancouver. Before the hierarchy of nationality and race was removed from the regulations, immigration from southern Europe, Central and South America, and Asia was pretty much confined to family sponsorship. In 1959, with economic conditions declining and Italian immigrants overtaking British in numbers, the Diefenbaker government passed an Order in Council excluding married children, brothers, and sisters from the list of eligible relatives. The Liberals, now in Opposition, jumped on this, claiming it was aimed primarily at Italians. The row in the House and the media persuaded the government to withdraw the new regulation.[13]

Of the million and a quarter immigrants admitted to Canada between 1946 and 1966, just over a third were sponsored relatives. Studies of immigrant integration have shown that family sponsorship can have practical benefits. Three generations of a family living together often result in a more productive and efficient family unit, as well as being an antidote for the loneliness of living in a new country. A 1967 change in the regulations narrowed the range of relatives eligible for family sponsorship, but at the same time introduced a new category of "nominated immigrants" for more distant relatives who can pass a relaxed version of the points system.

There was certainly a lot of public debate about immigration policy. Sections of organized labour opposed high immigration levels during periods of high unemployment, while religious groups and ethnic communities exposed bias in the administration of a supposedly racially neutral selection system – to mention just two sources of criticism. And there are always concerns about security threats, especially in taking in refugees. In the early days it was the Red Scare of the "commies";

nowadays it is the "terrorists" who are too easily conflated with Muslims. Nonetheless a remarkably strong political consensus supported an expansive and liberal immigration policy. Indeed the political parties competed for the pro-immigration vote. No parliamentarian thundered more about unfairness in the Liberal government's management of immigration than the leader of the Conservative Opposition, John Diefenbaker. Diefenbaker's German name added authenticity to the Conservatives' support of a "progressive" immigration policy. The Liberals did all they could to reap the political rewards of claiming ownership of a new, generous immigration policy that was bringing so many immigrants to Canada. For its part, the CCF and its successor party, the NDP, had a long history of opposing the ethnic bias and racism in Canadian immigration policy.

Underlying this political consensus were the rights revolution and the international winds of change identified in the two previous chapters as having a powerful impact on Canada's political culture in the immediate post-war years. King, in his 1947 statement on immigration policy, said that "[a]n alien has no 'fundamental human right' to enter Canada. This is a privilege."[14] On the heels of that statement, critics were jumping on the government for violating the rights of Canadian citizens to bring their family members to Canada, and denying aliens the right of due process of law both in determining their eligibility for entry to Canada and in deporting them from Canada. In the 1956 parliamentary debate on immigration, the Conservatives focused their attack on the government's failure to provide adequate safeguards for the rights of both citizens and non-citizens in immigration procedures. There was constant pressure to make the Immigration Appeals Board a more judicial, less executive-dominated body. A 1956 decision of the Supreme Court of Canada ruled that, in delegating authority to Special Inquiry Officers in the field to decide who was admissible, the government had breached a basic principle of administrative law.[15] The result was an Order in Council spelling out the precise classes of persons who were admissible to Canada. King notwithstanding, the rights revolution was judicializing the immigration process.

The decolonizing winds of change that blew away the distinction between the white Commonwealth and the non-white Commonwealth made it ridiculous for Canada to maintain that kind of distinction in its immigration preferences. Post-war Canada, unlike the cautious, newly autonomous Canada of the 1920s, aspired to be a leader in world affairs, especially at the United Nations, where formerly colonized countries were becoming the majority in the General Assembly. Immigration policy and refugee policy had to be in sync with these foreign policy ambitions. In the 1956 Suez Crisis, Lester Pearson, Canada's minister of external affairs and who had also served as president of the General Assembly, inspired the action that used UN peacekeepers to stop a British-French invasion of Egypt. For this Pearson received the Nobel Peace Prize and the admiration of Canadians who did not mind at all this sharp rebuff of British and French imperialism.

We take Canadian citizenship for granted today, but it is important to note that, of the old Commonwealth countries, Canada, with its 1946 Citizenship Act, was the first to establish the status of citizenship for its people, rather than their simply being British subjects domiciled in Canada. Imagine swearing in new Canadians at British-subject ceremonies! Paul Martin Sr, the author of the Citizenship Act, told how the inspiration for the Act came from a tour of the military cemetery at Dieppe: "The racial origins of the dead were so varied ... It struck me that herein lay the character of Canada, a land of people of diverse national origins."[16] Canadian citizenship went hand-in-hand with an immigration policy of opening Canada to the world.

The political consensus that developed around immigration was at the level of the "chattering classes" – federal politicians, religious leaders, lawyers, academics, writers, and journalists. It did not penetrate through the entire society. Pockets of robust racism remain. When they are heard from, they are often put down with much vehemence, arousing fears of illiberal "political correctness." In the 1970s the federal Parliament added the hate propaganda section to the Criminal Code, criminalizing speech aimed at arousing race-hatred.[17] In the 1980s the Supreme Court of Canada, in one of its early decisions on the Charter of Rights and Freedoms, upheld the legislation, accepting the legislature's concern about the social damage of hate-mongering as a justification for restricting the right to free speech – the very opposite position to that of the US Supreme Court.[18] Canada did not experience the rise of the anti-immigrant parties that have emerged in Europe as a response to increased immigration from Islamic countries. The closest Canada has come is a plank in the platform of the Reform Party that, King-style, warned against immigration that would "radically or suddenly alter the ethnic makeup of Canada."[19] A residue of that is found in the Conservative Party that absorbed the Reformers and dropped "Progressive" from its label. Even so, the Conservatives do their best to camouflage their immigration qualms because it is bad politics in Canada to be anti-immigration or tepid in response to refugee crises.

An important limitation of the political consensus on immigration was Quebec. Suspicion of immigration as an English plot to swamp the French is a long tradition, going back to colonial days. This traditional hostility to immigration lived on in Quebec. In the vigorous promotion of post-war immigration, Quebec, in Freda Hawkins's words, "remained a ghost at the banquet."[20] Of the three and a half million immigrants admitted to Canada between 1947 and 1971, only 15 per cent settled in Quebec, and of these only 5 per cent were francophones.[21] It took the heightened sense of agency engendered by Quebec's Quiet Revolution to turn Quebec from a grumbling recipient of Ottawa's immigration policy to an active creator of a Quebec immigration policy. In 1968 Quebec established its own Department of Immigration, sending representatives to Paris, Brussels, Beirut, and other areas of large French-speaking populations.

Under the Constitution, immigration is a concurrent field of legislation in which federal law is paramount. Although Quebec would have to comply with federal immigration law, it was able to mount an aggressive program to attract French-speaking immigrants to the province. Quebec would also use its control over education to ensure that new Canadians who settle in the province, be they anglophone or francophone, if they wish their children to attend state-supported schools, would be required to send them to French schools.

Francophone Quebec faces the challenge of surviving as a French-speaking island in a North American English-speaking sea. That challenge shaped its response to immigration and its implications. Diversity and pluralism were acceptable – within limits. The limit was the need – the absolute imperative – to maintain Quebec as a predominantly French-speaking society. Quebec's distinctiveness was now pretty well down to the French language. Its distinct system of civil law had long lost its panache as a popular badge of a distinct identity – although the province was developing its own version of the welfare state. Ironically, the third historic element of Quebec's distinctiveness, the Catholic religion, was giving way to a distinctly militant secularism that would become an obstacle to the reasonable accommodation of Islamic immigrants. What all of this adds up to is that "multiculturalism," with its implication that all cultures are equal, does not work as an ideal in a Quebec whose majority is committed to the superior claim of French over all other cultures.

It was the view of the royal commission, shared by the government and I am sure all Canadians, that there cannot be one cultural policy for

Canadians of British and French origin, another for the original peoples
and yet third for all others. For although there are two official languages,
there is no official culture, nor does any ethnic group take precedence over
any other ...

The individual's freedom would be hampered if he were locked for life
within a particular cultural compartment by the accident of birth or language ...

A policy of multiculturalism within a bilingual framework commends
itself to the government of Canada as the most suitable means of assuring
the cultural freedom of Canadians.[22]

These were the words of Pierre Elliott Trudeau, introducing his government's multiculturalism policy to the House of Commons on 8 October
1971.

The royal commission Trudeau referred to was the Royal Commission
on Bilingualism and Biculturalism. As it did its work, the commission
encountered a source of discontent in the country that had not been anticipated: new Canadians arriving in great numbers with neither a British
or French background resented the privileging of two cultures that B & B
implied. Pearson added two "ethnic" representatives to the commission
and one volume of the commission's report dealt with the contributions
of "other ethnic" groups to the country.[23] With the announcement of the
multiculturalism policy, Trudeau was continuing this effort to mollify
the growing numbers of non-British, non-French citizens by eliminating
the second "B" in the classic dualistic vision of Canada.

For Trudeau, rejecting biculturalism as official policy was more than
a clever political strategy to win the "ethnic" vote. It reflected his deep
underlying philosophy of human freedom. Philosophically Trudeau
had become a cosmopolitan man of the world. Culture was something
that should be freely adopted, not pushed on the individual by the
state. Language was an instrumental vehicle of communication that
could be separated from its cultural associations. Requiring all Canadians to speak at least one of Canada's official languages would give
them the freedom to function effectively in the political and economic
life of the country without forcing them to abandon an old culture or
adopt a new one. Thus, for Trudeau, bilingualism went hand-in-hand
with multiculturalism.

Many of those who reacted negatively to the multiculturalism announcement failed to notice Trudeau's emphasis on individual cultural freedom. The *Toronto Star*, Canada's largest-circulation newspaper,

and traditionally Liberal, was typical. "No immigrant," it thundered, "should be encouraged to think that Canada is essentially a chain of ethnic enclaves like the New Iceland Republic that once flourished on the shores of Lake Winnipeg."[24] Of course the last thing that Trudeau wanted was to encourage Canadians to lock themselves into ethnic enclaves. But Trudeau's idea that individuals freely choose their cultures seems to view, naively, the individual self as unformed by all kinds of societal influences. A school of Canadian liberal philosophy was forming around the writing of thinkers such as Charles Taylor, James Tully, and Will Kymlicka that considers belonging to a cultural tradition a crucial ingredient of a person's identity.[25] This is something that seemed to escape Trudeau in offering Aboriginal Canadians emancipation from their culture, and in being so disdainful of *Québécois* who feared the survival of a distinct francophone society in North America.

One thing certain about multiculturalism is that there is an enormous amount of talk about it and a great deal of ink spilled about it. It is one of those subjects on which virtually everyone has an opinion – although not likely an informed opinion. Jack Jedwab reports that 64 per cent of Canadians, when asked what actions the Government of Canada takes to promote multiculturalism, answered "didn't know."[26] As Yasmeen Abu-Laban observes, multiculturalism in Canada is a "symbolic policy," not a description of government actions or expenditures.[27] On the whole, "multiculturalism" is a positive symbol, especially in English-speaking Canada, whereas the "m" word is virtually taboo, or politically dangerous, in other countries that have policies and principles that support ethnic pluralism.

As concrete public policy – beyond the symbolism – there is very little to Canada's policy of multiculturalism. There was no immediate legislative follow-up to Trudeau's 1971 statement. The Canadian Multiculturalism Act was passed in July 1988 under the Mulroney government. Multiculturalism does not rate a line in Brian Mulroney's voluminous 1,100-word memoir. And no wonder! The Act is basically a little piece of rah-rah symbolism. It does not require anyone to do anything or prohibit anyone from doing anything, nor does it authorize funding for any specific program or group. The Act's "policy" section leads with a declaration that it is "the policy" of the Government of Canada to "recognize and promote the understanding that multiculturalism reflects the cultural and racial diversity of Canadian society and acknowledges the freedom of all members of Canadian society to preserve, enhance and share their cultural heritage."[28] The Act does not attempt a definition of "multiculturalism," which is just as well, given the complexity of the subject.

The only other significant recognition of multiculturalism in Canadian law is section 27 of the Canadian Charter of Rights and Freedoms, which states: "This Charter shall be interpreted in a manner consistent with the preservation and enhancement of the multicultural heritage of Canadians." Section 27 is a broad guideline to Canadian judges to take into consideration Canada's commitment to multiculturalism in interpreting the Charter. It is not itself the basis for any rights or freedoms. Justices of the Supreme Court of Canada rarely refer to it even when they are dealing with challenges to laws that privilege the religion of Canada's founding Europeans, the British and the French, such as Sunday closing laws or public funding for Catholic schools. Beginning with the 1970 appointment of Bora Laskin, the son of Russian Jews, the Supreme Court's bench has become multicultural, but it has not relied on section 27 in giving a generous and liberal interpretation of the Charter, including its equality rights.

The Multiculturalism Act authorizes the minister responsible for multiculturalism policy to "encourage and assist" ethno-cultural minority communities in various ways, and this includes providing some money. In the free-spending 1970s, without the authority of the Act, the government found sources of funding for ethnic groups – not billions, but millions. But those days are long gone – although they left a legacy of suspicion that vast amounts of taxpayers' money are being poured into folk festivals and the like. In his account of the Government of Canada's Multiculturalism Program, John Biles indicates that the largest expenditures have been for research and education, with support for twenty-eight chairs of ethnic studies in Canadian universities, many academic publications, and an ethnic studies journal and association. In fiscal year 2010/11, the government's multicultural grants program paid out $901,753 to support 94 events across Canada – peanuts in a multibillion-dollar budget.[29]

Multiculturalism as a positive symbol and an official policy of government is, however, limited to English-speaking Canada. All Quebec governments, whether federalist or separatist, have rejected multiculturalism since its adoption by the federal government in 1971. It is important to understand the reason for this. The majority of Quebecers identify with Quebec as a nation whose fundamental mission is to preserve Quebec as a distinct French-speaking society. Multiculturalism purports to treat all cultures as equal. For Quebec's governments and the majority of Quebec's people, that is unacceptable because they insist that the French language and whatever culture goes with it be privileged. Trudeau's multiculturalism would reduce the *Québécois* to one of Canada's many ethnic minorities.

Quebec's alternative to multiculturalism is "interculturalism." Interculturalism accepts the value of ethnic diversity, but with the condition that minority ethnic groups must integrate into the French culture of the host nation. Gérard Bouchard, the leading expositer of interculturalism, explains its difference from multiculturalism this way: whereas the federal government's multicultural policy "endorses the idea that there is no majority culture," the aim of interculturalism is "to manage in a pluralist spirit the relationship between the majority culture and the minority cultures."[30] The crucial point here is that the francophone majority in Quebec demands to be recognized not as a cultural minority in Canada, but as a political entity – a political nation with governmental powers whose overriding mission is and always has been the survival of its distinctive society.

For ethnic minorities living in "intercultural" Quebec, the experience is not that much different than the experience of minorities living in "multicultural" English Canada. Quebec, as already noted, has become much more willingly open to immigration than it ever was in the past. The proportion of immigrants to population has not shot up, but by the early 2000s it was at 11 per cent, compared with the 7–8 per cent it was stuck at for the earlier decades of the twentieth century.[31] Most of these recent immigrants have settled in the Montreal region, making that city feel and appear as multicultural as Toronto.

The minority that has felt the impact of Quebec's policy of privileging the French language and culture most severely are Anglo-Quebecers. Quebecers with a British background now constitute just over 10 per cent of Quebec's population – about half of what their proportion was half a century ago. Bouchard refers to Anglo-Quebecers as a "national minority" within Quebec. This is consistent with the fact that the right to use English in Quebec's courts and legislature is enshrined in Canada's founding Constitution. The special status of Quebec's English-speaking minority also reflects French Quebec's traditional dualist vision of Canada as a binational, English-French country. Most Anglo-Quebecers who did not want to live in a dominantly French society are long gone from the province. The great majority of those who remain are bilingual. Even so, their British name and background too often are barriers to a career in the provincial public service.

Accommodating a growing Muslim minority has posed the greatest challenge to Quebec's policy of "integrative pluralism." A society that has made secularism a fundamental value has difficulty accommodating Islamic citizens unaccustomed to confining their religious faith to the private realm. That is as true of contemporary France as it is of Quebec. The practice of some Muslim women of covering their face with a *niqab* or their hair with a head scarf in public causes a stir outside Quebec, but an even greater one in Quebec. Although 66 per cent of those responding to a recent survey in Quebec supported a ban on Muslim women covering their faces in public places, in the rest of Canada only 41.5 per cent did so. In 2008 Quebec launched a public inquiry led by Gérard Bouchard and Charles Taylor that brought forward recommendations for "a reasonable accommodation" with Muslim citizens.[32]

The integration of new citizens into Canadian society has been a concern of both the critics and supporters of multiculturalism. The critics' concern is that the policy will ghettoize the country by fostering insular ethnic communities. Supporters, however, believe that immigrants who are not pressured to cut all ties with their homelands or to discard the faith or cultural practices they brought with them will be more willing and more able to integrate into the mainstream society. In fact immigrants in Canada have shown high levels of integration in terms of participating in the political, social, and economic life of the country. But integration has not meant assimilation. Will Kymlicka puts it this way: "So while immigrant groups have increasingly asserted their right to express their ethnic particularity, they typically wish to do so within the public institutions of the English-speaking society (or French-speaking in Canada)."[33] Canada's multiculturalism policy might have little to do with this high level of integration. A comparative study of Canada and the United States – which does not have a multiculturalism policy – shows that "[r]ates of economic and social integration for comparable groups of immigrants are virtually identical in the two countries."[34] Again multiculturalism seems to be more of a symbol than a driving engine of policy. Another comparative study of Canadian and US experience in managing diversity shows that, setting aside the massive migration of Mexicans and other Hispanics into the United States – a challenge Canada has not had to face – the cliché of the Canadian mosaic versus the American melting pot does not hold up. Both countries have been liberal and effective in managing ethnic diversity.[35]

The interesting question, then, is why does the "m" word – multiculturalism – have such positive symbolic value in Canada, especially in English-speaking Canada? The answer to that question can be found, at least in part, in the subtitle of this book: Canada is "a country based on incomplete conquests." Earlier chapters of this book told the story of how the English-speaking settlers, once they became British North America's most powerful people, tried by political means to eliminate French Canada and Aboriginal Canada. In the case of French Canada, the aim of Lord Durham's report and its implementation by the colonial authorities was to meld the French Canadians into a single province that would come to be dominated by an English-speaking majority. Similarly the policy goal of colonial Canada's Gradual Civilization Act and, after Confederation, the Indian Act was to solve the "Indian problem" by dissolving the Indians into the mainstream society. In neither case did the policy succeed. French Canada, although mostly provincialized in Quebec, survived with a strong sense of its nationhood. The First Nations, Métis, and later the Inuit also maintained a strong sense of their being distinct nations or peoples. Trudeau's multiculturalism policy was a bid to reduce these "nations within" to minority cultures with the same status as the ethnic communities formed by new immigrants to Canada. Had the *Québécois* and the Aboriginal peoples accepted the status accorded them by multiculturalism, the incomplete conquests of Canada would have been completed.

But at the very time the Trudeau government was proclaiming multiculturalism, the "nations within" were telling it they were nations, not minority cultures. The options for Quebec's French majority after the Quiet Revolution was either a province with the special status and powers appropriate for the homeland of a founding people, or an independent state. In rejecting the Chrétien-Trudeau White Paper, the Indian leadership made it clear that their goal was to recover a nation-to-nation relationship with Canada. The key in both cases was that the "nations within" considered themselves political societies with a right to a significant measure of self-rule. Unlike immigrant groups, they had not come to Canada from another homeland – their homelands were in Canada. French Canada and Aboriginal Canada had no objection to multiculturalism's support of ethnic diversity – unlike the British settlers they had never yearned for a monocultural Canada. But cultural respect was no substitute for the political power they had to have over the matters most important to their peoples. If Canada was to be governed with the consent of its peoples and not by force, it would have to be multinational and multicultural.

It should not be surprising that Canada's multinational character was not, by any means, recognized by Canada's national government or by the majority of Canada's English-speaking population. The one-nation-one-state idea has a strong grip on the modern mind. As James Tully, one of the leading theorists of multinational democracies, explains, "multinational democracies often emerge out of the cocoon of societies in which the majority tends to understand itself as a single-nation democracy, even when this is historically inaccurate."[36] In their book on multinational democracies, Alain-G. Gagnon and Tully identify four examples of multinational democracies: Belgium, Canada, Spain, and the United Kingdom.[37] Although these four countries have different constitutional arrangements for recognizing the "nations within," in all of them the citizens who identify with the historic "nations within" also participate as full citizens in the political institutions of the larger multination. This means that those who identify with the smaller "nations within" have a dual citizenship: they identify with their historic nation – be it Flanders, Mi'kma'ki, Catalonia, or Scotland – and also with the larger nation, and the primary allegiance of many might be to their historic nation.

The only nation that Canadians with a British or American background or new Canadians from other parts of the world identify with is Canada, the nation-state they are proud to belong to, that represents them in the United Nations, and acts on their behalf in the international community of nation-states. But doesn't that nation have some ethnicity? Neil Bissoondath, who came to Canada from Trinidad, speaks for many new Canadians when he laments the uncertainty in answering that quintessential Canadian question: who are we?[38] "Lacking a full and vigorous response," Bissoondath finds that far too many define themselves with a hyphen as "West Indian-Canadians" or "Ukrainian-Canadians," whereas he simply wants to be a Canadian, not a "professional ethnic."

Part of the difficulty experienced by Bissoondath and many other Canadians like him is the tendency to deny recognition of Canada's British heritage. Trudeau's multiculturalism statement said that, in Canada, "although there are two official languages there is no official culture." Although that statement in a narrow sense might be legally true, it fails to recognize the reality of Canada's historical roots in British North America. That reality means that Canada's system of government is largely built on British foundations and that, outside Quebec, the dominant language of public life, including education, is English. Trudeau might have thought that a language can be completely divorced from its cultural context, but the reality is that a good deal of culture – values and traditions – adheres to language. As I have shown in Chapter 4, English-speaking settlers brought with them the seeds of a shared civic culture that holds together Canada's deeply diversified society. To the three original components of that shared civic culture – parliamentary democracy, constitutional government, and monarchy – three more components have been added: federalism, respect for ethnic diversity, and human rights. Participating in that shared civic culture provides a substantive answer to what it means to be a Canadian.

Monarchy might seem to have become a wobbly component of Canada's shared civic culture. Retaining a head of state who resides in Britain might appear to be out of sync with the expectations of Canadian nationalism. But much has been done to Canadianize the Crown in Canada. Most of the monarch's responsibilities – dignified and efficient – are exercised in Canada by Canadian representatives of the queen (the governor general, provincial lieutenant-governors, and territorial commissioners) selected by Canada's prime minister. The queen of Canada is also the queen of fifteen other realms, most of which are not British in their cultural heritage, and the head of a fifty-three nation multicultural Commonwealth of Nations. Many of the European immigrants to Canada come from constitutional monarchies or from republics that have experienced presidential heads of state much more autocratic than modern monarchs. The frequent filling of viceregal offices with Canadians from minority ethnic groups has given a multicultural flavour to the Canadian Crown. For Aboriginal Canada the Crown remains a unifying element in its relations with Canada. That certainly no longer can be said for francophone Quebec. Even so, it is interesting to observe the insignificant role that changing Quebec to a republic has played in the Quebec independence movement, and how little attention separatist constitutionalists give to working out how an elected president would co-habit with a prime minister in a Laurentide republic. It is also interesting to find, in the heavy season of constitutional reform into which Canada plunged in the mid-1970s, how little support there was for changing Canada from a constitutional monarchy to a republic. That surely had something to do with the fact that Canadian nationalists have been more afraid of Canada's becoming too American than being too British.

Multicultural Canada – with two of its foundational pillars insisting that the country is also multinational, and its English-speaking majority brimming with unfulfilled nationalism – was becoming a difficult country to figure out. There is no constitutional recipe book for a country whose peoples harbour such cross-cutting aspirations. After the

failure of the Victoria Charter to resolve Quebec's nationalist aspirations, neither the Trudeau government nor most Canadians outside
Quebec had any desire to return to the constitutional table. If there was
to be a return to constitutional negotiations, it would have to be forced
on the country by the majority of Quebecers. And that is exactly what
would happen next.

PART SIX

Seeking a Constitutional Fix

Chapter 14

Patriation:
Quebec's Loss, Aboriginal Gains

Fifteen November 1976 is a pivotal date in Canada's odyssey. On the evening of that day, as Canadians watched spellbound the televised coverage of the results of the Quebec provincial election, most were shocked and surprised when it became clear that René Lévesque's Parti Québécois had won. For the first time in any constitutional democracy, a secessionist party had come to power through democratic means.

In 1974 a PQ convention had made a commitment that, as soon as the party came to power, it would hold a referendum to ratify the constitution of an independent Quebec. Lévesque watered down the referendum commitment to mean that a PQ government would not make any moves towards independence until authorized to do so by a referendum.[1] The PQ's election campaign emphasized giving the province of Quebec good government, not an immediate declaration of independence.

Liberal premier Robert Bourassa's decision to call the 1976 election with another year left in the normal mandate handed the PQ its breakthrough opportunity. Not the least of the factors that influenced Bourassa's decision was the need to get another mandate before dumping the soaring costs of the 1976 Summer Olympics on the city of Montreal. But the deciding factor was the possibility that Pierre Trudeau might go ahead unilaterally with patriation of the Constitution, closing down any opportunity for Quebec to obtain the changes it sought in the division of powers. The Trudeau government had recovered its majority in the 1974 federal election. When the Speech from the Throne opening a new session of Parliament in the fall of 1976 included words indicating the federal government might proceed with unilateral patriation, Bourassa called the snap November election. Little did he know that, as events unfolded, it would be the Supreme Court of Canada, not a

Quebec Liberal government, that would stop a federal Liberal government from proceeding with unilateral patriation.

Bourassa had been rewarded for calling a snap election in 1973 with a Liberal landslide, winning 102 out of 108 seats. The PQ came out of that election with just six seats, one less than it took in 1971. But the PQ's popular vote had actually increased from 24 to 33 per cent. Bourassa was counting on the rejuvenation of the Union Nationale – which, along with the Créditistes, lost all their seats in 1973 – to take votes away from the PQ, and on the PQ's internal discord to cripple the party. It is the PQ's fate to be forever riven by a division between fundamentalists and more pragmatic sovereignists. Lévesque was always in the latter camp. In designing and delivering the party's message in the 1976 election campaign, the pragmatists prevailed. The architect of the PQ's winning campaign was Claude Morin, a long-time senior Quebec public servant who had joined the PQ in 1972. Morin suggested to Lévesque that "[m]aybe we should just run on a good government platform, promise to rid Quebecers of the arrogant and scandal-prone Liberals, and once we have established our credentials as prudent managers, we could hold a referendum on the future of Quebec."[2] Lévesque took Morin's advice and won the election. The pragmatic approach in the election might have made the PQ less scary to the Quebec electorate, but the PQ victory sure shook up the rest of Canada.

The coming to power in Quebec of a political party whose *raison d'être* was, in the popular lingo of English-speaking Canada, "to break up the country," ushered in a period of new constitutionalism. There was "a virtual explosion of conferences, seminars and publications on constitutional ailments and cures as the public-spirited and the self-seeking sought to get their views on the record."[3] This outburst of constitutional interest and discussion seemed to vindicate the conclusion of the Molgat-MacGuigan parliamentary committee that "Canadians now want a new constitution."[4] University of Toronto president John Evans, for example, invited concerned citizens to a week-long conference that produced a five-hundred-page book on constitutional options for Canada.[5]

Governments, too, wasted no time entering the "new constitutionism" playing field. In July 1977 Trudeau appointed a Task Force on Canadian Unity, chaired by John Robarts, the former Ontario premier who had hosted the 1967 Confederation for Tomorrow Conference in Toronto, and Jean-Luc Pépin, a former cabinet minister in the Trudeau government who at this time was heading the Anti-Inflation Board.

Pépin's constitutional orientation was poles away from Trudeau's. The mandate Trudeau gave the Task Force was to provide its own recommendations, not make recommendations to the government. The Task Force held hearings across the country, and put together a carefully crafted set of recommendations on the constitutional changes best calculated to satisfy Quebec and the rest of Canada. Pépin and Robarts submitted their final report in January 1979. Trudeau heard that their recommendations would produce a much more decentralized federation and a measure of special status for Quebec. When he was handed a copy of the report, his biographer, John English, tells us that "he tossed it immediately in the waste basket without reading it."[6]

It was the provincial premiers who opened up the constitutional conversation at the governmental level. In August 1976 they had come together in Edmonton in response to the federal government's renewed interest in patriating the Constitution. The premiers of the resource-rich western provinces voiced their deep concern about securing control over their natural resources. The context here was the shocking rise of oil prices by the Organization of the Petroleum Exporting Countries (OPEC) in 1973, and the Trudeau government's objective of sheltering Canadian consumers from soaring world prices by making oil produced in western Canada (mostly in Alberta) available at low prices to Canadian consumers (most of whom live in central Canada). Western Canada's alienation from a constitutional agenda that focused on accommodating Quebec nationalism might be overcome if Quebec supported the west's demands for enhanced provincial jurisdiction over natural resources.[7]

Alberta premier Peter Lougheed wrote to Trudeau summing up the premiers' position: they were not prepared to deal with patriation without a consensus on substantial increases in provincial powers. Bringing the Constitution home to Canada was going to involve some heavy federal-provincial negotiations. It was equally clear that, in the mid-1970s, Canada's economy had become as big an issue, if not a bigger one, for Canadians and their governments as the Constitution. So when the provincial premiers came to Ottawa in February 1977 to meet with Prime Minister Trudeau, it was the economic mess the country was in – stagflation, nearly double-digit levels of both unemployment and inflation – not the Constitution, that they talked about. The governments agreed on various common measures, including reducing public spending and eliminating jurisdictional overlap. Trudeau declared that the conference's success "marks the beginning of a process of more complete and purposeful intergovernmental consultation."[8] It should be noted that the "separatist" premier of Quebec, René Lévesque, participated in this relatively successful exercise in cooperative federalism.

The new PQ government was not backing away from its primary mission, but was in no rush to seek a referendum mandate for negotiating Quebec independence. In its first few months, it turned to a project it believed could be accomplished without constitutional change even though it was a crucial rationale of independence: making Quebec a thoroughly unilingual French-speaking society. On 1 April 1977 the government tabled a White Paper on language policy. Its lead author was the minister of cultural development, Camille Laurin, a psychiatrist and at one time a good friend of Pierre Trudeau. But the White Paper was built on a premise that was the very opposite of Trudeau's thinking about the relationship between language and culture. Laurin and his colleagues were imbued by an intellectual tradition that understood "thought, and therefore, culture" to be "inextricably linked with language."[9] Their White Paper began with a declaration that,

> [t]he Quebec we wish to build will essentially be French. The fact that the majority of its population is French will be clearly visible – at work, in communications, and in the country side. It will also be a country in which the traditional balance of power will be altered, especially in regard to the economy; the use of French will not merely be universalized to hide the predominance of foreign powers from the French population; this use will accompany, symbolize and support a reconquest by the French-speaking majority in Quebec of that control over the economy which it ought to have.

Dr Laurin, as political psychiatrist, prescribed this declaration as shock treatment for the anglophone minority and a means of removing a source of insecurity for the francophone majority.

The first bill to be introduced in Quebec's National Assembly – the renamed Legislative Assembly – set out a legislative framework for Laurin's recommendations. After weeks of debate and committee hearings, Bill 1 gave way to Bill 101, the Charte de la langue française. While still maintaining the basic principles of the White Paper, Bill 101 made compromises on some issues. Businesses with fewer than fifty employees were exempted from the requirement that French be the language of work. Signs in public places could be bilingual if they were targeting an ethnic group or business. Only the children of parents who had been educated in English in Quebec would have access to publicly supported English schools. Although this was more restrictive than the Bourassa Liberal government's Bill 22, which gave children who could pass an English-language test, including children of immigrants and migrants from other provinces, access to an English education in Quebec, Bill 101 ended the ordeal of language police examining five-year-olds for their proficiency in English. Still, it outraged Trudeau and many others in English Canada who believed in the right of parents to choose how their children are to be educated. Lévesque, whose input on Bill 101 inclined towards moderating its provisions, had a clause inserted offering access to Quebec's English schools to Canadians moving to Quebec from any province that reciprocated by offering access to French education to francophones migrating to that province from Quebec. That offer of reciprocity came to naught when the annual premiers' meeting that took place in New Brunswick in 1977 favoured a general resolution calling for a review of minority language education in Canada.

Camille Laurin's Bill 101 certainly administered the shock treatment to English-speaking Canada. It accelerated the exodus of Anglo-Quebecers: between 1976 and 1981, 130,000 English-speaking Quebecers left the province, "taking with them, their diplomas, their expertise, their bank accounts. It was quite the bloodletting."[10] Bill 101 heralded a shift in the balance of power in the Quebec economy, but it also ensured a change in the balance of economic power in Canada. The head offices of some of Canada's most important business corporations moved from Montreal to Toronto, making the Ontario capital the country's business capital. Although its immediate impact was to deepen the divide between English and French Canada, in the longer run it might be a factor in preserving the federation's unity. The Charte de la langue française would take a few blows, at its edges, from the Supreme Court of Canada, but its essentials would remain, and it is the law of Quebec today. If French Quebec could accomplish its fundamental aspiration of ensuring that it would be a predominantly French society by using powers available to it under the existing Constitution, the question arises: is its independence from Canada really necessary?

Faced with these initiatives of the provincial premiers and Quebec, Trudeau was ready to lead the country with a constitutional initiative of his own. In January 1977 he replied to Peter Lougheed that he could not accept the premiers' insistence that changes in the federal division of powers must be an integral part of any constitutional agreement. He had his officials beavering away on fashioning an approach to

constitutional reform that reflected his vision of Canada. In June 1978,
it was unveiled. Its first iteration took the form of a glossy booklet, covered with maple leaves, entitled "A Time for Action." Available in post
offices across the country, it summoned Canadians to a "renewal of the
Canadian federation." "A Time for Action" set out an agenda for a complete overhaul of the founding Constitution.[11] The reform process
would have two phases. Phase I would deal with matters the federal
government believed it could do unilaterally using the limited power
of constitutional amendment it had obtained in 1949. This phase would
include a statement of the federation's fundamental objectives, a Charter of Rights and Freedoms applying only to the federal government,
and a remodelling of the institutions of the federal government. The
provinces would be consulted, and they could opt into the Charter if
they wished, but their consent to this set of reforms was viewed as unnecessary. Matters requiring provincial consent would be dealt with
in phase II, as would Aboriginal rights and an amending formula.
Phase I was to be completed by 1 July 1979 and phase II by 1 July 1981,
so that a largely renovated Constitution could be brought home to
Canada on a Dominion Day marking the fiftieth anniversary of the
Statute of Westminster.

Close on the heels of the release of "A Time for Action," Bill C-60 was
introduced in Parliament giving formal legal expression to phase 1.
A parliamentary committee voted to seek the opinion of the Supreme
Court of Canada on whether the federal Parliament could make unilateral fundamental changes in the Senate. In 1980 the Court answered in
the negative – the same answer it would give Prime Minister Stephen
Harper when he referred a similar question to the Court a quarter of a
century later. For their part, however, the provincial governments were
not at all interested in Trudeau's initiative. By the time he got around
to discussing the Constitution with them, Bill C-60 had died on the
order paper.

Although it turned out to be a period piece, Bill-60 was an interesting
attempt to alter the fundamental nature of Canada's federal system.
Trudeau's two key proposals for remodelling institutions at the centre
were to replace the Senate with a House of the Federation jointly elected
by the House of Commons and the provincial legislatures, and to expand
the Supreme Court of Canada from nine to eleven judges appointed
in consultation with the provincial governments and ratified by the
House of the Federation. These proposals would have changed Canadian federalism from an inter-state model to an intra-state model. In an

intra-state federation, the interests of the units of the federation (provinces, states) are primarily represented and accommodated through national institutions, especially the upper house of the federal legislature. The American, German, and South African federations are leading examples. In an inter-state federation, negotiations between the central government and the governments of the federation's units are the primary process for accommodating national and local interests. As we saw in Chapter 9, the Canadian federation's fate was sealed in its first decade when, led by Ontario and Quebec, it became a thoroughly interstate federation. The lack of take-up on Trudeau's proposals shows that, for Canada, there was no turning back to a federalism that would diminish the role of provincial governments.

The Trudeau government's constitutional proposals were innovative in two other ways. One section of Bill C-60 attempted to codify some of the conventions of responsible government by spelling out the role of the governor general in the formation of a government after an election. It also formalized the governor general's five-year term. There was nothing new here – it was just an effort to put into formal law existing informal constitutional practices. But even this modest attempt at modernizing Canada's Constitution was too much for some commentators. It cost Trudeau the support of Eugene Forsey, the renowned constitutional expert whom Trudeau had appointed to the Senate. When a committee of the Canadian Bar Association proposed a non-monarchical head of state in its comprehensive proposal for a new Constitution, all hell broke loose and the committee's handiwork was repudiated by its parent organization. Clearly the time had not come even to touch the monarchical elements in Canada's Constitution.

The other innovative proposal, one with much better prospects, was proportional representation. Half the members of the House of the Federation were to be elected on the basis of proportional party representation in the provincial legislatures. In debating Bill C-60, the NDP proposed that, instead of a new upper house in the federal Parliament, an additional one hundred seats be added to the House of Commons on a regional basis allocated by proportional representation. Although nothing came of these proportional representation ideas at the time, they indicated some dissatisfaction with the existing simple plurality, first-past-the-post electoral system. Later on this would grow into a much broader-based public movement to have Canada follow most of the parliamentary world in adopting an electoral system that produces an elected legislature reflecting the political preferences of the people.

By the fall of 1978, the time had come for Canada's governments to return once again to intergovernmental negotiations on the Constitution. For negotiations to have a ghost of a chance of success, the agenda had to have a balance of federal and provincial concerns. And there was: when the first ministers convened in Ottawa at the end of October, the fourteen items on Prime Minister Trudeau's "Agenda for Change" covered both Ottawa's interest in a Charter of Rights and restructuring federal institutions as well as the provinces' interest in changes to the division of powers. A Continuing Committee of Ministers on the Constitution (CCMC), chaired by Saskatchewan's attorney general, Roy Romanow, and the federal minister of justice, Marc Lalonde, was mandated to work on the issues and develop proposals for a federal-provincial conference in February. This was a staggering task to be completed in a few months.

Three pan-Canadian Aboriginal organizations – the National Indian Brotherhood (NIB), representing status Indians; the Native Council of Canada, representing non-status Indians and Métis; and the Inuit Committee on National Issues – were invited to attend the October conference – as observers. NIB leader Noel Starblanket later remarked that he could have seen the proceedings just as well on television.[12] Although "A Time for Action" stated that "the renewal of the Federation must fully respect the legitimate rights of the native peoples," Aboriginal rights, however, did not make the list of fourteen items that Trudeau proposed for this round of constitutional negotiations.

Pierre Elliott Trudeau at this time was never more amenable to the provincial premiers' concerns. His stock, political and personal, was down. His government was only months away from the end of its five-year mandate, when it would have to call an election, and the polls showed his party well behind the Conservatives and their new leader, Joe Clark. The economy was still in bad shape, and his marriage had broken up. Pierre Trudeau was not riding high.

The provinces, on the other hand, were on the constitutional offensive. The Atlantic and western provinces were fired up about controlling the bounty from their petroleum resources. Decisions of a centralizing Supreme Court had much to do with this. The Court's decision in the 1967 *Offshore Mineral Rights Reference*[13] ruled that the federal government had ownership of the seabed immediately adjacent to the coastline and legislative control of natural resource development out to the international limit of the continental shelf. A decade later, the Court blocked Saskatchewan's attempt to capture the windfall gains generated by OPEC increases in the world price of oil. In the 1978

Canadian Industrial Gas & Oil Ltd case,[14] the Court, in a seven to two decision, held that Saskatchewan's "royalty surcharge" on petroleum producers was an unconstitutional indirect tax and encroached on the federal government's exclusive power over international and interprovincial trade. A year later, this time unanimously, the Court struck down a Saskatchewan plan to cut back on potash production in order to protect the interests of multinational companies operating mines in the United States and Saskatchewan.[15] Again the Court unanimously found that this was an unconstitutional provincial intrusion into international trade. The Supreme Court and the federal government seemed to be colluding to prevent the petroleum-producing provinces from enjoying the full benefit of their natural resources. Quebec's PQ government had not yet made a move to hold a referendum on independence, creating the illusion that, if it got enough at the federal-provincial bargaining table, the referendum might not take place.

Roy Romanow, Marc Lalonde, and their CCMC colleagues did not have much of a Christmas that year. Between November and early January 1979, they held three week-long meetings and spent much of the time in between crafting "best effort" solutions for contested issues. When the first ministers reassembled on 5 February, it was more like a meeting of the UN General Assembly than a gathering of Canadian politicians. Each premier headed a delegation that came with full-blown formal statements of their province's position. The fact that some of "the best efforts" drafts showed "a high degree of consensus and accommodation" was almost a miracle.[16]

At the meetings that led to Confederation, the proposals of the central Canadian politicians had set the agenda, while the Atlantic Canadian delegates bargained for modifications. A century later that could not happen. The provinces of the east and the west came to Ottawa in February 1979 with their own proposals. The centre of the country was deeply divided between a largely English-speaking Ontario that wanted nothing more than to preserve the federal union and a largely French-speaking Quebec that had elected a government whose constitutional priority was to break away from that union. The central government could not have been led by anyone more passionately committed to Canada's national unity than Pierre Elliott Trudeau, but it would have taken a statesman of superhuman capacity to bridge the gap between all these views of what Canada should be all about.

The clash of perspectives can be seen in the competing proposals on Senate reform. British Columbia had the most full-blown proposal: provincial government delegations voting as a bloc in a true House of the Provinces. The federal government proposed that half of the House of the Provinces be appointed by Ottawa. New Brunswick insisted that the Senate should continue as a national institution, with all of its members appointed by the federal government. Alberta, Quebec, and Newfoundland, rather than wanting provinces to have more power at the centre, wanted more power transferred to the provinces. And Saskatchewan, with an NDP government, favoured abolishing the Senate. The Senate was the most contentious issue in the Confederation debates. The constitutional conference in Ottawa in February 1979 gave every indication that there was no consensus on keeping the Senate as is or on any alternative for reforming or abolishing it. Those divergent views on Senate reform remain with us down to the present day.

In this 1978–79 effort at a comprehensive overhaul of the Constitution, Pierre Trudeau went as far as he would ever go in limiting federal power and increasing provincial power. That was still not very far. His government agreed in "best effort" drafts to limit, but not abandon, its power to spend money in areas of exclusive provincial jurisdiction, and to do the same thing with its declaratory power to take over public works in a province. The federal government also agreed to give up its anachronistic jurisdiction over divorce so that family law could be brought entirely under provincial control, and to transfer inland fisheries to provincial control. These concessions would eliminate some of the excessively centralist features of the original Constitution. But on the hot division-of-powers issue – control over natural resources – the feds gave very little. Ottawa was willing to clarify the provinces' power to develop their natural resources, but it would not agree to limits on its paramount power over the marketing of natural resources in interprovincial and international trade.

On other key issues – a constitutional charter of rights and freedoms, putting the principle of fiscal equalization in the Constitution, and a formula for amending the Constitution in Canada – there was still no consensus even among government leaders, who are more inclined to be accommodating than the people they represent. Canadians, though they didn't know it at the time, were going through a profound educational experience. Reluctantly they were learning that they were divided by very different understandings, very different visions, of the nature of Canada as a political community. Is it a country primarily based on two (or three) founding peoples? Or a country whose main constituent parts are ten equally important provinces? Or a bilingual democracy led by a strong national government supported by a majority of individual rights-bearing citizens? These are not the kind of differences that can be papered over with carefully crafted "best effort" solutions. No liberal-democratic state deeply divided on what the country is all about has successfully carried out comprehensive constitutional change unless facing a truly existential crisis. Leaders and citizens will make the compromises required to accommodate their differences only if they see them as the alternative to civil war or break-up. Canada was not there yet – although a successful Quebec referendum on separation might get them there in a hurry.

The February 1979 conference brought to an end the first era of new constitutionalism. Believe it or not, Canadians would have another go at comprehensive constitutional reform in the early 1990s. We Canadians are slow learners. But when Trudeau called an election on 26 March, he moved the next stage of the constitutional struggle into the arenas of raw politics: elections and a referendum.

Joe Clark's Progressive Conservatives "won" the May 1979 election. The Liberals built their campaign around Trudeau, who campaigned mostly on his agenda for constitutional reform. But many voters were tired of Trudeau and the Constitution. Joe Clark's victory was somewhat like Justin Trudeau's electoral triumph in 2015: a young novice leader defeating an experienced opponent. But there is one important difference. The young Trudeau would lead a majority government, whereas the May 1979 election did not give Joe Clark's party a majority in the House of Commons. The Conservatives won 136 seats to the Liberals' 114. The NDP elected 26 MPs, and more than likely would support the Liberals on a non-confidence vote. Six Créditistes from rural Quebec held the balance of power in a 282-seat House. Joe Clark's tragedy, and it was of his own making, was that he was in denial about the minority status of his government. He told Canadians: "I am proceeding on the assumption that the Progressive Conservative Party has won a mandate to govern. I intend to carry out that mandate." Clark would learn the hard way that, in a parliamentary democracy, the mandate to govern comes from Parliament.[17]

One of the two Quebec gladiators who had been at the centre of constitutional politics for over a decade now seemed to be leaving the scene. In the summer of 1979, Trudeau took his boys for a summer holiday and then with some friends left for a northern canoe trip. As leader of the Opposition he had little do, as Prime Minister Clark had decided not to have Parliament meet until October – the longest period in Canadian history before a newly elected Parliament's first meeting.

When the 31st Parliament finally met on 9 October, Trudeau seemed to be disengaging from the responsibilities of leadership. He began missing important party events. Then, on 20 November, he stunned his colleagues when he walked into the regular Wednesday caucus meeting and said, "It's all over."[18] He had decided to resign as party leader.

The other gladiator, René Lévesque, was now flying high. After the failure of the federal-provincial conference, he could focus on the PQ's constitutional program. On 1 November the PQ released *Quebec-Canada: A New Deal*, which for the first time spelled out what sovereignty-association meant.[19] René Lévesque's and Claude Morin's fingerprints were all over it. Quebec would have formal legal sovereignty, but would be in an economic union with Canada, regulated by an international treaty. In effect it was a mini European Union. There would be a council to manage the union and a court to adjudicate disputes arising under the treaty. On these two institutions Quebec and Canada would have equal representation. But on the monetary authority managing the common currency (the Canadian dollar), Quebec would be a junior partner. The idea was to soft-pedal Quebec separation as much as possible. Indeed "separate" and "independence" were banned from the PQ's lexicon.

Publication of PQ's constitutional plan paved the way for formulating the referendum question. In December, after a marathon drafting session by the cabinet, Lévesque announced the question that, said he, was "clear and frank." Here it is:

> The Government of Quebec has made public its proposal to negotiate a new agreement with the rest of Canada, based on the equality of nations.
>
> This agreement would enable Quebec to acquire the exclusive power to make its laws, administer its taxes and establish relations abroad – in other words sovereignty – and at the same time maintain with Canada an economic association including a common currency.
>
> Any change in political status resulting from these negotiations will be submitted to the people through a referendum.
>
> ON THESE TERMS, DO YOU AGREE TO GIVE THE GOVERN-MENT OF QUEBEC THE MANDATE TO NEGOTIATE THE PROPOSED AGREEMENT BETWEEN QUEBEC AND CANADA?

The "question" was frank in showing the PQ government's strategy of soft-pedalling separation. But asking for a mandate to negotiate a deal and promising a second referendum if the negotiation produced "a change in status" was less than lucid.

At the very time Lévesque's PQ government was preparing its referendum plan, the Clark Progressive Conservative government, with its eyes tightly closed, headed into the denouement of its political catastrophe. On 11 December Finance Minister John Crosbie presented his budget to the House of Commons. By raising new revenues and not increasing expenditures, Crosbie's budget imposed the fiscal discipline required to reduce a $9 billion deficit. One of the tax changes was an increase in the excise tax on transportation fuels from 7 to 18 cents. That increase was too much for the six Créditistes, and Crosbie admits that no serious attempt was made to work out a deal with them.[20] The Conservatives did not think the Liberals and NDP were prepared to bring the government down – and even if they did, with Trudeau out of the picture, they did not fear an election. But the Liberals fooled them. They quietly assembled all their troops while a handful of busy Tories remained out of Ottawa. On 13 December NDP finance critic Bob Rae moved a vote of non-confidence that carried 139 to 133. The Créditistes abstained.

The defeated Clark government called an election for 18 February 1980. A few days later, Pierre Trudeau dropped the other shoe. After a walk in the snow on the evening of 17 December, he had decided against retuning to politics. The next morning he woke up and said to himself, "My God, I made the wrong decision last night."[21] At a press conference later in the day, Trudeau announced his decision to resume the Liberal Party leadership. His duty to accept the draft of his party, he explained, was even stronger than his desire to return to private life.

Nineteen eighty marks another turning point in Canada's odyssey shaped by the fortunes of the two French-Canadian gladiators, Pierre Trudeau and René Lévesque. In February Trudeau won an election. In May Lévesque lost a referendum. The 1980 Liberal campaign was very different from the campaign of the year before. Trudeau's advisers managed to keep him relatively quiet on his constitutional ideals. As Stephen Clarkson puts it, the strategy was "Hiding the Charisma: Low Bridging the Saviour."[22] The Clark Conservatives offered much of the 1979 platform that they had not been able to implement in their short time in power. There were no leadership debates. The Liberals recovered their majority, increasing their share of the popular vote from 40 to 42 per cent, and taking all but one of Quebec's seventy-five seats – seven more than the previous year. The bad news for the Liberals and for the country was that they elected only two MPs west of the Ontario border – down one from 1979.[23]

On 15 April, the same day Trudeau spoke in the Speech from the Throne debate opening the new Parliament, Lévesque announced that the referendum would be held on 20 May. Under the rules Quebec's National Assembly established for the referendum, there would be official teams for the "yes" and "no" sides. Lévesque, of course, would captain the "yes" side, while Claude Ryan, the former editor of Le Devoir and now leader of the Liberal Party of Quebec, would lead the "no" side. The Quebec Liberal Party issued its constitutional proposals, in what came to be called the Beige Paper, early in 1980. Given the lead role Ryan had played in attacking the Victoria Charter, it is not surprising that the Beige Paper proposed increasing provincial powers, especially in the fields of social policy and culture. But the paper also called for increasing provincial participation in federal government institutions: a Federal Council, made up of provincial government appointees replacing the Senate, and a strong role for the provinces in selecting Supreme Court justices. Its general tenor was close to those of Henri Bourassa and the proposals of the Pépin-Robarts Task Force on National Unity. If Canada were to have a new Constitution based on federal-provincial negotiations, it is likely it would come close to the Beige Paper's approach.

Claude Ryan aside, the real leader of the federalist political forces – and everyone knew it – was Pierre Trudeau. Trudeau never repudiated the Beige Paper, but against Ryan's advice he gave the justice and inter-governmental portfolios to Jean Chrétien and sent him to work with Ryan in the referendum campaign. Chrétien and Ryan were not a happy couple. Trudeau invited the NDP to form a coalition with the Liberals. If NDP leader Ed Broadbent had accepted, he might well have given the federal government's referendum pitch more balance. But just as Crerar had turned down King's coalition invitation in 1921, so Broadbent declined Trudeau's invitation. It was Trudeau, then, who would carry the ball for the "yes" side.

Trudeau's most potent ally in the campaign was not another politician, but a group of mobilized women. The person who stirred them up was Lise Payette, a television star and ardent feminist who had joined Lévesque's cabinet. In an offhand remark, Payette decried how the Quebec education ministry's teaching materials depicted the good little girl Yvette who helps her mother with the dishes and learns sewing and needlework. That might not have got Payette into too much trouble – but she went on and rebuked Claude Ryan for marrying an Yvette. Oh dear! On 7 April, before the referendum campaign had really started, fifteen thousand women filled the Forum, the hallowed home of the Montreal Canadiens, cheering speaker after speaker – all supporting the "no" side. The Yvettes were a formidable force delivered into the federalists' hands by an errant separatist.

In the solemn, measured speech Trudeau delivered to a very hushed House of Common on 15 April he said that, if the "yes" side won – and at the time it was ahead in the polls – his government would not negotiate sovereignty-association with the Quebec government. On 2 May he spoke in Montreal to the Chambre de Commerce. With sarcasm and wit he poured ridicule on what the "yes" side thought was its trump card: that Quebecers could vote "yes" without fear of any immediate consequences. "From being separatists, they became *indépendantistes*. From *indépendantistes*, they turned into sovereignists," Trudeau taunted. He went on, his nasal voice rising, "fearing that the option was a little too clear, they moved on to sovereignty-association. Then, they hastened to assure us ... that they wouldn't do one without the other – they begged us to believe that they only wanted a mandate to negotiate them, not do them, because to do it, they would need a second referendum." Then he paused to twist the knife. "You've got to admit that for courage of conviction, for nobility of ideal, for spirit of decision, we've seen better!"[24]

Trudeau made two more speeches in the campaign. He spoke in Quebec City on 7 May and on 16 May at the Paul Sauvé Arena in Montreal, on the very stage where René Lévesque had wept with joy celebrating his party's historic victory on 16 November 1976. The Paul Sauvé speech was the real game-changer. In the words of journalists Robert Sheppard and Michael Valpy, Trudeau gave "an electrifying performance that reverberated throughout the province for days."[25] At the climactic moment of his speech, appearing to discard his written notes, he glared out at the audience and waited for a moment of calm. Then he spoke these words: "I know that I can make a solemn commitment that following a 'No' vote we will immediately take action to renew the Constitution and we will not stop until we have done that."[26] He went on to say that he made this "solemn declaration" to all Canadians in the other provinces, implying that he would not let the provincial governments prevent him from fulfilling this commitment. This was the first strong hint of Trudeau's determination, if necessary, to proceed unilaterally with constitutional reform.

Much ink has been spilt on whether Trudeau in this speech deliberately deceived Quebecers. Certainly the constitutional changes he would soon champion and see through to completion – a constitutional charter of rights, an all-Canadian constitutional amending formula, and constitutionalizing the principle of fiscal equalization – were not what Quebec nationalists had been looking for. Nor did they include the decentralizing proposals that Trudeau seemed to be taking seriously at the 1978–79 constitutional conferences, or that were in the report of his own Unity Task Force, or in the paper of his "no" side partner, the Quebec Liberal Party. Trudeau's defenders argue that anyone who had been paying attention would have known that Trudeau could never have had those kinds of changes in mind when he committed to constitutional renewal. That might be true. All the same, if Trudeau had talked briefly about what he meant by constitutional renewal, it is doubtful that his words would have brought that cheering crowd of Quebecers to its feet in the Paul Sauvé Arena on 16 May 1980. The one thing of which we can be sure is that Trudeau's performance that night gave rise to a popular Quebec myth of betrayal.

Four days later, the referendum took place. The turnout was massive: 85.6 per cent. The result for the people of Quebec was clear: 59.6 per cent voted "no" to sovereignty-association, while 40.4 per cent voted "yes." For the *Québécois*, the vote was much closer: it is estimated that a bare majority, perhaps 51 per cent, of francophones voted "yes." Christian Dufour refers to the referendum as "the essence of sovereignty: the enjoyment of the right to self-determination."[27] The 1980 Quebec referendum was the first time since their "conquest" by Britain and their abandonment by France that the *Québécois* had been consulted directly, if not clearly, on their future. The only clear thing about the result was that it was neither definitive nor final. Back in the Paul Sauvé Arena on the evening of 20 May, after the results were clear, René Lévesque his voice cracking with fatigue, led the crowd of five thousand in the singing of "Gens du pays." As the last notes died out he said simply, "*À la prochaine.*" Until next time.[28]

Trudeau was now in the driver's seat. He had risen from his political grave to win an election and defeat the separatists in the Quebec referendum. He was now more determined than ever to complete his constitutional mission, and with his political base never stronger, he might have launched his own constitutional initiative immediately. But no. Twenty days after the referendum he invited the provincial premiers to meet with him at 24 Sussex and crank up the rickety old machinery of federal-provincial negotiations. So the Continuing Committee of Ministers on the Constitution, this time captained by Jean Chrétien and Roy Romanow, was relaunched with instructions to come back with the makings of a deal to be sealed at a first ministers' conference in Ottawa after Labour Day.

Trudeau now felt much more in control of the agenda. He divided the items the CCMC was to work on into two lists: the People's List, whose main two items were a charter of rights and patriation, and a Governments' List consisting of division-of-powers issues and the Senate. The premiers smelled a rat – the possibility that, if there was no agreement on the Governments' list, Trudeau might proceed unilaterally with what came to be dubbed the People's Package. That threat haunted the intergovernmental process from beginning to end.

This second CCMC was an even bigger affair than the first. The band of ministers, officials, and experts – about three hundred in all – that, through the rainy summer of 1980, moved across the country from Montreal to Toronto to Vancouver was referred to by one participant as "Nathan Detroit's floating crap game."[29] Although the participants worked hard during the days and socialized hard in the evenings, building strong personal bonds, many must have sensed that they really did not have a snowball's chance in hell of making a deal.

The differences between Trudeau and most of the premiers, as well as among the premiers, were just too numerous and too fundamental. Trudeau had withdrawn the reductions in federal power he had conceded in the 1978–79 round. At the road show's first stop in Montreal, the Ottawa delegation weighed in with a major paper on the need for powers to strengthen the Canadian economic union. Alberta premier Peter Lougheed's government was immersed in negotiations with Ottawa over controlling the petroleum resources on which his province's economic future depended. At the constitutional table he pressed hard for the federal government to surrender some of the exclusive control over the marketing of natural resources that it had secured through decisions of the Supreme Court of Canada. British Columbia continued to insist that without a new Senate there could be no deal. At the other end of the country, Newfoundland and Labrador's Brian Peckford, a new boy at the table, pushed fiercely for control of the offshore fishery and the revenues from newly discovered offshore oil reserves. Ontario premier Bill Davis – whose province, since Premier Robarts's 1967 Confederation for Tomorrow Conference, was looked upon as a conciliator – was embarrassed by not being able to commit to offering his province's six hundred thousand francophones the right to use French in Ontario's courts and legislature. In Saskatchewan's Allan Blakeney and Manitoba's Sterling Lyon, the west provided two eloquent critics of the tendency of an entrenched constitutional bill of rights and freedoms to undermine parliamentary sovereignty. Blakeney and Lyon held back most of the premiers from supporting Trudeau's first constitutional renewal priority. New Brunswick's Richard Hatfield, however, had become an ardent fan of a constitutional bill of rights.

And where was Quebec in all this? Lévesque, post-referendum, was in the position of a poker player whose down card had been revealed and its value was too low to scare anyone else at the table. For the moment he was a political eunuch. Claude Morin, the clever strategist who was now his intergovernmental affairs minister, persuaded Lévesque and the PQ cabinet that the best Quebec could do in this next round of constitutional bargaining was to help the premiers build a common front against Trudeau. Their common ground would be opposition to federal unilateralism.

With all these cross-cutting currents and machinations, it was surely no wonder that the CCMC had nothing very positive to report to its leaders at the end of the summer. The four-day first ministers' meeting that began in the Ottawa Conference Centre on 8 September was surely the surliest and sourest in Canadian history. Its only rival for that dubious honour would occur fourteen months later. Two events on the Sunday before the conference opened cast a dark shadow over the proceedings to come. When the premiers, after arriving in Ottawa, gathered in Manitoba premier Lyon's hotel suite, Claude Morin passed around photocopies of a secret memorandum setting out the federal government's bargaining strategy. It had been prepared by Michael Kirby, the senior official in the federal intergovernmental affairs department. A separatist mole had leaked the Kirby memorandum to Morin. After setting out the various provincial proposals and how they might be handled in negotiations, Kirby's memorandum concluded: *"The probability of an agreement is not high. Unilateral action is therefore a distinct possibility."*[30] It then invoked Machiavelli's maxim that "there is nothing more difficult to arrange, more doubtful of success, and more dangerous to carry through than initiating changes in a state's constitution."[31] At the conference's opening banquet that evening hosted by Governor General Ed Schreyer (a former Manitoba premier), the premiers angrily accused Chrétien of bargaining in bad faith. Their biting jabs put Trudeau in a foul mood. When a cake to celebrate Saskatchewan premier Blakeney's fifty-fifth birthday was wheeled in, Trudeau turned his back on the celebration and shortly after stormed out of Rideau Hall, allegedly saying to his RCMP bodyguard, "Fuck off, and don't follow me home."[32]

For the next four days Canadians, through intense media coverage, for the very first time, were able to watch their political leaders debate constitutional reform. Many of the speeches they heard were eloquent, some even learned, but they did not hear a country coming together to adopt a renewed Constitution. Instead they heard profoundly different visions of their country and of the political institutions best suited for its governance. On Friday, after four days of public meetings, the premiers met with Prime Minister Trudeau in a private session at 24 Sussex. René Lévesque's delegation had prepared a paper attempting to synthesize the provincial positions. The premiers discussed it at a breakfast meeting in the Château Laurier, so that it became known as the "Château consensus."[33] It was much too slanted in the direction of further decentralizing the federation to have a hope of persuading Trudeau that it could be a basis for continuing negotiations. At half-past nine on the evening of 12 September, the premiers filed out of 24 Sussex, glum and silent. A "tired and testy" Trudeau wound up the conference, admitting its failure, but by no means throwing in the towel on his mission to renew the Constitution.[34] He would talk to his colleagues about what to do next.

When Trudeau met the Liberal caucus on 17 September, it was in a feisty mood, especially its Quebec contingent, who were still smarting over the abuse they had taken from the separatists in the May referendum (for example, being branded as traitors). They were all for unilateral action by the federal government and very much in favour of including the charter of rights in the federal initiative. "If you are going to do it," said Hazen Argue, a Saskatchewan senator, "let's go first class." In French that translated as *"Roulons en Cadillac."*[35] There was an intellectual argument that it would be adding insult to injury to include a constitutional charter of rights that would limit the power of provincial legislatures in a package that ignored provincial demands for increased powers. But the political argument that prevailed was that enshrining the fundamental rights of citizens in the Constitution had much more popular appeal than fine points of constitutional logic. Trudeau found his cabinet colleagues whom he met with the next day less exuberant than the caucus, but on balance very much in favour of a unilateral initiative that included patriation and a charter of rights and freedoms.

On 2 October the federal government booked network time for Trudeau to address the country. Trudeau's broadcast was competing with Mohammed Ali's fourth comeback fight, this time with Larry Holmes. Ali lost, but Trudeau won a very large audience's attention. In the style of France's General de Gaulle, he was appealing over the heads of political elites directly to the people. He would send a resolution of the Canadian Parliament to the British government requesting it to pass amendments to the Canadian Constitution. This would be the last time Canada would have to go to London to change its Constitution: the amendments would include a formula for amending the Constitution in Canada. Besides patriation, a constitutional charter of rights and freedoms would be added to Canada's Constitution, along with a section constitutionalizing the principle of fiscal equalization in the federation. These were the three components of his People's Package of constitutional reform. He would welcome provincial support for the package, but was fully prepared to proceed without them.

Trudeau was breaking the mould of Canada's constitutional politics. He was treating Canada according to his vision of the country: a democratic aggregation of individual citizens bound together by a common set of rights and freedoms, including the right to educate their children and deal with government in English and French, and governed primarily by a national government in Ottawa. Changes affecting the powers of the provinces would be made without their consent. The mechanism for refining the federal government's proposals would not be the traditional intergovernmental meetings, but televised public hearings before a committee of the Canadian Parliament. The provinces would be asked to consider the amending formula that was in the 1971 Victoria Charter requiring that amendments be supported by the legislatures of Ontario, Quebec, two Atlantic provinces, and two western provinces. But if negotiations over this formula became deadlocked, the federal government could take the formula directly to the people in a referendum and seek majorities in the four regions of the country. Trudeau knew the risk he was taking. "We could tear up the goddamn country by this action," he told the cabinet, "but we're going to do it anyway."[36] The next thirteen months would be the heaviest season of constitutional politics the country had ever seen – and that's saying something!

The populist character of the campaign for Trudeau's initiative had two dimensions. One was a heavy, government-financed advertising campaign. Television was a large part of that, as were massive and somewhat idiotic billboards all over the country showing iconic Canadian geese flying our Constitution back to Canada. And of course, the whole idea of a "People's Package" was a crude exercise in populist public relations. The other dimension was the Special Joint Committee on the Constitution. The committee had twenty-five members from both the Senate and the House of Commons: fifteen Liberals, ten Progressive

Conservatives, and two NDP MPs. Trudeau had secured NDP leader Ed Broadbent's support for his unilateral initiative, broadening the political base for his policy, but also giving the NDP some leverage in improving the package or preventing regressive changes in it. Between early November 1980 and late February 1981, the committee had fifty-six hearing days – all of them televised.[37] Its proceedings were an unprecedented opening up of Canada's constitutional process. But for individual citizens it was a continuation of spectator constitutionalism. The committee heard from six governments and ninety-three interest groups. The only individuals permitted to make submissions were five chosen by the political parties, two each by the Liberals and PCs and one by the NDP.

Although theoretically the parliamentary committee was to deal with all components of the People's Package, its focus was very much on the Canadian Charter of Rights and Freedoms. Most submissions were directed to strengthening and broadening the Charter. An environmental group, for example, wanted the rights of trees written into the Charter. As I learned from my own appearance before the committee, there was little interest in the role of courts in interpreting and enforcing the Charter. The Progressive Conservative Party invited me to be one of their two individual witnesses, not because I was a member of their party, but because of my knowledge of other countries' experience, especially that of the United States, with a constitutional bill of rights. Polling data indicating its overwhelming popularity made PCs on the committee reluctant to pour any cold water on the Charter. My evidence focused on how US experience showed that what a constitutional rights charter means depends very much on how the judiciary interprets it. This seemed to come as news to many members of the committee.

The Charter that came before the committee was already stronger and more extensive than any of the drafts considered in earlier stages of the constitutional process. It now had a robust and comprehensive equality clause (section 15) – robust in that it proclaimed every individual to be "equal before and under the law" and having "the right to the equal protection and benefit of the law without discrimination"; and comprehensive in identifying race, national or ethnic origin, colour, religion, sex, age, or mental or physical handicap as specific examples of unconstitutional discrimination. The right to equal benefit of the law – for instance, for handicapped people, added in response to submissions to the parliamentary committee – could require positive action by government. Such rights are sometimes referred to as "red rights," in contrast to "blue rights" that prohibit action by the state. The US Bill of Rights is made up entirely of "blue rights," reflecting the American revolutionary tradition that views the state as the enemy. The Canadian tradition, as we saw in the chapter on Confederation, is much more inclined to see the state as a necessary agent for social justice. A clause added to the equality section underlines that tradition by making it clear that positive discrimination aimed at the "amelioration of conditions of disadvantaged individual or groups" would be accepted under the Charter.

The parliamentary committee process resulted in a considerable strengthening of the Charter. The committee itself could only recommend changes in the draft, which Jean Chrétien would then take to cabinet. The most extensive changes accepted by the Trudeau government were a toughening up of the criminal justice sections. Especially important was the addition of a clause empowering judges to exclude evidence obtained by the police in a manner contrary to a citizen's rights if they thought the inclusion of such evidence would "bring the administration of justice" into disrepute. This provision was in line with US law and with recent recommendations of the Royal Commission of Inquiry into Certain Activities of the RCMP. Its inclusion in the Charter subjected police investigation practices to judicial scrutiny as never before, and has turned out to be the biggest single generator of Charter litigation. The submissions of civil liberties groups led to another important strengthening of the Charter: the general limitation clause at the beginning. Instead of a clause permitting government to violate Charter rights in emergencies or allowing parliamentary democracy to override constitutional rights, a new section 1 erected a higher standard for government actions or legislation to meet in order to justify violations of Charter rights: limits on rights would have to be "reasonable," "prescribed by law," and capable of being "demonstrably justified in a free and democratic society." That last phrase places the onus on government to justify actions or laws that violate any rights in the Charter. It subjects to judicial appraisal the government's rationale for policy decisions that adversely affect rights.

At one point in the proceedings, when solicitor-general Robert Kaplan was sitting in for Jean Chrétien, it appeared that the government would support entrenching property rights in the Charter. The Canadian Bill of Rights protects property rights, and property rights had been included in the charter contained in the 1978 Bill C-60. Its reinsertion would have been congenial to conservatives and thus broadened support for Trudeau's initiative. Most of the provinces were opposed, but the NDP's opposition was crucial. The NDP well knew how the property right in the US Constitution had been used to block the imposition of environmental regulations on privately owned property. Saskatchewan's NDP premier, Allan Blakeney, who was still being wooed by the Trudeau government to support its initiative, made it clear that reversing its acceptance of property rights was a precondition of any possible agreement with his government.[38] The Trudeau government preferred to keep the NDP and Saskatchewan onside than to woo the right.

The rejection of a constitutionally entrenched property right added to the Charter's distinctly Canadian character. In the same vein the inclusion of education rights for the French-speaking minorities in English Canada and the English-speaking minority in Quebec privileges groups in a distinctively Canadian, and un-American, manner. Similarly, section 27, which instructs judges to interpret the Charter "in a manner consistent with the preservation and enhancement of the multicultural heritage of Canada," reflects the celebration of multiculturalism as part of Canada's civic culture. A further section (#28), added at the end of the parliamentary committee process through intensive lobbying by women's organizations, states that the Charter rights "are guaranteed equally to male and female persons." The section was definitely overkill in terms of protection against sex discrimination, but it was a feel good concession to Canadian feminists. Exposure of charter-making to a parliamentary committee ensured that the Canadian Charter of Rights and Freedoms would be a thoroughly Canadian document.

While the parliamentary committee was busy receiving submissions on the Charter, unexpected action by Indigenous peoples was opening up the People's Package to an additional item of constitutional renewal. Canada's Aboriginal pillar was idle no more. Since the rejection of the federal White Paper in 1969, Aboriginal organizations had been working to be admitted to the constitutional renewal process. All they had been able to obtain from the federal and provincial governments, however, was observer status at the negotiating table and a promise from Prime Minister Trudeau that, after the People's Package phase was done, they would be invited to the table in phase 2 of the process. Needless to say, that would not satisfy the forces of Aboriginal nationalism that had been building up in the country for several decades.

Aboriginal constitutional concerns were both defensive and offensive. On the defensive side, treaty Indians opposed a patriation process cutting all Canadian ties to Britain that ignored treaty relations First Nations had entered into with the British Crown. Offensively, Indians, both status and non-status, Inuit, and Métis hoped to secure positive recognition of their rights in the constitutional reform process. The Indigenous peoples waged the defensive side of their campaign in London, and their effort to secure constitutional gains in Ottawa. Throughout, their efforts were plagued by lack of unity. This is not surprising, given the thin legitimacy of pan-Canadian organizations that represent peoples whose identity is primarily local and tribal, and the complexity of the issues involved. It is truly a political miracle that, despite these difficulties, Indigenous peoples achieved as much as they did in the patriation process.

The epicentre of Aboriginal mobilization was British Columbia, where meetings explaining the constitutional challenge took place across the province in the fall of 1980. George Manuel, whom we met at the beginning of Chapter 12, was now the grand chief of the Union of BC Indian Chiefs (UBCIC) and was still an articulate advocate for Aboriginal rights. Before Christmas, "hundreds of Indigenous peoples scraped together funds and boarded a train in Vancouver, which they called the Constitution Express."[39] The Express rolled across the country picking up supporters and publicity along the way. Its arrival in Ottawa with five hundred Indians on board was a major media event. Two days later, two thousand Indians attended a First Nations Assembly in the largest convention hall in Ottawa. "The Indians," in the words of Douglas Sanders, "had established a remarkable presence in Ottawa at a crucial time in the constitutional reform process."[40]

Aboriginal groups were divided about appearing before the joint parliamentary committee. The UBCIC had changed its mind, and now feared that entrenching their rights in Canada's Constitution would compromise Indian nations' claim to their political independence. The UBCIC would concentrate its efforts on an international campaign. Representatives of the Inuit, who are inclined to be less fundamentalist, favoured participating in the parliamentary committee process, as did the Yukon Council of Indians and the Dene Nation of the Northwest Territories. Eventually, after several weeks of dithering, National Indian Brotherhood president Del Riley agreed to go before the committee. With the strong support of the NDP caucus and the technical assistance of the Yukon Indians' counsel, Donald Rosenbloom, a fragile consensus was worked out among three national native groups, the National Indian Brotherhood, the Native Council of Canada, and the Inuit Committee on National Issues.

That agreement, reached in NDP leader Ed Broadbent's office, contained three proposed amendments. First and foremost was a new freestanding part of the Constitution, outside the Charter, which read as follows: "(1) The aboriginal and treaty rights of the aboriginal peoples of Canada are hereby recognized and affirmed. (2) In this Act, 'aboriginal peoples of Canada' includes the Indians, Inuit and Métis peoples of Canada." A second amendment to section 25 of the Charter stipulated that the rights and freedoms of Aboriginal peoples recognized by the 1763 Royal Proclamation should not be abrogated or derogated from by anything in the Charter. The third amendment provided that a future first ministers' conference discuss Aboriginal issues and involve Aboriginal representatives. On Friday, 30 January, leaders of the three federal political parties and the national Indigenous organizations agreed to a deal based on these three components.

The deal barely survived the weekend. Early the next week the Alberta chiefs unanimously rejected the deal and called for Del Riley's resignation. The BC chiefs had already shifted their effort to the international arena. A crucial point was whether Aboriginal gains in Canada's Constitution could be rolled back without the consent of Aboriginal peoples. When Jean Chrétien explained that any Aboriginal rights provisions would be subject to a constitutional amending formula in which Aboriginal peoples and their governments had no place, much of the Indigenous support for the deal disintegrated. Nevertheless, for the time being, the proposed amendments remained as additions to the People's Package.

The international campaign included a trip to New York, where interest in Indigenous matters was just beginning to make its way onto the United Nations agenda, and a submission by the Native Council of Canada to the Bertrand Russell Peace Tribunal in Amsterdam that resulted in a condemnation of Canada's treatment of Indigenous peoples and their exclusion from the constitutional process.[41] But most of the international effort was concentrated in London, where the National Indian Brotherhood opened an office and began lobbying MPs and members of the House of Lords to block passage of the Canadian government's constitutional proposals when they came before the British Parliament.

Several Aboriginal organizations initiated court cases arguing that Britain's treaty commitments to Indian nations in Canada created a trust relationship that required Aboriginal consent before Britain could sever its legal ties to Canada. The most significant was the Indian Association of Alberta's case, which was joined by native organizations from New Brunswick and Nova Scotia, so that the case related to both pre- and post-Confederation treaties. The case challenged the position the British Foreign Office had taken in its submission to the parliamentary committee chaired by Sir Anthony Kershaw that was looking into the constitutionality of the Trudeau government's plan to ask the Parliament at Westminster to ratify its proposals for constitutional change. The Foreign Office took the view that, since the Statute of Westminster, any Crown obligations to Indians in Canada had been passed on to the Crown in right of Canada. A Queen's Bench judge threw out a challenge to that view. The Alberta Indians appealed to the Court of Appeal, where the matter came before Lord Denning, a British judge renowned for his independence of mind and support for the underdog. Denning let the Indians down – gently. He found that, with Dominion autonomy the Crown had split, and the Crown in right of Canada was now the Indian nations' treaty partner, relieving the British Crown of any continuing treaty obligations. But he spoke warmly about the "rights and freedoms" originally guaranteed by the British Crown, and optimistically that "they should be honoured by the Crown in respect of Canada so long as the sun rises and the rivers flow. That promise must never be broken,"[42] he concluded.

Denning's words might be the most valuable result of the Indians' London lobby. Their efforts there received little media coverage in Canada, and that might be just as well. Non-Aboriginal Canadians regard themselves as former colonists who have got out from under imperial rule; they would not take kindly to efforts to promote British interference in Canadian affairs. No doubt there is a deep hypocrisy in that position: the insensitivity of white former colonists to the colonialism they have imposed on native peoples. But the reality is that, to advance its interests, Canada's Aboriginal pillar would have to rely on the influence it could bring to bear on an independent Canada, not on the interference of a former imperial power.

On 14 October, less than two weeks after Trudeau announced his constitutional initiative, the provincial premiers met in Toronto's Harbour Castle Hotel to consider their response. It soon emerged that six premiers were determined to oppose Trudeau's unilateralism, which they considered to be unconstitutional. But Ontario's Bill Davis was tired of the constitutional bickering and the holding up of patriation to get more powers for the provinces. With the Charter's enormous popularity and a provincial election looming, Davis decided that Canada's largest province would support Trudeau's resolution. New Brunswick's Richard Hatfield followed suit. Always a maverick, Hatfield was not inclined to line up with any group, and was a strong supporter of extending language rights to the large French minority in his province. As an NDPer, Saskatchewan's Allan Blakeney was somewhat uncomfortable in a gathering of premiers who, except for Lévesque, were of a conservative hue. He would see if he could get Trudeau to add something to his package that would strengthen provincial control of their natural resources. Nova Scotia's John Buchanan also wanted to keep the door open for making a deal with Trudeau. In February 1981, after negotiations between Blakeney and the Trudeau government had broken down, Nova Scotia and Saskatchewan turned the Gang of Six into the Gang of Eight.

Alberta's Peter Lougheed and Quebec's René Lévesque were the heart and soul of the provincial opposition. Lougheed's struggle with Ottawa over control of Alberta's petroleum resources had made him an advocate of federal decentralization and thus a natural ally of Quebec. That struggle reached its apex on 28 October 1980, when the federal government, as part of its budget, announced the National Energy Program (NEP), a highly interventionist policy aimed at protecting Canadians from escalating global oil prices, ensuring security of supply, and increasing Canadian ownership of oil and natural gas, as well as increasing federal taxes on these resources. It would prevent Alberta from benefiting from its new-found resources to the extent that Ontario and eastern provinces had cashed in on their resource wealth in mining and lumber in earlier days. The NEP was bitterly resented, not only in Alberta, but also in British Columbia and Saskatchewan. The Canadian nationalists who championed the NEP seemed oblivious to the damage it would do to national unity. As for Lévesque, he had rebounded from his referendum defeat and was well aware that no province more than his could be mobilized to oppose Ottawa's unilateralism, especially when it promised nothing for Quebec nationalists.

The Gang of Eight waged their battle on three fronts: in the Canadian political arena, in London, and in the Canadian courts. It was in the courts that they won enough to bring about important changes in the patriation package of constitutional reforms. Not surprisingly, Quebec's PQ government waged the most vigorous public relations campaign against the Trudeau initiative. Billboard and television advertisements featured a federal fist crushing the Quebec flag, with the warning "*Minute, Ottawa.*"[43] In Alberta radio talk shows cheered Lougheed's opposition. To show his opposition to the NEP, Lougheed cut down the flow of oil to other provinces. Bumper stickers proclaimed, "Let the

Eastern bastards freeze in the dark."[44] The country was deeply engaged
in the constitutional struggle, but its apparent divisions were puzzling.
Polls showed that large majorities loved the Charter, but also opposed
federal unilateralism; Davis, who supported Trudeau, would win a majority in the Ontario election; while Lévesque, who was bitterly opposed, would win a majority in the Quebec election. Most Canadians
did not want to choose between the Charter and federalism – they valued both.

The Gang of Eight decided that it was not enough simply to oppose
what Trudeau was offering. They had to come up with a positive alternative. This they did on 16 April 1981, with much fanfare, at the Château
Laurier in Ottawa. Their proposal was to patriate the Constitution with
an all-Canadian amending formula, but to hold off on other changes,
including the Charter of Rights, until the Constitution was in Canadian
hands. The amending formula they proposed had been suggested first
by Alberta's legislative assembly, then put before the intergovernmental meetings by Peter Lougheed in 1979. Because it was proposed at a
Vancouver meeting of the CCMC, it came to be known as the "Vancouver formula."[45] Under the formula, amendments affecting the whole
country – other than a few requiring provincial unanimity – would
need the support of the federal Parliament and the legislatures of two-
thirds of the provinces representing 50 per cent of the population.
Whereas the amendment rule in Trudeau's package gave both Ontario
and Quebec a veto over constitutional change, the numerical Vancouver
formula, on its face, respected western Canadians' strongly held belief
in the equality of the provinces. Because Ontario has close to 40 per cent
of Canada's population, the Vancouver formula came close to giving
that province a veto, but left Quebec very vulnerable to the power
of the English-speaking provinces. To make the formula palatable to
Quebec, it contained a clause allowing a dissenting province to opt out
of an amendment and receive fiscal compensation. Quebec, for example, could opt out of an amendment giving Ottawa jurisdiction over
post-secondary education and receive an amount of money equivalent
to what the federal government would pay to fund colleges and universities in English Canada. Although the Group of Eight's proposal did
not receive much notice at the time, it is the formula that, in the end,
made its way into Canada's patriated Constitution.

Signing on to the Gang of Eight's proposal was an agonizing decision
for René Lévesque. It meant that he was agreeing to patriate Canada's
Constitution on terms that offered no new powers or special status for

Quebec and in fact reduced Quebec's status by taking away its historic constitutional veto and imposing Charter limitations on its National Assembly. Just a few days earlier, his government had won a strong election victory, and the PQ had recovered much of its political momentum. But Lévesque stuck with the strategy of blocking the Trudeau initiative by allying with the dissenting provinces. Developments on the London and the judicial fronts indicated that this strategy might well pay off.

In London, Quebec established an early beachhead, and was soon joined by Alberta, British Columbia, and Saskatchewan, which cranked up their lobbying operations there. The target of these lobbying efforts was the parliamentary committee chaired by Sir Anthony Kershaw. The disaffected provinces got a big lift when the committee concluded that a request affecting Canada's federal structure should be conveyed with "at least that degree of Provincial concurrence ... as that required for a post-patriation amendment."[46] Jean Chrétien wasted no time filing a rebuttal. Pierre Trudeau recognized that Canadian nationalist sentiment was well past the point of welcoming this kind of British interference in Canadian affairs. He used the title of a newly released sci-fi film, *The Empire Strikes Back*, to show his disdain for the Kershaw report.

All this lobbying and scrapping in London, however, would turn out to be of no consequence because of litigation initiated in Canadian courts, culminating in a decision of the Supreme Court of Canada. Three provinces, Manitoba, Newfoundland, and Quebec, referred to their highest provincial courts the question of whether provincial consent was a constitutional requirement for a request by the federal Parliament to the British Parliament to amend the Canadian Constitution in the ways the federal government contemplated. By April 1981 all three courts had rendered their decisions: Manitoba's Court of Appeal (three judges to two) and Quebec's Court of Appeal (four judges to one) found that provincial consent was not a requirement, but all three judges of Newfoundland's Court of Appeal came to the opposite conclusion. This amount of division among provincial appellate courts on an issue of huge importance to the country meant that there had to be an appeal from these decisions to the Supreme Court of Canada.

Everything now came to a halt. Joe Clark, the leader of the Opposition, agreed to stop the Conservatives' filibuster of the government's resolution in the House of Commons, and Trudeau indicated that his government would not proceed with its initiative if the Supreme Court ruled that its unilateralism was unconstitutional. Through the spring, summer, and early fall of 1981, Canadians held their breath as governments made their submissions to the Supreme Court and the justices pondered their decision.

On the morning of 28 September the Supreme Court of Canada rendered its decision, for the first time ever, on live television. The television broadcast was a fiasco. Millions of viewers watched Chief Justice Bora Laskin mouth an executive summary of the Court's decision, but there was no sound – a justice's foot had disconnected the wire controlling the sound system.[47] The Court's opinion, when finally communicated to the country, was somewhat bewildering. Neither side appeared to have won. A seven-to-two majority held that, as a strict matter of law, there was no requirement of provincial consent for any request of the federal Parliament to the British Parliament to amend Canada's Constitution. But a majority of six judges held that, as a matter of constitutional convention, "a substantial measure of consent" was required for a request that involved changes affecting the powers of the provinces.

Constitutional conventions are the soft and murky side of the constitutional system. They are, in effect, ethical rules or principles about the proper exercise of legal powers, and they are important. As we saw in the chapter on Confederation, our system of responsible, democratic government depends on the observance of constitutional conventions. Now a Supreme Court majority was saying that both practice over the years and the principle of federalism require that, when the federal Parliament asks the British Parliament to amend Canada's Constitution on matters affecting the provinces, it must have substantial provincial support.

Courts can find that conventions exist, and they can say what those conventions require, but they do not enforce them – enforcement comes through the political process. The Supreme Court had given the Trudeau government a *legal* green light. It could go ahead, with the support of only two of the federation's ten provinces, and request the British Parliament to enact its resolution, and not have to worry about Canadian courts' nullifying what it had done by finding it illegal. But the Supreme Court had also given Trudeau's government a *political* red light. If his government were to proceed without substantial provincial support, it would be violating the principle of federalism, and the moral legitimacy of what it had done would be called into question. Trudeau never hesitated. He respected constitutional convention, and announced that he would try one more time to reach an agreement with the provincial premiers.

And so Prime Minister Trudeau and the ten provincial premiers, with their cabinet colleagues and aides, assembled once again in the first week of November 1981 in the Ottawa Conference Centre to attempt an agreement on the Constitution. This time the prospects of success had improved. Thanks to the Supreme Court's decision, the meeting did not have to achieve unanimity – a "substantial measure" of provincial support for a federal resolution was all that was required. Moreover, there was now a sense of desperation among the first ministers. They had been at this constitutional business for a very long time. The premiers, including René Lévesque, accepted that the patriation agenda of constitutional reforms would be short and would not embrace an entire constitutional make-over. The time for compromise was at hand. And in four November days, compromise was achieved. But it was a compromise that fell short, in that it did not include Quebec, French Canada's homeland.

The compromise that made patriation possible was Trudeau's agreement to give up the amending formula he favoured and support the premiers' Vancouver formula, and to have a section inserted in the Charter of Rights allowing legislatures to override Charter rights. In return, nine of the ten premiers gave up their effort to include in the patriation package increases in provincial powers and the restructuring of federal institutions, especially the Senate. The core of this deal was worked out by Jean Chrétien, Roy Romanow, and Ontario attorney general Roy McMurtry in the conference centre kitchen. The "kitchen accord" led to an agreement, made in the evening of the conference's third day, by premiers and officials of the English-speaking provinces meeting in their hotel suites in downtown Ottawa and using the phone to communicate with Chrétien and Trudeau at 24 Sussex, while the Quebec delegation slept at L'Auberge de la Chaudière, across the Ottawa River in Hull.[48] The impetus for the breakup of the Gang of Eight seems to have been the moment, just before the lunch break on the third day, when an exasperated Trudeau turned to Lévesque and, speaking in French, challenged him as a democrat to take their differences to the people in a referendum. Lévesque allegedly "jumped at the idea."[49] A referendum, though, was anathema to Lévesque's premier colleagues, and provided the grounds for cooking up a deal without him. What went on that evening of 4 November will long be discussed and debated in Canadian history. What we do know is that it gave rise to the myth of the "night of the long knives" that strengthened a sense of betrayal among Quebec nationalists.

Quebec appeared to have been betrayed by its Gang of Eight partners. Lévesque had agreed in April to accept as the general constitutional amending rule two-thirds of the provinces representing 50 per cent of the population. That rule denied Quebec a veto, but allowed it to opt out of an amendment and be fiscally compensated. Now, nine premiers, in order to make a deal with Trudeau, had agreed to drop fiscal compensation for an opting-out province. It was hard enough to get Trudeau to accept opting out – he hated "checkerboard federalism" – but he could not be budged on accepting fiscal compensation. Then, to make matters worse, the amending formula agreed to by Trudeau and the other premiers would have a section requiring all the provinces plus Ottawa to agree to a short list of matters, one of which was the amending formula itself. What Allan Blakeney often referred to as the "tyranny of unanimity" would lock in a formula adverse to Quebec's interests that would be difficult, if not impossible, to change.

Quebec would seem to have got some relief from the so-called notwithstanding clause that allows federal and provincial legislatures to override the Charter. But the override clause did not apply to the language rights in the Charter, and it was language rights – above all, minority language educational rights – that were most important to Quebec nationalists. Section 23 (1) (a) of the Charter gives children of English-speaking citizens who migrate to Quebec the right to have their children educated in Quebec's English schools. The PQ government's Bill 101, as we have seen, in order to limit the expansion of Quebec's English-speaking population, gives the right to attend English schools only to children of parents who had received their English education in Quebec. The imposition of the Charter's section 23 on Quebec meant that the province would no longer have full control over a vital part of its distinct culture. This was a very bitter pill for René Lévesque to swallow.

Soon after the first ministers' conference adjourned, the federal government, with the concurrence of the premiers of the English-speaking provinces, made changes in the agreement designed to make it more agreeable to Quebec. A province opting out of an amendment passed under the two-thirds-of-the-provinces/50-per-cent-of-the-population rule that "transfers provincial legislative powers relating to education or other cultural matters from provincial legislatures to Parliament" would receive "reasonable compensation."[50] And tacked on to the very end of the Constitutional Act, 1982 is section 59, which simply says that section 23 (1) (a) of the Charter will come into force only when authorized by the legislative assembly or government of Quebec. To this day, Quebec has not signalled its willingness to accept the Charter section that its francophone majority found most objectionable.[51] These last-minute efforts to accommodate Quebec went largely unnoticed, and did little to diminish the sense of betrayal felt by many *Québécois*.

The insertion in the Charter of a clause allowing legislatures to override Charter rights, while crucial for winning the support of the provincial premiers, was a difficult change for the public to understand. Section 33 of the Charter authorizes the federal parliament or a provincial legislature to attach to any Act a declaration that it operates "notwithstanding" a specific Charter right. Legislation with such a declaration could be used to immune legislation from judicial review when first enacted, or attached to a re-enactment of legislation found by the courts to contravene a Charter right. Saskatchewan's Blakeney and Manitoba's Lyon made the case for the "notwithstanding" clause in a closed session. They argued that it was needed to balance the judicial protection of rights with parliamentary democracy. A legislative override means that judges do not have the final word on how far rights should be stretched or how a right should be balanced against competing rights or social values. The override provides an alternative to stacking the courts with ideologically acceptable judges or amending the Constitution to overcome a decision that is deeply opposed by democratically elected governments.[52] Others have made the very opposite argument: what is the point of entrenching rights and freedoms if legislatures can override them?[53] Trudeau managed to get a five-year time limit attached to any use of the "notwithstanding" clause, but with the possibility of renewal, and to restrict its application to sections 2 and 7–15 of the Charter. This means it would not apply to democratic rights such as the right to vote, or to the language and mobility rights so essential to Trudeau's pan-Canadian nationalism. The pros and cons of the Charter's legislative override clause have been much debated at the theoretical level. But the reality is that the Charter's popularity has inhibited governments, except for Quebec's, from using it.

Besides the "notwithstanding" clause and their preferred amending formula, the premiers made two other gains in the package that emerged from the November conference. An affirmative action clause was attached to mobility rights, allowing provinces with below-average levels of employment to protect jobs from out-of-province job-seekers. This was put in primarily to meet Newfoundland's concern that employment opportunities created by offshore oil finds be preserved for the province's workforce. Finally, there was a change in the division of powers respecting natural resources. It was essentially the condition that NDP leader Ed Broadbent had exacted from Trudeau in exchange for supporting his constitutional initiative. It would add section 92a to the list of provincial powers in the original Constitution. Section 92a gives provincial legislatures exclusive jurisdiction over the exploration, conservation, and development of non-renewable, forestry resources, and electrical energy in the province. It also gives them a non-exclusive legislative power over the export of these resources to other provinces, and to levy any mode of taxation on natural resources. None of this really adds much to provincial powers, and falls well short of what Peter Lougheed and other premiers were trying to secure in earlier negotiations. The original Constitution made it clear that provinces own their natural resources. Section 92a removes doubts about a power the provinces already had. Giving provinces legislative power over interprovincial trade in their resources and power to levy indirect taxes on their resources, theoretically, increases their powers. But these additional powers are subject to paramount federal jurisdiction in the same fields. Section 92a is full of sound and fury signifying very little. The feds can still call the shots on what happens to provincial resources when they go into interprovincial or international markets, and how much money they want to take from the sale of these resources for the federal treasury.

When the first ministers' conference concluded on 5 November, it looked as if there were two other losers besides Quebec: women and Aboriginal peoples. When Prime Minister Trudeau announced that the legislative override would apply to section 28 – the section that states that the rights and freedoms in the Charter are guaranteed equally to males and females – the alliance of women who had lobbied to get the section into the Charter erupted in fury.[54] It took only a few days for their storm of protest to register with the premiers and the prime minister. The "notwithstanding" clause would not apply to section 28. Indeed section 28 has its own "notwithstanding" clause – its guarantee of sex equality stands, "notwithstanding" anything else in the Charter.

A similar pattern played out with the addition of section 34 (in the final text it is section 35) to the constitutional package: a free-standing section stating that the Aboriginal and treaty rights of the Aboriginal peoples of Canada are hereby recognized and affirmed.[55] At the November conference a number of premiers said they could not accept this provision because they did not know what was meant by Aboriginal rights, and were troubled by the fact that some of the Aboriginal leadership were opposed to it. So it was dropped from the accord issued at the end of the conference. This mobilized an Aboriginal lobby in Ottawa and demonstrations in a number of cities that persuaded the premiers to restore section 34 – but with one small change. The word "existing" would be added before "aboriginal and treaty rights." Rumour has it that this word was inserted at the insistence of Alberta's Peter Lougheed. At the time there was a concern among Aboriginal leaders that the insertion of "existing" was intended to ensure that the rights Aboriginal peoples enjoyed would be limited to what was available to them in 1981. The Métis Association of Alberta was the only Aboriginal organization that agreed with the new wording. Despite these fears, the recognition and affirmation of "existing aboriginal and treaty rights," as we shall see, adds significantly to the legal and political resources of Aboriginal peoples in Canada.

After these last changes in the patriation package of constitutional amendments, the politics of the process was over. All that remained was to complete the formalities. In early December 1981 both houses of Parliament passed resolutions supporting the package. The majority in the House of Commons was large, 246 in favour and only 24 opposed, made up of seventeen Progressive Conservatives, five Liberals, and two New Democrats. The next step took place at Westminster. With nine provinces supporting the Canadian Parliament's resolution, securing the Mother of Parliament's approval was not expected to be a problem. Twenty-seven of the thirty hours of discussion and debate on the bill were about Aboriginal peoples.[56] Lord Denning's judicial decision that Dominion autonomy had transferred responsibility for honouring treaties with native peoples from the British to the Canadian Crown was an important factor in preventing concerns about Indigenous peoples from being grounds for blocking the bill. It is interesting that British parliamentarians showed virtually no concern about Quebec's opposition. Perhaps they felt that talking about Quebec's position would smack too much of meddling in Canadian politics.

On 25 March 1982 the Canada Act completed its passage through the Westminster Parliament. The Act has just two substantive sections. Section 1 gives the Constitution Act, 1982, containing the amendments to the Canadian Constitution requested by the Parliament of Canada, the force of law in Canada on the day it is proclaimed. Section 2 cuts the umbilical cord between Canada and Britain. It states that "No Act of the

Parliament of the United Kingdom passed after the *Constitution Act, 1982* comes into force shall extend to Canada as part of its law." The final step took place in Ottawa on the grey and rainy morning of 17 April 1982, when Queen Elizabeth, at a table out in front of the Parliament Buildings, with millions of Canadians watching on television, proclaimed the Constitution Act, 1982 in force.

The Constitution Act, 1982 renamed the British North America Act, 1867 the "Constitution Act, 1867," and similarly renamed all past amendments to it.[57] But this new addition to our Constitution did not replace our founding Constitution. It simply tacked onto it a number of new components, the most important of which were the Canadian Charter of Rights and Freedoms, the recognition and affirmation of the Aboriginal and treaty rights of the Aboriginal peoples of Canada, and a set of rules (a formula) for amending the Constitution.

Patriation, bringing the Constitution to its homeland and severing Canada's final legal tie to the United Kingdom, was, in principle, something for non-Aboriginal Canadians, anglophone and francophone, to celebrate. French Canadians, to say the least, had never been keen on the British connection, and English-speaking Canadians, by the late twentieth century, had become such staunch Canadian nationalists that they did not squawk about removing references to the British connection from the titles of Canada's constitutional documents. The *Québécois*, the French-Canadian majority, would have welcomed patriation had it been accompanied by constitutional changes that give Quebec the powers and status appropriate for French Canada's homeland. That was why the Quebec government, even when it was led by federalist Liberals, held up patriation when it was on the brink of happening in 1964. Patriation eighteen years later, not only without any enhanced recognition of Quebec's place in Confederation, but also with the province subject to a Constitution that could be changed contrary to its wishes, was a very bitter pill for many *Québécois* to swallow. No wonder Quebec's National Assembly, on 25 November 1981, passed a decree by a 70 to 38 majority rejecting the Canadian Parliament's patriation resolution.

Quebec's National Assembly was the only provincial legislature to debate and vote on the patriation resolution before it went forward to London. In 1971, when the Victoria Charter was to be the basis for patriating the Constitution, the agreed-upon procedure was that Parliament and all the provincial legislatures would pass identical resolutions. Why was that procedure not followed in 1981? Was it because the prime minister did not want to draw attention to the division in the Canadian body politic? Would not affirming resolutions in the legislatures to which premiers are accountable have given the patriation package a deeper democratic root – what constitutional scholars call "autochthony"[58] – in Canada? It is to be noted that the constitutional amending system adopted through patriation requires affirmative resolutions of provincial legislatures.

The treatment Quebec received in Canada's highest court did not make the patriation pill any easier to swallow. At the same time the National Assembly was rejecting the patriation resolution, the Quebec government asked Quebec's Court of Appeal whether proceeding with the patriation amendments without Quebec's consent was "unconstitutional in the conventional sense." The Quebec Court of Appeal, whose judges are appointed by the federal government, answered in the negative, but not until 7 April 1982, ten days before the queen would proclaim the Constitution Act, 1982 in force. The Quebec government's appeal to the Supreme Court of Canada was not decided until 6 December 1982 – long after the horse was out of the barn. The Supreme Court, in an anonymous and unanimous decision, also answered the question in the negative, and in an intellectually unsatisfactory way. The Court applied one of Sir Ivor Jennings's three tests for the existence of a constitutional convention: "did the actors involved in the precedents believe they were bound by a rule." Because none of the politicians outside Quebec had explicitly acknowledged that Quebec's consent was necessary for an amendment affecting its powers, the Court concluded that there was no convention requiring Quebec's consent. The Court ignored Jennings's other two tests: the precedents, and the reason for the rule, and his statement that "[a] single precedent with a good reason may be enough to establish the rule." The precedents were clear: no amendment of Canada's Constitution that affected Quebec's powers had ever gone forward to London without Quebec's consent. And the reason for that rule went to the essential bargain of Confederation that French-speaking Canadians, in return for being subject to a federal Parliament in which English-speaking Canadians would have a majority, would have a province in which they were a majority, with the constitutionally secured powers needed to protect and advance their distinct society. It is difficult to avoid concluding that the Supreme Court's decision in the *Quebec Veto Reference* was based on a political rationale: not to render ethically illegitimate constitutional changes that the majority of Canadians were celebrating.[59] In the end, as we shall see, the convention of requiring Quebec's consent for constitutional amendments affecting its powers was re-established, as the politics of the country triumphed over the finding of its highest court of law.

Although patriation was a blow to much of the French majority in Quebec, it was a boon to the French-Canadian minority outside Quebec. Section 16 declares English and French to be "the official languages" of Canada and of New Brunswick, section 23 extends to French-speaking citizens in English-speaking Canada the right to have their children educated in French where their numbers warrant, and section 20 the right, where there is sufficient demand, to be served in French by offices or agencies of the federal government. The right to use French in provincial legislatures and courts, a right guaranteed to Quebec's English minority at the time of Confederation, retains a checkerboard pattern in Canada. That right, as we have seen, was "guaranteed" to French-speakers when Manitoba became a province, totally denied once English-speakers became a majority, and then revivified by the Supreme Court of Canada in 1979. The Charter of Rights extends the right to New Brunswick, where francophones constitute 35 per cent of the population, but not to Ontario, with the country's largest francophone minority, or to any of the other English-speaking provinces. That the extension of linguistic rights to francophones outside of Quebec went as far as it did in the patriation amendments reflects the Trudeauvian vision of a Canada in which its French dimension takes the form of making all of Canada, rather than just Quebec, the home for its French-speaking citizens. Popular as that vision might be with many English-speaking Canadians, it might be too little too late to satisfy the constitutional aspirations of the *Québécois*.

The great irony of patriation is that, although it was the culmination of a constitutional struggle that Quebec initiated, Quebec was its biggest loser, and Aboriginal peoples, who were excluded from negotiations, ended up being, if not patriation's biggest winners, at least its most unintended winners. That is not to say that patriation satisfied the constitutional aspirations of Aboriginal peoples. I noted that pan-Canadian Aboriginal lobbying organizations, in the end, did not support patriation. In any case, those organizations did not have mandates from the historic Amerindian nations, the Métis, or Inuit peoples to settle constitutional issues on their behalf.

If there was to be a satisfactory constitutional resolution of relations among Canada's three founding pillars, much work still lay ahead after patriation.

Chapter 15

The End of Mega Constitutional Politics?

On a raw fall day in November 1989, in an office at Queen's University in Kingston, Ontario, three political scientists struggled to carry out a job they had been asked to do by an organization called Canadians for a Unifying Constitution, a group of Canadian leaders in business, government, and academe. We three political science professors – yes, I was one of them – had been asked by this illustrious group to help them save the Meech Lake Accord.

The Accord was a package of proposed constitutional changes put together in 1987 by the country's first ministers that was widely viewed as the best chance there would ever be to change Canada's Constitution in a way that would accommodate the demands generated by Quebec nationalism – demands that patriation had ignored. Under the new post-patriation amending rules, the Accord had to be approved by the federal Parliament and all ten provincial legislatures. By the fall of 1989 the Accord had sailed through Parliament and most of the provincial assemblies, but not without arousing a great deal of public criticism. By the fall of 1989 public opposition seemed serious enough to block approval in the legislatures of Manitoba and New Brunswick, the two provinces that had not approved the Accord, and to persuade Newfoundland's legislature to rescind its approval. The new amending rules put a three-year time limit on the ratification process. Time was running out.

Our job was to write the copy for a glossy booklet that would rebut the many criticisms that had been made of the Meech Lake Accord. We three – Ron Watts, former Queen's principal and now director of Queen's University's Centre for Intergovernmental Affairs; Richard Simeon, a leading scholar of federal-provincial relations with a journalist's touch;

and I, a battered and bruised constitutional scholar-warrior – worked away on that grey November Sunday with a strong sense of crisis. Like so many Canadians we were convinced that this was our country's last chance. If Canadians could not ratify the most modest constitutional reforms put forward in a generation by a Quebec government and approved by Quebec's National Assembly, then Quebec likely would leave the federation.

Thousands of copies of our booklet, "Meech Lake: Setting the Record Straight,"[1] were rapidly distributed across the country. It probably had a larger readership than anything any of us had ever written. But it did not save the Meech Lake Accord. Neither did the efforts of many other Canadians. As we shall see, the Accord failed to gain approval in either Manitoba's or Newfoundland's legislatures within the time frame set by the amending rules. Even so, Quebecers did not vote to leave the federation, but in 1995 they came close to doing that – oh so close! Six years earlier we three academics, like so many Canadians, were convinced that without some major constitutional restructuring, Canada might come apart. And so, from 1987 to 1995, once again, mega constitutional politics – the political struggle of a deeply divided country to get a constitutional fix that makes everyone happy – dominated Canada's political agenda.

In our glossy little booklet, we three political scientists made no mention of one of the criticisms that the Meech Lake Accord encountered and that in the end proved fatal to its ratification: the absence in it of any reference to Aboriginal peoples. This was so despite the fact that, through the five years following patriation, constitutional politics in Canada had focused entirely on negotiations with Aboriginal peoples. The final negotiating session between first ministers and Aboriginal leaders ended in failure and frustration in March 1987, just a month before the negotiations that led to the Meech Lake Accord began. From the start, the shadow of that important unfinished business hung over the ill-fated Accord.

Section 37 of the Constitution Act, 1982 called for a first ministers' constitutional conference at which matters affecting Aboriginal peoples would be on the agenda. The conference was to take place within the first year following patriation, and representatives of Aboriginal organizations and delegates of the two northern territorial governments would be invited to participate. The conference took place in March 1983, and was entirely devoted to Aboriginal issues.[2] It resulted in an agreement to amend the Constitution by adding two subsections to section 35, the section that recognizes and affirms "aboriginal and treaty rights." One subsection makes it clear that any rights that exist or may be acquired by way of land claims agreements are treaty rights.[3] Back in the 1970s, when the federal government launched its "comprehensive land claims" policy, it would not dignify these agreements as "treaties." The designation of the rights agreed upon in these agreements as treaty rights gives these modern land claims agreements constitutional status and, in effect, entrenches them so they cannot be unilaterally rescinded or modified by any of the parties to them. This was a significant gain for Aboriginal peoples. The second addition guaranteed that Aboriginal and treaty rights apply equally to male and female persons.[4] For Aboriginal women who had suffered from the federal government's imposition of patrilineal regulations on First Nations communities, this was a progressive step towards correcting past injustices. The amendment was readily ratified by Parliament and all the provincial legislatures except Quebec's. Quebec had no objection to the content of the amendment, but rejected the legitimacy of the constitutional amending process that had been made law without its consent.

The extraordinary thing about the 1983 constitutional amendment is that, right up to the present day, it has been the one and only use of the general amending formula. All that debate and negotiation about the basic rule for amending the Constitution in Canada, from the 1920s to 1981, and then, after finally establishing the rule, it is used only once! And that once is not for a big constitutional reform, but for some small clarifications of the constitutional section recognizing the rights of Aboriginal peoples. That was surely not the expectation of the many participants in the long struggle to place custody of the Constitution in Canadian hands.

The 1983 conference also produced a new section 37 that called for at least two more constitutional conferences with agendas that included matters affecting Aboriginal peoples. Three more conferences did take place, in 1984, 1985, and 1987. All three dealt solely with Aboriginal issues, and had the same Aboriginal and territorial representation as the 1983 conference. All three focused on Aboriginal self-government, and all three were exercises in mutual frustration. It took three conferences to find out that it was not possible for Aboriginal and non-Aboriginal leaders to agree on how to make it clear that the right of Indigenous peoples to govern themselves was one of the Aboriginal rights recognized and affirmed in the Constitution. Federal, provincial, and territorial government leaders were not opposed to Aboriginal peoples' taking more control over governance in their communities. In 1983 a special parliamentary committee chaired by Keith Penner had issued a report proposing that First Nations be constitutionally recognized as a third order of government, with full powers to govern themselves within Canada.[5] John Munro, minister of Indian affairs in the Trudeau government, gave a favourable response to that proposal. At the conferences the federal government and many of the provinces were willing to have the Constitution grant an Aboriginal self-government right that would have legal effect for any Aboriginal people that successfully negotiated the details with the federal government and the government of the province in which it was located. Such a contingent right was unacceptable in principle, however, to Aboriginal people, who regard the right to govern themselves as inherent in their very existence as organized nations or peoples.

The concern about recognition of the "inherent right of self-government" was most important for the Assembly of First Nations, whose member nations had existed and governed themselves for centuries before the arrival of Europeans. These nations, as we saw in earlier chapters of this book, had not been conquered by France or Britain or by their colonists. The written text of the treaties that many of these nations made with the Crown contains words stating that the Aboriginal signatories had ceded all their rights in exchange for reserves, money, and other benefits. But, as we saw in Chapter 8, records show that no such surrendering of rights was agreed to in the treaty negotiations, nor did representatives of the Indigenous nations have any mandate to sign away their people's political independence. The Supreme Court of Canada would soon begin rendering decisions rejecting the written text of treaties as being definitive of what was agreed upon when treaties were negotiated.[6] Aboriginal participants in the constitutional conferences saw the contingent right on offer as implying that the legitimacy of any self-governing that their peoples might engage in stemmed from what was granted to them by Canada's federal and provincial governments. Aboriginal leaders were willing to have their nations and peoples negotiate with those governments the terms on which they would continue to exercise self-government in Canada, but they would not accept that Indigenous peoples had ever surrendered their responsibility for the governance of their societies and the lands and resources that sustain them. Although George Erasmus, the grand chief of the Assembly of First Nations, was perhaps the most eloquent expositor of the "inherent right," the Inuit and

Métis participants at the conferences held to the basic idea that responsibility for controlling their societies was inherent in the very existence and collective achievements of their societies.[7]

Non-Aboriginal Canadians watching the televised broadcasts of politicians and Aboriginal leaders debating what is a fundamental, existential matter must have found the proceedings somewhat bewildering, although some must also have found it educational. Like the author of this book, who only began to think about these matters fifteen years into his career as a political science professor and so-called constitutional expert, most Canadians had never thought about or read about how Aboriginal peoples came to be treated as subjects of Britain and Canada. It was clear that, at this point in Canada's odyssey, there could not be a meeting of minds on the question of the source of Aboriginal peoples' right to self-government. Still, it must be said that in no other county on the planet would Aboriginal and non-Aboriginal leaders engage so intently in a public discussion of this question. This is surely a consequence of Canada's being a country based on incomplete conquests.

Changes in political leadership and two elections propelled Canada into yet another round of mega constitutional politics. In February 1984 Pierre Trudeau took another walk in the snow and decided to resign from politics. This time he did not change his mind. John Turner, his successor as Liberal leader and prime minister, called a September election and lost badly to the Progressive Conservatives and their new leader, Brian Mulroney. In 1985 René Lévesque followed Trudeau into retirement, and his successor, Pierre-Marc Johnson, lost a December election to the Liberals led by a recycled Robert Bourassa. Mulroney and Bourassa both won big: Mulroney's Conservatives garnered just over 50 per cent of the popular vote, the first time that had been done since Diefenbaker's 1958 landslide, and 211 seats in a 282-member House; Bourassa's Liberals took 56 per cent of the popular vote and 99 of the 122 seats in the National Assembly. Both leaders had campaigned on promises to succeed where the two old gladiators, Lévesque and Trudeau, had failed, and to make the changes needed to bring Quebec back into Canada's constitutional family.

Gil Rémillard, a law professor at Université Laval, was the key to uniting Bourassa and Mulroney in an ambitious new constitutional project. Rémillard had been advising the Quebec Liberals on the constitutional plank in their platform as they approached the provincial election. In August 1985 Mulroney bought Rémillard to Ottawa as special constitutional adviser to his minister of justice, sending a signal to

Bourassa that they might make sweet constitutional music together. Rémillard cut short his one-year contract with the federal government to stand as a Liberal candidate in the Quebec election in December 1985. After the election Bourassa made Rémillard his minister of intergovernmental affairs. In May 1986, at a gathering of academics and government officials at Mont-Gabriel, a ski resort north of Montreal, Rémillard outlined Quebec's conditions for accepting the patriated Constitution. The list of constitutional changes contained just five items, all of them focused on securing Quebec's historic place in Confederation. Those five items became the basis of the Meech Lake Accord.

It took almost a year for Prime Minister Mulroney to feel confident enough about the first ministers' reaching agreement on Quebec's five points to summon them to a constitutional conference. Through that year, the Quebec government, with Mulroney's blessing, engaged in shuttle diplomacy, sending Rémillard to provincial capitals to explain and sell Quebec's agenda. All of this was done not secretly, but very quietly. A desperate fear of failure hung over the enterprise: if proposals as modest and as federalist as the Bourassa government's were not acceptable to the rest of Canada, then another drive in Quebec for much more radical change seemed sure to follow. Although the quiet, elitist nature of the negotiation was understandable, it would prove politically fatal.

By April 1987 Mulroney, keeping in close touch with Bourassa, thought the governments were close enough to a deal to invite the first ministers to a constitutional conference, not in the downtown Ottawa Conference Centre, but in the quieter setting of the government's conference centre on Meech Lake in Quebec's Gatineau Hills. There, on 31 April, Mulroney and the ten provincial premiers, behind closed doors and beyond the gaze of television cameras, agreed to proceeding with a set of constitutional amendments based on Quebec's five points. The first ministers met again in a marathon session in a government building in Ottawa to put the final touches on the text of what was officially now the proposed Constitution Act, 1987, but in popular parlance was known as the Meech Lake Accord. Now the public would find out what they had been up to.

The first of the five constitutional amendments proposed in the Accord was the most difficult to understand and by far the most controversial. It was designed to meet Quebec's desire to be recognized as a distinct society within Canada. It would become a new section 2 of

Canada's original Constitution – right after the first section, which states, "This Act may be cited as the *Constitution Act*, 1867." In the final text it read as follows:

2(1) The Constitution of Canada shall be interpreted in a manner consistent with
(a) the recognition that the existence of French-speaking Canadians, centred in Quebec but also present elsewhere in Canada, and English-speaking Canadians, concentrated outside Quebec but also present in Quebec, constitutes a fundamental characteristic of Canada; and
(b) the recognition that Quebec constitutes within Canada a distinct society.[8]

Notice that, to win the support of the governments of the English-speaking provinces, recognition of Quebec as a distinct society had to be preceded by a clause recognizing francophones outside Quebec and anglophones inside Quebec. Quebec was not to be described as French Canada's homeland. The proposed amendment affirmed the role of Quebec's legislature and government to "preserve and promote the distinct identity of Quebec," but did not confer additional powers on Quebec. Another subsection similarly affirmed the federal and provincial roles to preserve the fundamental characteristic of Canada referred to in subsection (1). It was to be a guide to citizens, governments, and, most important, courts on how to interpret the Constitution. The distinct society clause was not easily explained or understood. Canadians not enthusiastic about accommodating Quebec could, and did, read their worst fears into it.

The rest of the Accord was more straightforward. A section on immigration responded to Quebec's desire to entrench its immigration agreements with the federal government constitutionally by providing that possibility for all the provinces. The proposed Supreme Court amendment contained a touch of Quebec's special status: the federal government would be required to fill vacancies on the Court from lists submitted by provincial governments, but a vacancy in one of Quebec's three positions on the Court would be filled by a Quebec government nominee. The amendment would constitutionalize Quebec's representation on the Supreme Court bench that had been provided for in legislation since the Court's creation to ensure the participation of jurists knowledgeable about Quebec's distinct civil law system. A section on future federal-provincial shared-cost programs in areas of exclusive provincial responsibility entitled an opting-out province to fiscal compensation if it introduced a program of its own that met "national objectives." As for the amending formula, instead of restoring Quebec's veto, the veto power of all provinces was increased by adding Senate reform, the expansion of the northern territories, and the creation of new territories to the matters requiring unanimous provincial approval. Also, the fiscal compensation for provinces opting out of amendments under the 50-per-cent/two-thirds-of-the-provinces rule was extended to cover any transfer of jurisdiction to Ottawa, not just those relating to culture and education.

Only the amendments relating to the Supreme Court and the amending formula required approval of all the provinces. But the first ministers wanted the five components of the Accord to be adopted as a package. That meant the Meech Lake Accord would be subjected to the tyranny of unanimity: it would have to be supported by resolutions passed in the federal Parliament and the legislatures of all ten provinces. That had been the process planned for approval of the Victoria Charter. But, as we have seen, at the time of patriation, Prime Minister Trudeau and the nine premiers did not seek ratification of their deal by the provincial legislatures. The authors of the Meech Lake Accord, to put the matter mildly, underestimated how seeking approval of the Accord by elected legislative bodies would expose their constitutional handiwork to public scrutiny and discussion and make its adoption much more difficult. They were accustomed to the constitutional methods of elite accommodation: if the leaders make a deal, their people will follow. However, the democratic nature of Canada's constitutional culture had ratcheted up a notch or two. As Alan Cairns points out, adding a Charter of Rights and Freedoms meant that Canada's Constitution had become less of a governments' constitution and more of a citizens' constitution.[9] Many citizens did not take kindly to a bundle of constitutional amendments cobbled together by eleven men behind closed doors and put to the legislature on the basis that not a word could be changed. It was the undemocratic process that created the Meech Lake Accord, as much as its contents, that led to its final demise.

Under the new amending rules, the proposed amendments had to be approved in all the legislatures within three years of the first legislature's ratification. The three-year clock began ticking on 23 June 1987, when the Accord passed easily through Quebec's National Assembly

– not surprising, given that it had been shaped by the Bourassa government, which had a huge majority in the Assembly. That seemed to allow plenty of time to complete the process, and ratification started off well: Saskatchewan ratified in September, the House of Commons in October by a vote of 242 to 16, and Alberta in December. To bring Alberta premier Don Getty onside, Mulroney had to tack onto the end of the Accord an undertaking that, until Senate reform was accomplished, the federal government would appoint senators from provincial lists.[10]

A New Brunswick election in October and a Manitoba election in April 1988 upset the Meech Lake applecart. The constitution-makers had not taken into account the virtual certainty that provincial elections are bound to be held in any three-year period, and might well result in new governments taking power that did not participate in the intergovernmental agreement that produced the constitutional proposals. Indeed, elections during the ratification process might serve as a democratic check on the process. That is certainly what happened with the Meech Lake Accord. In the New Brunswick election, Liberal leader Frank McKenna, who, as Opposition leader, had serious issues with · the Accord, swept to power, winning all fifty seats in the legislature. The Ontario election held at the same time returned David Peterson's Liberals to power with a majority of seats. Peterson was a leading advocate of Meech Lake, but, in Ontario, the linchpin province, the Accord was not an election issue. In Manitoba, NDP premier Howard Pawley, a strong supporter of Meech Lake, was defeated in the legislature and called an April election in which Gary Filmon's Conservatives won a minority government. Filmon announced that he was in no hurry to ratify Meech Lake. Sharon Carstairs, whose Liberals came from nowhere to form the official Opposition and hold the balance of power, proclaimed that "Meech Lake is dead."[11]

The political winds outside Quebec were blowing strongly against Meech Lake. Much of the opposition came from Trudeau liberals. Pierre himself returned briefly to the political fray by buying a full page in Montreal's *La Presse* and the *Toronto Star* to denounce the Accord as a bungled and unnecessary attempt to accommodate those "perpetual losers," Quebec nationalists. The Accord, he screamed, would render the Canadian state "totally impotent," destined to be governed by "political eunuchs."[12] The rhetoric was extreme, but it inspired a wave of protest against the Accord from those who shared Trudeau's vision of Canada.

Feminists in English-speaking Canada were one of the noisiest and most effective groups mobilizing opposition to the Accord. Their hard-won victory in securing women's rights in the Charter was in jeopardy, they alleged, because of what a Quebec recognized as a distinct society might get up to. Anti-Meech sentiment was also strong farther left along the political spectrum. The Accord's providing for fiscal compensation for provinces opting out of federal shared-cost programs was the target of left-leaning Canadians who favoured a national welfare state over provincial rights. Left-of-centre opponents linked their concern about weakening the federal government's power to build the Canadian welfare state to their opposition to the free trade agreement the Mulroney government was negotiating with the United States. In their view, both would push Canada's political economy to the right. The Accord also had plenty of detractors on the right side of politics, especially in western Canada, where there was little support for the idea that Quebec had been hard done by at the time of patriation and had to be brought back into the constitutional family.

Despite the growing strength of the anti-Meech forces, by the fall of 1988 all the provinces except Manitoba and New Brunswick had ratified the Accord. In November Mulroney's Progressive Conservatives won re-election, albeit with a reduced majority. But the 1988 federal election was fought over free trade with the United States, not the Meech Lake Accord. Then, on 15 December, the Supreme Court of Canada rendered its decision in the Quebec sign case, with consequences that would prove fatal for the Meech Lake Accord. The Court found that the provision in Quebec's Bill 101 requiring that outdoor advertising be only in French violated the right to freedom of expression in the Charter, and could not be saved by the Charter's reasonable limits clause. The Court accepted that, in order to preserve Quebec's French face, it would be reasonable to require that signs be predominantly in French, but a total ban of English (and all other languages) was unnecessary. Bourassa's federalist-oriented government had discontinued the PQ's policy of attaching the Charter's override to every new piece of legislation, but it now found itself under tremendous pressure to use the override. On Sunday, 18 December, under the slogan "Ne touchez pas à la loi 101," nationalists staged the largest rallies since the 1980 referendum outside the building where Bourassa and his colleagues were meeting. The Bourassa government's decision to use the override but also to amend Bill 101 to allow multilingual lingual signage indoors did not douse the fires. It was not nearly enough change for English-speaking Canadians and a cowardly retreat for Quebec nationalists.

Bourassa's suggestion that there would have been no need to use the Charter override to restore unilingual French signs if the Meech Lake Accord were in place only made matters worse. That comment played right into the fears of Meech Lake's critics that the distinct society clause would enable Quebec to ride roughshod over the Charter of Rights. The day after the Bourassa government made its decision, Gary Filmon, who had been a staunch opponent of recognizing the French minority's language rights in Manitoba, withdrew the Meech Lake resolution from Manitoba's legislature. Trudeau's Charter, which was aimed at unifying the country, was generating the kind of English-French tribal warfare the country had not seen since the conscription crises. It was doing this not because English-speaking Canadians and francophone Quebecers were at odds over the rights and freedoms in the Charter, but because in the heat and passion of mega constitutional politics the Charter, as English Canada's icon, was clashing with Bill 101, the Charter of the French language, an icon of the *Québécois*.

After the Bourassa government used the override, the Meech Lake Accord's fortunes went steadily downhill. In the Newfoundland election of April 1989, another pro-Meech government went down to defeat. The Liberals, led by Clyde Wells, who promised to rescind his province's approval of the Accord, came to power. This did more than put a third province in the anti-Meech column. Clyde Wells, an articulate lawyer and excellent communicator, became a national leader of the anti-Meech side. In November Wells debated Prime Minister Mulroney on prime-time television. With his sonorous voice and honest face, he brought an aura of righteousness to his defence of citizens' rights and national fairness against the ambiguities of the Meech Lake Accord and its privileging of Quebec.

Public hearings in Manitoba produced a report calling for extensive changes in the Accord and in New Brunswick a call for a companion accord designed to provide constitutional security for those who felt threatened by Meech – especially linguistic minorities and women. On 5 April 1990 Newfoundland's legislature rescinded its approval of the Accord. With time running out, Mulroney had to do something to save Meech Lake. His first manoeuvre was to establish a House of Commons committee, chaired by Jean Charest, to conduct public hearings on New Brunswick's proposal of a companion accord. The committee managed to reach an all-party consensus in a 17 May report recommending a parallel accord designed to meet the concerns of the three dissenting provinces.[13] Among other things, it called for a declaration that the distinct society clause conferred no extra powers on Quebec or undermined the Charter. Not only was that kind of tinkering with the Accord utterly unacceptable to Quebec; it was also highly offensive to the Quebec nationalists Mulroney had recruited to his party, notably Environment Minister Lucien Bouchard, who resigned and began building a new federal party, the Bloc Québécois, to ensure that the voice of Quebec nationalism was heard in the House of Commons.

Mulroney, to use his own words, made one more desperate roll of the dice: he invited the provincial premiers to join him for dinner on Sunday, 3 June, at the Museum of Civilization. If the dinner showed some possibility of getting past the constitutional impasse, then the premiers would stay in Ottawa to see whether somehow they could pull a rabbit out of a hat and save Meech Lake. Mulroney's scouts, Senator Lowell Murray and Norman Spector, his senior adviser on federal-provincial relations, had completed a rush tour of provincial capitals, and although they did not think the situation was promising, neither did they consider it hopeless. So, Monday morning, the first ministers moved back for another round of negotiations in the country's constitutional arena, the Ottawa Conference Centre. In an important respect, this would differ from previous first ministers meetings. For the first time since Confederation, opposition leaders could join government leaders. This was obviously important for Manitoba's Filmon, who led a minority government and brought with him Liberal leader Sharon Carstairs and the new NDP leader, Gary Doer. Ontario premier David Peterson invited NDP leader Bob Rae and Conservative leader Mike Harris to be part of his province's delegation. The opposition politicians would not be at the negotiating table, but would be present for consultation. The Meech Lake experience was teaching Canadian politicians that, in a parliamentary democracy, constitutional success requires political consensus across party lines.

For six days and nights the first ministers laboured away in closed sessions in a windowless room on the fifth floor of the Conference Centre, connected by hand-held mobile telephones (as big as boots) to their officials and consulting teams in other parts of the Centre and in neighbouring hotels. There was tremendous excitement when, finally, the prime minister and premiers assembled in the flag-bedecked hall on the first floor of the Centre an hour and a half before midnight on Saturday, 9 June, to issue their final communiqué. It seemed that they *had* pulled a rabbit out of the hat. All would support Meech Lake, but on condition that, as soon as the Meech amendments were fully ratified, action would begin on a new parcel of additional amendments.[14] The new constitutional initiative would include an effort through public hearings to draft a new opening section of the Constitution stating what Canada is all about, development of a proposal for an elected Senate, amending the Charter to better protect linguistic minorities and women, resumption of constitutional meetings with Aboriginal peoples, working out the constitutional future of the northern territories, and looking again at the constitutional amending formula. What a big awkward rabbit! And what a load of additional constitution-making to take on!

The messy conditions attached to approving the Accord quickly became academic. Frank McKenna had done a complete turnaround and now fully supported the Meech Lake amendments; the New Brunswick legislature ratified the Accord on 15 June. But Clyde Wells affixed an asterisk beside his signature on the 9 July communiqué. He was committed only to submitting the Meech Accord "for appropriate legislative or public consideration and to use every possible effort to achieve decision prior to June 23, 1990." Premier Wells would not even say whether he himself would support the Accord. The Manitoba troika, Filmon, Carstairs, and Doer, said they would support the Accord. But on 12 June, when Filmon sought the unanimous consent of Manitoba's legislative assembly to skip the required two days' notice and proceed immediately to consider the Meech amendments, one hand was raised for the "nays." That hand belonged to Elijah Harper, and it held a feather. Harper was the sole Aboriginal member of the legislature. The legislature had been holding public hearings, and there were still thirty-five hundred witnesses, most of them Aboriginal, to be heard. All that was needed to shorten the hearings so that the legislature could vote on Meech Lake in time to meet the 23 June deadline was a majority vote, but none of the party leaders wanted to offend the Aboriginal peoples. Manitoba would not meet the deadline.

In Newfoundland, Premier Wells released his caucus from party discipline in voting on the Meech Lake Accord. The main advocates for the Accord were political leaders from mainland Canada, who flew to St John's to pitch Meech Lake to the Assembly: New Brunswick's McKenna, Ontario's Peterson, and Saskatchewan's Grant Divine, followed, finally, by Mulroney himself on 21 June. Wells kept delaying a vote to see what happened in Manitoba. On the afternoon of 22 June, with only a few hours to go, Lowell Murray announced on national television that the government was prepared to ask the Supreme Court of Canada to accept an extension of the deadline to 23 September, the date when Saskatchewan became the second province to ratify the Accord, but that the government would proceed with this only if Newfoundland ratified Meech Lake before the day was done.

The offer was clearly cynical and insulting to Newfoundlanders. The only reason Manitoba would get an extension that was refused for Newfoundland was that it was considered safer to offend Newfoundlanders than Aboriginal peoples. When Clyde Wells, a man of principle, heard this offer, he rose in the House to denounce it as "the final manipulation,"[15] and announced that the House would be adjourned without a vote. The Meech Lake Accord was dead.

The majority of Canadians did not break down in tears. An April poll reported that 59 per cent of respondents opposed Meech Lake – even in Quebec only 49 per cent supported the Accord. More troubling were polls showing that sovereignty-association, rejected by 60 per cent in 1980, was now favoured by two-thirds of Quebecers.

After the demise of the Meech Lake Accord, there was no doubt about where the largest of Canada's three founding pillars – now being referred to as the "rest of Canada," or ROC – stood on continuing the effort of constitutional reform. As I noted in an earlier volume, "[a]fter Meech, the commonest constitutional aspiration of the people in ROC was to put the Constitution in the freezer and get on with life."[16] But that was not going to happen. The two smaller pillars, Aboriginal Canada and French Canada – at least the part of it that dominated Quebec politics – still harboured strong and unsatisfied constitutional ambitions. At this point in Canada's odyssey most of the political leaders in English-speaking Canada believed they should not give up the effort to work out a grand solution to these unrequited constitutional ambitions that would be satisfactory to the entire country. And so, for the next twenty-eight months, from June 1990 until the Charlottetown Accord was put to a referendum in October 1992, the country engaged in a mega round of mega constitutional politics.

Aboriginal peoples pushed their way back onto the country's political agenda in April 1990, when the Mohawks of Kanesatake blocked a highway into the town of Oka, a few miles west of Montreal, to protest the town council's decision to encroach on a traditional Mohawk burying ground in order to add nine holes to the town's golf course. The Mohawk action is what Ojibwa scholar John Borrows calls a flashpoint event:

an event triggered by a disrespectful intervention authorized by a non-Aboriginal government that ignores a long-simmering but unresolved dispute with an Aboriginal community.[17] The Kanesatake people had been trying for years to establish their rights to the land they had lived on since the New France era, but had been denied access to both the comprehensive and specific claims processes. The Mohawks of Kahnawake, a larger Mohawk community on lands closer to Montreal, soon joined the Kanesatake Mohawks.[18] When the Quebec government resorted to police action, the Mohawks blockaded the approach to the Mercier Bridge, a main entry to Montreal from the south shore of the St Lawrence. By this time Aboriginal groups all across the continent were demonstrating support for the Mohawk people, threatening to block major transportation corridors. The Oka crisis did not end until September, when the federal government sent in the army to take down the barricades.

The Mohawks' action did not lead to a resolution of the issues underlying their conflict with Canada over sovereignty and land rights. The federal government continued to try to impose Indian Act governance on the communities. But the crisis did persuade Prime Minister Mulroney that a national commission of inquiry was urgently needed to look into Canada's relationship with Aboriginal peoples. He asked Brian Dickson, the recently retired chief justice of the Supreme Court of Canada, to consult with Aboriginal organizations and communities across the country on the commission's mandate and membership.

The Royal Commission on Aboriginal Peoples (RCAP) was established in August 1991. RCAP's terms of reference were comprehensive: it was to examine and make recommendations on all aspects of the relationship with Aboriginal peoples. Its composition was bicultural. Four commissioners would represent the main categories of Aboriginal peoples in Canada: George Erasmus, a former grand chief of the Assembly of First Nations; Viola Robinson, a former president of the Native Council of Canada, representing non-status Indians; Mary Sillett, a former vice-president of the Inuit Tapirisat of Canada; and Paul Chartrand, a university professor and leading Métis scholar. The three non-Aboriginal commissioners were René Dussault, a Quebec Court of Appeal judge; Bertha Wilson, a retired Supreme Court of Canada judge; and Allan Blakeney, the former NDP premier of Saskatchewan. Never before in any settler country had distinguished representatives of the native peoples and the newcomers sat down together to consider how the relationship between the two groups had evolved, where it was at in the present day, and how it might be improved in the future.

Former chief justice Dickson was an appropriate person to carry out the consultation that produced RCAP. Under his leadership the Supreme Court by 1990 was showing that it would take a very liberal approach to the recognition of Aboriginal and treaty rights in section 35 of the Constitution Act, 1982. In 1990 the Court delivered its first decisions on section 35 rights. In a case involving the right of Musqueam Indians in British Columbia to use their traditional fishing nets, the Court made it clear that the insertion of the word "existing" into section 35 did not mean that the constitutional rights of Aboriginal peoples were only those that had survived regulation by the laws of Canada's governments.[19] The Musqueam people's constitutional right to use traditional nets took priority over fishery regulations unless, after consultation with the Aboriginal people, the government could show that conservation of the fish stock required some limits on that right. In the *Sioui* case, decided at the same time, the Court rendered an important decision on treaty rights. Sioui was a descendant of Wyandot people who had fled to Quebec and settled on the north shore of the St Lawrence after the fall of Huronia.[20] The Court ruled that the treaty the Wyandot had made with the British Crown after the fall of New France gave them the right to cut trees for a traditional ritual and that right took precedence over Quebec provincial park regulations. Aboriginal peoples were not waiting for constitutional negotiations to clarify their rights. Through litigation they were beginning, with considerable success, to use the legal resources they had obtained at the time of patriation.

After the death of Meech Lake, Quebec would take the very opposite path to the one that had led to that Accord. Instead of quiet negotiations with the ROC leadership, Quebec's constitutional actions would be out in the open, highly public and democratic, and focused 100 per cent on Quebec's future without the slightest effort to anticipate how English-speaking Canada might respond to its plans. Constitutional action proceeded on two fronts. The first was a committee of the Quebec Liberal Party, chaired by Jean Allaire, a former Quebec City mayor. The Allaire committee, using the latest audio-video technology, held meetings in every constituency and consulted with business, union, and academic leaders, inviting input on Quebec's options now that the ROC had rejected its most modest proposals. The second was done in partnership with the Parti Québécois, now led by Jacques Parizeau. Bourassa and Parizeau, summoning up Quebec's French heritage, called it an "estates general." It took the form of a commission established by Quebec's

National Assembly with a mandate to consult with all the estates of the province on Quebec's future. The thirty-six-member commission included Quebec and federal politicians, and representatives of business, labour, the cooperative movement, education, the arts, and municipalities. It was chaired by two prominent francophone businessmen, Michel Bélanger and Jean Campeau. Beginning in November 1990 and on through the winter of 1991, it received submissions from six hundred groups and individuals in the province.

By March 1991 both the Allaire committee and the Bélanger-Campeau commission had completed their work and filed their reports. They were very much in harmony with each other. Allaire's basic formula for Quebec's future – political autonomy within a strengthened Canadian economic union – came very close to sovereignty-association.[21] The Allaire report laid out a detailed constitutional plan for a massive restructuring of Canada along decentralized lines, reducing Ottawa mainly to a manager of the economic union. The Allaire committee's recommendations, with only slight modifications, were approved by a Liberal Party convention in Montreal attended by 2,771 delegates. The Bélanger-Campeau commission exuded the confidence of a "national collectivity" that, with "serenity," could now choose its future.[22] It laid down a two-track process that was incorporated in Bill 150, passed by Quebec's National Assembly in May 1991.[23] One track would prepare for a referendum on Quebec sovereignty, to take place between 8 and 22 June or between 12 and 28 October 1992. Quebec would become sovereign one year to the day after a majority for the "yes" side. On the other track, a legislative committee was prepared to examine "any offer of a new constitutional partnership" made by the Canadian government – providing that offer was binding on Canada and the other provinces.

Allaire and Bélanger-Campeau embodied the full flowering of Quebec's Quiet Revolution. In them we can see the confidence of a modernizing society. Quebec's two leading political parties placed the leadership of its commission to look at the province's future in the hands of two successful French-speaking businessmen, a social category that scarcely existed before the Quiet Revolution and Bill 101. Allaire's nationalism was not anchored in nostalgia for a rural Catholic society, but was couched in the vision of a coherent society close to the people, able to compete and participate in an increasingly interdependent world. The Allaire proposals also reflected the Quiet Revolution's liberal side. The right of English-speaking communities to develop their cultural communities within Quebec was to be respected, and

Aboriginal peoples in Quebec were to be treated as "distinct nations entitled to their cultures, their language, their customs and traditions, as well as the right to direct the development of their own identity."[24] Indeed, the Quebec envisioned by Allaire was nearly a smaller version of what Canada was becoming: a multinational society that respected the rights of its cultural minorities.

Quebec's ultimatum that it would proceed with sovereignty unless the rest of Canada offered it an attractive alternative was seen as cheeky and arrogant outside Quebec. But it was an ultimatum that Brian Mulroney was not prepared to ignore, even though it came at a bad time for his government to plunge back into the constitutional maelstrom. Polls in 1990 showed support for the Mulroney government slipping below 20 per cent and falling rapidly. By September 1991 it had plummeted to 14 per cent. The Progressive Conservatives' opponents made sure that the goods and services tax (GST), introduced in 1991 to replace a hidden manufacturers' sales tax that was hindering Canadian exports, contributed to the government's unpopularity. The 1990s were turning out to be the most difficult decade Canada's economy had experienced since the Second World War.

Before the Quebec ultimatum, Mulroney took two disconnected initiatives. On 1 November 1990 he unveiled the Citizens' Forum on Canada's Future. The Forum's mandate was to give Canadians in all parts of the country and from all walks of life an opportunity to speak out on the future of their country. It was headed by Keith Spicer, Canada's first commissioner of official languages, at this time chairman of the Canadian Radio-television and Telecommunications Commission. Spicer was assisted by an "advisory group" of Canadian notables, and the Forum was to report its findings to the country by Canada Day, 1 July 1991. Before Spicer flew off to read poetry to the native people in Tuktoyaktuk, he acknowledged that the Forum had "a very high potential for fiasco." And he pretty much got that right. His advisers publicly bickered about what they were doing at the very time the Bélanger-Campeau commission was going serenely about its task of consulting the Quebec people. Nonetheless some four hundred thousand Canadians "spilled their guts out" about how they saw their country's future, but relatively few Quebecers were among the guts-spillers. Overall the ROC participants said they were interested in accommodating Quebec, but not at the price of sacrificing such cherished ideals as individual or provincial equality, and that they wanted a strong central government that, among other things, "will act with resolution to remedy the country's economic ills" and "help to unify its citizens."[25]

The second federal initiative was a more traditional joint parliamentary committee, chaired by Senator Gérald Beaudoin and Alberta MP Jim Edwards, with a mandate to examine and make recommendations on the process for amending Canada's Constitution. The Meech Lake experience shaped an overwhelming message in the submissions made to the committee: constitutional proposals that were the product of first ministers' negotiations would have no legitimacy. A number of submissions to Beaudoin-Edwards proposed a constituent assembly with various patterns of representation as a means of broadening the base for the development of constitutional proposals. But because Quebec would not participate in any constitutional process until the ROC came up with an offer, a constituent assembly would require a two-stage process: a first stage without Quebec and a second stage with Quebec. Although that seemed like an awkward process and was not recommended by Beaudoin-Edwards, the country was about to stumble through a process very much like that. The committee called for federal legislation to authorize a "consultative referendum" on constitutional proposals. Given that British Columbia already had legislation forbidding its legislature to act on constitutional proposals that had not been approved in a referendum, the consultative referendum would take place before legislative ratification. Beaudoin-Edwards recommended a double majority for a successful "yes" vote: an overall majority plus majorities in the country's four regions designated by the Victoria Charter – Atlantic Canada, Quebec, Ontario, and the West.

In the Speech from the Throne opening a new session of Parliament on 13 May 1991, a month before the Beaudoin-Edwards committee made its final report, the federal government announced its constitutional process. The cabinet would develop a set of constitutional proposals, not as a basis for negotiating with other governments, but as a step towards interlegislative negotiations. A parliamentary committee would take the federal proposals to meetings with the constitutional committees and commissions that a number of provinces had set up, or with provincial legislatures themselves. This approach would certainly broaden the process beyond intergovernmental negotiations, but it had its problems, the biggest of which was that Quebec would not be participating. Moreover, although the English-speaking provinces were willing to play the game of developing an offer for Quebec to consider – which in itself was a tribute to their national patriotism – they were not about to abandon their own constitutional priorities and walk lockstep in unison with Ottawa.

The Speech from the Throne came with a cabinet shuffle that saw Joe Clark, the former PC leader and prime minister who had been serving as Mulroney's external affairs minister, take over the new constitutional affairs portfolio. This was a positive step for the constitutional process. As Mulroney remarks in his memoirs,[26] because of his long absences from the country as external affairs minister, Clark was "in the enviable position" of not being associated with Meech Lake, the GST, or other issues that had harmed his government's popularity – and he was a westerner. One of Clark's first moves was to link Aboriginal peoples to the constitutional process. He encouraged the pan-Canadian Aboriginal organizations to consult with their constituent members and then interact with the federal parliamentary committee. Elijah Harper's feather demonstrated that Canada had clearly reached the point in its odyssey where major constitutional changes could neither ignore Aboriginal peoples nor be imposed on them.

On 24 September 1991 the federal government unveiled its package of constitutional proposals, *Shaping Canada's Future Together*.[27] And what a package it was: a potpourri with constitutional goodies for everyone. It included all of Meech Lake plus reforms the first ministers had promised to pursue once Meech Lake was passed, including Senate reform, Aboriginal self-government, Charter changes, and a Canada clause defining the country. There was also yet another effort to satisfy both those who wanted to decentralize the federation and those (like the Mulroney government) who wanted to strengthen Ottawa's economic powers. Although it would be greatly modified in the months of negotiations that lay ahead, the federal proposals under that soapy slogan would shape the agenda of the Charlottetown Accord that Canadians would be asked to approve in October 1992. One component of the federal government's package that did not require any formal constitutional change – and that most unfortunately for the country dropped out of sight for nearly a generation – was proposals to improve parliamentary democracy by relaxing party discipline and making Parliament less executive-dominated.

Shaping Canada's Future Together was now turned over to a parliamentary committee to shop around the country. The committee, chaired by Claude Castonguay, an experienced Quebec constitutionalist, and Manitoba MP Dorothy Dobbie, had strong Liberal and NDP representation as well as the governing Progressive Conservatives. Entirely missing were the two political parties that were rapidly becoming the strongest opposition parties in the country: Preston Manning's Reform Party in western Canada and Lucien Bouchard's Bloc Québécois. In the end, these were the parties that would tip the balance against the

Charlottetown Accord. Castonguay-Dobbie got off to a miserable start when it headed west and no one showed up at a meeting in Manitoba. At the end of November, Castonguay resigned for health reasons and Senator Beaudoin took his place.

Then NDP members of the committee had a bright idea. They suggested that the committee sponsor a series of public conferences in various regions of the country. The public conferences would bring together politicians (mostly federal), experts, interest-group leaders, and an increasingly popular Canadian species called "ordinary citizens."[28] The latter would be chosen from persons answering newspaper advertisements by the local independent research institution organizing the conferences. Five conferences in cities across the country, each focusing on a different cluster of issues, warmed up Canada's coldest winter months of 1992. The first was in Halifax, and dealt with that old Canadian chestnut, the division of legislative powers, enlivened this time by a concept that only Canadians could talk about in public: asymmetrical federalism. The question here was how far a federation could go in allowing one or several of its units more power than others. In Calgary the delegates debated the most hardy perennial of Canada's constitutional issues, Senate reform, and not surprisingly concluded with a strong consensus for an elected Senate. The Montreal conference evinced strong support for strengthening Canada as an economic union – that is, removing provincial barriers to the flow of commerce and labour across the country – but those of a leftish persuasion insisted that the economic union be balanced by a social union protecting Canada's social welfare programs. Toronto got the poetry assignment: defining what Canada is all about. If any consensus could be discerned in this conference, it was that Canada's deep diversity was coming to be seen as the core of Canadian identity. The Vancouver conference had the challenge of knitting together the outcomes of the first four conferences. It did this well enough to enable co-chair Rosalie Abella (later a justice of the Supreme Court of Canada), on behalf of "the little conference that could," to hand over a package of conclusions to the Beaudoin-Dobbie committee on 17 February 1992.

The parliamentary committee had just eleven days to modify the federal government's proposals in the light of what came out of the public conferences. The thirty-two MPs and senators, behind closed doors but connected to their party leaders by telephone – including, for some Liberals, their former leader, Pierre Trudeau – fought and bickered, but an hour before midnight on 18 February produced, with some dissents, a 125-page report entitled *A Renewed Canada*.[29] The changes had clearly diluted the conservative flavour of *Shaping Canada's Future*. Gone was the insertion of private property rights into the Charter as well a large new federal economic power, and a social union clause had been added.

The constitutional process was now at a critical point. Picture a democratic process of constitutional reform as taking the shape of an hourglass, with a wide stage of public discussion at the top, then narrowing down to a neck where detailed proposals are negotiated and drafted, then widening out to the public ratification stage through a referendum, and finally, approval by elected legislatures. By March 1992 that wide process of public discussion consultation was completed, and the time had come for a small representative group to work out detailed proposals. But there was a serious problem: the process of public consultation process had taken place in two totally separate political spaces, Quebec and the rest of Canada, and Quebec was unwilling to become involved in working out constitutional proposals with representatives of the ROC. Multilateral meetings involving the federal government, nine provinces, the two northern territories, and four pan-Canadian Aboriginal organizations was now the ROC's only way of moving to the next stage of the constitutional process.

The multilateral process, with each of the sixteen delegations entitled to have eight members participating in its work, involved a considerably larger group of people than first ministers' meetings. But there were serious problems with its Aboriginal participation. The Assembly of First Nations is a highly confederal organization with no mandate to commit historic and independent nations on their constitutional future. A further problem was the failure to include the Native Women's Association of Canada (NWAC). At a sixth public conference, held in Ottawa in March to consider Aboriginal issues, NWAC made a strong case for the separate representation of women at the constitutional table. When it was rebuffed, NWAC resorted to the courts to claim that its exclusion from the constitutional process violated the Charter. It lost in the Trial Division of the Federal Court, but on appeal was successful in getting a ruling from the Federal Court of Appeal that excluding NWAC from constitutional talks violated Indian women's right to freedom of expression. The decision was rendered in late August, just as the final details of the Charlottetown Accord were being settled. NWAC's exclusion likely reduced support for the Accord among Canadians who might otherwise have supported it.

The multilateral process's other weakness was its total domination by the provinces. It supported changes in the division of powers that had the potential for a massive decentralization of the Canadian federation. Through a process of "make a deal federalism," individual provinces could negotiate complete federal withdrawal from legislative fields such as labour market training, housing, and tourism. Joe Clark, unlike the ministers who led some of the provincial delegations, could not be sure that his prime minister and cabinet colleagues fully backed his efforts. There were rumours that Mulroney and his Quebec colleagues feared that Joe, a westerner and a conciliator, would succumb to the western provinces' insistence on a triple-E Senate – elected, effective, and equal representation for each province. Joe did not succumb, nor did Alberta, Manitoba, Saskatchewan, Newfoundland, or Nova Scotia back down from a fully triple-E remake of the Senate. It was Ontario premier Bob Rae who led the resistance to triple-E, knowing how unacceptable it would be to Quebec. No premier of *la belle province* could ever sell Quebecers the idea that their province was just a province like all the rest.

To break the deadlock over the Senate, Prime Minister Mulroney made a brief appearance on the constitutional stage. He invited the first ministers to have lunch with him at 24 Sussex Drive on 20 June, and succeeded in persuading them to have one more go at Senate reform. He then flew off to a G7 meeting in Munich, leaving Joe Clark to work with the premiers to break the Senate deadlock. At this point only the ROC premiers were participating; Premier Bourassa was still playing the show-me-your-offer game. It took a week, but Clark and nine premiers, now rejoined by the territorial and Aboriginal leaders, managed to make a deal on the Senate. The agreement they announced on 7 July was called the Pearson Accord because it had been put together not in the downtown Ottawa Conference Centre, but in the quieter confines of the Pearson Building, which houses the Department of External Affairs (later Foreign Affairs, now Global Affairs).

Poor Mike Pearson. It seems unfair to have put his name on such a messy and unwieldy plan for reforming the Senate. The proposal now was for a two big-E and one little-e Senate. Yes, it would be elected, by a "single transferable vote" system, which it is doubtful anyone understood. And the provinces would each have the same number of senators, none of whom could hold a cabinet position. But its effectiveness would be reduced in that it would no longer have the full legislative power the Senate has had since Confederation. On only one kind of issue could this reconstructed Senate veto the House of Commons: bills involving "fundamental tax policy changes directly related to natural resources." Readers should know where that point came from. Senate reform was aimed more than anything else at placating a west that "wanted in." The Pearson Accord Senate would hit that target right on, but it was bound to be an impossible sell in Quebec.

Quebec's premier Robert Bourassa was now at a critical juncture. If he refused to consider the constitutional proposals that were supported by the rest of Canada, he would be committed to an October referendum on Quebec sovereignty. By mid-summer 1992 Bourassa's flirtation with sovereignty was over. He knew that the proposals of his own party's Allaire report had no chance of being supported by the ROC. His only option was to enter the multilateral process and see whether he could make its emerging constitutional package more palatable to Quebec. On 4 August he accepted an invitation to have lunch with the other premiers at the prime minister's Harrington Lake summer home. Enough progress was made to have another lunch on 10 August. This set the stage for all of the delegations, now joined by Bourassa, to meet in the Pearson Building.

In four days, from 18 to 21 August, a deal was negotiated that Quebec was willing to take to its people in a referendum. Many small detailed changes were made in various components of the constitutional package, but the crucial compromise was over the Senate. Each of the ten provinces would have six senators and the northern territories one each, in an elected Senate reduced in size from 104 to 62. Bourassa had agreed to equality of the provinces in the Senate. In return he got a guarantee that, in a House of Commons expanded by 42 (to keep the total number of parliamentarians unchanged), no matter how much Quebec's proportion of the Canadian population might decline, Quebec would have 25 per cent of the seats. One other sweetener was thrown in: in addition to the Senate's power to block new taxes on resources, a majority of francophone senators could block legislation affecting the French language and culture. Otherwise, deadlocks between the two houses would be broken by a majority vote of the 62 senators and 337 MPs. The Senate's effectiveness would be a very small "e," and there would be a major departure from the principle of rep-by-pop in the House of Commons. This would not be an easy deal to sell to Canadians. But it was the deal that gave final shape to the proposals that would soon be submitted to the Canadian people.

On 28 August the delegations assembled in Charlottetown, PEI, the cradle of Confederation, for final touch-ups and a formal signing. The Charlottetown Accord was now on its way to a referendum,[30] which all along was the logical climax of this round of mega constitutional politics. Quebec was legislatively committed to a referendum on sovereignty or the Allaire proposals no later than 26 October. Alberta had joined British Columbia in requiring a referendum before any constitutional amendments could be considered by their legislatures. The Beaudoin-Edwards parliamentary committee considered a consultative referendum a good means of overcoming the democratic deficit in Canada's constitutional process. On 3 June the federal Parliament passed Bill C-81, setting up the machinery for a constitutional referendum.[31] Despite the near-inevitability of a referendum, the makers of the Charlottetown Accord appeared to have given no consideration to how well the package of proposals they were putting together might play out in such a vote. Their sixty-section Accord, sprinkled with asterisks marking loose ends to be tidied up through future negotiations, was singularly ill designed for a referendum in which the people would have only the choice of voting yes or no. A referendum did promise, whatever the result, to bring closure to a constitutional debate that many Canadians feared would never end.

A week after Charlottetown, Bourassa was successful in persuading 90 per cent of the delegates attending a Liberal Party convention to drop the Allaire proposals and amend Bill 150 so that Quebec could hold a 26 October referendum on the Charlottetown Accord. The federal government followed suit, authorizing a referendum in the rest of Canada on that day. British Columbia and Alberta were willing to participate in the referendum under federal legislation, rather than under their own statutes.

Although all Canadians would vote on the same set of constitutional proposals, the rules governing the conduct of the referendum campaign would differ between Quebec and the ROC. The competition in Quebec was limited to two committees, one each for the "yes" and "no" sides, one led by Bourassa and the Liberals, the other by Parizeau and the Parti Québécois. Expenditures for each side were limited to 50 cents per voter. Outside Quebec the campaign was much more wide open. There was no limit to the number of committees that could campaign for either side. The spending limit was 54 cents per voter in districts for which committees were registered; unregistered individuals and groups could not spend more than $5,000. The three main parliamentary parties, Liberals, Progressive Conservatives, and NDP, combined to form the main "yes" committee. But instead of having party leaders head the committee, they cast retired politicians and distinguished citizens in that role. That might have had something to do with the fact that Prime Minister Mulroney's popularity was at 11 per cent and falling. On the "no" side there was a much broader range of committees. Preston Manning's Reform Party and Liberal opposition parties in British Columbia and Manitoba (dedicated Trudeau-ites) were the only partisan committees. In addition a number of interest groups formed committees to attack parts of the Accord that were particularly objectionable to them.

Television was the principal communication medium. In televised debates – one in English-speaking Canada and one in Quebec – the "yes" side did not do badly. Most post-mortems thought the NDP's Audrey McLaughlin had not been bested by Reform's Preston Manning, and put Robert Bourassa slightly ahead on points in his toe-to-toe with Jacques Parizeau. The worst TV moment for the "yes" side was Mulroney's misfired scare tactic when he tore up a list of Quebec's gains in the Accord to show what would be left of Canada if the "no" side won. Pierre Trudeau's cameo appearance at the Montreal restaurant Maison Egg Roll seemed to be a huge lift for the "no" side. In the ten- or twenty-second clips that made up most of the TV coverage, it was much easier to trash a point in the Accord than to explain the Accord's complexities and ponderous prose. Also, it did not help that its sponsors could not produce an authoritative legal text of the Accord until the final two weeks of the campaign. A very effective "no"-side TV ad showed a trusty farmer coming out of his barn, saying he was not prepared to "trust a pig in a poke."

On 26 October 1992, 14 million Canadians – 75 per cent of eligible voters – for the first time in their country's history, cast ballots in a Canada-wide constitutional referendum. The result was not a surprise: 54 per cent voted against the Charlottetown Accord.[32] Both the west and Quebec voted "no." There were "yes" majorities in only four provinces – New Brunswick, Newfoundland, Ontario (by a whisker), and Prince Edward Island – and in the Northwest Territories. No rule had been promulgated as to what would count as a large enough win for the "yes" side to proceed to ratification in the country's legislatures, the final stage of the constitutional amending process. But that did not matter, given that the result was a clear victory for the "no" side.

It might seem strange that an Accord developed through a great deal of public discussion and supported by the federal, provincial, and territorial governments and the traditional opposition parties, as well as four Aboriginal organizations, was rejected by the majority of Canadians in the majority of provinces. But at this moment the principal opposition parties in national politics were the Bloc Québécois and the Reform Party, and they had played no part in making the Meech Lake Accord. These two parties opposed the Accord for fundamentally opposite reasons: for Reformers and many other westerners, it gave Quebec much too much; for the Bloc and many other Quebecers, it did not offer Quebec nearly enough. The guarantee to Quebec of a quarter of the seats in the House of Commons regardless of its population was as unacceptable to much of English Canada, but especially the west, and utterly inadequate to meet Quebec's aspiration to be recognized as the homeland of a founding people. More English-speaking Canadians might have supported the Accord had they been convinced that a "yes" vote was necessary to keep the country from breaking up. But polls showed that majorities of over 60 per cent in all parts of the country did not believe that a "no" win would boost the separatist cause. Moreover, all through the campaign, polls showed the "no" side well ahead in Quebec. This did not encourage voters outside Quebec to think that the Accord was a means of accommodating Quebec.

Canadians who might view the referendum defeat of the Charlottetown Accord as a lost opportunity to cure the county's constitutional discontents should be reminded of what the Accord would have saddled the country with had it been approved by the voters and ratified by the legislatures. First, they would have had an elaborate Canada clause at the beginning of the Constitution to guide judges' interpretations that included such dubious and unhelpful statements as "Canadians confirm the principle of the equality of the provinces at the same time as recognizing their diverse characteristics."[33] The Constitution would have subjected the federal division of powers to endless tinkering and added marshmallow clauses proclaiming that the country was an economic and social union without explaining what in practice that might mean. It would have provided a rinky-dink federal upper house based on the equality of provinces that would unlikely have made anyone happy and would have no longer been balanced by a lower house based on the principle of representation according to population.[34] And just to make sure our leaders never stopped talking about the Constitution, a first ministers' conference would have been required every year. No wonder so many who voted "yes" did so with their hand tightly clenching their nose!

Of course, there were some good things in the Accord. A small one was section 38, abolishing the federal government's power to disallow (that is, veto) or reserve (that is, hold up) provincial legislation. These imperial powers are completely inconsistent with Canada's federal system and have long been obsolete. Section 58 of the Accord would have accrued another smallish benefit to the northern territories. They would have been protected from provinces expanding northward into their terrain without their consent. Also, their path to becoming new provinces would have been eased by enabling Parliament to authorize new provinces without the unanimous provincial consent required under the existing Constitution.

The fifteen sections (sections 41–56) on Aboriginal peoples, a quarter of the Accord, were a big good feature showing how far non-Aboriginal Canada had moved in recognizing their rights. These sections acknowledged Aboriginal peoples' "inherent right of self-government within Canada," and laid out a process for negotiating it, called for a just and fair interpretation of treaty rights, promised better financing of Aboriginal communities, recognized Métis rights in Alberta and Saskatchewan, committed to an accord with the Métis Nation, and clarified that federal jurisdiction under section 91(24) applies to all Aboriginal peoples – a position the Supreme Court of Canada would endorse in 2016.[35] These provisions also had a down side. Tacking "within Canada" onto an inherent right was contradictory and insulting. The inherent right came with creation, not with Canada, and Aboriginal peoples, in their quiet and forgiving way, are not interested in leaving Canada. More seriously, many First Nations regard nation-to-nation treaties, not Canada's constitution-amending process, as the only legitimate way to regulate their relations with Canada. Although the Aboriginal sections of the Accord were not a target of the "no" campaign, polling stations on reserves reported a 60 per cent "no" vote.

The greatest benefit of the Charlottetown Accord experience was its value as a collective learning experience. The peoples who make up Canada learned that, as a sovereign people, they could act together only in a negative way. They could reject a grand new scheme for sharing citizenship in a political community called Canada, but they could not remodel that community in one bold and popular constitutional move. On a smaller scale, the peoples of Quebec were about to have a similar learning experience.

After the Charlottetown Accord went down, the phrase on everyone's lips in Canada outside Quebec was "constitutional exhaustion." Even in Quebec many were exhausted with constitutional debates and struggle. Dedicated sovereignists, however, were not done. The premise of the sovereignists' opposition to Charlottetown was that nothing short of independence was a satisfactory future for Quebec. Now their moment had come.

The table was set for a second Quebec referendum when the Parti Québécois, led by Jacques Parizeau, defeated Daniel Johnson's Liberals in the 1994 Quebec election. Johnson had taken over the Liberal leadership when Robert Bourassa retired from politics in January 1994. The PQ won seventy-seven seats to the Liberals forty-seven, while Mario Dumont's nationalist Action démocratique du Québec took one seat. But the popular vote was much closer, with the PQ garnering just half a per cent more than the Liberals. Although the election had hardly handed the new government a strong mandate for separation, Parizeau never hesitated to fulfil his election promise of having a referendum on Quebec independence within eight to ten months of coming to office.[36]

Parizeau had become a dedicated and straightforward Quebec sovereignist. Just two months after the election, he unveiled a bill that amounted to a declaration of Quebec independence. It would come into force a year after a majority "yes" vote in a referendum on the question: "Are you in favour of the Act passed by the National Assembly declaring the sovereignty of Quebec?" The Act would authorize Quebec to negotiate an economic union with Canada, but that would not be a condition of Quebec's political independence. Parizeau was for sovereignty on the rocks – no conditions attached.

But the premier did not get his way. When the province went into a massive process of public consultation, it quickly became clear that Parizeau had a rival for Quebec leadership: none other than Lucien Bouchard, leader of the Bloc Québécois, which had done so well in the 1993 federal election that it now formed the Official Opposition in Ottawa, and Bouchard was a devotee of sovereignty-association. Bouchard, with his softer option and more congenial personality, had more appeal to nationalists than the more doctrinaire Parizeau. At the very time Parizeau was announcing his bold referendum plan, Bouchard was suddenly inflicted with a strange flesh-eating bacteria that required the amputation of his left leg. His quick and gallant recovery from this tragedy only added to his charisma. By April, Parizeau, sensing that his bold approach was losing ground, postponed the referendum

scheduled for June until the fall. On 12 June he met with Bouchard and
Mario Dumont to work out a common referendum policy. The three
leaders agreed they would work together for Quebec sovereignty, but
on condition that, after a "yes" win, Quebec would negotiate an economic and political partnership with Canada. That agreement produced the following question for the referendum now scheduled for
30 October: "Do you agree that Quebec should become sovereign, after
having made a formal offer to Canada of a new Economic and Political
Partnership within the Bill respecting the future of Quebec and of the
agreement signed on June 12, 1995?"[37]

The question was more convoluted than Parizeau and most
Canadians had wanted, but it was bolder and less conditional than the
1980 question. The attempt to negotiate a political and economic partnership with Canada after a referendum win did not have to be successful. Quebec's sovereignty was conditional only on making the
effort. The question was framed in a way that assumed Quebec could
become a sovereign independent state through its own declaration, an
assumption that was soon to be challenged in the courts. The reference
to a *political* partnership, not just an economic partnership, with Canada
reflects the influence of the European Union on the soft sovereignists'
thinking. Bouchard and those attracted to his vision had in mind a two-
nation EU. Citizens of an independent Quebec, like citizens of EU
member states, would have joint citizenship, continuing to be Canadian
citizens. And like much of the EU, Quebec and Canada would share a
common currency, the Canadian dollar. It was a smooth and relatively
painless path to Quebec independence, but a most improbable one. The
likelihood was next to zero that a Canadian government could sell such
a scheme to Canadians outside Quebec or be willing to partner with a
much smaller nation (and former province) in a diarchy responsible for
managing key aspects of economic policy.

All through this year when Quebec was engaged in working out its
referendum plan, the eyes and ears of Canadians outside Quebec were
riveted on the province. Some were aghast that the possible breakup of
their country was so near at hand. Others, especially in western Canada,
were angry and prone to display their independence by muttering "let
the SOBs go." Some simply dreaded the prospect of their country's returning to yet another round of painful and divisive constitutional debates that surely would follow a "yes" win. It was frustrating simply to
watch and wait.

The "yes" side had a bolder option to sell than in 1980. That, however, was balanced by their advantage in leadership. Brian Mulroney

had retired from politics in 1993, and his successor, Kim Campbell, had led the Progressive Conservatives to the most ignominious political defeat in Canadian political history.[38] The PCs were reduced from a huge majority of 210 to just two seats in the House of Commons. Jean Chrétien, the new federal prime minister and leader of a Liberal government with a solid majority, was a passionate Quebec federalist and an able administrator, but he did not have the charisma of his mentor, Pierre Trudeau. The dominant personality of the referendum campaign was Lucien Bouchard. Only the Quebec premier could captain the "yes" side, but Parizeau had the good sense to keep Bouchard in the spotlight and designate him as Quebec's chief negotiator with Canada after a sovereignist win.

With just a week to go in the campaign and the "yes" side ahead by six points, Chrétien succumbed to the urging of "no" captain Daniel Johnson and, in a speech in the Montreal suburb of Verdun, promised to recognize Quebec as a distinct society, restore Quebec's constitutional veto, and transfer power over labour market training to Quebec.[39] This desperate "Hail Mary" move was supplemented by the organization of a huge rally in Montreal's downtown Place du Canada in support of national unity. The busing in from Ontario of many of the demonstrators probably breached Quebec referendum rules. The banners and bumper stickers of the demonstrators read, "My Canada includes Quebec." Canadian patriotism was alive and well. We cannot be sure about it, but this rally of patriotic Canadians on the weekend before the vote might have tipped the balance for the "no" side. The referendum was that close.

It was not until 10 p.m. on Monday, 30 October, that the "no" side edged ahead, with 50.6 per cent of the slightly more than five million Quebecers (94 per cent of eligible voters) who voted checking "no" on their ballot. If thirty-two thousand of them had voted the other way, the sovereignists would have won. If they had, the only thing we can be sure of is that chaos and confusion would have immediately followed. Prime Minister Chrétien had made it clear that the Canadian government was not prepared to accept a "yes" win as leading immediately to Quebec's becoming an independent state. Minister of National Defence David Collenette had Canadian armed forces prepared to protect federal property in Quebec from a sovereignist takeover. The appearance of Canadian soldiers in the streets would not have a soothing effect. Anglo hotheads in Montreal and in towns along the Quebec side of the Ottawa River had been threatening to partition their communities from a sovereign Quebec. Their collision with sovereignists celebrating in the streets had the potential for communal violence. Up north the James Bay Cree had made it clear that it would take armed force to make them part of a sovereign Quebec. The "no" win, narrow though it was, meant that, in the aftermath of the referendum, we Canadians did not have to test the limit of our tradition of civility, our capacity for resolving deep differences peacefully without resorting to violence.

The issues that must be resolved if the majority of Quebecers vote to leave Canada do not make an easy agenda. For starters, there is the question of boundaries. It is not at all clear in ethics or law that Quebec north of the Eastmain River, which was added to the province of Quebec in 1912 and where the majority of the population is Aboriginal, should be part of an independent Quebec. But Quebec sovereignists have never conceived of an independent Quebec having anything other than the existing boundaries of the province of Quebec. An equally challenging question concerns Quebec's share of Canada's national debt. In 1995 Quebec's provincial debt per capita was considerably larger than that of any other province. Could the new Quebec state assume its proportionate share of Canada's national debt without facing bankruptcy? Would the Canadian government have a mandate to transfer Quebec's share of the national debt to the rest of Canada? How would federal public works in Quebec enter into the accounting? And then there is the matter of securing and maintaining a transportation corridor connecting Atlantic Canada to the rest of Canada. Those on both sides of the barricades who talk glibly and simplistically about Quebec's leaving Confederation should think carefully about these kinds of issues. "Breaking up the country" is a poor metaphor for fundamental change within a long-established democratic federation.

On 30 October 1995 Premier Parizeau was anything but gracious in his concession speech. "It is true that we were beaten," he admitted. Then he asked, "By whom?" and answering his own question, said, "money and ethnic votes."[40] Surely the more telling lesson to take from Quebec's second referendum was that the people of Quebec had learned much the same lesson as the people of Canada had imbibed three years earlier. As the sovereign people of a multinational, multicultural society, Quebecers could say "no" to a new plan for their future together, but they could not positively embrace a new political order.

Chapter 16

The Three Pillars Continue Their Odyssey

In 2017, when Canadians celebrate the 150th anniversary of Confederation, let us not make the mistake of thinking that 1867 is when the
Canadian story began. Confederation is certainly a big chapter in that
story for the two largest pillars on which the country rests, English
Canada and French Canada, though not for its smallest but oldest pillar, Aboriginal Canada, which did not participate in Confederation.
Canada's odyssey began over a century earlier, when Britain took control of New France and made peace with France's Amerindian allies.
After the American Revolution, British settlers quickly became the
dominant population of British North America. Although Britain and
its colonists had the numbers and the arms that might have induced
them to attempt to eliminate the *Canadiens* and the Indian nations,
for reasons explored in the opening chapters of this book they did not
do so. Instead they formed relations with the French settlers and Aboriginal peoples that bore the seeds of the complex society that Canada
would become.

At Confederation the French Canadians and the British North
American colonists formed a parliamentary federal state based on a
written Constitution – something Britain itself has never had. For the
next century, as we have seen, that state grew and changed incremen-
tally, including in its relations with Aboriginal peoples, until the late
1960s, when the nationalist aspirations of all three pillars pushed the
country into an effort at what would have amounted virtually to a new
founding. But despite a series of heroic attempts – successive rounds of
mega constitutional politics – we did not pull it off. Since the final fling,
the 1995 Quebec referendum, the country has settled back into the normal life of a settled constitutional democracy.

In these conditions of normality, the Constitution is not before us morning, noon, and night. Still, constitutional change continues, "in bits and pieces," to use the words of Daniel Elazar.[1] Changes take place, not through the kind of grand democratic social contract by which the English political philosopher John Locke envisaged a people founding a political society, but through Edmund Burke's organic evolutionary process. Burke thought of a society's constitution as the collection of laws, institutions, political practices, and principles that serves the people well enough to be passed along to future generations. Some will need to be fixed or even discarded as a society evolves. For societies moving along a Burkean path, constitutional change is incremental, the test of what is worth keeping is pragmatic, and consent is mostly implicit.

This concluding chapter deals with the bits and pieces of constitutional change that have occurred since the country stopped engaging in mega constitutional politics. Over the past two decades there have been plenty of changes in the way we Canadians are governed, some of them good, some problematic, and some downright regressive, especially the operation of parliamentary democracy. The three foundational pillars adjust their relations to one another as they continue their odyssey together.

Let us begin with Quebec, the homeland of Canada's French pillar. One might have thought that, after coming so close to success in the 1995 referendum, the separatists would have quickly pushed for another. But the very opposite happened. The loss took the wind out of the sovereignists' sails. The Parti Québécois managed to stay in power until 2003, and formed a minority government in 2012 that lasted only two years. The PQ continues to be torn apart by the historic tension between fundamentalists committed to an immediate referendum and pragmatists who prefer to wait until there are "winning conditions." It would be foolish to think that those conditions will never come, but the prospects are not good for their developing soon. Now the generational divide is reversed from the PQ's heyday: the old are keener supporters of Quebec independence than the young. And the future belongs to the young.

It is doubtful that the decline in support for Quebec separatism has anything to do with post-referendum constitutional moves aimed at placating Quebec nationalists. Foremost among those were attempts to fulfil the key component of the Meech Lake Accord: recognizing Quebec as a distinct society. Less than a month after the 1995 referendum, the House of Commons passed a motion introduced by Prime Minister Jean Chrétien that the House would be guided by "the reality that Quebec is a distinct society within Canada."[2] Not to be outdone, in 1997 the premiers of the English-speaking provinces and heads of the territorial governments issued a declaration, the so-called Calgary Accord, that, "All provinces, while diverse in their characteristics, have equality of status."[3] Finally, in 2007 the House of Commons passed a motion, introduced by Prime Minister Stephen Harper, "That this House recognize that the Québécois form a nation within a united Canada."[4] The Calgary statement was more like a red flag than a peace offering, and the Harper statement was actually a putdown for separatist Quebec nationalists who view all the people within the present boundaries of Quebec as forming the Quebec nation.

The Chrétien government also tinkered with the constitutional amending formula in order to deliver on Chrétien's referendum campaign promise to restore Quebec's veto on constitutional amendments. Early in 1996 the House of Commons passed legislation stipulating that ministers of the Crown could not introduce a resolution to support amendments under the 50-per-cent-of-the-population/two-thirds-of-the-provinces rule unless these amendments were supported by legislatures or referendums in five regions of the country – Atlantic Canada (two provinces representing 50 per cent of the population), British Columbia, Ontario, Quebec, and the prairie provinces (two provinces representing 50 per cent of the population).[5] In purely legal terms this statute binds only the federal executive, and can be rescinded by a future Parliament. But imagine the political risk a prime minister would take by having the Act overridden in order to shove through an amendment that was unpopular in one of the country's regions.

Canadians have found that the general procedure for amending the Constitution – the federal Parliament plus seven provinces representing 50 per cent of the population – is virtually unusable. It has been used only once, in 1983 to clarify the section 35 guarantee of Aboriginal and treaty rights. Since then, political leaders have shied away from using it because of the well-grounded fear that it would open up another divisive round of mega constitutional politics. But three other parts of the amending formula have provided fertile soil for constitutional amendments. These are section 43, for amendments that apply to one or more, but not all, the provinces; section 44, empowering the federal Parliament to pass legislation in relation to the executive government, the Senate, and House of Commons in matters not subject to the general procedure or the unanimity rule; and section 45, empowering provinces to amend their constitutions in matters not subject to the unanimity requirement. Section 43, the so-called bilateral amending formula,[6] was used in 1997 to remove the guarantee of the Protestant minority's schools in Quebec. Although the amendment was an occasion for some debate in the House of Commons, it was approved by a unanimous vote in Quebec's National Assembly, reflecting the secularization of Quebec society. Section 43 has also been used to recognize the strength of francophone Canada outside Quebec. A 1993 amendment made New Brunswick Canada's only officially bilingual and bicultural province, reflecting the fact that people of *Acadien* descent constitute 34 per cent of the province's population. The *Acadiens* have come a long way back since their expulsion from British North America nearly a quarter of a millennium ago.[7]

In this era of post–mega constitutional politics, the Supreme Court of Canada has made much more significant contributions to developing the Constitution than the formal amending process. None of its contributions has been more important than the decision it rendered in 1998, three years after the Quebec referendum, on the question of whether Quebec (or any other province) had the right under Canadian or international law to secede unilaterally from Canada. The question submitted to Quebecers in the 1995 referendum in effect claimed such a right. With the referendum campaign still in progress, a Quebec judge ruled that unilateral secession would be unconstitutional, but refused to grant an injunction to stop the referendum. Stéphane Dion, a new recruit to the Chrétien government, who, as a Université de Montréal political science professor, had written a series of public letters challenging Premier Bouchard, felt strongly that on this crucial question of the right to unilateral secession the air should be cleared.[8] His urging led to questions on the legality of unilateral secession being referred to the Supreme Court.

No federation finds it easy even to talk about secession, let alone set out legal rules for a seceding unit to follow. The preamble to Australia's Constitution states that the Australian states "have agreed to unite in one indissoluble union," while the preamble of the American Constitution refers to the people of the United States forming "a perfect union," and, as the Civil War so amply showed, made no provision for states that might wish to leave that union. In 1997 Canada ventured into the uncharted territory of the constitutional rules of secession because Dion and his colleagues, facing Premier Bouchard's threat to hold yet another Quebec sovereignty referendum as soon as "winning ways" prevailed, saw the potential for chaos and violence in the conflicting assumptions and lawlessness of 1995.

On 20 August 1998 the Supreme Court of Canada, in a unanimous unsigned opinion, rendered its path-breaking decision.[9] It answered the two key questions in the negative: neither Canadian constitutional law nor international law supported Quebec's right to secede unilaterally following a majority vote of the Quebec people in favour of secession. As citizens of a federal country, the justices reasoned, Quebecers participate in building two majorities, one national and one provincial. Both majorities must participate in a change as fundamental as the secession of a province. Besides, democracy in Canada cannot be reduced to simple majority rule. The rights and interests of minorities – English-speaking Canadians in Quebec, French-speaking Canadians outside Quebec – and of Aboriginal peoples must be respected. And, most fundamentally, the rule of law requires that the secession of a province be effected through the legally prescribed rules for amending the Canadian Constitution. The Court held that the right to the self-determination of peoples in international law gives rise to a right to secede only for a people suffering oppressive colonial subjugation. Such conditions, the Court said, "are manifestly inapplicable in Quebec under existing circumstances."[10]

As with its decision in the 1980 *Patriation* case, the Court gave something to both sides. In the event of a referendum resulting in "a decision of a clear majority of the population of Quebec on a clear question to pursue secession," the other participants in Confederation have a duty to negotiate the terms of secession with Quebec. The aim of the negotiations would be to attempt through good-faith bargaining to honour the clearly expressed desire of Quebecers to secede in a manner that is fair to the rights and interests of all Canadians affected by the secession. The Court did not say what would or should happen if the negotiations failed. Presumably it hoped the international community would use the Court's decision as a standard for assessing whether recognition should be denied Quebec if it asserted its independence after a failed negotiation. Nor did the Court attempt to define what would constitute a clear question or a clear majority. Those are political questions the Court said that are best left to the political actors involved. Although the Supreme Court's creative statecraft aroused academic criticism, it seemed to serve the political purpose of giving both sides something to cheer about. Premier Bouchard assessed the Court's creation of a duty on the part of the ROC to negotiate after a "yes" win as "comforting to the sovereignist project," while Prime Minister Chrétien said the decision meant that Canada was not a prison for Quebec, but that it also established "a barrier that you have to go over before secession."[11]

The final act in the drama over the right to secede came in 1999, when Stéphane Dion introduced the Clarity Act in the House of Commons.[12] The Act asserts that the House of Commons has the right to decide whether a question relating to secession is sufficiently clear to trigger the duty to negotiate. The House of Commons is also to decide whether the clear question was approved by a clear majority. The Act does not specify how big the majority must be to be clear, but the implication is that 50 per cent plus one vote would not be enough. This remains a bone of contention. Bouchard's PQ government was returned to power in 1998 despite winning less of the popular vote than Jean Charest's Liberals. In 2000 Bouchard fired back at the Clarity Act with Quebec's Self-Determination Act asserting that "the Quebec people has the inalienable right to freely decide the political regime and legal status of Quebec."[13] The Quebec Act asserts that 50 per cent of valid voters plus one constitutes a majority in a referendum on Quebec's future.

Fortunately for the peace, order, and good government of Canada, the country has not had to find out what would happen if the federal Clarity Act and Quebec's Self-Determination Act met on the constitutional battlefield. Lucien Bouchard never found his "winning conditions," nor did his successors as PQ premiers, Bernard Landry and Pauline Marois. But the Acts stand in the statute books as indicators of the ugly circumstances that would confront Canadians should Quebec sovereignists win a future referendum.

The most significant changes in Canada's constitutional arrangements over the past quarter of a century have concerned the country's Aboriginal pillar. The right of Indigenous peoples to govern their own societies is no longer a contested right in Canada – or in the world. In the 1990s, following the lead of the Royal Commission on Aboriginal Peoples, the federal government opened up the land claims process to include self-government. In 2007, 143 countries endorsed the United Nations Declaration of the Rights of Indigenous Peoples. Article 3 of that Declaration recognizes that the world's Indigenous peoples (with populations totalling over three hundred million) have the right to self-determination, by virtue of which "they freely determine their political status and freely pursue their economic, cultural and social development."[14] Canada was not among the countries adopting the Declaration, but in 2010 the Harper government agreed to support the Declaration. The difficulties in moving forward with fulfilling this right in Canada are now more practical than ideological – the willingness of the federal and provincial governments to resource Aboriginal communities adequately, and the capacity of Aboriginal communities to discharge effectively the responsibilities of governance.

Canada's Inuit people have had the least difficulty in taking advantage of the federal government's willingness to couple self-government with land issues in negotiating modern treaties with Indigenous peoples. In 1993 the Tunngavik Federation of Nunavut reached an agreement with Canada on land and self-government, covering the entire eastern Arctic.[15] The agreement was preceded by a 1992 referendum in which the Northwest Territories people, by a 69 per cent majority, approved carving out a new territory called Nunavut, containing one-third of Canada's land mass.

The Inuit opted for a public form of self-government embracing all who live in the territory. Because Nunavut's twenty-five thousand Inuit constitute 85 per cent of the territorial population, they are bound to play a major role in its governance. That governance is a parliamentary/cabinet system adapted to Inuit tradition. In Nunavut, elections and the legislative process operate without political parties. Candidates run on their individual merit, and the legislature aims at reaching consensus in its deliberations. Inuktitut is the working language of government. Government is not just decentralized but deconcentrated, with centres of authority distributed to a number of settlements in the territory.[16] In return for surrendering their native title over their entire homeland, the Inuit enjoy ownership under Canadian law of 11 per cent (three hundred and fifty thousand square kilometres) of the territory, lands they selected because of their importance for traditional and contemporary economic pursuits.

Three other Inuit communities have made modern treaty-like agreements with Canada. The Inuit of Nunavik in northern Quebec, as noted earlier, joined with the James Bay Cree in being parties to Canada's first land claims agreement in 1975. With the concurrence of the provincial government, the eleven thousand Inuit, who are the dominant population in Quebec's far north, have taken over most governmental responsibilities, including health, education, social welfare, and municipal government. In 1984 representatives of the forty-five hundred Inuvialuit people of the Mackenzie River delta signed the first land claim to be settled in the Northwest Territories. In addition to gaining ownership rights to ninety-one thousand kilometres for Inuvialuit settlements, the Inuvialuit have harvesting rights and an important role in a special conservation regime across the Arctic north slope. In 2005 the eight thousand Inuit people of northern Labrador entered into an agreement with Canada and the province of Newfoundland and Labrador modelled on Nunavut. Northern Labrador is now Nunatsiavut, governed by an elected parliament. The agreement was ratified by a large majority of the region's people, by the federal Parliament, and by Newfoundland and Labrador's Legislative Assembly.

By 2005, 95 per cent of the Inuit people in Canada were living under agreements with Canada that they have consented to, that enable them to retain their identity, and that give them considerable power to secure and advance their economic interests. Life under these agreements is far from heaven on earth. Many practical issues remain to be resolved, but the solutions must now come from communities that have advanced significantly along the path of self-determination and decolonization.

The native peoples the white man called Indians and whom we now refer to as First Nations, numbering over eight hundred thousand – about 60 per cent of Canada's Aboriginal population – have not found it as easy as the Inuit to enter into land and self-government agreements. The first to do so were the fourteen communities that form the Council of Yukon Indians. In 1993 the Council, representing six thousand people – 20 per cent of Yukon's population – signed an umbrella agreement establishing a land selection process and a menu of self-government responsibilities that serve as parameters for each First Nation to enter into a treaty with Canada and Yukon. By 2015 all but three of the Yukon First Nations had made treaties under the agreement. Reaching final agreements has been facilitated by the pragmatism of Indian leaders who, like Inuit negotiators, have accepted clauses in which they cede, lease, and surrender their Aboriginal rights in return for the rights recognized in their treaties.[17]

It is not surprising that the Nisga'a in British Columbia were the first Aboriginal nation south of the sixtieth parallel to negotiate a modern treaty covering land and self-government issues. It was the Nisga'a who instigated the landmark court case that began to turn federal policy around in 1973. In 1998 Nisga'a negotiators signed an agreement with representatives of the federal and BC governments that recognizes the authority of the Nisga'a government over a wide range of subjects, including policing and public order, environmental protection, education, health, social welfare, language, and culture.[18] Unlike the governments of the Inuit self-governing territories, the Nisga'a government is an Aboriginal government organized on traditional lines, with most responsibilities administered by four villages. Although the several hundred non-Nisga'a people living in the area do not have the full rights of the five thousand Nisga'a citizens, they can participate in administering services that directly and significantly affect them.

The Nisga'a agreement required the Nisga'a people to accept some tough compromises.[19] The agreement recognizes Nisga'a ownership of just over 8 per cent of the lands they claimed as traditional territory. But that land does include the villages where they live and where they engage in farming, forestry, fishing, and other essential economic activities. In most subject areas on which the Nisga'a can make laws, Nisga'a law must give way if it is in conflict with federal or provincial law. But in matters crucial to their identity and culture, such as their constitution, citizenship, language, and management of Nisga'a-owned lands, Nisga'a law is supreme and prevails over federal or provincial laws. The toughest pill for the Nisga'a to swallow was an extinguishment clause, insisted on by the federal government, in which the Nisga'a accepted the agreement as "full and final settlement in respect of Aboriginal rights, including Aboriginal title." No wonder the agreement was approved by only 51 per cent of the 2,384 eligible Nisga'a voters in the ratifying referendum.

The agreement also had to be ratified in the federal Parliament and the British Columbia legislature. It won approval in both legislatures, but not without a good deal of debate that focused mostly on the recognition of the sovereign legislative power of the Nisga'a in matters essential to their culture and self-governance. That sliver of Aboriginal sovereignty was too much for some legislators to swallow. Gordon Campbell, leader of the Liberal Opposition in the BC Legislative Assembly, launched a court challenge to the agreement's recognition of Nisga'a sovereignty. In a landmark decision, Justice Williamson of the BC Supreme Court rejected Campbell's challenge,[20] ruling that forming federal and provincial legislatures at the time of Confederation did not exhaust legislative power in Canada and extinguish the right of Aboriginal peoples to govern their own societies. Aboriginal societies retained at least some of their sovereignty.

Few First Nations are willing to make the compromises the Nisga'a accepted. That is certainly true in British Columbia, the province which historically boycotted the historic treaty process and as a result has more First Nations peoples living on their lands without recognition of their title than any other Canadian jurisdiction. In 1993 the BC government, the federal government, and the Congress of First Nations established the British Columbia Treaty Commission to facilitate and monitor treaty-making on land and self-government issues.[21] To date only four of the fifty-four BC First Nations eligible to use the process have entered into final agreements.

Similarly, the Dehcho Dene, the largest First Nation in the Northwest Territories, have not been able to reach an agreement with Canada. That leaves the lands through which a Mackenzie Valley pipeline might be built, approximately a quarter of the territory, subject to an unsettled claim. The Dehcho Dene aim to establish a public government for all who live in their part of the territory. In 2002 they entered into an Interim Agreement with Canada that gives them a decisive voice in any new resource development in their territory.[22] How this resilient northern native nation, whose declaration of nationhood four decades ago had such an impact on Canadian Aboriginal policy, settles its issues with Canada will have a huge bearing on the future of the Northwest Territories.

Elsewhere in Canada, some First Nations have the will and capacity to push ahead on their own, unilaterally asserting their authority in areas such as education, family welfare, and policing, making bilateral arrangements with provincial and federal governments on recognizing and funding these initiatives. The Kahnawake Mohawks in Quebec and the Mi'kmaq of Nova Scotia are leading examples. But the great majority of Canada's First Nations are too small to take on major governance responsibilities. Without political reorganization such as the establishment of tribal, regional, or provincial councils, there cannot be significant progress towards self-government, and that reorganization can only be done by the First Nations themselves.

Equally important is adequate funding. The federal government, for some time, has been willing to dismantle the Indian Act and let provincial governments and First Nations governments assume responsibility for services such as education, health, and social welfare that up to now have been funded by Ottawa. But for more than a century those services have been grossly underfunded, with damaging consequences for First Nations people. It would be extremely unwise for First Nations governments to assume responsibility for the basic public services needed by their people without being adequately resourced. Adequate resources must be a combination of transfer payments along the lines of the equalization grants to provinces and much greater access to revenues from developments on their historic lands.

The situation and prospects of the Métis, the third category of Aboriginal peoples recognized in Canada's Constitution, are markedly different from those of the Indians and Inuit. Besides the communities formed by the descendants of the Red River Métis, other Métis with a different ethnogenesis[23] have established Métis national organizations in all the western provinces. Only in Alberta have the Métis secured a land base for their communities. In 1989, the Alberta-Métis Settlements Accord gave their eight settlements a firmer legal base for their land and autonomy in local affairs. Elsewhere, provincial Métis organizations provide a range of educational, cultural, and legal services to their members, and in some provinces, notably Saskatchewan, they have taken important first steps towards having recognized governmental responsibilities.[24]

In 2013 the Supreme Court of Canada rendered its decision in a case concerning a charge that the federal government's delay in implementing the commitment in section 31 of the Manitoba Act, 1870 to grant 1.4 million acres of land to Métis children breached its constitutional duty.[25] The Supreme Court majority concluded with the declaration that "the federal Crown failed to implement the land grant provision set out in s. 31 of the *Manitoba Act, 1870* in accordance with the honour of the Crown."[26] That declaration was the remedy sought by the plaintiff, the Manitoba Métis Federation. Negotiations concerning some kind of compensation are still in process. But no amount of money will compensate the Métis nation for the harm done to it by the shoddy and insensitive way that the Macdonald Conservative and subsequent Mackenzie Liberal governments went about fulfilling Canada's constitutional obligation to the Métis nation, whose elected leaders led the treaty-like process that established Manitoba. The whole point of section 31 was to give the Métis a land base close to established Métis families living along the Red and Assiniboine rivers on which future generations of Métis could build a new farming economy.[27]

A major unresolved issue is securing a consensus on who are the Métis. According to Statistics Canada, Canada's Métis population rocketed from 204,000 in 1996 to just under 390,000 ten years later.[28] This spectacular increase was the result of a census policy of self-identification. At one time, "half-breed" was a census category, but until 1996 there had never been one for "Métis." Introducing that category was probably prompted by section 35 of the Constitutional Act, 1982, which recognizes three categories of Aboriginal peoples: Indians, Inuit, and Métis.

In *Powley* (2003), the Supreme Court of Canada defined Métis in a case involving a father and son charged with hunting moose without a licence near Sault Ste Marie, Ontario. The Powleys claimed that, as Métis, they had a constitutional right to hunt that overrode Ontario regulations. In deciding the case in the Powleys' favour, the Court gave the following definition of Métis: "The term Métis in s. 35 does not encompass all individuals with mixed Indian and European heritage, rather it refers to distinctive peoples who, in addition to their mixed ancestry, developed their own customs, way of life, and recognizable group identity separate from Indian or Inuit and European forebears."[29]

The Supreme Court's definition extended the Métis designation far beyond the descendants of the historic Métis nation led by Riel and Dumont to persons with mixed European and Indigenous heritage who live in communities that do not identify as Indian or Inuit. Métis scholar Chris Andersen argues that not only does this open up the Métis category to indefinite expansion; it also perpetuates the mistaken and racist idea that being a "half-breed," a person of mixed blood, is what defines a Métis. It is their historical nation-building and nation-maintaining experience, he argues, that differentiates Métis from Indians. Many Indians, status and non-status, are of mixed Aboriginal and non-Aboriginal ancestry. To be fair, prudent, and true to our history, Canada might have to unpack the Métis category as a catch-all for every Canadian with some Aboriginal heritage who does not identify as Indian or Inuit.

The Supreme Court of Canada, as the *Powley* case demonstrates, continues to be a major player in the resurgence of Aboriginal peoples. This is true in other common law countries with colonized native peoples within. The high courts of Australia, New Zealand, and the United States are now playing an important role in shaping the rights of Indigenous peoples in their countries. Indeed the Supreme Court of Canada's decision in *Calder*, which was instrumental in changing Canada's Aboriginal policy in the 1970s, was the crucial precedent in the Australian High Court's *Mabo* decision, which changed Australian policy in the 1990s.[30] For Indigenous peoples, as small minorities within democratic countries, resorting to the courts to vindicate rights and defend interests makes good sense, especially when the courts are rooted in the common law tradition of judicial independence and law development, and their judges are no longer soaked in the racism of earlier settler generations. The courts in all four common law countries, in varying degrees, have been relatively liberal in responding to the legal claims of Aboriginal peoples. Their decisions have often been out front of elected politicians, forcing changes in the policies of their governments. But their agency as instruments of full decolonization is limited. They are still the "white man's courts," not only in their composition, but also in the justices' belief that Indigenous peoples are subject to the overriding sovereignty of the settler state.

The Supreme Court of Canada has made its most important contributions to advancing Aboriginal rights in its decisions relating to native title. The Court's 1997 decision in *Delgamuukw* confirmed that native title was one of the existing Aboriginal rights recognized in section 35 of the Constitution Act, 1982, and spelled out some of its features.[31] Native title is communal, rather than individual. It confers on the society that it has full ownership of the land and its resources, including subsurface minerals. That was the good news. But much of the Court's treatment of native or Aboriginal title has dealt with its limitations. First, Aboriginal people cannot sell any part of their lands on the private market; native title land can be sold only to the Crown – that is, the Government of Canada. A second limitation smacks of paternalism: the Aboriginal people that hold native title can develop the land in nontraditional ways, providing a development does not undermine their historic attachment to the land. The Supreme Court gave two examples of what it would not allow a native community to do to its own lands: strip-mine a hunting ground or pave over a burial ground for a parking lot. A third limitation underlines the continuing colonialism in the Court's thinking. In common law, native title is understood as a "burden" on the Crown's sovereignty, and in discharging the Crown's – that is, the federal or provincial government's – responsibilities to the larger community, there might be compelling and substantial circumstances that could make an infringement of native title justifiable. Chief Justice Lamer, who wrote the principal majority opinion, asserted somewhat casually that "the development of agriculture, forestry, mining, hydroelectric power, the general economic development of the interior of British Columbia, protection of the environment or endangered species, the building of infrastructure and the settlement of foreign populations" – any of these – "can justify the infringement of aboriginal title."[32] The Court's purpose in fashioning this new law, the chief justice explained, was "to reconcile the pre-existence of aboriginal society with the sovereignty of the Crown."[33]

The Supreme Court did not determine whether the Gitskan and Wet'suwet'en peoples who had initiated the *Delgamuukw* case had native title to what they claimed to be their historic lands. They would have to go back to a trial court for a determination of their claim or enter into a land claims negotiation with the federal and provincial governments. Putting the very existence of their homeland in the hands of a non-Aboriginal judge would be costly and risky. On the other hand, the federal government's insistence on extinguishing native title made the land claims process very unattractive. The question then arose: what legal protection is there for lands of an Aboriginal nation when ownership of its lands has not been recognized by a Canadian court or government? The Supreme Court dealt with that issue in a trio of cases in the early 2000s.

The Haida Nation, which has not negotiated a land treaty with Canada, raised this question when the BC government issued permits to lumber companies to harvest trees on its homeland, Haida Gwai, formerly called the Queen Charlotte Islands.[34] The Supreme Court reasoned that, if the government was under no obligation to protect the interests of Aboriginal people during the long process of validating native title, then, when title was finally recognized, much of what the people value in their lands might have been destroyed. The "honour of the Crown" requires that, in these circumstances, governments have a duty to consult with the Aboriginal people to see if the project could proceed in a way that accommodates their interests and minimizes damage. In a companion case, involving the Taku River Tlingit Nation, where a company wanted to reopen a mine and build a road to it over land to which the Tlingit claimed native title, the Court applied its doctrine of the duty to consult.[35] It meant that Tlingit representatives had the right to participate in the environmental assessment process and to liaise with decision-makers on other issues of concern to them. A year later, in *Mikisew*, the Court extended the "duty to consult" to the so-called off-reserve lands the nations that signed the historic treaties are alleged to have "surrendered."[36]

A duty to consult native owners and try to accommodate their interests before pushing through projects on their lands might be better than nothing, but it is still a far cry from affirming Aboriginal peoples' constitutional right to protect and develop their lands and resources. The blockbuster decision of the Supreme Court that took a major step in that direction came in 2014 in a case brought to the courts by the Xeni Gwet'in First Nation, one of six bands of the Tsilhqot'in Nation that for centuries have lived in the mountainous interior of northwest British Columbia.[37] The case was triggered by a flashpoint incident when the

Xeni Gwet'in blockaded a bridge to stop a forest company from logging on their lands. Eventually the case went before Judge David Vickers of the British Columbia Supreme Court, the province's highest trial court, to determine whether the Tsilhqot'in people have Aboriginal title to the area in question, approximately 5 per cent of what the Tsilhqot'in regard as their traditional territory. It took Judge Vickers five years to study the claim area and hear evidence from elders, historians, and other experts. In the end he decided that the Tsilhqot'in had title to a large portion of the claimed area. When Judge Vickers's decision was upheld by the Supreme Court of Canada in 2014, it granted a declaration that the Tsilhqot'in people had native title to most of the land they claimed. It was the first time a Canadian court had settled a dispute about native title. Until *Tsilhqot'in*, Aboriginal peoples had always settled native title claims through negotiations with government – negotiations that always resulted in the extinguishment of native title.

In addressing the rights of the Aboriginal landowners, the Supreme Court recognized that their governing authorities have "the right to proactively use and manage the land."[38] The appropriate role of non-Aboriginal governments in this context – the role that is consonant with the honour of the Crown – is not to lean on the Aboriginal owners to accommodate projects proposed by outside commercial interests, but to work with the Aboriginal people in the management of their land with the aim of increasing the benefits they can derive from it. Industrial development on native title lands may occur so long as the Aboriginal community has determined that the project is a desirable use of their lands. Such projects may involve partnerships with other governments or the private sector. As for the federal or provincial governments' power to infringe on the rights of native title holders, the Court in *Tsilhqot'in* dropped the blasé tone evident in *Delgamuukw* about what could justify an infringement of native title holders' rights. This time it held that the justification requires circumstances that, from the perspectives of both Aboriginal people and the general public, make a compelling case for overriding a constitutional right. In no way did the harvesting of trees by the forestry company in the Tsilhqot'in territory meet that standard.

It is significant that *Tsilhqot'in* was a unanimous decision supported by an eight-judge panel, five of whom where Harper government appointments. The case might well mean that many First Nations with unsettled land claims will prefer to go to court to secure recognition of their native title, rather than negotiate a settlement with the federal and provincial governments. The Supreme Court's recognition of the Tsilhqot'in people's ownership of their lands comes without any extinguishment attached. So long as Ottawa's comprehensive land claims policy insists on extinguishment of native title, First Nations' leaders will have a hard time convincing their people that it is better to negotiate than to litigate.

At Confederation, Aboriginal peoples were left out. Now, a century and a half later, the country is engaged in an effort to achieve "reconciliation" with Aboriginal peoples. Reconciliation has been the focus of public discussion and policy since the historic apology to Aboriginal peoples in the House of Commons on 11 June 2008, when Prime Minister Harper, admitting the tragic mistakes of policy in the past, said, "Today we recognize this policy of assimilation was wrong, has caused great harm, and has no place in our country."[39] The parliamentary apology led to the establishment of the Truth and Reconciliation Commission (TRC), whose final report at the end of 2015 has had a tremendous educational impact on the country. The TRC has given Canadians a detailed Call for Action that lays out ninety-four specific ways in which we can "reverse the legacy of residential schools and advance the process of Canadian reconciliation."[40]

News stories about Aboriginal peoples are staple items every day in the mass media. Moving ahead with reconciliation is a non-partisan concern embraced by most Canadians. But the focus is nearly always on the injustices of the past: residential schools, missing and murdered native women, the sixties scoop, and so on. Educating the non-Aboriginal public about the mistakes and tragedies of the past no doubt builds support for doing better in the future. But guilt and sorrow, in themselves, do not produce effective changes in policy. There is a real danger that policy changes needed to deal with the fundamental aspiration of Aboriginal peoples to recover responsibility for the well-being of their societies and access to the resources that can enable them to discharge that responsibility effectively will receive little attention. There is a real danger that reconciliation might mean getting Aboriginal peoples to accept the political and economic status quo in return for exposing the truths about the bad things of the past and a bit of financial compensation for the suffering. Tucked away in the Truth and Reconciliation Commission's ninety-four calls for action is #43: full adoption of the UN Declaration on the Rights of Indigenous Peoples. That Declaration contains the commitments to self-government and control of homeland resources. Those essential aspirations require dealing with the hard stuff: power, money, natural resources. There is no sign yet that dealing with that hard stuff is on the agenda even of a government headed by a prime minister like Justin Trudeau, who has stated in his mandate letter to all of his ministers that, "No relationship is more important to me and to Canada than the one with Indigenous Peoples."[41]

Like its relations with Aboriginal peoples, Canada's federal system has changed over the past twenty years without any formal constitutional amendments. Canadians have scarcely noticed the most significant structural change because it involves Canada's three northern territories, where less than 1 per cent of the country's population resides. The three territories, Yukon, the Northwest Territories, and Nunavut, although not provinces, have assumed more and more of the responsibilities and status of provinces. When the provinces formed the Council of the Federation in 2003 as an instrument for coordinating relations between the units of the federation and the central government, it had thirteen members: the ten provinces plus the three northern territories. This consolidated the practice of including territorial governments as regular participants in intergovernmental affairs, a political realm that is more important in Canada than in any of the world's other federations.

In Yukon and the Northwest Territories provincehood was for a long time a constitutional aspiration of many non-Aboriginal citizens. But the territories are not likely to gain that status in the foreseeable future. The main reason is demography. Their white settler populations have never been large, while their Aboriginal populations have remained significant and politically active, and generally more interested in Aboriginal self-government than in being citizens of a Canadian province. The combined population of all three northern territories in 2015 was 107,000, less than 80 per cent of Canada's smallest province, Prince Edward Island. As Gordon Robinson pointed out some years ago, giving full provincial status to three territories whose combined population is smaller than PEI's would be a very hard sell to Canadians, whose Constitution operates with an amending formula based on the equality of provinces.[42] In these territories across the top of Canada, there is absolutely zero interest in becoming a single province. Each of the three territories has its own distinct demographic composition and interests. Yukon and the Northwest Territories, where the federal government has devolved control over land and resources, come closer than Nunavut to having the full powers of a province. In Nunavut, except for the 11 per cent of the territory that the lands claim agreement brought under Inuit ownership, Ottawa retains control over lands and resources.[43]

First Nations constitute only 15 per cent of the Yukon's population, but half of the NWT's. With major land and self-government issues still unresolved, the NWT's constitutional structure is far from settled. Nunavut, with a dominant Inuit population and a constitutional settlement with Canada, continues the struggle to make self-government work well. Maximizing self-government and ensuring a voice in national affairs, especially in matters affecting the Canadian north, rather than provincehood, are viable goals for Canada's vast, but thinly populated northern territories.

The Council of the Federation in some ways was a throwback to Honoré Mercier's Inter-Provincial Conference of 1887. Quebec premier Jean Charest, anxious to show that he led a Quebec government committed to renewing the federation, rather than trying to break it up, was a leading player in establishing the Council. Although the federal government is not a member, the prime minister is invited to attend its annual meeting, which always attracts a good deal of media attention if only because it is held on slow news days in the summer. Prime Minister Paul Martin attended the Council's first meeting, in 2003, and the provinces managed to extract a commitment from him to transfer $41 billion to them for health care over the next ten years. No doubt that had something to do with Stephen Harper's acting more like Sir John A. Macdonald, who spurned the premiers' invitation to their conference in 1887. Harper did meet with the premiers and territorial leaders three times, but mainly to discuss the economy, not to negotiate the size of federal fiscal transfers. Harper much preferred negotiating fiscal deals one-on-one with individual premiers to getting beaten up by them in public.

By the time Harper became prime minister, fiscal federalism – which is more important than the Constitution in determining how the federation actually operates – was moving in an ideological direction that he very much favoured. In the 1990s the Chrétien Liberals reduced the size of fiscal transfers to the provinces and removed most of the conditions on how the provinces must spend them. The era when Ottawa used its fiscal power to push the provinces into mounting the programs of Canada's welfare state were over.[44] Provinces would continue to rely on substantial transfers of federal money to carry on their health care, post-secondary education, and social welfare programs, but that money would come in the form of block grants with very few strings attached. With health care, the important string would be meeting the five conditions of the Canada Health Act, which requires a single, public-payer medicare system for all Canadians. For the Chrétien Liberals, reducing the size of these transfers was driven by deficit-cutting fiscal policy. For the Harper Conservatives, ideology was as important as fiscal prudence in continuing the shift in fiscal federalism the Liberals had initiated. It was a policy that made the federal government fiscally smaller and respected provincial autonomy – both ideological principles of the Conservatives. John Ibbitson reports that, by the end of Harper's third mandate, federal revenues as a share of gross domestic product were at 14.1 per cent, the lowest since 1958.[45] A permanent legacy of the Harper government's decade of power might well be a reduction in the fiscal size of Canada's central government.

A 1999 agreement entered into by the federal government and all the provinces except Quebec put the breaks on federal policy-making in fields that are primarily provincial responsibilities. The Social Union Framework Agreement (SUFA) requires that any *new* federal social policy initiatives that are to be funded through federal transfers to the provinces must be approved by a majority of provinces, and opting-out provinces must receive federal funding for their own programs providing they satisfy "Canada-wide objectives."[46] The federal government can also distribute benefits such as the Chrétien government's Millennial Scholarships directly to citizens, but provinces must be consulted on the design of such programs before they are introduced. Even though these SUFA restrictions on the federal spending power exceed what was offered in the Meech Lake Accord, they went too far in legitimizing federal initiatives in fields of provincial jurisdiction for the sovereignist government that was still in power in Quebec to sign up. SUFA shows what can be done by way of restructuring the federation without a formal amendment of the constitutional text. It adapts fiscal federalism to the political and economic conditions of the times, and, like all conventions, it depends on politics, not law, for its enforcement.

Two bits and pieces of unfinished constitutional business remain matters of concern to many Canadians: the Supreme Court of Canada and the Senate. The Supreme Court was on the agenda of constitutional reform from the beginning of the mega constitutional era. In the 1970s Senate reform became western Canadians' constitutional priority. The Constitution Act, 1982, containing the only actual amendments achieved through the many years of mega constitutional politics, did not deal with the Supreme Court or Senate directly, but it did establish rules for changing these institutions in the future. Up to 1982 the Supreme Court could be changed by a simple amending statute of Parliament. That year, the Court was, in effect, constitutionalized. Under the amending formula, most changes to the Court are now subject to the two-thirds-of-the-provinces/50-per-cent-of-the-population rule, while changes in its "composition" require approval of Parliament and all the provinces.

The Constitution Act, 1982 also subjected the Senate to the new amending formula: changes to the Senate's powers or to the method of selecting senators are subject to the two-thirds/50-per-cent rule. In another part of the amending formula, for the first time since Confederation the Senate had its powers reduced. On amendments dealing with its powers or methods of selection and other amendments requiring provincial agreement, the Senate has only a suspensory veto – it may hold up an amendment for one hundred and eighty days, but after that the amendment becomes law without the Senate's consent. In effect this means that the Senate no longer has the power to prevent substantial changes in its structure or powers, or even its abolition.

Although the Senate's role in constitutional change has been reduced, the Supreme Court of Canada continues to be a powerful player in the evolution of Canada's Constitution. In recent years the Court has decided important cases with respect to itself and the Senate.

In 2014 the Court found (six to one) that the Harper government's appointment of Marc Nadon, a supernumerary – that is, partially retired – judge of the Federal Court of Appeal to one of the three Quebec positions on the Court was invalid.[47] Nadon had practised law in Quebec earlier in his career, but at the time of his appointment he did not. In the Court majority's view, that meant Nadon did not meet the eligibility criteria set out in section 6 of the Supreme Court Act for Quebec positions on the Court: being among the judges of Quebec's superior court or "among the barristers or advocates of the Province of Quebec." The majority justified its decision by taking a purposive approach to interpreting the legislation: "The purpose of s. 6 is to ensure not only civil law training and experience on the Court, but also to ensure that Quebec's distinct legal traditions and social values are represented on the Court, thereby enhancing the confidence of the people of Quebec in the Supreme Court as the final arbiter of their rights."[48] The Court also ruled that Parliament could not pass legislation changing the eligibility rules so that a person who at any time has been a barrister or advocate in Quebec could fill a Quebec position on the Court. Patriation recognized that the Supreme Court as "the guardian of the Constitution" is a fundamental premise of the Constitution.[49] No longer can the Court's fundamental features be changed by an ordinary Act of Parliament.

The Supreme Court also turned back an attempt to get around the constitutional rule that changing the method of selecting senators requires the approval of Parliament and seven provinces. The Harper government referred to the Court its plan to establish, by federal legislation, "consultative elections" in the provinces and territories to help the prime minister advise the governor general on Senate picks. The government argued that, so long as the prime minister was not bound by the elections, this did not amount to a change in the selection system. The Court saw through this subterfuge: "In our view, the argument that introducing consultative elections does not constitute an amendment to the Constitution privileges form over substance."[50] Prime ministers would feel politically bound to select election winners, so even though the text of the Constitution would not be changed, the effect would be to change the Senate from an appointed to an elected body, and that would amount to a significant change in the Senate's fundamental nature and role. The Court also found that changing the tenure of senators from a continuous term until retirement at age seventy-five to renewable eight-year terms amounted to a fundamental change in the Senate because it would threaten the independence of senators who sought a renewal of their appointment.

In the *Senate Reference*, the Supreme Court justices wrote an essay on the constitutional amending process established in Part V of the Constitution Act, 1982. In their view, the amending procedure must apply to anything that changes "the architecture of the Constitution" – how the different parts of the Constitution work together. A Senate with an elected mandate, in their view, was bound to change that architecture. Applying this idea, they said "the entire process by which Senators are selected" must be subject to the Constitution's general amending procedure.[51] The breadth of the Court's language sent shivers up the spines of those who want to reform the selection process for both the Senate and the Supreme Court.

Justin Trudeau's government likely has found a method of reforming the way senators and Supreme Court justices are selected without amending the Constitution. In both cases the aim is to remove the dominant influence of patronage or ideology and establish a merit system of selection. For the Senate, the government has created a five-person independent advisory board – three federal members with two-year terms plus two ad hoc members from the province or territory where a vacancy is being filled – that will create a shortlist of "five non-partisan and meritorious" persons to fill vacancies.[52] For the Supreme Court, Prime Minister Trudeau has announced the establishment of a seven-person

Independent Advisory Board to assist the government in filling vacancies on the Court.[53] The board consists of a retired judge nominated by the Canadian Judicial Council, two lawyers nominated by the Canadian Bar Association and the Federation of Law Societies, a legal scholar nominated by the Council of Canadian Law Deans, and three persons, two of whom must not be lawyers, nominated by the minister of justice. The board's mandate is actively to seek out candidates and encourage them to apply and to provide the prime minister with merit-based recommendations of three to five "functionally bilingual" candidates.

With much less fanfare, Prime Minister Harper introduced a similar reform for selecting governors general, provincial lieutenant-governors, and territorial commissioners. In 2012 Harper established the Advisory Committee on Vice-Regal Appointments, which grew out of an ad hoc search committee he used in 2010 to select Governor General David Johnston. In addition to the queen's Canadian secretary, who chairs the committee, the committee has two other permanent federal "delegates": persons, one anglophone and one francophone, knowledgeable about the role of the queen's representatives in Canada. For appointing lieutenant-governors and territorial commissioners, two individuals from the appropriate jurisdiction are temporarily added to the committee. The committee searches out promising candidates, soliciting names from a broad range of sources. It reviews the capabilities and accomplishments of the persons suggested, and produces a short list of those it considers to be outstanding. The prime minister makes his selection from that list after hearing the committee's reasons for their top choices.

All three of these reforms have been carried out in the Burkean manner, adapting important institutions of government to a society fed up with excessive partisanship and anxious to see citizens chosen for important offices on the basis of their qualifications for the job. None of the three purports to bind the constitutional appointing authority nor have any been incorporated in legislation that might attract a constitutional challenge. Whether these new procedures for assisting prime ministers in selecting senators, Supreme Court justices, and representatives of the queen become constitutional conventions depends on whether successor governments follow them. The possibility of that happening depends on how well the results of the new procedures are viewed by the public and the politicians. The proof of the pudding will be in the eating.

Improving the selection process for senators and Supreme Court justices is important constitutional business that can be tackled without plunging the country into another sweaty round of constitutional politics. An even more important piece of institutional malfunctioning that needs to be addressed is the sorry state Canada's parliamentary democracy at the national level has fallen into in recent years. The formal shell of responsible parliamentary government remains intact: the government of Canada continues to be led by politicians who command the confidence of the House of Commons. But power has become concentrated as never before in the hands of the prime minister and his political aides. Between elections, especially under majority governments, debate and discussion in the House of Commons, the people's house, has been rendered virtually irrelevant. Government has become more presidential than parliamentary – but presidential without the check and balance of an independent legislature. The tendency to concentrate power in the office of prime minister is a built-in hazard of parliamentary systems. Placing the command of the executive branch of government in the hands of politicians who have a majority in the elected chamber of the legislature provides stability and clear direction, but that virtue courts the vice of excessive government control of the legislature. A 2004 international study of the concentration of power in the office of prime ministers in twenty-seven parliamentary democracies put Canada at the very top of the table.[54]

Note that this finding that Canada leads the parliamentary world in centralizing power in the prime minister's office was before the Harper era. Indeed this tendency began in Pierre Trudeau's era. The work of political scientist Donald Savoie – in particular, his *Governing from the Centre*, published in 1999 – analyses the centralizing trend through the late 1960s to the end of the century.[55] Savoie focuses on the role of central agencies, especially the Privy Council Office (PCO) and the Prime Minister's Office (PMO), in reducing the role of departments and coordinating policy at the centre. In Chapter 12 we saw how that process affected the making of Aboriginal policy.

In terms of undermining the role of Parliament and MPs, the most important factors have been the tightening of party discipline and the growth in the size and the power of the PMO. Under Pierre Trudeau the PMO more than tripled in size. The PMO was, and is, staffed by mostly young people who have never been civil servants nor run for Parliament. They are chosen primarily for their loyalty to the prime minister and his party. Their mission is, above all, the re-election of the government. More than anything else, it is the age of television, when political opinion is shaped more by short sound bites than by newspaper columns, that has made governments feel the need to manage their message to the voters through a communication strategy. Managing the message is the number one job of the PMO. But managing communications inevitably spills over into policy-making – not on the day-to-day running of government, but on the big, politically controversial files. And, as they say, it's the "kids in short pants" – the government's spin-doctors – not party whips, who tell cabinet ministers, MPs, and senators what they can say – and do. Party discipline in the House of Commons is tightening up as MPs are treated not as legislators or policy-makers, but as soldiers under their general's marching orders in a perpetual political campaign.[56]

The decline of parliamentary democracy reached it lowest point in the Harper era. *Irresponsible Government*, written by Brent Rathgeber, who left the Conservative caucus to sit as an independent MP, provides a succinct but thorough account of how badly parliamentary democracy was broken in the Harper years.[57] The sorry litany includes the unprecedented curtailment of debate, the tight partisan control and stifling of parliamentary committees, the bundling together of dozens of unrelated subjects in omnibus bills to prevent careful consideration of legislation, control by the PMO of MPs' answers in Question Period, the irrelevance of cabinet in policy-making, and the control of what cabinet ministers, MPs, and senators could communicate to the media. Stephen Harper had no democratic mandate to undermine parliamentary democracy so grievously. It is not at all evident that these practices were necessary to carry out the policy mandate that his supporters gave him. It is clear that his autocratic, unparliamentary way of governing had much to do with his political defeat.

The change of government resulting from the October 2015 election should serve as a corrective for much of what undermined the proper functioning of parliamentary democracy in the Harper era. Prime Minister Trudeau, conscious of the fact that his party has a majority in the House of Commons, has promised to govern in a way that is respectful of all MPs. Beginning on his swearing-in day, he has shown a commitment to cabinet government. Stephen Harper's autocratic style is not part of the Conservative values his party espouses, so there is reason to believe there will be all-party support for abandoning the worst practices of the Harper government.

Beyond the corrective behaviour expected from a change of government, some fundamental problems need attention in order to revivify Canada's parliamentary democracy. First, there is that big elephant in the room of our democracy, the PMO. It is something of a johnny-come-lately in the structure of government, emerging as a major power base in the late 1960s, unplanned and unheralded, its place in governing shaped by political practice, not law. In the 1980s the Mulroney government added "political staffers" exempt from civil servant status and protocols to the offices of cabinet ministers. The fact that, except for the Diefenbaker and Clark interludes, the Liberals had governed since 1940 led Mulroney's Progressive Conservatives to believe, not unreasonably, that the top echelons of the public service were thoroughly Liberalized. It was thought that authorizing ministers to hire individuals who shared their policy inclinations would balance the advice they would get from the public service. Political staffers in ministers' offices and the PMO are an invasive species in Ottawa. As with all invasive species, there is a danger of exempt political staff extending their influence too far and undermining the role of the permanent and professional public service.

But the PMO and political staffers are here to stay. Justin Trudeau clearly attaches great importance to the staff he has recruited for his office. They have been profiled and discussed in the media as much as the members of his cabinet. Although the PMO and political staffers are now part of government, the shame is that the Supreme Court of Canada denied this fact in a decision it rendered in 2011, when it upheld lower court decisions that overturned the access to information commissioner's granting access to information in ministers' offices and the PMO.[58] The right of citizens to access governmental information applies to records or documents under the control of "government institutions." The Supreme Court found, eight judges to one, that neither ministers' offices nor the PMO are "government institutions." Justice Louis LeBel, in a strong dissenting opinion, pointed out that there is no exemption from access to information for material that is too political. It is hard to understand how ministers' offices and the PMO, which are paid for by taxpayers, could not be government institutions. Most commentators today would rank the PMO as the most powerful component of the federal government.

Let us hope that the Trudeau government will live up to its commitment to accountability and transparency by following Justice Lebel's analysis and amend the Access to Information Act to overcome the Supreme Court's decision. Of course there are conversations and meetings that are highly political and that the government has every right to keep private. But the public, which pays for what is being done by political staffers, has a right to know whom it is paying for, what their jobs are, how much it all costs, and to have access to records of the research the staff carry out or commission, including surveys of public opinion. If any of that is too politically embarrassing for political leaders, they should do it on their party's own dime.

A second fundamental flaw at the very base of our parliamentary democracy is the illiteracy of Canadians about the so-called unwritten conventions of the Constitution. As was pointed out in the chapter on Confederation, crucial principles, rules, and practices that make Canada a parliamentary democracy are not spelled out in the text of Canada's Constitution. A citizen, or a school child learning to be a citizen, will look in vain in the Constitution for some mention of a prime minister or cabinet or of the essential principle of our democracy: that Canadians are to be governed by ministers who are responsible to Parliament and supported by a majority in the elected legislature. In theory, political leaders and citizens are supposed to carry knowledge of these "unwritten conventions" around in their heads. Whatever reality that theory had a century and a half ago, it is baloney today. During the 2008 prorogation crisis, Ipsos Reid reported that 51 per cent of Canadians believed the prime minister of Canada is directly elected by the people. That prompted me to write that, "the time has come to bring those spooky unwritten constitutional conventions down from the attic of our collective memory and try to see if we can pin them down in a manner that is publicly accessible and politically consensual."[59] New Zealand and the United Kingdom have done that with the production of cabinet manuals providing online, succinct, well-written statements of the important principles, rules, and practices of parliamentary and cabinet government. In 2011 a group of Canada's leading constitutional scholars, senior representatives of all five parliamentary parties, and retired senior governmental and parliamentary officials recommended that the Government of Canada produce a Canada Manual.[60]

The contents of a cabinet manual are not meant to be enforceable in the courts. It is best that this part of the Constitution be developed through an informal governmental and political process, not handed over to the judiciary. In Canada, as in New Zealand and the United Kingdom, production of a cabinet manual must begin with the cabinet secretariat. Canada's secretariat, the PCO, already has a *Manual of Official Procedure of the Government of Canada*, a cumbersome compendium, many hundreds of pages long, containing some of the material that should go into a cabinet manual and much that deals with ceremonial procedures and protocols that should not. Although the PCO could launch and manage the process of producing a cabinet manual, it would be wise to follow the United Kingdom and consult with constitutional experts, invite input from parliamentarians, and road-test it with the media to ensure that the final product is well-informed, non-partisan, and written in a style that makes it easily accessible to citizens, landed immigrants, teachers, and students.

The principal benefit of having a document like a cabinet manual accessible online is increasing the constitutional literacy of Canadians. Looking through the chapter headings of the United Kingdom's cabinet manual we see headings such as

* elections and government formation;
* the prime minister, ministers, and the structure of government;
* ministers and parliament;
* collective cabinet decision-making; and
* ministers and the civil service.

None of these matters is covered in the written text of Canada's Constitution, yet knowledge of them is essential for intelligent citizenship. The unavailability of such knowledge is a substantial "democratic deficit." The prime minister (or provincial premier) who gives the green light to the production of a Canadian cabinet manual will have made an important contribution to improving the quality of democratic life in Canada.

Finally, there is now the possibility of electoral reform at the federal level. Changing the way Canadians elect the House of Commons and provincial legislatures has been on the country's constitutional agenda since the 1970s. In 2005, 57.7 per cent of British Columbia voters in a referendum approved the single transferable vote system recommended by a citizens' assembly for that province – just short of the 60 per cent threshold the government required for a successful "yes" vote.[61] In that same year a majority of voters in Prince Edward Island rejected a proposed mixed member proportional system for their province, as did Ontario voters in 2007. It is not surprising that, despite those setbacks at the provincial level, there continues to be great interest in Canada in establishing an electoral system that produces legislatures better reflecting the will of the people than elections based on the simple plurality, winner-take-all system. That system made more sense when elections were contested by only two parties. But for nearly a century

Canada has had multiparty political contests at both the federal and provincial levels. With a multitude of candidates in the constituency contests, the simple plurality system means that a candidate supported by a third or less of the people might be elected and the votes of the majority of the people in the riding count for nothing. This can result, and often does, in a party supported by less than 40 per cent of the electorate winning a majority of seats in the House of Commons or a provincial legislature. Indeed Stephen Harper's Conservatives and Justin Trudeau's Liberals both formed "majority governments" with less than 40 per cent of the popular vote.

These kinds of skewed outcomes have persuaded most of the parliamentary democracies in the Western world and the Commonwealth to use electoral systems that provide a fair degree of proportionality. The United Kingdom, India, and Canada remain the main outliers. Recent political science research shows that the concentration of power in the office of prime minister and the electoral system are the greatest sources of dissatisfaction with the quality of democracy in Canada.[62] These two sources of discontent are related. The first-past-the-post electoral system makes it possible for elections to result, as we have seen, in "false majority" governments. False majority governments need not stifle parliamentary debate, but the temptation and opportunity to do so is there. It will be interesting to see if Justin Trudeau lives up to his promise to respect Parliament's deliberative role.

Mr Trudeau promised that, if elected, he would take steps to ensure that the 2015 election was the last one based on the first-past-the-post system. That makes him the first leader of one of the "old-line" parties (Conservatives and Liberals) that have governed at the federal level since Confederation to break with the system that for so long has been so favourable to those parties – and so unfavourable to all other parties. At the time of writing, a parliamentary committee is consulting with Canadians and assessing alternative reforms. The Liberal government has not committed to act on the committee's recommendations or to put a proposed new system to a referendum. There is tremendous pressure, and not just from the Conservatives, to ask the people themselves to approve a change in how they perform their one essential act in our democracy: voting in parliamentary elections. That pressure will be difficult to resist.

Just over two hundred and fifty years ago, France, in the Peace of Paris that ended the Seven Years' War, handed over its North American "possessions" to Britain. A year later Britain made a treaty at Niagara that secured peace with twenty-four Amerindian nations by recognizing their ownership of much of the territory France had ceded. After those foundational treaties, British settlers first trickled in, then, in the wake of the American Revolution, flooded in, adding mightily to the number already in Newfoundland and Nova Scotia and making English-speaking people the dominant majority in what we now call Canada. Even though the nation-building vision of those English-speaking colonials was a British North America in which there was no enduring place for *Canadiens* or Aboriginal peoples, Britain and its successor state Canada did not conquer these peoples by military means or succeed in having them disappear through policies of assimilation. In that sense conquest was incomplete, and the "nations within" survived. Over time – in the case of Aboriginal peoples, a very long time – that reality has come to be recognized, not by all who make up English-speaking Canada, but by most of its leaders, as a permanent defining feature of Canada.

Canada, going forward, must be governed as a multinational democracy. Even though that idea has not yet been firmly embraced by the people, it is essential to the three founding pillars that share country and citizenship. As the odyssey continues, there will be plenty of problems making a country based on three distinct societal pillars work well, but at least we have learned not to try to fix the problems all at once.

A country built on such diverse foundations might seem rather shaky. But compared with what is going on in the rest of the world these days, Canada looks pretty solid. Political scientists who measure these things tell us that Canada is among only 21 of 164 countries to receive a score of zero on the State Fragility Index.[63] If there is validity in that finding, it is a tribute to the civic culture Canadians have come to share. This is the glue that holds the country together.

Of parliamentary government, the monarchy, and constitutionalism – the three components of the civic culture the Loyalists brought with them to British North America at the end of the eighteenth century – constitutionalism has turned out to be the strongest. Constitutionalism requires that those who wield government power, be it a powerful monarch or a popular prime minister, are subject to limits requiring the observance of proper procedures of government and respect for the rights and interests of citizens. Aboriginal societies had long enjoyed constitutional government, and by the 1700s so did Britain. Constitutionalism became much more robust after Confederation, when limits on government were written into a constitutional text and enforced by an independent judiciary. The Supreme Court of Canada has emerged as a powerful institution of governance in applying constitutional limits on governments – to uphold federalism and to protect the rights of citizens, including the rights of official language minorities and the rights of Aboriginal peoples. At times this vigorous judicial restraint of popular government has prompted some to say Canada is in danger of becoming a jurocracy. Nonetheless the strength of constitutionalism in Canada's civic culture provides the basis for a trustful relationship between the country's two demographically small pillars, Aboriginal Canada and French Canada, and the English-speaking majority.

The version of parliamentary government that Britain provided for its settlers in Nova Scotia and later for the Loyalists could hardly be called democratic, so meagre was the power and the social base of the elected chamber. Nonetheless the parliamentary model of government, with its close linkage of executive and legislative power, became a permanent feature of government in Canada. Pressure from the colonists made the elected legislature become the powerhouse of government, and with the expansion of the franchise the essential institution of Canadian democracy. In modern times, as governments have come to behave like powerful corporations peddling their brand and keeping their members "on message," the quality of parliamentary democracy has declined. The most recent federal election indicates that Canadians want to arrest that democratic slippage.

Monarchy, the third element of Canada's civic culture that came with British settlers, has deep roots in the country's history, although it no longer has deep popular support. However, the thorough Canadianization of the Crown and the strong performance of those who represent it in Canada and, of course, of the monarch herself have deprived Canadian republicans of ammunition. Anti-Americanism, the Canadian equivalent of the anti-British sentiment that fuels Australian republicanism, does not make dumping the queen for a presidential head of state a popular cause in Canada. For many First Nations people, the Crown continues to be an important basis of their allegiance to Canada. Although it no longer performs that function for the Québécois, it is not a significant source of nationalist discontent. The Crown's viceregal representatives bring grace and warmth to Canadian public life, and the queen ties the country to a global and multicultural Commonwealth of monarchical and republican nations. Monarchy is here to stay.

Confederation added a new element to Canada's civic culture: federalism. At first, for English-speaking leaders such as our first prime minister, dividing sovereign power between two levels of governments was a temporary compromise, but within a few years it became an iconic principle of government. Despite the intentions of some of its founders, Canada became the most federal country in the world. Nowhere else are relations between the central government and the governments of the federation's units so constantly in the news or do intergovernmental relations play such a prominent role in national policy-making. A federal ethic permeates the Canadian political psyche. As Aboriginal peoples assert and gain self-governing responsibilities, federal relations must expand to accommodate this third division of sovereign power. The democratic governments of cities, especially Canada's big cities, which deliver the essential services of everyday life where most Canadians live, seek more direct involvement in making the policies that shape those services and for more fiscal capacity of their own. In the twenty-first century, Canadian federalism is mutating into multilevel governance.

In the aftermath of the Second World War, Canada's political culture underwent a profound change. The country took a leading role in establishing the United Nations and building a post-war world based on the equality of peoples. As it did so, its leaders and, to an increasing extent the Canadian people, embraced a belief in universal human rights that challenged the racist assumptions of earlier generations. This gave rise to what Michael Ignatieff has called a "rights revolution."[64] The recognition, codification, and judicial enforcement of fundamental civil and political rights has added another component to Canada's civic culture. The ethical thinking that inspired the rights revolution has spilled over into relations with Aboriginal peoples and has had much to do with reversing their colonization and recognizing their rights in the Canadian Constitution.

In the 1950s, coincidentally with the rights revolution, an egalitarian principle of social justice – fiscal equalization – was injected into the operation of Canada's federal system. The idea of maintaining an equal minimal level of well-being for citizens wherever they live in the country became another enduring addition to Canada's civic culture. From the beginning, there have been many disputes about how the fiscal transfers within the federation should be calculated, but the basic principle that the parts of the federation experiencing good economic times should help those that are not remains intact. It is a principle that builds on Canada's social democratic roots and distinguishes the Canadian federation from the American. Unlike Americans, Canadians, through fiscal equalization, gain some shelter from the biting winds of global capitalism.

The final addition to Canada's civic culture is the product of that second quiet revolution which made English-speaking Canada less British and more multicultural. The same currents of thought that underlay the rights revolution supported the changes in immigration policy that have created a more multicultural Canada. Canadian multiculturalism is more evident in the celebration of it than in actual numbers. The ancestral backgrounds of a large majority of Canadians are still British and French. But in no other country in the world is ethnic diversity so much a part of its citizens' sense of identity. Although Quebec, officially, aspires to be intercultural, rather than multicultural, it embraces diversity as never before – so long as it is not at the expense of the majority French culture. Popular enthusiasm for Canada's welcoming of Syrian refugees is countrywide and evidence of the degree to which support for ethnic diversity has become part of Canada's civic culture and national identity.

All of the ingredients of the civic culture that I have identified have to do with constitutional developments, institutions, and government. What might be more fundamental in forming a bond of unity among French, Aboriginal, and English-speaking Canadians is the physical beauty and grandeur of the northern country we share and treasure. That is in our songs and in our souls, and more than anything else makes us a people.

Notes

Chapter 1

1 Peter H. Russell, *Constitutional Odyssey: Can Canadians Become a Sovereign People?* 3rd ed. (Toronto: University of Toronto Press, 2004).
2 Constitution written in upper case refers to the written text of what is regarded as a county's highest law. When lower case is used, constitution refers to the informal practices, conventions, judicial decisions, laws, and treaties that regulate how a country is governed and that form its constitutional system. Britain has a constitution, but not a Constitution.
3 See Peter H. Russell, *Recognizing Aboriginal Title: The Mabo Case and Indigenous Resistance to English Settler Colonialism* (Toronto: University of Toronto Press, 2006), 139.

Chapter 2

1 R.H. Mahon, *Life of General the Hon. James Murray* (London: John Murray, 1921), 195–238.
2 See Fred Anderson, *The War that Made America: A Short History of the French and Indian War* (New York: Penguin Books, 2006), 212–14; C.P. Stacey, *Quebec 1759: The Siege and the Battle* (Toronto: Macmillan, 1959), 164; William Wood, *The Fight for Canada: A Naval and Military Sketch from the History of the Great Imperial War* (London: Archibald Constable, 1904), 292–4.
3 Gordon Donaldson, *Battle for a Continent: Quebec, 1759* (Toronto: Doubleday Canada, 1973), 117.
4 Fintan O'Toole, *White Savage: William Johnson and the Invention of America* (Albany: State University of New York Press, 2005), 209.
5 James Thomas Flexner, *Mohawk Baronet: A Biography of Sir William Johnson* (Syracuse, NY: Syracuse University Press, 1959), 125–6.

6 Ibid,, 205–9; O'Toole, *White Savage*, 204–10.

7 Flexner, *Mohawk Baronet*, 213–19.

8 Adam Short and Arthur G. Doughty, *Documents Relating to the Constitutional History of Canada, 1819–1828* (Ottawa: King's Printer, 1907), 6–7, 21–8.

9 Geoffrey Plank, *An Unsettled Conquest: The British Campaign Against the People of Acadia* (Philadelphia: University of Pennsylvania Press, 2001), 141–9; W.L. Morton, *The Kingdom of Canada: A General History from Earliest Times*, 2nd ed. (Toronto: McClelland & Stewart, 1969), 135–6.

10 J.M. Bumsted, *The Peoples of Canada: A Pre-Confederation History* (Toronto: Oxford University Press, 1992), 125–6.

11 James E. Candow, *The Lookout: A History of Signal Hill* (St John's: Creative Publishers, 2011), 49–51.

12 Hilda Neatby, *Quebec: The Revolutionary Age, 1760–1791* (Toronto: McClelland & Stewart, 1966), chap. 2; Mason Wade, *The French Canadians, 1760–1967* (Toronto: Macmillan, 1968), chap. 2.

13 A.L. Burt, *The Old Province of Quebec*, vol. 1, *1760–1778* (Toronto: McClelland & Stewart, 1968).

14 Ibid., 35.

15 Short and Doughty, *Documents Relating to the Constitutional History of Canada*.

16 Ibid.; the Proclamation can also be found in Canada, *Canada 125: Its Constitutions, 1763–1982* (Ottawa: Canada Communications Group, 1992), 85–9.

17 Guy Frégault, *La guerre de conquête* (Montreal: Fider, 1955), 9.

18 Burt, *Old Province of Quebec*, 1, 82.

19 See Mahon, *Life of General the Hon. James Murray*.

20 G.P. Browne, "Murray, James," in *Dictionary of Canadian Biography*, vol. 4 (Toronto: University of Toronto Press, 1979), 569–78.

21 Wade, *French Canadians*, 57.

22 Neatby, *Quebec*, 53.

23 André Vachon, "Briand, Jean-Olivier," in *Dictionary of Canadian Biography*, vol. 4 (Toronto: University of Toronto Press, 1979), 94–102.

24 Browne, "Murray, James."

25 Mahon, *Life of General the Hon. James Murray*, 346.

26 Burt, *Old Province of Quebec*, 115.

27 G.P. Browne, "Carleton, Guy, 1st Baron Dorchester," in *Dictionary of Canadian Biography*, vol. 5 (Toronto: University of Toronto Press, 1983), 141–54.

28 Neatby, *Quebec*, 102.

29 Ibid., 104.

30 Browne, "Carleton, Guy," 144.

31 Neatby, *Quebec*, 102.

32 *Campbell v. Hall*, 1 Cowp. (1774).

33 Ibid., 54.

34 R. Coupland, *The Quebec Act: A Study in Statesmanship* (Oxford: Clarendon Press, 1925), 98–9.

35 Ibid., 104.

36 The text of the Quebec Act can be found in Short and Doughty, *Documents Relating to the Constitutional History of Canada*, 401–5; and in Canada, *Canada 125*, 89–94.

37 Eliot A. Cohen, *Conquered into Liberty: Two Centuries of Battles Along the Great Warpath that Made the American Way of War* (New York: Simon & Schuster, 2011), 134.

38 Neatby, *Quebec*, 159–60.

39 Cohen, *Conquered into Liberty*, 135–60.

40 Nicole Stoffman, "What Did the Habitants Think of the British Regime?" (undergraduate essay, Department of Political Science, University of Toronto, 2013).

41 Browne, "Carleton, Guy," 146.

42 Cohen, *Conquered into Liberty*, 160.

Chapter 3

1 O'Toole, *White Savage*, 221.

2 See Richard White, *The Middle Ground: Indians, Republics and Empires in the Great Lakes Region, 1650–1815* (New York: Cambridge University Press, 1991).

3 David Hackett Fischer, *Champlain's Dream* (Toronto: Vintage Canada, 2009).

4 See Francis Jennings, *The Invasion of America: Indians, Colonialism and the Cant of Conquest* (Chapel Hill: University of North Carolina Press, 1975).

5 Flexner, *Mohawk Baronet*, 260.

6 James Sullivan, ed., *The Papers of Sir William Johnson*, vol. 3 (Albany: New York University Press, 1921–62).

7 Arthur Pound, *Johnson of the Mohawks* (New York: Macmillan, 1930), 331–8.

8 There are many biographies of Sir William Johnson. I have drawn heavily on those written by James Thomas Flexner, M.W. Hamilton, Julian Gwyn, Fintan O'Toole, Arthur Pound, and William L. Stone, listed in the bibliography.

9 O'Toole, *White Savage*, 244.

10 Anderson, *War That Made America*, 180–1.

11 Flexner, *Mohawk Baronet*, 256.

12 Canada, *Canada 125*, 85–8.

13 Brian Slattery, *The Land Rights of Indigenous Canadian Peoples as Affected*

by the Crown's Acquisition of Their Territories (Saskatoon: University of Saskatchewan, Native Law Centre, 1979), 192.

14 John Borrows, "Wampum at Niagara: The Royal Proclamation, Canadian Legal History, and Self-Government," in *Aboriginal and Treaty Rights in Canada: Essays on Law, Equality, and Respect for Difference*, ed. Michael Asch (Vancouver: UBC Press, 1997), 162.

15 Donald Braider, *The Niagara (Rivers of America)* (New York: Holt, Rinehart & Winston, 1972).

16 Flexner, *Mohawk Baronet*, 266.

17 Borrows, "Wampum at Niagara," 163.

18 Quoted in ibid., 164.

19 Sullivan, *Papers of Sir William Johnson*, vol. 2, 228; see also William L. Stone, *The Life and Times of Sir William Johnson*, 2 v. (Albany, NY: J. Munsell, 1865).

20 Canada, *Canada 125*, 64.

21 O'Toole, *White Savage*, 264.

22 Louis Chevrette, "Pontiac," in *Dictionary of Canadian Biography*, vol. 3 (Toronto: University of Toronto Press, 1974).

23 O'Toole, *White Savage*, 273–9.

24 Flexner, *Mohawk Baronet*, 331.

25 Fintan O'Toole, *White Savage*, 323.

Chapter 4

1 Ann Jarvis Boa, ed., *My Eventful Life: Stephen Jarvis U.E., 1756–1840* (Montreal: Price Patterson, 2002), 104.

2 Walter Stewart, *True Blue: The Loyalist Legend* (Toronto: Collins, 1985), 119.

3 Ibid., 120.

4 Boa, *My Eventful Life*, 111–12.

5 Bumsted, *Peoples of Canada*, 56–9, 118–20.

6 Ibid., 121–5.

7 See A.G. Bradley, *The United Empire Loyalists: Founders of British Canada* (London: Thornton Butterworth, 1932); and Maya Jasanoff, *Liberty's Exiles: American Loyalists in the Revolutionary World* (New York: Alfred Knopf, 2011).

8 Bradley, *United Empire Loyalists*, 138.

9 Jasanoff, *Liberty's Exiles*, chap. 5.

10 Stewart, *True Blue*, 128.

11 Ibid., chap. 9.

12 Justus A. Griffin, *A Pioneer Family: Ancestors and Descendants of Richard Griffin* (Hamilton, ON: Griffin and Richmond, 1924), 24–9.

13 Bradley, *United Empire Loyalists*, 147–55.

14 Robert S. Allen, *His Majesty's Indian Allies: British Indian Policy in Defence of Canada, 1774–1815* (Toronto: Dundurn Press, 1992), 62.

15 Jasanoff, *Liberty's Exiles*, 194.

16 W.P.M. Kennedy, *The Constitution of Canada, 1534–1937: An Introduction to Its Development, Law and Custom*, 2nd ed. (Oxford: Oxford University Press, 1938), 85.

17 Gerald M. Craig, ed., *Lord Durham's Report* (Montreal; Kingston, ON: McGill-Queen's University Press, 2007), 138.

18 See Fernand Ouellet, *Lower Canada 1791–1840: Social Change and Nationalism* (Toronto: McClelland & Stewart, 1980).

19 Aileen Dunham, *Political Unrest in Upper Canada, 1815–1836* (Toronto: McClelland & Stewart, 1963).

20 David Smith, *The Canadian Senate in Bicameral Perspective* (Toronto: University of Toronto Press, 2003).

21 See Nathan Tidridge, *Prince Edward, Duke of Kent: Father of the Canadian Crown* (Toronto: Dundurn Press, 2013).

22 Ibid., 90.

23 For an overview, see J.R. Miller, "Aboriginal Peoples and the Crown," in *Canada and the Crown: Essays on Constitutional Monarchy*, edited by D. Michael Jackson and Philippe Lagassé, 255–69 (Montreal; Kingston, ON: McGill-Queen's University Press, 2013).

24 John Borrows, *Canada's Indigenous Constitution* (Toronto: University of Toronto Press, 2010), 196–8.

25 John Locke, *The Second Treatise of Government* (1689; repr., New York: Liberal Arts Press, 1952), 55.

Chapter 5

1 See E.A. Cruikshank, ed., *The Correspondence of Lieutenant Governor John Graves Simcoe*, vol. III, *1794–1795* (letters of Richard Cartwright, William Jarvis, and Alexander McKee on the Battle of Fallen Timbers) (Toronto: Ontario Historical Society, 1925); and Allen, *His Majesty's Indian Allies*, 83.

2 See Colin G. Calloway, *Crown and Calumet: British Indian Relations, 1783–1815* (Norman: University of Oklahoma Press, 1953).

3 Allen, *His Majesty's Indian Allies*, 52–4; see also William L. Stone, *Life of Joseph Brant-Thayendanegea*, vol. 1 (New York: Alexander V. Blake, 1865); and James W. Paxton, *Joseph Brant and His World: 18th Century Mohawk Warrior and Statesman* (Toronto: Lorimer, 2008), 47–8.

4 Ibid., 73–4.

5 Allen, His *Majesty's Indian Allies*, 84.

6 R. David Edmunds, *Tecumseh and the Search for Indian Leadership* (New York: Pearson/Longman, 2007).

7 Allen, *His Majesty's Indian Allies*, 71.

8 See Edmunds, *Tecumseh and the Search for Indian Leadership*.

9 On the events leading to the War of 1812, see Carl Benn, *The War of 1812* (Toronto: Osprey, 2010); Troy Bickham, *The Weight of Vengeance: The United States, the British Empire and the War of 1812* (New York: Oxford, 2012); J. Mackay Hitsman, *The Incredible War of 1812*, updated by Donald E. Graves (Montreal: Robin Brass Studio, 1999); and Alan Taylor, *The Civil War of 1812* (New York: Knopf, 2010).

10 Allen, *His Majesty's Indian Allies*, 111–12.

11 Ibid., 115.

12 Ibid., 116.

13 Edmunds, *Tecumseh and the Search for Indian Leadership*, 145.

14 Taylor, *Civil War of 1812*, 10.

15 See Carl Benn, *The Iroquois in the War of 1812* (Toronto: University of Toronto Press, 1998).

16 Donald B. Smith, *Sacred Feathers: The Reverend Peter Jones (Kahkewaquonaby) & the Mississauga Indians* (Lincoln: University of Nebraska Press, 1982).

17 Benn, *Iroquois in the War of 1812*, 145.

18 Pierre Berton, *The Invasion of Canada, 1812–1813* (Toronto: Anchor Canada, 1980), 110.

19 Benn, *War of 1812*, 47.

20 James Laxer, *Tecumseh and Brock* (Toronto: Anansi, 2012), 146.

21 Hitsman, *Incredible War of 1812*, 81.

22 Berton, *Invasion of Canada*, 248.

23 Robert Malcomson, *Capital in Flames: The American Attack on York, 1813* (Montreal: Robin Brass Studio, 2008), 190.

24 J. Mackay Hitsman, *The Incredible War of 1812*, 172–3; Edmunds, *Tecumseh and the Search for Indian Leadership*.

25 Allen, *His Majesty's Indian Allies*, chap. 7.

26 Bickham, *Weight of Vengeance*, 243–61.

27 Canada, Royal Commission on Aboriginal Peoples, *Report*, vol. 1 (Ottawa: Canada Communications Group, 1996), 153–5.

28 Ontario, Ipperwash Inquiry, *Report*, vol. 1, *Investigation and Findings* (Toronto: Queen's Printer for Ontario, 2007), 25–8.

29 Peter Lockyer, "The Gunshot Treaty," *Watershed: Life in Northumberland, Prince Edward County and Quinte*, Fall 2012, 48–51.

30 Allen, *His Majesty's Indian Allies*, 184.

31 Canada, Royal Commission on Aboriginal Peoples, *Report*, vol. 1, 144.

32 Robin Fisher, *Contact and Conflict: Indian European Relations in British Columbia, 1774–1890* (Vancouver: UBC Press, 1977), 51.

33 Ibid., 66–7.

34 Slattery, *Land Rights of Indigenous Canadian Peoples*, 164.

35 Sydney Harring, *White Man's Law: Native People in Nineteenth-Century Canadian Jurisprudence* (Toronto: University of Toronto Press, 1998), 24–6; Russell, *Recognizing Aboriginal Title*, 90.

36 See Russell, *Recognizing Aboriginal Title*, chap. 4.

37 See Smith, *Sacred Feathers*.

38 Kennedy, *Constitution of Canada*, 150.

39 Edward S. Rogers, "The Algonquian Farmers of Southern Ontario, 1830–1845," in *Aboriginal Ontario: Historical Perspectives on the First Nations*, ed. Edward S. Rogers and Donald B. Smith, 122–66 (Toronto: Dundurn Press, 1994).

40 Peter S. Schmalz, *The Ojibwa of Southern Ontario* (Toronto: University of Toronto Press, 1991), 145.

41 Canada, Royal Commission on Aboriginal Peoples, *Report*, vol. 1, 145.

42 Harring, *White Man's Law*, 33.

43 Canada, Royal Commission on Aboriginal Peoples, *Report*, vol. 1, 146.

Chapter 6

1 Alfred D. Decelles, *The "Patriotes" of '37*, Chronicles of Canada 25 (Toronto: Glasgow, Brook, 1916), 16.

2 J.G.M. Clarke, *The Honourable Jonathan Sewell: Background, Career and Family, 1766–1839* (Toronto: Self-published, 1993), 26–30.

3 Kennedy, *Constitution of Canada*, 89.

4 Hans Kohn, *Nationalism: Its Meaning and History* (Toronto: D. Van Nostrand, 1955), 23.

5 Craig, *Lord Durham's Report*, 13.

6 Helen Taft Manning, *The Revolt of French Canada, 1800–1835* (Toronto: Macmillan, 1962), 60.

7 Decelles, *"Patriotes" of '37*, 14–15.

8 Ibid., 15.

9 Ouellet, *Lower Canada*, 93.

10 Manning, *Revolt of French Canada*, 151–4.

11 Adam Short and Norah Story, *Constitutional Documents Relating to the Constitutional History of Canada, 1819–1828* (Ottawa: King's Printer, 1925), 125–6.

12 Decelles, *"Patriotes" of '37*, 26.

13 Kennedy, *Constitution of Canada*, 103.

14 See Ouellet, *Lower Canada*, chaps 3–7.

15 Ibid., 137.

16 W.P.M. Kennedy, ed., *Statutes, Treaties and Documents of the Canadian Constitution, 1713–1929* (Oxford: Oxford University Press, 1930), 277; English translation.

17 Ouellet, *Lower Canada*, 222.

18 Manning, *Revolt of French Canada*, 244–5.

19 Kennedy, *Constitution of Canada*, 105.

20 Kennedy, *Statutes, Treaties and Documents*, 262.

21 Ibid., 279–80.

22 Ouellet, *Lower Canada*, 267.

23 See Liora Salter, "The Complex Relationship between Commissions of Inquiry and Public Controversy," in *Commissions of Inquiry: Praise or Reappraise?* ed. Allan Manson and David Mullan, 185–210 (Toronto: Irwin Law, 2003).

24 Kennedy, *Constitution of Canada*, 110

25 Ibid., 55.

26 Kennedy, *Statutes, Treaties and Documents*, 342–3.

27 Decelles, *"Patriotes" of '37*, 60.

28 John Sewell, *Mackenzie: A Political Biography of William Lyon Mackenzie* (Toronto: James Lorimer, 2002), chap. 2.

29 See Graeme Patterson, "An Enduring Canadian Myth: Responsible Government and the Family Compact," in *Interpreting Canada's Past*, vol. 1, *Before Confederation*, ed. J.M. Bumsted, 230–47 (Toronto: Oxford University Press, 1986).

30 Gerald M. Craig, "Strachan, John," in *Dictionary of Canadian Biography*, vol. 9 (Toronto: University of Toronto Press, 1976).

31 See Dunham, *Political Unrest in Upper Canada*, chap. 6.

32 Ibid., 101.

33 See Constitutional Act of 1791, sections III and XXII, in Short and Doughty, *Documents Relating to the Constitutional History of Canada, 1759–1791*, 694–708.

34 Dunham, *Political Unrest in Upper Canada*, chap. 5.

35 Gerald M. Craig, *Upper Canada: The Formative Years, 1784–1841* (Toronto: McClelland & Stewart, 1963), 122.

36 Ibid., 202.

37 See William Kilbourn, *The Firebrand: William Lyon Mackenzie and the Rebellion in Upper Canada* (Toronto: Clarke, Irwin, 1956).

38 Ibid., 47–9.

39 Craig, *Upper Canada*, 192, 205.

40 Ibid., 139.

41 See Albert Schrauwers, *"Union Is Strength": W.L. Mackenzie, the Children of Peace, and the Emergence of Joint Stock Democracy in Upper Canada* (Toronto: University of Toronto Press, 2009).

42 Craig, *Upper Canada*, 228–9.

43 Kilbourn, *Firebrand*, 157.

44 Ouellet, *Lower Canada*, 294.

45 Decelles, *"Patriotes" of '37*, 77.

46 Ibid., 99.

47 Most of the details that follow are taken from Kilbourn, *Firebrand*, chap. 13.

48 Ouellet, *Lower Canada*, 318–21.

49 Chester New, *Lord Durham* (Oxford: Oxford University Press, 1929), 299–320.

50 Ibid., 313–19.

51 Quoted in Kennedy, *Constitution of Canada*, 167. For the text of Lord Durham's official commission, see Craig, *Lord Durham's Report*, 3–5.

52 New, *Lord Durham*, 391.

53 Ouellet, *Lower Canada*, 322.

54 Sewell, *Mackenzie*, 160.

55 New, *Lord Durham*, 409.

56 Kennedy, *Statutes, Treaties & Documents*, 367–71.

57 New, *Lord Durham*, 464.

58 Ibid., 467, 490.

59 Kennedy, *Constitution of Canada*, 168.

60 Craig, *Lord Durham's Report*, 48.

61 Ibid., 49.

62 Phillip A. Buckner, *The Transition to Responsible Government: British Policy in British North America, 1815–1850* (Westport, CT: Greenwood Press, 1985), 5.

63 Craig, *Lord Durham's Report*, 140.

64 Ibid., 149.

65 Ibid., 29.

66 Ibid., 31.

67 Ibid., 148.

68 Ibid., 68.

69 Ibid., 158.

70 John Stuart Mill, "Considerations on Representative Government," in *John Stuart Mill: On Liberty and Other Essays*, ed. John Grey (Oxford: Oxford University Press, 1991), 428.

71 Lord Acton, *Essays on Freedom and Power* (Gloucester, MA: Peter Smith, 1972), 158–60.

72 Kennedy, *Statutes, Treaties and Documents*, 433–45.

73 J.M.S. Careless, *The Union of the Canadas: The Growth of Canadian Institutions 1841–1857* (Toronto: McClelland & Stewart, 1967), 15.

74 Union Act, 1840, section XL.

75 Ibid., section LIX.

76 Buckner, *Transition to Responsible Government*, 261–2.

77 Kennedy, *Constitution of Canada*, chap. 13.

78 Kennedy, *Statutes, Treaties and Documents*, 389.

79 William Lawson Grant, *The Tribune of Nova Scotia: A Chronicle of Joseph Howe* (Toronto: Glasgow, Brook, 1915), 57–8.

80 Jacques Monet, *The Last Cannon Shot: A Study of French-Canadian Nationalism, 1837–1850* (Toronto: University of Toronto Press, 1969), 68.

81 See John Ralston Saul, *Louis-Hippolyte LaFontaine & Robert Baldwin* (Toronto: Penguin, 2010).

82 Ibid., 112–27.

83 Monet, *Last Cannon Shot*, 111.

84 Careless, *Union of the Canadas*, 52.

85 Kennedy, *Constitution of Canada*, 217–29.

86 Trevor Lloyd, *The British Empire, 1558–1995*, 2nd ed. (Oxford: Oxford University Press, 1996), 163.

87 Buckner, *Transition to Responsible Government*, 309.

88 Kennedy, *Statutes, Treaties and Documents*, 405.

89 Buckner, *Transition to Responsible Government*, 298.

90 Careless, *Union of the Canadas*, 119.

91 Monet, *Last Cannon Shot*, 266.

92 Ibid.

93 Saul, *Louis-Hippolyte LaFontaine & Robert Baldwin*, 185.

94 Buckner, *Transition to Responsible Government*, 308.

95 Lorne C. Callbeck, *The Cradle of Confederation: A Brief History of Prince Edward Island from Its Discovery in 1534 to the Present Time* (Fredericton, NB: Brunswick Press, 1964), 163.

96 St John Chadwick, *Newfoundland: Island into Province* (Cambridge: Cambridge University Press. 1967), 17.

97 Careless, *Union of the Canadas*, 156.

98 See Pierre Savard and Paul Wycznski, "Garneau, François-Xavier," in *Dictionary of Canadian Biography*, vol. 9 (Toronto: University of Toronto Press, 1976)

99 Monet, *Last Cannon Shot*, 129.

Chapter 7

1 Quoted in David A. Wilson, *Thomas D'Arcy McGee*, vol. 2 (Montreal; Kingston, ON: McGill-Queen's University Press, 2007), 29.
2 Janet Ajzenstat et al., eds., *Canada's Founding Debates* (Toronto: Stoddart, 1999), 232.
3 Wilson, *Thomas D'Arcy McGee*, vol. 2, 27.
4 Wilson, *Thomas D'Arcy McGee*, vol. 1, 221.
5 Ibid., 359.
6 Wilson, *Thomas D'Arcy McGee*, vol. 2, 6.
7 Kennedy, *Constitution of Canada*, 284.
8 Union Act Amendment Act, 17 & 18 Victoria, c. 118, 1954.
9 J.M.S. Careless, *Brown of the Globe*, vol. 2 (Toronto: Macmillan, 1963), 109.
10 Ibid., 128.
11 Quoted in Donald Creighton, *The Road to Confederation: The Emergence of Canada, 1863–1867* (Toronto: Macmillan, 1964), 69.
12 Ibid., 32.
13 Callbeck, *Cradle of Confederation*, 185.
14 Chadwick, *Newfoundland*, 20–2.
15 Quoted in P.B. Waite, *The Life and Times of Confederation, 1864–1867: Politics, Newspapers, and the Union of British North America* (Toronto: University of Toronto Press, 1962), 68.
16 Christopher Moore, *1867: How the Fathers Made a Deal* (Toronto: McClelland & Stewart, 1998), 217–26.
17 Careless, *Brown of the Globe*, vol. 2, 154.
18 Quoted in Creighton, *Road to Confederation*, 121; italics in original.
19 Ibid., 116.
20 Careless, *Brown of the Globe*, vol. 2, 155.
21 Michael Crummey, "The Circus Comes to Charlottetown: The Accidental Birth of a Nation," *Walrus* 11, no. 7 (2014): 50–61.
22 Richard Gwyn, *John A., the Man Who Made Us: The Life and Times of John A. Macdonald* (Toronto: Random House Canada, 2007), 174–5.
23 Moore, *1867*, 99.
24 Gwyn, *John A.*, 311.
25 The resolutions can be found in Kennedy, *Constitutional Documents of Canada*, 541–7.
26 The leading account of these conventions is Andrew Heard, *Canadian Constitutional Conventions: The Marriage of Law & Politics*, 2nd ed. (Toronto: Oxford University Press, 2014).
27 See Peter H. Russell and Lorne Sossin, eds., *Parliamentary Democracy in Crisis* (Toronto: University of Toronto Press, 2009).

28 Ibid., 142.

29 Peter H. Russell, "The Principles, Rules and Practices of Parliamentary Government: Time for a Consolidation," *Journal of Parliamentary and Political Law* 6, no. 2 (2012): 353–64.

30 See, for instance, the speech of John Rose, in Canada, *Parliamentary Debates on Confederation of the British North American Provinces*, 3rd Sess., 8th Provincial Parliament of Canada (Quebec City: Hunter Rose, 1865), 387.

31 See W.R. Lederman, "The Independence of the Judiciary," *Canadian Bar Review* 34 (1956): 1148–58.

32 See Peter H. Russell, *The Judiciary in Canada: The Third Branch of Government* (Toronto: McGraw-Hill/Ryerson, 1987), chap. 8.

33 Walter Bagehot, *The English Constitution* (London: Fontana, 1963).

34 Moore, *1867*, 152.

35 The relevant sections of the Constitution Act, 1867 are 56, 57, and 90.

36 The more American and republican term "senate" was adopted later, at the London Conference.

37 Kennedy, *Constitution of Canada*, 263.

38 Ajzenstat et al., *Canada's Founding Debates*, 77.

39 G.P. Browne, ed., *Documents on the Confederation of British North America* (Toronto: McClelland & Stewart, 1969), 133.

40 Ibid., 80.

41 See Smith, *Canadian Senate in Bicameral Perspective*.

42 Janet Ajzenstat, *The Once and Future Democracy: An Essay in Political Thought* (Montreal; Kingston, ON: McGill-Queen's University Press, 2003), 74–7.

43 See A.I. Silver, *The French-Canadian Idea of Confederation, 1864–1900* (Toronto: University of Toronto Press, 1982).

44 Ralph C. Nelson et al., "Canadian Confederation as a Case Study in Community Formation," in *The Causes of Confederation*, ed. Ged Martin, 50–85 (Fredericton, NB: Acadiensis Press, 1990).

45 Ajzenstat et al., *Canada's Founding Debates*, 230–1.

46 Canada, Royal Commission on Aboriginal Peoples, *Report*, vol. 1, 158–9.

47 Ibid., 145.

48 Gwyn, *John A.*, 153.

49 See the last paragraph of Chapter 5.

50 Edward Said, *Culture and Imperialism* (New York: Vintage Books, 1994), 10.

51 George F.G. Stanley, *A Short History of the Canadian Constitution* (Toronto: Ryerson Press, 1969), 79.

52 Ajzenstat et al., *Canada's Founding Debates*, 295.

53 Ibid., 308.

54 Ibid., 282–3.
55 Ibid., 289.
56 Waite, *Life and Times of Confederation*, 142.
57 Ibid., 143.
58 Quoted in Creighton, *Road to Confederation*, 215.
59 Ibid., 372.
60 Chadwick, *Newfoundland*, 22.
61 Quoted in Creighton, *Road to Confederation*, 235.
62 Quoted in Frederick Jones, "'The Antis Gain the Day': Newfoundland and Confederation," in Martin, *Causes of Confederation*, 143.
63 Waite, *Life and Times of Confederation*, 235.
64 Ibid., 245.
65 Moore, *How the Fathers Made a Deal*, 180.
66 J. Murray Beck, *Joseph Howe*, vol. 2, *The Briton Becomes Canadian* (Montreal; Kingston, ON: McGill-Queen's University Press, 1983), 185.
67 Moore, *How the Fathers Made a Deal*, 180.
68 Waite, *Life and Times of Confederation*, 254.
69 Ibid., 263–7.
70 Ibid., 270–1.
71 Ibid., 275.
72 Gwyn, *John A.*, 387.
73 Kennedy, *Constitution of Canada*, 314.
74 Italics added. The exclusivity of the provinces' legislative powers appears in the *Rough Draft of the London Conference for British North America Bill*, but even the *Final Draft of the British North America Bill* does not use the word "exclusive" in referring to the federal Parliament's legislative authority. See Browne, *Documents on the Confederation of British North America*.
75 Creighton, *Road to Confederation*, 423, 240, and 323.

Chapter 8

1 Deanna Christensen, *Ahtahkakoop: The Epic Account of a Plains Cree Chief, His People, and Their Struggle for Survival, 1816–1896* (Altona, MB: Friesens, 2000), 691.
2 R. Louis Gentilove and Geoffrey Maythews, eds., *Historical Atlas of Canada*, vol. 2, *The Land Transformed, 1800–1891* (Toronto: University of Toronto Press, 1993), plate 5.
3 Canada, Royal Commission on Aboriginal Peoples, *Report*, vol. 1, 13.
4 On the uncertainty of the boundaries, see Slattery, *Land Rights of Indigenous Canadian Peoples*, 184–9.

5 Richard Gwyn, *Nation Maker: Sir John A. Macdonald: His Life, Our Times* (Toronto: Random House Canada, 2011), 75.

6 Kennedy, *Constitution of Canada*, 326.

7 Ibid.

8 Gwyn, *Nation Maker*, 100–1.

9 Dan Asfar and Tim Chodan, *Louis Riel* (Edmonton: Folklore, 2003), 35.

10 W.L. Morton, *Manitoba: A History* (Toronto: University of Toronto Press, 1967), 63.

11 Ibid., 77.

12 John O'Farrell, *Irish Families in Ancient Quebec Records* (Mayo, QC: Our Lady of the Shrine, 1967), 7.

13 Thomas Flanagan, *Louis "David" Riel: Prophet of the New World* (Toronto: University of Toronto Press, 1979), 17–26.

14 Asfar and Chodan, *Louis Riel*, 14.

15 Maggie Siggins, *Riel: A Life of Revolution* (Toronto: HarperCollins, 1994), 101.

16 Ibid., 79.

17 Ibid., 111.

18 Morton, *Manitoba*, 68.

19 Siggins, *Riel*, 112–13.

20 Asfar and Chodan, *Louis Riel*, 51.

21 For the full list, see Siggins, *Riel*, 115–16.

22 Gerhard J. Ens and Joe Sawchuck, *From New Peoples to New Nations: Aspects of Métis History and Identity from the Eighteenth to the Twenty-first Centuries* (Toronto: University of Toronto Press, 2016), 100.

23 Morton, *Manitoba*, 131.

24 George F.G. Stanley, *The Birth of Western Canada: A History of the Riel Rebellions* (Toronto: University of Toronto Press, 1936), 78–9.

25 Siggins, *Riel*, 123–4.

26 Asfar and Chodan, *Louis Riel*, 57.

27 Stanley, *Birth of Western Canada*, 84.

28 Asfar and Chodan, *Louis Riel*, 61.

29 Siggjns, *Riel*, 139–40.

30 Asfar and Chodan, *Louis Riel*, 66.

31 Siggins, *Riel*, 142.

32 Ibid., 150–1.

33 Stanley, *Birth of Western Canada*, 98.

34 Asfar and Chodan, *Louis Riel*, 91.

35 Ibid., 100.

36 Siggins, *Riel*, 169.

37 Stanley, *Birth of Western Canada*, 113.

38 Siggins, *Riel*, 176.

39 Gwyn, *Nation Maker*, 133.

40 Siggins, *Riel*, 178.

41 Gwyn, *Nation Maker*, 133–4.

42 Morton, *Manitoba*, 141.

43 Manitoba Act, 1871, section 31.

44 *Manitoba Métis Federation v. A.G. Canada & A.G. Manitoba*, (2013) 1 S.C.R. 623.

45 Manitoba Act, 1871, sections 22 and 23.

46 Siggins, *Riel*, 187.

47 Gwyn, *Nation Maker*, 149.

48 Asfar and Chodan, *Louis Riel*, 126.

49 Gwyn, *Nation Maker*, 267.

50 Asfar and Chodan, *Louis Riel*, 154.

51 Kennedy, *Constitution of Canada*, 335–6.

52 Margaret A. Ormsby, *British Columbia: A History* (Toronto: Macmillan, 1958), 247–8.

53 Arthur J. Ray, Jim Miller, and Frank Tough, *Bounty and Benevolence: A History of Saskatchewan Treaties* (Montreal; Kingston, ON: McGill-Queen's University Press, 2000), 62.

54 Quoted in John R. Wunder, *"Retained by The People": A History of American Indians and the Bill of Rights* (New York: Oxford University Press, 1994), 29.

55 Keith Sinclair, *A History of New Zealand* (Harmondsworth, UK: Penguin, 1959), chap. 6.

56 Russell, *Recognizing Aboriginal Title*, 108–11.

57 See Jacques Barzun, *Race: A Study in Superstition* (New York: Harper & Row, 1937).

58 Ray, Miller, and Tough, *Bounty and Benevolence*, 94–5.

59 John L. Tobias, "Canada's Subjugation of the Plains Cree, 1879–1885," in *Sweet Promises: A Reader on Indian-White Relations in Canada*, edited by J.R. Miller (Toronto: University of Toronto Press, 1991), 213.

60 See Olive Patricia Dickason, *Canada's First Nations: A History of Founding Peoples from Earliest Times* (Toronto: McClelland & Stewart, 1992), chap. 19.

61 Robert J. Talbot, *Negotiating the Numbered Treaties: An Intellectual and Political Biography of Alexander Morris* (Saskatoon: Purich, 2009), 66.

62 Ibid., 46.

63 Canada, *Report of the Royal Commission on Aboriginal Peoples*, vol. 1, 158–9.

64 These words are used in all the numbered treaties, the texts of which are available at the web site of Indigenous and Northern Affairs Canada, at https://www.aadnc-aandc.gc.ca/eng/1370373165583/1370373202340.

65 See Michael Asch, *On Being Here to Stay: Treaty and Aboriginal Rights in Canada* (Toronto: University of Toronto Press, 2014), 85–99.

66 Treaty 7 Elders, *The True Spirit and Original Intent of Treaty 7* (Montreal; Kingston, ON: McGill-Queen's University Press, 1996), 199–200.

67 Supreme Court of Canada, *R. v. Sioui*, (1991) 1 S.C.R. 1025.

68 See D.J. Hall, *From Treaties to Reserves: The Federal Government and Native Peoples in Territorial Alberta, 1870–1905* (Montreal; Kingston, ON: McGill-Queen's University Press, 2015), 80–5.

69 Except for Treaty 5, whose gift was $5 per head, the same as for their near neighbours, the Treaty 1 and 2 peoples, whose gift was raised to $5 in the 1875 revision of their treaties.

70 See John Leonard Taylor, "Canada's Northwest Indian Policy in the 1870s: Traditional Premises and Necessary Innovations," in *The Spirit of the Alberta Indian Treaties*, 3rd ed., edited by Richard T. Price, 3–8 (Edmonton: University of Alberta Press, 1999).

71 See Sarah Carter, *Lost Harvests: Prairie Indian Reserve Farmers and Government Policy* (Montreal; Kingston, ON: McGill-Queen's University Press, 1990).

72 Talbot, *Negotiating the Numbered Treaties*, 109.

73 Treaty 7 Elders, *True Spirit and Original Intent of Treaty 7*, 226.

74 See Hugh A. Dempsey, *Indian Tribes of Alberta* (Calgary: Glenbow Museum, 1997).

75 An Act for the gradual enfranchisement of Indians, the better management of Indian affairs, to extend the provision of the Act 31st Victoria, Chapter 42, Statutes of Canada, 20 Vict., c. 6, s. 10.

76 Ibid., s. 12.

77 Quoted in John S. Milloy, *A National Crime: The Canadian Government and the Residential School System, 1879–1986* (Winnipeg: University of Manitoba Press, 1999), 6.

78 *Cherokee Nation v. Georgia*, 30 US (5 Pe.) 1 (1831). For a discussion of Chief Justice Marshall's jurisprudence, see Russell, *Recognizing Aboriginal Title*, 92–9.

79 J.R. Miller, *Skyscrapers Hide the Heavens: A History of Indian-White Relations in Canada*, 3rd ed. (Toronto: University of Toronto Press, 2000), 198.

80 Canada, Parliament, House of Commons, *Debates*, 30 March 1876, 933.

81 Ibid., 929.

82 Canada, Royal Commission on Aboriginal Peoples, *Report*, vol. 1, 292.

83 Ibid., 283.

84 Ibid., 294–5.

85 "Text of Harper's residential schools apology," *Globe and Mail*, 11 June 2008.

86 Russell, *Recognizing Aboriginal Title*, 262.
87 Milloy, *National Crime*, xiv.
88 See Donald B. Smith, *Mississauga Portraits: Ojibwa Voices from Nineteenth-Century Canada* (Toronto: University of Toronto Press, 2013).
89 Canada, Royal Commission on Aboriginal Peoples, *Report*, vol. 1, 338.
90 Ibid., 294–5.
91 See Russell McGregor, *Imagined Destinies: Aboriginal Australians and the Doomed Race Theory, 1880–1939* (Melbourne: Melbourne University Press, 1997).
92 Milloy, *National Crime*, 70–1.
93 See Mark Abley, *Conversations with a Dead Man: The Legacy of Duncan Cameron Scott* (Vancouver: Douglas & McIntyre, 2013).
94 Canada, Royal Commission on Aboriginal Peoples, *Report*, vol. 1, 335.
95 Ibid., 349.
96 Milloy, *National Crime*, 246–51.
97 Quoted in Canada, Royal Commission on Aboriginal Affairs, *Report*, vol. 1, 357.
98 Ibid., 357.
99 Quoted in ibid., 365.
100 See Canada, Indigenous and Northern Affairs Canada, "Treaty Texts: Treaty No. 6"; available online at https://www.aadnc-aandc.gc.ca/eng/1370373165583/1370373202340.
101 James Daschuk, *Clearing the Plains: Disease, Politics of Starvation and the Loss of Aboriginal Life* (Regina: University of Regina Press, 2014), 101.
102 Ibid., 114.
103 Tobias, "Canada's Subjugation of the Plains Cree," 215.
104 Peter Dodson, *Little Pine and Lucky Man: A History 1866–1885* (Little Pine and Lucky Man First Nations, SK: Peter Dodson, 2003), 33.
105 Rudy Wiebe, *Big Bear* (Toronto: Penguin Canada, 2008), 122–3.
106 Tobias, "Canada's Subjugation of the Plains Cree," 225.
107 The pass system was never given any legislative base; see Canada, Royal Commission on Aboriginal Peoples, *Report*, vol. 1, 296–7.
108 Siggins, *Riel*, 328.
109 Ibid., 356.
110 Gwyn, *Nation Maker*, 436.
111 Asfar and Chodan, *Louis Riel*, 188.
112 Joseph Boyden, *Louis Riel & Gabriel Dumont* (Toronto: Penguin Canada, 2013), 79.
113 Flanagan, *Louis "David" Riel*, 136.
114 Siggins, *Riel*, 371.

115 Ibid., 372.
116 Gwyn, *Nation Maker*, 448.
117 Christensen, *Ahtahkakoop*, 499.
118 For details of these events, see A. Blair Stonechild, "The Indian View of the 1885 Uprising," in Miller, *Sweet Promises*, 258–76.
119 Siggins, *Riel*, 402.
120 Stonechild, "Indian View of the 1885 Uprising," 270.
121 J.R. Miller, "The Northwest Rebellion of 1885," in Miller, *Sweet Promises*, 256.
122 Stonechild, "Indian View of the 1885 Uprising," 273.
123 See Donald Purich, *The Métis* (Saskatoon: Purich Publishing, 1988), 110.
124 James Morrison, *Treaty Research Report: Treaty No. 9 (1905–1906)* (Ottawa: Indian and Northern Affairs Canada, 1986), 6.
125 *St Catherine's Milling and Lumber Company v. The Queen*, 1889, 14 Appeal Cases, 47.
126 Harring, *White Man's Law*, 138.
127 *Cooper v. Stuart*, (1889) App. Cas., 286.
128 John Long, *Treaty No. 9: Making the Agreement to Share the Land in Far Northern Ontario in 1905* (Montreal; Kingston, ON: McGill-Queen's University Press, 2010), 333.
129 For the list, see ibid., 12.
130 Kenneth Coates, *Treaty Research Report – Treaty 10 (1906)* (Ottawa: Indian and Northern Affairs Canada, 1986), 5.
131 Ibid., 12.
132 René Fumoleau, *As Long As the Land Shall Last: A History of Treaty 8 and Treaty 11, 1870–1939* (Toronto: McClelland & Stewart, 1973), 165.
133 Canada, Royal Commission on Aboriginal Peoples, *Report*, vol. 1, 78.
134 For a good account of their ecology, see Hugh Brody, *The Other Side of Eden: Hunters, Farmers and the Shaping of the World* (Vancouver: Douglas & McIntyre, 2000).
135 Slattery, *Land Rights of Indigenous Canadian Peoples*, 108.
136 Ibid., 153.
137 Shelagh D. Grant, *Arctic Justice: On Trial for Murder, Pond Inlet, 1923* (Montreal; Kingston, ON: McGill-Queen's University Press, 2002), 24–5.
138 Ibid., 80.
139 Quoted in Canada, Royal Commission on Aboriginal Peoples, *The High Arctic Relocation* (Ottawa: Canada Communications Group, 1994), 44.
140 *Re Eskimo*, (1939) S.C.R. 104.
141 Canada, Royal Commission on Aboriginal Peoples, *High Arctic Relocation*, 42.

142 Ibid., 105.
143 Ibid., 34.

Chapter 9

1 Wade, *French Canadians*, 416–17.
2 Silver, *French Canadian Idea of Confederation*, 156.
3 Wade, *French Canadians*, 419.
4 Pierre Dufour and Jean Hamelin, "Mercier, Honoré," in *Dictionary of Canadian Biography*, vol. 12 (Toronto: University of Toronto Press, 1990).
5 Wade, *French Canadians*, 417.
6 Ramsay Cook, *Canada and the French-Canadian Question* (Toronto: Macmillan, 1966), 48.
7 Russell, *Constitutional Odyssey*, 34–5.
8 Christopher Armstrong, *The Politics of Federalism: Ontario's Relations with the Federal Government, 1867–1942* (Toronto: University of Toronto Press, 1981), 13.
9 Margaret Evans, *Sir Oliver Mowat* (Toronto: University of Toronto Press, 1992), 62–4.
10 Armstrong, *Politics of Federalism*, 21.
11 Ibid., 11.
12 Evans, *Sir Oliver Mowat*, 148–9.
13 R. MacGregor Dawson, *The Government of Canada*, 4th ed. (Toronto: University of Toronto Press, 1963), 142.
14 Ibid., 53–4.
15 Robet C. Vipond, *Liberty and Community: Canadian Federalism and the Failure of the Constitution* (Albany: State University of New York Press, 1991), 54–5.
16 Ibid., 59.
17 Quoted in ibid., 62; italics in original.
18 Evans, *Sir Oliver Mowat*, 156–60.
19 Ibid., 171.
20 Coen G. Pierson, *Canada and the Privy Council* (London: Stevens & Sons, 1960), 9.
21 Peter H. Russell, *The Supreme Court of Canada as a Bilingual and Bicultural Institution* (Ottawa: Queen's Printer for Canada, 1969), 13–17.
22 Quoted in ibid., 17.
23 (1878), 2 S.C.R. 70, in Peter H. Russell, Rainer Knopff, and Ted Morton, eds., *Federalism and the Charter: Leading Constitutional Decisions* (Ottawa: Carleton University Press, 1989), 31.
24 Ibid., 32.

25 7 App. Cas. 96, in ibid., 37.
26 Ibid., 113; Peter H. Russell et al., eds., *The Court and the Constitution: Leading Cases* (Toronto: Emond/Montgomery, 2008), 36.
27 John A. Saywell, *The Lawmakers: Judicial Power and the Shaping of Canadian Federalism* (Toronto: University of Toronto Press, 2002), 100.
28 Ibid., 102.
29 Proceedings of the Inter-Provincial Conference held in the city of Quebec (microfilm), 20–28 October 1887, available online at https://archive.org/details/cihm_07519.
30 Cook, *Canada and the French-Canadian Question*, 48–9.
31 Armstrong, *Politics of Federalism*, 30–1.
32 *Liquidators of the Maritime Bank of Canada v. Receiver General of New Brunswick*, (1892) A.C. 443, in Russell, Knopff, and Morton, *Federalism and the Charter*, 52.
33 Ibid., 441–2.
34 *Attorney General of Ontario v. Attorney General of Canada*, (1896) A.C. 348, in Russell, Knopff, and Morton, *Federalism and the Charter*, 53.
35 *Attorney General of Ontario v. Attorney General of Canada*, 360.
36 Ibid., 361.
37 Janice Staples, "Consociationalism at the Provincial Level: The Erosion of Dualism in Manitoba, 1870–1890," in *Consociational Democracy*, edited by Kenneth McRae (Toronto: McClelland & Stewart, 1974), 290–3.
38 See Charles R. Epp, *The Rights Revolution: Lawyers, Activists, and Supreme Courts in Comparative Perspective* (Chicago: University of Chicago Press, 1998).
39 Wade, *French Canadians*, 424.
40 *Barrett v. City of Winnipeg*, (1891) S.C.R. 374.
41 *City of Winnipeg v. Barrett*, (1892) A.C. 445, 454.
42 *Brophy v. Attorney General of Manitoba*, (1895) A.C. 202.
43 Morton, *Kingdom of Canada*, 389–90.
44 Oscar D. Skelton, *The Day of Sir Wilfrid Laurier: A Chronicle of Our Own Time* (Glasgow: Brook & Company, 1916), 171.
45 André Siegfried, *The Race Question in Canada* (New York: D. Appleton, 1907), 1.
46 See, for instance, J.R. Seeley, *The Expansion of England* (London: Macmillan, 1906).
47 Casey Murrow, *Henri Bourassa and French-Canadian Nationalism: Opposition to Empire* (Montreal: Harvest House, 1968), 16.
48 Quoted in Joseph Schull, *Laurier: The First Canadian* (Toronto: Macmillan, 1965), 384.

49 André Pratte, *Wilfrid Laurier* (Toronto: Penguin, 2013), 84–5.

50 Schull, *Laurier*, 452.

51 Pratte, *Wilfrid Laurier*, 152.

52 Gwyn, *Nation Builder*, 564.

53 Pratte, *Laurier*, 178.

54 Quoted in ibid., 183.

55 Ibid.

56 Murrow, *Henri Bourassa*, 77.

57 *Ottawa Separate Schools Trustees v. Mackell*, (1917) A.C. 62, in Russell, Knopff, and Morton, *Federalism and the Charter*, 605.

58 J.L. Granatstein, *The Greatest Victory: Canada's One Hundred Days, 1918* (Toronto: Oxford University Press, 2014), 61.

59 J.L. Granatstein and J.M. Hitsman, *Broken Promises: A History of Conscription in Canada* (Toronto: Oxford University Press, 1977), 46.

60 Ibid., 63.

61 Robert Craig Brown, *Robert Laird Borden: A Biography*, vol. 2, *1914–1937* (Toronto: Macmillan, 1980), 70.

62 Schull, *Laurier*, 581.

63 Granatstein and Hitsman, *Broken Promises*, 66.

64 Brown, *Robert Laird Borden*, 109.

65 Ibid., 100.

66 Robert Bothwell, Ian Drummond, and John English, *Canada, 1900–1945* (Toronto: University of Toronto Press, 1987), 158.

67 Schull, *Laurier*, 604.

68 Granatstein and Hitsman, *Broken Promises*, 89.

69 Granatstein, *Greatest Victory*, 80.

70 Lawrence LeDuc et al., *Dynasties and Interludes: Past and Present in Canadian Electoral Politics* (Toronto: Dundurn, 2010), 109.

71 Ibid., 120.

72 Peter H. Russell, *Two Cheers for Minority Government: The Evolution of Canadian Parliamentary Democracy* (Toronto: Emond/Montgomery, 2009), 15–16.

73 Kennedy, *Constitution of Canada*, 372–3.

74 Morton, *Kingdom of Canada*, 441.

75 Bothwell, Drummond, and English, *Canada*, 234.

76 Dawson, *Government of Canada*, 53.

77 Bothwell, Drummond, and English, *Canada*, 242–3.

78 Armstrong, *Politics of Federalism*, 146.

79 Ibid., 147–8.

80 *British Coal Corporation v. The Queen*, (1935) A.C. 500.

81 *Edwards v. Canada*, (1930) A.C. 124.

82 *In Re The Board of Commerce Act, 1919*, (1922) A.C. 191, in Russell, Knopff, and Morton, *Federalism and the Charter*, 61.

83 *Toronto Electric Commissioners v. Snider*, (1925) A.C. 396, in Russell, Knopff, and Morton, *Federalism and the Charter*, 73.

84 *Attorney General of Canada v. Attorney General of Ontario*, (1937) A.C. 327, in Russell, Knopff, and Morton, *Federalism and the Charter*, 104.

85 *A.G. Canada v. A.G. Ontario (Labour Conventions Reference)*, in Russell, Knopff, and Morton, *Federalism and the Charter*, 110.

86 W.H. McConnell, "The Judicial Review of Prime Minister Bennett's 'New Deal,'" *Osgoode Hall Law Journal* 6, no. 1 (1968): 39–86.

87 Alan C. Cairns, "The Judicial Committee and Its Critics," *Canadian Journal of Political Science* 4, no. 3 (1971): 301–45.

88 Canada, Parliament, Senate, *Report to the Honourable Speaker Relating to the Enactment of the B.N.A. Act, 1867* (Ottawa: J.O. Patenaude, 1939).

89 Canada, Royal Commission on Dominion-Provincial Relations, *Report* (Ottawa: King's Printer, 1940).

90 Quoted in Kenneth McRoberts, *Quebec: Social Change and Political Crisis*, 3rd ed. (Toronto: McClelland & Stewart, 1988), 80.

Chapter 10

1 Desmond Morton, *When Your Number's Up: The Canadian Soldier in the First World War* (Toronto: Random House, 1983), 174.

2 W. Kaye Lamb, "Canada," in *The Canadian Encyclopaedia*, vol. 1 (Edmonton: Hurtig, 1985), 261–2.

3 Quoted in Carl Berger, "The True North Strong and Free," in *Nationalism in Canada*, edited by Peter H. Russell (Toronto: McGraw-Hill Ryerson, 1966), 3.

4 Ibid., 11–12.

5 Gwyn, *Nation Maker*, 384.

6 Patrice Dutil, "Macdonald, His 'Ottawa Men' and the Consolidation of Prime Ministerial Power (1867–1873)," in *Macdonald at 200: New Reflections and Legacies*, edited by Patrice Dutil and Roger Hall, 282–310 (Toronto: Dundurn, 2014).

7 David Wilson, "Macdonald and the Fenians," in Dutil and Hall, *Macdonald at 200*, 94–114.

8 Gwyn, *Nation Maker*, chap. 12.

9 Ibid., 308.

10 See Ian Macdonald, "Foreign Investment: Villain or Scapegoat?" in Russell, *Nationalism in Canada*, 178–202; and John Dales, "Protection, Immigration and Canadian Nationalism," in Russell, *Nationalism in Canada*, 164–77.

11 David W. Delainey and J.C. Herbert Emery, "The National Policy's Impact on the West: A Reassessment," in Dutil and Hall, *Macdonald at 200*.

12 Gwyn, *Nation Builder*, 309.

13 Ninette Kelley and Michael J. Trebilcock, *The Making of the Mosaic: A History of Canadian Immigration Policy*, 2nd ed. (Toronto: University of Toronto Press, 2010), 64.

14 Donald Kerr and Deryck Holdsworth, eds., *Historical Atlas of Canada: Addressing the Twentieth Century*, vol. 3 (Toronto: University of Toronto Press, 1990), plate 27.

15 Kelley and Trebilcock, *Building the Mosaic*, 69.

16 Kerr and Holdsworth, *Historical Atlas of Canada*, plate 27.

17 Kelley and Trebilcock, *Making of the Mosaic*, 121.

18 Quoted in ibid., 122.

19 Ibid., 142.

20 Ibid., 139.

21 Constance Backhouse, *Colour-Coded: A Legal History of Racism in Canada* (Toronto: University of Toronto Press, 1999), 3.

22 Canada, *Statutes of Canada 1885*, 47/48 Vic, c. 40, s. 2.

23 W. Peter Ward, *White Canada Forever: Popular Attitudes and Public Policy towards Orientals in British Columbia* (Montreal; Kingston, ON: McGill-Queen's University Press, 1978), 40.

24 Canada, Parliament, House of Commons, *Debates*, 3rd Session, 5th Parliament, 4 May 1885, 1588.

25 Ibid.

26 See Barzun, *Race*, chap. 4.

27 Canada, Parliament, House of Commons, *Debates*, 3rd Session, 5th Parliament, 4 May 1885, 1589.

28 Timothy J. Stanley, "'The Aryan Character of the Future of British North America': John A. Macdonald, Chinese Exclusion, and the Invention of Canadian White Supremacy," in Dutil and Hall, *Macdonald at 200*, 122–5.

29 Quoted in ibid., 128.

30 Kelley and Trebilcock, *Making of the Mosaic*, 145.

31 Ward, *White Canada Forever*, 80.

32 Ibid., 65.

33 Kelley and Trebilcock, *Making of the Mosaic*, 99.

34 *Cunningham v. Tommy Homa*, (1903) A.C. 151.

35 *Union Colliery Company v. Bryden*, (1899) A.C. 580, at 587.

36 Quoted in Ward, *White Canada Forever*, 66.

37 Ibid., 69.

38 Kelley and Trebilcock, *Making of the Mosaic*, 150.

39 Hugh Johnston, *The Voyage of the Komagata Maru: The Sikh Challenge to Canada's Colour Bar* (Vancouver: UBC Press, 1989), 4.

40 Ward, *White Canada Forever*, 61.

41 Kelley and Trebilcock, *Making of the Mosaic*, 153.

42 Quoted in Ward, *White Canada Forever*, 91.

43 Kelley and Trebilcock, *Making of the Mosaic*, 252, 168,

44 Ibid., 213.

45 Ibid., 157.

46 Ibid., 203.

47 See Irving Abella and Harold Troper, *None Is Too Many: Canada and the Jews of Europe, 1933–1948* (Toronto: Lester & Orpen Dennys, 1982).

48 Ward, *White Canada Forever*, 164.

49 Granatstein, *Greatest Victory*, 60.

50 Ibid., 80.

51 Quoted in ibid., 82.

52 Dawson, *Government of Canada*, 49.

53 Pratte, *Wilfrid Laurier*, 149.

54 Morton, *Kingdom of Canada*, 441.

55 Quoted in Bothwell, Drummond, and English, *Canada*, 237.

56 Dawson, *Government of Canada*, 53.

57 Bothwell, Drummond, and English, *Canada*, 374–5, 446.

58 Ibid., 238.

59 John Holmes, "Nationalism in Canadian Foreign Policy," in Russell, *Nationalism in Canada*, 207.

60 Kenneth McNaught, *The Penguin History of Canada* (London: Penguin Books, 1988), 260.

61 Quoted in Robert MacDougall, "The All-Red Dream: Technological Nationalism and the Trans-Canada Telephone System," in *Canadas of the Mind: The Making and Unmaking of Canadian Nationalisms in the Twentieth Century*, edited by Norman Hilman and Adam Chapnick (Montreal; Kingston, ON: McGill-Queen's University Press, 2007), 54.

62 Ibid., 57.

63 Quoted in Frank Peers, "The Nationalist Dilemma in Canadian Broadcasting," in Russell, *Nationalism in Canada*, 255.

64 *In re Regulation and Control of Radio Communication in Canada*, (1932) A.C. 304, in Russell, Knopff, and Morton, *Federalism and the Charter*, 93.

65 Peers, "The Nationalist Dilemma in Canadian Broadcasting," 253–4.

66 Ibid., 255.

67 MacDougall, "All-Red Team," 47.

68 Hugh MacLennan, *Two Solitudes* (Toronto: McClelland & Stewart, 1945), 4.

69 See Abraham Rotstein, "The 20th Century Prospect: Nationalism in a Technological Society," in Russell, *Nationalism in Canada*, 341–63.

70 *Attorney General of Canada v. Ontario* (Employment and Social Insurance Act Reference), (1937) A.C. 356, in Russell, Knopff, and Morton, *Federalism and the Charter*, 97.

71 Canada, Royal Commission on Dominion-Provincial Relations, *Report*, Book 2, 25.

72 Paul Gérin-Lajoie, *Constitutional Amendment in Canada* (Toronto: University of Toronto Press, 1950), 108.

73 Desmond Morton, *A Short History of Canada*, 6th ed. (Toronto: Penguin Canada 2006), 215.

74 Canada, Parliament, House of Commons, *Debates*, 5th Session, 18th Parliament, 8 September 1939, 36.

75 Granatstein and Hitsman, *Broken Promises*, 171.

76 Bothwell, Drummond, and English, *Canada*, 325.

77 See Max Nemni and Monique Nemni, *Young Trudeau: Son of Quebec, Father of Canada, 1919–1944* (Toronto: McClelland & Stewart, 2006).

78 Peter H. Russell, *The First Summit and the Atlantic Charter* (St John's, NL: Atlantic Charter Foundation, 2011), 4.

Chapter 11

1 Fraser Isbister, "Asbestos 1949," in *On Strike: Six Key Labour Struggles in Canada, 1919–1949*, edited by Irving Abella (Toronto: James Lorimer, 1975), 168.

2 Giles Beausoleil, "History of the Strike at Asbestos," in *The Asbestos Strike*, edited by Pierre Elliott Trudeau, 143–82 (Toronto: Lewis & Samuel, 1974).

3 Isbister, "Asbestos 1949," 163.

4 Irving Abella, "Introduction," in Abella, *On Strike*, xiv.

5 Gérard Dion, "The Church and the Conflict in the Asbestos Industry," in Trudeau, *Asbestos Strike*, 214.

6 Beausoleil, "History of the Strike at Asbestos," 168–9.

7 David Kwavnick, ed., *The Tremblay Report* (Toronto: McClelland & Stewart, 1973), 50.

8 John English, *Citizen of the World: The Life of Pierre Elliott Trudeau*, vol. 1, *1919–1968* (Toronto: Knopff Canada, 2006), 201.

9 Pierre Elliott Trudeau, "The Province of Quebec at the Time of the Strike," in Trudeau, *Asbestos Strike*, 50.

10 Ibid., 66.

11 See Max Nemni and Monique Nemni, *Trudeau Transformed: The Shaping of a Statesman, 1944–1965* (Toronto: McClelland & Stewart, 2011), 225–31.

12 Daniel Poliquin, *René Lévesque* (Toronto: Penguin Books, 2009), 53.

13 Ibid., 58.

14 Nemni and Nemni, *Trudeau Transformed*, 399.

15 McRoberts, *Quebec*, 131.

16 Poliquin, *René Lévesque*, 67–8.

17 McRoberts, *Quebec*, 131–9.

18 Bothwell, Drummond, and English, *Canada*, 273.

19 David Clark Mackenzie, *Inside the Atlantic Triangle: Canada and the Entrance of Newfoundland into Confederation, 1939–1949* (Toronto: University of Toronto Press, 1986), 201–2.

20 Ibid., 217.

21 British North America Act, 1949, (No.1).

22 *Attorney General of Ontario v. Attorney General of Canada*, (1947) A.C. 128.

23 Canada, Parliament, House of Commons, *Debates*, 1st Session, 21st Parliament, 21 September 1949, 661.

24 Ibid., 313–14.

25 Russell, *Judiciary in Canada*, 112–17.

26 Gérin-Lajoie, *Constitutional Amendment in Canada*, xiv.

27 Ibid., xvii.

28 British North America Act, 1949, (No.2).

29 J.A. Corry, "Constitutional Trends and Federalism," in *Evolving Canadian Federalism*, edited by A.R.M. Lower et al. (Durham, NC: Duke University Press, 1958), 103.

30 Boswell, Drummond, and English, *Canada*, 136.

31 Ibid., 143.

32 Ibid., 148.

33 British North America Act, 1951.

34 Boswell, Drummond, and English, *Canada*, 222.

35 Constitution Act, 1982, section 36.

36 Michael Ignatieff, *The Rights Revolution* (Toronto: Anansi, 2000).

37 United Nations Charter, Article 1 (1).

38 Quoted in MacLennan, *Toward the Charter*, 74.

39 Ibid., 100.

40 See Russell, Knopff, and Morton, *Federalism and the Charter*, 299.

41 (1959) S.C.R. 265.

42 *Saumur v. Quebec*, (1953) S.C.R. 299.

43 *Switzman v. Elbling and Attorney General of Quebec*, (1957) S.C.R. 285.

44 Russell, Knopff, and Morton, *Federalism and the Charter*, 323.

45 MacLennan, *Toward the Charter*, 110.

46 Ibid., 147.

47 Quoted in Guy Favreau, *The Amendment of the Constitution of Canada* (Ottawa: Queen's Printer, 1965), 27.
48 Ibid., appendix 3.
49 Quoted in D.V. Smiley, *Canada in Question: Federalism in the Eighties*, 3rd ed. (Toronto: McGraw-Hill Ryerson, 1980), 10.
50 See Russell, *Recognizing Aboriginal Title*, 141.
51 Quoted in Graham Fraser, *PQ: René Lévesque and the Parti Québécois in Power* (Toronto: Macmillan, 1984), 32.
52 Quoted in Russell, *Constitutional Odyssey*, 78.
53 English, *Citizen of the World*, 416.
54 Russell, *Two Cheers for Minority Government*, 32.
55 McRoberts, *Quebec*, 139.
56 Bothwell, Drummond, and English, *Canada*, 285.
57 Canada, "Federalism for the Future: A Statement of Policy by the Government of Canada, the Constitutional Conference, 1968, Ottawa, February 5, 6, and 7" (Ottawa: Queen's Printer, 1968).
58 Fraser, *PQ*, 48.
59 Richard Simeon, *Federal-Provincial Diplomacy: The Making of Recent Policy in Canada* (Toronto: University of Toronto Press, 1972), 122.
60 Kenneth McRae, ed., *Consociational Democracy: Accommodation in Segmented Societies* (Toronto: McClelland & Stewart, 1974).
61 Fraser, *PQ*, 55.
62 Bothwell, Drummond, and English, *Canada*, 374.
63 Canada, Royal Commission of Inquiry into Certain Activities of the Royal Canadian Mounted Police, *Second Report*, vol. 2 (Ottawa: Queen's Printer, 1981), 919–20.
64 Simeon, *Federal-Provincial Diplomacy*, 120.
65 Ibid., 121.
66 See Russell, *Constitutional Odyssey*, 74–6.
67 Canada, Special Joint Committee of the Senate and House of Commons on the Constitution of Canada, *The Constitution of Canada: Final Report* (Ottawa: Queen's Printer, 1972), 15.

Chapter 12

1 George Manuel and Michael Posluns, *The Fourth World: An Indian Reality* (Toronto: Collier-Macmillan, 1974).
2 Ibid., 94.
3 Peter H. Russell, "Aboriginal Nationalism – Prospects for Decolonization," *Pacifica Review* 8, no. 2 (1996): 60.

4 United Nations Charter, Article 1(2).
5 Manuel and Posluns, *Fourth World*, 236.
6 Ibid., 245.
7 Ibid.
8 *Delgamuukw v. British Columbia*, (1997), 3 S.C.R. 1010, para. 186.
9 Canada, Royal Commission on Aboriginal Peoples, *Report*, vol. 1, 309.
10 Canada, Parliament, House of Commons, *Debates*, 2nd Session, 21st Parliament, 21 June 1950, 3393.
11 Canada, Royal Commission on Aboriginal Peoples, *Report*, vol. 1, 311.
12 Augie Fleras and Jean Leonard Elliott, *The Nations Within: Aboriginal-State Relations in Canada, the United States and New Zealand* (Toronto: Oxford University Press, 1992), 150–1.
13 Canada, Royal Commission on Aboriginal Peoples, *Report*, vol. 1, 299–300.
14 H.B. Hawthorn, ed., *A Survey of the Contemporary Indians of Canada: Economic, Political, Educational Needs and Policies*, vol. 1 (Ottawa: Indian Affairs Branch, 1966).
15 Ibid., 13.
16 Sally Weaver, *Making Canadian Indian Policy: The Hidden Agenda, 1968–1970* (Toronto: University of Toronto Press, 1981), 20–4.
17 See Donald J. Savoie, *Governing from the Centre: The Concentration of Power in Canadian Politics* (Toronto: University of Toronto Press, 1999).
18 Weaver, *Making Canadian Indian Policy*, 54.
19 Ibid., 62.
20 Thomas R. Berger, *Fragile Freedoms: Human Rights and Dissent in Canada* (Toronto: Clarke, Irwin, 1981), chap. 8.
21 Weaver, *Making Canadian Indian Policy*, 81.
22 Quoted in ibid., 82; emphasis in original.
23 Ibid., 114.
24 Canada, Department of Indian Affairs and Northern Development, "Statement of the Government of Canada on Indian Policy" (Ottawa, 1969).
25 Ibid., 2.
26 Ibid., 3.
27 Ibid.
28 Ibid., 7.
29 Ibid., 6.
30 Ibid., 9.
31 Weaver, *Making Canadian Indian Policy*, 174.
32 Harold Cardinal, *The Unjust Society* (Edmonton: Hurtig, 1969).
33 Russell Means, *Where White Men Fear to Tread: The Autobiography of Russell Means*, with Martin J. Wolf (New York: St Martin's Griffin, 1995), 228–30.

34 Ibid., 293.
35 Claudia Orange, *The Treaty of Waitangi* (Wellington: Allen & Unwin, 1987).
36 Michael King, *Nga Iwe O Te Motu: 1000 Years of Maori History* (Auckland: Reed Books, 2001), 96.
37 Russell, *Recognizing Native Title*, 159–60.
38 Weaver, *Making Canadian Indian Policy*, 182.
39 Quoted in Berger, *Fragile Freedoms*, 232.
40 Quoted in ibid., 242.
41 *Calder et al. v. Attorney General of British Columbia*, (1973) S.C.R. 313, 404.
42 Ibid., 328.
43 Gérard La Forest, "Reminiscences of Aboriginal Rights at the Time of the *Calder* Case and Its Aftermath," in *Let Right Be Done: Aboriginal Title, the Calder Case, and the Future of Indigenous Rights*, edited by Hamer Foster, Heather Raven, and Jeremy Webber, 55–8 (Vancouver: UBC Press, 2007).
44 See Kent McNeil, *Common Law Aboriginal Title* (Oxford: Clarendon Press, 1989).
45 See Mel Watkins, ed., *Dene Nation: The Colony Within* (Toronto: University of Toronto Press, 1977), 3–4.
46 *Tsihlqot'in Nation v. British Columbia*, 2014 SCC 44.
47 Boyce Richardson, *Strangers Devour the Land* (Toronto: Macmillan of Canada, 1975), 298.
48 *James Bay and Northern Quebec Agreement*, 13.
49 For an analysis of the agreement, see Canada, Royal Commission on Aboriginal Peoples, *Report*, vol. 2, part 2, 720–2.

Chapter 13

1 Canada, Parliament, House of Commons, *Debates*, 3rd Session, 20th Parliament, 1 May 1947, 2646.
2 Canada, Parliament, House of Commons, *Debates*, 1st Session, 27th Parliament, 14 October 1966, 8651.
3 See José Igartua, *The Other Quiet Revolution: National Identities in English Canada, 1945–71* (Vancouver: UBC Press, 2006).
4 Kelley and Trebilcock, *Making of the Mosaic*, 318.
5 Ibid., 342.
6 Gerald E. Dirks, *Canada's Refugee Policy: Indifference or Opportunism?* (Montreal; Kingston, ON: McGill-Queen's University Press, 1977), appendix A.
7 Garth Stevenson, *Building Nations from Diversity: Canadian and American Experience Compared* (Montreal; Kingston, ON: McGill-Queen's University Press, 2014), 168.

8 Kelley and Trebilcock, *Making of the Mosaic*, 343.

9 Dirks, *Canada's Refugee Policy*, 201.

10 Kerr and Holdsworth, *Historical Atlas of Canada*, vol. 3, "Canada 1891–1961: An Historical Overview," plate 1.

11 Dirks, *Canada's Refugee Policy*, 142–3.

12 Freda Hawkins, *Canada and Immigration: Public Policy and Public Concern* (Montreal; Kingston, ON: McGill-Queen's University Press, 1972), 49.

13 Kelley and Trebilcock, *Making of the Mosaic*, 336.

14 Canada, Parliament, House of Commons, *Debates*, 3rd Session, 20th Parliament, 1 May 1947, 2646.

15 *Attorney General of Canada v. Brent*, (1956) S.C.R. 318.

16 Paul Martin, "Citizenship and the People's World," in *Belonging: The Meaning and Future of Canadian Citizenship*, edited by William Kaplan (Montreal; Kingston, ON: McGill-Queen's University Press, 1993), 66.

17 Canada, *Criminal Code*, sections 318–20.

18 *R. v. Keegstra*, (1990) 3. S.C.R. 697.

19 John Ibbitson, *Stephen Harper* (Toronto: McClelland & Stewart, 2015), 64.

20 Hawkins, *Canada and Immigration*, 79.

21 Kelley and Trebilcock, *Making of the Mosaic*, 364.

22 Canada, Parliament, House of Commons, *Debates*, 3rd Session, 28th Parliament, 8 October 1971, 8642.

23 John English, *Just Watch Me: The Life of Pierre Elliott Trudeau, 1968–2000* (Toronto: Vintage Canada, 2010), 142.

24 Quoted in ibid., 146.

25 See Charles Taylor, *Reconciling the Solitudes: Essays on Canadian Federalism and Nationalism* (Montreal; Kingston, ON: McGill-Queen's University Press, 1993); James Tully, *Strange Multiplicity: Constitutionalism in an Age of Diversity* (Cambridge: Cambridge University Press, 1995); and Will Kymlicka, *Multicultural Citizenship: A Liberal Theory of Minority Rights* (Oxford: Clarendon Press, 1995).

26 Jack Jedwab, "Introduction," in *The Multiculturalism Question: Debating Identity in 21st Century Canada*, edited by Jack Jedwab (Montreal; Kingston, ON: McGill-Queen's University Press, 2014), 4.

27 Yasmeen Abu-Laban, "Reform by Stealth: The Harper Conservatives and Canadian Multiculturalism," in Jedwab, *Multiculturalism Question*, 150.

28 Statutes of Canada, 1988, c. 31, section 3(1).

29 John Biles, "The Government of Canada's Multicultural Program: Key to Canada's Inclusion Reflex," in Jedwab, *Multiculturalism Question*, 11–52.

30 Gérard Bouchard, *Interculturalism: A View from Quebec* (Toronto: University of Toronto Press, 2012), 64.

31 Ibid., 8.
32 Gérard Bouchard and Charles Taylor, *Building the Future: A Time for Reconciliation, Report of the Consultation Commission on Accommodation Practices Related to Cultural Differences* (Quebec City: Gouvernement du Québec, 2008).
33 Kymlicka, *Multicultural Citizenship*, 15.
34 Jeffrey G. Reitz, "Multicultural Policies and Popular Multiculturalism in the Development of Canadian Immigration," in Jedwab, *Multiculturalism Question*, 113.
35 Stevenson, *Building Nations from Diversity*.
36 James Tully, "Introduction," in *Multinational Democracies*, edited by Alain-G. Gagnon and James Tully (Cambridge: Cambridge University Press, 2001), 3.
37 Gagnon and Tully, *Multinational Democracies*.
38 Neil Bissoondath, "A Question of Belonging: Multiculturalism and Citizenship," in *Belonging: The Meaning and Future of Canadian Citizenship*, edited by William Kaplan (Montreal; Kingston, ON: McGill-Queen's University Press, 1993), 377.

Chapter 14

1 Fraser, *PQ*, 65.
2 Poliquin, *René Lévesque*, 137.
3 Alan C. Cairns, "The Politics of Constitutional Renewal in Canada," in *The Politics of Constitutional Change in Industrial Nations: Redesigning the State*, edited by Keith G. Banting and Richard Simeon (Toronto: University of Toronto Press, 1985), 102.
4 See Chapter 11.
5 *Options Canada* (Toronto: University of Toronto, 1977).
6 English, *Just Watch Me*, 384.
7 Roy Romanow, John Whyte, and Howard Leeson, *Canada ... Notwithstanding: The Making of the Constitution, 1976–1982* (Toronto: Carswell/Methuen, 1984), 3.
8 Ibid., 7.
9 Quoted in Fraser, *PQ*, 97.
10 Poliquin, *René Lévesque*, 144.
11 Canada, Prime Minister's Office, "A Time for Action: Toward the Renewal of the Canadian Federation" (Ottawa: Government of Canada, 1978).
12 Douglas E. Sanders, "The Indian Lobby," in *And No One Cheered: Federalism, Democracy and the Constitution Act*, edited by Keith G. Banting and Richard Simeon (Toronto: Methuen, 1983), 304.

13 *Reference re Offshore Mineral Rights of British Columbia*, (1967) S.C.R. 1967, in Russell, Knopff, and Morton, *Federalism and the Charter*, 145.

14 *Canadian Industrial Gas & Oil Ltd. v. Saskatchewan*, (1978) 2 S.C.R. 545, in Russell, Knopff, and Morton, *Federalism and the Charter*, 188.

15 *Central Canada Potash and Attorney General of Canada v. Saskatchewan*, (1979) 1 S.C.R. 42, in Russell, Knopff, and Morton, *Federalism and the Charter*, 205.

16 Romanow, Whyte, and Leeson, *Canada ... Notwithstanding*, 53.

17 Quoted in Russell, *Two Cheers for Minority Government*, 36.

18 English, *Just Watch Me*, 413.

19 Quebec, *Québec-Canada: A New Deal* (Quebec City: Éditeur official, 1979).

20 John C. Crosbie, *No Holds Barred: My Life in Politics* (Toronto: McClelland & Stewart, 1997), 181.

21 English, *Just Watch Me*, 437.

22 Stephen Clarkson, *The Big Red Machine: How the Liberal Party Dominates* (Vancouver: UBC Press, 2005), 87.

23 Lawrence LeDuc et al., *Dynasties and Interludes: Past and Present in Canadian Electoral Politics* (Toronto: Dundurn, 2010), 323, table 8.4.

24 Fraser, *PQ*, 225.

25 Robert Sheppard and Michael Valpy, *The National Deal: The Fight for a Canadian Constitution* (Toronto: Macmillan, 1982), 32.

26 Quoted in ibid., 33.

27 Christian Dufour, *A Canadian Challenge*, 85.

28 Fraser, *PQ*, 236.

29 Sheppard and Valpy, *National Deal*, 42.

30 Quoted in ibid., 55.

31 Ibid. Machiavelli, writing in an era when states rarely had a written constitution, said that it was initiating "a new order of things" that was so difficult, dangerous, and so on to carry out.

32 English, *Just Watch Me*, 474.

33 Romanow, Whyte, and Leeson, *Canada ... Notwithstanding*, 101.

34 Sheppard and Valpy, *National Deal*, 63.

35 Quoted in Stephen Clarkson and Christina McCall, *Trudeau and Our Times*, vol. 1, *The Magnificent Obsession* (Toronto: McClelland & Stewart, 1990), 292.

36 Quoted in English, *Just Watch Me*, 479.

37 Romanow, Whyte, and Lesson, *Canada ... Notwithstanding*, 247–8.

38 Ibid., 126.

39 Louise Mandell and Leslie Hall Pinder, "Tracking Justice: The Constitution Express to Section 35 and Beyond," in *Patriation and Its Consequences: Constitution Making in Canada*, edited by Lois Harder and Steve Patten (Vancouver: UBC Press, 2015), 189.

40 Sanders, "Indian Lobby," 313.

41 Mandell and Pinder, "Tracking Justice," 188.
42 Quoted in Sanders, "Indian Lobby," 323.
43 Sheppard and Valpy, *National Deal*, 184.
44 English, *Just Watch Me*, 488.
45 Romanow, Whyte, and Leeson, *Canada ... Notwithstanding*, 87.
46 Quoted in Russell, *Constitutional Odyssey*, 117.
47 For an account of the fiasco and how CBC reporter Mike Duffy enabled commentators to discuss the decision, see Peter H. Russell, "The *Patriation* and *Quebec Veto References*: The Supreme Court Wrestles with the Political Part of the Constitution," *Supreme Court Review*, 54 (2011): 70–1.
48 See Ron Graham, *The Last Act: Pierre Trudeau, the Gang of Eight, and the Fight for Canada* (Toronto: Penguin Canada, 2012).
49 English, *Just Watch Me*, 505.
50 Constitution Act, 1982, section 40.
51 Ibid., section 59.
52 See Peter H. Russell, "Standing Up for Notwithstanding," *Alberta Law Review* 29, no. 2 (1991): 293–309.
53 See John D. Whyte, "On Not Standing for Notwithstanding," *Alberta Law Review* 28, no. 2 (1989–90): 348–57.
54 See Penny Kome, *The Taking of Twenty-Eight: Women Challenge the Constitution* (Toronto: Women's Press, 1983).
55 In the constitutional text, "aboriginal" is in lower case, but since the Royal Commission on Aboriginal Peoples it has been considered disrespectful to use aboriginal in lower case because that connotes a generic or racial category, whereas "Aboriginal" with a capital is meant to be a political category.
56 Mandell and Pinder, "Tracking Justice," 196.
57 For instance, the British North America Act, 1871 is renamed the Constitution Act, 1871. For all the renamings, see the schedule attached to the Constitution Act, 1982.
58 See K.C. Wheare, *The Constitutional Structure of the Commonwealth* (Oxford: Clarendon Press, 1960), chap. 4.
59 See Marc E. Gold, "The Mask of Objectivity: Politics and Rhetoric in the Supreme Court of Canada," *Supreme Court Review* 7 (1985): 455–510.

Chapter 15

1 Canadians for a Unifying Constitution in cooperation with The Friends of Meech Lake, "Meech Lake: Setting the Record Straight" ([Chelsea, QC], 1990).
2 For an account of this conference and the three that followed, see David C. Hawkes, *Aboriginal Peoples and Constitutional Reform: What Have We*

Learned? (Kingston: Queen's University, Institute of Intergovernmental Relations, 1989).

3 Constitution Act, 1982, section 35 (3).

4 Ibid., section 35 (4).

5 Canada, Parliament, House of Commons, Special Committee on Indian Self-Government, *Report* (Ottawa, 1983).

6 The first case is *R. v. Sioui*, (1990) S.C.R. 1025, in Russell et al., *Court and the Constitution*, 439–40.

7 For an account of how First Nations, Inuit, and Métis think about their right to self-government, see Canada, Royal Commission on Aboriginal Peoples, *Report*, vol. 2, part 1, 108–19.

8 For the text of the Meech Lake Accord, see Patrick J. Monahan, *Meech Lake: The Inside Story* (Toronto: University of Toronto Press, 1991), appendix 2.

9 Alan C. Cairns, *Charter versus Federalism: The Dilemmas of Constitutional Reform* (Montreal; Kingston, ON: McGill-Queen's University Press, 1992).

10 See "The Meech Lake Communiqué, 30 April 1997," in Monahan, *Meech Lake*, appendix 2.

11 Ibid., 151.

12 Quoted in Russell, *Constitutional Odyssey*, 139.

13 Canada, Parliament, House of Commons, Special Committee to Study the Proposed Companion Resolution to the Meech Lake Accord, *Report* (Ottawa, May 1990).

14 The June communiqué is in Monahan, *Meech Lake*, appendix 4.

15 Quoted in Monahan, *Meech Lake*, 234.

16 Russell, *Constitutional Odyssey*, 154.

17 Peter H. Russell, "Oka to Ipperwash: The Necessity of Flashpoint Events," in *This Is an Honour Song: Twenty Years since the Blockades*, edited by Leanne Simpson and Kiera L. Ladner, 29–46 (Winnipeg: Arbeiter Ring, 2010).

18 See Geoffrey York and Loreen Pindera, *People of the Pines: The Warriors and the Legacy of Oka* (Boston: Little, Brown, 1991).

19 *R. v. Sparrow*, (1990) 1 S.C.R. 1075, in Russell et al., *Court and the Constitution*, 411.

20 *R. v. Sioui*, (1990) S.C.R. 1025.

21 Quebec Liberal Party, Constitutional Committee, *A Quebec Free to Choose* (Montreal: Quebec Liberal Party, 1991).

22 Quebec, Commission on the Political and Constitutional Future of Quebec, *Report* (Quebec City, 1991).

23 An Act Respecting the Process for Determining the Political and Constitutional Future of Quebec, section 1.

24 Quebec Liberal Party, Constitutional Committee, *Quebec Free to Choose*, 32.

25 Canada, Citizens' Forum on Canada's Future, *Report* (Ottawa, 1991), 47.

26 Brian Mulroney, *Memoirs, 1939–2003* (Toronto: McClelland & Stewart, 2007).

27 Canada, *Shaping Canada's Future Together: Proposals* (Ottawa: Supply and Services Canada, 1991).

28 For an account of the conferences, see Russell, *Constitutional Odyssey*, 177–81.

29 Canada, Parliament, Special Joint Committee of the Senate and House of Commons on a Renewed Canada, *A Renewed Canada* (Ottawa, 1992).

30 For the text of the Charlottetown Accord, see Russell, *Constitutional Odyssey*, appendix.

31 For a summary of the Referendum Act and a discussion of Canada's previous experience with referendums, see Patrick Boyer, *Direct Democracy in Canada: The History and Future of Referendums* (Toronto: Dundurn, 1996).

32 For a tabulation of the vote by province and territory, see Russell, *Constitutional Odyssey*, 227.

33 "Consensus Report on the Constitution: Final Text, Charlottetown, August 28, 1992 (Charlottetown Accord)," section 1(h).

34 The main exception is section 41(b) of the Constitution Act, 1982, which guarantees that a province's representation in the House of Commons will never be less than its number of senators. Only Prince Edward Island has benefited from this.

35 See *Daniels v. Canada*, 2016 SCC 12.

36 The text was reproduced in the *Globe and Mail*, 7 December 1994.

37 Russell, *Constitutional Odyssey*, 232–3.

38 See LeDuc et al., *Dynasties and Interludes*, chap. 11.

39 Lawrence Martin, *Iron Man: The Defiant Reign of Jean Chrétien* (Toronto: Viking Canada, 2003), 128.

40 André Picard, "Parizeau promises to 'exact revenge' for sovereignist loss," *Globe and Mail*, 31 October 1995.

Chapter 16

1 Daniel J. Elazar, "Constitution-making, the Pre-eminently Political Act," in *Redesigning the State: The Politics of Constitutional Change*, edited by Keith G. Banting and Richard Simeon (Toronto: University of Toronto Press, 1985), 244.

2 Susan Delacourt, "PM offers Quebec distinct status," *Globe and Mail*, 28 November 1995.

3 Brian Laghi and Graham Fraser, "Premiers develop unity plan," *Globe and Mail*, 15 September 1997.

4 Ibbitson, *Stephen Harper*, 249.
5 Constitutional Amendment Act, 1996; Statutes of Canada, 1996, chap. 1.
6 Dwight Newman, "Understanding the Section 43 Bilateral Amending Formula," in *Constitutional Amendment in Canada*, edited by Emmett Macfarlane, 147–63 (Toronto: University of Toronto Press, 2016).
7 Constitutional Amendment Proclamation, 1993 (New Brunswick).
8 Stéphane Dion, *Straight Talk: Speeches and Writings on Canadian Unity* (Montreal; Kingston, ON: McGill-Queen's University Press, 1999).
9 *Reference re Secession of Quebec*, (1998) 2 S.C.R. 217, in Russell et al., *Court and the Constitution*, 541.
10 Ibid., para. 138.
11 Edward Greenspan and Anne McIlroy, "PM and Bouchard square off," *Globe and Mail*, 22 August 1998.
12 (2000) Statutes of Canada, chap. 26.
13 (2001) Statutes of Quebec, chap. 46, s. 2.
14 For the text and a discussion of the Declaration, see James (Sa'ke'j) Henderson, *Indigenous Diplomacy and the Rights of Indigenous Peoples: Achieving UN Recognition* (Saskatoon: Purich, 2008).
15 Jens Dahl, Jack Hicks, and Peter Jull, eds., *Nunavut: Inuit Regain Control of Their Land and Their Lives* (Copenhagen, International Work Group for Indigenous Affairs, 2000).
16 Jack Hicks and Graham White, *Made in Nunavut: An Experiment in Decentralized Government* (Vancouver: UBC Press, 2015).
17 See Christopher Alcantara, *Negotiating the Deal: Comprehensive Land Claims Agreements in Canada* (Toronto: University of Toronto Press, 2013).
18 Canada, British Columbia, Nisga'a Nation, *Nisga'a Final Agreement* (1999).
19 See Tracie Lea Scott, *Postcolonial Sovereignty? The Nisga'a Final Agreement* (Saskatoon: Purich, 2012).
20 *Campbell v. A.G. British Colubia*, (2000) 189 D.L.R. 333.
21 See Christopher McKee, *Treaty Talks in British Columbia*.
22 *Deh Cho First Nations Interim Resource Development Agreement* (2003), available online at https://www.aadnc-aandc.gc.ca/eng/1100100025103/1100100025111.
23 See Ens and Sawchuck, *From New Peoples to New Nations*.
24 See, for instance, Janique Dubois, "From Service Providers to Decision Makers: Building a Métis Government in Saskatchewan," in *Métis in Canada: History, Identity, Law & Politics*, edited by Christopher Adams, George Dahl, and Ian Peach, 433–62 (Edmonton: University of Alberta Press, 2013).
25 *Manitoba Métis Federation Inc. v. Canada*, 2013 SCC 14.

26 Ibid., para. 154.

27 See Paul L.A.H. Chartrand, "Aboriginal Rights: The Dispossession of the Métis," *Osgoode Hall Law Journal*, 29, no. 3 (1991): 463–82.

28 Chris Andersen, *"Métis": Race, Recognition, and the Struggle for Indigenous Peoplehood* (Vancouver: UBC Press, 2014), 74.

29 *R. v. Powley*, 2003 SCC 43, para. 10.

30 See Russell, *Recognizing Aboriginal Title*.

31 *Delgamuukw v. British Columbia*, (1997) 3 S.C.R. 1010.

32 Ibid., para. 165.

33 Ibid., para. 186.

34 *Haida Nation v. British Columbia*, (2004) 3 S.C.R. 511, in Russell et al., *Court and the Constitution*, 462.

35 *Taku River Tlingit First Nation v. British Columbia*, (2004) 3 S.C.R. 350.

36 *Mikisew Cree First Nation v. Canada*, (2005) 3 S.C.R. 388.

37 *Tsilhqot'in Nation v. British Columbia*, 2014 SCC 44.

38 Ibid., para. 94.

39 Meagan Fitzpatrick and Linda Nguyen, "We are sorry," *Gazette* (Montreal), 12 June 2008.

40 Truth and Reconciliation Commission of Canada, *Calls to Action* (Winnipeg, 2015), 1.

41 Justin Trudeau, "Mandate Letter" (Ottawa, 13 November 2015), para. 7.

42 Gordon Robertson, *Northern Provinces: A Mistaken Goal* (Montreal: Institute for Research on Public Policy, 1985).

43 See Alistair Campbell and Kirk Cameron, "Constitutional Development and Natural Resources in the North," in *Governing the North American Arctic: Sovereignty, Security, and Institutions*, edited by Dawn Alexandrea Berry, Nigel Bowles, and Halbert Jones, 180–99 (New York: Palgrave Macmillan, 2016).

44 See Douglas M. Brown, "Fiscal Federalism: Searching for Balance," in *Canadian Federalism: Performance, Effectiveness and Legitimacy*, edited by Herman Bakvis and Grace Skogstad (Toronto: Oxford University Press, 2008), 72–80.

45 Ibbitson, *Stephen Harper*, 269.

46 First Ministers, "A Framework Agreement to Improve the Social Union for Canadians" (Ottawa, 4 February 1999), available online at http://www.scics.gc.ca/english/conferences.asp?a=viewdocument&id=638.

47 *Reference re Supreme Court Act*, (2014) 1 S.C.R. 433.

48 Ibid., para. 49.

49 Ibid., para. 89.

50 *Reference re Senate Reform*, (2014) 1 S.C.R. 704, para. 52.

51 Ibid., para. 65.

52 Joanna Smith, "Liberals take first step in Senate overhaul," *Globe and Mail*, 4 December 2015.

53 Canada, Prime Minister, "New Process for Judicial Appointments to the Supreme Court of Canada," News release (Ottawa, 2 August 2016).

54 Eoin O'Malley, "The Power of Prime Ministers: Results of an Expert Survey," *International Political Science Review* 28, no. 1 (2007): 7–27.

55 Savoie, *Governing from the Centre*.

56 See Alison Loat and Michael MacMillan, *Tragedy in the Commons: Former Members of Parliament Speak Out about Canada's Failing Democracy* (Toronto: Random House, 2014).

57 Brent Rathgeber, *Irresponsible Government: The Decline of Parliamentary Democracy in Canada* (Toronto: Dundurn, 2014).

58 *Canada (Information Commissioner) v. Canada*, (2011) 2 S.C.R. 306.

59 Peter H. Russell, "Learning to Live with Minority Parliaments," in *Parliamentary Democracy in Crisis*, edited by Peter H. Russell and Lorne Sossin (Toronto: University of Toronto Press, 2009), 148.

60 See Peter Russell and Cheryl Milne, *Adjusting to a New Era of Parliamentary Democracy* (Toronto: University of Toronto, Faculty of Law, Asper Centre for Constitutional Rights, 2011).

61 For a discussion of these voting systems, see Law Reform Commission of Canada, *Renewing Democracy: Debating Electoral Reform in Canada* (Ottawa, 2002).

62 Lawrence LeDuc and Jon H. Pammett, "Attitudes toward Democratic Norms and Practices: Canada in Comparative Perspective," in *Canadian Democracy from the Ground Up: Perspectives and Performance*, edited by Elizabeth Gidengil and Heather Bastedo (Vancouver: UBC Press, 2014), table 1.4, 29.

63 Elizabeth Gidengil and Heather Bastedo, "Introduction," in Gidengil and Bastedo, *Canadian Democracy from the Ground Up*, 3.

64 Ignatieff, *Rights Revolution*.

Bibliography

Books and Journals

Abella, Irving. "Introduction." In *On Strike: Six Key Labour Struggles in Canada, 1919–1949*. Edited by Irving Abella, xi–xv. Toronto: James Lorimer, 1975.

Abella, Irving, and Harold Troper. *None Is Too Many: Canada and the Jews of Europe, 1933–1948*. Toronto: Lester & Orpen Dennys, 1982.

Abley, Mark, *Conversations with a Dead Man: The Legacy of Duncan Cameron Scott*. Vancouver: Douglas & McIntyre, 2013.

Abu-Laban, Yasmeen. "Reform by Stealth: The Harper Conservatives and Canadian Multiculturalism." In *The Multicultural Question: Debating Identity in 21st Century Canada*. Edited by Jack Jedwab, 149–72. Montreal; Kingston, ON: McGill-Queen's University Press, 2014.

Acton, Lord. *Essays on Freedom and Power*. Gloucester, MA: Peter Smith, 1972.

Ajzenstat, Janet, *The Once and Future Democracy: An Essay in Political Thought*. Montreal; Kingston, ON: McGill-Queen's University Press, 2003.

Ajzenstat, Janet, Paul Romney, Ian Gentiles, and William D. Gairdner, eds. *Canada's Founding Debates*. Toronto: Stoddart, 1999.

Alcantara, Christopher. *Negotiating the Deal: Comprehensive Land Claims Agreements in Canada*. Toronto: University of Toronto Press, 2013.

Allen, Robert S. *His Majesty's Indian Allies: British Indian Policy in Defence of Canada, 1774–1815*. Toronto: Dundurn, 1992.

Andersen, Chris. *"Métis": Race, Recognition, and the Struggle for Indigenous Peoplehood*. Vancouver: UBC Press, 2014.

Anderson, Fred, *The War that Made America: A Short History of the French and Indian War*. New York: Penguin Books, 2006.

Armstrong, Christopher. *The Politics of Federalism: Ontario's Relations with the Federal Government, 1867–1942*. Toronto: University of Toronto Press, 1981.

Asch, Michael. *On Being Here to Stay: Treaty and Aboriginal Rights in Canada.*
Toronto: University of Toronto Press, 2014.

Asfar, Dan, and Tim Chodan. *Louis Riel.* Edmonton: Folklore, 2003.

Backhouse, Constance. *Colour-Coded: A Legal History of Racism in Canada.*
Toronto: University of Toronto Press, 1999.

Bagehot, Walter. *The English Constitution.* London: Fontana, 1963.

Barzun, Jacques. *Race: A Study in Superstition.* New York: Harper & Row, 1937.

Beausoleil, Giles. "History of the Strike at Asbestos." In *The Asbestos Strike.*
Edited by Pierre Elliott Trudeau, 143–82. Toronto: Lewis & Samuel, 1974.

Beck, J. Murray. *Joseph Howe,* vol. 2, *The Briton Becomes Canadian.* Montreal;
Kingston, ON: McGill-Queen's University Press, 1983.

Benn, Carl. *The Iroquois the War of 1812.* Toronto: University of Toronto Press,
1998.

Benn, Carl. *The War of 1812.* Toronto: Osprey, 2010.

Berger, Carl. "The True North Strong and Free." In *Nationalism in Canada.*
Edited by Peter H. Russell, 3–26. Toronto: McGraw-Hill Ryerson, 1966.

Berger, Thomas, *Fragile Freedoms: Human Rights and Dissent in Canada.* Toronto:
Clarke, Irwin, 1981.

Berton, Pierre. *The Invasion of Canada, 1812–1813.* Toronto: Anchor Canada,
1980.

Bickham, Troy. *The Weight of Vengeance: The United States, the British Empire and
the War of 1812.* New York: Oxford, 2012.

Biles, John, "The Government of Canada's Multiculturalism Program: Key
to Canada's Inclusion Reflex." In *The Multiculturalism Question: Debating
Identity in 21st Century Canada.* Edited by Jack Jedwab, 11–52. Montreal;
Kingston, ON: McGill-Queen's University Press, 2014.

Bissoondath, Neil. "A Question of Belonging: Multiculturalism and
Citizenship." In *Belonging: The Meaning and Future of Canadian Citizenship.*
Edited by William Kaplan, 368–87. Montreal; Kingston, ON: McGill-
Queen's University Press, 1993.

Borrows, John. *Canada's Indigenous Constitution.* Toronto: University of Toronto
Press, 2010.

Borrows, John. "Wampum at Niagara: The Royal Proclamation, Canadian
Legal History, and Self-Government." In *Aboriginal and Treaty Rights in
Canada: Essays on Law, Equality, and Respect for Difference.* Edited by Michael
Asch, 173–207. Vancouver: UBC Press, 1997.

Bothwell, Robert, Ian Drummond, and John English. *Canada, 1900–1945.*
Toronto: University of Toronto Press, 1987.

Bouchard, Gérard. *Interculturalism: A View from Quebec.* Toronto: University of
Toronto Press, 2012.

Bouchard, Gérard, and Charles Taylor. *Building the Future: A Time for Reconciliation, Report of the Consultation Commission on Accommodation Practices Related to Cultural Differences*. Quebec City: Gouvernement du Québec, 2008.

Boyden, Joseph. *Louis Riel & Gabriel Dumont*. Toronto: Penguin Canada, 2013.

Boyer, Patrick. *Direct Democracy in Canada: The History and Future of Referendums*. Toronto: Dundurn, 1996.

Bradley, A.G. *The United Empire Loyalists: Founders of British Canada*. London: Thornton Butterworth, 1932.

Brody, Hugh. *The Other Side of Eden: Hunters, Farmers, and the Shaping of the World*. Vancouver: Douglas & McIntyre, 2000.

Brown, Douglas M. "Fiscal Federalism: Searching for Balance." In *Canadian Federalism: Performance, Effectiveness and Legitimacy*. Edited by Herman Bakvis and Grace Skogstad, 63–88. Toronto: Oxford University Press, 2008.

Brown, Robert Craig. *Robert Laird Borden: A Biography*, vol. 2, *1914–1937*. Toronto: Macmillan, 1980.

Browne, G.P. "Carleton, Guy, 1st Baron Dorchester." In *Dictionary of Canadian Biography*, vol. 5. Toronto: University of Toronto Press, 1983.

Browne, G.P., ed. *Documents on the Confederation of British North America*. Toronto: McClelland & Stewart, 1969.

Browne, G.P. "Murray, James." In *Dictionary of Canadian Biography*, vol. 4. Toronto: University of Toronto Press, 1979.

Buckner, Phillip A. *The Transition to Responsible Government: British Policy in British North America, 1815–1850*. Westport, CT: Greenwood Press, 1985.

Bumsted, J.M. *The Peoples of Canada: A Pre-Confederation History*. Toronto: Oxford University Press, 1992.

Burt, A.L. *The Old Province of Quebec*, vol. 1, *1760–1778*. Toronto: McClelland & Stewart, 1968.

Cairns, Alan C. *Charter versus Federalism: The Dilemmas of Constitutional Reform*. Montreal; Kingston, ON: McGill-Queen's University Press, 1992.

Cairns, Alan C. "The Judicial Committee and Its Critics." *Canadian Journal of Political Science* 4, no. 3 (1971): 301–45.

Cairns, Alan C. "The Politics of Constitutional Renewal in Canada." In *The Politics of Constitutional Change in Industrial Nations: Redesigning the State*. Edited by Keith G. Banting and Richard Simeon, 95–145. Toronto: University of Toronto Press, 1985.

Callbeck, Lorne C. *The Cradle of Confederation: A Brief History of Prince Edward Island from Its Discovery in 1534 to the Present Time*. Fredericton, NB: Brunswick Press, 1964.

Calloway, Colin G. *Crown and Calumet: British Indian Relations, 1783–1815*. Norman: University of Oklahoma Press, 1953.

Campbell, Alastair, and Kirk Campbell. "Constitutional Development and Natural Resources in the North." In *Governing the North American Arctic: Sovereignty, Security, and Institutions*. Edited by Dawn Alexandrea Berry, Nigel Bowles, and Halbert Jones, 180–99. New York: Palgrave Macmillan, 2016.

Canada. *Canada 125: Its Constitutions, 1763–1982*. Ottawa: Canada Communications Group, 1992.

Canada. "Federalism for the Future: A Statement of Policy by the Government of Canada, the Constitutional Conference, 1968, Ottawa, February 5, 6, and 7." Ottawa: Queen's Printer, 1968.

Canada. *Parliamentary Debates on Confederation of the British North American Provinces*, 3rd Sess., 8th Provincial Parliament of Canada. Quebec City: Hunter Rose, 1865.

Canada. *Shaping Canada's Future Together: Proposals*. Ottawa: Supply and Services Canada, 1991.

Canada. Citizens' Forum on Canada's Future. *Report*. Ottawa, 1991.

Canada. Department of Indian Affairs and Northern Development. "Statement of the Government of Canada on Indian Policy." Ottawa, 1969.

Canada. Parliament. House of Commons. Special Committee on Indian Self-Government, *Report*. Ottawa, 1983.

Canada. Parliament. House of Commons. Special Committee to Study the Proposed Companion Resolution to the Meech Lake Accord, *Report*. Ottawa, May 1990.

Canada. Parliament. Senate. *Report to the Honourable Speaker Relating to the Enactment of the B.N.A. Act, 1867*. Ottawa: J.O. Patenaude, 1939.

Canada. Parliament. Special Joint Committee of the Senate and House of Commons on a Renewed Canada. *A Renewed Canada*. Ottawa, 1992.

Canada. Parliament. Special Joint Committee of the Senate and House of Commons on the Constitution of Canada. *The Constitution of Canada: Final Report*. Ottawa: Queen's Printer, 1972.

Canada. Prime Minister. "New Process for Judicial Appointments to the Supreme Court of Canada." News release, Ottawa, 2 August 2016.

Canada. Prime Minister's Office. "A Time for Action: Toward the Renewal of the Canadian Federation." Ottawa, 1978.

Canada. Royal Commission of Inquiry into Certain Activities of the Royal Canadian Mounted Police. *Second Report*, vol. 2. Ottawa: Queen's Printer, 1981.

Canada. Royal Commission on Aboriginal Peoples. *The High Arctic Relocation*. Ottawa: Canada Communications Group, 1994.

Canada. Royal Commission on Aboriginal Peoples. *Report*. Ottawa: Canada Communications Group, 1996.

Canada. Royal Commission on Dominion-Provincial Relations. *Report*. Ottawa: King's Printer, 1940.

Canada, British Columbia, and Nisga'a Nation. *Nisga'a Final Agreement.* 1999.

Canadians for a Unifying Constitution, in cooperation with The Friends of Meech Lake. "Meech Lake: Setting the Record Straight." [Chelsea, QC], 1990.

Candow, James E. *The Lookout: A History of Signal Hill.* St John's, NL: Creative Publishers, 2011.

Cardinal, Harold. *The Unjust Society.* Edmonton: Hurtig, 1969.

Careless, J.M.S. *Brown of the Globe,* 2 v. Toronto: Macmillan, 1963.

Careless, J.M.S. *The Union of the Canadas: The Growth of Canadian Institutions, 1841–1857.* Toronto: McClelland & Stewart, 1967.

Carter, Sarah. *Lost Harvests: Prairie Indian Reserve Farmers and Government Policy.* Montreal; Kingston, ON: McGill-Queen's University Press, 1990.

Chadwick, St John. *Newfoundland: Island into Province.* Cambridge: Cambridge University Press. 1967.

Chartrand, Paul L.A.H. "Aboriginal Rights: The Dispossession of the Métis." *Osgoode Hall Law Journal,* 29, no. 3 (1991): 463–82.

Chevrette, Louis. "Pontiac." In *Dictionary of Canadian Biography,* vol. 3. Toronto: University of Toronto Press, 1974.

Christensen, Deanna. *Ahtahkakoop: The Epic Account of a Plains Cree Chief, His People, and Their Struggle for Survival, 1816–1896.* Altona, MB: Friesens, 2000.

Clarke, J.G.M. *The Honourable Jonathan Sewell: Background, Career and Family, 1766–1839.* Toronto: Self-published, 1993.

Clarkson, Stephen. *The Big Red Machine: How the Liberal Party Dominates.* Vancouver: UBC Press, 2005.

Clarkson, Stephen, and Christina McCall. *Trudeau and Our Times,* vol. 1, *The Magnificent Obsession.* Toronto: McClelland & Stewart, 1990.

Coates, Kenneth. *Treaty Research Report: Treaty No. 10 (1906).* Ottawa: Indian and Northern Affairs Canada, 1986.

Cohen, Eliot A. *Conquered into Liberty: Two Centuries of Battles Along the Great Warpath that Made the American Way of War.* New York: Simon & Schuster, 2011.

Cook, Ramsay. *Canada and the French-Canadian Question.* Toronto: Macmillan, 1966.

Corry, J.A. "Constitutional Trends and Federalism." In *Evolving Canadian Federalism.* Edited by A.R.M. Lower et al., 92–125. Durham, NC: Duke University Press, 1958.

Coupland, R. *The Quebec Act: A Study in Statesmanship.* Oxford: Clarendon Press, 1925.

Craig, Gerald M. "John Strachan." In *Dictionary of Canadian Biography,* vol. 9. Toronto: University of Toronto Press, 1976.

Craig, Gerald M., ed. *Lord Durham's Report.* Montreal; Kingston, ON: McGill-Queen's University Press, 2007.

Craig, Gerald M. *Upper Canada: The Formative Years, 1784–1841*. Toronto: McClelland & Stewart, 1963.

Creighton, Donald. *The Road to Confederation: The Emergence of Canada, 1863–1867*. Toronto: Macmillan, 1964.

Crosbie, John C. *No Holds Barred: My Life in Politics*. Toronto: McClelland & Stewart, 1997.

Cruikshank, E.A., ed. *The Correspondence of Lieutenant Governor John Graves Simcoe*, vol. 3, *1794–1795*. Toronto: Ontario Historical Society, 1925.

Crummy, Michael. "The Circus Comes to Charlottetown: The Accidental Birth of a Nation." *Walrus* 11, no. 7 (2014): 50–61.

Dahl, Jens, Jack Hicks, and Peter Jull, eds. *Nunavut: Inuit Regain Control of Their Land and Their Lives*. Copenhagen: International Work Group for Indigenous Affairs, 2000.

Dales, John. "Protection, Immigration and Canadian Nationalism." In *Nationalism in Canada*. Edited by Peter H. Russell, 164–77. Toronto: McGraw-Hill Ryerson, 1966.

Daschuk, James. *Clearing the Plains: Disease, Politics of Starvation and the Loss of Aboriginal Life*. Regina: University of Regina Press, 2014.

Dawson, R. MacGregor. *The Government of Canada*, 4th ed. Toronto: University of Toronto Press, 1963.

Decelles, Alfred D. *The "Patriotes" of '37*, Chronicles of Canada 25. Toronto: Glasgow, Brook, 1916.

Delainey, David L., and J.C. Herbert Emery. "The National Policy's Impact on the West: A Reassessment." In *Macdonald at 200: New Reflections and Legacies*. Edited by Patrice Dutil and Roger Hall, 223–50. Toronto: Dundurn, 2014.

Dempsey, Hugh A. *Indian Tribes of Alberta*. Calgary: Glenbow Museum, 1997.

Dickason, Olive Patricia. *Canada's First Nations: A History of Founding Peoples from Earliest Times*. Toronto: McClelland & Stewart, 1992.

Dion, Gérard. "The Church and the Conflict in the Asbestos Industry." In *The Asbestos Strike*. Edited by Pierre Elliott Trudeau, 205–26. Toronto: Lewis & Samuel, 1974.

Dion, Stéphane. *Straight Talk: Speeches and Writings on Canadian Unity*. Montreal; Kingston, ON: McGill-Queen's University Press, 1999.

Dirks, Gerald E. *Canada's Refugee Policy: Indifference or Opportunism?* Montreal; Kingston, ON: McGill-Queen's University Press, 1977.

Dodson, Peter. *Little Pine and Lucky Man: A History, 1866–1885*. Little Pine and Lucky Man First Nations, SK: Peter Dodson, 2003.

Donaldson, Gordon. *Battle for a Continent: Quebec, 1759*. Toronto: Doubleday Canada, 1973.

Dubois, Janique. "From Service Providers to Decision Makers: Building a Métis Government in Saskatchewan." In *Métis in Canada: History, Identity,*

Law & Politics. Edited by Christopher Adams, George Dahl, and Ian Peach, 433–62. Edmonton: University of Alberta Press, 2013.

Dufour, Pierre, and Jean Hamelin. "Mercier, Honoré." In *Dictionary of Canadian Biography*, vol. 12. Toronto: University of Toronto Press, 1990.

Dunham, Aileen. *Political Unrest in Upper Canada, 1815–1836*. Toronto: McClelland and Stewart, 1963.

Dutil, Patrice. "Macdonald, His 'Ottawa Men' and the Consolidation of Prime Ministerial Power." In *Macdonald at 200: New Reflections and Legacies*. Edited by Patrice Dutil and Roger Hall, 282–310. Toronto: Dundurn, 2014.

Edmunds, R. David. *Tecumseh and the Search for Indian Leadership*. New York: Pearson/Longman, 2007.

Elazar, Daniel J. "Constitution-making, the Pre-eminently Political Act." In *Redesigning the State: The Politics of Constitutional Change*. Edited by Keith G. Banting and Richard Simeon, 232–48. Toronto: University of Toronto Press, 1985.

English, John. *Citizen of the World: The Life of Pierre Elliott Trudeau*, vol. 1, *1919–1968*. Toronto: Knopff Canada, 2006.

English, John. *Just Watch Me: The Life of Pierre Elliott Trudeau*, vol. 2, *1968–2000*. Toronto: Vintage Canada, 2010.

Ens, Gerhard J., and Joe Sawchuck. *From New Peoples to New Nations: Aspects of Métis History and Identity from the Eighteenth to the Twenty-first Centuries*. Toronto: University of Toronto Press, 2016.

Epp, Charles R. *The Rights Revolution: Lawyers, Activists, and Supreme Courts in Comparative Perspective*. Chicago: University of Chicago Press, 1998.

Evans, A. Margaret. *Sir Oliver Mowat*. Toronto, University of Toronto Press, 1992.

Favreau, Guy. *The Amendment of the Constitution of Canada*. Ottawa: Queen's Printer, 1965.

First Ministers, "A Framework Agreement to Improve the Social Union for Canadians" (Ottawa, 4 February 1999), available online at http://www.scics.gc.ca/english/conferences.asp?a=viewdocument&id=638.

Fischer, David Hackett. *Champlain's Dream*. Toronto: Vintage Canada, 2009.

Fisher, Robin. *Contact and Conflict: Indian European Relations in British Columbia, 1774–1890*. Vancouver: UBC Press, 1977.

Flanagan, Thomas. *Louis "David" Riel: Prophet of the New World*. Toronto: University of Toronto Press, 1979.

Fleras, Augie, and Jean Leonard Elliott. *The Nations Within: Aboriginal-State Relations in Canada, the United States and New Zealand*. Toronto: Oxford University Press, 1992.

Flexner, James Thomas. *Mohawk Baronet: A Biography of Sir William Johnson*. Syracuse, NY: Syracuse University Press, 1959.

Fraser, Graham. *PQ: René Lévesque & The Parti Québécois in Power.* Toronto: Macmillan, 1984.

Frégault, Guy. *La guerre de conquête.* Montreal: Fider, 1955.

Fumoleau, René. *As Long As the Land Shall Last: A History of Treaty 8 and Treaty 11, 1870–1939.* Toronto: McClelland & Stewart, 1973.

Gagnon, Alain-G., and James Tully, eds. *Multinational Democracies.* Cambridge: Cambridge University Press, 2001.

Gentilove, R. Louis, and Geoffrey J. Mathews, eds. *Historical Atlas of Canada,* vol. 2, *The Land Transformed, 1800–1891.* Toronto: University of Toronto Press, 1993.

Gérin-Lajoie, Paul. *Constitutional Amendment in Canada.* Toronto: University of Toronto Press, 1950.

Gold, Mark E. "The Mask of Objectivity: Politics and Rhetoric in the Supreme Court of Canada." *Supreme Court Review* 7 (1985): 455–510.

Granatstein, J.L. *The Greatest Victory: Canada's One Hundred Days, 1918.* Toronto: Oxford University Press, 2014.

Granatstein, J.L., and J.M. Hitsman. *Broken Promises: A History of Conscription in Canada.* Toronto: Oxford University Press, 1977.

Graham, Ron. *The Last Act: Pierre Trudeau, the Gang of Eight, and the Fight for Canada.* Toronto: Penguin Canada, 2012.

Grant, Shelagh D. *Arctic Justice: On Trial for Murder, Pond Inlet, 1923.* Montreal; Kingston, ON: McGill-Queen's University Press, 2002.

Grant, William Lawson. *The Tribune of Nova Scotia: A Chronicle of Joseph Howe.* Toronto: Glasgow, Brook, 1915.

Griffin, Justus A. *A Pioneer Family: Ancestors and Descendants of Richard Griffin.* Hamilton, ON: Griffin and Richmond, 1924.

Gwyn, Richard. *John A., The Man Who Made Us: The Life and Times of John A. Macdonald.* Toronto: Random House Canada, 2007.

Gwyn, Richard. *Nation Maker: Sir John A. Macdonald: His Life, Our Times.* Toronto: Random House Canada, 2011.

Hall, D.J. *From Treaties to Reserves: The Federal Government and Native Peoples in Territorial Alberta, 1870–1905.* Montreal; Kingston, ON: McGill-Queen's University Press, 2015.

Harring, Sidney L. *White Man's Law: Native People in Nineteenth-Century Canadian Jurisprudence.* Toronto: University of Toronto Press, 1998.

Hawkes, David C. *Aboriginal Peoples and Constitutional Reform: What Have We Learned?* Kingston, ON: Queen's University, Institute of Intergovernmental Relations, 1989.

Hawkins, Freda. *Canada and Immigration: Public Policy and Public Concern.* Montreal; Kingston, ON: McGill-Queen's University Press, 1972.

Hawthorn, H.B.. ed. *A Survey of the Contemporary Indians of Canada: Economic, Political, Educational Needs and Policies*. Ottawa: Indian Affairs Branch, 1966.

Heard, Andrew. *Canadian Constitutional Conventions: The Marriage of Law & Politics*, 2nd ed. Toronto: Oxford University Press, 2014.

Henderson, James (Sa'ke'j). *Indigenous Diplomacy and the Rights of Indigenous Peoples: Achieving UN Recognition*. Saskatoon: Purich, 2008.

Hicks, Jack, and Graham White. *Made in Nunavut: An Experiment in Decentralized Government*. Vancouver: UBC Press, 2015.

Hitsman, J. MacKay. *The Incredible War of 1812*. Montreal: Robin Brass Studio, 1999.

Ibbitson, John. *Stephen Harper*. Toronto: McClelland & Stewart, 2015.

Igartua, José. *The Other Quiet Revolution: National Identities in English Canada, 1945–71*. Vancouver: UBC Press, 2006.

Ignatieff, Michael. *The Rights Revolution*. Toronto: Anansi, 2000.

Isbister, Frank. "Asbestos 1949." In *On Strike: Six Key Labour Struggles in Canada, 1919–1949*. Edited by Irving Abella, 163–78. Toronto: James Lorimer, 1975.

Jasanoff, Maya. *Liberty's Exiles: American Loyalists in the Revolutionary World*. New York: Alfred Knopf, 2011.

Jedwab, Jack. "Introduction." In *The Multiculturalism Question: Debating Identity in 21st Century Canada*. Edited by Jack Jedwab, 1–10. Montreal; Kingston, ON: McGill-Queen's University Press, 2014.

Jennings, Francis. *The Invasion of America: Indians, Colonialism, and the Cant of Conquest*. Chapel Hill: University of North Carolina Press, 1975.

Johnston, Hugh. *The Voyage of the Komagata Maru: The Sikh Challenge to Canada's Colour Bar*. Vancouver: UBC Press, 1989.

Jones, Frederick. "'The Antis Gain the Day': Newfoundland and Confederation." In *The Causes of Confederation*. Edited by Ged Martin, 142–7. Fredericton, NB: Acadiensis Press, 1990.

Kelley, Ninette, and Michael J. Trebilcock. *The Making of the Mosaic: A History of Canadian Immigration Policy*, 2nd ed. Toronto: University of Toronto Press, 2010.

Kennedy, J.P.M. *The Constitution of Canada, 1534–1937: An Introduction to Its Development Law and Custom*, 2nd ed. Oxford: Oxford University Press, 1938.

Kennedy, J.P.M., ed., *Statutes, Treaties and Documents of the Canadian Constitution, 1713–1929*. Oxford: Oxford University Press, 1930.

Kerr, Donald, and Deryk Holdsworth, eds. *Historical Atlas of Canada*, vol. 3, *Addressing the Twentieth Century*. Toronto: University of Toronto Press, 1990.

Kilbourn, William. *The Firebrand: William Lyon Mackenzie and the Rebellion in Upper Canada*. Toronto: Clarke, Irwin, 1956.

King, Michael. *Nga Iwe O Te Motu: 1000 Years of Maori History*. Auckland: Reed Books, 2001.

Kohn, Hans. *Nationalism: Its Meaning and History*. Toronto: D. Van Nostrand, 1955.

Kome, Penny. *The Taking of Twenty-Eight: Women Challenge the Constitution*. Toronto: Women's Press, 1983.

Kravnick, David, ed. *The Tremblay Report*. Toronto: McClelland & Stewart, 1973.

Kymlicka, Will. *Multicultural Citizenship: A Liberal Theory of Minority Rights*. Oxford: Clarendon Press, 1995.

La Forest, Gérard. "Reminiscences of Aboriginal Rights at the Time of the *Calder* Case and Its Aftermath." In *Let Right Be Done: Aboriginal Title, the Calder Case, and the Future of Indigenous Rights*. Edited by Hamer Foster, Heather Raven, and Jeremy Webber, 55–8. Vancouver: UBC Press, 2007.

Lambe, W. Kaye. "Canada." In *The Canadian Encyclopaedia*, vol. 1. Edmonton: Hurtig, 1985.

Law Reform Commission of Canada. *Renewing Democracy: Debating Electoral Reform in Canada*. Ottawa, 2002.

Laxer, James. *Tecumseh and Brock*. Toronto: Anansi, 2012.

Lederman, W.R. "The Independence of the Judiciary." *Canadian Bar Review* 34 (1956): 769–809, 1139–79.

LeDuc, Lawrence, Judith I. McKenzie, Jon H. Pammett, and André Turcotte. *Dynasties and Interludes: Past and Present in Canadian Electoral Politics*. Toronto: Dundurn, 2010.

LeDuc, Lawrence, and Jon Pammett. "Attitudes toward Democratic Norms and Practices: Canada in Comparative Perspective." In *Canadian Democracy from the Ground Up: Perspectives and Performance*. Edited by Elizabeth Gidengil and Heather Bastedo, 22–40. Vancouver: UBC Press, 2014.

Lloyd, Trevor. *The British Empire, 1558–1995*, 2nd ed. Oxford: Oxford University Press, 1996.

Loat, Alison, and Michael MacMillan. *Tragedy in the Commons: Former Members of Parliament Speak Out about Canada's Failing Democracy*. Toronto: Random House, 2014.

Locke, John. *The Second Treatise of Government*. New York: Liberal Arts Press, 1952.

Long, John. *Treaty No. 9: Making the Agreement to Share the Land in Far Northern Ontario in 1905*. Montreal; Kingston, ON: McGill-Queen's University Press, 2010.

Macdonald, Ian. "Foreign Ownership: Villain or Scapegoat?" In *Nationalism in Canada*. Edited by Peter H. Russell, 178–202. Toronto: McGraw-Hill Ryerson, 1966.

MacDougall, Robert. "The All-Red Dream: Technological Nationalism and the Trans-Canada Telephone System." In *Canadas of the Mind: The Making and Unmaking of Canadian Nationalisms in the Twentieth Century*. Edited by Norman Hilman and Adam Chapnick, 46–52. Montreal; Kingston, ON: McGill-Queen's University Press, 2007.

Mackenzie, David Clark. *Inside the Atlantic Triangle: Canada and the Entrance of Newfoundland into Confederation, 1939–1949*. Toronto: University of Toronto Press, 1986.

MacLennan, Christopher. *Toward the Charter: Canadians and the Demand for a National Bill of Rights, 1929–1960*. Toronto: University of Toronto Press, 2002.

MacLennan, Hugh. *Two Solitudes*. Toronto: McClelland & Stewart, 1945.

Mahon, R.H. *Life of General the Hon. James Murray*. London: John Murray, 1921.

Malcomson, Robert. *Capital in Flames: The American Attack on York, 1813*. Montreal: Robin Brass Studio, 2008.

Mandell, Louise, and Leslie Hall Pinder. "Tracking Justice: The Constitution Express to Section 35 and Beyond." In *Patriation and Its Consequences: Constitution Making in Canada*. Edited by Lois Harder and Steve Patten, 180–202. Vancouver: UBC Press, 2015.

Manning, Helen Taft. *The Revolt of French Canada, 1800–1835*. Toronto: Macmillan, 1962.

Manuel, George, and Michael Posluns. *The Fourth World: An Indian Reality*. Toronto: Collier-Macmillan, 1974.

Martin, Lawrence. *Iron Man: The Defiant Reign of Jean Chrétien*. Toronto: Viking Canada, 2003.

Martin, Paul. "Citizenship and the People's World." In *Belonging: The Meaning and Future of Canadian Citizenship*. Edited by William Kaplan, 364–78. Montreal; Kingston, ON: McGill-Queen's University Press, 1993.

McConnell, W.H. "The Judicial Review of Prime Minister Bennett's 'New Deal.'" *Osgoode Hall Law Journal* 6, no. 1 (1968): 39–86.

McGregor, Russell. *Imagined Destinies: Aboriginal Australians and the Doomed Race Theory, 1880–1939*. Melbourne: Melbourne University Press, 1997.

McNaught, Kenneth. *The Penguin History of Canada*. London: Penguin Books, 1988.

McNeil, Kent. *Common Law Aboriginal Title*. Oxford: Clarendon Press, 1989.

McRae, Kenneth, ed. *Consociational Democracy: Accommodation in Segmented Societies*. Toronto: McClelland & Stewart, 1974.

McRoberts, Kenneth. *Quebec: Social Change and Political Crisis*, 3rd ed. Toronto: McClelland & Stewart, 1988.

Means, Russell. *Where White Men Fear to Tread: The Autobiography of Russell Means*, with Martin J. Wolf. New York: St Martin's Griffin, 1995.

Mill, John Stuart. "Considerations on Representative Government." In *John Stuart Mill: On Liberty and Other Essays*. Edited by John Grey. Oxford: Oxford University Press, 1991.

Miller, J.R. "Aboriginal Peoples and the Crown." In *Canada and the Crown: Essays on Constitutional Monarchy*. Edited by D. Michael Jackson and Philippe Lagassé, 255–69. Montreal; Kingston, ON: McGill-Queen's University Press, 2013.

Miller, J.R. "The Northwest Rebellion of 1885." In *Sweet Promises: A Reader on Indian-White Relations in Canada*. Edited by J.R. Miller, 243–58. Toronto: University of Toronto Press, 1991.

Miller, J.R. *Skyscrapers Hide the Heavens: A History of Indian-White Relations in Canada*, 3rd ed. Toronto: University of Toronto Press, 2000.

Milloy, John. *A National Crime: The Canadian Government and the Residential School System, 1879–1986*. Winnipeg: University of Manitoba Press, 1999.

Monahan, Patrick. *Meech Lake: The Inside Story*. Toronto: University of Toronto Press, 1991.

Monet, Jacques. *The Last Cannon Shot: A Study of French-Canadian Nationalism, 1837–1850*. Toronto: University of Toronto Press, 1969.

Moore, Christopher. *1867: How the Fathers Made a Deal*. Toronto: McClelland & Stewart, 1998.

Morrison, James. *Treaty Research Report: Treaty No. 9 (1905–1906)*. Ottawa: Indian and Northern Affairs Canada, 1986.

Morton, Desmond. *When Your Number's Up: The Canadian Soldier in the First World War*. Toronto: Random House, 1983.

Morton, W.L. *The Kingdom of Canada: A General History from Earliest Times*, 2nd ed. Toronto: McClelland & Stewart, 1969.

Morton, W.L. *Manitoba: A History*. Toronto: University of Toronto Press, 1967.

Mulroney, Brian. *Memoirs, 1939–2003*. Toronto: McClelland & Stewart, 2007.

Murrow, Casey. *Henri Bourassa and French-Canadian Nationalism: Opposition to Empire*. Montreal: Harvest House, 1968.

Neatby, Hilda. *Quebec: The Revolutionary Age, 1760–1791*. Toronto: McClelland & Stewart, 1966.

Nelson, Ralph C., Walter C. Sunderland, Ronald H. Wagenberg, and E. Donald Biggs. "Canadian Confederation as a Case Study in Community Formation." In *The Causes of Confederation*. Edited by Ged Martin, 50–85. Fredericton, NB: Acadiensis, 1990.

Nemni, Max, and Monique Nemni. *Trudeau Transformed: The Shaping of a Statesman, 1944–1965*. Toronto: McClelland & Stewart, 2011.

Nemni, Max, and Monique Nemni. *Young Trudeau: Son of Quebec, Father of Canada, 1919–1944*. Toronto: McClelland & Stewart, 2006.

New, Chester. *Lord Durham*. Oxford: Oxford University Press, 1929.

Newman, Dwight. "Understanding the Section 43 Amending Formula." In *Constitutional Amendment in Canada*. Edited by Emmett Macfarlane, 147–63. Toronto: University of Toronto Press, 2016.

O'Farrell, John. *Irish Families in Ancient Quebec Records*. Mayo, QC: Our Lady of the Shrine, 1967.

O'Malley, Eoin. "The Power of Prime Ministers: Results of an Expert Survey." *International Political Science Review* 28, no. 1 (2007): 7–27.

Ontario. Ipperwash Inquiry. *Report*, vol. 1, *Investigation and Findings*. Toronto: Queen's Printer for Ontario, 2007.

Options Canada. Toronto: University of Toronto, 1977.

Orange, Claudia. *The Treaty of Waitangi*. Wellington, NZ: Allen & Unwin, 1987.

O'Toole, Fintan. *White Savage: William Johnson and the Invention of America*. Albany: State University of New York Press, 2005.

Ormsby, Margaret A. *British Columbia: A History*. Toronto: Macmillan, 1958.

Ouellet, Fernand. *Lower Canada, 1791–1840: Social Change and Nationalism*. Toronto: McClelland & Stewart, 1980.

Patterson, Graeme. "An Enduring Canadian Myth: Responsible Government and the Family Compact." In *Interpreting Canada's Past*, vol. 1, *Before Confederation*. Edited by J.M. Bumsted, 230–47. Toronto: Oxford University Press, 1986.

Paxton, James W. *Joseph Brant and His World: 18th Century Mohawk Warrior and Statesman*. Toronto: Lorimer, 2008.

Peers, Frank. "The Nationalist Dilemma in Canadian Broadcasting." In *Nationalism in Canada*. Edited by Peter H. Russell, 252–70. Toronto: McGraw-Hill Ryerson, 1966.

Pierson, Coen G. *Canada and the Privy Council*. London: Stevens & Sons, 1960.

Plank, Geoffrey. *An Unsettled Conquest: The British Campaign Against the People of Acadia*. Philadelphia: University of Pennsylvania Press, 2001.

Poliquin, Daniel. *René Lévesque*. Toronto: Penguin Books, 2009.

Pound, Arthur. *Johnson of the Mohawks*. New York: Macmillan, 1930.

Pratte, André. *Wilfrid Laurier*. Toronto: Penguin, 2013.

Purich, Donald. *The Métis*. Saskatoon: Purich, 1988.

Quebec. *Québec-Canada: A New Deal*. Quebec City: Éditeur official, 1979.

Quebec. Commission on the Political and Constitutional Future of Quebec. *Report*. Quebec City, 1991.

Quebec Liberal Party. Constitutional Committee. *A Quebec Free to Choose*. Montreal: Quebec Liberal Party, 1991.

Rathgeber, Brent. *Irresponsible Government: The Decline of Parliamentary Democracy in Canada*. Toronto: Dundurn, 2014.

Ray, Arthur J., Jim Miller, and Frank Tough. *Bounty and Benevolence: A History of Saskatchewan Treaties*. Montreal; Kingston, ON: McGill-Queen's University Press, 2000.

Reitz, Jeffrey G. "Multiculturalism Policies and Popular Multiculturalism in the Development of Canadian Immigration." In *The Multiculturalism Question: Debating Identity in 21st Century Canada*. Edited by Jack Jedwab, 107–26. Montreal; Kingston, ON: McGill-Queen's University Press, 2014.

Richardson, Boyce. *Strangers Devour the Land*. Toronto: Macmillan of Canada, 1975.

Robertson, Gordon. *Northern Provinces: A Mistaken Goal*. Montreal: Institute for Research on Public Policy, 1985.

Rogers, Edward S. "The Algonquian Farmers of Southern Ontario, 1830–1845." In *Aboriginal Ontario: Historical Perspectives on the First Nations*. Edited by Edward S. Rogers and Donald B. Smith, 122–66. Toronto: Dundurn, 1994.

Romanow, Roy, John Whyte, and Howard Leeson. *Canada ... Notwithstanding: The Making of the Constitution, 1976–1982*. Toronto: Carswell/Methuen, 1984.

Rotstein, Abraham. "The 20th Century Prospect: Nationalism in a Technological Society." In *Nationalism in Canada*. Edited by Peter H. Russell, 341–63. Toronto: McGraw-Hill Ryerson, 1966.

Russell, Peter H. "Aboriginal Nationalism – Prospects for Decolonization." *Pacifica Review* 8, no. 2 (1996): 57–71.

Russell, Peter H. *Constitutional Odyssey: Can Canadians Become a Sovereign People?* 3rd ed. Toronto: University of Toronto Press, 2004.

Russell, Peter H. *The First Summit and the Atlantic Charter*. St John's, NL: Atlantic Charter Foundation. 2011.

Russell, Peter H. *The Judiciary in Canada: The Third Branch of Government*. Toronto: McGraw-Hill/Ryerson, 1987.

Russell, Peter H. "Learning to Live with Minority Parliaments." In *Parliamentary Democracy in Crisis*. Edited by Peter H. Russell and Lorne Sossin, 136–49. Toronto: University of Toronto Press, 2009.

Russell, Peter H. "Oka to Ipperwash: The Necessity of Flashpoint Events." In *This Is an Honour Song: Twenty Years since the Blockades*. Edited by Leanne Simpson and Kiera L. Ladner, 29–46. Winnipeg: Arbeiter Ring, 2010.

Russell, Peter H. "The *Patriation* and *Quebec Veto References*: The Supreme Court Wrestles with the Political Part of the Constitution." *Supreme Court Review*, 54 (2011): 69–76.

Russell, Peter H. "The Principles, Rules and Practices of Parliamentary Government: Time for a Consolidation." *Journal of Parliamentary and Political Law* 6, no. 2 (2012): 353–64.

Russell, Peter H. *Recognizing Aboriginal Title: The Mabo Case and Indigenous Resistance to English Settler Colonialism.* Toronto: University of Toronto Press, 2006.

Russell, Peter H. "Standing Up for Notwithstanding." *Alberta Law Review* 29, no. 2 (1991): 293–309.

Russell, Peter H. *The Supreme Court of Canada as a Bilingual and Bicultural Institution.* Ottawa: Queen's Printer for Canada, 1969.

Russell, Peter H. *Two Cheers for Minority Government: The Evolution of Canadian Parliamentary Democracy.* Toronto: Emond/Montgomery, 2009.

Russell, Peter H., Rainer Knopff, Thomas M.J. Bateman, and Janet L. Hiebert, eds. *The Court and the Constitution: Leading Cases.* Toronto: Emond/Montgomery, 2008.

Russell, Peter, Rainer Knopff, and Ted Morton, eds. *Federalism and the Charter: Leading Constitutional Decisions.* Ottawa: Carleton University Press, 1989.

Russell, Peter H., and Cheryl Milne. *Adjusting to a New Era of Parliamentary Democracy.* Toronto: University of Toronto, Faculty of Law, Asper Centre for Constitutional Rights, 2011.

Russell, Peter H., and Lorne S. Sossin, eds. *Parliamentary Democracy in Crisis.* Toronto: University of Toronto Press, 2009.

Said, Edward. *Culture and Imperialism.* New York: Vintage Books, 1994.

Salter, Liora. "The Complex Relationship between Commissions of Inquiry and Public Controversy." In *Commissions of Inquiry: Praise or Reappraise?* Edited by Allan Manson and David Mullan, 185–210. Toronto: Irwin Law, 2003.

Sanders, Douglas E. "The Indian Lobby." In *And No One Cheered: Federalism, Democracy and the Constitution Act.* Edited by Keith G. Banting and Richard Simeon, 301–32. Toronto: Methuen, 1983.

Saul, John Ralston. *Louis-Hippolyte LaFontaine & Robert Baldwin.* Toronto: Penguin, 2010.

Savard, Pierrel, and Paul Wyczynski. "Garneau, François-Xavier." In *Dictionary of Canadian Biography,* vol. 9. Toronto: University of Toronto Press, 1976.

Savoie, Donald J. *Governing from the Centre: The Concentration of Power in Canadian Politics.* Toronto: University of Toronto Press, 1999.

Saywell, John T. *The Lawmakers: Judicial Power and the Shaping of Canadian Federalism.* Toronto: University of Toronto Press, 2002.

Schmalz, Peter S. *The Ojibwa of Southern Ontario.* Toronto: University of Toronto Press, 1991.

Schrauwers, Albert. *"Union Is Strength": W.L. Mackenzie, the Children of Peace, and the Emergence of Joint Stock Democracy in Upper Canada.* Toronto: University of Toronto Press, 2009.

Schull, Joseph. *Laurier: The First Canadian*. Toronto: Macmillan, 1965.

Scott, Tracie Lea. *Postcolonial Sovereignty? The Nisga'a Final Agreement*. Saskatoon: Purich, 2012.

Seeley, J.R. *The Expansion of England*. London: Macmillan, 1906.

Sewell, John. *Mackenzie: A Political Biography of William Lyon Mackenzie*. Toronto: James Lorimer, 2002.

Sheppard, Robert, and Michael Valpy. *The National Deal: The Fight for a Canadian Constitution*. Toronto: Macmillan, 1982.

Short, Adam, and Arthur G. Doughty. *Documents Relating to the Constitutional History of Canada, 1759–1791*. Ottawa: King's Printer, 1907.

Short, Adam, and Norah Story. *Constitutional Documents Relating to The Constitutional History of Canada, 1819–1828*. Ottawa: King's Printer, 1925.

Siegfried, André. *The Race Question in Canada*. New York: D. Appleton, 1907.

Siggins, Maggie. *Riel: A Life of Revolution*. Toronto: HarperCollins, 1994.

Silver, A.I. *The French-Canadian Idea of Confederation, 1864–1900*. Toronto: University of Toronto Press, 1982.

Simeon, Richard. *Federal-Provincial Diplomacy: The Making of Recent Policy in Canada*. Toronto: University of Toronto Press, 1972.

Sinclair, Keith. *A History of New Zealand*. Harmondsworth, UK: Penguin, 1959.

Skelton, Oscar D. *The Day of Sir Wilfrid Laurier: A Chronicle of Our Own Time*. Glasgow: Brook & Company, 1916.

Slattery, Brian. *The Land Rights of Indigenous Canadian Peoples as Affected by the Crown's Acquisition of Their Territories*. Saskatoon: University of Saskatchewan, Native Law Centre, 1979.

Smiley, D.V. *Canada in Question: Federalism in the Eighties*, 3rd ed. Toronto: McGraw-Hill/Ryerson, 1980.

Smith, David E. *The Canadian Senate in Bicameral Perspective*. Toronto: University of Toronto Press, 2003.

Smith, Donald B. *Mississauga Portraits: Ojibwa Voices from Nineteenth-Century Canada*. Toronto: University of Toronto Press, 2013.

Smith, Donald B. *Sacred Feathers: The Reverend Peter Jones (Kahkewaquonaby) & the Mississauga Indians*. Lincoln: University of Nebraska Press, 1982.

Stacey, C.P. *Quebec 1759: The Siege and the Battle*. Toronto: Macmillan, 1959.

Stanley, George F.G. *The Birth of Western Canada: A History of the Riel Rebellions*. Toronto: University of Toronto Press, 1936.

Stanley, George F.G. *A Short History of the Canadian Constitution*. Toronto: Ryerson Press, 1969.

Stanley, Timothy J. "'The Aryan Character of the Future of British North America': John A. Macdonald, Chinese Exclusion and the Invention of

Canadian White Supremacy." In *Macdonald at 200: New Reflections and Legacies*. Edited by Patrice Dutil and Roger Hall, 115–40. Toronto: Dundurn, 2014.

Staples, Janice. "Consociationalism at the Provincial Level: The Erosion of Dualism in Manitoba, 1870–1890." In *Consociational Democracy*. Edited by Kenneth McRae, 288–99. Toronto: McClelland & Stewart, 1974.

Stevenson, Garth. *Building Nations from Diversity: Canadian and American Experience Compared*. Montreal; Kingston, ON: McGill-Queen's University Press, 2014.

Stewart, Walter. *True Blue: The Loyalist Legend*. Toronto: Collins, 1985.

Stoffman, Nicole. "What Did the Habitants Think of the British Regime?" Undergraduate essay, Department of Political Science, University of Toronto, 2013.

Stone, William L. *The Life and Times of Sir William Johnson*, 2 v. Albany, NY: J. Munsell, 1865.

Stone, William L. *Life of Joseph Brant-Thayendanegea*, 2 v. New York: Alexander V. Blake, 1865.

Stonechild, A. Blair. "The Indian View of the 1885 Uprising." In *Sweet Promises: A Reader on Indian-White Relations in Canada*. Edited by J.R. Miller, 258–76. Toronto: University of Toronto Press, 1991.

Sullivan, James, ed. *The Papers of Sir William Johnson*. Albany: New York University Press, 1921–62.

Talbot, Robert J. *Negotiating the Numbered Treaties: An Intellectual and Political Biography of Alexander Morris*. Saskatoon: Purich, 2009.

Taylor, Alan. *The Civil War of 1812*. New York: Knopf, 2010.

Taylor, Charles. *Reconciling the Solitudes: Essays on Canadian Federalism and Nationalism*. Montreal; Kingston, ON: McGill-Queen's University Press, 1993.

Taylor, John Leonard, "Canada's Northwest Indian Policy in the 1870s: Traditional Premises and Necessary Innovations." In *The Spirit of the Alberta Indian Treaties*, 3rd ed. Edited by Richard T. Price, 3–8. Edmonton: University of Alberta Press, 1999.

Tidridge, Nathan, *Prince Edward, Duke of Kent: Father of the Canadian Crown*, Toronto: Dundurn, 2013.

Tobias, John L. "Canada's Subjugation of the Plains Cree, 1879–1885." In *Sweet Promises: A Reader on Indian-White Relations in Canada*. Edited by J.R. Miller, 212–40. Toronto: University of Toronto Press, 1991.

Treaty 7 Elders. *The True Spirit and Original Intent of Treaty 7*. Montreal; Kingston, ON: McGill-Queen's University Press, 1996.

Trudeau, Justin. "Mandate Letter." Ottawa, 13 November 2015.

Trudeau, Pierre Elliott. "The Province of Quebec at the Time of the Strike." In
    The Asbestos Strike. Edited by Pierre Elliott Trudeau, 1–81. Toronto: Lewis &
    Samuel, 1974.
Truth and Reconciliation Commission of Canada. *Calls to Action*. Winnipeg, 2015.
Tully, James. "Introduction." In *Multinational Democracies*. Edited by Alain-G.
    Gagnon and James Tully, 1–33. Cambridge: Cambridge University Press, 2001.
Tully, James. *Strange Multiplicity: Constitutionalism in an Age of Diversity*.
    Cambridge: Cambridge University Press, 1995.
Vachon, André. "Briand, Jean-Olivier." In *Dictionary of Canadian Biography*,
    vol. 4. Toronto: University of Toronto Press, 1979.
Vipond, Robert C. *Liberty and Community: Canadian Federalism and the Failure of
    the Constitution*. Albany: State University of New York Press, 1991.
Wade, Mason. *The French Canadians, 1760–1967*. Toronto: Macmillan, 1968.
Waite, P.B. *The Life and Times of Confederation, 1864–1867: Politics, Newspapers,
    and the Union of British North America*. Toronto: University of Toronto Press,
    1962.
Ward, W. Peter. *White Canada Forever: Popular Attitudes and Public Policy to-
    wards Orientals in British Columbia*. Montreal; Kingston, ON: McGill-Queen's
    University Press, 1978.
Watkins, Mel, ed. *Dene Nation: The Colony Within*. Toronto: University of
    Toronto Press, 1977.
Weaver, Sally. *Making Canadian Indian Policy: The Hidden Agenda, 1968–1970*.
    Toronto: University of Toronto Press, 1981.
Wheare, K.C. *The Constitutional Structure of the Commonwealth*. Oxford:
    Clarendon Press, 1960.
White, Richard. *The Middle Ground: Indians, Republics, and Empires in the Great
    Lakes Region, 1650–1815*. New York: Cambridge University Press, 1991.
Whyte, John D. "On Not Standing for Notwithstanding." *Alberta Law Review*
    28, no. 2 (1989–90): 348–57.
Wiebe, Rudy. *Big Bear*. Toronto: Penguin Canada, 2008.
Wilson, David A. *Thomas D'Arcy McGee*, 2 v. Montreal; Kingston, ON: McGill-
    Queen's University Press, 2007.
Wilson, David A. "Macdonald and the Fenians." In *Macdonald at 200: New
    Reflections and Legacies*. Edited by Patrice Dutil and Roger Hall, 94–114.
    Toronto: Dundurn, 2014.
Wood, William. *The Fight for Canada: A Naval and Military Sketch from the
    History of the Great Imperial War*. London: Archibald Constable, 1904.
Wunder, John R. *"Retained by The People": A History of American Indians and the
    Bill of Rights*. New York: Oxford University Press, 1994.
York, Geoffrey, and Loreen Pindera. *People of the Pines: The Warriors and the
    Legacy of Oka*. Boston: Little, Brown, 1991.

Judicial Decisions

A.G. Canada v. A.G. Ontario, (1937) A.C. 327.

A.G. Canada v. A.G. Ontario, (1937) A.C. 356.

A.G. Ontario v. A.G. Canada, (1896) A.C. 348.

British Coal Corporation v. The Queen, (1935) A.C. 500.

Brophy v. A.G. Manitoba, (1895) A.C. 202.

Calder et al. v. A.G. British Columbia, (1973) S.C.R. 313.

Campbell v. A.G. British Columbia, (2000) 189 D.L.R. 333.

Campbell v. Hall, 1 Cowp. 204 (1774).

Cherokee Nation v. Georgia, 30 US (Pe.) 1 (1831).

Citizens Insurance Company v. Parsons, (1881), 7 App. Cas. 96.

City of Winnipeg v. Barrett, (1892) A.C. 445.

Cunningham v. Tommy Hoffa, (1903) A.C. 151.

Delgamuukw v. British Columbia, (1979) 3 S.C.R. 1010.

Edwards v. Canada, (1930) A.C. 124.

Haida Nation v. British Columbia, (2004) 3 S.C.R. 511.

Hodge v. The Queen, (1883), 9 App. Cas. 177.

In Re Regulation and Control of Radio Communication in Canada, (1932) A.C. 304.

In Re The Board of Commerce Act, 1919, (1922) A.C. 191.

Liquidators of the Maritime Bank of Canada v. Receiver General of New Brunswick,
    (1892) A.C. 437.

Manitoba Métis Federation Inc. v. Canada, (2013) 1 S.C.R. 623.

Mikisew Cree First Nation v. Canada, (2005) 3 S.C.R. 388.

Ottawa Separate Schools Trustee v. Mackell, (1917) A.C. 62.

R. v. Powley, (2003) 2 S.C.R. 207.

R. v. Sioui, (1991) 1 S.C.R. 1025.

Re Eskimo, (1939) S.C.R. 104.

Reference re Legislative Authority to Alter or Replace the Senate, (1980) 1 S.C.R. 54.

Reference re Secession of Quebec, (1998) 2 S.C.R. 217.

Russell v. The Queen, (1882), 7 App. Cas. 829.

Saumer v. Quebec, (1953) S.C.R. 599.

Severn v. The Queen, (1878) 2 S.C.R. 70.

Switzman v. Elbling and A.G. Quebec, (1957) S.C.R. 285.

Taku River Tlingit First Nation v. British Columbia, (2004) 3 S.C.R. 350.

Toronto Electric Commissioners v. Snider, (1925) A.C. 396.

Tsilhqot'in Nation v. British Columbia, (2014) 2 S.C.R. 256.

Union Colliery Company v. Brydon, (1899) A.C. 580.

Index